Queenship and Power

Series Editors
Charles E. Beem
University of North Carolina
Pembroke, NC, USA

Carole Levin
University of Nebraska
Lincoln, NE, USA

This series focuses on works specializing in gender analysis, women's studies, literary interpretation, and cultural, political, constitutional, and diplomatic history. It aims to broaden our understanding of the strategies that queens—both consorts and regnants, as well as female regents—pursued in order to wield political power within the structures of male-dominant societies. The works describe queenship in Europe as well as many other parts of the world, including East Asia, Sub-Saharan Africa, and Islamic civilization.

More information about this series at
http://www.palgrave.com/gp/series/14523

Kelly Digby Peebles • Gabriella Scarlatta
Editors

Representing the Life and Legacy of Renée de France

From *Fille de France* to Dowager Duchess

Editors
Kelly Digby Peebles
Clemson University
Clemson, SC, USA

Gabriella Scarlatta
University of Michigan–Dearborn
Dearborn, MI, USA

ISSN 2730-938X   ISSN 2730-9398   (electronic)
Queenship and Power
ISBN 978-3-030-69120-2   ISBN 978-3-030-69121-9   (eBook)
https://doi.org/10.1007/978-3-030-69121-9

This Palgrave Macmillan imprint is published by the registered company Springer Nature Switzerland AG.
The registered company address is: Gewerbestrasse 11, 6330 Cham, Switzerland

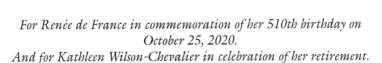

For Renée de France in commemoration of her 510th birthday on October 25, 2020.
And for Kathleen Wilson-Chevalier in celebration of her retirement.

ACKNOWLEDGMENTS

This collection on the life and legacy of Renée de France originated in a series of panels offered at the Kings and Queens conference organized by the Royal Studies Network (2017 in Madrid, 2018 in Winchester, and 2019 in Catania). We sincerely thank founding director Ellie Woodacre and the conference organizers who offered us the perfect venue in which to investigate Renée de France's legacy from multiple perspectives and disciplines. Many important ideas originated at the three conferences and much precious feedback was gathered.

We want to express our heartfelt gratitude to our *amie et collègue* Kathleen Wilson-Chevalier who has presented her papers on Renée with us and who has helped us all along in the conception and creation of this volume. Her invaluable assistance, unwavering encouragement, and erudite knowledge on Renée and her sister Claude de France have inspired and nurtured this project all along.

We also want to thank our copywriter Leah Eschrich, for helping us with the final stages of the volume assembly. We are grateful to the series editors, Charles Beem and Carole Levin, and to all our contributors for our friendly exchange of ideas and their enthusiasm for this project, and also to the anonymous reader who provided precious feedback on how to enrich it.

We would like to thank our respective institutions, Clemson University and the University of Michigan-Dearborn, for their financial and intellectual support and for their continuous encouragement in our scholarly pursuits. In times of difficult financial constraints, it is heartening to be continuously encouraged and funded to conduct research in France and

viii   ACKNOWLEDGMENTS

Italy and present papers at international conferences. We also want to acknowledge the Archivio di Stato di Modena, Daniela Cereia at the Archivio di Stato di Torino, and Juliette Jestaz at the Bibliothèque historique de la ville de Paris, for welcoming our queries and our research in their impressive facilities, as well as Karin Maag and Paul Fields at Calvin College's H. Henry Meeter Center for hosting the 2016 French Paleography Workshop, skillfully taught by Tom Lambert and supported by the Sixteenth-Century Society and Conference.

Kelly thanks her family—John, Lucy, and Brady—for their unflagging love and support, and most especially for their patience, resilience, silliness, and tenderness when her research took her overseas or required her to work long hours. She thanks her parents, Rosemary and Mike Digby, for being such wonderful parents, grandparents, neighbors, copyeditors (thanks, mom!), and travel companions. And she thanks her writing coach, Cassie Premo Steele, for creating our powerful support network of women writers, including Sondos Abdelgawad, Heidi Sherman, Liz Vogel, Shirley Smith, Casey Moore, Chantalle Verna, and Colette Cann.

Kelly also thanks Salvador Oropesa and the Department of Languages at Clemson University for supporting the publication of this volume and the international travel for conference presentations and archival research from which this work developed. She also wishes to thank Clemson University's College of Architecture, Arts, and Humanities and her colleague, Caroline Dunn in the history department, for hosting the Kings and Queens V conference in Greenville, South Carolina, in 2016, where she presented her first paper on Renée de France and first experienced the welcoming atmosphere of the Royal Studies Network.

Gabriella is very grateful to Marty Hershock, Dean of the College of Arts, Sciences, and Letters, for his continuous encouragement and gift of time to pursue her research abroad and to write. Her gratitude also goes to the Office of Research and Sponsored Programs for a generous grant that allowed her to travel to conferences and to visit the Italian archives. Without the generosity, collegial encouragement, and support of all involved at the University of Michigan-Dearborn, this volume could not have been published.

Finally, Gabriella wants to thank her family—Greg, Sierra, Leah, Graham, Peter, and Vittoria—for their constant encouragement and unconditional love throughout this entire journey, from Michigan to France to Ferrara and back! She is extremely appreciative to have a family who warmly embraces her pursuits and is always eager to help.

CONTENTS

NOTES ON CONTRIBUTORS

Eleonora Belligni is Associate Professor of Early Modern History at the University of Turin, Italy. Her research focuses on the Renaissance, the Reformation, and the Counter-Reformation in Europe. She has been working on the history of ideas and of political and religious culture of Early Modern Europe—Spain, England, France, Dalmatia, and small Italian States (Ferrara, Venice, and Rome). Her interests range widely: literature and rhetoric, cultural history and history of political thought, gender history, history of childhood and education, and history of economics. Among her books, *Renata di Francia. Un'eresia di corte* (Utet, 2011) analyzes the heretical court of Renée de France, duchess of Ferrara, as a part of an extended religious and political network.

Guillaume Berthon is *maître de conférences* at the University of Toulon (Laboratoire Babel) and received his PhD at the Université Sorbonne (2010). He is a specialist of Renaissance French literature and book history. He is the author of two books on Clément Marot: *L'Intention du Poète. Clément Marot "autheur"* (Garnier, 2014) and *Bibliographie critique des éditions de Clément Marot (ca. 1521–1550)* (Droz, 2019).

Cyril Cvetkovic is preparing a thesis in History on the court of Renée de France in Montargis at *Centre d'études supérieures de la Renaissance* (University of Tours/CNRS) under the direction of Professor Benoist Pierre. He is employed by the Château royal de Montargis as PhD student-researcher and benefits from a *CIFRE* grant from the National Association for Research and Technology in France.

Robert J. Hudson is Associate Professor of French at Brigham Young University. His research focuses primarily on the lyric and poetic traditions of Renaissance France, exploring an undercurrent of earthy Gallicism within the Italian-influenced imitative verse of vernacular poets from the reign of François I. His articles on Clément Marot, Maurice Scève, Pontus de Tyard, and Pierre de Ronsard appear in venues such as *Romanic Review*, *French Forum*, *Nottingham French Studies*, and the *Centre for Reformation and Renaissance Studies*. He is finishing a manuscript under contract with ACMRS for an English-language translation and critical edition of Clément Marot's *Verse Epistles*.

Kelly Digby Peebles is Associate Professor of French and Director of Language & International Health at Clemson University, South Carolina. She teaches French language, culture, civilization, and literature, as well as health humanities. Her research centers on French literary and historical works by and about Renée de France, women and gender issues, book history, and illness narratives in Early Modern France. Her recent published works include the critically edited translation, *Jeanne Flore, Tales and Trials of Love*, volume 33 in the series *The Other Voice in Early Modern Europe* (CRRS and Iter, 2014), a biographical entry on Renée de France in *Literary Encyclopedia*, and several journal articles and book chapters, including "Clément Marot's and Renée de France's Voyages: Political Exile to Spiritual Transformation" in *Women in French Studies*, "Embodied Devotion: the Dynastic and Religious Loyalty of Renée de France (1510–1575)," in *Royal Women and Dynastic Loyalty*, edited by Caroline Dunn and Elizabeth Carney (Palgrave Macmillan, 2018), and "Reincarnating the Forgotten Francis II: from Puerile Pubescent to Heroic Heartthrob," in *Remembering Queens and Kings in Early Modern England and France*, edited by Estelle Paranque (Palgrave Macmillan, 2019). She also is preparing the forthcoming volume *Portraits of Renée de France: Letters, Documents, and Literary Works* with Gabriella Scarlatta for inclusion in the series the Other Voice in Early Modern Europe (ACMRS Press and Iter).

Marzia Pieri is Professor of Theater and Spectacles at the University of Siena, Italy, and a former fellow at The Harvard University Center for Italian Renaissance Studies in Florence. Her publications include *La scena boschereccia nel Rinascimento italiano* (1983), *La nascita del teatro moderno* (1989), and *Il teatro di C. Goldoni* (1993), as well as various critical editions of Goldoni's plays and articles on Italian theater.

Gabriella Scarlatta is Professor of French and Italian and Associate Dean of the College of Arts, Sciences, and Letters at the University of Michigan–Dearborn. She teaches French and Italian literature, culture, and civilization, in particular the Medieval and Renaissance periods. Her research focuses on Renée de France and her circle, the French and Italian Petrarchan and Neo-Petrarchan court poets, early women writers and intellectuals, and the theoretical intersections of gender and genre. Her recent publications include "Gender, Power, and Sexuality in Betussi's and Brantôme's *Illustrious Women*," in *Royal Studies Journal, Ruling Sexualities Special Edition* (2019); *The* Disperata: *from Medieval Italy to Renaissance France* (2017); *Representing Heresy in Early Modern France*, co-edited with Lidia Radi (2017); "Philippe Desportes," in *Literary Encyclopedia*, and "Beheading the Elegy: Genre and Gender on the Scaffold of Bologna," in *Italica*. She is also preparing the forthcoming volume *Portraits of Renée de France: Letters, Documents, and Literary Works* with Kelly Peebles, for inclusion in the Other Voice series (ACMRS Press and Iter).

Roger S. Wieck is Melvin R. Seiden Curator and Department Head of Medieval and Renaissance Manuscripts at The Morgan Library & Museum in New York. Previously, he held curatorial positions at the Walters Art Museum, Baltimore, and the Houghton Library of Harvard. His books on royal manuscripts include *The Primer of Claude de France: MS 159, The Fitzwilliam Museum, Cambridge* (2012; with C. J. Brown and E. König); *The Prayer Book of Claude de France: MS M.1166, The Pierpont Morgan Library, New York* (2010); and *The Prayer Book of Anne de Bretagne: MS M.50, The Pierpont Morgan Library, New York* (1999).

Kathleen Wilson-Chevalier is Art History Professor Emerita at The American University of Paris. Trained as a Fontainebleau specialist, she has published a catalogue on French Renaissance prints, edited books (*Royaume de fémynie*, with Eliane Viennot; *Patronnes et mécènes en France à la Renaissance, Femmes et fonctions à la cour de France*, with Caroline zum Kolk), and written articles on French women of rank and their artistic patronage. Recent publications examine commissions associated with two Bourbon princesses, Jeanne de France and Louise de Bourbon-Montpensier, but especially the piety and patronage of Queen Claude de France, intertwined with those of her mother, Anne de Bretagne, and her sister, Duchess Renée.

Dick Wursten is an independent scholar and an inspector of religious education in Flanders. He lives and works in Antwerp, Belgium. His research focuses on the interplay between theology, history, and culture, with a preference for early sixteenth-century France. In his book *Clément Marot and Religion. A Reassessment in the Light of His Psalm Paraphrases* (2010), he shows how deeply Marot's translations—and its author— were embedded in the European movement of learned Humanists.

LIST OF FIGURES

LIST OF TABLES

CHAPTER 1

Introduction: Renée de France's Life and Legacy

Kelly Digby Peebles and Gabriella Scarlatta

Renée de France was born to King Louis XII and Anne de Bretagne on October 25, 1510, at the Château de Blois, where she was soon baptized at the Chapelle Saint-Calais. She was the third of four children born to the couple, of whom only two survived to adulthood: Renée and her elder sister, Claude de France, who became queen consort to their father's successor, François I. Detailed manuscript accounts of Renée's baptism call attention to the broader European contexts that would later define the contours of her adult life.[1] Her godfather, the Milanese *condottiero*, Marshal of France, and Governor of Asti and Milan, Gian Giacomo Trivulzio, carried the newborn *fille de France* down a tapestry-lined path

---

[1] *Le Baptême de Renée de France en 1510. Compte des frais et préparatifs*, ed. Pauline Matarasso (Paris: CNRS Éditions, 2011).

K. D. Peebles (✉)
Clemson University, Clemson, SC, USA
e-mail: kpeeble@clemson.edu

G. Scarlatta
University of Michigan–Dearborn, Dearborn, MI, USA
e-mail: geschric@umich.edu

1

from the castle to the royal chapel, assisted by her sister Claude.[2] Behind
them followed Renée's two godmothers, Anne de France, Dowager
Duchess of Bourbon and a *fille de France* herself, and her governess,
Georgette de Montchenu, also known as Madame du Bouchage, whose
husband was a close advisor to Louis XII.[3] Anne de France had personally
overseen the baptismal preparations, ordering the construction of a two-
tiered wooden platform three steps high on which the font stood beneath
a fabric pavilion.[4] The temporary structure was swathed in *fleur de lys*-
embroidered tapestries, while the young princess was swathed in an
ermine-lined white damask blanket, both carefully crafted to call attention
to the royal and ducal heritage of her parents. Other attendants included
Mademoiselle de Bourbon (Louise de Bourbon), the Princesse d'Orange
(Claude de Chalon), Madame de Nevers (Marie d'Albret), ladies-in-
waiting of Claude, and Anne de France, as well as ambassadors representing the courts of Emperor Maximilian I, King Ferdinand II of Aragon and
Castile, and the Duke of Ferrara (Alfonso I d'Este), among other Italian

[2] Trivulzio had begun fighting for the French under King Charles VIII and had captured
Milan for Renée's father. See Michael Mallet and Christine Shaw, *The Italian Wars,
1494–1559* (New York: Routledge, 2014), 49–50. Named Marshal of France by Louis XII in
1499, François I retained him in his service on his accession in 1515. See R. J. Knecht,
Renaissance Warrior and Patron. The Reign of Francis I (Cambridge: Cambridge University
Press, 1994), 43.

[3] Ymbert de Batarnay, Sieur du Bouchage, was a lifelong statesman who served Kings Louis
XI, Charles VIII, Louis XII, and François I. Charles VIII named him governor of his and
Anne de Bretagne's son Charles-Orland. Although Renée's care was soon conferred to
Michelle de Saubonne, baronne de Soubise after Madame du Bouchage's death in August
1511, it seemed that Monsieur du Bouchage continued to play a role in her life, as he was
later charged with overseeing the care of François I's and Claude's children, Louise,
Charlotte, and François, as well as that of Renée. See Bernard de Mandrot, *Ymbert de
Batarnay, Seigneur du Bouchage. Conseiller des Rois Louis XI, Charles VIII, Louis XII et
François Ier (1438–1523)* (Paris: Alphonse Picard, 1886), 182–184 and 269. See also Pauline
Matarasso, "Claude ou Renée? Les lettres d'Anne de Bretagne à Mme du Bouchage,"
Mémoires de la Société d'histoire et d'archéologie de Bretagne, 74 (1996): 453–459.
Interestingly, Monsieur and Madame du Bouchage are the grandparents of Diane de Poitiers
through their daughter Jeanne de Batarnay. On the social significance of baptism and the
choice of godparents, see Guido Alfani and Vincent Gourdon, "Spiritual Kinship and
Godparenthood: An Introduction," *Spiritual Kinship in Europe, 1500–1900*, ed. Guido
Alfani and Vincent Gourdon (Cham, Switzerland: Palgrave Macmillan, 2012), 1–43. They
note that the "ternary" model for choosing godparents was typical in France, with females
given two godmothers and one godfather, 8.

[4] Matarasso, *Le Baptême*, 41. For a discussion of a similar ceremonial platform, see Peebles's
Chap. 11.

city states, their presence foreshadowing negotiations for Renée's hand in marriage.[5] Though a relatively intimate affair in comparison to other court ceremonies, including Renée's own wedding, her baptism nonetheless reveals how such events were carefully orchestrated to publicly display social networks and solidify overlapping personal and political relationships. As Tracy Adams writes, Anne de France was "a master of politics," having learned to govern with her husband, Pierre de Bourbon, during her brother Charles VIII's minority all "while outwardly conforming to norms of female comportment."[6] And by this time, she had earned a significant reputation for fostering young women at her court, among them Marguerite d'Autriche and Louise de Savoie, teaching them essential skills to ensure their future success in navigating social hierarchies and governing a household, including how to establish and preserve morality, faith, and family tradition.[7] At Renée's baptism, those in closest proximity to the young *fille de France* were those who had the closest personal relationships with her parents, and the young women observing the ceremony were active participants by carrying the infant's blanket and other sacred objects, learning firsthand from this ritual.[8] That ritual, as Guido Alfani notes, "realizes not only the spiritual birth of the new Christian but also his social

[5] *Négotiations diplomatiques entre la France et l'Autriche durant les trente premières années du XVI* siècle, ed. André Le Glay (Paris: Imprimerie royale, 1845), 367–368n2. Le Glay includes a prose description of the baptism ceremony ostensibly authored by Jean Caulier, ambassador to Margaret of Austria, though no source is provided.

[6] Tracy Adams, "Fostering Girls in Early Modern France," in *Emotions in the Household, 1200–1900*, ed. Susan Broomhall (Cham, Switzerland: Palgrave Macmillan, 2008), 103–118, and "Rivals or Friends? Anne de Bourbon and Anne de Bretagne," *Women in French Studies* Special Issue (2010): 46–61, 49.

[7] Adams, 48. See also Pauline Matarasso, *Queen's Mate. Three Women of Power in France on the Eve of the Renaissance* (Burlington, VT: Ashgate, 2001), 36. Though here she focuses on Anne de France, Matarasso also discusses the courts of Anne de Bretagne and Louise de Savoie. Elodie Lequain also discusses Anne de France's "school" for young noblewomen, focusing at length on the education of her own daughter, Suzanne de Bourbon, "La maison de Bourbon, 'escolle de vertu et de perfection'. Anne de France, Suzanne de Bourbon et Pierre Martin," *Médiévales*, 48 (Printemps 2005): 39–54.

[8] Among the young women mentioned by name, Claude de Chalon would marry the Comte de Nassau five years later, and Marie d'Albret, who had married Charles II de Clèves, Comte de Nevers, in 1504, gave birth to their son François in 1516. Though not specifically mentioned in the ambassador's dispatch, Anne de France's daughter, Suzanne de Bourbon, was of a similar age and had married Charles III, Duke of Bourbon, in 1505. After the birth of their son in 1517, François I was chosen as his godfather and namesake, though their relationship would later disintegrate. See Knecht, *Renaissance Warrior*, 203.

birth," thereby creating a lasting spiritual kinship that "put members of different social classes in relation with one another [...] to establish ties at every level of the social ladder."[9] In fact, in a collection of lessons composed for her daughter, Suzanne de Bourbon, to prepare her for her future roles as wife and mother, Anne de France writes of the significance of these relationships, urging her to "carefully consider who will baptize [your children] and instruct them in the church and who will bring them up, because whoever it is must be wise and honorable."[10] Through this ceremony, Renée's parents were thus shaping their daughter's future social network and forging bonds to support her as she grew older.

By late 1513, Renée's parents had discussed marriage to one of Maximilian's and Ferdinand's mutual grandsons.[11] However, her mother's death on January 9, 1514, her sister's May 1514 marriage to her father's presumed heir, François d'Angoulême, followed by her father's death on January 1, 1515, and the subsequent accession of her brother-in-law as François I led to a reordering of the crown's priorities and a consequential shifting of Renée's prominence in the royal hierarchy in favor of Claude's and François's children.[12] Several primary documents survive in manuscript and in print related to Renée's childhood and coming of age. Ambassadors' dispatches and account books paint a picture of her birth and baptism, while multiple marriage contracts, correspondence, and ephemeral pamphlets elucidate the celebrations surrounding her wedding. The increasing prominence of her public profile during the sixteenth century is confirmed by literary and artistic works produced by equally celebrated writers and artists. Her image was captured in a richly decorated manuscript by the illuminator known as the Master of Claude de France[13] and in a drawing by the celebrated portrait artist Jean Clouet, which is

[9] Guido Alfani, "Introduction," *Fathers and Godfathers: Spiritual Kinship in Early-Modern Italy* (Abingdon: Taylor & Francis Group, 2009), 3 and 10.

[10] Anne de France, *Lessons for My Daughter,* ed. and trans. Sharon L. Jansen (Cambridge: D. S. Brewer, 2004), 60.

[11] See the dispatches of Pedro de Quintana, King Ferdinand's ambassador to France and to the Holy Roman Empire, in December 1513. "Henry VIII: December 1513," in *Letters and Papers, Foreign and Domestic, Henry VIII, Volume 1, 1509–1514,* ed. J. S Brewer (London: His Majesty's Stationery Office, 1920), 1102–1121.

[12] François I charged Monsieur du Bouchage with negotiating the marriage of Renée and Charles of Austria (the future Charles V) in 1515. Francis's and Claude's first child, Louise de France, was born later that year and subsequently engaged to him. See de Mandrot, *Ymbert de Batarnay,* 249 and 272.

[13] Roger Wieck discusses these images in Chap. 3.

now housed in the Musée Condé in Chantilly (Fig. 1.1). Renée's 1528 wedding was celebrated by court poet Clément Marot, *valet de chambre* to François I, in an epithalamium that evokes the musical and choreographic revelry of a royal wedding, but also acknowledges the difficult situation of a young princess whose dynastic marriage and imminent departure for her husband's foreign land were motivated by geo-political and military concerns associated with decades of war with Italy.[14] Inspired by the bellicose subtext of the union, the poet represents the groom, Ercole d'Este, future Duke of Ferrara, Modena, and Reggio (whose father's ambassador had attended Renée's baptism), as a virile warrior and alludes to the deliberate joining of two dynasties and political bodies—Valois France and Estense

Fig. 1.1 Jean Clouet. Portrait of Renée of France, ca. 1519. Chantilly, Musée Condé, Inv. MN28. © RMN-Grand Palais/Art Resource, NY. (Photo: Michel Urtado)

[14] On the subtext of the Italian Wars, see Gabriel Braun, "Le Mariage de Renée de France: une inutile mésalliance. 28 juin 1528," *Histoire, économie et société* 7, no. 2 (1988): 147–168.

Ferrara—as an armed invasion of the young bride's physical body.[15] Paradoxically, the poet also notes that it was precisely that fear-provoking encounter that held the promise of mutual prosperity and interdependence through the couple's offspring. Sure enough, Renée's and Ercole's union would ultimately produce five offspring: Anne, Alfonso, Lucrezia, Eleonora, and Luigi. In fact, their firstborn, Anne, would effectively retrace her mother's journey across the Alps twenty years later for her own marriage to François de Lorraine, a socially brilliant match that would be arranged by Renée's nephew, King Henri II.

Renée's baptism and marriage were marked with elaborate pomp and circumstance that clearly established the importance of her rank and publicly commemorated higher order political negotiations. As was often the case for royal couples, several months after the festivities, Renée left her home to set up court alongside that of her husband in Ferrara, accompanied by a significant entourage of French courtiers. This highly symbolic journey, which Christiane Coester terms the "bridal voyage,"[16] began with the ritualized public staging of the bride's and groom's first meeting. In Renée's case, this occurred at the château de Saint-Germain-en-Laye[17] and culminated with her crossing of the Alps, representing both geo-political and cultural borders. As this journey progressed, the bride "changed from daughter to wife, from one family to another, and she therefore changed not only her legal status but also her frame of cultural reference."[18] As Giulia Calvi further explains, "women marrying into foreign dynasties brought with them a dynastic capital made of status, wealth, material culture, court rituals and etiquette, religion as well as their own entourage."[19]

[15] On Marot's portrayal of the marriage, see Kelly D. Peebles, "Renée de France's and Clément Marot's Voyages: Political Exile to Spiritual Liberation," *Women in French* Special Issue 7 (2018): 33–60. In 1555, the Italian poet Bernardo Zane will also commemorate this union in a powerful image joining the two fertile rivers, the Po and the Seine. See Gabriella Scarlatta's Chap. 7.

[16] "Crossing Boundaries and Traversing Space. The Voyage of the Bride in Early Modern Europe," in *Moving Elites: Women and Cultural Transfers in the European Court System*, ed. Giulia Calvi and Isabelle Chabot (Florence: European University Institute, 2010), 9–20.

[17] Their first encounter is described in *Le triumphant et tresnoble mariage de treshaulte et trespuissante princesse Madame Renee de France fille du Roy de France Loys douziesme de ce nom faict avec le Duc de Ferrare en la ville et cité de Paris* (s.l.: s.n., 1528). The only extant copy of this imprint is located at the Bibliothèque historique de la ville de Paris, 12-Rés-0567. The library's rare book curator, Juliette Jestaz, kindly photographed this pamphlet for us.

[18] Coester, "Crossing Boundaries," 9.

[19] Giulia Calvi, "Introduction," in Calvi and Chabot, *Moving Elites*, 1.

This certainly was Renée de France's case when she left France, where she had come of age alongside her royal nieces and nephews, including the future King Henri II. Guido Guerzoni contends that by surrounding herself with a predominantly French entourage, she established a "French Court in the middle of nowhere,"[20] but her circle was far from homogeneous, for Renée also continued to cultivate the heterodox ideas that had characterized the French court during her youth. Orphaned before the age of four, Renée had developed a close relationship with her cousin, Marguerite de Navarre, who was known for her support of reform-minded individuals and espousal of evangelical ideas, and with whom Renée continued to correspond during her years in Ferrara.[21]

After settling in Ferrara, where Renée came to be known as Renata di Francia or Madame Renea, despite—and perhaps also inspired by—the unfamiliar, though vibrant, cultural surroundings, she continued to exploit her status as a *fille de France* and to associate with diverse intellectuals. The palaces of Schifanoia and San Francesco, as well as nearby Consandolo and Belriguardo, were a venue for political, religious, and diplomatic discussions, and they also functioned as a meeting space for a constellation of orthodox and heterodox personalities, many of whom were considered to be dubious or dangerous. As many other women of power, including her foremothers, Anne de Bretagne, Anne de France, and Louise de Savoie, she exercised various forms of power and influence in public and private spaces and took full advantage of her dynastic network as she established herself in her new duchy.[22] Renata's acquaintances, activities, and suspected beliefs led to her forced profession of the Catholic faith in 1554, when her cousin, King Henri II, sent the Grand Inquisitor

---

[20] Guido Guerzoni, "Strangers at Home. The Courts of Este Princesses between XVth and XVIIth Centuries," in Calvi and Chabot, *Moving Elites*, 141–156, 154.

[21] On Marguerite's and Renée's correspondence, see Jules Bonnet, "Marguerite d'Angoulême, Reine de Navarre et Renée de France (1535–1536)," *Bulletin historique et littéraire* 37, no. 3 (15 March 1888): 113–123. On Marguerite's faith, see Jonathan Reid, *King's Sister – Queen of Dissent: Marguerite de Navarre and Her Evangelical Network (1492–1549)* (Leiden: Brill, 2009). On female religious influences in Renée's early years, see Kathleen Wilson-Chevalier's Chap. 2.

[22] For a discussion of the sources of power and how elite women exercised power, see Theresa Earenfight, "A Lifetime of Power: Beyond Binaries of Gender," in *Medieval Elite Women and the Exercise of Power, 1100–1400: Moving Beyond the Exceptionalist Debate*, ed. Heather J. Tanner (Cham, Switzerland: Palgrave Macmillan, 2019): 271–293.

of France, Mathieu Ory, to Ferrara in order to oversee her interrogation.[23] Although Renée's correspondence reveals the extent of the distress provoked by this incident, she maintained a correspondence with Jean Calvin until the end of his life, seeking his counsel both before and after her husband's death in 1559.[24]

These connections grew stronger still during Renée's dowager years. On the death of her husband on October 3, 1559, her eldest son, Alfonso II d'Este, rose to power as the Duke of Ferrara, and Renée experienced a subsequent reduction in monetary allowances and personnel allotted to her as staff.[25] As Renée outlived her husband, her own court was not completely dissolved following Ercole's death, but rather, her daughter-in-law's court existed in parallel to hers for a short time,[26] and in mid-1560, Renée had begun to explore a return to France. In November 1560, the dowager duchess reunited with the French court and her firstborn daughter, Anne d'Este, who was by then Duchess of Guise and a close companion of both the Queen Mother, Catherine de Medici, and of the queen, her husband's niece, Mary Stuart, Queen of Scots. Renée arrived in Orléans just weeks before the untimely death of King François II and subsequent accession of the young Charles IX, where the court was preparing for a meeting of the Estates General to debate increasing religious, political, and economic tension.[27] Renée spent her last fifteen years at her château in Montargis, a geographically strategic location for troop movements during the Wars of Religion. There, displaying the royal *fleur de lys* of her

[23] Emmanuel Rodocanachi, *Renée de France, duchesse de Ferrare* (Paris: Ollendorff, 1896), 237–252.

[24] See, for example, Calvin's letters to Renée from July 1560 and early 1561. Edouard Cunitz, Johann-Wilhelm Baum, and Eduard Wilhelm Eugen Reuss, eds., *Ioannis Calvini opera quae supersunt omnia, Volumen XVIII*, (Brunsvigae: Schwetschke et filium, 1863), 147–148, 315–316.

[25] Guerzoni, "Strangers at Home," 141–156. Guerzoni notes that she received "33.500[...] annually up to 1555," and then "after the hiatus of 1558–9, during which her allowance dropped to 21.500," she later "received 38.250 in 1562, before her definitive return to France," 154.

[26] Guerzoni, "Strangers at Home," 156. Unlike her predecessors, Eleonora d'Aragona (wife of Ercole I), Anna Sforza, and Lucrezia Borgia (first and second wives respectively of Alfonso I), Renata outlived the duke.

[27] Renée traces her journey from Ferrara to Orléans, from September to November 1560, in a series of letters to Alfonso. See Odette Turias, *Renée de France, Duchesse de Ferrare, témoin de son temps: 1510–1575, Tome I* (PhD diss, Université de Tours, 2005), 333–341. See also Peebles's Chap. 11 in this volume.

Valois heritage prominently in the great hall of her château, as Androuet du Cerceau illustrates in his architectural drawings of Montargis, she continued to participate both in court life and in the French Calvinist network.[28] Much as in Ferrara, Renée's *domaine* became a veritable sanctuary for religious and political refugees from both sides of the conflict.[29] In the mid-1560s, prominent voices within the French Calvinist network, in particular Théodore de Bèze and Pierre Viret, adopted Renée as a symbolic figurehead of their cause by praising her leadership and public service in published book dedications, and her own correspondence from this time amply confirms their laudatory comments.[30]

While Renée's "heretical" court is closely examined in Eleonora Belligni's (2011) biography,[31] she has not yet earned the scholarly attention that has been devoted to her mother, Anne de Bretagne, to her cousin, Marguerite de Navarre, nor even to her own sister, Claude de France. However, Renée's life and legacy invite critical reflection from a variety of disciplines, and this volume aims to fill this lacuna by examining the many roles that Renée/Renata adopted, embodied, or had forced upon her—including *fille de France*, Duchess of Ferrara, and later, Dowager Duchess and *châtelaine* of Montargis—and to elucidate the abundant visual and textual evidence that celebrates her qualities and bears

---

[28] See the image reproduced on the front cover from Jacques Androuet du Cerceau, *Le Premier volume des plus excellents bastiments de France. Auquel sont designez les plans de quinze bastiments, & de leur contenu: ensemble les elevations & singularitez d'un chascun* (Paris: pour Jacques Androuet du Cerceau, 1576). For a detailed discussion of Androuet du Cerceau's renovations of the château de Montargis and its gardens, see Cyril Cvetkovic's Chap. 12.

[29] See Renée Burlamacchi in her *Memoirs Concerning her Father's Family*, in *Sin and Salvation in Early Modern France: Three Women's Stories*, ed. Colette Winn, ed. and trans. Winn and Nicholas Van Handel, The Other Voice in Early Modern Europe, 53 (Toronto: Iter Press, 2017), 43–54.

[30] Théodore de Bèze, *Recueil des opuscules. C'est à dire. Petits Traictez de M. Jean Calvin. Les uns reveus et corrigez sur le Latin, les autres translatez. Nouvellement de Latin en Français* (Geneva: Baptiste Pinereul, 1566), *2r–*5r, and Pierre Viret, *De l'Estat, de la conférence, de l'authorité, puissance, prescription & succession tant de la vraye que de la fausse Église, depuis le commencement du monde, & des Ministres d'icelles & de leurs vocations & degrez* (Lyon: Claude Senneton, 1565), *iir–*viiiv. For further discussion of Renée's role of symbolic figurehead in Bèze's dedication, see Peebles, "Embodied Devotion: The Dynastic and Religious Loyalty of Renée of France (1510–1575)," in *Royal Women and Dynastic Loyalty*, ed. Caroline Dunn and Elizabeth Carney (Cham, Switzerland: Palgrave Macmillan, 2018), 123–137.

[31] *Renata di Francia (1510–1575) Un'eresia di corte* (Turin: UTET, 2011).

witness to her hardships. These collected essays offer a comprehensive (yet far from exhaustive) look at her participation in and influence on cultural and intellectual life in sixteenth-century France and Italy: her generous patronage of artists, scholars, and other literati; the adversities that Renée encountered due to her support for heterodox voices; her unflagging spirit of resilience, tolerance, and charity despite those difficulties; and her astute cultivation of social, religious, and diplomatic connections, particularly between Valois France and Estense Ferrara, but also within broader European politico-religious networks.

Arranged chronologically in order to trace the trajectory of Renée's life, each chapter focuses on activities associated with her role(s) at a specific stage in her life, for example, the development of her religious faith in her childhood, her support of artists and literati made possible by her social status as Duchess of Ferrara, and her epistolary diplomacy that developed from her political connections as a French royal, which was further enhanced by the social freedom she enjoyed in her dowager years. This collection also demonstrates the breadth of Renée's legacy by investigating cultural artifacts facilitated by her patronage and inspired by her life story, including French and Italian poetry, theater, landscape architecture, and visual arts, and its chapters represent a variety of methodological approaches, including bibliographical and textual studies, art history, gender studies, religious studies, and literary criticism.

The first chapters in this volume examine Renée's early years, beginning with Kathleen Wilson-Chevalier's analysis of Anne de Bretagne's educational, economic, financial, and religious legacy to her daughters Claude and Renée. As notorious court chronicler Pierre de Brantôme observes of Anne, "sa court estoit fort belle escole pour les Dames, car elle les faisoit bien nourrir et sagement; et toutes, à son modelle, se faisoyent et se façonnoyent très-sages et vertueuses" (her court was a very fine school for Ladies, for she nourished them well and wisely; and all of them, following her example, behaved and presented themselves as very wise and virtuous).[32] Indeed, Wilson-Chevalier firmly establishes the emotional and intellectual role of this environment on Renée's adult life and the way in which she would later structure her own court, where she would exercise charitable and protective actions toward the religiously persecuted. This

---

[32] Pierre de Brantôme, sieur de Bourdeille, *Recueil des Dames, poésies, et tombeaux*, ed. Etienne Vaucheret (Paris: Gallimard, 1991), 13–14. All translations in this chapter are the editors'.

chapter focuses in particular on the influence of Renée's governess, Michelle de Saubonne, Baronne de Soubise, and on the liberal religious upbringing of the young princesses, who, from early childhood, were surrounded by trusted people and prelates engaged in religious reform in an effort to cultivate a "learned, rejuvenated Church." Furthermore, their mother struggled to control her natal duchy of Brittany and to ensure her daughters' status as *filles de France* despite the French king's strategic machinations and other religious and political conflicts that ultimately thwarted her attempts, resulting in Renée's lengthy legal proceedings against the French crown to reclaim her birthright of Brittany.

Roger Wieck's chapter guides us through Renée's physical and spiritual growth by examining the textual and pictorial contents of a primer commissioned during her childhood. He demonstrates how the purposeful structure of this richly illuminated and jewel-like treasure juxtaposes portraits of the book's owner with prayers. Beginning with the most basic, memorized devotions and progressing to prayers recited in adulthood, some of which were customary, while others were unique to Renée's life story, this book offers a fascinating glimpse into how Renée learned to read and to recite her catechism. Her spiritual growth in adulthood is further examined in Dick Wursten's contribution, a study of Renée's correspondence with noted reformer and spiritual leader of Geneva, Jean Calvin. Five years after Renée's marriage and subsequent departure from France, court poet Clément Marot retraced her journey across the Alps to Ferrara in the aftermath of the *Affaire des Placards*, a controversial incident involving the public display of broadsheets criticizing papal abuses and the Catholic sacrament of the Eucharist. Marot arrived in Ferrara in April 1535, seeking refuge at Renée's court, likely on the insistence of Marguerite de Navarre, though his sojourn was interrupted just a year after his arrival by an event that Wursten terms the "Ferrarese imbroglio." Marot and other perceived "heretics" were pursued by the local inquisitor following a protest against the idolatry of mass during Lent. Wursten pursues a new line of inquiry by deconstructing the long-established historiography related to this event and calling into question the widely held belief that Jean Calvin was not only involved, but also personally met Renata and befriended her at that time. By examining primary sources, or getting back to the basics, so to speak, Wursten proposes a reassessment of Calvin's and Renée's relationship. Clément Marot continues to be at the center of Guillaume Berthon's study, in which he investigates the literary afterlife of the "Ferrarese imbroglio" in Marot's poetry. This chapter identifies and compares extant witnesses of two poems written during Marot's stay in Italy, offering a critical edition and textual analysis of both. Berthon examines the larger politico-religious situation, Renée's personal situation, and the thematic evolution of the poems between their initial composition for Renée and their dissemination to a wider public. One poem anticipates the birth of Renée's third child and posits an apocalyptic vision of Christ's return amidst the current turmoil of the Church, while the second, written after Marot fled Ferrara in the wake of the imbroglio, excoriates the materialism of Venice, a city that gilded its churches, but neglected its poor. Berthon demonstrates that Renée's influence is ever present in the poems, but in an effort to secure royal patronage, their heterodox backdrop necessarily faded as the political tides changed. In the following chapter, Robert Hudson also examines Marot's poetry written under Renée's auspices, but in contrast highlights the blithesome side of the poet's tone, language, and style during this period. Hudson considers the physical surroundings of Renée's court and argues that the gardens of her Belvedere, an island retreat on the Po river, represent a veritable *locus amoenus*. For Marot, this lush Italian backdrop inspired a lyrical evolution, a self-professed shift in poetic style made possible by Renée's patronage and protection.

The atmosphere of Renata's court, brimming with intellectual debates over humanistic and religious matters, was particularly receptive to new ideas and reformed opinions about traditional Church dogmas. The wide variety of religious backgrounds welcomed within this space led to the consumption and circulation of new literary and artistic models in constantly evolving ways. Gabriella Scarlatta's chapter analyzes how four fairly unknown texts portray Renata: Gianbattista Giraldi Cinzio's *Le Fiamme* and his sonnet "Donna, che togli con gentil costume," Bernardo Zane's sonnet "Alla Signora Madama e Duchessa di Ferrara Reniera da Este," Suor Girolama Castellani's *canzone*, "Pensier, che pur mi desti a l'alta impresa," and Orazio Brunetto's dedication in his *Lettere di Horatio Brunetto*. Despite their formal and stylistic diversity, Renata emerges consistently in these works as a guiding light and a beacon for her community. Although this role is seldom recognized by scholars, Scarlatta demonstrates that Renata was persistently sung as one who aids and comforts the religiously and politically persecuted from all walks of life. All four writers highlight Renata's influential and unwavering work, as well as her unobtrusive mediation between the kings of France, the Habsburg emperor, and the Este dynasty, all the while drawing strength from the intellectual enterprises of her tolerant humanistic circle. Analysis of the authors' backgrounds and close readings of their texts in this chapter reveal that Renata inspired genuine respect and praise from the diverse group of individuals that surrounded her and her family. Giraldi's work is also examined in Marzia Pieri's chapter, where the author explores more closely his relationship as Ercole II's secretary and playwright with the duchess. Tracing the powerful female tradition of patronage from her mother, Anne de Bretagne, and godmother Anne de France to Louise de Savoie and the latter's daughter, Marguerite de Navarre, Pieri shows the ways in which Renata's involvement enriched the Este cultural and intellectual legacy in Ferrara. Renata was particularly fond of theater, from the writing and reading of plays to their staging and production, and Pieri demonstrates her affinities with Giraldi, including personally experiencing the Counter-Reformation's invasive demands. After offering a short history of the theater (and its stagnation) in Ferrara under Ercole I and Alfonso I, Pieri observes a theatrical renaissance thanks to Ercole II's and Renata's patronage and advocacy: the number of representations and the use of Italian increased, and theater became a family affair as the young Este children acted in a play to entertain Pope Paul II. Furthermore, through his *œuvre*, Giraldi built and reinvigorated the Este theater and stage with strong female protagonists that embodied Renata's and her close friends' lives and stories. Indeed, Pieri argues that a close reading of Giraldi's work reveals a strong and stoic *duchessa* on equal footing, both intellectually and politically, with the Duke.

While Eleonora Belligni's Italian-language biography brought renewed scholarly interest to Renée de France and the heterodox voices associated with her court, her contribution to this volume approaches Renée's biography in light of a specific fragment of women's history: the concept of "simulated celibacy," which she defines as a set of habits and bearings designed to give the appearance that Renata remained unmarried. According to Belligni, in her role as *subventrix*, Renata developed a much broader perspective on religious and political matters, surrounding herself with the diverse ideas of humanists, former academics, school teachers, and writers, a motivated collective network that subsisted in large part thanks to her financial and political support, even during Ferrara's darkest hours. Due to her substantial capital and independence, Renata was able to intervene in local politics and family affairs, often through conflict resolution, charitable activities, and the distribution of offices and charges.[33] Belligni examines Renata's significant place in this limited phenomenon as she successfully exploited simulated celibacy not only to take a leading role in religious dissent, but also to remain somewhat independent of her husband, his duchy, and his culture.

According to Kathleen Wilson-Chevalier, art played a key role in breaking down prevailing and oversimplified binary oppositions. This chapter offers a critical reassessment of Renata's image by analyzing a variety of artistic media connected with the Estense ducal court and other female and male ruling kin, including silver plaques and tapestries depicting scenes from well-known European *roman sentimentaux* and frescoes that adorned the Belriguardo residence, known in French as the Belvedere, a site that also figures in Hudson's study. This chapter fleshes out Renée's profile as a formidably resilient French princess during an uncomfortably complex age of religious and political change and argues that due to her commanding rank and particularly fine education, Renée assumed a more important place in Ferrara's tendentially tolerant mainstream culture than has generally been acknowledged. Indeed, as Kelly Peebles's chapter demonstrates, Renée adeptly relied on her hierarchical rank in order to reclaim her place within the French court after the 1559 death of her husband. Furthermore, as Jean Calvin points out to Renée in correspondence from that time, widowhood paired with her royal status would afford her even greater freedom to pursue an agenda of religious and political tolerance and encourage change in those areas.

Beginning with both textual and visual representations of the Estates General in Orléans that took place in late 1560 and early 1561 soon after Renée's return to France, Kelly Peebles's contribution examines how Renée exploited the figurative "platform," so to speak, of her royal status in order to shape her public image on the physical platform created for that assembly. Renée's conspicuous image in depictions of this event signals her importance on the stage of European politics. Peebles analyzes Renée's strategy of epistolary diplomacy in her correspondence with Jean Calvin and English ambassador to the French court, Nicholas Throckmorton, to highlight how she exploited affective relationships,

---

[33] According to Rosanna Gorris, Renée's annual revenue consisted of 10,000 *écus* from her French territories, and her dowry from François I amounted to 50,000 *écus*, "'D'un château l'autre': La Corte di Renata di Francia a Ferrara (1528–1560)," in *Il Palazzo di Renata*, ed. Loredana Olivato (Ferrara: Corbo editore, 1997), 139–169, 140.

religious affinities, and socio-political status in order to influence public policy. At a time of increasingly violent conflict between Protestant and Catholic factions, Renée drew from her close ties to individuals on both sides of the politico-religious divide, including her son-in-law, François de Guise, in order to advocate for change. This divide accompanied Renata's last years of her life journey. Indeed, upon her return to Montargis, the dowager duchess found a castle in much need of repair, as Cyril Cvetkovic explains in the last chapter. Nonetheless, there, she regularly evoked the principles of goodness, charity, justice, and peace, qualities that in turn contributed to the construction of an image faithful to her own ideal of a royal princess. By analyzing the socio-cultural role of landscape architecture, Cvetkovic demonstrates how gardens visually represented new courtly norms and practices and the need for material representation of noble identity. Thus, the grounds of the château of Montargis, its architectural program, and its construction works efficiently expressed Renée's royal rank and signaled her authority over the surrounding territory in a very public manner. As the first War of Religion was beginning to ignite, this was a crucial strategy for reaffirming her status in her native France, a strategy that was, Cvetkovic contends, quite compatible with her Calvinist leanings.

While many moments of Renée's life were marked with elaborate ceremony to establish their momentous nature—her birth, marriage, and return to France, among many others—interestingly, she declined any celebration of her life's end. Unlike her contemporary, Jeanne de Navarre, who publicly renounced Catholicism on Christmas of 1560,[34] there is no archival evidence to suggest that Renée made a public statement of conversion to the reformed religion. However, Renée's own Testament, written in the hand of the reformed pastor, Daniel Toussaint, suggests that she did convert in practice and privately, if not formally and publicly. Indeed, several boldly affirmed statements offer poignant insight into Renée's religious faith. She first states that "nous sommes sauvés par foy non par nos oeuvres" (we are saved by faith and not by our works). She then continues by embracing the new commandment, "le sommaire de la loy est que nous

---

[34] For a brief overview, see *Jeanne d'Albret. Letters from the Queen of Navarre with* an Ample Declaration, ed. Kathleen M. Llewellyn, Emily E. Thompson, and Colette H. Winn (Tempe, Arizona: ACMRS Press and Iter, 2016), 3–4. For a more extensive biography, see Nancy L. Roelker, *Queen of Navarre, Jeanne d'Albret: 1528–1572* (Cambridge, Massachusetts: Belknap, 1968), 154.

aimions nostre Dieu de tout nostre coeur, et nos prochains comme nous-mesmes" (the sum of the law is that we must love our God with all our heart and our neighbors as ourselves) and by proclaiming "qu'il est beso-ing de prier Dieu souvent qu'il nous soit propice et nous pardonne nos défauts" (that it is necessary to pray to God often so that he might look on us favorably and forgive our sins). Renée then goes on to reject the tradi-tional Catholic sacraments, with the exception of "le baptesme par lequel nous somme visiblement introduicts en l'Eglise, et admoneste de [...] nos peches [...] et aussi la Saincte-Cène qui est la nourriture de ceux qui ont desja profité en l'Eglise" (baptism, through which we are visibly presented to the Church and admonished for [...] our sins [...] and also Communion, which nourishes those who have already embraced the Church).[35] Finally, explicitly proscribing that her passing be commemorated, Renée writes of her wish for a simple burial, "sans pompes et cérémonies qui ne profitent aux morts et ont peu de force pour consoler et instruire les vivans" (with-out pomp and ceremony, which do not benefit the deceased and have little effect in consoling and edifying the living).[36] Casting aside ephemeral entrapments, Renée crafts her legacy according to those values she held most dear—"l'union et concorde"—and urges her children "qu'en par-faite amitié et exemple de toute vertu, ils facent en leur maison perpétuer la mémoire d'une générosité illustre et toujours recommandable" (that with perfect love and as an example of true virtue, they fashion their homes to project an illustrious and commendable generosity). Nearly seventy years earlier, Anne de France, writing with "perfect natural love" to her daughter, Suzanne de Bourbon, and expecting "imminent, sudden, and early death," states: "devote yourself completely to acquiring virtue. Behave so that your reputation may be worthy of perpetual memory: whatever you do, above all, be truly honest, humble, courteous, and loyal."[37] Renée's testament echoes her godmother's statement almost word for word, as if she, too, is writing *Lessons* to her children, thereby placing herself and her offspring in that long line of strong royal women.

[35] Charmarie Jenkins Webb, *Royalty and Reform: The Predicament of Renée de France, 1510–1575* (Ph.D. diss., Tufts University, 1969), 587–588. Webb transcribes the original document, written in the hand of reformed pastor Daniel Toussaint, which is housed in the Archivio di Stato in Turin, Sezione I, Palazzo Castello, Archives des Princes de Genevois et de Nemours, Paquet 8, Category 5.

[36] Webb, *Royalty and Reform*, 592.

[37] Anne de France, *Lessons*, 25 and 31.

BIBLIOGRAPHY

PRIMARY SOURCES

Albret, Jeanne d'. 2016. *Letters from the Queen of Navarre with* An Ample Declaration. Edited and translated by Kathleen M. Llewellyn, Emily E. Thompson, and Colette H. Winn. Tempe, Arizona: ACMRS Press and Iter.

Androuet du Cerceau, Jacques. 1576. *Le Premier volume des plus excellents bastiments de France. Auquel sont designez les plans de quinze bastiments, & de leur contenu: ensemble les elevations & singularitez d'un chascun.* Paris: pour Jacques Androuet du Cerceau.

Anne de France. 2004. *Lessons for My Daughter.* Edited and translated by Sharon L. Jansen. Cambridge: D. S. Brewer.

Bèze, Théodore de. 1566. *Receuil des opuscules. C'est à dire. Petits Traictez de M. Jean Calvin. Les uns reveus et corrigez sur le Latin, les autres translatez. Nouvellement de Latin en Français.* Geneva: Baptiste Pinereul.

Brantôme, Pierre de, sieur de Bourdeille. 1991. *Recueil des Dames, poésies, et tombeaux.* Edited by Etienne Vaucheret. Paris: Gallimard.

Burlamacchi, Renée. 2017. Memoirs Concerning her Father's Family. In *Sin and Salvation in Early Modern France: Three Women's Stories,* ed. Colette Winn, ed. and trans. by Winn and Nicholas Van Handel, 43–54. Tempe, Arizona: ACMRS Press and Iter.

Calvin, Jean. 1863. *Ioannis Calvini opera quae supersunt omnia, Volumen XVIII.* Edited by Edouard Cunitz, Johann-Wilhelm Baum, and Eduard Wilhelm Eugen Reuss. Brunsvigae: Schwetschke et filium.

Le Baptême de Renée de France en 1510. Compte des frais et préparatifs. 2011. Edited by Pauline Matarasso. Paris: CNRS Éditions.

Letters and Papers, Foreign and Domestic, Henry VIII, Volume 1, 1509–1514. 1920. Edited by J. S. Brewer. London: His Majesty's Stationery Office.

Le triumphant et tresnoble mariage de treshaulte et trespuissante princesse Madame Renee de France fille du Roy de France Loys douziesme de ce nom faict avec le Duc de Ferrare en la ville et cité de Paris. 1528. N.p.: n.p.

Négotiations diplomatiques entre la France et l'Autriche durant les trente premières années du XVIᵉ siècle. 1845. Edited by André Le Glay. Paris: Imprimerie royale.

Viret, Pierre. 1565. *De l'Estat, de la conférence, de l'authorité, puissance, prescription & succession tant de la vraye que de la fausse Église, depuis le commencement du monde, & des Ministres d'icelles & de leurs vocations & degrez.* Lyon: Claude Senneton.

SECONDARY SOURCES

Adams, Tracy. 2008. Fostering Girls in Early Modern France. In *Emotions in the Household, 1200–1900*, ed. Susan Broomhall, 103–118. Cham, Switzerland: Palgrave Macmillan.

———. 2010. Rivals or Friends? Anne de Bourbon and Anne de Bretagne. *Women in French Studies Special Issue*: 46–61.

Alfani, Guido. 2009. *Fathers and Godfathers: Spiritual Kinship in Early-Modern Italy*. Abingdon: Taylor & Francis Group.

Alfani, Guido, and Vincent Gourdon. 2012. Spiritual Kinship and Godparenthood: An Introduction. In *Spiritual Kinship in Europe, 1500–1900*, ed. Guido Alfani and Vincent Gourdon, 1–43. Cham, Switzerland: Palgrave Macmillan.

Belligni, Eleonora. 2011. *Renata di Francia (1510–1575). Un'eresia di corte.* Turin: UTET.

Bonnet, Jules. 1888. Marguerite d'Angoulême, Reine de Navarre et Renée de France (1535–1536). *Bulletin historique et littéraire* 37 (3): 113–123.

Braun, Gabriel. 1988. Le Mariage de Renée de France: une inutile mésalliance. 28 juin 1528. *Histoire, économie et société* 7 (2): 147–168.

Calvi, Giulia. 2010. Introduction. In *Moving Elites: Women and Cultural Transfers in the European Court System*, ed. Giulia Calvi and Isabelle Chabot, 1–5. Florence: European University Institute.

Coester, Christiane. 2010. Crossing Boundaries and Traversing Space. The Voyage of the Bride in Early Modern Europe. In *Moving Elites: Women and Cultural Transfers in the European Court System*, ed. Giulia Calvi and Isabelle Chabot, 9–20. Florence: European University Institute.

Earenfight, Theresa. 2019. A Lifetime of Power: Beyond Binaries of Gender. In *Medieval Elite Women and the Exercise of Power, 1100–1400: Moving Beyond the Exceptionalist Debate*, ed. Heather J. Tanner, 271–293. Cham, Switzerland: Palgrave Macmillan.

Gorris, Rosanna. 1997. 'D'un château l'autre': La Corte di Renata di Francia a Ferrara (1528–1560). In *Il Palazzo di Renata*, ed. Loredana Olivato, 139–169. Ferrara: Corbo editore.

Guerzoni, Guido. 2010. Strangers at Home. The Courts of Este Princesses between XVth and XVIIth Centuries. In *Moving Elites: Women and Cultural Transfers in the European Court System*, ed. Giulia Calvi and Isabelle Chabot, 141–156. Florence: European University Institute.

Knecht, R.J. 1994. *Renaissance Warrior and Patron. The Reign of Francis I.* Cambridge: Cambridge University Press.

Lequain, Élodie. 2005. La maison de Bourbon, 'escolle de vertu et de perfection'. Anne de France, Suzanne de Bourbon et Pierre Martin. *Médiévales* 48: 39–54.

Mallet, Michael, and Christine Shaw. 2014. *The Italian Wars, 1494–1559.* New York: Routledge.

Mandrot, Bernard de. 1886. *Ymbert de Batarnay, Seigneur du Bouchage. Conseiller des Rois Louis XI, Charles VIII, Louis XII et François Ier (1438–1523)*. Paris: Alphonse Picard.

Matarasso, Pauline. 1996. Claude ou Renée? Les lettres d'Anne de Bretagne à Mme du Bouchage. *Mémoires de la Société d'histoire et d'archéologie de Bretagne* 74: 453–459.

Peebles, Kelly D. 2018a. Embodied Devotion: The Dynastic and Religious Loyalty of Renée of France (1510–1575). In *Royal Women and Dynastic Loyalty*, ed. Caroline Dunn and Elizabeth Carney, 123–137. Cham, Switzerland: Palgrave Macmillan.

———. 2018b. Renée de France's and Clément Marot's Voyages: Political Exile to Spiritual Liberation. *Women in French Special Issue* 7: 33–60.

Reid, Jonathan. 2009. *King's Sister – Queen of Dissent: Marguerite de Navarre and Her Evangelical Network (1492–1549)*. Leiden: Brill.

Rodocanachi, Emmanuel. 1896. *Renée de France, duchesse de Ferrare*. Paris: Ollendorff.

Roelker, Nancy L. 1968. *Queen of Navarre, Jeanne d'Albret: 1528–1572*. Cambridge, MA: Belknap.

Turias, Odette. 2005. *Renée de France, Duchesse de Ferrare, témoin de son temps: 1510–1575*. Ph.D. diss., Université de Tours.

Webb, Charmarie Jenkins [Blaisdell]. 1969. *Royalty and Reform: The Predicament of Renée de France, 1510–1575*. Ph.D. diss., Tufts University.

CHAPTER 2

Anne de Bretagne, Claude de France, and the Roots of Renée's *Persona*

Kathleen Wilson-Chevalier

A Florentine ambassador recounts that on May 25, 1510, the future Renée de France emitted a signal from within Queen Anne de Bretagne's womb.[1] Exactly five months later, Renée emerged into a realm governed by her father King Louis XII, teeming with great ladies of clout. In many a European court, princesses were poised as the head of households over which and from which they ruled, generally alongside their princely kin.[2]

---

[1] Alessandro Nasi's account involves King Louis XII, Queen Anne de Bretagne, the defunct Cardinal d'Amboise and Florimond Robertet. Giuseppe Canestrini and Abel Desjardins, eds., *Négociations diplomatiques de la France avec la Toscane*, vol. II (Paris: Imprimerie Nationale, 1861), 507; cited by Pauline Matarasso, *Queen's Mate. Three Women of Power in France on the Eve of the Renaissance* (Aldershot: Ashgate, 2001), 259n24.

[2] Nadine Akkerman and Birgit Houben, eds., *The Politics of Female Households. Ladies-in-Waiting across Early Modern Europe* (Leiden and Boston: Brill, 2014); Caroline zum Kolk and Kathleen Wilson-Chevalier, *Femmes à la cour de France. Charges et fonctions XVe-XIXe siècle* (Villeneuve d'Ascq: Presses Universitaires du Septentrion, 2018).

K. Wilson-Chevalier (✉)
The American University of Paris, Paris, France
e-mail: kchevalier@aup.edu

© The Author(s), under exclusive license to Springer Nature
Switzerland AG 2021
K. D. Peebles, G. Scarlatta (Eds.), *Representing the Life and Legacy of Renée de France*, Queenship and Power,
https://doi.org/10.1007/978-3-030-69121-9_2

21

Anne de Bretagne is henceforth recognized as a "major woman of State,"[3] and it was hard to match the spectacular aura of her royal court, which reflected and refracted her power. Like all power though, Anne's was predicated on an unstable balancing act.[4] Twice queen, but sovereign duchess, too, Anne built upon models of exemplary ladies of her caliber, with whom she had much in common yet who could at any moment pose a threat, especially because she lacked a male heir in the land of Salic law. Having brilliantly mastered the rules of the beastly courtly game, Anne was bent on transmitting her painstakingly acquired skills to her heiresses, Renée and her older sister Claude. Both were raised around their mother's (lost) tapestries of Christine de Pisan's *City of Ladies,* and the broader universe haunted by these privileged *filles de France* afforded copious gendered lessons to be absorbed.[5] Amboise, a major castellar base that Anne and her progeny frequented throughout their lives, had been the hub of the (unnamed) regency of one of Renée's godmothers, Anne de France, during Queen Anne's first marriage.[6] The elder Anne was a formidable woman of power in her own right. At the summit of the numerous princesses also groomed in her orbit were the reigning regent of the Low Countries, Marguerite d'Autriche, and the rising political star Louise de Savoie, chatelaine of Amboise from 1500.[7] When death hovered over

[3] Michel Nassiet, "Anne de Bretagne, A Woman of State," in *The Cultural and Political Legacy of Anne de Bretagne. Negotiating Convention in Books and Documents,* ed. Cynthia J. Brown (Cambridge: D.S. Brewer, 2010), 163–175.

[4] Theresa Earenfight, "A Lifetime of Power: Beyond Binaries of Gender," in *Medieval Elite Women and the Exercise of Power, 1100–1400. Moving beyond the Exceptionalist Debate,* ed. Heather J. Tanner (Palgrave Macmillan, 2019), 271–293, convincingly frames monarchical power as "a family affair."

[5] Antoine Le Roux de Lincy, *Vie de la reine Anne de Bretagne, femme des rois de France Charles VIII et Louis XII,* vol. IV (Paris: L. Curmer, 1861), 79; Susan Groag Bell. *The Lost Tapestries of the City of Ladies. Christine de Pizan's Renaissance Legacy* (Berkeley, Los Angeles, London: University of California Press, 2004), 144–145.

[6] Most recently, Lucie Gauguin, *Amboise un Château dans la ville* (Tours and Rennes: Presses universitaires François-Rabelais de Tours, Presses universitaires de Rennes, 2014). Her other godmother was her governess Madame du Bouchage; Pauline Matarasso, *Le Baptême de Renée de France en 1510. Compte des frais et préparatifs* (Paris: CNRS Éditions, 2011), 68.

[7] Tracy Adams, "Fostering Girls in Early Modern France," in *Emotions in the Household, 1200–1900,* ed. Susan Broomhall (New York: Palgrave Macmillan, 2008), 103–118, on the concept and widespread practice of fostering. Thierry Crépin-Leblond and Monique Chatenet, eds., *Anne de France: art et pouvoir en 1500* (Paris: Picard, 2014); Aubrée David-Chapy, *Anne de France, Louise de Savoie, inventions d'un pouvoir au féminin* (Paris: Classiques

Anne de Bretagne, whose second reign radiated out from the nearby castle of Blois, the queen confided her daughters and her possessions to Louise (or so Louise proclaimed).[8] Only Anne's political acumen could have led her to gamble on Louise, set to rise to power alongside her beloved son King François I and Anne's elder daughter Claude. After Anne de Bretagne expired in early 1514, not yet thirty-seven, the futures of her precious daughters were unsure. Would the pawns she had set in place suffice to protect the thirty-seven-year-old Louise's young "wards"?

Queen/Duchess Anne's impending successor Claude was only fourteen at her mother's demise, and the future Duchess of Ferrara, Renée, not quite three years and three months old. A worthy maternal dynasty had fortunately girded their way. Anne's short-lived mother Marguerite de Foix-Navarre, already afflicted with the absence of a male heir,[9] had been well groomed by her own mother Éléonore, queen regnant of Navarre for almost twenty-five years.[10] Prior to the Breton *États'* ratification of female succession on February 8, 1486, acting regent Anne de France had been pressuring Marguerite to accept a royal marriage for her nine-year-old daughter Anne.[11] Before her decease the following May, Pierre Le Baud had dedicated to Marguerite his *Genealogie des tres anciens roys, ducs et princes qui, au temps passé, ont regy et gouverné ceste royalle principauté de*

Garnier, 2016), and "La 'Cour des Dames' d'Anne de France à Louise de Savoie: un espace de pouvoir à la rencontre de l'éthique et du politique," in *Femmes à la cour de France*, 49–65; Zita Rohr, "Rocking the Cradle and Ruling the World: Queens' Households in Late Medieval and Early Modern Aragon and France," in *Royal and Elite Households in Medieval and Early Modern Europe: More Than Just a Castle*, ed. Theresa Earenfight (Boston: Brill, 2018), 309–337.

[8] Nadine Kuperty-Tsur, "Le Journal de Louise de Savoie, nature et visées," in *Louise de Savoie 1476–1531*, ed. Pascal Brioist, Laure Fagnart, and Cédric Michon (Tours and Rennes: Presses universitaires François-Rabelais and Presses universitaires de Rennes, 2015), 270.

[9] Elizabeth L'Estrange, *Holy Motherhood. Gender, dynasty and visual culture in the later middle ages* (Manchester: Manchester University Press, 2008), 219ff; Joris Corin Heyder, "Les *Heures* de Marguerite de Foix: sources artistiques d'un atelier Nantais presque inconnu," in *Nantes flamboyante, (1380–1530)*, ed. Nicolas Faucherre and Jean-Marie Guillouët (Nantes: Société archéologique et historique de Nantes et de la Loire-Atlantique, 2014), 123–139.

[10] Elena Woodacre, *The Queens Regnant of Navarre. Succession, Politics, and Partnership, 1274–1512* (New York: Palgrave Macmillan, 2013), 109–130.

[11] Julien Havet, "Mémoire adressé à la dame de Beaujeu sur les moyens d'unir le duché de Bretagne au domaine du roi de France," *Revue historique*, 25 (1884): 276.

Bretagne, justifying the rule of women in Breton history.[12] In late 1498, in the wake of the Italian wars and as she was completing the negotiation of her strong second marriage contract, Anne commissioned three tombs, including a magnificent Franco-Italian sepulcher honoring the mother who had asserted her rights (Fig. 2.1) as well as the father from whom her duchy of Brittany accrued.[13] Alone, (until recent catastrophe) the mother-daughter pair continued to command over the damaged west window of the cathedral of Nantes, dated to the period when Anne lavishly transferred Marguerite's remains from there to the Carmelite convent upon finalization of the tomb in 1507.[14] When its chief sculptor Michel Colombe carved his Janus-like self-portrait on the reverse of the youthful *Allegory of Prudence* (Fig. 2.2), symbolizing an ancient male past, he gave added importance to the political virtue placed near the head of the wise mother whose success Anne unceasingly labored to repeat.[15] By then, she was fully engaged in a battle over her duchy with Louis XII, the father of her extant progeny, and her second royal consort who coveted her territory no less than her first, Charles VIII. Like Marguerite d'Autriche, Louise de Savoie was insistently claiming the same political virtue for herself and her daughter Marguerite, too.[16] Understanding that Claude and Renée's future paths would be daunting, Anne shouldered a support team with the responsibility of ensuring her daughters' political and religious fortitude (another virtue on the Nantes tomb). A highly competent household, and

[12] Geneva, Bibliothèque de Genève, ms. fr. 131. Jean-Christophe Cassard, "L'histoire en renfort de la diplomatie: la Genealogie des roys, ducs et princes de Bretaigne de Pierre Le Baud (1486)," *Mémoires de la Société d'histoire et d'archéologie de Bretagne*, 62 (1985): 67–95.

[13] Jean-Marie Guillouët, "Michel Colombe," and fig. 51: "Deux Vertus...," in *Tours 1500 Capitale des arts*, exh. cat. Tours, musée des Beaux-Arts, ed. Béatrice de Chancel-Bardelot et al. (Paris: Somogy, 2012), 186, 216; and "Les ducs de Bretagne et le couvent des Carmes de Nantes," in *Le Cœur d'Anne de Bretagne*, ed. Laure Barthet and Camille Broucke, exh. cat. château de Châteaubriant (Milan: SilvanaEditoriale, 2014), 67–69.

[14] Françoise Gatouillat, "Une grande commande de la reine Anne de Bretagne: la verrière occidentale de la cathédrale Saint-Pierre de Nantes," in *Nantes flamboyante (1380–1530)*, ed. Faucherre and Guillouët, 158–159.

[15] On this virtue singled out by Christine de Pisan in her *Le Livre de Prudence*, see *La Vertu de prudence entre Moyen Âge et âge classique*, ed. Evelyne Berriot-Salvadore, Catherine Pascal, François Roudaut and Trung Tran (Paris: Classiques Garnier, 2012), especially Nathalie Dauvois's chapter "Prudence et politique chez les grands rhétoriqueurs: Janus bifrons," 55–71.

[16] Tracy Adams, "Louise de Savoie, la prudence et la formation des femmes diplomates vers 1500," in *Louise de Savoie*, 29–38; Mary Beth Winn and Kathleen Wilson-Chevalier, "Louise de Savoie, ses livres, sa bibliothèque," 239-240; Charlotte Bonnet, "Louise de Savoie et François Demoulins de Rochefort," 254–255.

Fig. 2.1   Jean Perréal, Michel Colombe, and Girolamo Paciarotti. "Marguerite de Foix, duchesse de Bretagne and her coat of arms," Tomb of the Duke and the Duchess of Brittany. Nantes, Cathedral, completed 1507. (Photos: Kathleen Wilson-Chevalier)

Fig. 2.2   Michel Colombe. "Allegory of Prudence," Tomb of the Duke and the Duchess of Brittany. Nantes, Cathedral, completed 1507. (Photos: Kathleen Wilson-Chevalier)

staunch allies, stood forward to continue her fight to empower her daughters beyond death.[17] Importantly, even the path toward Renée's heterodox court had been traced.

THE POWER OF A PROACTIVE HOUSEHOLD

In January 1499, Anne's marriage contract with King Louis XII adroitly reasserted her control over Brittany.[18] Ten months later, Claude, her first viable daughter, was born. Despite the princess's public engagement in 1506 to the heir apparent François de Valois/Angoulême, the conflicting marital strategies of her parents, centered around the transmission of the Breton duchy, remained unresolved at Anne's death. Their tug-of-war reached its peak in 1505, when Anne abandoned the Loire Valley and regained her duchy in a huff. A flurry of letters ensued, most penned by her faithful financial officer Jacques de Beaune, already by her side at the marriage contract signature, and Anne's young wardrobe mistress, secretary, and confidante Michelle de Saubonne.[19] After these able servants negotiated Anne's return to Louis's court with the king and François's mother Louise, the political, cultural, and religious role of Michelle, Madame de Soubise from 1506,[20] only grew. Simultaneously, Anne's temporal and spiritual interests were increasingly intertwined with de Beaune's extensive clan.[21] The queen/duchess had built a strong support network that was henceforth neatly braided into her own and her daughters' fates.

[17] On her court and that of Claude, Monique Chatenet, *La Cour de France au XVIᵉ siècle. Vie sociale et architecture* (Paris: Picard, 2002), and Caroline zum Kolk, "The Household of the Queen of France in the Sixteenth Century," *The Court Historian* 14, no. 1 (June 2009): 3-22.

[18] Michel Nassiet, "Les traités de mariage d'Anne de Bretagne," in *Pour en finir avec Anne de Bretagne?*, ed. Dominique Le Page (Nantes: Conseil général de Loire-Atlantique, 2004), 74-81, and "Anne de Bretagne," 165-166.

[19] Alfred Spont, *Semblançay (?-1527): la bourgeoisie financière au début du XVIᵉ siècle* (Paris: Librairie Hachette & Cⁱᵉ, 1895), 76 and 85-100; Pauline Matarasso, "Seen through a squint: the letters of Jacques de Beaune to Michelle de Saubonne. June to September 1505," *Renaissance Studies*, 11, no. 4 (1997): 343-357.

[20] Spont, *Semblançay*, 88n2; 1507 for Jacques Santrot, *Les doubles funérailles d'Anne de Bretagne, reine et duchesse (9 janvier-19 mars 1514)* (Rennes: Presses universitaires de Rennes, 2014), 592.

[21] Spont, *Semblançay*, 75-76; Bernard Chevalier, "Tours en 1500, une capitale inachevée," in *Tours 1500*, 32-34.

Anne's 1499 marriage contract stipulated that her "nearest and true heirs" would succeed her, even foreseeing the eventual inheritance of her duchy by her second child, male or female: so Renée.[22] From January 9 to March 23, 1514, double funerals—the most elaborate ever to celebrate a French queen—prolonged the unequal royal/ducal tug-of-war over her intention to perpetuate an independent Breton line.[23] Anne's household first participated in the grandiose processions that accompanied her body to the royal abbey of Saint-Denis, and then, no longer accompanied by the royal court, transported the sovereign duchess's heart to the Carmes in Nantes. Her fine cardiotaph was interred between her parents' bodies in the underground vault, where Anne had discretely placed Duchess Marguerite on Duke François's heraldic right. Louis XII proceeded to transfer Anne's parents' hearts to the Orléans chapel in Paris[24]—a counter move that signaled his determination to strip control of Brittany from his daughter the future queen and his "treschere et tresamee fille Renee" (as he referred to her on October 25, 1510, the day she was born).[25] In July 1514, upon the death of Chancellor Philippe de Montauban, who had conveyed Anne's heart to Brittany, Louis suppressed the Breton chancellery, which Anne had immediately reinstated when her first spouse died. Then, on Renée's fourth birthday October 25, 1514, he handed the administration of the duchy over to heir apparent François.[26] Prudent Anne had envisioned inimical assaults, and sometime in 1514 her household launched a remarkable communication campaign. Today, nearly forty illuminated manuscripts subsist in two different versions, all with textual and pictorial variations:[27] mostly Pierre Choque's *Commemoracion et advertissement de la mort de la très chrétienne et souveraine dame, madame Anne, deux fois reine de France, duchesse de Bretagne*, but the *Trespas de l'hermine regrettée* too.[28] Among the recipients designated as spiritual kin,

---

[22] Nassiet, "Les Traités de mariage," 75-76.

[23] Santrot, *Doubles Funérailles*.

[24] Santrot, *Doubles Funérailles*, 195.

[25] From the king's *lettres patentes:* Matarasso, *Le Baptême*, 5.

[26] Dominique Le Page, *Finances et politique en Bretagne au début des temps modernes, 1491-1547* (Vincennes: Institut de la gestion publique et du développement économique, 1997), 28-29; Dominique Le Page and Michel Nassiet, *L'Union de la Bretagne à la France* (Morlaix: Éditions Skol Vreizh, 2003), 147 (assuming Claude's weakness and consent).

[27] Santrot, *Doubles Funérailles*, 285-458.

[28] Also Pierre-Gilles Girault, *Les funérailles d'Anne de Bretagne, reine de France. L'Hermine regrettée* (Montreuil: Gourcuff Gradenigo, 2014); Elizabeth A. R. Brown, Cynthia J. Brown

two were foreign queens, Catherine of Aragon (probably)[29] and Catherine de Foix/Navarre[30]; at least four copies relate to the Bourbon clan, then headed by Renée's godmother the duchess of Bourbon Anne de France and the dowager duchess of Bourbon-Vendôme Marie de Luxembourg.[31] "Dame royalle," Louise de Savoie received her tardy copy only once she had become "Mère du roy."[32]

Several of the numerous extant miniatures open a fascinating window onto the multifaceted heritage that Anne bestowed upon her daughters. The sole dedicatory image (Fig. 2.3), that of Claude's personal copy of the *Commemoracion*,[33] squarely positions Anne's heiresses at the very core of this posthumous maneuver. Her herald Pierre Choque, shown with two companions bearing the queen's arms, offers Claude his account of the funeral ceremonies from which the royal family was proscribed. Below, the first line of text insists on her status as the "daughter of a king, a queen, and a duchess," while above, the gold sacralizing canopy and the fleur-de-lis insist on her unsurpassable royal rank (higher than her consort's, in fact). The rather generic women in mourning could possibly foreground great ladies of the court, including Renée's godmother, paying homage to the *filles de France*. Yet the six female mourners are almost certainly the leading *dames* and *damoiselles* of the queen's household, highlighted by both text and subsequent miniatures, and charged, alongside her male "servants," with the continuity of Anne's female line. To Claude's lower right, the matron could well be the first woman mentioned in the

and Jean-Luc Deuffic, "Qu'il mecte ma povre ame en celeste lumiere," *Les funérailles d'une reine Anne de Bretagne (1514)* (Turnhout: Brepols, 2013).

[29] Alternatively, Henry VIII's sister Margaret Tudor, Queen of Scotland ("Noble royne, fille et femme de roy."), Santrot, *Doubles Funérailles*, 292-293. Anne is designated as "Vostre parente, [t]ante et prochainne parente": Brussels, Bibliothèque royale Albert Iᵉʳ, ms. IV.521.

[30] "Noble dame yssue de Foueix, royalle lignee… / Vostre parente en qui est le renom" (Paris, BnF, ms. fr. 5095). Santrot, *Doubles Funérailles*, 292-293.

[31] The future constable Charles de Bourbon (not Santrot's identification), "Vostre parente" (Paris, BnF, ms. fr. 5096); Marie de Luxembourg, dowager duchess of Bourbon-Vendôme (Paris, Arsenal 5224) ["Perdu avez la grant royne et duchesse / Vostre cousine…"] and Renée de Bourbon, abbess of Fontevraud "vostre bonne cousine" (Paris, BnF 5100); and an unspecified "Noble dame yssue de Bourbon, royalle lignee … vostre bonne cousine" (Nantes, Bibliothèque municipale, coll. Lajarriette, ms. 653). Santrot, *Doubles Funérailles*, 287-288, 290, 295.

[32] "Vostre parente": Paris, BnF, ms. fr. 5094. Two other Savoie recipients were "cousins" Duke Charles II de Savoie and Louise's half-brother René. Santrot, *Doubles Funérailles*, 293 and 300.

[33] Paris, BnF, ms. fr. 25158, fol. 3v.

Fig. 2.3 Maître des Entrées parisiennes (Jean Coene IV?). "Pierre Choque Offering His *Commemoracion* to Claude de France." Paris, Bibliothèque nationale de France, MS. Français 25158, fol. 3v. Source: BnF

narration of the ceremonies, the "dame d'honneur de la noble royne," Jacqueline d'Astarac, dame de Mailly.[34] It was the latter's husband, the king's ambassador to Savoy Antoine de Mailly, who produced the divine sign said to announce the moment of Anne's death—one of the standard illustrations in these manuscripts, tasked with broadcasting the miraculous status of a blessed queen.[35] Slightly above Claude, to her left, appears her three-year-old sister Renée, not yet old enough for mourning dress it would seem. The little princess is depicted gesturing toward a lady who in turn, she too from above, gestures back to her: most credibly Madame "de Soubize" [Soubise], the woman cited directly after Madame de Mailly. Surrounded by a cluster of court ladies dressed in black, and perhaps two of the men of learning who contributed epitaphs to these volumes, Michelle de Saubonne figures as the eminence grise of the now motherless princesses. The preceptor of her famed granddaughter Catherine de Parthenay later recounted that shortly before Anne's death, the queen had made de Soubise the surrogate mother of Renée.[36] Hagiographic though the text and its editor may be, Renée's tight bond to one of her mother's most trusted ladies is beyond the shadow of a doubt. The moment illustrated in this miniature becomes a fundamental one in the narrative of Renée's life which, from a pictorial point of view, begins here. Michelle would be exiled from the royal court in July 1518, three and a half years into Claude's queenship, in the months following the birth of the dauphin, henceforth the heir to Brittany for François I and Louise.[37] The act surely reflects the pair's fear of Madame de Soubise's superior ability to defend the interests and moral values that her former mistress meant to transmit to the *gouverante*'s young protégée(s). What exactly were these?

[34] Santrot, *Doubles Funérailles*, 346 and figs. VI, VII, VIII, IX, X, XI.
[35] Santrot, *Doubles Funérailles*, 25-28, 514 and 566-567.
[36] Jules Bonnet, ed., *Mémoires de la vie de Jean de Parthenay-Larchevêque sieur de Soubise* (Paris: Léon Willem, 1879), 5-6.
[37] This date is justified below.

ANNE DE BRETAGNE AND PRELATES ENGAGED
IN RELIGIOUS REFORM

The Petit Palais version of the anonymous *Trespas de l'hermine regrettée* places emphasis on the religious side of the funeral ceremonies, with an insistence on sacred books.[38] Two of its magnificent vellum sheets picture Philippe de Luxembourg, the Bishop/Cardinal du Mans, in front of Notre-Dame de Paris as he receives Anne's catafalque.[39] The same power-ful prelate appears again at Saint-Denis (Fig. 2.4), where he buries Anne in the extraordinary cope she had gifted to the abbey—the most magnifi-cent it ever received.[40] Choque specifies that Louis XII chose the French monarchical burial site, so the queen's donation ensured the lasting visibil-ity of her Breton emblems on royal ground. The illumination gives promi-nence to the cope's ermine (associated in a number of these miniatures with royal and ducal crowns), an emblem that confounded Anne and Claude.

Anne is generally perceived as rigidly traditional in the realm of reli-gion. Is it possible that she and her direct entourage were actually favoring a learned, rejuvenated Church? The aging Philippe de Luxembourg was one of the earliest reforming bishop/cardinals of France. His promotion of the reform of Chazal-Benoît precedes that of the up-and-coming reforming bishop Guillaume Briçonnet the Younger (1470-1535).[41] Briçonnet, a nephew of Jacques de Beaune, had been Anne's almoner since 1496, and he rose to the status of first almoner in 1513.[42] In 1511, the queen/duchess and Philippe de Luxembourg had worked hand-in-hand to reconcile Louis XII and Pope Julius II during the Council of Pisa, where Briçonnet and his brother Denis were active alongside their father (long-attached to Anne), too.[43] Together with his mentor Jacques Lefèvre

---

[38] Paris, Petit Palais, coll. Dutuit, ms. 665; fol. 5v for the importance of books.

[39] Dutuit, ms. 655; fol. 27v and fol. 28r.

[40] Dutuit, ms. 655; fol. 36r.

[41] Jean-Marie Le Gall, *Les moines au temps des réformes: France, 1480-1560* (Seyssel: Champ Vallon, 2001), 39-40, 49, 101-102.

[42] Santrot, *Double funérailles*, 527.

[43] Sandrot, *Double funérailles*, 454-455. On Guillaume Briçonnet the Elder's tight relation with Anne, see Bernard Chevalier, *Guillaume Briçonnet (v.1445-1514). Un cardinal-ministre au début de la Renaissance* (Rennes: Presses Universitaires de Rennes, 2005), 172-175. On the Briçonnet brothers and Claude de France, Kathleen Wilson-Chevalier, "Denis Briçonnet et Claude de France: l'évêque, les arts et une relation (fabriste) occultée," in *Les Evêques, les*

Fig. 2.4 Jean Pichore. "Philippe de Luxembourg and Pierre Choque at the Burial of Anne de Bretagne at Saint-Denis," in the *Trespas de l'hermine regrettée*. Paris, Petit Palais, Musée des Beaux-Arts de la Ville de Paris, ms. Dutuit 665, fol. 36r. © IRHT-CNRS/Petit Palais

d'Étaples,[44] whom he had called to his side at Saint-Germain-des-Près in 1508, Guillaume Briçonnet the Younger led the reform of the abbey with the help of the king and the queen, whose confessor Geoffroy Boussard intervened in 1513. Driving Briçonnet and Lefèvre's action was an apocalyptic world view shared with the monks of Saint-Vincent du Mans, reformed by the Bishop/Cardinal du Mans in 1500.[45] Briconnet's religious stance was hence crystal clear when he officiated at Anne's last funeral mass on February 15, 1514, on the outskirts of Paris at Notre-Dame-des-Champs, just before her body was spectacularly welcomed by his ally the bishop/cardinal at Notre-Dame.

Philippe de Luxembourg's ties to Anne's successor Queen Claude are patent too. The young queen acted in favor of Church reform almost as soon as she rose to the throne. In 1516, Pope Leo X appointed Cardinal de Luxembourg papal legate charged with monastic reform, and Giles of Viterbo, who was in contact with Jacques Lefèvre d'Étaples, worked with her confessor Louis Chantereau to reform the recalcitrant Augustinians of Paris.[46] In August, Claude chose the elderly bishop/cardinal to officiate at her May 10, 1517, coronation at Saint-Denis (Fig. 2.5),[47] while Jacques de Beaune choreographed the ceremony. The occasion was again celebrated in manuscripts, illustrated by the "Master of the Paris Entries" workshop responsible for Claude's earlier frontispiece (Fig. 2.3). They repeatedly refer to Claude as "royne et duchesse," "femme de roy, fille aisnee de France et heritiere de Bretaigne" and specify that "Monsieur le Legat, cardinal du Mans" wore her mother's extraordinary ermine-laden

lettres et les arts, ed. Gary Ferguson and Catherine Magnien, *Seizième Siècle*, 11 (2015): 95-118.

[44] Chevalier, *Briçonnet*, 324-325, and Chevalier, "Tours en 1500," 34.

[45] Guy Bedouelle, *Lefèvre d'Étaples et l'Intelligence des Ecritures* (Geneva: Droz, 1976), 57-60; Guy-Marie Oury, *Histoire religieuse de la Touraine* (Tours: CLD Normand & Cie., 1975), 153; Le Gall, *Les Moines*, 77, 143, 199.

[46] Sheila M. Porrer, *Jacques Lefèvre d'Étaples and The Three Maries Debates* (Geneva: Droz, 2009), 26; Bernard Barbiche and Ségolène de Dainville-Barbiche, "Les légats *a latere* en France et leurs facultés aux XVIᵉ et XVIIᵉ siècles," in *Archivum Historiae Pontificiae*, Vol. 23 (1985): 100; Kathleen Wilson-Chevalier, "Claude de France and the Spaces of Agency of a Marginalized Queen," in *Women and Power at the French Court, 1483-1563*, ed. Susan Broomhall (Amsterdam: Amsterdam University Press, 2018), 155-161.

[47] Paris, BnF, ms. fr. 5750, fol. 19v. One of six extant manuscripts discussed in Myra D. Orth, *Renaissance Manuscripts: The Sixteenth Century* (London & Turnhout: Harvey Miller Publishers, 2015), II, fig. 19, 88-91; on the heraldic double crown, Santrot, *Doubles Funérailles*, 155.

Fig. 2.5 Maître des Entrées parisiennes (Jean Coene IV?). "Philippe de Luxembourg Officiating at Claude de France's Coronation Mass." Paris, Bibliothèque nationale de France, MS. 5750, fol. 19v. Source: BnF

cope as he performed mass.[48] At this point in time, before Luther's impact revolutionized the parameters of religious change, major emphasis was placed on exemplary bishops as leaders of Church reform. The queen's "masterpiece" Morgan Library prayer book is replete with meritorious prelates in the image of Philippe de Luxembourg (and Guillaume and Denis Briçonnet), for whom the literacy of the priesthood was a primary concern; and it cannot be coincidental that the volume foregrounds St. Claude (fol. 35v and fol. 36r), soon followed by St. Julian of Le Mans (fol. 39r), who is then directly followed by St. René (fol. 39v), all three associated with books. This unique, highly personal girdle book, worn around the queen's waist, is generally dated near the time of Claude's coronation,[49] and God places a crown on the head of the pious Virgin of the Assumption (fol. 23v). Like the Virgin at the moment of her coronation (fol. 24r), these saintly figures shine with the light of Christ that Lefèvre d'Étaples considered to illuminate his *Commentaire des épîtres de Paul*, completed in the prophetic climate of reform at Saint-Germain-des-Près. The uncommon prayer accompanying these images of the crowned Virgin concludes with an invocation to "protect the petitioner [the queen] 'against all enemies.'"[50] From which flank might threats have come?

QUEEN/DUCHESS ANNE, MADAME DE SOUBISE, AND THEIR DAUGHTERS

In 1528, François I acknowledged in writing the services that Madame de Soubise (†1549) had rendered to Queen Anne, the deceased Queen Claude, and Renée (whose birth Michelle accompanied and in whose name she intervened after Anne's death).[51] Anne's daughters' households

---

[48] Cynthia J. Brown, *Pierre Gringore. Les Entrées royales à Paris de Marie d'Angleterre (1514) à Claude de France (1517)* (Geneva: Droz, 2005), 279, 282-285 (transcribed from Paris, BnF, ms. fr. 5750).

[49] New York, ML MS M.1166. Roger S. Wieck and Cynthia J. Brown, *The Prayer Book of Claude de France. MS M.1166. The Pierpont Morgan Library, New York* (Luzern: Quaternio Verlag, 2010), 175, 190-193. Maxence Hermant, "Le Maître de Claude de France," in *Tours 1500*, 263-267, and Eberhard König, *The Book of Hours of Claude de France* (Ramsen: Heribert Tenschert, 2012), 16-26, on prayer books as girdle books.

[50] Wieck and Brown, *Prayer Book*, 213.

[51] Marcel Giraud-Mangin, "Michelle de Saubonne. Dame d'atour d'Anne de Bretagne," *Mémoires de la Société d'histoire et d'archéologie de Bretagne*, 16 (1946): 85: "[...] en considération des bons et agréables services qu'elle a faits, tant à la reine Anne qu'à la feue reine Claude et qu'elle fera à Mme Renée," citing an archival act dated September 14, 1528.

were interlocked at the end of her life, their shared accounts overseen by Jacques de Beaune's son Guillaume, their mother's most direct financial officer since 1491, dispatched to Genoa shortly after Claude's birth to select the marble for the Nantes tomb.[52] Historians have misdated the moment Louise de Savoie and her son ousted Madame de Soubise from court.[53] Three epistles enacting her disgrace were dispatched from Angers. In the king's mother's missive, Louise enquires about [her grandchildren] "monseigneur le daulphin et mes petites filles."[54] The hostile dismissal thus took place in 1518, not 1515, during a royal progress to Brittany, the duchy surely at the core of this concerted move, and Michelle's dismissal but one of a litany of curbs on Claude's power effected by François and Louise. It follows, though, that Madame de Soubise was by Renée's side uninterruptedly for nearly the first eight years of her life. The attempt of "Madame la régente" [Louise] to impose the precedence of her own daughter Marguerite over "Madame Renée" may be related to Michelle's continued championing of Anne's daughters at the time of Claude's belated coronation.[55] Prior to her departure, Michelle replied to Louise (July 11, 1518), mentioning Jacques de Beaune as a witness to the truth of her assertions and specifying that she would leave court with her mother-in-law and "her daughter." She had three daughters, however; and her eldest, Anne de Parthenay (at most three years older than Renée),[56] figures as one of Claude's ladies-in-waiting in 1523.[57] Did Anne help negotiate her mother's return to court four years after Claude's death, when Renée hinged her acceptance of a marriage to the future duke of Ferrara on permission that her former mentor be allowed to re-integrate her household? Madame de Soubise figured as Renée's official lady of honor in Ferrara in 1529, her daughters Charlotte and Renée the first

---

[52] Paris, BnF, Clairambault 835, fol. 2025-2030; Santrot, *Double Funérailles*, 517-518, 592; Guillouët, in *Tours 1500*, 216, citing Flaminia Bardati for his identification with "Guillaume Bonino."

[53] Beginning with Bonnet, *Mémoires*, 6n2; Matarasso, *Le Baptême*, 74-76.

[54] Giraud-Mangin, "Michelle de Saubonne," 82, citing copies of five letters preserved at the castle of Blain (now with the other letters at the Médiathèque Louis Aragon in Nantes); Matarasso, "Seen through a squint."

[55] Bonnet, *Mémoires*, 6.

[56] V.-M. Saulnier and Rosanna Gorris "Anne de Parthenay," in *Dictionnaire des lettres françaises. Le XVIe siècle*, ed. George Grente (Paris: Fayard, 2001), 908.

[57] BnF, ms. fr. nouv. ac. 9175, fol. 367-370.

ladies-in-waiting listed in the duchess's retinue.[58] Clément Marot's Ferrarese epistle to Michelle, contemporaneous to his epistles and epigrams for her daughters Anne and Renée, attests to his long trajectory by Madame de Soubise's side.[59]

Until at least mid-1518, Madame de Soubise's protection of humanists had long-term effects on the combined education of the royal princesses and her own daughters. Remarkably, the earliest, and two of the only three extant (religious) primers made for princes and princesses in Renaissance France, are those of Claude, no later than 1506, and of Renée, no later than 1517, the second written in the highly legible humanistic script of Claude's prayer book and book of hours.[60] The poet Clément Marot credited Madame de Soubise with having introduced his father Jean Marot to court.[61] The elder Marot produced some of his most important texts for Anne, beginning with his *Vraye disant advocate des dames* in 1506,[62] the year the empowerment of Claude catapulted to the top of her mother's agenda. Jean Pichore was simultaneously completing his illustrations of Antoine Dufour's *Vies des femmes célèbres* for Anne. Though written in male voices, both volumes placed a great number of famed women before female eyes.[63] During their formative years, even before they could read, both of Anne's daughters, and the Parthenay sisters, would have been able to view therein a large number of heroines, both good and bad: learned in

---

[58] Paris, BnF, Clairambault 835, fol. 2047. My thanks to Caroline zum Kolk for her assistance with these documents.

[59] See Guillaume Berthon's Chap. 5 in this volume.

[60] Maxence Hermant, "L'héritage d'Anne de Bretagne et Claude de France," in *Trésors royaux La bibliothèque de François Iᵉʳ*, ed. by Maxence Hermant (Rennes: Presses Universitaires de Rennes, 2015), 226, n° 108. For Claude's, see Roger S. Wieck, Cynthia J. Brown and Eberhard König, *The Primer of Claude de France. MS 159, The Fitzwilliam Museum, Cambridge. Commentary to the Facsimile Edition* (Luzern: Quaternio Verlag, 2012); for Renée's, see Wieck's chapter in this volume.

[61] Georges Guiffrey, ed., *Clément Marot. Œuvres* (Geneva: Slatkine Reprints, 1969), *Epistres*, III, 388; Guillaume Berthon, *L'Intention du poète Clément Marot "autheur"* (Paris: Classiques Garnier, 2014), 46, n. 4.

[62] Cynthia J. Brown, *The Queen's Library: Image-making at the court of Anne of Brittany, 1477-1514* (Philadelphia: University of Pennsylvania Press, 2011), 166-180, with additional examples.

[63] Nantes, musée Dobrée, ms. 17. Sophie Cassagnes-Brouquet, *Un manuscrit d'Anne de Bretagne. Les* Vies des femmes célèbres *d'Antoine Dufour* (Rennes: Éditions Ouest-France, 2007); Anneliese Pollock Renck, "Les Vies des Femmes Célèbres: Antoine Dufour, Jean Pichore, and a Manuscript's Debt to an Italian Printed Book," *The Journal of the Early Book Society*, 18 (2015): 158-180.

Greek and Latin like Nicostrata, credited with the invention of many of the Latin characters (fol. 21v); treacherous like Athalia, capable of killing her own offspring (fol. 27v); outspoken like Hortensia, shown announcing to the Triumvirate that women without representation will not finance their wars (fol. 44r). In keeping with the spirit of the *Enseignements* that Renée's godmother Anne de France was penning for her daughter Suzanne de Bourbon,[64] Anne de Bretagne and her confidante knew that discernment was a crucial tool for staying afloat in the perilous waters of court life. Hence an alignment of Amazon queens and queens as Amazons (Marpesia, Orithyia, Penthesilea, Semiramis, Thomyris, and Zenobia to name but a few) braced ladies and *damoiselles*, including Queen Anne's and Michelle's daughters, for their battles in and between courtly power centers. Minerva (fol. 11v), the goddess of Wisdom (often associated with Janus and Prudence),[65] was fittingly cast in the androgynous Amazonian mold.

CLAUDE, RENÉE, AND MARGUERITE D'ALENÇON/NAVARRE: A DURABLE SPIRITUAL BOND

Continuity colored the humanist program initially fostered at Anne's court, and Jean Marot seems to have composed a series of works, finished or unfinished, for Claude.[66] Then in his *Temple de Cupido*, plausibly sometime between 1516 and 1519, his son Clément identified himself as "Facteur de la Royne" [Claude]; and he may well have intended for her his *Espitre de Maguelonne*.[67] If Clément's poetry was shaped under the

---

[64] On the ritualized "emotional performance" that the two Annes shared: Tracy Adams, "Rivals or Friends?: Anne de Bourbon and Anne de Bretagne," *Women in French Studies*, Special Issue (2010): 46-61. On the Machiavellian edge to Anne de France's writings: Rohr, "Rocking the Cradle."

[65] Dauvois, "Prudence et politique," 62-71.

[66] Published in 1533 or 1534 as the *Recueil Jehan Marot*: Ellen Delvallée, "Le Recueil Jehan Marot: un manuscrit inachevé et perdu édité par Clément?" *Ad Hoc* 6 (2017) https://adhoc.hypotheses.org/presentation-de-la-revue-ad-hoc

[67] Berthon, *L'Intention*, 49-59 and 93-94, Mary McKinley, "Marot, Marguerite de Navarre et 'l'Epistre du despourveu," in *Clément Marot "Prince des poëtes françois" 1496-1996*, ed. Gérard Defaux and Michel Simonin (Paris: Honoré Champion, 1997), 620-621, identifies "Ferme Amour"/Claude as a female patron willing to take the poet into her service (at an earlier date). My thanks to Kelly Peebles for this reference. On the *Maguelonne* text, differently, Richard Cooper, "Picturing Marot," in *Book and Text in*

influence of the circle of Meaux,[68] the budding author neatly fit into the nascent evangelical clusters orbiting around the late Queen Anne, Madame de Soubise, and then Claude and Renée. Logically too, as courtly dynamics evolved, the younger Marot addressed his *Epistre du despourveu* to Marguerite d'Alençon (later Navarre), seemingly encouraged by his father to seek entry into the duchess's service around 1519.[69] Marguerite's tight bond to Claude has been of scarce interest to historians, often dismissive of the short-lived queen. Yet together, Queen Claude and her sister-in-law—and even Marguerite's mother Louise de Savoie, until politics prevailed—had been promoting religious reform since early in the new reign.[70]

Following Claude's premature death in 1524, both Jean and Clément Marot composed texts in her honor[71]; and Guillaume Briçonnet's renowned correspondence with Marguerite d'Alençon addressed the latter's deep grief.[72] Less known is the Erasmian Antonio Brucioli's account of Battista della Palla sighting a distressed Marguerite mourning Claude in the cathedral of Lyon (which bore a heavy Bourbon mark). The encounter spawns an imaginary dialogue over bodily resurrection between the deceased queen and Marguerite, in which Claude recalls her friendship, concord and very tight kinship with Marguerite, based on shared divine

France, 1400–1600: Poetry on the Page, ed. Adrian Armstrong and Malcolm Quainton (Aldershot: Ashgate, 2006), 53-71.

[68] Jonathan A. Reid, *King's Sister—Queen of Dissent. Marguerite of Navarre (1492-1549) and Her Evangelical Network* (Leiden and Boston: Brill, 2009), I, 73n81; Dick Wursten, *Clément Marot and Religion. A Reassessment in the Light of his Psalm Paraphrases* (Leiden and Boston: Brill, 2010), 7-21.

[69] McKinley, "Marot."

[70] Wilson-Chevalier, "Denis Briçonnet" and "Quelle 'trinité royale'? Reine, roi, régente et sœur de roi: Claude de France, François Ier, Louise de Savoie et Marguerite de Navarre," in *"La dame de cœur." Le patronage religieux des reines et des princesses XIIIe-XVIIe siècle*, ed. Murielle Gaude-Ferragu and Cécile Vincent-Cassy (Rennes: Presses Universitaires de Rennes, 2016), 123-136; Benoist Pierre, "L'entourage religieux et la religion de Louise de Savoie," in *Louise de Savoie*, 117-141; duplicating the misattribution of the dedication of Louis Chantereau's *La Vie et les miracles de saincte Véronique* to Louise, not Claude, 126.

[71] *Les Deux Recueils*, ed. Gérard Defaux and Thierry Mantovani (Geneva: Droz, 1999), 227-230, for Jean Marot's *Deploration de la feue Royne Claude de France* and *Epitaffe de la feue Royne Claude de France*; and Gérard Defaux, *Clémént Marot. Œuvres poétiques complètes* (Paris: Bordas, 1990), I, 371, for Clement's *De la Royne Claude*.

[72] *Guillaume Briçonnet and Marguerite d'Angoulême. Correspondance 1521-1524*, ed. Christine Martineau and Michel Veissiere (Geneva: Droz, 1979), II, 144.

and human beliefs.[73] The Italian's presentation of an apocalyptic discourse uttered by Claude, attuned to her interaction with the reforming circle around Arcangela Panigarola in Milan in 1518, may have inspired Marguerite's first literary work, her *Dialogue en forme de vision nocturne*.[74] The text, revolving around the death of Claude's daughter Charlotte, who quickly followed her mother to the tomb, can be related to a drawing of the effigies of mother and daughter on their mortuary bed (Fig. 2.6).

The accompanying Latin and French epitaphs have been attributed to the Italian humanist Théocrène (Benedetto Tagliacarne), tutor to at least some of the children, and a secretary of the king and queen of Navarre, Étienne Clavier, both of whom were in contact with Marot.[75] As for Brucioli, after this initial text conjoining Claude and Marguerite, he dedicated works to François I (1532), Marguerite (1534 and 1536), whom he never actually met, and finally Renée (1538), who extended her protection to the Nicodemite over a series of years.[76] At the end of her life Renée joined this evangelical chorus, recalling the impact of her older sister's death, experienced as God's punishing his children and suffered to the extreme: "Jay de la divinité du bon père celleste entremeles des chatimens envers les enfans quil aime me rendit poupille des lenfence ensuyvit encores le décès de la Royne Claude Madame et seure aynee que Je senti Jusques a extremité" (I have received from the divinity of the good celestial father the mixed punishments of the children that he loves, rendering me a ward

---

[73] Richard Cooper, "Marguerite de Navarre et la réforme italienne," in *Marguerite de Navarre 1492-1992*, ed. Nicole Cazauran and James Dauphiné (Paris: Eurédit, 2006), I, 163-165, citing a particularly significant passage from Brucioli's *Dialoghi* published in 1526 (and 1529): "Strettissima parente, et charissima et fedele et compagna, con laquale in somma concordia, del medesimo parere delle divine et humane cose, vivuta sempre sono, essendo uno et il medesimo animo stato sempre di ambidue, come se l'una nell'altra vivesse" (fol. 47v).

[74] Cooper, "Marguerite de Navarre et la réforme italienne," 164-165. Wilson-Chevalier, "Denis Briçonnet," for Claude and Panigarola.

[75] Rémi Jimenes, ed., *Geoffroy Tory de Bourges libraire et imprimeur humaniste (1480-1533)* (Tours: Presses Universitaires François-Rabelais, 2019), 131, fig. 25; Girault, *Les Funérailles*, 55; Pierre Jourda, "Un humaniste italien en France: Theocrenus (1480-1536)," *Revue du Seizième siècle*, 16 (1929): 40-57.

[76] Cooper, "Marguerite de Navarre," I, 169-173; Eleonora Belligni, *Renata di Francia (1510-1575). Un eresia di corte* (Turin: UTET Libreria, 2011), 185 and 156.

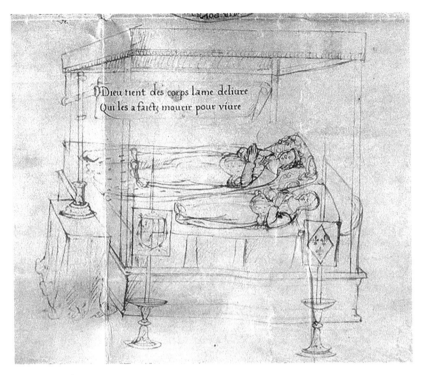

Fig. 2.6 Étienne Clavier? "Epitaphs and the Gisants of Queen Claude de France and Charlotte de France on Their Deathbed." ©Bibliothèques d'Agglopolys, Communauté d'Agglomération de Blois, Ms 245

from infancy, also followed by the death of Queen Madame Claude my older sister which affected me to the extreme).[77]

Returning to Madame de Soubise, it was she who in 1512 incited Anne de Bretagne to employ Jean Lemaire de Belges as her secretary and historiographer, and that very year he began dedicating works to Claude, or Anne and Claude.[78] In honor of her mother's obsequies he went on to

[77] From one of the many iterations of Renée's testament; Fontana, *Renata di Francia*, III, 324.
[78] Cynthia J. Brown, "Like Mother, Like Daughter: The Blurring of Royal Imagery in Books for Anne de Bretagne and Claude de France," in *Cultural and Political Legacy*, 105-108, 113-114; Santrot, *Doubles Funérailles*, 561-562; Delvallée, "Le Recueil" for Lemaire's influence on Marot father and son.

offer his earlier treatise on ancient and modern funeral ceremonies to "Madame Claude premiere fille de france et de bretaigne."[79] Did Michelle, whose wisdom and political acumen were supposedly lauded by Guillaume Budé,[80] also introduce to the queen/duchess the Hellenist Germain de Brie, who had rubbed shoulders with Erasmus in Venice in 1508 and who corresponded at length with both Erasmus and Budé?[81] Two years before supplying funeral epitaphs to Pierre Choque, de Brie offered Anne a Latin poem on the sinking of her fine vessel the *Cordelière*, published in January 1513, then translated into French by the aforementioned Pierre Choque for Anne.[82] Choque addressed to Claude after her rise to the throne a version of the manuscript with new poems, written in the fine humanistic script of her religious books, again a sign of the humanist culture in which Anne and Michelle's young daughters bathed.[83] The dedicatory page stages a crowned queen/duchess of Brittany (Fig. 2.7). Heavy emphasis is placed on the virtue of Justice: the word is spelled out, and both the queen and the allegorical rendition extend a raised sword with a not-quite-visible tip (echoing *Justice*'s intentionally blunted sword on the Nantes tomb).[84] Choque's *Incendie de la Cordelière* dedication is to "dame Claude Royne de france *et duchesse de Bretaigne*" [my emphasis] (fol. 4r). Between his act of translation (before January 9, 1514) and the fabrication of this manuscript (after January 1, 1515), Louis XII made François de Valois/

---

[79] *Jean Lemaire de Belges Œuvres*, ed. Jean-Auguste Stecher (Geneva: Slatkine Reprints, 1969), 270-292; Santrot, *Doubles Funérailles*, 104-105.

[80] Bonnet, *Mémoires*, V, citing her granddaughter Catherine de Parthenay.

[81] Marie Madeleine de la Garanderie, "Les épitaphes latines d'Anne de Bretagne, par Germain de Brie," *Annales de Bretagne*, 74, no. 3 (1967): 390-394.

[82] On the vessel, Max Guérout, "A quoi ressemble la nef la Cordelière?," in *Anne de Bretagne. Une histoire, un mythe*, ed. Didier Le Fur (Paris: Somogy, 2007), 104-111; on the poem, De la Garanderie, "Les épitaphes," 389. Paris, BnF ms. fr. 1672, for an early version; *Humbert de Montmoret, Germain de Brie, Pierre Choque, L'incendie de* La Cordelière, ed. Sandra Provini (La Rochelle: Rumeur des Ages, 2004); Michael Jones, "Les manuscrits d'Anne de Bretagne Reine de France, Duchesse de Bretagne," *Mémoires de la Société d'Histoire et d'Archéologie de Bretagne*, 60 (1978): 612n88; Brown, "Like Mother," 109-111.

[83] Now Paris, BnF, NAF 28882: "Ce present traicte par moy desdiee a vostre sacree mère me confiant a vostre clemence vous presente" (fol. 4v).

[84] Kathleen Wilson-Chevalier, "Claude de France: Justice, Power & the Queen as Advocate for Her People," in *Textual and Visual Representations of Power & Justice in Medieval France. Manuscripts and Early Printed Books*, ed. Rosalind Brown-Grant, Anne D. Hedeman, and Bernard Ribémont (Burlington, VT: Ashgate, 2015), 243, figs. 11.1-11.2.

Fig. 2.7 Maître de la Chronique scandaleuse? "Pierre Choque Presenting His *Incendie de la Cordelière to a Duchess/Queen.*" Paris, Bibliothèque nationale de France, MS. Français 28882, fol. 5r. Source: BnF

Angoulême administrator of the Breton duchy, diminishing the power of the scepter here relegated to the queen/duchess's left hand.

The period around Claude's coronation seems to have been particularly portentous. A double page in her miniscule prayer book (Fig. 2.8) highlights her Breton roots via her mother's favored St. Ursula,[85] represented in front of the maritime empire foregrounded in de Brie and Choque's texts. Ursula's pious (and literate) court of maidens was probably conceived around 1517, also possibly the date of Claude's Book of Hours with its crowned Cs, which includes not only Latin mottoes but, rather precociously, Greek ones too.[86] The year 1517 is also presented as a turning point in the career of Louise de Savoie's almoner François Demoulins: he had begun corresponding with Erasmus, sought a French translation of his *In Praise of Folly*, and introduced Guillaume Budé to the king.[87] At Louise's request, he was preparing a magnificent manuscript, the *Vie de la belle et clere Magdalene* (Paris, BnF, ms. fr. 24955), in humanistic script, it too replete with Latin and Greek. To this end, he consulted with the evangelical scholar Lefèvre d'Étaples who, around the time of Claude's coronation, dedicated to François I his controversial treatise on Mary Magdalen. Further editions were addressed to Demoulins (1518) and Denis Briçonnet (1519).[88]

Was Madame de Soubise's disgrace sealed in Autumn 1517, around the royal contestation of Renée's hierarchical precedence at her sister's coronation? On October 11, a month before this regal ceremony placed the scepter of power back in the queen's dexter hand (Fig. 2.5), François I reinforced the status of his sister Marguerite, Duchess of Alençon, bestowing on her person the duchy of Berry.[89] Sometime thereafter, Marguerite received a manuscript constructed around a musical mass, *La Messe de Sainte Anne*, composed to encourage the realm to pray to the traditional

---

[85] A fleet already plays an important role in the depiction of St. Ursula in the prayer book of the ill-fated Charles-Orland, no later than 1495 (Morgan Library, MS M50, fol. 17v). In Jean Bourdichon's *Grandes Heures d'Anne de Bretagne* (Paris, BnF, ms. lat. 9474), completed in 1508, the saint bears the Breton banner (fol. 3r).

[86] Roger S. Wieck, *Miracles in Miniature. The Art of the Master of Claude de France* (New York: The Morgan Library & Museum, 2014), 6-7. König, *Book of Hours of Claude*, 10-11, suggests a dating in the 1520s and "Protestant tendencies" perceptible in the borders.

[87] Bonnet, "Louise de Savoie et François Demoulins de Rochefort," 255-256.

[88] Porrer, *Lefèvre d'Étaples*, 33 and 491.

[89] *Ordonnances des rois de France. Catalogue des actes de François I*[er] (Paris: Imprimerie nationale, 1887), I, 128, n° 742.

Fig. 2.8 Master of Claude de France. "St. Ursula and Her Maidens," Prayer Book of Claude de France. New York, Morgan Library Ms M. 1166, fol. 46v-47r. Gift of Mrs. Alexandre P. Rosenberg in memory of her husband Alexandre Paul Rosenberg, 2008. (Photographic credit: The Morgan Library and Museum)

protectress of infertile women to come to her aid.[90] Its frontispiece (Fig. 2.9) bears a clear dedication to "Marguerite de France Duchesse d'Allençon et de Berry," whose arms are prominently displayed beneath a crowned female figure commanding over the scene from her throne. Yet the ecclesiastical author is arguably offering his work not to an enthroned Marguerite, as is generally supposed, but rather to her brother the kneeling king shown extending his hand. The enthroned figure would then be Queen Claude, already blessed with two girls and perhaps even the dauphin. Actively seconded by her ladies, she recommends to St. Anne the worried childless dedicatee singled out to her right. The ensuing text,

[90] Paris, BnF, ms. fr. 1035, fol. 1v. Myra D. Orth, "Manuscrits pour Marguerite," in *Marguerite de Navarre*, I, 89. The text and music are studied in depth in Michael Alan Anderson, *St. Anne in Renaissance Music* (Cambridge: Cambridge University Press, 2014), Chap. 7. My conclusions differ from theirs.

Fig. 2.9 "The Author Offering his Manuscript to François Ier in the Presence of Claude de France and Marguerite duchesse d'Angoulême et de Berry," *La Messe de Sainte-Anne*. Paris, BnF, ms. fr. 1035, fol. 1v. Source: BnF

seemingly colored by the "spirit of blackmail" around royal posterity that has been linked to Church reformers,[91] dovetails with the apocalyptic vision of the Briçonnet brothers. Just before urging Marguerite to request that "monseigneur reverendissime mon seigneur le legat" approve the mass, the author (Denis?) specifies that his brother (Guillaume?) asked him to pray for Marguerite at three pilgrimage sites dedicated to St. Anne (3v-4r). The patron saint of childbirth is then associated with an illumi-nated plea to the kings and princes of Christianity to launch a crusade against the Turks (5r). Anne's royal lineage ("lignee royalle iudaicque") is next linked to "la royne ma souueraine dame et mes dames du royal sang de France" (5v); aided by the supplications of French subjects (6v), royal ladies will procreate and ensure peace among princes and kings. The theme of universal peace through wedlock had already been so dear to Anne de Bretagne that she arranged imperial marriages for little Renée right up to her death.[92]

In Rome, Denis Briçonnet, then being avidly sought out by the reform-ing abbess Panigarola, played an active role in the negotiations of the papal/royal marriage that followed the baptism of the dauphin on April 16, 1518, at which Anne de France served as godmother once again. Written shortly after the birth of the dauphin (February 28), Panigarola's March 10, 1518, missive, however, contains an allusion to the bishop's being slandered before Louise de Savoie.[93] The reform movement was floundering at court, and *La Messe de Sainte Anne* was plausibly commis-sioned as a bridge to the Valois-Angoulême. On June 6, the royal family appeared in unison at the king and the queen's entries into Angers, the capital of Louise's duchy of Anjou. Guillaume Briçonnet ("Bishop of Lodève") rode amid the participating ecclesiastics; and two days later the legate *a latere* Marco Cornaro was feted.[94] On June 28, François penned a letter from Angers ordering the replacement of "madame de Soubize" as Renée's governess; June 29, Claude was forced to do the same; and June

---

[91] Le Gall, *Les Moines*, 112: "le milieu réformateur paraît avoir exercé un vrai chantage à la postérité royale."

[92] Matarasso, *Queen's Mate*, 270-275.

[93] Eugenio Giommi, *La monaca Arcangela Panigarola, madre spirituale di Denis Briçonnet (1512-1520). L'attesa del "pastore angelico" annunciato dell'"Apocalypsis Nova" del Beato Amedeo fra il 1514 et il 1520*, tesi di laurea (Florence: Università degli Studi di Firenze, Facoltà di Lettere e Filosofia, 1968), 127ff.

[94] Armand Parrot, *Voyage du roi François Ier à Angers, en 1518* (Angers: Imp. Cosnier et Lachèse, 1858), 18-19.

30, Louise confirmed the transferal of her charge to "madame la contesse de Tonnerre" [Françoise de Rohan]. By foregrounding St. Anne, the Briçonnet/Lefèvre circle was reaching out to the official Royal Trinity— François and Louise, but especially Marguerite. Are these the very circumstances that pushed Lefèvre d'Étaples to turn his attention to the saint? Sometime during the same year he had himself depicted presenting to Marguerite's mother Louise, her almoner Demoulins by his side, his controversial *Petit livret faict à l'honneur de Madame Saincte Anne*, which undermined the very saint honored in the musical mass.[95] In 1519, the now Erasmian Demoulins was promoted grand almoner of France.[96] Renée had lost her governess, but the prominence of evangelical ideas was on the rise and the bond between Claude, Renée, and Marguerite tightened.

CONTEXTUALIZING EARLY DEPICTIONS OF RENÉE DE FRANCE

If princes and princesses were taught to read around the age of seven,[97] then 1517 becomes the most probable year for Claude's commission (in tandem with Madame de Soubise?) of Renée's prayer book-cum-primer.[98] Like Claude's own illuminated prayer books, Renée's is attributed to the artist to whom her sister's name has accrued: "The Master of Claude de France." The sisters' three religious manuscripts devolve from works commissioned by Anne de Bretagne. Their spirit, however, has evolved. In Renée's very first book, the traditional prayers are accompanied by rarer invocations, the implications of which remain to be explained. From a pictorial point of view, Renée's manuscript differs notably from the late fifteenth-century primer of Anne's ill-fated son Charles-Orland (1492–1495), in which his mother figures twice. The slightly older motherless Renée, instead, plays an exceptionally independent and proactive role in her unusually high number of appearances on the vellum stage, moving from an initial portrait of sorts, fol. 6r (Fig. 3.1), to idealized images (as Charles-Orland) of the princess she would become (fol. 8r; fol.

[95] Paris, Bibl. de l'Arsenal 4009, fol. 1v; Porrer, *Lefèvre d'Étaples*, 62-84.
[96] Bonnet, "Louise and Demoulins," 256-262.
[97] Marie Madeleine Fontaine and Elsa Kammerer, "Nourrir et instituer l'enfant," in *Enfants de la Renaissance*, ed. Caroline zum Kolk (Luçon: In fine éditions d'art, 2019), 52-58.
[98] See Wieck's chapter in this volume; for bibliography on the Master, notes 35 and 69.

8v, Fig. 3.3), fol. 9v (Fig. 3.4) and fol. 13v. The depiction of her confession differs from that of her mother Anne [Fig. 3.9]: a pure young princess kneels in close proximity to her namesake St. René, the exemplary bishop of Claude's prayer book, here shown blessing his protégée (Fig. 3.3). Lefèvre's insistence that confession should be from one Christian to another, heartfelt, and directly to God seems to inflect the image.[99] Sanctity was being closely scrutinized, and Renée's book reduces the male and female saints adorning Charles-Orland's primer to a single important female protagonist: the Mary Magdalen then being dissected by Lefèvre,[100] shown on fol. 11r embracing the cross. Demoulins, in his perhaps contemporaneous life of Magdalen, affirms that she is correctly referred to as "Apostola," because a messenger of Jesus Christ.[101] Logically, then, it is also the "belle et clere Magdalene" who appears on the heraldic right of St. Peter on fol. 6v, boldly penning her own text as the Apostles compose their Creed. In a comparable vein, Renée's prayers twice conjure up a vision of Christ, first perceived directly on the other side of her prie-Dieu, descending to earth (Fig. 3.4), then, on fol. 13r, bathing her humble yet pure princessly figure in his divine light. The evolution from his more distant appearance to Charles-Orland (fol. 31v) is notable, much in the spirit of the Veronica da Binasco illustrations sent from Milan to Claude in 1518.[102] Could Renée's future motto, IN CRISTO SOL RENATA,[103] already be nascent here?

The patronage of the first "portrait" of the infant Renée in prayer (Fig. 3.1) is surely imputable to Claude, plausibly seconded by de Soubise. What, though, triggered the creation of the finest extant rendition of the princess, the Chantilly drawing by Jean Clouet?[104] Although historians

[99] Philip Edgcumbe Hughes, *Lefèvre Pioneer of Ecclesiastical Renewal in France* (Grand Rapids: William B. Eerdmans Publishing Company, 1984), 93.
[100] Porrer, *Lefèvre d'Étaples*. Lefèvre began writing a text on the saints in 1519, but abandoned it to avoid controversy, Hughes, *Lefèvre*, 96.
[101] Paris, BnF, ms. fr. 24955, fol. 51v: "C'est bien raison que Magdalene qui a esté messagiere de iesus christ soit nommee Apostola. Eve nostre mère, diffamant le sexe feminin, apporta les nouuelles de triste mort, et Magdalene sauuant et reparant l'honneur des dames apporta les nouuelles de resurrection et de ioyeuse vie."
[102] In Isidoro de Isolanis, *Inexplicabilis mysterii gesta B. Veronicae virginis*, Paris, BnF, Rés. Vélins 2743; Wilson-Chevalier, "Denis Briçonnet."
[103] Kelly D. Peebles, "Embodied Devotion: The Dynastic and Religious Loyalty of Renée de France (1510-1575)," in *Royal Women and Dynastic Loyalty*, ed. Caroline Dunn and Elizabeth Carney (New York: Palgrave Macmillan, 2018), 123-137.
[104] Chantilly, musée Condé, inv. MN 28.

date it uncertainly between 1519 and 1524, it is undeniably one of the earliest high-quality Clouet crayons depicting figures at the French royal court. Did François I and his mother request it as they negotiated the second official marriage treaty involving Renée, which promised her to the Margrave of Brandenburg,[105] or did Claude impel this image too? Tendentially, women, but first and foremost mothers, oversaw the production and exchange of children's portraits[106]; and six comparable extant drawings figure the royal children, minus the youngest, Marguerite de France, born in June 1523. All logically date from before Claude's death in July 1524, like the related oil paintings of the Dauphin François (Antwerp), Charlotte (Minneapolis and Chicago), Madeleine (London, Weiss Gallery), and Charles (Orléans).[107] The stylistic similarity of these panels to Clouet's painting of Marie d'Assigny (Edinburgh) has been noted; and it has been suggested that such portraits project a serene and humble "evangelical conception of being."[108] Marie d'Assigny (or d'Acigné) was one of Claude's ladies-in-waiting, as was Madeleine d'Astarac, whose crayon portrayal must have been made during Claude's lifetime too.[109] Kin to Anne's lady of honor Madame de Mailly, Madeleine's first spouse was the son of Anne's half-brother François II d'Avaugour, charged with her scepter at the Saint-Denis obsequies. Was the "Mademoiselle Anne de Bretagne Damoiselle D'Avaugour" who figured among Renée's "dames et damoiselles" in 1525 the daughter of

---

[105] Alexandra Zvereva, *Portraits dessinés de la cour des Valois. Les Clouet de Catherine de Médicis* (Paris: Arthena, 2011), fig. 21, 210; Zvereva, "Louise de Savoie," 192-201; Mathieu Deldicque, *Clouet. Le Miroir des dames* (Dijon: Éditions Faton, 2019), 22-23; Gabriel Braun, "Le mariage de Renée de France avec Hercule d'Esté: une inutile mesalliance. 28 juin 1528," *Histoire, économie et société*, 7, no. 2 (1988): 148.

[106] Zvereva, *Portraits dessinés*, 117. Like Alexandra Zvereva (*Les Clouet de Catherine de Médicis. Chefs-d'œuvre graphiques du musée Condé* [Paris and Chantilly: Somogy éditions d'art and musée Condé, château de Chantilly, 2002], 62, fig. 20), Deldicque, *Le Miroir*, 24 and 22, nonetheless hypothesizes a commission from François I of the portraits of his children, to which he links that of Renée.

[107] Deldicque, *Le Miroir*, 24, for a reproduction of the painting of Madeleine, who later corresponded with Renée. She is surely younger than four.

[108] Étienne Jollet, *Jean & François Clouet* (Paris: Éditions de la Lagune, 1997), 169-172, tying this "conception évangélique de l'être" to Marguerite de Navarre.

[109] Chantilly, MN 230; dated ca. 1523 in Zvereva, *Les Clouet de Catherine*, 125, fig. 56. Another of Claude's ladies-in-waiting drawn by Clouet at an early date is Anne de La Tour, dame de Turenne (Florence, inv. 14930 F).

Madeleine?[110] Anne d'Avaugour went on to serve Claude's youngest daughter Marguerite de France, Renée's lifelong ally, until at least 1547. Artistic clusters could be shaped by lasting household loyalties.

EVANGELICAL HUMANISM, SPIRITUAL, AND POLITICAL FORTITUDE

When Anne de Graville had herself depicted around 1521 offering her *Beau romant des deux amans Palamon et Arcita* to Claude de France, Renée was at least ten and logically part of Claude's suite. Graville had the queen represented under a canopy bearing (as usual) the emblems of both France and Brittany, accompanied by three ladies-in-waiting caught in animated debate.[111] The Parthenay memoirs assert that Renée's surrogate mother Madame de Soubise knew "the true religion" at an early date and raised her young children accordingly.[112] Initially, this was perforce the evangelical humanism propounded by Erasmus and Lefèvre, both of whom were laboring to reform the Church.[113] In 1521, Marguerite d'Alençon was operating in tandem with Claude's court, alongside the reputed evangelical Anne de Graville, seen as a lady-in-waiting to Claude but without firm proof, and Anne Boleyn, who after almost seven years by the queen's side, remained attached to the ideas of Lefèvre d'Étaples for the rest of her life.[114] Forty years later, in a conversation with the English Ambassador Throckmorton after she returned to France, by then a correspondent of Calvin, Renée recalled her acquaintance with Queen Elizabeth's mother when she was serving her sister Claude.[115] Claude's circle of *damoiselles* disseminated new religious sensitivities, even abroad.

[110] Paris, BnF, Clairambault 835, fol. 2031; Gallica http://archivesetmanuscrits.bnf.fr/ ark:/12148/cc13947q/cd0e225.
[111] Paris, Arsenal, ms. 5116, fol. 1v. The volume also contains the *Espistre de Maguelonne* (see note 67).
[112] Bonnet, *Mémoires*, 7.
[113] Bonnet, *Mémoires*, V. On the interrelations of the two scholars, Bernard Roussel, "Lefèvre d'Etaples et Erasme: une amitié critique," in *Jacques Lefèvre d'Étaples*, ed. Jean-François Pernot *(1450?-1536)* (Paris: Champion, 1995), 23-54.
[114] Kathleen Wilson-Chevalier, "Queen Claude of France," 95-96; "Spaces of Agency," 160-161.
[115] Gustave Masson, "L'histoire du protestantisme français étudiée au Record Office," *Bulletin de l'Histoire du protestantisme français*, 17, no. 11 (1868): 545n1: "Theyre was an old accqueyntans betwixt the Queen hyr mother and me, when she was on of my syster Queen Claudes mayds of honor." See "Elizabeth: January 1561, 1-10," in *Calendar of State*

No caesura ensued. After Claude's premature death, the spirit of Christian humanism colored the education of the royal children at court. No later than early 1526, a free translation of Erasmus's *Institution d'un prince jusqu'à l'âge d'adolescence* was illuminated for the three royal sons and their tutor.[116] That year, it is purported, Lefèvre d'Étaples, after perilous attacks and a period of forced exile, was called to Blois by the king, where he became the preceptor of Madeleine and Charles, at least. Two years later, around the time Renée left for Ferrara, he published a *Liber Psalmorum* to teach the six-year-old Charles Latin, then in 1529 two others, a *Vocabulaire du Psaultier* dedicated to both of his young pupils, and a *Grammatographia* to Madeleine alone.[117] All three were published anonymously, the need for dissimulation ever more pressing.[118] This meshed easily with the concept of "juste ypocrisy," already an integral part of the education of young maidens, as Christine de Pisan and Anne de France's writings prove.[119]

Madame de Soubise's role as an active protectress of "heretics" by Renée's side has been well circumscribed in Ferrara in the mid-1530s, when secrecy was becoming an ever more critical tool for survival.[120] Regarding great ladies and Church reform, her impact has been judged second only to that of Marguerite de Navarre, and she has been identified as the first noblewoman of high rank to convert.[121] After her second involuntary return to her Parc-Soubise domain in 1536, she is credited with

Papers Foreign: Elizabeth, Volume 3, 1560-1561, ed. Joseph Stevenson (London: Her Majesty's Stationery Office, 1865), 489-490. *British History Online*, accessed September 23, 2019, http://www.british-history.ac.uk/cal-state-papers/foreign/vol3/pp480-495. Adams, "Fostering Girls," 113.

[116] Patricia Stirnemann, in *L'Art du Manuscrit de la Renaissance en France*, ed. Cécile Scaillérez and Patricia Stirnemann (Chantilly: musée Condé and Somogy éditions d'art, 2001), 26-29, fig. 6. For a slightly different reading, Wilson-Chevalier, "Queen Claude of France," 109-110.

[117] Jeanne Veyrin-Forrer, "Simon de Colines, Imprimeur de Lefèvre d'Étaples," in Pernot, *Lefèvre d'Etaples*, 110-117.

[118] Jacob Vance, *Secrets: Humanism, Mysticism, and Evangelism in Erasmus of Rotterdam, Bishop Guillaume Briçonnet, and Marguerite de Navarre* (Leiden: Brill, 2014).

[119] Rohr, "Rocking the Cradle," relates Pisan's notion of "juste ypocrisy" to Anne de France.

[120] See Belligni, *Renata di Francia*, and Gabriella Scarlatta's and Roger Wieck's chapters in this volume.

[121] Nancy L. Roelker, "Les femmes de la noblesse huguenote au XVIᵉ siècle," *Bulletin de la Société de l'Histoire du Protestantisme Français* (1974): 231.

having furthered the spread of Protestantism in the Bas-Poitou.[122] Perhaps her compulsory distance from courtly centers of governance facilitated this bold alignment with religious change. Renée, instead, remained in the vortex of power until the end of her life, and contradictory loyalties—royal, ducal, and religious—perforce complexified her fundamentally ("Fabriste") tolerant stance.[123]

Just as Anne de Bretagne remained stifled during her first reign, young Queen Claude was unable to prevent her father and her spouse's imperialistic absorption of Brittany or to impose her conceit of state. To make matters worse, Claude's lady of honor, whose wages were three times those of Anne de Parthenay in 1523, was Françoise de Foix/Châteaubriant, her spouse's very public mistress, whose presence sapped her household at its very core.[124] Such a model appealed to male rulers, as Ercole d'Este later demonstrated through his relationship with Renée's lady-in-waiting Madame de Noyant.[125] Yet Marguerite de Foix/Bretagne had modeled for her daughter and her granddaughters not only political but also sexual fortitude; and Anne's Spanish motto NON MUDERA ("she will not change"), revitalized by Claude in her Book of Hours, harks back to their royal Navarrais roots.[126] The devise urges steadfastness, a comportment that permeates the final image of Anne de Graville's *Palamon et Arcita* translation for "her sovereign mistress" (Fig. 2.10). A princess donning the ermine of a French queen, discretely supported by two alert ladies-in-waiting, boldly confronts a group of four courtly gentlemen, delivering to them a lecture on perfect love while denouncing the counterfeit love of her day.[127] The preceding story, however, recounts the deadly conflict of two knights, just as tensions were peaking between the king and his constable, Bourbon. Claude is arguably charged with pleading the cause of

---

[122] "Chronique d'histoire régionale: Société d'émulation de la Vendée. 1925, La Roche-sur-Yon," *Revue d'histoire de l'Église de France*, 12, no. 55 (1926): 269.

[123] Leonardo De Chirico and Daniel Walker, *Lealtà in tensione: un carteggio protestante tra Ferrara e l'Europa (1537-1564) Giovanni Calvino, Renata di Francia* (Caltanissetta: Alfa e Omega, 2009). See Dick Wursten's chapter in this volume.

[124] Zvereva, *Portraits dessinés*, 265, fig. 165, accepts the identification of a crayon at the Uffizi as a representation of Madame de Châteaubriant around 1520.

[125] See my chapter "Under the Rubble" in this volume.

[126] Charles Sterling, *The Master of Claude, Queen of France. A Newly Defined Miniaturist* (New York: H.P. Kraus, 1975), 8; König, *The Book of Hours*, 37-44.

[127] The last line on the folio reads: "J'entens aymant d'ung amytié par faicte / Non pas de celle aujourd'huy contrefaicte." See Wilson-Chevalier, "Spaces of Agency," 160-163 for bibliography and further contextualization.

Text on the manuscript image:

£ vo⁹compter du io² ne de la nuyt
tout ce ppos ne me fiet ne me duyt
Si mon subiet en parle en aultre sorte
A qui le feist de cela me rapporte
Il me suffist que cellup qui mentent
pense combiē vng vray cueur est cōtēt
Dauoir ce bien dōt la longue attendue
Luy feist souffrir iadis mainte venue
Jentens aymant dung amytie par fucte
Non pas de celle auiourdhuy cōtrefaicte.

Fig. 2.10 Master of Anne de Graville. "Queen Hippolyta Lecturing on Perfect Love to a Group of Gentlemen," *Roman de Palamon et Arcita*. Paris, Bibliothèque de l'Arsenal, MS. 5116, fol. 68. Source: BnF

political reconciliation with her husband the king, too. Renée was perforce familiar with this manuscript and its author; and she demonstrated throughout her life that she had absorbed Graville's model for her royal sister who, like the ancient Hortensia, remains resilient yet firm.

RESISTING WOMEN

The night preceding Claude's death, the queen/duchess "accepted" to bequeath Brittany to her children according to their gendered order of birth, beginning with her son the dauphin and including her daughters, were all the royal sons deceased.[128] Clément Marot's subsequent epitaph suggests that death brought Claude relief from the battles that had incessantly plagued her life,[129] that of Brittany among those doomed. Ambassadorial accounts are contradictory; nothing proves the common conviction that Claude was weak. Her parents had espoused Claude de Seyssel's concept of a "consultative" monarchy,[130] and Claude surely continued to embrace their political stance, implying collaboration with the powerful Bourbon clan. The most remarkable expression of the alliance between the Valois/Breton sisters and Renée's godmother Anne de France occurred in July 1515, when the royal court was celebrated as François I embarked on his first Italian campaign. Duchess Anne masterminded an entry into Moulins, followed four days later by a well-documented and highly elaborate one into Lyon, a territory under Bourbon sway. Scaffolds on both water and land highlighted not only the king, but also Anne's crucial protégé, the constable Charles de Bourbon and the fifteen-year-old queen and her little sister, staged as heiresses enabling the Italian campaign.[131] As early as May 1517, though, Anne de France and Louise de Savoie locked horns over what the former perceived to be the dishonorable Valois-Angoulême treatment of Charles.[132] The subterranean male/

[128] The verb in quotation marks is used by Le Page and Nassiet, *L'Union*, 153. Transcribed by Jean-Alexis Néret, *Claude de France: femme de François Iᵉʳ: 1499-1524* (Paris: Les Éditions de France, 1942), 191-192: "dame Claude, par la grâce de Dieu reine de France, duchesse de Bretagne," and so on.

[129] Defaux, *Œuvres complètes*, I, 371: "Esprit lassé de vivre en peine, & dueil, / Que veulx tu plus faire en ces basses Terres ? / Assez y as vescu en pleurs, & Guerres, / Va vivre en paix au Ciel resplendissant, / Si complairas à ce corps languissant, / Sur ce fina par Mort, qui tout termine, / Le Lys tout blanc, la toute noire Hermine, / Noire d'ennuy, & blanche d'innocence."

[130] Nicole Hochner, *Louis XII. Les déréglements de l'image royale (1498-1515)* (Seyssel: Champ Vallon, 2006), for example, Chap. 6: "Une philosophie du partage," 216-244.

[131] Anne-Marie Lecoq, *François Iᵉʳ imaginaire, symbolique et politique à l'aube de la Renaissance française* (Paris: Macula, 1987), 144-145, 188-207; Orth, *Renaissance Manuscripts*, II, fig. 65, 219-222.

[132] Guillaume de Marillac, "Vie du connétable Charles de Bourbon de 1490 à 1521," in *Choix de Chroniques et mémoires sur l'histoire de France, XVIᵉ siècle*, ed. J.-A.-C. Buchon (Paris: Panthéon Littéraire, 1861), 124-184. For a resumé of the dynastic confrontation

female Breton/Bourbon affiliation was still effective the following April, when Anne de France presented the dauphin at the baptismal font. Yet the demolition of the feudal empire fortified by the dowager duchess and the duke de Bourbon proceeded inexorably; and the young Renée perforce experienced the slow ripping to bits of her brilliant godmother's domain. The lesson could only have enhanced her sense of caution, made her ever-more-inclined to a "juste ypocrisy" that would help her surmount the adversity that would traverse her life. Prior to her departure for Ferrara in 1528, the heavy-handed royal mother/son team managed to snatch both Breton and Bourbon lands. Yet Queen Anne's intent regarding her sovereign territory remained so self-evident that when her second daughter married Ercole II d'Este, she was forced to renounce her rights to Brittany (as were her d'Avaugour kin). The tug-of-war was dormant, not resolved. If Anne died when Renée was a mere infant, her profile as a "bonne duchesse," grounded in a genuinely clement Breton fiscal policy, still lives on.[133] Following their father's death, Claude, Queen of France and Duchess of Brittany, "The all white lily, the all black ermine / Black with lassitude, & white with innocence," remained for a decade the closest kin and lady of highest rank in Renée's life. Unable to transmit an independent Brittany to her sister, Claude gave her an unassailable gift: the superior model of a princess motivated by charitable evangelical humanist ideals and revered by her subjects—no mean task.[134] Brantôme, whose aunt and grandmother had belonged to Anne's court, traces an unequivocal line of descent: from mother, "the true Mother of the poor," to daughter, "very good and very charitable," to daughter/sister, "real *fille de France*, true in goodness and charity." The word "charity" recurs abundantly in his depiction of Renée, whom he had encountered in both Ferrara and France[135]; and visual and/or literary proof confirms his assertions. The first historiated initial of a missal made for Anne's ally Philippe de Luxembourg depicts St. Julian healing a blindman at the Le Mans gate, while the saint's entourage draws

between the two courts, see Philippe Hamon, "Charles de Bourbon, connétable de France (1490-1527)," in *Les Conseillers de Francois Ier*, ed. Cédric Michon (Rennes: Presses universitaires de Rennes, 2011), 95-97.

[133] Le Page and Nassiet, *L'Union*, 130-136.

[134] Wilson-Chevalier, "Spaces of Agency," 165-166.

[135] Pierre de Bourdeille, seigneur de Brantôme, *Recueil des Dames, poésies et tombeaux*, ed. Étienne Vaucheret (Paris, Gallimard "La Pléiade," 1991): "la vraye Mere des pauvres," 16; "très-bonne et très-charitable, et fort douce à tout le monde," 171; "bien fille de France, vraie en bonté et charité," 176.

the destitute commoner to the attention of a governor, crowned.[136] A comparable vision of monarchical responsibility infuses Claude's prayer book illumination of a model St. Louis, a young king pictured distributing alms (fol. 37r). Similarly, the highly personalized "Epistre envoyée de Venize à Madame la Duchesse de Ferrare," dedicated by the fleeing Clément Marot to Renée in 1536, contrasts the painted and gilded luxury of Venetian churches to the "ymaiges vives" (living images) of "Les pouvres nudz, palles & languissans" (the nude, pale, and languishing poor), cast as more appropriate recipients of their misspent wealth.[137] Along with more generic lessons learned from great ladies of rank, this is the specific dynastic, political, and religious model (buttressed by the feared wisdom of Madame de Soubise) heralded by Renée de France.

The *Journal d'un bourgeois de Paris* narrates the belated funeral of Claude in November 1524, announcing miracles performed by the queen's body and noting that she had been "highly loved during her lifetime and after her death."[138] Renée, fourteen, had learned to stand up to Louise de Savoie;[139] funereal rank positioned her after the regent, yet she preceded her ally and sister-in-law Marguerite. Her governess Françoise de Rohan countess of Tonnerre still by her side, Renée was fully armed for independent battle and would never relinquish her conviction, as Brantôme puts it, that the "awful" Salic law (*ceste méchante loy salique*) had prevented her from ruling France.[140] While her strong unorthodox religious beliefs caused her considerable grief, they fortified her determination to rule her domains with equity. The year before she left for Italy, her mother's ally

---

[136] Le Mans, BM ms 0254; imprecisely dated between 1495-1503 (see http://initiale.irht. cnrs.fr/codex/2698, with bibliography). The *Healing of a Blindman* on fol. 4r (https://www.pop.culture.gouv.fr/notice/enluminures/D-006914) accompanies the beginning of Psalm 138 (my thanks to Elizabeth L'Estrange for her assistance) and seems to reflect the psalm's insistence, line 6, on the Lord's regard for the lowly.

[137] Defaux, *Clément Marot*, II, 102-105: "Temples marbrins y font & y adorent / Images peinctz, qu'à grandz despens ilz dorent / Et à leurs pieds, helas, sont gemissans / Les pouvres nudz, palles & languissans. / Ce sont, ce sont, telles ymaiges vives / Qui de ces grans despenses excessives / Estre debv[r]oient aournées et parées / Et de nos yeulx les autres separées" (lines 39-46).

[138] Reprinted in Michel Nassiet, "Les reines héritières: d'Anne de Bretagne à Marie Stuart," in *Femmes et pouvoir politique. Les princesses d'Europe XVe-XVIIIe siècle*, ed. Isabelle Poutrin et Marie-Karine Schaub (Rosny-sous-Bois: Éditions Bréal, 2007), 144-145.

[139] Kelly Digby Peebles, "Renée de France's and Clément Marot's Voyages: Political Exile to Spiritual Libération," *Women in French Studies* Special Issue 7 (2018): 40–42.

[140] Brantôme, *Recueil des Dames*, 174.

Jacques de Beaune, Semblançay, fell to the unblunted sword of "Justice" wielded by François I and his mother Louise. Duchess, Renée took numerous risks to protect her subjects, particularly those condemned by what to her eyes was an unjust Church, and to further reconciliation no matter one's religious beliefs. From the 1540s, the seat of her court in exile was the Este *delizia* of Consandolo. Even after its very location had fallen into oblivion, the memory of Renea, a heretical duchess who did not disdain the Virgin, endured.[141] NON MUDERA. Never give up. In the early 1570s, she and Anne d'Este, her no less determined and even-more-learned daughter, pressured the French Crown to regain the Breton heritage that, to their mind, was rightfully theirs.[142] Like that of other successful Renaissance princesses, Renée de France's superior education hinged on a broad collaborative team. Figuring at the very top of the list of the many capable individuals who helped shape her steadfast and resilient *persona* are her mother Anne and her sister Claude. Thus, from Nantes (Fig. 2.2) to Ferrara (Chaps. 10 and 11) and beyond, *Prudence/Minerva* stood by Renée's side as she doggedly labored to wield her agency and patronage to good end.

BIBLIOGRAPHY

PRIMARY SOURCES

MANUSCRIPTS

Geneva, Bibliothèque de Genève: ms. fr. 131: Pierre Le Baud, Genealogie des roys, ducs et princes de Bretaigne
Le Mans, BM: ms 0254: Missal of Philippe de Luxembourg
Nantes, musée Dobrée: ms. 17: Antoine Dufour, Vies des femmes célèbres
New York, The Morgan Library and Museum:
    MS M50: The Prayer Book of Charles-Orland
    MS M.1166: The Prayer Book of Queen Claude de France

---

[141] Elena Marescotti *et al. La delizia estense di Consandolo* (Consandolo: l'Associazione Ricerche Storiche di Consandolo, 2008); Emanuel Rodocanachi, *Renée de France, une protectrice de la réforme en France et en Italie* (Paris, P. Ollendorf, 1896), 297 for her commission of a gold and enamel Virgin as late as 1556; 309-311 on her generosity.

[142] Brantôme, *Recueil des Dames*, 174; Rodocanachi, *Renée*, 481-482; Christiane Coester, *Schön wie Venus, mutig wie Mars Anna d'Este Herzogin von Guise und von Nemours (1531-1607)* (Munich: R. Oldenbourg, 2007), 207-210.

Paris, Bibliothèque de l'Arsenal: MS 5116: Anne de Graville, Beau romant des deux amans Palamon et Arcita
Paris, Bibliothèque nationale de France:
Clairambault 835: Officiers des Maisons des roys, reynes, enfans de France et de quelques princes du sang
MS Français 1035: La Messe de Sainte Anne
MS Français 1672: Pierre Choque, Traduction du poème sur la "combustion" de la nef nommée la Cordelière
MS Français 5750: Le sacre, couronnement, triumphe et entrée de la très cretienne royne et duchesse, ma souveraine dame et maistresse, madame Claude de France
MS Français 14116: Le sacre, couronnement, triumphe et entrée de la trescretienne royne et duchesse... madame Claude de France
MS Français 24955: François Demoulins de Rochefort, La vie de la belle et clere Magdalene
MS Français 24955: François Demoulins de Rochefort, La vie de la belle et clere Magdalene
MS Français 25158: Pierre Choque, Commemoracion et advertissement de la mort de... Madame Anne, deux foiz royne de France, duchesse de Bretaigne
MS Latin 9474: Jean Bourdichon, Horae ad usum Romanum, dites Grandes Heures d'Anne de Bretagne
NAF 9175, fol. 367-370: Officiers domestiques de la Reyne Claude de France
NAF 28882: Pierre Choque, Le combat de la "Cordelière"
Vélins 2743: Isidoro de Isolanis, Inexplicabilis mysterii gesta B. Veronicae virginis
Paris, Petit Palais, coll. Dutuit, MS 665: Trespas de l'hermine regrettée

IMPRINTS

Bonnet, Jules, ed. 1879. *Mémoires de la vie de Jean de Parthenay-Larchevêque sieur de Soubise*. Paris: Léon Willem.
Brantôme, Pierre de Bourdeille, seigneur de. 1991. In *Recueil des Dames, poésies et tombeaux*, ed. Étienne Vaucheret. Paris: Gallimard.
Briçonnet, Guillaume, and Marguerite d'Angoulême. 1975–79. In *Correspondance 1521–1524*, ed. Christine Martineau and Michel Veissiere, vol. 2. Geneva: Droz.
Canestrini, Giuseppe, and Abel Desjardins, eds. 1861. *Négociations diplomatiques de la France avec la Toscane*. Vol. II. Paris: Imprimerie Nationale.
"Elizabeth: January 1561, 1-10." In *Calendar of State Papers Foreign: Elizabeth, Volume 3, 1560-1561*. Edited by Joseph Stevenson. London: Her Majesty's Stationery Office, 1865. *British History Online*. http://www.british-history.ac.uk/cal-state-papers/foreign/vol3/pp480-495.

Gringore, Pierre. 2005. In *Pierre Gringore. Les Entrées royales à Paris de Marie d'Angleterre (1514) à Claude de France (1517)*, ed. Cynthia J. Brown. Geneva: Droz.

de Isolanis, Isidoro. 2004. In *Vita della Beata Veronica da Binasco*, ed. Giacomo Ravizza. Pavia: Seminario Vescovile di Pavia.

Lemaire de Belges, Jean. 1969. In *Oeuvres*, ed. Jean-Auguste Stecher. Slatkine Reprints: Geneva.

Marot, Clément. 1990–1993. In *Clémént Marot. Œuvres poétiques complètes*, ed. Gérard Defaux, vol. 2. Paris: Bordas.

———. 1969. In *Clément Marot. Œuvres*, ed. Georges Guiffrey, vol. 5. Slatkine Reprints: Geneva.

Marot, Jean. 1999. In *Les Deux Recueils*, ed. Gérard Defaux and Thierry Mantovani. Geneva: Droz.

Ordonnances des rois de France. Catalogue des actes de François 1er. 1887. *Tome 1: 1ᵉʳ janvier 1515-31 décembre 1530*. Paris: Imprimerie nationale.

Voyage du roi François Iᵉʳ à Angers, en 1518. Edited by Armand Parrot. Angers: Imp. Cosnier et Lachese, 1858.

SECONDARY SOURCES

Adams, Tracy. 2008. Fostering Girls in Early Modern France. In *Emotions in the Household, 1200-1900*, ed. Susan Broomhall, 103–118. New York: Palgrave Macmillan.

———. 2010. Rivals or Friends?: Anne de Bourbon and Anne de Bretagne. *Women in French Studies* 1: 46–61.

———. 2015. Louise de Savoie, la prudence et la formation des femmes diplomates vers 1500. In *Louise de Savoie 1476-1531*, ed. Pascal Brioist, Laure Fagnart, and Cédric Michon, 29–38. Tours and Rennes: Presses universitaires de François Rabelais and Presses universitaires de Rennes.

Akkerman, Nadine, and Birgit Houben, eds. 2014. *The Politics of Female Households. Ladies-in-Waiting across Early Modern Europe*. Leiden and Boston: Brill.

Anderson, Michael Alan. 2014. *St. Anne in Renaissance Music*. Cambridge: Cambridge University Press.

Barthet, Laure, and Camille Broucke, eds. 2014. *Le Cœur d'Anne de Bretagne*. Milan: Silvana Editoriale. Exhibition catalog.

Barbiche, Bernard, and Ségolène de Dainville-Barbiche. 1985. Les légats a latere en France et leurs facultés aux XVIᵉ et XVIIᵉ siècles. *Archivum Historiae Pontificiae* 23: 93–165.

Bedouelle, Guy. 1976. *Lefèvre d'Etaples et l'Intelligence des Ecritures*. Geneva: Droz.

Bell, Susan Groag. 2004. *The Lost Tapestries of the City of Ladies. Christine de Pizan's Renaissance Legacy*. Berkeley, Los Angeles, London: University of California Press.

Belligni, Eleonora. 2011. *Renata di Francia (1510-1575). Un eresia di corte.* Turin: UTET.

Berriot-Salvadore, Evelyne, Catherine Pascal, François Roudaut, and Trung Trans, eds. 2012. *La Vertu de prudence entre Moyen Âge et âge Classique.* Paris: Classiques Garnier.

Berthon, Guillaume. 2014. *L'Intention du poète Clément Marot "autheur.".* Paris: Classiques Garnier.

Bonnet, Charlotte. 2015. Louise de Savoie et François Demoulins de Rochefort. In *Louise de Savoie 1476-1531,* ed. Pascal Brioist, Laure Fagnart, and Cédric Michon, 253–262. Tours and Rennes: Presses universitaires François-Rabelais and Presses universitaires de Rennes.

Braun, Gabriel. 1988. Le mariage de Renée de France avec Hercule d'Esté: une inutile mesalliance. 28 juin 1528. *Histoire, économie et société* 7 (2): 147–168.

Brown, Cynthia J. 2010. Like Mother, Like Daughter: The Blurring of Royal Imagery in Books for Anne de Bretagne and Claude de France. In *The Cultural and Political Legacy of Anne de Bretagne. Negotiating Convention in Books and Documents,* ed. Cynthia J. Brown, 101–122. Cambridge: D.S. Brewer.

———. 2011. *The Queen's Library: Image-making at the Court of Anne of Brittany, 1477–1514.* Philadelphia: University of Pennsylvania Press.

Brown, Elizabeth A. R., Cynthia J. Brown, and Jean-Luc Deuffic, eds. 2013. *Qu'il mecte ma povre ame en celeste lumiere. Les funérailles d'une reine Anne de Bretagne (1514).* Pecia. Le livre et l'écrit, 2012, 15. Turnhout: Brepols.

Cassagnes-Brouquet, Sophie. 2007. *Un manuscrit d'Anne de Bretagne. Les Vies des femmes célèbres d'Antoine Dufour.* Rennes: Éditions Ouest-France.

Cassard, Jean-Christophe. 1985. L'histoire au renfort de la diplomatie: la généalogie des Roys, Ducz et Princes Royaulx de Bretaigne, de Pierre Le Baud. *Mémoires de la Société d'histoire et d'archéologie de Bretagne* 62: 67–95.

de Chancel-Bardelot, Béatrice, Pascal Charron, Pierre-Gilles Girault, and Jean-Marie Guillouët, eds. 2012. *Tours 1500. Capitale des arts.* Paris and Tours: Somogy and Tours, musée des Beaux-Arts. Exhibition catalog.

Chatenet, Monique. 2002. *La Cour de France au XVI͏ᵉ siècle. Vie sociale et architecture.* Paris: Picard.

Chevalier, Bernard. 2005. *Guillaume Briçonnet (v.1445-1514). Un cardinal-ministre au début de la Renaissance.* Rennes: Presses Universitaires de Rennes.

———. 2012. Tours en 1500, une capitale inachevée. In *Tours 1500 Capitale des arts,* ed Chancel Bardelot et al., 21-36. Paris and Tours: Somogy and Tours, musée des Beaux-Arts.

"Chronique d'histoire régionale: Société d'émulation de la Vendée. 1925, La Roche-sur-Yon." *Revue d'histoire de l'Eglise de France* 12, no. 55 (1926): 269.

Coester, Christiane. 2007. *Schön wie Venus, mutig wie Mars. Anna d'Este Herzogin von Guise und von Nemours (1531-1607).* Munich: R. Oldenbourg.

Cooper, Richard. 2006a. Marguerite de Navarre et la réforme italienne. In *Marguerite de Navarre 1492-1992. Actes du colloque international de Pau*, ed. Nicole Cazauran and James Dauphiné, vol. 2, 2nd ed., 159–188. Paris: Eurédit.

————. 2006b. Picturing Marot. In *Book and Text in France, 1400–1600: Poetry on the Page*, ed. Adrian Armstrong and Malcolm Quainton, 53–71. Aldershot: Ashgate.

Crépin-Leblond, Thierry, and Monique Chatenet, eds. 2014. *Anne de France: art et pouvoir en 1500*. Paris: Picard.

Dauvois, Nathalie. 2012. Prudence et politique chez les grands rhétoriqueurs: Janus bifrons. In *La Vertu de prudence entre Moyen Âge et âge classique*, ed. Evelyne Berriot-Salvadore, Catherine Pascal, François Roudaut, and Trung Tran, 55–71. Paris: Classiques Garnier.

David-Chapy, Aubrée. 2016. *Anne de France, Louise de Savoie, inventions d'un pouvoir au féminin*. Paris: Classiques Garnier.

De Chirico, Leonardo, and Daniel Walker. 2009. *Lealtà in tensione: un carteggio protestante tra Ferrara e l'Europa (1537-1564) Giovanni Calvino, Renata di Francia*. Caltanissetta: Alfa e Omega.

De la Garanderie, Marie-Madeleine. 1967. Les épitaphes latines d'Anne de Bretagne, par Germain de Brie. *Annales de Bretagne* 74 (3): 377–396.

Defaux, Gérard, and Thierry Mantovani, eds. 1999. *Les deux recueils Jehan Marot de Caen, poëte et escripvain de la royne Anne de Bretagne, et depuis valet de chambre du treschretien roy François premier*. Geneva: Droz.

Deldicque, Mathieu. 2019. *Clouet. Le Miroir des dames*. Dijon: Éditions Faton. Exhibition catalog.

Delvallée, Ellen. 2017. "Le Recueil Jehan Marot: un manuscrit inachevé et perdu édité par Clément?" *Ad Hoc* 6. https://adhoc.hypotheses.org/presentation-de-la-revue-ad-hoc

Earenfight, Theresa. 2019. A Lifetime of Power: Beyond Binaries of Gender. In *Medieval Elite Women and the Exercise of Power, 1100-1400. Moving beyond the Exceptionalist Debate*, ed. Heather J. Tanner. Cham, Switzerland: Palgrave Macmillan.

Fontaine, Marie Madeleine, and Elsa Kammerer. 2019. Nourrir et instituer l'enfant. In *Enfants de la Renaissance*, ed. Caroline zum Kolk, 52–58. Luçon: In fine éditions d'art. Exhibition catalog.

Gatouillat, Françoise. 2014. Une grande commande de la reine Anne de Bretagne: la verrière occidentale de la cathédrale Saint-Pierre de Nantes. In *Nantes flamboyante (1380-1530). Actes du colloque au Château des ducs de Bretagne, Nantes, 2011*, ed. Nicolas Faucherre and Jean-Marie Guillouët, 155–167. Nantes: Société archéologique et historique de Nantes et de la Loire-Atlantique.

Gauguin, Lucie. 2014. *Amboise un château dans la ville*. Tours and Rennes: Presses universitaires François Rabelais de Tours, Presses universitaires de Rennes.

Giommi, Eugenio. 1968. *La monaca Arcangela Panigarola, madre spirituale di Denis Briçonnet (1512-1520). L'attesa del "pastore angelico" annunciato dell'"Apocalypsis Nova" del Beato Amedeo fra il 1514 et il 1520, tesi di laurea.* Florence: Università degli Studi di Firenze, Facoltà di Lettere e Filosofia.

Giraud-Mangin, Marcel. 1946. Michelle de Saubonne. Dame d'atour d'Anne de Bretagne. *Mémoires de la Société d'histoire et d'archéologie de Bretagne* 16: 69–89.

Girault, Pierre-Gilles. 2014. *Les funérailles d'Anne de Bretagne, reine de France. L'Hermine regrettée.* Montreuil: Gourcuff Gradenigo. Exhibition catalog.

Guérout, Max. 2007. A quoi ressemble la nef la Cordelière? In *Anne de Bretagne Une histoire, un mythe*, ed. Pierre Chotard, 104–111. Paris and Nantes: Somogy and Château des ducs de Bretagne—Musée d'histoire de Nantes. Exhibition catalog.

Guillouët, Jean-Marie. 2012. Michel Colombe. In *Tours 1500 Capitale des arts*, ed. Béatrice de Chancel-Bardelot, Pascal Charron, Pierre-Gilles Girault, and Jean-Marie Guillouët, 186–191. Paris: Somogy. Exhibition catalog.

———. 2014. Les ducs de Bretagne et le couvent des Carmes de Nantes. In *Le Cœur d'Anne de Bretagne*, ed. Laure Barthet and Camille Broucke, 61–69. Milan: SilvanaEditoriale. Exhibition catalog.

Hamon, Philippe. 2011. Charles de Bourbon, connétable de France (1490-1527). In *Les Conseillers de François I*er, ed. Cédric Michon, 95–97. Rennes: Presses universitaires de Rennes.

Havet, Julien. 1884. Mémoire adressé à la dame de Beaujeu sur les moyens d'unir le duché de Bretagne au domaine du roi de France. *Revue historique* 25 (2): 275–287.

Hermant, Maxence. 2012. Le Maître de Claude de France. In *Tours 1500 Capitale des arts*, ed. Béatrice de Chancel-Bardelot, Pascal Charron, Pierre-Gilles Girault, and Jean-Marie Guillouët, 263–267. Paris and Tours: Somogy and musée des Beaux-Arts. Exhibition catalog.

———. 2015. L'héritage d'Anne de Bretagne et Claude de France. In *Trésors royaux: la bibliothèque de François I*er, ed. Maxence Hermant, 209–215. Rennes: Presses Universitaires de Rennes.

Heyder, Joris Corin. 2014. Les *Heures* de Marguerite de Foix: sources artistiques d'un atelier Nantais presque inconnu. In *Nantes flamboyante (1380-1530)*, ed. Nicolas Faucherre and Jean-Marie Guillouët, 123–139. Nantes: Société archéologique et historique de Nantes et de la Loire-Atlantique.

Hochner, Nicole. 2006. *Louis XII. Les dérèglements de l'image royale (1498-1515).* Seyssel: Champ Vallon.

Hughes, Philip Edgcumbe. 1984. *Lefèvre Pioneer of Ecclesiastical Renewal in France.* Grand Rapids: William B. Eerdmans Publishing Company.

Jimenes, Rémi, ed. 2019. *Geoffroy Tory de Bourges libraire et imprimeur humaniste (1480-1533).* Tours: Presses universitaires François-Rabelais. Exhibition catalog.

Jollet, Étienne. 1997. *Jean & François Clouet.* Paris: Éditions de la Lagune.

Jones, Michael. 1978. Les manuscrits d'Anne de Bretagne Reine de France, Duchesse de Bretagne. *Mémoires de la Société d'Histoire et d'Archéologie de Bretagne* 50: 43–81.

Jourda, Pierre. 1929. Un humaniste italien en France: Theocrenus (1480-1536). *Revue du Seizième siècle* 16: 40–57.

König, Eberhard. 2012. *The Book of Hours of Claude de France.* Ramsen: Heribert Tenschert.

Kuperty-Tsur, Nadine. 2015. "Le Journal de Louise de Savoie, nature et visées. In *Louise de Savoie 1476-1531,* ed. Pascal Brioist, Laure Fagnart, and Cédric Michon, 263-276. Tours and Rennes: Presses universitaires François Rabelais and Presses universitaires de Rennes.

Lecoq, Anne-Marie. 1987. *François Ier imaginaire. Symbolique et politique à l'aube de la Renaissance française.* Paris: Macula.

L'Estrange, Elizabeth. 2008. *Holy Motherhood. Gender, Dynasty and Visual Culture in the Later Middle Ages.* Manchester: Manchester University Press.

Le Gall, Jean-Marie. 2001. *Les moines au temps des réformes: France, 1480-1560.* Seyssel: Champ Vallon.

Le Page, Dominique. 1997. *Finances et politique en Bretagne au début des temps modernes, 1491-1547.* Vincennes: Institut de la gestion publique et du développement économique.

———, ed. 2004. *Pour en finir avec Anne de Bretagne?* Nantes: Conseil général de Loire-Atlantique.

Le Page, Dominique, and Michel Nassiet. 2003. *L'Union de la Bretagne à la France.* Morlaix: Éditions Skol Vreizh.

Le Roux de Lincy, Antoine. 1861. *Vie de la reine Anne de Bretagne, femme des rois de France Charles VIII et Louis XII.* Vol. IV. Paris: L. Curmer.

Marescotti, Elena, et al. 2008. *La delizia estense di Consandolo.* Consandolo: l'Associazione Ricerche Storiche di Consandolo.

Marillac, Guillaume de. 1861. Vie du connétable Charles de Bourbon de 1490 à 1521. In *Choix de Chroniques et mémoires sur l'histoire de France, XVIe siècle,* ed. J.-A.-C. Buchon, 124–184. Paris: Panthéon Littéraire.

Masson, Gustave. 1868. L'histoire du protestantisme français étudiée au Record Office. *Bulletin de l'Histoire du protestantisme français* 17 (11): 542–555.

Matarasso, Pauline. 1997. Seen through a squint: the letters of Jacques de Beaune to Michelle de Saubonne. June to September 1505. *Renaissance Studies* 11 (4): 343–357.

———. 2001. *Queen's Mate. Three Women of Power in France on the Eve of the Renaissance.* Aldershot: Ashgate.

———. 2011. *Le Baptême de Renée de France en 1510. Compte des frais et préparatifs.* Paris: CNRS Éditions.

McKinley, Mary. 1997. Marot, Marguerite de Navarre et 'l'Epistre du despourveu.'. In *Clément Marot "Prince des poëtes françois" 1496-1996. Actes du Colloque international de Cahors en Quercy 21-25 mai 1996*, ed. Gérard Defaux and Michel Simonin, 615–626. Paris: Honoré Champion.

Nassiet, Michel. 2004. Les traités de mariage d'Anne de Bretagne. In *Pour en finir avec Anne de Bretagne?* ed. Dominique Le Page, 71–81. Nantes: Conseil général de Loire-Atlantique.

———. 2007. Les reines héritières: d'Anne de Bretagne a Marie Stuart. In *Femmes et pouvoir politique. Les princesses d'Europe XVe-XVIIIe siècle*, ed. Isabelle Poutrin and Marie-Karine Schaub, 134–143. Rosny-sous-Bois: Éditions Bréal.

———. 2010. Anne de Bretagne, A Woman of State. In *The Cultural and Political Legacy of Anne de Bretagne. Negotiating Convention in Books and Documents*, ed. Cynthia J. Brown, 163–175. Cambridge: D.S. Brewer.

Néret, Jean-Alexis. 1942. *Claude de France: femme de François Ier: 1499-1524*. Paris: Les Éditions de France.

Orth, Myra D. 2006. Manuscrits pour Marguerite. In *Marguerite de Navarre 1492-1992. Actes du colloque international de Pau*, ed. Nicole Cazauran and James Dauphiné, vol. 2, 2nd ed., I, 85-105. Paris: Eurédit.

———. 2015. *Renaissance Manuscripts: The Sixteenth Century*. Vol. 2. London & Turnhout: Harvey Miller Publishers.

Oury, Guy-Marie. 1975. *Histoire religieuse de la Touraine*. Tours: CLD Normand & Cie.

Peebles, Kelly D. 2018a. Embodied Devotion: The Dynastic and Religious Loyalty of Renée de France (1510-1575). In *Royal Women and Dynastic Loyalty*, ed. Caroline Dunn and Elizabeth Carney, 123–137. New York: Palgrave Macmillan.

Peebles, Kelly Digby. 2018b. Renée de France's and Clément Marot's Voyages: Political Exile to Spiritual Libération. *Women in French Studies* 7: 33–60. https://doi.org/10.1353/wfs.2018.0002.

Pierre, Benoist. 2015. L'entourage religieux et la religion de Louise de Savoie. In *Louise de Savoie 1476-1531*, ed. Pascal Brioist, Laure Fagnart, and Cédric Michon, 117–141. Tours and Rennes: Presses universitaires François-Rabelais and Presses universitaires de Rennes.

Porrer, Sheila M. 2009. *Jacques Lefèvre d'Étaples and The Three Maries Debates*. Geneva: Droz.

Provini, Sandra, ed. 2004. *Humbert de Montmoret, Germain de Brie, Pierre Choque. L'Incendie de La Cordeliere*. La Rochelle: Rumeur des Anges.

Reid, Jonathan A. 2009. *King's Sister—Queen of Dissent. Marguerite of Navarre (1492-1549) and Her Evangelical Network. 2 vols*. Leiden and Boston: Brill.

Renck, Anneliese Pollock. 2015. Les Vies des Femmes Célèbres: Antoine Dufour, Jean Pichore, and a Manuscript's Debt to an Italian Printed Book. *The Journal of the Early Book Society* 18: 158–180.

Roelker, Nancy L. 1974. Les Femmes de la noblesse huguenote au XVIe siècle. In "Actes du colloque l'Amiral de Coligny et son temps (Paris, 24-28 octobre 1972)." Special issue, *Bulletin de la Société de l'Histoire du Protestantisme Français*, 227–250. http://www.jstor.org/stable/24297204.

Rohr, Zita. 2018. Rocking the Cradle and Ruling the World: Queens' Households in Late Medieval and Early Modern Aragon and France. In *Royal and Elite Households in Medieval and Early Modern Europe: More Than Just a Castle*, ed. Theresa Earenfight. Boston: Brill.

Roussel, Bernard. 1995. Lefèvre d'Etaples et Erasme: une amitié critique. In *Jacques Lefèvre d'Étaples (1450?-1536). Actes du colloque d'Étaples les 7 et 8 novembre 1992*, ed. Jean-François Pernot, 23–54. Paris: Champion.

Santrot, Jacques. 2014. *Les doubles funérailles d'Anne de Bretagne, reine et duchesse (9 janvier-19 mars 1514)*. Rennes: Presses Universitaires de Rennes.

Saulnier, V.-L., and Rosanna Gorris. 2001. Anne de Parthenay. In *Dictionnaire des lettres françaises. Le XVIe siècle*, ed. Georges Grente, 908. Paris: Fayard.

Scailliérez, Cécile, and Patricia Stirnemann, eds. 2001. *L'Art du manuscrit de la Renaissance en France*. Chantilly and Paris: musée Condé and Somogy éditions d'art. Exhibition catalog.

Spont, Alfred. 1895. *Semblançay (?-1527): la bourgeoisie financière au début du XVIe siècle*. Paris: Librairie Hachette & Cie.

Stecher, Jean-Auguste, ed. 1969. *Jean Lemaire de Belges Œuvres*. Geneva: Slatkine Reprints.

Sterling, Charles. 1975. *The Master of Claude, Queen of France. A Newly Defined Miniaturist*. New York: H.P. Kraus.

Vance, Jacob. 2014. *Secrets: Humanism, Mysticism, and Evangelism in Erasmus of Rotterdam, Bishop Guillaume Briçonnet, and Marguerite de Navarre*. Leiden: Brill.

Veyrin-Forrer, Jeanne. 1995. Simon de Colines, Imprimeur de Lefèvre d'Étaples. In *Jacques Lefèvre d'Etaples (1450 ?-1536). Actes du colloque d'Etaples les 7 et 8 novembre 1992*, ed. Jean-François Pernot, 97–117. Paris: Honoré Champion.

Wieck, Roger S. 2014. *Miracles in Miniature. The Art of the Master of Claude de France*. New York: The Morgan Library & Museum.

Wieck, Roger S., Cynthia J. Brown, and Eberhard König. 2012. *The Primer of Claude de France. MS 159, The Fitzwilliam Museum, Cambridge. Commentary to the Facsimile Edition*. Luzern: Quaternio Verlag.

Wieck, Roger S., and Cynthia J. Brown. 2010. *The Prayer Book of Claude de France. MS M.1166. The Pierpont Morgan Library, New York*. Luzern: Quaternio Verlag.

Wilson-Chevalier, Kathleen. 2015a. Claude de France: Justice, Power & the Queen as Advocate for Her People. In *Textual and Visual Representations of Power & Justice in Medieval France. Manuscripts and Early Printed Books*, ed. Rosalind Brown-Grant, Anne D. Hedeman, and Bernard Ribémont, 241–272. Burlington: Ashgate.

———. 2015b. Denis Briçonnet et Claude de France: l'évêque, les arts et une relation (fabriste) occultée. In Les Evêques, les lettres et les arts, ed. Gary Ferguson and Catherine Magnien. Special issue, Seizième Siècle 11, 95–118.

———. 2016. Quelle 'trinité royale'? Reine, roi, régente et sœur de roi: Claude de France, François Ier, Louise de Savoie et Marguerite de Navarre. In "La dame de cœur." Le patronage religieux des reines et des princesses XIIIe-XVIIe siècle, ed. Murielle Gaude-Ferragu and Cécile Vincent-Cassy, 123–136. Rennes: Presses Universitaires de Rennes.

———. 2017. Queen Claude of France and Her Entourage: Images of Religious Complaint and Evangelical Reform. In Representing Heresy in Early Modern France, ed. Lidia Radi and Gabriella Scarlatta, 93–129. Toronto: Centre for Reformation and Renaissance Studies.

———. 2018. Claude de France and the Spaces of Agency of a Marginalized Queen. In Women and Power at the French Court, 1483-1563, ed. Susan Broomhall, 139–172. Amsterdam: Amsterdam University Press.

Winn, Mary Beth, and Kathleen Wilson-Chevalier. 2015. Louise de Savoie, ses livres, sa bibliothèque. In Louise de Savoie 1476-1531, ed. Pascal Brioist, Laure Fagnart, and Cédric Michon, 235–252. Tours and Rennes: Presses universitaires de François Rabelais and Presses universitaires de Rennes.

Woodacre, Elena. 2013. The Queens Regnant of Navarre. Succession, Politics, and Partnership, 1274-1512. New York: Palgrave Macmillan.

Wursten, Dick. 2010. Clément Marot and Religion. A Reassessment in the Light of His Psalm Paraphrases. Leiden and Boston: Brill.

zum Kolk, Caroline. 2009. The Household of the Queen of France in the Sixteenth Century. The Court Historian 14 (1): 3–22.

zum Kolk, Caroline, and Kathleen Wilson-Chevalier. 2018. Femmes à la cour de France. Charges et fonctions XVe-XIXe siècle. Villeneuve d'Ascq: Presses Universitaires du Septentrion.

Zvereva, Alexandra. 2002. Les Clouet de Catherine de Médicis. Chefs-d'œuvre graphiques du musée Condé. Paris and Chantilly: Somogy. Exhibition catalogue.

———. 2011. Portraits dessinés de la cour des Valois. Les Clouet de Catherine de Médicis. Paris: Arthena.

———. 2015. 'Chose qui me donne de la peine et continuel travail plus que je ne vous puis dire': Louise de Savoie et les recueils de portraits au crayon. In Louise de Savoie 1476-1531, ed. P. Brioist, L. Fagnart, and C. Michon, 183–204. Tours and Rennes: Presses universitaires François-Rabelais and Presses universitaires de Rennes.

CHAPTER 3

The Primer of Renée de France

Roger S. Wieck

One of the treasures of Modena's Biblioteca Estense Universitaria is a small manuscript prayer book written in a clear humanist script and hand-somely decorated with twelve miniatures (five of which include portraits of a young girl) and a rich series of floral or vegetal borders on every page (Figs. 3.1, 3.2, 3.3, and 3.4).[1] Toward the end of the manuscript is a prayer for "the soul of your servant King Louis, my father, and the soul of

---

[1] Modena, Biblioteca Estense Universitaria, MS Lat. 614 = α.U.2.28. While a treasure of the library, the manuscript is still missing, the result of a theft in 1994. Complete photography, taken prior to the theft, enabled facsimiles to be published in print and on CD-ROM. See Ernesto Milano, *Commentario al codice* Les petites prières de Renée de France: *Lat. 614 = α.U.2.28, Biblioteca Estense Universitaria, Modena* (Modena: Il Bulino, 1998), Ernesto Milano and Myra Orth, *Das Blumengebetbuch der Renée de France: Biblioteca Estense Universitaria, Modena, Lat. 614 = α.U.2.28* (Luzern: Faksimile Verlag, 1998), and Mauro Bini, *Les petites prières de Renée de France: Biblioteca Estense Universitaria, Modena, α.U.2.28 = Lat. 614* (Modena: Il Bulino and Y. Press, 2004). I, alas, have never seen the original, but have relied on the facsimiles. See the appendix for a complete description of the manuscript, including provenance and citations.

R. S. Wieck (✉)
The Morgan Library & Museum, New York, NY, USA
e-mail: rwieck@themorgan.org

K. D. Peebles, G. Scarlatta (eds.), *Representing the Life and Legacy of Renée de France*, Queenship and Power,
https://doi.org/10.1007/978-3-030-69121-9_3

Ve Maria gratia ple
na dominus tecum
benedicta tu in mulieribus et
benedictus fructus ventris tui
Iesus. Sancta Maria mater
dei ora pro nobis peccatorib'
Amen.

Fig. 3.1   Master of Claude de France (and, for the portrait, possibly Jean Perréal or Jean Clouet). *Annunciation* and *Renée Praying*, from the Primer of Renée de France, ca. 1515–17. Modena, Biblioteca Estense Universitaria, MS Lat. 614 = α.U.2.28, fols. 5v-6. (Photographic credit: The Morgan Library & Museum)

your servant Queen Anne, my mother."[2] In early sixteenth-century France, the time and place the manuscript was created, there were only two people on earth who could recite such a prayer: Claude de France and her younger sister, Renée, who were the two daughters of King Louis XII and his queen, Anne de Bretagne. When Anne died on January 9, 1514, and Louis on January 1, 1515, their two children, Claude and Renée, were orphans. At the death of her father, the sixteen-year-old Claude, who had

---

[2] The full text of this prayer reads: "Inclina Domine aure[m] tuam ad preces nostras quibus misericordiam supplices deprecamur, ut animam famuli tui Ludovici Regis patris mei, et animam famule tue Anne Regine matris mee, quas de hoc seculo migrare iussisti in pacis ac lucis regione constituas, et sanctorum tuoru[m] iubeas esse confortes. Per Christum Dominum nostrum. Amen" (Incline your ear, O Lord, to our prayers through which as supplicants we beg your mercy, so that you will establish the soul of your servant King Louis, my father, and the soul of your servant Queen Anne, my mother, whom you have ordered to depart from this world, in the region of peace and light, and order them to be the consorts of your saints), fols. 19-19v.

Fig. 3.2 Master of Claude de France. *Supper at Emmaus*, from the Primer of Renée de France, ca. 1515–17. Modena, Biblioteca Estense Universitaria, MS Lat. 614 = α.U.2.28, fol. 7v. (Photographic credit: The Morgan Library & Museum)

married François d'Angoulême in 1514, became queen of France as the wife of King François I. In the portraits within the Modena manuscript, especially in the first, more exact one (Figs. 3.1, 3.3, 3.4), the young girl depicted is far too young to be Queen Claude. At sixteen, Claude is also too old for a book that starts off with the Pater noster (Our Father), Ave Maria (Hail Mary), and Credo (Apostles' Creed), prayers she had

Fig. 3.3 Master of Claude de France. *Renée Confessing*, from the Primer of Renée de France, ca. 1515–17. Modena, Biblioteca Estense Universitaria, MS Lat. 614 = α.U.2.28, fol. 8v. (Photographic credit: The Morgan Library & Museum)

Oce me domine viam
in qua ambulem, ego
enim sum paruula ignorans
progreffum meum. Da mihi

Fig. 3.4 Master of Claude de France. *Renée Praying to Christ*, from the Primer of Renée de France, ca. 1515–17. Modena, Biblioteca Estense Universitaria, MS Lat. 614 = α.U.2.28, fol. 9v. (Photographic credit: The Morgan Library & Museum)

memorized as a young girl from the primer her mother had given her around 1505.[3] By default this leaves Renée as the only candidate for the person depicted within the manuscript and for whom the book would have thus been made. This essay examines the book's textual and pictorial

[3] Cambridge, Fitzwilliam Museum, MS 159, according to Roger S. Wieck, Cynthia J. Brown, and Eberhard König, *The Primer of Claude de France: MS 159, The Fitzwilliam Museum, Cambridge* (Luzern: Quaternio, 2012).

contents as well as the artist who painted the illuminations; the analysis helps reveal the particular circumstances surrounding its commission.

The Modena manuscript is, in part, a primer. It is a book made to teach Renée to read and, at the same time, a book from which she could learn her basic catechism. It begins with the Our Father, Hail Mary (Fig. 3.1), and Apostles' Creed, followed by Grace before Meals (Fig. 3.2) and the Confiteor (the Act of Confession), which is here, as is sometimes the case, preceded by the Misereatur, a form of absolution (Fig. 3.3).[4] These five prayers were among the most basic of all Catholic devotions, ones that were memorized, as mentioned above, by all at an early age.[5] They are then followed by five groups of "grown-up" devotions (ones not to be memorized), some of which were well known and popular, while others are quite rare and possibly unique to this manuscript. These start with a pair of prayers for wisdom, "Doce me Domine" (Fig. 3.4) and "Domine Deus omnipotens."[6]

Next is the group of devotions that begin with "O Crux ave spes unica," a prayer to the true cross, which is followed by "Iesus autem transiens" (Luke 4:30), words used in a number of charms; "Subveniat mihi Domine," a rare and possibly unique prayer for mercy; and "Actiones nostras quesumus Domine," a popular prayer asking God's assistance before any action.[7] The third section contains a short prayer to one's guardian angel, "Salve sancte custos" (based on the Introit from the Mass for Guardian Angels); "Benedic anima mea," a quotation of Psalm 102:1; the Gloria Patri; and the popular "Salva nos Domine."[8] Next is the group with a long, rare, and possibly unique prayer of praise, "Laudo et glorifico te

---

[4] The Misereatur (May Almighty God have mercy), for example, is recited along with (a longer version of) the Confiteor at the start of every Mass.

[5] Primers in the Middle Ages and Renaissance were school or prayer books from which children learn to read and to pray. Usually thin, they might include an ABC, Our Father, Hail Mary, Apostles' Creed, Grace before and after Meals, and other elementary devotions. See Kathryn M. Rudy, "An Illustrated Mid-Fifteenth-Century Primer for a Flemish Girl: British Library, Harley MS 3828," *Journal of the Warburg and Courtauld Institutes* 69 (2006): 51–94, with generous citations to earlier literature.

[6] "Doce me Domine" (Teach me, Lord), "Domine Deus omnipotens" (Lord God omnipotent).

[7] "O Crux ave spes unica" (Hail, O Cross, our only hope), "Iesus autem transiens" (But Jesus passing through), "Subveniat mihi Domine" (May the Lord help me), "Actiones nostras quesumus Domine" (Direct, we beseech you, O Lord, our actions).

[8] "Salve sancte custos" (Hail holy guardian), "Benedic anima mea" (Bless the Lord, O my soul), *Gloria patri* (Glory be to the Father), "Salva nos Domine" (Save us, O Lord).

Domine"; the Te Deum, a popular hymn attributed, as the rubric informs us, to Sts. Ambrose and Augustine; and "Deus qui contritorum non despicis," a popular prayer in times of tribulation, which is derived from the votive Mass of the same theme.[9] The concluding group includes John's Gospel lesson In principio (John 1:1–14), which is the reading from the third (main) Mass on Christmas Day that regularly appears in books of hours, followed here by the customary "Protector in te sperantium Deus"; the prayer for the souls of King Louis XII and Queen Anne de Bretagne, "Inclina Domine aurem tuam," which is a standard prayer for the dead, extracted from a Mass for the Dead, that allows for the insertion of the names of particular persons; and French versions of the Ten Commandments, the Five Commandments of the Church, and the Apostles' Creed.[10] Lacking in the Latin Apostles' Creed at the front of the manuscript, but present here in the French version are rubrics attributing the creed's individual Twelve Articles of Faith to particular apostles. The manuscript would have been commissioned for Renée shortly after the death of Louis, sometime (as will be discussed below) between 1515 and 1517, as an appropriate book for a five- to seven-year-old reader.

For a thin book, it is richly illuminated. Flowers or fruit on gold ground decorate the borders for each of the thirty-seven pages of the manuscript. The twelve miniatures range in size from full- to half-page.[11] These twelve images mark the major textual divisions within the book as outlined above: God Blessing (at the Our Father), Annunciation and Renée Praying (Hail Mary; Fig. 3.1), Apostles Writing Their Articles of Faith (Apostles' Creed), Supper at Emmaus (Grace Before Meals; Fig. 3.2), Renée Praying (Misereatur), Renée Confessing (Confiteor; Fig. 3.3), Renée Praying to Christ ("Doce me Domine"; Fig. 3.4), Mary Magdalene Adoring the Cross ("O Crux ave spes unica"), Guardian Angel ("Salve sancte custos"),

[9] "Laudo et glorifico te Domine" (I praise and honor you, O Lord), Te Deum (You, O God, we praise), "Deus qui contritorum non despicis" (O God, who despises not the sighs of the contrite).

[10] In principio (In the beginning), "Protector in te sperantium Deus" (O God, protector of all who trust in you), "Inclina Domine aurem tuam" (Incline your ear, O Lord). See note 2 for the complete prayer in both Latin and English.

[11] The *Liber Iesus* (Milan, Biblioteca Trivulziana, MS 2163), a small codex of fourteen leaves produced for the education of Massimiliano Sforza (1493–1530), son of Ludovico il Moro, contains only four miniatures and three historiated initials. See Jonathan J.G. Alexander, Pier Luigi Mulas, and Marzia Pontone, *Grammatica del Donato e Liber Iesus: due libri per l'educazione di Massimiliano Sforza* (Modena: Panini, 2016). The complete manuscript is viewable on the website of the Archivio Storico Civico e Biblioteca Trivulziana.

Renée Praying to Christ ("Laudo et glorifico te Domine"), and John on Patmos (In principio).

Relative to the number of miniatures and to the slenderness of the book, there are an unusually high number (five) of portraits of its owner. Prayer books of the period intended to include portraiture normally have but one. In the first (fol. 6; Fig. 3.1) Renée appears as a young girl with chubby cheeks, between the ages of five and seven, wearing a gold brocade dress. In the remaining four (fols. 8, 8v, 9v, and 13; Figs. 3.3, 3.4), she is depicted as a young teenager wearing a light pink dress with voluminous bombard sleeves. The age difference between the first portrait and the other four, which are alike and form a group, is purposeful. In the first she is portrayed at the age when she received her primer (five, six, or seven years old). Contemplating the image of the Annunciation on the facing page, Renée is shown praying the Ave Maria, not from the book that lies open but ignored before her, but from memory. As she continues to grow, into a young adult who, having sinned, will confess and seek absolution, she will say longer and more complex prayers, not from memory, but from her prayer book.

The artist of the book is an illuminator known as the Master of Claude de France.[12] He is named after the two jewel-like manuscripts, a prayer book owned by the Morgan Library & Museum (MS M.1166; Figs. 3.5, 3.6), and a book of hours (Ramsen, Heribert Tenschert, Antiquariat Bibermühle) that Renée's older sister, Claude, commissioned for herself in the years when she became queen (in 1515) and was crowned (in 1517).[13] Active as an independent artist from 1508 till the early 1520s, the Claude

---

[12] The artist was baptized by Charles Sterling. See Sterling, *The Master of Claude, Queen of France. A Newly Defined Miniaturist* (New York: H.P. Kraus, 1975).

[13] For Claude's prayer book, see Roger S. Wieck and Cynthia J. Brown, *The Prayer Book of Claude de France: MS M.1166, The Pierpont Morgan Library, New York* (Luzern: Quaternio, 2010). For her book of hours, see Eberhard König, *The Book of Hours of Claude de France* (Ramsen: Antiquariat Bibermühle, 2012). The book of hours, the "bestseller" of the late Middle Ages and Renaissance, was a prayer book used by the laity that contained, at its heart, the eponymous Hours of the Blessed Virgin Mary. See Victor Leroquais, *Les livres d'heures manuscrits de la Bibliothèque nationale*, 4 vols. (Paris: [s. n.] and Macon: Protat Frères, 1927–1943); Roger S. Wieck, Laurence R. Poos, Virginia Reinburg, and John Plummer, *Time Sanctified: The Book of Hours in Medieval Art and Life* (New York: George Braziller, 1988); and Roger S. Wieck, *Painted Prayers: The Book of Hours in Medieval and Renaissance Art* (New York: George Braziller, 1997).

Fig. 3.5 Master of Claude de France. *Virgin and Child with St. John the Baptist*, with the coat of arms of Queen Claude de France in the lower border, and *Annunciation to Joachim*, from the Prayer Book of Claude de France, ca. 1515–17. New York, Morgan Library & Museum, MS M.1166, fols. 15v-16. Gift of Mrs. Alexandre P. Rosenberg in memory of her husband Alexandre Paul Rosenberg, 2008. (Photographic credit: The Morgan Library & Museum)

Master, who was based in Tours, illuminated (in whole or in part) approximately thirty manuscripts, commissions from royals or their courtiers.[14] The artist's style is one of fineness and delicacy. His palette exhibits a subtle range of soft purples, mauves, and roses. He preferred to work on a small scale, painting in tiny stippled brushstrokes. His short figures are almost childlike, and they express themselves with quiet, restrained gestures. His miniatures are infused with sweetness. Forms tend to be less detailed and more abstracted. His borders are usually filled with flowers

[14] For a review of the artist's career, including a list of all his known works, see Roger S. Wieck and Francisco Trujillo, *Miracles in Miniature: The Art of the Master of Claude de France* (New York: Morgan Library & Museum, 2014).

Fig. 3.6   Master of Claude de France. *Annunciation*, with the coat of arms of Queen Claude de France in the lower border, from the Prayer Book of Claude de France, ca. 1515–17. New York, Morgan Library & Museum, MS M.1166, fol. 18v. Gift of Mrs. Alexandre P. Rosenberg in memory of her husband Alexandre Paul Rosenberg, 2008. (Photographic credit: The Morgan Library & Museum)

(Figs. 3.1, 3.2, 3.3, and 3.4), antique candelabras (Fig. 3.5), or Italianate architectural frames (Fig. 3.6). Although he trained under Jean Bourdichon (1457–1521) and derives much of his style from that *peintre du roi*, he was also influenced by Jean Poyer (fl. 1465–ca. 1503) and the Master of the della Rovere Missals (Jacopo Ravaldi?; fl. ca. 1475–1505). In Renée's primer, the figures of the Virgin and the Archangel Gabriel (Fig. 3.1), Christ and his two disciples (Fig. 3.2), the bishop who hears Renée's confession (Fig. 3.3), and the standing Christ (Fig. 3.4) are characteristic of the artist's short figures with relatively large heads, which render the figures doll- or childlike. Typical of his palette are the subtle blues and pale lilacs seen in the robes worn by Gabriel, Christ and his disciples, and the bishop hearing Renée's confession. The quiet gestures of Gabriel, Christ at Emmaus, and the bishop are also characteristic. The close similarities in style and iconography between the Annunciation in Renée's primer (Fig. 3.1) and that in the prayer book that helped define his style (Fig. 3.6) make it easy to attribute both creations to the same artist. The flowers and plants that fill the borders in Renée's primer, foliage that the artist learned to paint from Bourdichon, are one of the three main styles with which he adorns his borders.[15]

At the tender age at which she received it, Princess Renée was far too young to have commissioned the primer herself. Convincing evidence points to her older sister, Claude, as the most likely patron of the manuscript. There are four main arguments. First is the artist. Between the time she became queen in 1515 and she was crowned in 1517, Claude de France, as mentioned above, commissioned two manuscripts for herself— a prayer book and a book of hours—both painted by the Master of Claude de France. This artist obviously occupied a special place in her heart. This was most likely due to a gift from her mother. Around 1508, at the time when her own *Grandes Heures* (Paris, Bibliothèque nationale de France, MS lat. 9474) illuminated by official court artist Jean Bourdichon came into her possession, Anne commissioned for the nine-year-old Claude her own book of hours (called the "Hachette Hours" after a previous owner, André Hachette; Ireland, private collection).[16] Around 1508, Anne could

---

[15] In the summer of 2019, as I was completing this article, the Metropolitan Museum of Art (Cloisters Collection) in New York acquired a previously unknown manuscript by the Master of Claude de France that contains an amazing thirty-nine portraits of flowers (acc. no. 2019.197).

[16] For Anne's *Grandes Heures*, see *Grandes Heures d'Anne de Bretagne/Great Hours of Anne of Brittany*, ed. Monica Miró (Barcelona: Moleiro, 2008–10). For Claude's ca. 1508 Book of Hours, see Wieck, *Miracles in Miniature*, 28–30, 78, figs. 38–40.

recognize that her daughter at the age of nine had outgrown the primer she had given her some three years prior, around 1505 (Cambridge, Fitzwilliam Museum, MS 159). Anne commissioned Claude's book of hours from the Master of Claude de France, who was just then emerging from Bourdichon's workshop and establishing himself as an independent illuminator. So when Claude became queen and started to think about commissioning her own books of devotion, she turned to that artist whom her mother had employed to paint her first "grown-up" book of hours, the one Anne gave to Claude around 1508.[17] While treating herself to a pair of new codices (the Morgan Library Prayer Book and the Tenschert Book of Hours), Claude also thought of her younger sister, Renée, who, around five years old, was the age when Claude had received her primer from Anne. Claude thus commissions a book for Renée, fittingly for her age a primer, from an artist who was clearly a favorite of hers.

The second piece of evidence that points to Claude as the patron of Renée's primer is the prayer for the souls of Louis and Anne, "Inclina Domine aurem tuam." The same prayer can be found in exactly one other manuscript: Claude's book of hours (not, of course her ca. 1508 one, but the one she commissioned ca. 1515–17).[18] It is only natural to conclude that the person who asked for this prayer to be included in her book of hours—Queen Claude herself—would be the same person to ask that it also be included in a manuscript that was being made at the same time for Louis and Anne's other orphan, Claude's young sister, Renée. Such a personal devotion would have been composed in the first instance at the command of the queen herself.

The third reason to think that it was Claude who commissioned Renée's primer is the book's model. Around 1495, Anne de Bretagne, then queen to Charles VIII, commissioned a primer for the dauphin, Charles-Orland

---

[17] Books of hours for adults lack those very devotions that comprise a primer, namely, ABC, Our Father, Hail Mary, Apostles' Creed, Act of Confession, and Grace before and after Meals. For references detailing the traditional contents of a book of hours, see note 13.

[18] In Claude's book of hours, the prayer appears appropriately at the end of the Office of the Dead (slight differences between it and the version in Renée's primer are in **bold**): "Inclina Domine aurem tua[m] ad preces nostras quibus misericordiam **tuam** supplices deprecamur, ut animam famuli tui Ludovici Regis patris mei, et animam famulae tue Annae Reginae matris meae, **et animas omnium fidelium defunctorum**, quas de hoc seculo migrare iussisti in pacis ac lucis regione constituas, et sanctorum tuorum iubeas esse confortes." König, *The Book of Hours of Claude de France*, fol. 119. Claude's version includes "the souls of all the faithfully departed," a phrase lacking in Renée's Primer.

(New York, Morgan Library & Museum, MS M.50).[19] It consists of the Pater noster, Ave Maria, Apostles' Creed, Graces before and after Meals, the Confiteor, and numerous additional devotions, concluding with a prayer for wisdom. It is decorated with thirty-four miniatures by Jean Poyer (a rough contemporary of Jean Bourdichon). Strong textual and pictorial parallels between the two books indicate that the Primer of Charles-Orland was clearly the model for Renée's primer. The Ave Maria in both is illustrated by an Annunciation (Figs. 3.1 and 3.7). Grace before Meals in both is illustrated by the Supper at Emmaus (Figs. 3.2 and 3.8). Not only is this a relatively rare subject in manuscript illumination, but the two versions are also similar enough for one to argue that Jean Poyer's composition (Fig. 3.8) provided direct inspiration to the Master of Claude de France (Fig. 3.2) for his version. Apparently, Queen Claude lent the Primer of Charles-Orland itself to the Claude Master for him to study and "copy." The Confiteor in Charles-Orland's primer shows Anne de Bretagne at Confession (Fig. 3.9); the same prayer in Renée's primer shows the princess doing the same thing (Fig. 3.3). Finally, the earlier manuscript includes a prayer for wisdom illustrated with an image of Charles-Orland Praying to Christ (Fig. 3.10). Similarly, Renée's primer also includes a prayer for wisdom illustrated with an image of Renée Praying to Christ (Fig. 3.4). In Charles-Orland's primer, he is depicted not at the age he was when he was given his codex (around three-years-old), but as a young man, a teenager, in a kind of portrait at a projected age.[20] Similarly, Renée is not depicted at the age when she was given her book, but as a young, teenaged woman. Finally, it should be noted that the two codices are very close in size: Renée's primer measures 122 × 88 mm; Charles-Orland's 125 × 80 mm (both may have suffered some trimming).

The fourth piece of evidence pointing to Claude as the one who commissioned Renée's primer is that the Modena manuscript is not a "one-off." Indeed, it is one of the group of three manuscripts that Claude commissioned at this time, each of which had as its model or inspiration a manuscript already in her possession. These three earlier manuscripts had been commissioned by her mother and thus she would have had great

---

[19] Roger S. Wieck, with K. Michelle Hearne, *The Prayer Book of Anne de Bretagne: MS M.50, The Pierpont Morgan Library, New York* (Luzern: Faksimile Verlag, 1999).
[20] Sadly, Charles-Orland never reached the age of his projected portrait; he died in 1495, shortly after his third birthday.

Fig. 3.7   Jean Poyer. *Annunciation*, from the Primer of Charles-Orland, ca. 1495. New York, Morgan Library & Museum, MS M.50, fol. 1v. Purchased by J. Pierpont Morgan (1837–1913) in 1905. (Photographic credit: The Morgan Library & Museum)

Fig. 3.8   Jean Poyer. *Supper at Emmaus*, from the Primer of Charles-Orland, ca. 1495. New York, Morgan Library & Museum, MS M.50, fol. 8. Purchased by J. Pierpont Morgan (1837–1913) in 1905. (Photographic credit: The Morgan Library & Museum)

Fig. 3.9   Jean Poyer. *Anne de Bretagne Confessing*, from the Primer of Charles-Orland, ca. 1495. New York, Morgan Library & Museum, MS M.50, fol. 10v. Purchased by J. Pierpont Morgan (1837–1913) in 1905. (Photographic credit: The Morgan Library & Museum)

Fig. 3.10 Jean Poyer. *Charles-Orland Praying*, from the Primer of Charles-Orland, ca. 1495. New York, Morgan Library & Museum, MS M.50, fol. 31. Purchased by J. Pierpont Morgan (1837–1913) in 1905. (Photographic credit: The Morgan Library & Museum)

emotional attachment to them, especially in those painful years immediately following Anne's death.[21] Thus, as we have seen, when Claude decided to have a primer made for Renée, she turned to the one Anne had commissioned for her son the dauphin, Charles-Orland, a book that Claude had inherited as part of her mother's library. When Claude commissioned her prayer book (Figs. 3.5 and 3.6), she was inspired for its decorative scheme by the primer (Cambridge, Fitzwilliam Museum, MS 159) her mother had given her as a young girl. That primer is unusually decorated: its twelve text pages are illustrated not with miniatures, but with historiated borders (margins containing narrative figures); the manuscript contains only two full-page miniatures (one at the front and one at the back). With a sense either of nostalgia toward that book or of commemoration of her mother—or both—Claude filled her prayer book with historiated borders (such as seen on the right side of Fig. 3.5). In a most unusual decorative layout for its time, ninety-seven of its 104 pages are illustrated by historiated borders. It is unusual because in the late Middle Ages and Renaissance, historiated borders customarily play a secondary role to that of miniatures incorporated into the text area proper. (The prayer book also includes seven large and twenty-seven small square miniatures, about which more below.) For the texts of her prayer book, as well as for those in the book of hours she commissioned at the same time, Claude turned to the "Hachette Hours," the *Horae* her mother had given her around 1508, as a model. The "Hachette Hours" contains a Calendar; Gospel Lessons; John's Passion; Obsecro te and O intemerata; Hours of the Virgin intermixed with the Hours of the Conception of the Virgin, of the Cross, and of the Holy Spirit; Penitential Psalms and Litany; Office of the Dead; and a long series of suffrages (short devotions to individual saints) and a few miscellaneous prayers. In fact, the texts of the "Hachette Hours" are what would result if one combined Claude's prayer book with her book of hours. Indeed, except for a single prayer, the suffrages in the "Hachette Hours" perfectly match those in Claude's prayer book.[22]

---

[21] I have previously explored the theory of manuscripts originally commissioned by Anne de Bretagne as inspirations for specific commissions on the part of Claude in Wieck, *Miracles in Miniature*, and "Tours 1500," in *Manuscripts in the Making: Art & Science. Volume One*, ed. Stella Panayotova and Paula Ricciardi (London: Harvey Miller, 2017), 135–43.

[22] Among the suffrages, the prayer to the Holy Face (Salve sancta facies), which is included in the prayer book, is absent in the "Hachette Hours." The suffrages in the manuscripts, while fairly typical of late medieval prayer books produced in northern France, do contain a few atypical saints, but understandable considering the manuscripts' owner: Louis (King

Pictorially, too, there are affinities between the "Hachette Hours" and Claude's prayer book and book of hours. The suffrages in the "Hachette Hours" are illustrated with small square miniatures featuring bust-length portraits of saints; the suffrages in the prayer book are illustrated in the same way, with small square miniatures of bust-length saints. Each text page in the "Hachette Hours" is framed by a field of gold upon which are painted armillary spheres, bird wings painted in lilac, tightly knotted cordelières, and scrolls inscribed with the motto *Non mudera*.[23] These were the devices of Anne de Bretagne. Claude adopted these devices; she filled the borders of her Book of Hours with them, imitating the "Hachette Hours." The unusual device-filled borders in the Book of Hours and the equally unusual historiated borders of the Prayer Book were specifically requested by the queen of her illuminator; she participated in these two commissions more closely than was usual.[24] Had he had his own way, the artist would have filled the borders with the flowers, as in Renée's Primer (Figs. 3.1, 3.2, 3.3, and 3.4), antique candelabras (Fig. 3.5), or Italianate architectural frames (Fig. 3.6) that he much preferred.

Renée's Primer thus has a complex history and is part of a complicated story. It is one of three small codices, all of which were commissioned by Claude at the same time, as she began her reign as queen, and all were illuminated by the queen's favored artist. All three commissions hark back to manuscripts in the queen's possession, books that had been commissions from her mother. The situation can be diagrammed as follows (Table 3.1):

Louis IX of France, naturally popular among French royalty; he was the namesake of Claude's father, Louis XII), Renatus (patron saint of Claude's young sister), Ursula (a Breton princess to whom Anne de Bretagne and Claude had special attachment), and Helena (mother of Emperor Constantine who discovered the true cross, relics of which were in the royal family's Sainte-Chapelle in Paris).

[23] On these elements, see also Kathleen Wilson-Chevalier, Chap. 2 in this volume.
[24] Claude's use of earlier manuscripts as inspiration for her commissions is not without precedent. In the late fourteenth century, for example, Jean, duc de Berry, so coveted the "Savoy Hours" (which survives in fragmentary state in New Haven, Yale University, Beinecke Rare Book and Manuscript Library, MS 390) owned by his brother King Charles V of France that he commissioned his first book of hours, the *Petites Heures* (Paris, Bibliothèque nationale de France, MS lat. 18014), in imitation of it; see Wieck, "The Savoy Hours, Bibliophilic Jealousy, and the Manuscript Patronage of Jean, Duc de Berry," in *Die Savoy Hours/The Savoy Hours/Les Heures de Savoie*, ed. Roger S. Wieck and Raymond Clemens (Luzern: Quaternio Verlag, 2017), 115–46.

Table 3.1   Claude's commissions ca. 1515–17

Claude's commissions ca. 1515–17:	Modeled on:
Book of hours	"Hachette Hours"
Ramsen	Ireland
Prayer book	Primer of Claude
Morgan M.1166	Fitzwilliam 159
Primer of Renée	Primer of Charles-Orland
Modena Lat. 614	Morgan M.50

It is possible, however, that the story of the relationship between Renée and the Master of Claude de France did not stop with her first book. In 2013, a small book of hours, an otherwise unknown work by the Claude Master, appeared on the art market.[25] It is richly illuminated with fourteen large and twenty-nine small miniatures painted by the artist in his characteristic style (Fig. 3.11). The manuscript has close textual affinities with the "adult" prayers in the Modena Primer. There is thus a strong possibility that Renée, having fallen in love with the work of the Claude Master from her primer, turned to the same artist when she came to commission her first "adult" book of hours.

To return to Renée's primer, its contents are completely traditional and fall in line with those of the two other primers discussed in this essay (that of Claude de France and that of Charles-Orland). Created between 1515 and 1517, it and its contents predate the time when, in the 1520s, Martin Luther's Protestant ideas began to circulate in France.[26] As the provenance

[25] London, Christie's, November 20, 2013, lot 56, illus. The manuscript, which failed to sell at the auction, was later bought by its present owner by private treaty.

[26] Even the presence of such texts as the Ten Commandments, Five Commandments of the Church, and Apostles' Creed in French at the end of Renée's primer is typical of its time; similar devotions in French occur in books of hours published in Paris such as a 1506 *Horae* printed by Thielman Kerver and in a ca. 1510 edition by Gillet and Germaine Hardouin; see Hugh William Davies, *Catalogue of a Collection of Early French Books in the Library of C. Fairfax Murray*, 2 vols. (London: s.n., 1910), 301–303, no. 266, and 312, no. 272. A random sampling of some of the Morgan Library's printed *Horae* reveals that, in the late fifteenth and early sixteenth centuries, the Penitential Psalms and the Apostles' Creed in French make regular appearance; they occur in Thielman Kerver editions of October 28, 1498 (PML 126016/ChL 1513R), of September 16, 1499 (PML 78955/ChL 1513T), and of June 20, 1500 (PML 129150/ChL 1514M); and in an edition October 1, 1505, of Guillaume Anabat for Germaine Hardouin (PML 586). The title page of the last book even mentions "cum pluribus orationibus tam in gallico q[uam] in latino" (with many prayers in French as well as in Latin).

Fig. 3.11 Master of Claude de France. *Angel with the Eucharist* and *Tortured Christ*, from a book of hours, after 1515–17. Private collection, fols. 26v-27. © Christie's Images Limited, 2020

indicates (see the appendix), Renée took her first book with her when she moved to Ferrara following her marriage to Ercole II d'Este, Duke of Ferrara, in 1528. As other contributions in this volume relate, Renée became an important supporter of the Protestant Reformation, an ally of John Calvin, and a convert—to Ercole's huge dismay. Perhaps because it did not conform to her new beliefs, or perhaps because it was indeed a children's book, Renée, in any case, when she left Ferrara and returned to France in 1560 following the death of her husband the previous year, did not take the primer with her.

APPENDIX

"Primer of Renée de France"
Modena, Biblioteca Estense Universitaria, MS Lat. 614 = α.U.2.28.
France, Tours, ca. 1515–1517.
Vellum, 26 leaves, 122 × 88 (87 × 51) mm, 1 column, 17 lines, in Latin
and French, in *littera humanistica textualis*, 3 full-page, 7 three-quarter-
page, and 2 half-page miniatures, and 37 four-sided borders with flowers
or fruit on gold ground, illuminated by the Master of Claude de France
(while the portrait on fol. 6 is painted by another hand, possibly Jean
Clouet or Jean Perréal) (Fig. 3.1).

Table 3.2 Prayers and accompanying images in the *Primer of Renée de France*

Text	Image
Blank vellum leaves (fol. 1 with eighteenth-century Italian inscription giving Renée's ownership and stamped "B.E.") (fols. 1–4)	
Pater noster (5)	God Blessing (4v)
Ave Maria (6)	Annunciation (5v; Fig. 3.1)
	Renée Praying (6; Fig. 3.1)
Apostles' Creed (7-7v)	Apostles Writing (6v)
Grace Before Meals (7v-8)	Supper at Emmaus (7v; Fig. 3.2)
Misereatur (8-8v)	Renée Praying (8)
Confiteor (8v-9)	Renée Confessing (8v; Fig. 3.3)
Doce me Domine; Domine Deus omnipotens (9v-10v)	Renée Praying to Christ (9v; Fig. 3.4)
O Crux ave spes unica; Subveniat mihi Domine; Actiones nostras quesumus Domine (11-11v)	Mary Magdalene Adoring the Cross (11)
Salve sancte custos; Benedic anima mea; Salva nos Domine (12-12v)	Guardian Angel (12)
Laudo et glorifico te Domine; Te Deum; Deus qui contritorum non despicis (13-17)	Renée Praying to Christ (13)
In principio; Protector in te sperantium Deus; Inclina Domine aurem tuam; 10 Commandments (in French); 5 Commandments of the Church (in French); Apostles' Creed (in French) (17v-22v)	John on Patmos (17v)
Blank vellum leaves (fol. 23 stamped "B.E."; fol. 26v annotated "L. 614/α.U.2.28") (23-26v)	

Provenance:
Commissioned for Renée de France by her older sister, Queen Claude de France, in Tours, between 1515 and 1517; taken by Renée to Ferrara following her marriage to Ercole II d'Este, Duke of Ferrara, in 1528; left by Renée in Ferrara after her return to France in 1560 following the 1559 death of her husband (and not among those books burned by the Inquisition after her departure); remained at the castle in Ferrara (presumably as part of the "guardaroba ducale") when the Estense library was transferred to Modena in 1598; added to fol. 1 in the eighteenth century is a provenance annotation attributed to Estense librarian Ludovico Antonio Muratori: "Renea de Valois/moglie di Ercole 2°/4° Duca di Ferrara/figlia di Luigi XII./Re di Francia detto/il giusto, e di Anna/di Brettagna, e/sorella della moglie/di Francesco p[r]imo Re di Francia"; transferred from Ferrara to Modena, May 6, 1780 (*Registro di libri ricevuti dal 30 Dicembre 1773 al 29 Maggio 1781*, A. II. 925 & 935; shelf mark changed from "VII, G. 10" to "Lat. 614" and later augmented with "α.U.2.28"); stolen from the exhibition, "Recitare la devozione: Pregare nel segreto," at Montecassino Abbey in 1994 and still missing.

Citations:
Cavedoni 1864, 313–22; Fontana 1889–1899, I, 31–33; Müntz 1902, 81–82, illus. pp. 80, 81, 82; Michel 1905–29, IV/2, 741; "Pubblicazioni di carattere bibliografico" 1906, 298–99, illus. pp. 298, 299, 300; Carta and Bertoni 1907; Fumagalli 1913, 80–82, no. 362; Fava 1925, 127–29; Fava and Salmi 1950–73, II, 167–69, tav. LXII; Muzzioli 1953, 457–58, no. 739; Plummer 1982, 100; Biblioteca estense 1987, 26, 182, Tavv. CXXXI–CXXXIV; Avril and Reynaud 1993, 319, 322; Milano 1998; Milano and Orth 1998; Wieck 1999, 151–52, 214–15; Bini 2004; Wieck 2007, 267, 270, 271, Fig. 6; Wieck 2010a, 181, 201, 227, 234, 237, 285, Fig. 9; Wieck 2010b, 188, 189, Fig. 6; de Chancel-Bardelot et al. 2012, 266; König 2012, 29–33, 44, 52, 53, 57, 58, 61–62, 63, 70, 133, illus. pp. 28, 32, 57; Wieck, Brown, and König 2012, 125, 127, 151–52, 167–68, Fig. 7; Hand 2013, 33, 179–80, 181–82, 183, 184, 223, Fig. 4.4; Wieck 2014, 10, 38–40, 43, 54, 60 n. 7, 74, 78, Figs. 49, 51; D'Urso 2016, 209; Wilson-Chevalier 2016, 126; Wieck 2017b, 139–40, 141; Hermant and Toscano 2018, 20; Wieck 2018, 227, 229 n. 6.

Bibliography

Primary Sources

Manuscripts

Grandes heures d'Anne de Bretagne, BnF MS lat. 9474.
Hachette Hours, Private Collection.
Liber Iesus, Biblioteca Trivulziana, MS 2163.
Primer of Charles-Orland, The Morgan Library & Museum, MS M.50
Primer of Renée de France, Biblioteca Estense Universitaria, MS Lat. 614
= α.U.2.28
Prayer Book of Claude de France, The Morgan Library & Museum, MS M.1166.
The Primer of Claude de France, The Fitzwilliam Museum, MS 159.

Imprints and Reproductions

Bini, Mauro, ed. 2004. *Les petites prières de Renée de France: Biblioteca Estense Universitaria, Modena, α.U.2.28 = Lat. 614.* Modena: Il Bulino and Y. Press. CD-ROM.
König, Eberhard. 2012. *The Book of Hours of Claude de France.* Ramsen: Antiquariat Bibermühle.
Milano, Ernesto, and Myra D. Orth. 1998. *Das Blumengebetbuch der Renée de France: Biblioteca Estense Universitaria, Modena, Lat. 614 = α.U.2.28.* Luzern: Faksimile Verlag.
Miró, Monica, ed. 2008–10. *Grandes Heures d'Anne de Bretagne/Great Hours of Anne of Brittany.* Barcelona: Moleiro.
Wieck, Roger S., with a contribution by K. Michelle Hearne. 1999. *The Prayer Book of Anne de Bretagne: MS M.50, The Pierpont Morgan Library, New York.* Luzern: Faksimile Verlag.

Secondary Sources

Alexander, Jonathan J.G., Pier Luigi Mulas, and Marzia Pontone. 2016. *Grammatica del Donato e Liber Iesus: due libri per l'educazione di Massimiliano Sforza.* Modena: Panini.
Avril, François, and Nicole Reynaud. 1993. *Les manuscrits à peintures en France, 1440–1520.* Paris: Flammarion.
Biblioteca estense, Modena. 1987. Florence: Nardini.

Carta, Francesco, and Giulio Bertoni. 1920. *Les petites prières de Renée de France.* Modena: Orlandini & Fils. First reproduced 1907.

Cavedoni, Celestino. 1864. Descrizione di un libriccino di divozione che appartenne a Madama Renea di Francia, moglie di Ercole II d'Este, duca di Ferrara, Modena e Reggio. *Atti e Memorie delle RR. Deputazioni di Storia Patria per le provincie modenesi e parmensi* 2: 313–322.

de Chancel-Bardelot, Béatrice, Pascale Charron, Pierre-Gilles Girault, and Jean-Marie Guillouët, eds. 2012. *Tours 1500: Capitale des arts.* Paris: Somogy.

Davies, Hugh William, Comp. 1910. *Catalogue of a Collection of Early French Books in the Library of C. Fairfax Murray.* 2 vols. London: s.n.

D'Urso, Teresa. 2016. La diffusion du style *all'antica* à Tours: De Jean Bourdichon au Maître de Claude de France. In *Art et société à Tours au début de la Renaissance: Actes du colloque "Tours 1500, art et sociéte'à Tours au début de la Renaissance" organisé au CESR du 10 au 12 mai 2012,* ed. Marion Boudon-Machuel and Pascale Charron, 197–211. Turnhout: Brepols.

Fava, Domenico. 1925. *La Biblioteca Estense nel suo sviluppo storico, con il catalogo della mostra permanente e 10 tavole.* Modena: G. T. Vincenzi e Nipoti di D. Cavallotti.

Fava, Domenico, and Mario Salmi. 1950–73. *I manoscritti miniati della Biblioteca Estense di Modena.* 2 vols. Florence: Electra Editrice.

Fontana, Bartolommeo. 1889–99. *Renata di Francia, duchessa di Ferrara, sui documenti dell'archivio estense, del mediceo, del Gonzaga e dell'archivioi secreto vaticano.* 3 vols. Rome: Forzani.

Fumagalli, Giuseppe. 1913. *L'arte della legatura alla corte degli Estensi, a Ferrara e a Modena, dal sec. XV al XIX. Col catalogo delle ligature pregevoli della Biblioteca Estense di Modena.* Florence: T. de Marinis &c.

Hand, Joni M. 2013. *Women, Manuscripts and Identity in Northern Europe, 1350–1550.* Farnham: Ashgate.

Hermant, Maxence, and Gennaro Toscano. 2018. Le livre d'heures de Frédéric d'Aragon, un chef-d'oeuvre franco-italien enluminé en Touraine. *Art de l'enluminure* 64: 4–30.

Leroquais, Victor. 1927–43. *Les livres d'heures manuscrits de la Bibliothèque nationale.* 4 vols. Paris: [s. n.] and Macon: Protat Frères.

Michel, André. 1905–29. *Histoire de l'art depuis les premiers temps chrétiens jusqu'à nos jours.* 9 vols. Paris: A. Colin.

Milano, Ernesto. 1998. *Commentario al codice* Les petites prières de Renée de France*: Lat. 614 = α.U.2.28, Biblioteca Estense Universitaria, Modena.* Modena: Il Bulino.

Müntz, Eugène. 1902. Les miniatures françaises dans les Bibliothèques italiennes. *La Bibliofilia* 4 (3/4): 73–83.

Muzzioli, Giovanni. 1953. *Mostra storico della miniatura, Palazzo Venezia: Catalogo.* Florence: Sansoni.

Plummer, John, with the assistance of Gregory Clark. 1982. *The Last Flowering: French Painting in Manuscripts, 1420–1530, from American Collections.* New York: Pierpont Morgan Library.

1906. Pubblicazioni di carattere bibliografico e intorno alla storia dell'arte tipografica. *La Bibliofilia* 8 (7/8): 298–300.

Rudy, Kathryn M. 2006. An Illustrated Mid-Fifteenth-Century Primer for a Flemish Girl: British Library, Harley MS 3828. *Journal of the Warburg and Courtauld Institutes* 69: 51–94.

Sterling, Charles. 1975. The Master of Claude, Queen of France. A Newly Defined Miniaturist. New York: H.P. Kraus.

Wieck, Roger S. 1997. *Painted Prayers: The Book of Hours in Medieval and Renaissance Art.* New York: George Braziller.

———. 2007. The Primer of Claude de France and the Education of the Renaissance Child. In *The Cambridge Illuminations: The Conference Papers,* ed. Stella Panayotova, 267–277. London: Harvey Miller.

———. 2010. The Prayer Book of Claude de France. In *The Medieval Book: Glosses from Friends & Colleagues of Christopher De Hamel,* ed. Richard A. Linenthal, James H. Marrow, and William Noel, 183–195. Leiden: Brill | Hes & De Graaf.

———. 2017. The Savoy Hours, Bibliophilic Jealousy, and the Manuscript Patronage of Jean, Duc de Berry. In *Die Savoy Hours/The Savoy Hours/Les Heures de Savoie,* ed. Roger S. Wieck and Raymond Clemens, 115–146. Luzern: Quaternio Verlag.

———. 2017. Tours 1500. In *Manuscripts in the Making: Art & Science. Volume One,* ed. Stella Panayotova and Paula Ricciardi, 135–143. London: Harvey Miller.

———. 2018. The Book of Hours. In *Splendour of the Burgundian Netherlands: Southern Netherlandish Illuminated Manuscripts in Dutch Collections,* ed. Anne Margreet W. As-Vijvers and Anne S. Korteweg, 222–229. Zwolle: W Books.

Wieck, Roger S., and with Essays by Laurence R. Poos, Virginia Reinburg and John Plummer. 1988. *Time Sanctified: The Book of Hours in Medieval Art and Life.* New York: George Braziller.

Wieck, Roger S., and with a Contribution by Cynthia J. Brown. 2010. *The Prayer Book of Claude de France: MS M.1166, The Pierpont Morgan Library, New York.* Luzern: Quaternio.

Wieck, Roger S., and with a Contribution by Francisco H. Trujillo. 2014. *Miracles in Miniature: The Art of the Master of Claude de France.* New York: Morgan Library & Museum.

Wieck, Roger S., Cynthia J. Brown, and Eberhard König. 2012. *The Primer of Claude de France: MS 159, The Fitzwilliam Museum, Cambridge.* Luzern: Quaternio.

Wilson-Chevalier, Katherine. 2016. 'Trinités royales' et 'quadrangle d'amour': Claude de France, Marguerite de Navarre, François Ier, Louise de Savoie et la réforme fabriste de l'Église. In "La dame de coeur": Patronage et mécénat religieux des femmes de pouvoir dans l'Europe des XIVe-XVIIe siècles, ed. Murielle Gaude-Ferragu and Cécile Vincent-Cassy, 123-136. Rennes: Presses Universitaires.

CHAPTER 4

Back to Basics: Rereading the "Ferrarese Imbroglio" of 1536 in Light of Primary Sources

Dick Wursten

In April–May 1536, Jean Calvin, at the age of 26, stayed for a short time in Ferrara, probably together with Louis du Tillet, a friend and cleric.[1] No

[1] The Du Tillet family is closely linked to the French Court. Louis's grandfather had served Louise de Savoie, mother of King François Ier, and his father had become "valet de chambre du Roy" and "greffier en chef" of the Parlement de Paris. Louis du Tillet received Calvin at his home after he left Paris in 1533, and for a while they walked the same road, both literally and spiritually. In 1537 however, Louis decided to return to France and became canon of the Angoulême cathedral. In subsequent correspondence Calvin accuses his friend of defection. Du Tillet, however, argues that Calvin's approach at reforming the church had proven counterproductive, and thus was not according to God's will. See Alexandre César Crottet, *Correspondance française de Calvin avec Louis du Tillet chanoine d'Angoulême et curé de Claix: sur les questions de l'église et du ministère évangélique: découverte parmi les manuscrits de la Bibliothèque nationale de France, et publiée pour la première fois* (Paris: Cherbuliez, 1850).

D. Wursten (✉)
Independent Scholar, Antwerp, Belgium
e-mail: dick@wursten.be

one doubts this statement. It's an established fact. However, why he went, what he did, how long he stayed, and with whom he spoke is unknown. There is no documentary evidence to fill in the picture with more detail, and Calvin himself never referred to this trip, not even casually. This is also an established fact. It's only after Calvin's death, in the sketch of his life by Théodore de Bèze (published in 1564, 1565, and 1575) that the trip is mentioned, still without detail, but informing us that he was received by Renée de France, Duchess of Ferrara, whose court at the time was a haven for French refugees suspected of "heresy," and that this meeting made a deep impression on the duchess. To accept this information at face value, as is generally done, is naïve. Bèze's "Life of Calvin" basically is an apologetic document, not a "biography," which is discussed further below.[2] Nevertheless, a complete mythology has been woven around Calvin's stay in Ferrara, including vivid accounts of his activity there. Much of this mythology was constructed in the nineteenth century, but its impact is still perceptible today, and not only in popular writing.[3] In the leanest version, Bèze's statement is repeated, generally with the reference that Calvin served as a secretary to the duchess. In the longer version, Calvin teaches the true religion (often capitalized), privately in the duchess's chambers and publicly in sermons, attacking the authority of the Pope and denouncing Holy Mass as an abomination, resulting in an investigation by the Ferrarese inquisitor, who arrests a number of "heretics." Calvin himself barely gets away.[4] It is quite odd that an event about which hardly anything is known developed into such an eventful story.

---

[2] Irene Backus warns historians to be "careful before they treat any of these writings as documentary evidence about Luther, Calvin, Zwingli or Bèze. In this instance, chronological proximity does not mean greater accuracy. One should beware of making statements such as 'Bèze, Calvin's biographer says […].'" *Life Writing in Reformation Europe: Lives of Reformers by Friends, Disciples and Foes* (Aldershot: Ashgate, 2008), viii. For more detail, see below.

[3] For examples of popular writing consult the Internet; success is guaranteed by searching "Calvin and Ferrara." For an example in recent scholarly literature, see David Steinmetz's excellent thematic monograph, *Calvin in Context* (Oxford: Oxford University Press, 2010), where he notes: "Renée welcomed the scholarly refugees to her court and there is some reason to believe that she offered Calvin a position as secretary […],"10.

[4] The most imaginative version is that of Jean-Henri Merle d'Aubigné, *Histoire de la Réforme en Europe au temps de Calvin*, 8 vols. (Paris: Michel Lévy Frères, 1862–1877). On his motives, see vol. III, 251–254 and vol. V, 537–582. He mixes real events with excerpts from Calvin's letters, books, and sermons; he postdates events and adds dialogues, graphic descriptions, and action scenes to construct a lively portrait of a young Calvin as self-confident in his instruction of the duchess and continuously solicited by prominent French court-

It is time for a reassessment, not only because the historical truth has its rights, but also because legends and myths impede the vision of what really happened. To achieve this, I will first summarize the events that took place in Ferrara in the spring of 1536. It was an eventful period, well documented and thoroughly researched, but Calvin did *not* play a part in it. This, as I will show, is also an established fact, but scholars have been reluctant to accept it. After having cleared the field, I will reconstruct how it was possible for Calvin to be perceived as a prominent agent in the Ferrarese imbroglio of 1536, in which he did not participate. Taken together this deconstruction and reconstruction will shed new light on the true relationship between Calvin and the duchess.

LENT IN FERRARA, 1536

In Ferrara, on Good Friday, April 14, 1536, Jehannet de Bouchefort, a singer of the ducal chapel, left the church ostentatiously during a religious service just before the Adoration of the Cross.[5] This caused a scandal, and the local inquisitor, an official of the duke's administration, started an investigation. It soon became clear that the French court of the duchess was a hotbed of religious freethinkers, who in those days were often labeled "Lutherans," but in reality, there was a wide variety of reformations taking place, both within and outside of the official Church.[6]

iers for biblical teaching and counseling. Although criticized by fellow historians, this account became an international success, mainly in the United States. See John B. Roney, *The Inside of History: Jean Henri Merle d'Aubigné and Romantic Historiography* (Westport, Connecticut: Greenwood Press, 1996).

[5] I only sketch the outline of this affair. For a detailed account, see Claude A. Mayer, *Le départ de Marot de Ferrare*, BHR 17 (1956), 197–221. Mayer's study includes a complete overview and evaluation of strengths and weaknesses of previous studies, in particular Jules Bonnet, Bartolommeo Fontana, and Emanuel Rodocanachi, though some elements, including the number and exact names of the prisoners, remain unclear. Relevant archival documents were published by Bartolommeo Fontana, *Renata di Francia duchessa di Ferrara: sui documenti dell'archivio Estense, del Mediceo, del Gonzaga e dell'Archivio secreto vaticano*, 3 vols (Rome: Forzani, 1889–1899), interpretive notes have caused confusion. Later research by Rosanna Gorris and Eleonora Belligni has not significantly altered Mayer's reconstruction, but added personal details, such as the role of ladies-in-waiting and the position of Lyon Jamet.

[6] On this fundamental semantic problem, see Anne Overell, *Italian Reform and English Reformations, c.1535–c.1585* (Aldershot: Ashgate, 2008): "There was infinite variety in the experiments we call 'reform.' They could be bold or secretive, individual or communal, progressive or reactionary, 'Catholic' or 'Protestant.' All over Europe there were faltering

Asked for names, Bouchefort kept his mouth shut. Other witnesses were
called and testified to lively discussions in private chambers, which intensi-
fied during Lent, about issues that were contentious and far from innocuous in the 1530s, such as the authority of the Church and the pope, the
need for Confession, whether or not man had free will, and so on. It soon
became apparent that religious refugees from France dominated these discussions. They had left France because of the repression following the
infamous *Affaire des Placards* of October 1534 through January 1535,
during which broadsheets attacking Holy Mass as the abomination of
abominations were distributed. Although the duke was aware of this situation, he offered shelter to many of them, and both he and his wife
engaged several in their court, including the aforementioned Bouchefort.
Before entering the ducal chapel, the latter was a singer in the royal chapel
of the King of France (*chantre de la chambre et valet de garde-robbe du
roi*).[7] The same goes for the court poet, Clément Marot (enrolled as secretary to the duchess) and Lyon Jamet (one of the duke's private secretaries, at that time on diplomatic mission in Rome). All three figured on the
list of "criminals, wanted for heresy," which was published in January
1535 in France. As a matter of fact, they were sentenced to death by
default. Apparently, the duke didn't mind, as long as they did not cause
any trouble.[8] So, together with an ever-increasing number of similar religious refugees, Bouchefort had lived peacefully in the "French enclave" in

expressions, uncertain identities," 1. For a summary of events leading to the *Affaire des
placards* and subsequent suppression, see Dick Wursten, *Clément Marot and Religion. A
Re-assessment in the Light of his Psalm Paraphrases* (Leiden: Brill, 2010), 21–53.
   [7] Charmarie Jenkins Webb (Blaisdell), *Royalty and Reform: The Predicament of Renée de
France, 1510–1575* (PhD diss., Tufts, 1969), 98, referring to the *Catalogue des actes de
François Ier*, III, 475, 688; VII, 136, 175. On Bouchefort, a talented and well-paid singer of
the royal chapel, see Christelle Cazaux, *La Musique à la cour de François Ier* (Paris, 2002),
344–346, and John T. Brobeck, "Musical Patronage in the Royal Chapel of France under
Francis I (r. 1515–1547)," *Journal of the American Musicological Society* 48, no. 2 (1995):
214–215. Bouchefort published two *chansons à quatre*, four-part songs (Attaingnant, RISM
1530/4).
   [8] Explicitly so in a letter of the duke to his ambassador in Paris, Feruffini, dated May 5,
1536. The duke knew that Jehannet was accused of heresy, but if Jehannet would live "bene
et christianamente," he saw no harm in appointing him. "Desideravemo che la cosa non
procedesse piu oltra et lui si trovasse senza colpa, ma essendo occorso chel venerdi santo,
havendo noi fatto cantar qui in una chiesa il pascio et essendo ogniuno secondo il costume
andato ad adorare la croce el predetto gianetto, non solo non vi ando, ma per quanti da molti
ne fu referto, si parti con demonstrare di dispregiare et di tener [poco] Conto de la fede di
Christo […]." Fontana, *Renata*, vol. I, 318–320. French translation in Jules Bonnet, "Les

Ferrara for almost a year, protected by the duchess and tolerated by the duke, until that ominous moment during Holy Liturgy, when the singer apparently could no longer reconcile it with his conscience that he had to kneel in front of the cross, acknowledging it as a salutary object, singing hymns, such as "Pange lingua gloriosa."[9] To him, this must have felt like idolatry, an abomination. And, he was not the only one, as the inquisitor found out. People very close to the duchess seemed to be implicated. One witness mentions the names of two of Renée's secretaries: Clément Marot and Jean Cornillau, noting that it was common knowledge that these were inveterate "Lutherans." Asked what or who had caused this sudden uproot of heretical activity during Lent, the witness referred to "a man of the religious order of hermits preaching in Madame's court," and he added:

> before this preacher came, the women at court were very devout, but after being exposed to his preaching they hardly wished even to appear pious; they instead began to pass judgment on religious matters, claiming that listening to sermons was a waste of time, as was attending the Office of the Holy Virgin.[10]

The account of a second witness confirmed the image of Renée's court as a breeding ground for free-thinking heretics. This witness adds a physical description of one of the most zealous preachers: "a small Frenchman who had received a post as Madame's secretary." He is sure that this preacher had the back of Madame's personal almoner.[11] Pressed once more for his

premières persecutions à la cour de Ferrare," *Bulletin de la Société de l'Histoire du Protestantisme françaus* 39 (1890): 173–174.

[9] This is the official hymn for this celebration. Next to the adoration of the cross ("Crux fidelis") the faithful are also called to adore the blessed Sacrament ("Tantum ergo Sacramentum"). The ducal chapel at the time consisted of 14 or 15 professional singers. Choirmaster was "Maistre Jhan."

[10] Minutes of the interrogation of April 29: "[...] quondam virum religiosum ordinis hermitarum predicatorem in curia madamae, quem credit virum pessimum, et pro certo ex audito, quod predicavit non esse orandum quia orations facte sunt frivole nullius momentj et quod antequam iste vir predicator esset aut predicaret in curia, ille mullieres erant devotissimae sed postquam ille predicavit non pene volunt videre religiosos aut existimare res ecclesiasticas, et dicunt quod orare erat amissio temporis, similiter dicere officium Beate Virginis et similia." Fontana, *Renata*, vol. II, ix–x.

[11] "[...] cum quodam gallo parve stature cuius nomen ignorat sed ferebat[ur] habere locum Secretarij madame [...]." Fontana, *Renata*, vol. I, 324. Two secretaries were already identified as heretics in the first interrogation (April 28): Marot and Cornillau. So perhaps there is no need to look any further. For this, see Blaisdell, *Royalty*, 96. The name of Agostino

name, the witness replied "that he had heard he was a religious fugitive from France, and thinks a schoolteacher living in the county of Ferrara might have more information."[12] Various arrests followed and more were to come. Even Renée's position was threatened. She asked support from her royal family members, François I and Marguerite de Navarre, and from Anne de Montmorency, the Grand Marshall of France. They reacted almost immediately. Diplomatic missions by highly skilled French ambassadors followed one after another. They claimed that the Ferrarese Inquisitor had no jurisdiction over French citizens. The Pope was persuaded to join in this game. He issued a "Breve" in which he demanded that the prisoners (or the accused?) be tried by an ecclesiastical court, and thus should be transported to the papal city of Bologna. The duke did not comply, neither with the pope nor with the French, resulting in a gridlock. The investigation slowed down, Clément Marot could not be found, and the mysterious "preacher from the order of the hermits" also seemed to have vanished into thin air. The effort of the duke to collect incriminating evidence from France via his Ambassador to Paris, Girolamo Feruffini, proved less than fruitful. Montmorency and the king informed him that patience was running thin. Finally, the duke gave in, asked and got permission from the Pope to release the prisoners into the hands of the French authorities, and in August 1536, they were handed over to the French Ambassador to Venice, George de Selve, Bishop of Rodez. The dust settled soon thereafter. In a joint venture, the French, with support from the Pope, had triumphed over the duke and his inquisitor.

Foliati is mentioned in the registers of the duchess as "confesseur et prédicateur de Madame" (Madame's confessor and preacher). Emmanuel Rodocanachi, *Renée de France, duchesse de Ferrare. Une protectrice de la Réforme en Italie et en France* (Paris: Ollendorff, 1896), 107.

[12] "Et interrogatus cuius vocis sit ac fame dictus gallus dicit se audivisse quod ex Francia aufugerit propter hereses lutheranas, et quod credit *se audivisse* a quodam gallo instructore scolarium habitante in contracta *Zecche* civitatis Ferrariae qui de omnibus meliorem dabit informationem." Fontana, *Renata*, vol. I, 324–325, with emendations based on a copy, for explanations of which, see Fontana, *Renata*, vol. II, vii, note 1. Blaisdell knows of no school in Ferrara. See *Royalty*, 96. Eleonora Belligni, based on research by Chiara Francescini, suggests that in 1535, Renée had started an elite boys' school, where Francesco Paladini and François Richardot were teachers. *Evangelismo, Riforma ginevrina e nicodemismo: l'esperienza religiosa di Renata di Francia* (Cosenza: Brenner, 2008), 169. If correct, this information might be conducive to a new understanding of the role of Richardot in Ferrara. See more below.

RELIGION? IT'S POLITICS

What the above account makes clear is that eradication of heresy (to which all actors were committed) apparently was not the real issue in this Ferrarese imbroglio. If it were, then all parties, both ecclesiastical and civil (the French, the Ferrarese, and the pope) would simply have congratulated the duke on the arrest of some notorious heretics and would have joined forces to have them executed. Instead, they all excelled in obstructing one another's initiatives. What *seems* a religious imbroglio *is* in fact a political showdown. Pope Paul III, formerly known as Alessandro Farnese, also uses the affair as an opportunity to strengthen his position vis-à-vis the Duke of Ferrara.[13] One should not forget that in 1536, the tension between the two superpowers of the day, the Habsburg and Valois dynasties, represented respectively by Charles V and François I, rose by the day. A war seemed imminent, and one of the fronts would be in Northern Italy. Ercole's position was extremely difficult. Through his marriage with Renée, he was supposed to be loyal to the French. The Pope, on the other hand, used the proximity of the victorious Habsburg army, which was returning via Italy after the conquest of Tunis,[14] to put pressure on him to join the Habsburg League against the French. The French on their side had already invaded Savoy-Piedmont and were very interested in Milan. They wanted to be sure of the duke's loyalty. In April 1536, many observers were sure that the outbreak of war was only a matter of time. In the diplomatic jousting to avoid war and/or to win ground without actually having to wage war, the Pope (Alessandro Farnese) played a crucial role, and—as a shrewd politician—he profited from it. In all this, Ercole was a minor player, caught between the two superpowers and not able to keep pace with the diplomatic skills of the French and the pope. In the end, he had to comply to a solution concocted by the French ambassadors and Pope Paul III, regarding his domestic affairs. In 1536, an open confrontation between the two superpowers on Italian soil was averted, but the Savoy region and Turin remained French. It's in the corridors of this

---

[13] Before and after this affair, and as I suggest, *during* this affair, the diplomatic contacts between Ferrara and the Papal state had only one issue: both the duke and the Pope claimed Modena and Reggio. Ercole's father, Alfonso I, thought he had settled the issue for good with Pope Clement VII (Giuliano de Medici), but in 1535 the new Pope, Paul III (Alessandro Farnese), had reopened the case again. Only in 1539, Ercole succeeded in settling this dispute with the Pope, but at a very high financial price.

[14] Charles V had celebrated his triumph "over the infidel" in Rome on April 5, 1536.

diplomatic tug-of-war that the Ferrarese imbroglio was both instrumentalized and settled.[15] It became apparent that the link between Ferrara and France was no longer tenable, and Ercole reluctantly gave up his political independence and joined the Habsburg League. To conclude this episode, after another outburst of "heresy" at Renée's court in 1541, Ercole banished his wife to Consandolo, a castle located about 15 miles from Ferrara; the size of her French court was systematically diminished; her correspondence was intercepted; and Renée became more and more isolated. Ironically, the return to a more "normal" life was prompted by a visit to Ferrara by Pope Paul III in the spring of 1543. He had to be received and entertained properly, and he admonished the duke to recall his wife and live together as a marital couple. In the many vicissitudes of the duchess, it is remarkable that this Pope (from the house of Farnese) on two occasions contributed *effectively* to finding a way out (1536) or to establishing a *modus vivendi* (1543) in situations where Renée felt wedged between loyalty to her husband and deeply felt inner convictions (loyalty to France, and to her faith).[16]

CALVIN IN FERRARA: THE BIRTH OF A MYTH

Considering the facts, one wonders why in the nineteenth century, almost all scholars conducting archival research in Ferrara made Calvin a main actor in a play of which the script doesn't even contain his name. The answer is simple: based on the standard biography of Calvin, they were sure he *had* played a role, so his name *had* to be in the script. They simply

---

[15] For this, see Robert J. Knecht, *Renaissance warrior and Patron: The Reign of Francis I* (Cambridge: Cambridge University Press, 1996), chapter 16, "Montmorency's triumph." See also David Potter, *Renaissance France at War: Armies, Culture and Society c. 1480–1560* (Rochester: Boydell Press, 2008), 33–37. Focusing on Ercole's position, Charmarie Blaisdell makes similar observations about his "liberal attitude in matters of religion," noting that he was "faithful to Rome, as long as it did not obstruct his objectives as a Renaissance Prince," and pointing out the "relative weight of the matter of heresy." "Politics and Heresy in Ferrara, 1534–1559," *Sixteenth-Century Journal* 6, no. 1 (1975): 72 and 77. Writing for a popular audience, Mary Hollingsworth focuses on Ippolito d'Este, Ercole's brother and his ambassador at the French court, in *The Cardinal's Hat: Money, Ambition, and Everyday Life at the Court of a Borgia Prince* (New York: Overlook Press, 2004).

[16] Often Renée's letters to the Pope, in which she expresses her gratitude toward him for intervening on her behalf, are considered diplomatic or hypocritical. Considering what Pope Paul III did for her, I suggest abstaining from this kind of evaluation, at least concerning her letters from this period.

hadn't found it, at least not yet. Historical research is a complex exercise. There is always more context than one is aware of, and at the same time many of the relevant facts are unknowable, both on the level of the factual history itself (i.e., we don't know all the relevant facts) and on the level of interpretation (i.e., we can't look into the hearts and minds of people in order to identify what they were really thinking, feeling, and experiencing). However, without an interpretation, all facts and texts remain mute. So, one has to risk an interpretation, starting with the knowledge one has, while constantly being aware that the margin for error is immense. It is clear that in this case, something must have gone wrong. Therefore, it might be useful to start from scratch, trying to differentiate between fact and fiction, and then trying to determine what these scholars overlooked, didn't know, or misinterpreted.

THE FACTS

Calvin was in Ferrara. That is a certainty, not because the trip is mentioned in all accounts of Calvin's life, for that in itself is no guarantee, since these accounts were written after Calvin's death in 1564, but because there is an independent eye-witness: the Ferrarese physician and Professor of Medicine, Johannes Sinapius.[17]

An Eye-Witness

In a letter dated September 1, 1539, Sinapius refers to their first meeting in Ferrara in 1536. The letter is a eulogy on Calvin's qualities as a spiritual mentor, friend, and surprisingly, as marriage broker. In this letter, he expresses his wish to meet Calvin again, and then writes: "certainly, at the

---

[17] Johannes Sinapius (Johann Senff, 1505–1560) was an eminent Hellenist and medical doctor. He had taught Greek in Heidelberg and, recommended by Erasmus, had pursued his medical studies at the University of Ferrara. He became Renée's personal physician and tutor to her children. In 1545, he returned to Germany. He corresponded intensely with Simon Grynaeus. His wife, Françoise de Boussiron de Grand-Ry, was one of Renée's ladies-in-waiting. Calvin had played a role in convincing Françoise to accept Sinapius as her husband (1538). Their home seemed to have been one of the *foyers* where religious issues were discussed. His wife was certainly one of Calvin's informers and kept him posted about developments in Ferrara. On this, see John Flood and David Shaw, *Johannes Sinapius (1505–1560). Hellenist and Physician in Germany and Italy* (Geneva: Droz, 1997), in particular 92–95.

time when you were here, a few years ago, you actually concealed yourself from me like the Silenus of Alcibiades."[18]

The reference to Alcibiades's Silenus evokes a passage in Plato's *Symposium*, where Alcibiades compares Socrates to a Silenus, which is on the outside ugly and unattractive, but on the inside full of godly treasures. This comparison tells us that at the time of their meeting in Ferrara, Sinapius had no clue that he was talking to someone special. This is not surprising. In 1536, Sinapius was a professor of medicine at the university and personal physician to Renée, an insider so to speak. Calvin was a visitor, not yet known as a writer and theologian, traveling under the pseudonym of Charles d'Espeville.[19] Apparently, he did not present himself prominently. Unfortunately, Sinapius doesn't mention a date. However, this can be reconstructed.

The Timeframe

Based on two established dates, we can say with certainty that the trip must have taken place between March 15 and June 12, 1536. The first date (*terminus post quem*) is based on the fact that in March 1536, Calvin was in Basel, assisting with the preparation of the first edition of his *Institutio*, published by Thomas Platter d.d. March 15, 1536. In a semi-autobiographical section in the preface to his "Commentary on the Psalms," published in Latin in 1557, and in French in 1558,[20] Calvin

---

[18] "Quando sane illo quo adfuisti tempore, superioribus annis, revera me sicuti Alcibiades Silenus quispiam latuisti." Flood and Shaw, *Johannes Sinapius*, Letter 36, 186. In Plato's *Symposium*, Alcibiades compares Socrates to a statue of Silenus, ugly and hollow on the outside, but inside it is full of tiny golden statues of the gods (Symposium 216e–217a). The Silenus's comparison is applied to the moral and spiritual domain by Erasmus in his very popular Adagium "Sileni Alcibiadis." See Desiderius Erasmus, *Adagiorum chiliades* (Basel: Froben, 1540), III iii 1 (nr. 2201), 482–491. The metaphor is also used by Rabelais in his preface to *Gargantua* (1534). Another reference to their original meeting in Ferrara can be found in the letter from Sinapius to Calvin of December 5, 1553, in which he informs Calvin of the death of his wife: "A primo die quo nos olim Ferrariae vidimus et salutavimus […]." Flood and Shaw, *Johannes Sinapius*, Letter 61, 204.

[19] That Calvin traveled using this pseudonym is based on the note about his visit to Ferrara in Jean-Papire Masson, *Vita Ioannis Calvini auctore Papirio Massono* (Paris: s.n., 1620), 11–12.

[20] *Semi*-autobiographical because without this prefix the term would be anachronistic, and we might miss the framing of the story. Calvin has an ulterior motive when he inserts fragments of his personal life in this preface. In it, he postulates a more than general likeness (analogy) between what happened to David (and Israel) and what was happening to God's

informs the reader that he left Basel immediately after having finished the work on the *Institutio*: "discessu brevis," or in French, "incontinent après."[21] Unfortunately, he doesn't say where he went. The second date (*terminus ante quem*) is also established. On June 12, 1536, he is in Paris with his brother Antoine to arrange family affairs.[22] After subtracting the time needed for those quite long journeys, it seems plausible to accept a stay in Ferrara somewhere in April and/or May 1536. The duration cannot be determined.

A Timid Intellectual?

In the same preface, Calvin explains his motives for the publication of the *Institutio* in 1536. Only 26 years of age, a licentiate in law since 1532, he had exiled himself from France and had no regular job. Theologically he was an auto-didact. In the preface, he explains that he wrote this book as an apology for those who were persecuted in France as a result of the repression following the *Affaire des Placards*.[23] This is also why he addressed the dedicatory epistle preceding the first edition of the *Institutio* to the French king. Calvin saw it as his duty as an intellectual to take their defense. This had nothing to do with vainglory. To demonstrate his humility, he notes that even in Basel he never made it public that he, John Calvin, was the author of that book. He lived a hidden life there.[24] This is,

church in the sixteenth century. For this, see Barbara Pitkin, "Imitation of David: David as a paradigm for faith in Calvin's exegesis of the Psalms," *Sixteenth-Century Journal* 24, no. 4 (1993): 843–863. Herman J. Selderhuis, *Calvin's Theology of the Psalms* (Grand Rapids: Baker, 2007) also recalls Calvin's far-reaching identification of Calvin with David. He also underlines the asylum or exile motive, which is one of the ways in which he himself (and the refugee community in Geneva) could recognize themselves in the mirror of the Psalms.

[21] Calvin refers to his *Christianae religionis Institutio* (Basel: Thomas Platter, 1536); the full title of which is mentioned in note 25. For the publication of this book and Calvin's departure from Basel, see Jean Calvin, *In librum psalmorum Commentarius* (Geneva: Robert Estienne, 1557), iiir. In French, see Jean Calvin, *Commentaires sur le livre des Pseaumes* ([Geneva]: Conrad Badius, 1561), iiiir–iiiiv.

[22] June 12, 1536, signature on a deed of sale in Paris, June 22, 1536, similar activity in Noyon.

[23] He stresses that the first edition was not a multi volume "Summa theologiae," but "seulement un petit livret" ("breve dumtaxat enchiridion"), only exposing the typical topics of any catechism. This is an understatement: the Basel *Institutio* is a 514-page *in-octavo* imprint.

[24] A little bit hard to believe for someone who succeeds in having the illustrious Thomas Platter print a 514-page book, proudly carrying his name on the front page: "Christianae

as Calvin continues in his preface, the reason why he left Basel "immediately after" the *Institutio* was published, and why he kept concealing his
identity "everywhere else until he arrived in Geneva," where he was
engaged by Guillaume Farel to become a "minister" of God's Church.[25]
This is the moment when he ceases to be anonymous and comes into the
spotlight. The period "everywhere else until" includes his stay in Ferrara.
So, in Ferrara, he was not a self-confident preacher, not the Reformer he
would become, but a young scholar, traveling under the pseudonym of
Charles d'Espeville, who wanted to write books explaining the gospel to
defend the faithful against calumny. That is the maximum one can say
about the young Calvin. It appears that he was still waiting to see what
God had in mind for him. After Ferrara, things began to move very quickly.
After having settled his affairs in Paris in June 1536,[26] he tried to return to
Strasbourg to continue his life. He imagined it to be tranquil and studious,
serving the faithful with his mind.[27] Things turned out differently: "His
job found him in Geneva." There he became a teacher (i.e., professor) and
a little later, a preacher. It will take some more time—roughly from 1540
onward—before he really emerges as one of the leaders of the Swiss and
French Reformation.

   This simple sketch of the young Calvin makes it quite unlikely that he
was in any way actively involved in the Ferrarese imbroglio, even though
it is not impossible that he was in Ferrara during that time. He was too

religionis institutio, totam fere pietatis summam, & quicquid est in doctrina salutis cognitu
necessarium: complectens: omnibus pietatis studiosis lectu dignissimum opus, ac recens editum: Praefatio ad Christianissimum regem Franciae, qua hic ei liber pro confessione fidei
offertur / Ioanne Calvino Noviodunensi authore." Calvin, *In librum psalmorum*, iiir.

   [25] "Or que je n'eusse point ce but de me montrer et acquerir bruit, je le donnay bien cog-
noistre parce qu'incontinent apres je me retirai de là: joint mesmement que personne ne
sceut là que j'en fusse l'auteur: comme aussi partout ailleurs je n'en ai point fait de semblant,
et avoye deliberé de continuer de mesme jusqu'à ce que finalement maistre Guillaume Farel
me retient à Genève [...]." Calvin, *Commentaires*, iiiir–iiiiv.

   [26] He had already broken financially with the Church in 1534 abandoning his right on the
revenue of a Prebend at Noyon Cathedral. From Ferrara, he went to Paris to cut the last ties
that bound him to France leaving the care for the family fortune to his brother Antoine.

   [27] Some phrasing from the preface with the *caveat* this is also "image building," but there
must be a grain of truth in it to sound plausible: "Strasbourg, où je vouloye lors me retirer;"
"quelques estudes particulieres, auxquelles je me vouloye reserver libre;" "mon repos et la
tranquillite d'estudes que je cherchoye." Calvin, *Commentaires*, iiiir–iiiiv. Perhaps he went to
Ferrara with this kind of career in mind?

"bashful and timid" for this kind of action.[28] And even then, had he participated, Sinapius certainly would have remembered it, and Calvin himself would have had no reason to be ashamed of mentioning it. On the contrary, he would have used it in his image-building: "Already as a young man I confessed to the Truth and suffered for it."[29] *Quod non.* Although an *argumenta e nihilo* should be distrusted, this one does not seem inappropriate.

THE LIFE OF CALVIN (VIA BÈZE)

The next references to Calvin's trip can be found in Bèze's (and Colladon's) *posthumous* accounts of Calvin's life. The earliest account is written by Bèze in 1564, shortly after Calvin's death. Bèze relates the story, beginning with the year 1534. It is clear that Bèze is familiar with Calvin's own account of this episode in the "Preface to the Psalms." The framing is similar, but Ferrara is now explicitly mentioned as a destination and some details are even given, of which the relevant ones are italicized below:

Therefore, he left France in 1534, and in this same year had printed in Basel his first *Institution* as an apology addressed to the late King François, first of that name, for the poor persecuted faithful upon whom was wrongly applied the title Anabaptists, to excuse in the eyes of the Protestant Princes the persecution to which they were subjected. He also made a trip to Italy where he *saw Madame the Duchess of Ferrara*, still living today thanks to God, who, having seen and heard him *from then on knew him for what he was*, and ever since up to the time of his death *loved and honored him as an excellent agent of the Lord*. On his return from *Italy at which he only glanced*, he passed through this city of Geneva [...].[30]

---

[28] See Calvin's introspective words regarding his temperament in the same preface: "[...] je me recognoy estre timide, mol et pusillanime de ma nature [...]." Calvin, *Commentaires*, iiiir–iiiiv.

[29] Calvin, *Commentaires*, iiiir–iiiiv.

[30] "En fin voyant le povre estat du royaume de France, il delibera de s'en absenter pour vivre plus paisiblement et selon sa conscience. Il partit donques de France l'an 1534, et ceste mesme annee fit imprimer, à Basle, sa premiere Institution, comme un Apologetique adressé au feu roi François, premier de ce nom, pour les povres fideles persecutes, auxquels à tort on imposoit le nom d'Anabaptistes, pour s'excuser envers les princes Protestants des persecutions qu'on leur faisoit. Il fit aussi un voyage en Italie, où il vit Madame la duchesse de Ferrare, encores aujourd'huy vivante, graces à Dieu; laquelle l'ayant veu et ouy, dès lors jugea ce qui en estoit, et toujours depuis jusques à sa mort, l'a aimé et honoré, comme un excellent organe du Seigneur. A son retour d'Italie, laquelle il ne fit que voir, il passa à la bonne heure

Although Bèze says that Calvin stayed in Italy/Ferrara for only a very short time, he does suggest that Calvin actually met with Renée and that this meeting was the beginning of a lifelong friendship. Even more, the duchess already recognized Calvin's authority as a god-sent man, that is, "excellent organe du Seigneur." But now, we must be on the alert. As already signaled, Bèze is not a biographer in the modern sense. He is Calvin's successor, and France is torn apart by the religious conflict concerning how to rebuild and govern the Church of God. Many factions were struggling for power, and signs indicated that the conflict might take a violent turn. We are on the brink of the French Wars of Religion.[31] The pamphlet press flourished. So, writing that John Calvin died a godly man, which is the main message of the first "Vita," was not simply a matter of supplying the population with correct information. It was a strategic move in Geneva's public relations policy in which Calvin is not a saint (God forbid!), but a man who lived an exemplary life and whose vision of the Church was God-inspired. The biographical elements that Bèze adds to this account serve to underline that Calvin practiced what he preached, so to speak, and that people willingly or unwillingly recognized his authority. The reference to Ferrara is part of this apologetic offensive in propaganda warfare. In other words, Bèze is a spin doctor. Everyone in France knew who Renée was and for what she stood. Things in Ferrara had gone from bad to worse, especially since Ercole and the new order of the Jesuits had joined forces. In 1554, the Inquisition had filed a complaint for heresy against Renée. To save her life, she had to take Holy Communion publicly. After the death of her husband in 1559, she returned to France and withdrew to her castle in Montargis, transforming her court once more into a safe place for the persecuted, not discriminating as to the cause of persecution, much to the irritation of her spiritual adviser, Jean Calvin. That this formidable woman respected Calvin is a signal that the Reformed faction

---

par ceste ville de Genève [...]." Théodore de Bèze, *Commentaires de M. Jean Calvin, sur le livre de Josué. Avec une préface de Theodore de Besze, contenant en brief l'histoire de la vie et mort d'iceluy. Il a aussi deux tables: l'une des matieres singulieres contenues esdits Commentaires, l'autre des tesmoignages de l'Escriture saincte alleguez et proprement appliquez par l'autheur* (Geneva: François Perrin, 1564), vr. For other editions, see the bibliography. This text was also printed and sold separately as *Discours de M. Théodore de Besze, contenant en bref l'histoire de la vie et mort de Maistre Jean Caluin avec le Testament et derniere volonté dudict Calvin.* Irene Backus, *Life Writing in Reformation Europe* (Aldershot: Ashgate, 2008), 126.

[31] Historians divide the outbursts of violence between Roman Catholics and Protestants in France between 1562 and 1598 into six wars.

had support in high places. Moreover, it was true. Renée valued Calvin's advice, though she did not always follow his lead. However—and this is what we are looking for—this does not imply that their relationship *started* with an *actual meeting* in Ferrara in 1536, as Bèze suggests.

Already in 1565, a new edition appeared, this time probably in collaboration with Colladon.[32] In this edition, we read that Calvin went to Italy *with a companion*, whom the context reveals to be Louis du Tillet.[33] The last and definitive edition of Bèze's *Life of Calvin* was written in Latin and published in 1575. It's far more detailed than the earlier editions. New and noteworthy elements from this *Vita* are italicized below:

> Calvin, after publishing [the first edition of the *Institutio*], and thereby, as it were, performing his duty to his country, *felt an inclination to visit the Duchess of Ferrara*, a daughter of Louis XII, whose piety was then greatly spoken of, and at the same time *to salute Italy as from a distance*. He accordingly visited the duchess, and, in so far as the state of the times permitted, confirmed her in her zeal for the true religion. Therefore, she valued him very highly while he was alive, and having survived him, *she also gave a brilliant example of how grateful she was having known the deceased*.
>
> *He left Italy, which he—as he used to say—*had only entered in order to leave it, *and returned to France* [...].[34]

---

[32] About the complex question of authorship, see Backus, *Life Writing*, 128–130. This Vita is not translated into French until 1681. It is attached as a preface to Bèze's edition of a selection of Calvin's Correspondence, and later also to editions of the *Institutio*. The intended readers are scholars.

[33] "De Basle Calvin avec son dit compagnon vint en Italie et demeurèrent quelque temps à Ferrare." Théodore de Bèze, *Commentaries de M. Iea Calvin sur le livre de Iosué. Avec une Preface de Theodore de Besze, contenant en brief l'histoire de la vie et mort d'iceluy: augmentée depuis la premiere edition deduite selon l'ordre du temps quasi d'an en an* (Geneva: François Perrin, 1565), bir–biv. In this edition more anecdotical material is present, and a chronology is introduced. Strictly speaking it is not even entirely certain that Du Tillet really accompanied Calvin to Ferrara. In their correspondence, which chronologically follows the events, see Crottet, *Correspondence française de Calvin*, where the trip to Italy is not mentioned at all. Also, Colladon's "factual" additions are not particularly trustworthy.

[34] "Edito hoc libro suaque velut praestita patriae fide, Calvinum visendae Ferrariensis Ducis Ludovici XII. Francorum regis filiae, cuius tum pietas celebrabatur, simulque Italiae veluti procul salutandae desiderium incessit. Illam igitur vidit, simulque quantum id illum facere praesens rerum status sinebat, in vero pietatis studio confirmavit, ut eum postea vivum semper unice dilexerit, ac post quoque superstes gratae in defunctum memoriae specimen ediderit luculentum. Ceterum ex Italia, in cuius fines se ingressum esse dicere solebat ut inde exiret [...]." *Ioannis Calvini Epistolae et Responsa, quibus interiectae sunt insignium in eccle-*

This passage contains several interesting elaborations: for the first time, Bèze suggests that Calvin went to Ferrara *with a plan*, that is, meeting the duchess, for he states that he "felt an inclination to visit the duchess." The wording of Renée's appreciation is extended with the intriguing statement that Renée gave *a brilliant example of her gratitude toward Calvin*, even after his death in 1564. As with the previous elaborations, it is highly unlikely that new information had suddenly surfaced. Bèze is still a spin doctor and probably only tries to enhance the basic idea of Calvin's being Renée's spiritual mentor to drive his message home. He claims that Renée not only was grateful for, but also remained faithful to, Calvin's advice until her own death in June 1575. The "brilliant example" might also refer to her Testament, in which she prohibited that she be buried with any pomp and circumstance, be it royal or ecclesiastical. The phrase itself replaces the previous statement that "the Duchess, who is still alive," cherished Calvin's advice. Often overlooked are two other additions. The first stipulates that Calvin not only wanted to visit Renée, but also *wished to salute Italy as from a distance*. No great plans, nothing definitive. The second addition is the introduction of a quote by Calvin referring to his stay in Ferrara: "He left Italy, which he—as he used to say—had only entered in order to leave it." These two phrases replace the previous statement about "Italy at which he only glanced." In content they are interchangeable: Calvin was in Italy only for a very short time and was not particularly fond of it. However, the fact that Bèze introduces this appreciation as if he quotes Calvin gives more weight to the conclusion. Although unverifiable, the quote might be authentic, especially after deconstructing the myth. In the end, this might well be the most correct factual description of Calvin's visit to Ferrara: he was there, did not like what he found, and he left.

It is clear what Bèze is doing, though perhaps unconsciously. He uses elements from the later relationship between Renée and Calvin and projects them onto the supposed beginning of their relationship in Ferrara in 1536. This procedure will be copied again and again in the nineteenth century, making it possible that the young Calvin became a central agent in the Ferrarese imbroglio of Lent 1536.

---

sia Dei vivorum aliquot etiam epistolae. Eiusdem I. Calvini Vita a Theodoro Beza Genevensis ecclesiae ministro accurate descripta. (Geneva: Pierre Saint-André, 1575), "Vita," [16].

The Myths Revisited

After having cleared the field, it's time to revisit the myth about Calvin in Ferrara and take a fresh look at how Renée and Calvin came into contact, as well as to discern what their correspondence really is about.

Calvin in Ferrara

It's clear that in his *Vita,* Bèze sowed the seeds for the creation of the myth: Calvin might have saluted Italy from a distance, but he went to Ferrara with the explicit purpose of meeting the duchess. And, according to Bèze, when they do meet, the duchess is so impressed that this became the beginning of a lifelong friendship in which Calvin played the role of mentor and spiritual coach. As demonstrated earlier, the *relationship* between the two is not fictional, but the rest is. However, it is easy to imagine how this myth can begin to grow, in particular when Calvin's star begins to rise in the era of Reformed Romantic historiography. He was the hero of faith and the mentor of a woman descended from royalty, whose life captures the imagination. And this scheme delivers even better when it is combined with the Ferrarese imbroglio of 1536, in which he can play a heroic role. One would be well-advised to remember that neither Calvin nor Bèze ever mention the Ferrarese imbroglio, much less that Calvin played a part in it. For storytellers, however, this combination offers the advantage that there is something worth telling. Basically, this is precisely what Merle d'Aubigné did with great virtuoso in volume V of his *Reformation History.*[35] The only problem, as we saw, is that Calvin is not mentioned in that script. Well, this is what *we* know from *our* vantage point. This is not what a nineteenth-century researcher knew. He honestly believed that Calvin was in Ferrara and played a role in the imbroglio. The origin of this conviction might well have been a casual remark by Ludovico Muratori, an eighteenth-century Modenese historian, an annalist of the Vatican and Estense archives. Writing about the events of the year 1536, Muratori states:

> According to the Annalist Spondano, the archheretic John Calvin (who in the previous year had come to Ferrara and had lived there undercover) infected Renee, daughter of Louis XII and Duchess of Ferrara, in such a way

[35] See note 4.

with his errors that no one could draw the venomous poison from her heart. But in this year this wolf was exposed and has taken refuge in Geneva. I am assured by one who has seen the acts of the Inquisition in Ferrara that this pestiferous troublemaker was put in prison; but while he was being conducted from Ferrara to Bologna he was set free by armed men.[36]

The first part of the statement echoes the standard story of Bèze, albeit in the jargon of a Roman Catholic. The second part triggered many historians to start an investigation, but to no avail, as the mysterious document could not be found. The one who really cloaked himself in this matter is Bartolommeo Fontana (1835–1901), who searched all the archives to find evidence that Calvin really was there and was implicated in the imbroglio.[37] Although he also did not find that piece of evidence, the damage was done. Calvin was, if you will, smuggled into the heart of the Ferrarese imbroglio. The fact is that the other documents dug up by Fontana, and by others who remain unidentified, gave historians and other critics plenty of opportunities to fill in names: "the hermit who so zealously preached," must have been Calvin. Though Calvin was no hermit, the problem could be resolved by suggesting that he might have disguised himself as a hermit. Should this not prove to be convincing, there remained that "little Frenchman, who was also secretary to Madame."[38] In the last decades of

[36] "Secondo l'annalista Spondano, nell' anno precedente venuto a Ferrara l'eresiarca Giovanni Calvino, sotto abita finto talmente infettò Renea figlia de re Lodovico XII, e duchessa di Ferrara, degli errori suoi, che non si pote mal trarle di cuore il bevuto veleno. Ma nel presente anno veggendosi scoperto questo lupo, se ne fuggi a Genevra. Vengo assicurato da chi ha veduto gli atti dell' inquisizion di Ferrara, che si pestifero mobile fu fatto prigione." Lodovico Antonio Muratori, *Annali d'Italia ed alter opere varie*, vol IV: 1358–1687 (Rome, 1838), 374. The original edition is in twelve volumes, 1744–1749. See also Blaisdell, *Royalty*, 136–140.

[37] In addition to the three-volume biography of Renée, Fontana also published *Documenti dell'Archivio Vaticano e dell'Estense circa il soggiorno di Calvino a Ferrara* (Rome: Forzani, 1889–1899).

[38] One example: "Faut-il reconnaître, dans cet interlocuteur véhément Calvin ou plutôt Marot, inspiré et stimulé par Calvin? *Quoi qu'il en soit, directement ou indirectement, c'était toujours la voix de Calvin qui se faisait entendre.* Ses arguments convainquirent sans peine Renée, déjà plus qu'à demi gagnée." Rodocanachi, *Une protectrice*, 108. People who followed this identification also implicitly accepted that Calvin must have been Renée's secretary for a while. This explains why until today even scrupulous historians write that Calvin "for a time served as a *secretary* to the Duchess." Steinmetz, *Calvin in Context*, 10. See note 3. In some reconstructions, the cleric Louis du Tillet is made the foremost preacher and Calvin "dressed up like his assistant." This is based on Jean-Papire Masson: "et si clericum

the nineteenth century, a true Franco-Italian *Historikerstreit* ignited, in which both parties, notwithstanding their disputes, agreed on two things: first of all, Calvin did play an important role in the Ferrarese imbroglio of 1536, and second, he had a huge influence on Renée. They only disagreed in the evaluation of these events. For Protestant historians, this is the story of their hero, the herald of the True Faith, who yields neither to enmity nor to persecution, and in the end—with or without imprisonment and subsequent to narrow escape—triumphantly returned to Geneva. For Roman Catholic historians, the same elements form the story of the "arch-heretic" John Calvin, who corrupted the duke's wife with his perverse teachings, and unfortunately, managed to escape. Much havoc could have been prevented, had he then been brought to trial, they implicitly state. Since theological opinions are often connected with deep emotions, it does not come as a surprise that differences of opinion were not perceived as a signal that it was time to reformulate the research question. On the contrary. One fantastical life is placed over and alongside another. Both parties dug in deep and a veritable trench warfare began. On this point, the nineteenth century echoes the sixteenth in many ways, for the publication of Bèze's account of Calvin's life provoked the publication of another "Life of Calvin," not to celebrate the exemplary life of a godly man, but to destroy that image utterly, using all literary means available. I am referring here to Jerome Bolsec's "anti-vita," *Histoire de la vie, mœurs, actes, doctrine et mort de Jean Calvin, jadis grand ministre de Genève* (Lyon, 1577). With this book, Bolsec, a Carmelite who had converted to Protestantism, earned a living as physician, studied medicine in Ferrara, and for a while was personal almoner to Renée de France, settled an old score with Calvin, with whom he had fallen out on the topic of predestination in 1551. He had experienced how the so-called timid Calvin could morph into a bulldog when he felt personally attacked. This "anti-vita" has more of a satirical tone than that of serious historiography, but it was read by many Roman Catholics as the pure and simple truth about Calvin. It was republished many times in the sixteenth and seventeenth centuries and re-edited with annotations several times in the nineteenth century.[39]

---

sacerdoti inservientem agebat." *Vita Ioannis Calvini*, 11–12. On Masson and his source (François Bauduin, ex-secretary of Calvin), see Backus, *Life Writing*, 169–181.

[39] On Bolsec and his vita, see Backus, *Life Writing*, 153–162. An excellent summary is given by Alister McGrath, who writes that according to Bolsec, "Calvin was irredeemably tedious and malicious, bloodthirsty and frustrated. He treated his own words as if they were the word of God, and allowed himself to be worshipped as God. In addition to frequently

Muratori certainly knew it, and in his novella *Castellio gegen Calvin oder Ein Gewissen gegen die Gewalt* (1936), Stefan Zweig is still tributary to Bolsec.

RENÉE AND CALVIN

Only one topic remains to be addressed. If Calvin and Renée did not meet in Ferrara, how did they get acquainted, when did their correspondence begin, and what issue may have triggered it? With the new arrangement of facts, after the above deconstruction of the old myths, and without the looming presence of Calvin the Reformer obscuring the view, other people become visible: Renée's courtiers, and in particular, her ladies-in-waiting. These were not docile followers, but rather agents. In other words, they thought for themselves, acted, and even took risks. Not only the inquisitor, but also the duke finds it difficult to cope with this phenomenon. And, next to the courtiers, there are the scholars of the University of Ferrara, the painters, the poets, and the musicians. In the first half of the sixteenth century, Ferrara still was a thriving Renaissance city. So, it will not come as a surprise that these men and women, who corresponded with the entire world, also were perfectly capable of contacting Calvin if they had questions or wanted his advice. But in this case, we can be even more precise. We know who contacted Calvin, and we also know the occasion on which this happened.

The archives of Geneva house the draft of a letter written by Calvin to Renée. It is not dated, but it's clear that this is the first time that Calvin writes to the duchess.[40] The fact that in this letter Calvin does not even

---

falling victim to his homosexual tendencies, he had a habit of indulging himself sexually with any female within walking distance." *A Life of John Calvin* (Oxford: Blackwell, 1993), 16–17. Others who wrote a (partisan) *Vita Calvini* are Jean-Papire Masson (1620), Jacques Desmay (1621), Jacques Le Vasseur (1633), and Cardinal Richelieu (1651). For this, see Backus, *Life Writing*, chapters 4 and 5.

[40] Geneva BPU, Ms. fr. 196, 79–81. Aimée-Louis Herminjard, *Correspondance des réformateurs dans les pays de langue française*, vol. 7 (Geneva and Paris: Georg & Cie, 1886), 307–319 (ep. 1058). *Calvini opera quae supersunt omnia, Vol. XI*, ed. Edouard Cunitz, Johann-Wilhelm Baum, and Eduard Wilhelm Eugen Reuss, 323–333. *Lettres de Jean Calvin, recueillis pour la première fois et publiées d'après les manuscrits originaux*, vol. I, ed. and trans. Jules Bonnet (Paris: Librairie de C. Meyrueis et compagnie, 1854), 43–56. *Letters by John Calvin. Compiled from the Original Manuscripts and edited with Historical Notes*, ed. Jules Bonnet and trans. David Constable (Edinburgh: Thomas Constable and Co., 1855) vol. I, 295–306. Some date this letter to 1541 (Cunitz et al. and Bonnet), others in 1537

casually refer to a previous meeting in Ferrara, nor does he refer to the tumultuous events that had happened there, is notable. For us, this does not come as a surprise: they had not met, and Calvin's stay in Ferrara was not a memorable event for him. But of course, it did trouble historians, in particular those who supported an early date for this letter of summer 1537, which is very close to the events. As we begin to read this letter, it becomes even more apparent that Calvin feels impelled to go to great lengths to justify that he dares to write a letter to the duchess. This makes it even more improbable that he ever spoke with her before, let alone that Renée had already accepted Calvin as her spiritual guide, as Bèze claimed in his *Vita*.[41] Exit myth, one would say. However, the possibility of a falsification of a cherished theory not only causes stress but can also lead to cognitive dissonance. To overcome this nagging feeling that something is not right, many interpreters resorted to a kind of "close reading" to press the text to say the things that they wanted to hear. Of course, they honestly believed that they only made explicit what was implicit. One phrase in particular seemed amenable to this purpose, a phrase at the end of the first paragraph, part of the "captatio benevolentiae." Calvin writes: "Dadvantaige, j' ay congneu en vous une telle crainte de Dieu et fidele affection a luy obeir [...]" (I have observed in you such fear of God and such disposed faithfulness of obedience that [...]).[42] This quite general

(Doumergue, Herminjard). In the new edition of Calvin's correspondence, *Opera omnia denuo recognita*, Series VI: *Epistolae*, vol. I: 1530-sept. 1538 (Genève: Droz, 2005), edited by Cornelis Augustijn et al., this letter is reprinted with a material description, introduction, summarizing translation, and footnotes, 218–232. Based on internal evidence (e.g., paper mark, reference to some books Calvin encloses), the editors suggest summer 1537 as the date of composition, 219. Bèze also included this letter, translated into Latin, in his selection of Calvin's epistles, *Epistolae et Responsa*, 151–155, the same edition that premiered the final version of his "Calvini vita."

[41] It is too simple a solution to claim that these apologies are usual courtesies, that is, epistolary politeness when writing to people in high places, and should not be taken literally. It is perfectly possible to be polite and at the same time refer to previous commitments. The reader may decide for himself while considering the first line: "Madame, je vous supplie humblement de vouloir prendre en bonne part la hardiesse que j'ay eu de vous escripre ces presentes [...]." Cunitz et al., *Calvini opera, Vol. XI*, 323. In Constable's translation, "Madame,—I humbly beseech you that you would take in good part my boldness in writing these present [...]," Bonnet and Constable, *The Letters of John Calvin, Vol. 1*, 295. Why use such a strong term as "hardiesse" (boldness, brutality) if they were already on speaking terms since Ferrara? And exponentially so, if Renée had already recognized Calvin as "organe de Dieu," as Bèze suggests?

[42] English translation, Constable, *Letters by John Calvin*, Vol. 1, 296.

observation is then interpreted as a reference to their meeting in Ferrara in 1536. The English translation of "connaître en vous" as "to observe in you," already gets one off on the wrong foot by suggesting physical proximity. A more neutral translation, such as "I have known in you," meaning "I know you to be," or even more straightforwardly, "I know that you are god-fearing etc. [...]," does not imply that a personal meeting took place. It was common knowledge that the duchess was a pious woman. The phrase itself is a perfect build-up in order to remind the duchess of her duty as a Christian princess to act according to God's will, which Calvin, as a chosen minister of God, is going to reveal to her.

This is a well-known and often-cited letter. The issue at stake is very similar to the issue for which Jehannet de Bouchefort and Jean Cornillau had risked their lives in 1536 during Lent in Ferrara while attending Holy Mass (even more surprisingly, Calvin does not refer to the events in Ferrara, not even in passing). I paraphrase the question first because it is easily misunderstood. Protestants and secular historians often have great difficulty understanding the proper meaning of terms like "ouïr la Messe," that is, to attend Mass, and "faire communion," or to take communion, receiving the Host. In those days, the laity generally participated only by proxy in the rite of Holy Communion. The priest and the deacon performed the ceremony, the latter representing the people during communion, the former acting on behalf of God. So, one can perfectly attend Mass without taking communion or receiving the Host.[43] The question at stake in Ferrara is that Renée and her court did attend Mass, but apparently

---

[43] "[...] maistre Francoys, [...] vous avoit persuadé, qu'il ne seroit pas maulvays apres avoir ouy la messe de faire quelque communion laquelle servit de la cene de nostre Seigneur [...]," Cunitz et al., *Calvini opera, Vol. XI*, 324. In Constable's translation: "[...] Master François, [...] had persuaded you that it would not be a bad thing, after having heard mass, to hold some sort of communion, which must be somehow the Supper of our Lord," Bonnet and Constable, *The Letters of John Calvin, Vol. 1*, 296. In the summary of the new edition of Calvin's letters, Richardot's advice is summarized as: "attendance of the Lord's Supper is permissible after hearing the Mass," 219. See note 40. This oversimplifies the issue suggesting there already existed a standardized way of celebrating the Lord's Supper. However, in 1537, reform-oriented clergy is still experimenting how to do that properly. Many in France believed it was possible to reform Holy Mass without abolishing the ritual of the Catholic Liturgy. Only the words of the consecration had to be corrected ("christlich bessern," as Luther called it). Of course, the people had to participate in the ritual, receiving both bread and wine. At the court of Marguerite de Navarre, this is how Holy Mass was celebrated, with Gérard Roussel as officiating priest. Calvin's attack on Roussel (one of the *Epistolae Duae*) dates from the same period.

organized a kind of private service afterward in which they "took communion." It's not entirely clear how this was organized, but they viewed
this as a celebration of the "Lord's Last Supper." François Richardot,
Madame's almoner, had claimed that this indeed was the proper thing to
do.[44] One of the ladies-in-waiting, however, had refused to attend Mass.[45]
The duchess had withdrawn her goodwill from the lady and warned others
not to cause scandal. The history of Jehannet de Bouchefort seemed to
repeat itself, and this time the duchess was determined to nip it in the bud,
much to the dismay of Madame de Pons, also known as Anne de Parthenay.
In one way or another—by letter or vis-à-vis, for many people from Ferrara
passed through Geneva on their way to France or the Upper-Rhine cities—she had informed Calvin about the situation and asked him to address
this question, suggesting that the duchess was also eager to hear his opinion. This is the question that Calvin is going to address: Is it allowed for a
biblically informed Christian, such as the duchess (and many of her courtiers) to hear Mass (i.e., to attend the service, listen to the words of the
consecration, see the elevated Host, kneel, etc.) and then afterward in a

[44] François Richardot (1507–1574) was an Augustinian hermit, who had studied theology
in Paris, where he became a professor in 1529. In the early 1530s, he disappears from the
radar. It is rumored that he became a "Lutheran." What is certain is that the Pope discharged
him from his monastic vows and that he spent some time as a secular priest in Rome. It is
generally assumed that he arrived in Ferrara in May 1537, in the retinue of Vittoria Colonna.
He became Renée's personal almoner, a position he held until 1544. Then he returned to
France. He became Bishop of Arras (as successor of Granvelle), and preached at the Funeral
of Charles V. He was confessor to Margaret of Parma. The only biography available is written
by Abbé Léon Duflot, *Un Orateur du XVIe siècle. François Richardot, évêque d'Arras* (Arras:
Sueur-Charruey, 1898), a specimen of Roman Catholic historiography (apologetic, thus
minimizing his "heretical" period). Protestant historians generally blindly endorse Calvin's
negative judgment of this man. Only recently a more nuanced approach is tried, in which
Richardot is sketched as a pastoral orator, with a strong biblical foundation, who tries to
preach a message that unites people. See Gustaaf Janssens, "'*Superexcellat autem misericordia
iudicium.*' The Homily of François Richardot on the Occasion of the Solemn Announcement
of the General Pardon in the Netherlands (Antwerp, July 16, 1570)," *Public Opinion and
Changing Identities in the Early Modern Netherlands. Essays in Honour of Alastair Duke*, ed.
Judith Pollman and Andrew Spicer (Leiden: Brill, 2007), 107–124. In my opinion, it is not
impossible that he is that mysterious "man of the religious order of hermits preaching in
Madame's court" in 1536. See notes 10 and 12 in this chapter.

[45] Often identified as Françoise de Boussiron (Sinapius's wife), but without concrete evidence. Also, in the new edition of this letter, mentioned in note 40. One should be aware
that this is how myths are born. Renée's court was a royal court. She had a considerable
dowry, and when she arrived from France, her retinue consisted of 126 people.

way "take communion," which serves as a celebration of the Last Supper of the Lord?

Calvin's answer is simple: the Mass is an abomination and attending Mass is a sacrilege, so it is simply forbidden for a Christian to attend it. In fact, the wording used by Calvin echoes the wording in the *Placards* of 1534 and in the *Epistolae Duae* of 1537.[46] Richardot is wrong, and the lady in question does not deserve scorn, but praise. The strict position is that not only is the taking of communion (i.e., receiving the consecrated Host) out of the question, but being present when others do that is also considered a sin. One is guilty by contamination, a word that Calvin uses a lot in an almost literal, physical sense, and it is also a favorite with inquisitors, who refer to heresy as a contagious illness. So, Calvin strongly advises the Duchess not to listen to Richardot. He is a hypocrite, corrupt, money wolf, and a completely untrustworthy person, for when people disagree with Calvin, he always takes this personally and reacts with vehement attacks *ad hominem*. He urges the duchess to take a firm stand and to reject the Mass openly and totally. To do this is a holy duty for any god-fearing woman and a divine calling for a princess. Renée's reaction to this letter is unknown, but it can be inferred from her actions. Richardot remained in service, and he did so until 1544.

CONCLUSION

Some reticence and caution seem advisable when addressing the relationship between Calvin and Renée. Seen from Renée's side, there is certainly respect. In the first letter, dating from 1553, she asks Calvin for suitable husbands for two of her ladies-in-waiting.[47] He is a spiritual guide, yes, but only up to a certain degree, and he is one with whom she argues when she doesn't agree with him. And he certainly did not have a monopoly on advice. Labeling their relationship as a close friendship is thus incorrect. The characterization is from the wrong category. It's not sentimental.

---

[46] On further discussion of these *Epistolae*, see note 48.

[47] Cunitz et al., *Ioannis Calvini, Vol. XIV*, letter number 1832. The *Opera omnia* contain two letters directly addressed to Calvin, both dating from the last period of her life (as a widow): Vol. XX, letter numbers 4085, 4206. They deal with problems she had with the ministers Calvin sent to her in Montargis (on her request). Based on other letters, there must have been more, although much of the stream of information was indirectly (messengers, visitors). Sixteenth-century scholars and politicians were excellent networkers. On these letters, see also Kelly Peebles, Chap. 11.

Calvin is a man with a mission, and he corresponds with a woman who has power and is related to the French king. He needs her more than she him. In this respect, the first letter is telling. *In nuce*, all Calvin's letters are there. As a thread through his entire correspondence run the words spoken by the prophet Elijah urging the people of Israel to take a stand, to choose: "How long will you go limping between two different opinions? If the Lord is God, follow him, but if Baal, then follow him" (1 Kings 18:21).[48] The topics might change over the years, but the scope is the same. In other words, he urges the duchess to stop dissimulating, to take a stand against the abomination, to profess her Protestant faith, and to denounce the Church of the antichrist, the Pope. In short, he urges her to become a member of his party, for that is what he believes that God expects from her. When in 1554 the duchess is quite literally pressed by the Jesuits and the inquisitor to receive communion publicly, he is very disappointed and angry that she succumbed to the pressure. He castigates her verbally in his next letter, dated February 1555. He professes, of course, that it is sent "with love" and that it is for the best that she repent.[49] The summative

---

[48] This text is quoted on the title page of the *Epistolae duae*, published in January 1537. According to Calvin, "Vera pietas veram confessionem parit" (true piety cannot exist without public profession). The *Epistolae duae* (Basel: [Balthasar Lasius and Thomas Platter], 1537) have revealing titles: *Epistolæ duæ de rebus hoc sæculo cognitu apprime necessariis*. Prior, *De fugiendis impiorum illicitis sacris, et puritate Christianæ religionis observanda*. Altera, *De christiani hominis officio in sacerdotiis papalis ecclesiæ vel administrandis, vel abiiciendis*. The letter to Roussel has an apocalyptic tone, noting that if attending Mass is already a contamination, administering it is a crime above all abominations: sacrilege. In the *Petit traicté monstrant que c'est que doit faire un homme fidèle congnoissant la verité de l'évangile, quand il est entre les papistes* (Geneva: Jean Girard, 1543), the advice is even more precise: if emigration is impossible and one cannot keep away from any manifestation of the papist religion, a Christian must constantly confess this sin and ardently pray to God to show the way out. See Cunitz et al., *Calvini opera, Vol. VI*, 570–571. To his first letter, he added some of his recent tracts on the topic at hand, which were likely these. Thus, Renée knew what to do. For a more profound analysis, see Dick Wursten, *Clément Marot and Religion*, 410–415.

[49] Calvin to Renee, February 2, 1555: "Et de faict le diable en a tellement faict ses triomphes, que nous avons ete contrainte de gémir et baisser la teste, sans nous enquerir plus outre," Cunitz et al., *Calvini opera, Vol. XV*, 418. Constable's English translation reads: "And indeed the devil has so triumphed over us, that we have been constrained to groan over it, hold down our heads, and make no further enquiries," Bonnet and Constable, *Letters of John Calvin*, Vol. 3, 130. Calvin's messages to other Protestant leaders about the duchess's action also express his disappointment. He refers to Psalm 146:3, "Do not put your trust in princes," in his letter to Farel of November 1554: "De Ducissa Ferrariens tristis nuncius ac certior quam vellem, minis et probris victam cecidesse. Quid dicam nisi rarum in proceribus esse constantiae exemplum?" (Of the Duchess of Ferrara, we have sad tidings, and more

conclusion by Charmarie Blaisdell, who devoted a separate study to Calvin's correspondence to "women in high places," might suffice:

> Of all Calvin's letters to women, his letters to Renée most closely resemble letters of spiritual counsel [...]. Yet, in Renée's case too, his political motives seem obvious: he worked to keep her along the straight and arduous path to the Reformed faith for the purposes of keeping the movement alive in Italy and establishing the Reformed church officially in France. Again and again in Calvin's letters to Renée, we see him become impatient and exasperated with her reluctance to profess openly her Protestant beliefs.[50]

In the end, his interest in Renée—as in all other women (and men!) in high places—was not personal, only occasionally pastoral (this he left to his ministers sent from Geneva), but always political. The way Bèze in his "Life of Calvin" used the link between Calvin and Renée corresponds exactly with how Calvin himself viewed this relationship: it was useful for the propagation of the Reformation.

BIBLIOGRAPHY

PRIMARY SOURCES

Bolsec, Jérôme-Hermès. 1577. *Histoire de la vie, mœurs, actes, doctrine et mort de Jean Calvin, jadis grand ministre de Genève recueilly par M. Hierosme Hermes Bolsec Docteur médecin à Lyon.* Lyon: Jean Patrasson.
———. 1580. *De Ioannis Calvini, magni quondam Geneuensium ministri, vita, moribus, rebus gestis, studijs, ac denique morte historia.* Köln: Ludwig Alectorius and Haeredes Jacobi Soteri.
Calvin, Jean. 1536. *Christianae religionis institutio, totam ferè pietatis summā, & quicquid est in doctrina salutis cognitu necessarium, complectens: omnibus pietatis studiosis lectu dignissimum opus, ac recens editum.* Basel: Thomas Platter and Balthasar Lasius.
———. 1537. *Epistolæ duæ de rebus hoc sæculo cognitu apprime necessariis. Prior, De fugiendis impiorum illicitis sacris, et puritate Christianæ religionis observanda.*

certain than I could have wished. Overcome by threats and outrages she has fallen off. What can I say, except that an example of constancy is rare among princes?), Cunitz et al., *Calvini opera, Vol. XV*, 297–298.

[50]Blaisdell, "Calvin's Letters to Women: The Courting of Ladies in High Places," *Sixteenth-Century Journal* 13, no. 3 (1982), 84.

Altera, *De christiani hominis officio in sacerdotiis papalis ecclesiæ vel adminis-trandis, vel abiiciendis*. Basel: Balthasar Lasius and Thomas Platter.

———. 1543. *Petit traicté monstrant que c'est que doit faire un homme fidèle cong-noissant la verité de l'évangile, quand il est entre les papistes*. Geneva: Jean Girard.

———. 1557. *In librum Psalmorum, Johannis Calvini commentarius*. Genève: R. Estienne.

———. 1561. *Commentaires de M. Jean Calvin sur le livre des Pseaumes. Ceste traduction est tellement reveuë, et si fidelement conferee sur le latin, qu'on la peut juger estre nouvelle. Avec une table fort ample des principaux points traittez és Commentaires*. Genève: Conrad Badius.

———. 1854. *Lettres de Jean Calvin, recueillis pour la première fois et publiées d'après les manuscrits originaux, Vol. 1*. Ed. and trans. Jules Bonnet. Paris: Librairie de C. Meyrueis et compagnie.

———. 1855. *Letters by John Calvin. Compiled from the Original Manuscripts and edited with Historical Notes, Vol. 1*. Ed. Jules Bonnet and trans. David Constable. Edinburgh: Thomas Constable and Co.

———. 1858. *Letters by John Calvin. Compiled from the Original Manuscripts and edited with Historical Notes, Vol. 3*. Ed. Jules Bonnet and trans. Marcus Robert Gilchrist. Philadelphia: Presbyterian Board of Publication.

———. 1863–1900. *Calvini opera quae supersunt omnia*. Ed. Edouard Cunitz, Johann-Wilhelm Baum and Eduard Wilhelm Eugen Reuss, 59 vols. Braunschweig: Schwetschke et filium.

———. 2005. *Ioannis Calvini Opera omnia denuo recognita et adnotatione critica instructa notisque illustrata*. Series VI: *Epistolae*. Volumen I (1530-Sep. 1538). Edited by Cornelis Augustijn, Frans Pieter Van Stam, Christoph Burger, Paul Estié, August Den Hollander, Maarten Stollk, Mirjam Van Venn, and Jasper Vree. Genève: Droz.

———. 2008. *Ioannis Calvini Opera Omnia denuo recognita et adnotatione crit-ica instructa notisque illustrata*. Series IV: *Scripta didactica et polemica*. Volumen IV: *Epistolae duae* (1537) et *Deux discours* (Oct. 1536). Ed. Erik Alexander De Boer and Franc Pieter Van Stam. Geneva: Droz.

de Bèze, Théodore. 1564a. *Discours de M. Théodore de Besze, contenant en bref l'histoire de la vie et mort de Maistre Iean Calvin avec le Testament et derniere volonté dudict Calvin. Et le catalogue des livres par luy composez*. Geneva: François Perrin.

———. 1564b. *Commentaires de M. Jean Calvin, sur le livre de Josué. Avec une préface de Theodore de Besze, contenant en brief l'histoire de la vie et mort d'iceluy. Il y a aussi deux tables: l'une des matieres singulieres contenues esdits Commentaires, l'autre des tesmoignages de l'Escriture saincte alleguez et proprement appliquez par l'autheur*. Geneva: François Perrin.

———. 1564c. *Joannis Calvini in librum Josue brevis commentarius, quem paulo ante mortem absolvit. Addita sunt quædam de eiusdem morbo et obitu*. Geneva: François Perrin.

———. 1565. *Commentaires de M. Iean Calvin sur le livre de Iosué. Avec une Preface de Theodore de Besze, contenant en brief l'histoire de la vie et mort d'iceluy: augmentée depuis la premiere edition deduite selon l'ordre du temps quasi d'an en an. Il y a aussi deux tables: l'une des matieres singulieres contenues esdits commentaires, l'autre des tesmoignages de l'Escriture saincte alleguez et proprement appliquez par l'autheur.* Geneva: François Perrin.

———. 1575. *Ioannis Calvini epistolae et responsa, quibus interiectae sunt insignium in ecclesia Dei vivorum aliquot etiam epistolae. Eiusdem I. Calvini Vita a Theodoro Beza Genevensis ecclesiae ministro accurate descripta.* Geneva: Pierre Saint-André.

Erasmus, Desiderius. 1540. *Adagiorum chiliades.* Froben: Basel.

———. 1992. *Adages: II vii 1 to III iii 100.* Ed. and trans. R.A.B. Mynors. Vol. 34 of *The Collected Works of Erasmus.* Toronto: University of Toronto Press.

Herminjard, Aimée-Louis, ed. 1866–1897. *Correspondance des réformateurs dans les pays de langue française.* 9 vols. Geneva and Paris: Georg & Cie.

Masson, Jean-Papire. 1620. *Vita Ioannis Calvini auctore Papirio Massono,* 11–12. Paris: s.n.

SECONDARY SOURCES

Backus, Irene. 2008. *Life Writing in Reformation Europe: Lives of Reformers by Friends, Disciples and Foes.* Aldershot: Ashgate.

Belligni, Eleonora. 2008. *Evangelismo, riforma ginevrina e nicodemismo: l'esperienza religiosa di Renata di Francia.* Cosenza: Brenner.

———. 2011. *Renata di Francia (1510–1575). Un'eresia di corte.* Turin: UTET.

Blaisdell, Charmarie Jenkins. 1975. Politics and Heresy in Ferrara, 1534–1559. *Sixteenth-Century Journal* 6 (1): 67–93.

———. 1982. Calvin's Letters to Women: The Courting of Ladies in High Places. *Sixteenth-Century Journal* 13 (3): 67–84.

Bonnet, Jules. 1872. Clément Marot à la cour de Ferrare, 1535–1536. *Bulletin de la Société de l'histoire du Protestantisme français* 21: 159–168.

———. 1885a. Calvin à Ferrare, Avril 1536? *Bulletin de la Société de l'histoire du Protestantisme français* 34: 327–331.

———. 1885b. Clément Marot à Vénise et son abjuration à Lyon. *Bulletin de la Société de l'histoire du Protestantisme français* 34: 289–303.

———. 1890. Les premières persécutions à la cour de Ferrara. *Bulletin de la Société de l'histoire du Protestantisme français* 39: 169–180, 289–302.

———. 1892. Calvin à Ferrare (1535–1536). *Bulletin de la Société de l'histoire du Protestantisme français* 41: 171–191.

Bouwsma, William J. 1988. *John Calvin. A Sixteenth-Century Portrait.* New York: Oxford University Press.

Brobeck, John T. 1995. Musical Patronage in the Royal Chapels of France under Francis I (r. 1515–1547). *Journal of the American Musicological Society* 48: 187–239.

Cazaux, Christelle. 2002. *La Musique à la cour de François Ier*. Paris: École nationale des Chartes.

Cottret, Bernard. 1995. *Calvin: Biographie*. Paris: Éditions Jean-Claude Lattès.

Crottet, Alexandre César. 1850. *Correspondance française de Calvin avec Louis du Tillet* chanoine d'Angoulême et curé de Claix: *sur les questions de l'église et du ministère évangélique: découverte parmi les manuscrits de la Bibliothèque nationale de France, et publiée pour la première fois*. Paris: Cherbuliez.

Doumergue, Émile. 1899–1927. *Jean Calvin: les hommes et les choses de son temps*. 7 vols. Paris and Lausanne: Bridel.

Duflot, Léon. 1898. *Un Orateur du XVIe siècle. François Richardot, évêque d'Arras*. Arras: Sueur-Charruey.

Flood, John L., and David J. Shaw. 1997. *Johannes Sinapius (1505–1560). Hellenist and Physician in Germany and Italy*. Geneva: Droz.

Fontana, Bartolommeo. 1885. *Documenti dell'Archivio Vaticano e dell'Estense circa il soggiorno di Calvino a Ferrara*. Rome: R. Società Romana di Storia Patria.

———. 1889–1899. *Renata di Francia duchessa di Ferrara: sui documenti dell'archivio Estense, del Mediceo, del Gonzaga e dell' Archivio secreto vaticano*. 3 vols. Rome: Forzani.

Gorris, Rosanna. 1997. 'Un franzese nominato Clemente': Marot à Ferrare. In *Clément Marot "prince des poëtes françois" 1496–1996. Actes du colloque international de Cahors–en–Quercy, 21–25 mai 1996*, ed. Gérard Defaux and Michel Simonin, 339–364. Paris: Champion.

———. 2006. 'Va lettre, va … droict à Clément': Lyon Jamet, sieur de Chambrun, du Poitou à la ville des Este, un itinéraire religieux et existentiel. In *Les Grands Jours de Rabelais en Poitou. Actes du colloque international de Poitiers (30 août-1er septembre)*, ed. Marie-Luce Demonet and avec la collaboration de Stéphan Geonget, 145–172. Geneva: Droz.

Hollingsworth, Mary. 2004. *The Cardinal's Hat: Money, Ambition, and Everyday Life in the Court of a Borgia Prince*. New York: The Overlook Press.

Janssens, Gustaaf. 2007. 'Superexcellat autem misericordia iudicium.' The Homily of François Richardot on the Occasion of the Solemn Announcement of the General Pardon in the Netherlands (Antwerp, 16 July 1570). In *Public Opinion and Changing Identities in the Early Modern Netherlands. Essays in Honour of Alastair Duke*, ed. Judith Pollman and Andrew Spicer, 107–124. Leiden: Brill.

Knecht, Robert J. 1996. *Renaissance Warrior and Patron: The Reign of Francis I*. Cambridge: Cambridge University Press.

Mayer, Claude A. 1956. Le Départ de Marot de Ferrare. *Bibliothèque d'humanisme et Renaissance* 18 (2): 197–221.

McGrath, Alister E. 1993. *A Life of John Calvin: A Study in the Shaping of Western Culture*. Malden, MA: Blackwell.

Merle d'Aubigné, Jean-Henri. 1862–1877. *Histoire de la Reformation en Europe au temps de Calvin*. 8 vols. Paris: Michel Lévy Freres.

Muratori, Lodovico A. 1776. *Delle antichita estensi ed italiane. Trattato di Ludovico Antonio Muratori bibliotecario del serenissimo signor Duca di Modena. Continuazione della Parte II*. Naples: Gaetano Castello.

————. 1838. *Annali d'Italia ed altre opere varie. Volume IV dall'anno 1358 all'anno 1687*. Milan: Fratelli Ubicini.

Naphy, William G. 1994. *Calvin and the Consolidation of the Genevan Reformation*. New York: Manchester University Press.

Nicholls, David. 1996. Heresy and Protestantism, 1520–1542: Questions of Perception and Communication. *French History* 10: 182–205.

Overell, Anne. 2008. *Italian Reform and English Reformations, c.1535–c.1585*. Aldershot: Ashgate.

Pitkin, Barbara. 1993. Imitation of David: David as a Paradigm for Faith in Calvin's Exegesis of the Psalms. *Sixteenth Century Journal* 24 (4): 843–863.

Potter, David. 2008. *Renaissance France at War: Armies, Culture and Society c. 1480–1560*. Rochester: Boydell Press.

Rodocanachi, Emmanuel. 1896. *Renée de France duchesse de Ferrare. Une protectrice de la Réforme en Italie et en France*. Paris: Ollendorff.

Roney, John B. 1996. *The Inside of History: Jean Henri Merle d'Aubigné and Romantic Historiography*. Westport, Connecticut: Greenwood Press.

Selderhuis, Herman J. 2007. *Calvin's Theology of the Psalms*. Grand Rapids: Baker.

Steinmetz, David. 2010. *Calvin in Context*. Oxford: Oxford University Press.

Stjerna, Kirsi. 2009. *Women and the Reformation*. Malden, MA: Wiley-Blackwell.

Webb, Charmarie Jenkins [Blaisdell]. 1969. *Royalty and Reform: The Predicament of Renée de France, 1510–1575*. PhD diss., Tufts University.

Wursten, Dick. 2010. *Clément Marot and Religion. A Re-assessment in the Light of His Psalm Paraphrases*. Leiden/Boston: Brill.

CHAPTER 5

The Duchess and the Poet: Rereading Variants of Two Poems Written in Exile by Clément Marot to Renée de France in Relation to Ongoing Diplomatic Negotiations (1535–1538)

Guillaume Berthon
Translated by William Kemp, Judyt Landstein
and Robert J. Hudson

Renée de France played a significant role in the wake of the *Affaire des Placards* of October 1534, for her court offered a place of refuge to many of those fleeing the violent repression in Paris. On rereading the list of

I would like to thank William Kemp and Judyt Landstein most warmly and kindly for the translation of this text, as well as Robert J. Hudson for his translation of the poems by Marot and his contemporaries into elegant English verses. Through their comments, their kindness and their patience, Kelly Peebles and Gabriella Scarlatta have also greatly helped to improve this article from all points of view, and I am very grateful to them.

G. Berthon (✉)
Université de Toulon, Babel, France

those condemned, whose names had been publicly announced on January 25, 1535 (New Style), among other "Heretics," we encounter a certain Clément Marot. Though unlike those others, his name appears without any qualifying adjectives pointing to his position or occupation, offering us a glimpse of Marot's notoriety among his contemporaries.[1] In fact, Marot, who later claimed that he was at Blois on the night of October 17–18, immediately set off for southwest France and the court of Marguerite de Navarre. He was arrested in Bordeaux on November 27, but if we are to believe the account described in his *coq-à-l'âne*, written in Venice in July 1536, he was able to escape by concealing his identity.[2] Doubtless on the recommendation of Marguerite de Navarre, he departed for Italy, passing first through Languedoc and Provence before arriving at the court of Ferrara in March or April of 1535, where the duchess granted him an annual salary of 200 *livres tournois*.[3] The poet stayed in Ferrara for a little more than a year before seeking refuge once again in Venice around June 1536, and finally returning to France in late 1536, stopping first in Lyons, the site of his public confession and abjuration.

Poetically speaking, this Ferrarese "parenthesis" was a particularly fruitful period. Marot attempted to carve out a place of honor for himself alongside Renée, becoming the animator of court festivities and sending multiple poems to King François I, the Dauphin, and the Queen of Navarre to maintain a vicarious presence at the court of France despite his physical absence. He also took it on himself to enliven French poetic life from afar by inventing new challenges, such as the blazon competition.[4] After returning to France and publishing his *Œuvres* in Lyons in the summer of 1538, the poet included only a fraction of the fruits of his exile

---

[1] See Gabrielle Berthoud, "Les ajournés du 25 janvier 1535," *Bibliothèque d'Humanisme et Renaissance* 25, no. 2 (1963): 312. This most interesting list, as well as some pieces about the *Affaire des Placards*, can be found in Ms. 202 (189b) at Soissons. It also contains a version of one of the two texts that I will be studying in this chapter.

[2] Clément Marot, *Œuvres poétiques complètes*, ed. Gérard Defaux, II, 109, v. 134–164 and Mayer, *Clément Marot*, (Paris: Nizet, 1972), 267–269.

[3] Giulio Bertoni, "Documenti sulla dimora di Clément Marot a Ferrara," in *Mélanges de philologie offerts à Jean-Jacques Salverda de Grace*, 9–10 and Rosanna Gorris Camos, "'Un Franzese nominato Clement': Marot à Ferrare," in *Clément Marot "Prince des poëtes François" 1496–1996. Actes du Colloque international de Cahors en Quercy, 1996*, ed. Gérard Defaux and Michel Simonin (Paris: Champion, 1997), 342.

[4] See Guillaume Berthon, "L'invention du blason: retour sur la genèse d'un genre (Ferrare, 1535)," in *Anatomie d'une anatomie. Nouvelles recherches sur les blasons anatomiques du corps féminin*, ed. Julien Goeury and Thomas Hunkeler (Geneva: Droz, 2018), 135–156.

among those works. However, a bit earlier, in March of that same year, he did include an ample selection of them in a manuscript offered to Anne de Montmorency, whom the king had just elevated to the position of Constable of France. This manuscript is now known as the "Chantilly manuscript," due to its current place of conservation, the Château de Chantilly.[5]

As Marot's compositions in 1535–1536 were destined both for the ducal court of Ferrara and for the royal court of France, the poet modified his poems to tailor them to the reader, whether Renée or her husband the Duke of Ferrara, the King of France, the Dauphin, the Queen of Navarre, or the Constable Anne de Montmorency. He also systematically revised large parts of his works before circulating them officially. This is especially evident in the Chantilly manuscript.[6] Revisions to a piece offered to Renée in July 1535 in celebration of her third pregnancy as she was awaiting the little Lucrezia, as well as to an epistle that Marot sent to her from Venice in July 1536, result in two contrasting versions. Dick Wursten refers to these as "Janus-faced poems," for one version espouses a militant evangelism that is violently anti-papal and lambasts all forms of idolatry, while the other adopts a less aggressive approach condemning materialism and the enemies of the Muses.[7]

This duality has led to editorial mix-ups, although the former *Avant-naissance* was less mistreated than the Venetian *Epistle*. In the latter case, the older editions of Marot are more trustworthy. First, Georges Guiffrey, aware of only a small portion of the manuscript versions, including a single one of the *Epistle*, provided a faithful version of the text available to him. He was followed almost a century later by Claude A. Mayer, whose editions turn out to be the most complete and most rigorous in their attention to variants. Gérard Defaux, in his widely diffused two-volume edition

---

[5] See *Recueil inédit offert au connétable de Montmorency en mars 1538 (Manuscrit de Chantilly)*, ed. François Rigolot (Geneva: Droz, 2010).

[6] In addition to the two examples that I will be studying, there exist other stylistic variations in a few texts for which a version dating back to the moment of composition have come down to us as well as a later version. See the example of the Epistle to the Dauphin, printed as a pamphlet probably by François Juste at Lyons in 1536. Guillaume Berthon and William Kemp, "L'épître de Marot au dauphin (1536): le virage courtisan de François Juste," *Bulletin du bibliophile* 2 (2012): 367–373. It was inserted into the manuscript offered to Montmorency in 1538.

[7] Dick Wursten, *Clément Marot and Religion. A Reassessment in the Light of His Psalm Paraphrases* (Leiden: Brill, 2010), 40–50. This chapter stems in reality from an idea of Dick Wursten. I agree globally with his interpretation.

from the early 1990s, attempted to knit all of the different versions together, taking as his base text the Chantilly manuscript or the printed version based thereon, but also including the diverse readings from various manuscripts that had been carefully noted by Mayer. According to Defaux, his approach offered a "more correct" and "more revealing" text.[8] In the most recent edition of Marot's poetry, François Rigolot reproduces Defaux's peculiar assemblage, though he also includes the Chantilly version in its entirety in an annex.[9] In brief, today's reader, who may not have access to Guiffrey's or Mayer's older editions (now difficult to find), has access to almost none of the various versions of these two poems addressed to Renée and does not benefit from the most recent findings.

Above and beyond these tricky textual problems, these "two-faced" poems have led to contrasting interpretations. Several critics have seen in the militant text the "original" text of the *Epistle*, the result of spiritual complicities between the poet and Renée, and have considered the other version as a later rewriting, one that was toned down in accordance with the constable's "timorous Catholicism."[10] Others, including Paulette Leblanc, maintain the importance of both poems, pointing out that they are "equally interesting because they reflect two oscillating extremes in Marot's religious satire, depending on the public he was addressing."[11] Others yet have seen "two parallel and complementary versions," "a sort of original diptych" where neither of the sides represents Marot's true point of view, thus inflecting his verses occasionally toward Anne de Montmorency's orthodoxy, while at other times in the direction of Renée's more radical religious sensibilities.[12]

The aim of this chapter is twofold. On the one hand, I first describe all known manuscript versions of these two poems in order to understand

---

[8] Marot, *Œuvres poétiques complètes*, II, 880.

[9] Marot, *Œuvres poétiques complètes*, II, 565–568 (Defaux assemblage) and 631–634 (Chantilly). In his edition of the Chantilly manuscript alone (*Recueil inédit offert au connétable de Montmorency*), Rigolot gives the Chantilly version, but the Defaux assemblage is given in the Annex (305–309).

[10] Mayer, *Clément Marot*, 290 (1st quote), 361, 405; Defaux in his edition of the *Œuvres poétiques complètes*, II, 880 (2nd quote) and 953.

[11] Paulette Leblanc, *La poésie religieuse de Clément Marot* (Paris: Nizet, 1955), 188n2.

[12] Frédéric Tinguely (whose citations have been extracted), "Marot et le miroir vénitien," in *Clément Marot "Prince des poëtes François,"* 377. See also Robert Mélançon, "La personne de Marot," also in *Clément Marot "Prince des poëtes François,"* 518–520.

both the circumstances within which they were written and the sources that were followed in their publication. After investigating this to the greatest extent possible, the philological step of a rigorous critical edition will help us to better interpret the relationship of these textual variants to the political and diplomatic context of Renée's court in 1535–1536, that Dick Wursten elucidates in his contribution to this volume. Thus, this chapter aims to resolve a critical question: what do the more heterodox versions of Marot's poems tell us about his faith and that of the duchess who so generously offered him refuge from religious persecution?

INVENTORY AND DESCRIPTION OF THE MANUSCRIPTS

Several poems composed in Ferrara were printed in France before Marot's return from exile, while others were printed on his return.[13] But to my knowledge, neither of the two compositions under discussion were printed during Marot's lifetime († 1544). However, these two poems did circulate in manuscript form, as all the copies date from the sixteenth century (with one exception: MS. Fr. 22,558, housed at the Bibliothèque nationale de France (BnF)).

Several details lead us to believe that the diffusion of these poems was probably quite limited. First of all, sixteenth-century publishers were not aware of the Venetian *Epistle*, as it was first printed in the nineteenth century. Moreover, the *Avant-naissance* was not printed before 1547 in Poitiers, three years after Marot's death, along with many other unpublished works.[14] The poet's rivals also seem to have had no knowledge of either of these two texts, for they never mention them and concentrate their attacks elsewhere, claiming that a handful of pieces from his exile reveal the poet's "Lutheran" tendencies, as do the first epistle to King François I, written in Ferrara, and the enigmatic epistle to two sisters "joinctes par charité" (joined by charity), or the second *coq-à-l'âne*.[15] Marot's most important rival, François de Sagon, led the polemic, stating:

> [...] je m'en rapporte à toy
> et à l'escript qu'en adressas au Roy,

[13] A list of these poems is provided in the appendix to this chapter.
[14] Clément Marot, *Epigramme faictz à l'imitation de Martial* (Poitiers: Jean and Enguilbert de Marnef, September 27, 1547), in-8°. All references to the original editions of Marot are given in accordance with my *Bibliographie critique*.
[15] Marot, *Œuvres poétiques complètes*, II, 78–91.

Françoys du nom premier, chef de noblesse. [...]
    Ce n'est pas tout [:] ton epistre aux deux seurs,
Dont trop de gens ont esté possesseurs,
Se plaingnoit trop à grant tort de justice [...].
    Dedens Paris ces epistres j'ouy,
Dont je ne fus grandement resjoy:
Puis je les vey sans plus longues enquestes
Entre les mains d'ung maistre des requestes,
Mais je n'en sceu avoir prest ny octroy,
Pource que l'une avoit despleu au Roy.[16]

([...] this case to you I bring
All for the verse you addressed to our King,
François the first of this name, noble head. [...]
This is not all [:] your epistle addressed
To two sisters, now by many possessed,
Complains too much to the harm of justice [...]
Within Paris these epistles I hear,
Of which I'm not greatly rejoiced I fear:
Then I saw them without further inquests
In the hands of a Master of Requests,
But unto me no loan nor trade could bring,
Because the one had so displeased our King.)

Sagon's diatribe states clearly that certain texts written during the poet's exile were circulating in France ("Dont trop de gens ont esté possesseurs"), but always from hand to hand; it is possible to hear them read without being able to obtain a copy. If the *Avant-naissance* and the Venetian *Epistle* to Renée appear to have evaded the reaches of Sagon and his friends, it is likely that they received a similar diffusion, as evidenced by surviving manuscripts.

One of these manuscripts, that known as the Chantilly manuscript, deserves special treatment. The short lapse of time between the constable's nomination on February 10, 1538, and the date of the manuscript (March 1538, New Style) suggests that the editing was done rapidly, which the lack of ornamentation confirms. Still, Marot was able to review

---

[16] *Deffense de Sagon Contre Clement Marot*, Paris, Pierre Vidoue, [ca. 1537], in-8°, from the facsimile published by Émile Picot, *Querelle de Marot et Sagon* (Geneva, Slatkine Reprints, 1969), f. B 3r°-v°.

his text and make changes of varying importance, from a simple lexical variant to the complete rewriting of certain passages. The title page of the manuscript reveals the poet's aim: *Recueil des dernieres Œuvres de Clement Marot, non imprimees. Et premierement Celles qu'il fit durant son exil, et depuis son retour* (*Collection of the most recent works of Clement Marot that have not been printed, especially all those that he wrote during his exile and since his return*). Thus, the manuscript contains a selection of unedited texts composed during his stay in Italy (1535–1536) and after his return to France (1536–1538). It is probable that the poet wanted to stay in the good graces of the powerful constable and to demonstrate to Montmorency that he, the suspected poet, was not averse to letting him read texts that had been the subject of lively criticism during his exile. However, he cautiously excised three polemical pieces that had caught the attention of Sagon and his cohorts, replacing them by other, less controversial pieces. Among these are our two poems in more moderate versions than those appearing in other manuscript versions. Apart from the Chantilly manuscript, we now know of two versions of the *Avant-naissance* and four of the Venetian *Epistle*, though it is always possible that other copies may still come to light, whether in a library or on the book market.

L'Avant-naissance du troisième enfant de la duchesse de Ferrare (Prenatal Poem Awaiting the Birth of the Third Child of the Duchess of Ferrara)

We begin by examining the simplest of the two cases, the *Avant-naissance*, of which we know of two manuscripts in addition to the one conserved at Chantilly: Ms. Fr. 2370 at the BnF (f. 48r–49r) and Ms. 202 held in the Municipal Library at Soissons (f. 169v–171r).[17] These two manuscripts, copied in the sixteenth century, are quite similar, and we can read descriptions, albeit incomplete, of the pieces contained therein on Jonas, the IRHT's online database.[18] The pieces that were copied are relatively homogeneous with respect to chronology and genre. In both instances,

---

[17] I wish to thank Claire Sicard for obtaining for me the pictures of the corresponding leaves in the Soissons manuscript.

[18] URL: http://jonas.irht.cnrs.fr. Work on the contents of the two manuscripts is still in progress but at the time of consultation, 113 documents had been described in the Ms. 2370 and 38 in the Ms. 202, to which can be added 25 other documents described in the *Catalogue général des manuscrits des bibliothèques publiques de France*, ed. Henry Martin (Paris: Plon, 1885), 128–130. However, for this last manuscript, the most complete description is to be found in the hand-written census made by Françoise Féry-Hue (scanned and attached to the

the assembled pieces reflect the poetic esthetics of the 1530s, an atmosphere dominated by Marot and several other poets, including Mellin de Saint-Gelais, Claude Chappuys (above all, in the Ms. fr. 2370), and Marguerite de Navarre, though there were also a great number of anonymous compositions. The poems mix traditional eroticism—either chaste or obscene—with subjects inspired by events of the times, especially in Ms. 202. These include epitaphs of illustrious characters who died in the second half of the 1530s, various contemporary anecdotes, echoes in verse or in prose of major events, such as the *Affaire des Placards* of October 1534, the execution of Thomas More in July 1535, and that of Anne Boleyn in May 1536, the invasion of Provence by Charles V in June 1536, and the festivities surrounding the marriage of James V of Scotland with Madeleine de France in December 1536 through January 1537.

It is not easy to garner clues from the assembled pieces to situate the copy more exactly, since the two manuscripts are not true codicological units, that is, they are made up of independent quires assembled at an uncertain date and show traces of different hands on variable supports, for example, a mixture of paper and parchment in the case of Ms. Fr. 2370, in particular.[19] However, in both cases, no datable piece is later than 1538, and those whose composition is easy to date are mostly from the years 1534–1537. Also, in both manuscripts, the poems written by Marot— whose name is very often cited in the title—offer original readings, which seem related to an earlier version prior to those of the printed tradition, established by the poet himself.[20] In short, despite the necessary reservations that such studies involve, we can hypothesize that the version of the *Avant-naissance* that they provide resembles the copy that must have circulated just after its composition. If I speak of the version in the singular and not of the versions in the plural, this is due to the fact that the study of the variants clearly demonstrates that these two manuscripts provide two versions that derive from a unique prototype. Readings for verses 51–60 are nearly identical, with numerous errors typical of each one.

The version of the *Avant-naissance* that appears in the Chantilly manuscript is manifestly the result of the poet's rewriting of a text composed in

Jonas notice), describing more than 150 documents as well as a complete codicological description of the manuscript.

[19] The Marot pieces, however, do appear in homogeneous quires. My most sincere thanks to Marco Veneziale for his aid in describing this manuscript.

[20] See Claude Mayer's remarks, concerning manuscript 202. *Bibliographie des œuvres de Clément Marot, Volume I: Manuscripts,* (Geneva: Droz, 1954), 67.

1535, a rewriting that can most likely be dated to February–March 1538. If this version, radically different in lines 51–60, existed and circulated as early as the summer of 1535, it would doubtless have been transmitted in one or more manuscripts. However, it is only in 1547 that it is to be found in a printed edition, that of Poitiers. All later printed editions of the sixteenth century have retained this reading.

The Epistle Written in Venice to the Duchess of Ferrara

In the case of the Venetian *Epistle*, there is a greater number of known manuscripts. At this writing, we know of four in addition to the Chantilly manuscript: two at the BnF, one at Harvard, and another at Lausanne. The first, Ms. Fr. 4967 held by the Bibliothèque nationale de France (f. 291v–293v), was discovered by Georges Guiffrey and published in the third volume of his Marot edition in 1881. It is probably the one that represents the oldest version of the text. The last parts of this manuscript contain a vast collection of verses copied in the sixteenth century by an anonymous scribe. Numerous and judicious corrections have been inserted by a second hand. Among these texts, none seems to be later than 1537.[21] The Marot poems included here were unpublished at that time, and most all of them date from the years of his Italian exile. The neat chronological and thematic coherence leads us to advance the hypothesis that the manuscript must have been copied shortly after the poems were composed.[22] So, it is reasonable to conclude that, despite its numerous errors, the text of the *Epistle* in this manuscript is close to the one that was circulating just after its composition. The reading of verse 40, "Images peinctz qu'à grandz despens ilz dorent" (Painted icons at a great cost they guild), is more satisfying from a rhetorical point of view, since it prepares the opposition in verses 43–45 of the poor who are "ymaiges vives" (living icons).

---

[21] See the complete list of documents given by the *Catalogue* of the BnF and Mayer, *Bibliographie*, I 63–65. See also Guillaume Berthon and Jérémie Bichüe, "Le manuscrit poétique, de l'exercice à l'œuvre: le cas du manuscrit français 4967 de la BnF," in *Le Manuscrit littéraire à la Renaissance. Cahiers V.-L. Saulnier 37* (Paris: PUPS, 2020), which contains a detailed description of the manuscript and thoughts on the unedited pieces concerning the Marot-Sagon quarrel (1535–1537).

[22] We must recognize that the pieces in verse contained in the last part of the manuscript (the one I am discussing) show systematically the intervention of a second hand. This person has reread all the texts and has corrected them in a judicious manner.

This variant sets it off from the manuscripts of Harvard and of Lausanne, which can be linked to another prototype and were copied later. The Lausanne manuscript is actually a three-leaf manuscript copy inserted into an exemplar of Marot's *Œuvres*, printed by Dolet, that belonged to Charles Du Mont. Aimé-Louis Herminjard published a transcription of it in the sixth volume of his *Correspondance des réformateurs*.[23] Herminjard simply states that the copy was "written towards the end of the sixteenth century, and probably in Geneva."[24] Inserting unedited, transcribed pieces by hand into printed editions of the same author was a typical bibliographic practice at the end of the seventeenth century.[25] The three leaves in the Lausanne manuscript seem to come from a slightly earlier period, for the handwriting is more consistent with that of the end of the sixteenth century or early seventeenth century, when the text was copied from an earlier manuscript (recalling that the *Epistle* was not printed before the nineteenth century).

The Harvard manuscript was purchased by the Houghton Library in 1981 and described by François Rouget in 2006.[26] According to Rouget, the Houghton manuscript must have been copied in the last quarter of the sixteenth century by someone in the entourage of Marguerite de France, daughter of François I and Claude de France and Renée de France's niece,

---

[23] *Correspondance des Réformateurs dans les pays de langue française*, ed. Aimé-Louis Herminjard (Geneva, Basel, and Paris: H. Georg, M. Levy, and G. Fischbacher, 1866–1897), VI, 448–455. I want to express my thanks to Estelle Doudet for having succeeded in relocating the original leaves that seemed to have been lost. They are now conserved in the Archives Cantonales Vaudoises (P SVG G 174 Variétés littéraires, Frédéric Chavannes, 1844–1881), unfortunately without the edition of the *Œuvres* by Marot into which they had been inserted.

[24] Herminjard, *Correspondance*, 449n2.

[25] See two such examples in my *Bibliographie critique*, 1539/1 (copy of the Count of Hoym) and 1541/6 (Rothschild copy). On this practice, see Jean-Marc Chatelain, *La Bibliothèque de l'honnête homme. Livres, lecture et collections en France à l'âge classique* (Paris: BnF, 2003), 139.

[26] Houghton Library, Harvard University, Ms. Fr. 337, f. 120v°-123v°. See François Rouget, "Marguerite de Berry et sa cour en Savoie d'après un album de vers manuscrits," *Revue d'histoire littéraire de France* 106, no. 1 (2006): 3–16. F. Rouget was unaware that the Du Mont pièce published by Herminjard was simply a few leaves inserted into an edition and not a complete anthology and thought that the Harvard manuscript was the copy published by Herminjard. By comparing the two texts, Daniele Speziari had previously suspected that the two texts were not identical. "Clément Marot 'ferrarese,' nel ducato di Savoia e alla corte di Grancia: l'esempio des ms. Fr. 337 della Houghton Library, Università di Harvard e del ms. di Chantilly," in *Schifanoia* 40–41 (2011): 112–113. Many thanks to Daniele Speziari for having sent me reproductions of the Harvard manuscript.

who later became Duchess of Savoy in 1559.[27] In addition to Marot's *Epistle* and a few other poems, the lines included are mostly from the 1560s and 1570s. The presence of the Marot piece can probably be explained by Marguerite's relations with the poet during her youth at the French court, a connection referred to in one of Marot's epistles.[28] Furthermore, during her lifetime, she was able to protect the poet's tomb in the cathedral of Turin from destruction, though it was rapidly destroyed after her death.[29] Thus, the authority of the text of the Venetian *Epistle* is quite strong, despite the relatively late date of the manuscript copy.

Finally, the BnF Ms. Fr. 22,558 is in a category by itself. The copyist appears to have selected a certain number of passages from the *Epistle*, amounting to 48 lines out of 126. The result is a disjointed and flawed text, one that offers almost no new readings, but rather clear corruptions. The manuscript is part of an ensemble of three volumes composed at the end of the seventeenth century by François-Roger de Gaignières.[30] It is likely that this well-known collector and antiquarian, or perhaps one of his collaborators, wished to cite this text. Since it did not appear in any of the printed editions of the time, he selected only the most characteristic passages, in particular the pointed barbs against the papacy, as the excerpts stop at verse 66. We again recognize the working habits of the bibliophiles and savants from the seventeenth and eighteenth centuries, excessively eager to reveal unedited texts and curiosities. The eight most virulent lines of the *Avant-naissance* were collected in the same manner in the middle of the seventeenth century by the historian Jean Le Laboureur.[31]

Alongside these four manuscripts, the Chantilly manuscript also offers a version of the Venetian *Epistle* that was revised by the poet in early 1538,

---

[27] The name of one of these people, Louis de Rochefort, at once doctor and poet, shows up regularly. See Rosanna Gorris Camos, "L'insaisissable Protée: Ludovic Demoulin de Rochefort, médecin, poète et bibliophile entre Turin et Bâle," in *Pouvoir médical et fait du prince au début des temps modernes*, ed. Stéphane Velut et Jacqueline Vons (Paris: De Boccard, 2011), 147–209.

[28] Marot, *Œuvres poétiques complètes*, 330–332 ("Voyant que la Royne ma Mere ...").

[29] See Dick Wursten and Jetty Janssen, "New light on the location of Clément Marot's tomb and epitaph in Turin," *Studi Francesi* 161 (LIV-II, 2010): 293–303, especially 297–298.

[30] See the study of Anne Ritz-Guilbert, *La Collection Gaignières: un inventaire du royaume au XVIIᵉ siècle* (Paris: CNRS editions, 2016).

[31] They show up at the end of the *Mémoires de Messire Michel de Castelnau Seigneur de Mauvissière, Tome Premier*, ed. Jean Le Laboureur (Paris: P. Lamy, 1659), 747. Le Laboureur does not mention his source.

following the same principles as the *Avant-naissance*. However, this rewriting is much more significant, for in addition to rephrasing certain verses, the poet completely eliminates 27 lines (verses 33–38 and 46–66), displaces a block of eight other lines (verses 77–84 in the original text become 35–42 in the Chantilly version), and inserts seven entirely new lines (verses 33–34, 43–44, 52–54).

INTERPRETING THE VARIANTS

In sum, in the case of the *Avant-naissance,* just as in that of the Venetian *Epistle,* it is likely that the manuscript tradition in all its diversity—with the exception of the Chantilly manuscript—gives a faithful image of the texts that circulated at the time of their composition, that is, roughly at the time when they were written for Renée de France. The Chantilly manuscript, on the other hand, represents a version that the poet reworked in February–March 1538, specifically for the Constable Anne de Montmorency.

A major variant in the *Avant-naissance* confirms this hypothetical chronology. Let us recall the context in which Marot wrote his poem. Even though the duchess had only been pregnant for a short time—she would give birth to Lucrezia in December—Marot decided to compose a genethliac poem in the tradition of Virgil's fourth eclogue, which associates the birth of an exceptional child to the return of the Golden Age. The text also celebrates Marot's arrival in Ferrara as the beginning of a new era. In fact, since arriving in Ferrara in March–April 1535, the poet had to find a way to distinguish himself before the ducal couple. This explains the unusual anticipation demonstrated by titling three manuscripts as an "Avant-naissance" rather than as a poem composed "for the day of birth," as the etymology of the word *genethliac* would indicate. Marot chose not to await the birth of the child before highlighting his skill to the duchess. Given this anticipation, he was able to introduce a few amusing innovations compared to the Virgilian model. For example, verses 15–16 underscore the family's impatience—which the poet shares—and verses 69–70 reveal the poet's fear that such an appealing depiction of the life awaiting the child could entice it to enter the world prematurely.

In this context, the variants in lines 29–32 are most revealing. The Ms. Fr. 2370, located at the BnF and identical to the Soissons manuscript apart from two errors, reads as follows:

Puys je suis seur et on le congnoistra
Qu'à ta naissance avecques toy naistra
Don de vertu en ton ame logé
Si tu tiens rien de ceulx qui t'ont forgé.

(And I am sure, which will by all be sworn,
That at your birth, with you will too be born
Gift of virtue within your soul engorged
If anything comes from those who you forged.)

Ever a good court poet, Marot is careful in his treatment of both the duke and the duchess, depicting both as paragons of virtue. This poem likely coincides with his composition of a *dizain*, or ten-line stanza, for each of them, both of which were printed in Lyons before the end of 1535, and demonstrate the same strategy[32]:

Dixain à ses amys, quant en laissant la Royne de Navarre fut receu en la maison et estat de ma dame Renee, Duchesse de Ferrare.
Mes amys, j'ay changé ma Dame,
Une aultre a dessus moy puissance,
Nee deux foys de nom et d'ame,
Enfant de Roy par sa nayssance,
Enfant du Ciel par congnoissance,
De celluy qui la saulvera.
De sorte quant l'aultre sçaura,
Comme je l'ay telle choysie,
Je suys bien seur qu'elle en aura
Plus d'ayse que de jalousie.

(My friends, a new Lady I've claimed,
Another assumes the high place,
Two times born, in soul and when named,
Daughter of a King by her race,
Daughter of Heaven, knowing grace,
In Him who salvation did earn.
Such that when the other shall learn,

---

[32] Although the critical editions of Marot's works still give the date of 1537 as that of the first appearance of these two texts, in fact they were already present in the 1535 edition printed in Lyons by Denis de Harsy (text following the copy held at the Rutgers University Library, New Brunswick, NJ, USA: PQ1637 .M3A6 1535, f. M2v°-M3r°). See the list in the annex for further details.

How I did choose her, we will see,
I'm convinced that her heart will yearn
With more delight than jealousy.)

**Dixain au Duc de Ferrare par Clement Marot à son arrivee
Mil.ccccxxxv.**
Quant la vertu congneust que la fortune,
Me conseilloit abandonner la France,
Elle me dist, cherche terre opportune
Pour mon recueil, et pour ton asseurance.
Incontinent (prince) j'eu esperance
Qu'il feroit bon devers toy se retraire
Qui tous enfans de vertu veulx attraire,
Pour decorer ton palays sumptueux.
Et que plaisir ne prendroys à ce faire,
Si tu n'estoys toy mesmes vertueux.

(When Virtue did learn the counsel of Fortune,
That I should soon leave and abandon France,
She said to me, find a land opportune
For my welcome, and for your assurance.
Straight away (Prince) I had hoped that by chance
It might be choice if near you I retreat,
Since all children of virtue there do meet,
To decorate your most ornate house thus.
And no pleasure could you take to us greet,
If you were not yourself most virtuous.)

As these poems demonstrate, Marot handles his compliments with considerable skill in relation to the personality of husband and wife. For the duke, he describes virtues typical of a Renaissance prince involving his openness, as well as his artistic and cultural undertakings. For the duchess, the themes are much less standard. The poet begins by working through the name of Renée and its evangelical resonances ("Nee deux foys de nom et d'ame"), before going on to her motto: "Enfant de Roy par sa nayssance, / Enfant du Ciel par congnoissance," which echoes in French her *impresa* "Di real sangue nata / In Christo sol Renata" that she had stamped on at least one of her bindings, as Kelly Peebles has recalled.[33] The apogee of his *dizain* is a display of courtly rhetoric on the subject of the inconstant lover, ludically transposed onto the spiritual level. What strikes us at first is the spiritual complicity set up in the first exchanges between the poet and the duchess.

In the Chantilly manuscript, however, lines **29–32** of the *Avant-naissance* reads as follows, with changes highlighted in italics:

> Puis je suis seur (et on le congnoistra)
> Qu'à ta naissance, avecques toy naistra
> *Esprit docile, et cueur sans taiche amere*
> *Si tu tiens rien, du costé de la mere.*

> (And I am sure, which will by all be sworn,
> That at your birth, with you will too be born
> *A docile soul, heart where no bile does hide,*
> *If anything comes from your Mother's side.*)

The omission of any reference to the child's father, the Duke of Ferrara, is noticeable elsewhere in this manuscript (pp. **25–26**), since the *dizain* addressed to him appears here in the following iteration:

> **À Madame de Ferrare.**
> Quant la vertu congnut que la fortune
> Me conseilloit *d'*abandonner la France
> Elle me dit, cherche terre opportune
> Pour mon recueil et pour ton asseurance
> Incontinant *dame* j'euz esperance
> Qu'il feroit bon devers toy se retraire
> Qui tous enfans de vertu veulx attraire
> Pour decorer *ta maison sumptueuse*
> Et *qui* plaisir ne prendrois à ce faire
> Si tu n'estoys toy mesmes *vertueuse.*

> (When Virtue did learn the counsel of Fortune,
> That I should soon leave and abandon France,
> She said to me, find a land opportune
> For my welcome, and for your assurance.

[33] Kelly D. Peebles, "Embodied Devotion: The Dynastic and Religious Loyalty of Renée de France (1510–1575)," in *Royal Women and Dynastic Loyalty*, ed. Caroline Dunn and Elizabeth Carney (New York: Palgrave Macmillan, 2018), 123–137, 126–127.

Straightway (Lady) I had hoped that by chance
It might be choice if near you I retreat,
Since all children of virtue there do meet,
To decorate your most ornate house thus.
And no pleasure could you take to us greet,
If you were not yourself most virtuous.)

All mention of the duke has been eliminated in these two texts, and only the duchess remains. It is she who is now the unique example of virtue at the court of Ferrara. The silence with regard to Ercole, which is manifestly a frontal attack, is for Marot a way of clearly backing Renée in the events of 1535–1536.

In point of fact, the relationship between the duke and the duchess had already deteriorated prior to the arrival of the poet at court, and it disintegrated still further as a result of the successive confrontations surrounding the personality of Michelle de Saubonne, Baronne de Soubise.[34] The scheming baroness had served as governess to the young Renée de France up to 1518, when she was banished from court. In 1528, when Renée married the duke, the baroness was called to the duchess's side.[35] By February–March 1536, the duke had obliged her to leave the court.[36] One other important factor was the imbroglio of April–August 1536, concerning the scandal created by the singer Jehannet de Bouchefort on Good Friday, which Dick Wursten's contribution explores. The escalating aggression in 1535–1536 led, with the backing of Montmorency, to a temporary victory for Renée.[37]

By erasing all his reverences to the Duke of Ferrara in the Chantilly manuscript and leaving only the expression of his attachment to Renée, Marot conspicuously highlights that, in February–March 1538, his unique aim was to please the duchess and the constable who had faithfully backed her. The variation in lines 29–32 that we just observed confirms the

---

[34] Charmarie Jenkins Blaisdell, "Politics and Heresy in Ferrara, 1534–1559" *Sixteenth-Century Journal* 6, no. 1 (1975): 67–93, especially 73–75.

[35] On Michelle de Saubonne, see also Chap. 2 by Kathleen Wilson-Chevalier.

[36] Eleonora Belligni, *Renata di Francia (1510–1575). Un'eresia di corte* (Turin: UTET, 2011), 88–89. See also Rosanna Gorris Camos, "'Donne ornate di scienza e di virtù': donne e francesi alla corte di Renata di Francia," *Schifanoia* 28–29 (2005): 175–205, especially 179–181.

[37] Blaisdell, "Politics and Heresy in Ferrara," 76–79 and Belligni, *Renata di Francia*, 135 and 142.

anteriority of the text recorded in the Paris and the Soissons manuscripts vis-à-vis the Chantilly manuscript. This invalidates the idea that Marot might have written two different versions of his text from the start, one *esoteric*, intended for Renée and her entourage, and another *exoteric*, intended for the court of France. It is only after the diplomatic events of 1535–1536 that the variants were introduced.

What is true for the variants concerning the duke is also true for the variants in the religious sphere, because there is no hybrid manuscript combining the signs of reverence for the duke with the passage against the Papacy and call for a regenerated Church. At the end of the first version of the *Avant-naissance* (lines 51–60), Marot seizes the occasion to announce a new apocalypse, "Viens escouter verité revellee" (Come listen to all the truths now revealed), that the "caphards" (hypocrites) had tried for too long to hide: the Fall of Babylon the Great, represented by the Pope and his "triple cockscomb," and the coming of the reign of Christ in the midst of "torments."[38] This prediction is replaced in 1538 by a call for the cultural Golden Age promoted by King François I, a prediction that had the effect of moving the *Epistle*'s center of gravity from the palace of Ferrara to the court of France.

Once again, the case of the Venetian *Epistle* is a bit more complex. In both versions, Marot lambasts severely the materialism of the Venetians (line 80 or 38, according to the version): "Puis sont vivans à la loy d'Epicure" (Then they are living according to the Epicurian law), spending more to gild their churches than to aid the poor, celebrating the body and neglecting the spirit.[39] As Frédéric Tinguely has underscored, castigating Venice is a leitmotif going back at least to Jean Lemaire de Belges and Jean Marot, during the period when they were promoting the war against the City of the Doges. In the first version (lines 47–48), Marot underlines the accusation of idolatry by recalling the divine interdiction of "graven images" (Exodus 20.4), and he extends this fault to all of Christianity (lines 50–52), with the exception of a handful of believers truly converted to God "alone" (lines 53–56). He ends by a vibrant paraphrase of Apocalypse (17.1–2), referring to the "great whore," which he identifies with the papacy.[40] This entire passage is excised from the Chantilly

---

[38] For the scriptural references for this passage, see Wursten, *Clément Marot and Religion*, 40–41, and Michael Andrew Screech, *Marot évangélique* (Geneva: Droz, 1967), 114–116.
[39] Screech, *Marot évangélique*, 111–112.
[40] For the repercussions of the identification, see Screech, *Marot évangélique*, 112–114.

manuscript. In that iteration, the poet contents himself with knitting together a few more verses criticizing Venetian materialism. The Chantilly version does, nevertheless, unfold in a more rigorous way. A rapid introduction to the astonishing spectacle of the city built on a lagoon (lines 1–10) leads into an indignant tirade against the display of splendors to the detriment of the most elementary Christian charity (lines 11–54). The poet picks up his description of the city where he left off, inserting an occasional satirical jab (lines 55–95), before concluding with praise for the duchess (lines 95–106). In the first version, the virulent diatribe against the deep-seated idolatry of Christianity (lines 50–66) blunts somewhat the force of his second denunciation of materialism (lines 77–84, already amply developed in lines 11–48).

It is necessary to read once again the textual variants in relation to the evolving context of the poem's diffusion. In July 1536, a date backed up by two manuscripts, there is no reason for Marot not to continue writing against the Roman Church in the same satirical vein that he had employed one year earlier during Renée's pregnancy. It is true that Pope Paul III had helped Renée in the conflict with her husband over the Good Friday scandal.[41] But the duchess could accept a temporary and political alliance with the Pope without changing her inner convictions. On the other hand, Ercole d'Este, who dreamed of being a princely Mæcenas heading a court of artists, was probably very unhappy with the poet's vigorous condemnation of his extravagant expenditures! But Marot, who had taken refuge[42] in Venice a month earlier—"many days," he writes vaguely at the beginning of his *Epistle*—had no reason to be kind to the person who had had two compatriots arrested: first, the singer Jehannet de Bouchefort, then Renée's secretary Jean Cornillau. Both were subsequently handed over to the local inquisitor, who brought accusations against them.[43]

---

[41] See in this volume the chapter by Dick Wursten who notes that the Pope came once again to Renée's aid in 1543.

[42] We do not know the exact circumstances that led to Marot's departure for Venice. Claude Mayer hypothesizes that Marot was the escaped prisoner that several letters mention, especially the one addressed by Filippo Rodi, the ambassador of the Duke of Ferrara in Rome, to his master on June 30, 1536. *Clément Marot*, 331–333. This hypothesis is interesting but solid proof is lacking.

[43] See Mayer, *Clément Marot*, 319–335, Charmarie Blaisdell Webb, "Politics and Heresy," 76–79, and *Royalty and Reform: The Predicament of Renée de France, 1510–1575* (PhD diss., Tufts University, 1969), 92–115 and 120–123; see also Dick Wursten's contribution to this volume.

In February–March 1538, Marot was back in France and had regained his position as the king's *valet de chambre*. The country was exhausted after the invasion of Provence by the army of Charles V, and the Pope was working to bring peace between King François I and the Emperor.[44] These negotiations led to the peace of Nice in June 1538, the main mediator of which was none other than Anne de Montmorency himself.[45] It would have been difficult, under such circumstances, to recite the couplet referring to "la paillarde et grande meretrice" (that great and abominable whore), regardless of the constable's religious opinions at the time. Indeed, I have tried elsewhere to demonstrate that those opinions should not to be judged in accordance with his later orthodoxy and that the Chantilly manuscript displays in numerous places that the constable was ready to accept reasonable criticisms of Church abuses.[46] Marot persists, therefore, in his criticism of material riches as opposed to a lack of charity. He was surely aware that his reputation as a Lutheran was well established by that time, as evidenced by many contemporary epistolary exchanges.[47] The public abjuration that he had to endure in December 1536, had not fooled anyone. In these circumstances, he must have wanted to use the manuscript now at Chantilly as a sort of firewall by offering to the constable himself a collection of the unpublished poems that had provoked the well-known controversies during his exile, by which Marot offered Montmorency the opportunity to judge for himself. The constable could, if he so wished, read how Marot had confided to Renée his indignation at the corruption of the Church, indignation in which the more radical barbs had nevertheless been blunted. The main points, however, remain present, beginning with the spiritual complicity that joined the poet and the "twice-born princess," which Montmorency surely would not have missed.

---

[44] See Robert J. Knecht, *Un Prince de la Renaissance. François Ier et son royaume*, tr. Patrick Hersant (Paris: Fayard, 1998), 341–342.

[45] See Guillaume Berthon, "L'année politique et poétique 1538. De l'événement (la paix de Nice) aux recueils," in *La Muse de l'éphémère. Formes de la poésie de circonstance de l'Antiquité à la Renaissance*, ed. Aurélie Delattre et Adeline Lionetto (Paris: Classiques Garnier, 2014), 359–373.

[46] See Guillaume Berthon, *L'Intention du Poète*, 490–494, where an example is cited in which the Sorbonne is mocked in the Chantilly manuscript, but the lines were prudently withdrawn from the Lyonnaise edition appearing only a few months later in 1538.

[47] Mayer, *Clément Marot*, 313–314, 320–322, 397–398, 471–472.

CONCLUSION

Before letting the poems speak for themselves and encouraging the reader to observe the subtle metamorphoses of the poet's compositions, I would like to offer a few general conclusions to this study of the two "Janus-faced" poems.

In order to interpret these textual variants, it is necessary to rely on precise and rigorous critical editions based on the original documents, both manuscripts and imprints, which the two most recent editions of Marot's complete works do not always permit. This point is all the more important in the case of Marot, as it is well-known that he always took advantage of every new possibility of publication to revise and adapt his writings for a new audience, depending on new circumstances and according to variations in his humor and taste.[48]

At the same time, it is necessary to place the texts and their variants within a fully grounded context that extends beyond the area of religious polemic. As Dick Wursten's contribution to this volume amply demonstrates, the principal forces behind the imbroglio of April–June 1536 were above all political and diplomatic before also becoming religious, and the counter-intuitive alliances that were formed cannot be superimposed reliably on confessional divisions. In the battle against the duke, Renée received the support of the whole court of France: King François I, Marguerite de Navarre and Montmorency, all of whom were concerned that the duke's offensive not lead to the decline of French influence in Ferrara and more generally in Italy, as well as the support of Pope Paul III, who was eager to maintain his substantial friendship with Marguerite and to prevent any new incursion of French troops into Northern Italy.[49]

However mysterious it may have been, Marot's departure for Venice cannot be explained simply by his religious convictions: it was also and above all the result of the wider conflict between the duke and the duchess, itself provoked by an unstable equilibrium between the King of France, the Emperor Charles V, and the Pope in the Duchy of Ferrara. Marot's heterodoxy is not the only cause of the duke's enmity. After all, did not Ercole retain Lyon Jamet at his side, even though the latter probably

---

[48] See the numerous examples I give in *L'Intention du Poète*, 343–352, 507–513.
[49] Belligni, *Renata di Francia*, 134 and Blaisdell, "Politics and Heresy in Ferrara," 77.

shared the same faith as the poet?[50] Similarly, to interpret the textual choices in Chantilly manuscript that Marot offered to Montmorency in light of the latter's "rigid Catholicism" is to make it impossible to understand the extent to which that particular collection reveals more about the poet's beliefs than do the *Œuvres* that he published officially a few months later in Lyons.

In the end, the study of the manuscripts and a few contemporary iterations of the two most heretical poems—those attested by the manuscript tradition, though excluding the Chantilly version—leads to the conclusion that these texts are the ones that circulated at the time, and they are surely similar to those that Renée read. These versions reflect quite clearly the mindset of Marot in 1535–1536, after his flight in the wake of the *Affaires des Placards* and with the encouragement of the heterodox atmosphere of Renée's court. Once back on the more dangerous grounds of the court of France in 1537–1538, Marot did not hesitate to reshape his words and thoughts, disguising his provocative line against the "caphards," but without abandoning the essentials. Although he boasted to have learned the meaning of prudence at the school of Ferrara, he always refused to write what he did not believe, preferring ellipsis to hypocrisy.[51] In this way, the removal of any praise for Ercole from his poems written during his exile in Ferrara was just another way of reaffirming his strict fidelity to the person of Renée, the "Daughter of France," trapped on the inhospitable banks of the Po, or rather, in the striking words of the Song of Songs (2:2), "ce lys au milieu des espines" (this lily among brambles).[52]

---

[50] In *Renata di Francia*, 139, Belligni mentions that the duke's ambassador to the King of France wrote concerning Jamet that he was still "più imbrattato del Cornilao" (more tarnished than Cornillau), Renée's secretary who had been imprisoned.

[51] He thus declares in his Epistle to the Dauphin, printed in Lyons probably before the death of the young man: "Depuis ung peu je parle sobrement, / Car ces Lombars avec qui je chemine / M'ont fort appris à faire bonne myne, / À ung mot seul de Dieu ne deviser, / À parler peu, et à poultronniser. / Dessus ung mot une heure je m'arreste, / S'on parle à moy, je respons de la teste" ([...] for a while, soberly I now speak, / For these Lombards, with whom I share the route, / Have taught me to a fair face cast about, / Not one sole word about God vocalize, / To coldly speak, and then to *poltronize.* / Even one word and from speaking I rest, / If one bids me, then I will nod at best). See Berthon, *Bibliographie critique*, 1536/6. On this more prudent attitude on Marot's part and his refusal to write the confession of orthodox faith that was expected of him, see Wursten, *Clément Marot and Religion*, 44–50.

[52] Marot, *Recueil inédit*, 233. This text comes at the end of the Ferrara period in the Chantilly manuscript.

APPENDIX

List of Texts Composed in Exile and Known by an Immediate
Printed Publication (1535–1536)

References are given according to the *Œuvres poétiques complètes* edited by Gérard Defaux; bibliographical references are given according to my own *Bibliographie critique*.

Three epigrams (II 251 and 296–297: "De ceulx qui tant de mon bien se tourmentent," "Mes amys, j'ay changé ma Dame" and "Quant la vertu congneust que la fortune") were published in: 1535/3—*La Suyte de l'Adolescence clementine*—[Lyons, Denis de Harsy], [after april] 1535, in-16°.

The first epistle to the King written in Ferrara (II 80–86, "Je pense bien que ta magnificence") was published in: 1536/1—*L'Adolescence clementine*—Antwerpen, [Martin Lempereur] for Jean Steels, 1536, in-16°.

The first epistle to Renée (II 77–78, "En traversant ton pays planturreux") was published in: 1536/2—*L'Adolescence* clementine—[Lyons, Denis de Harsy], 1536, in-16°.

The epistle to the Dauphin (II 116–118, "En mon vivant n'apres ma mort avec") was published in: 1536/6—*Double d'une epistre, envoyée par Clement Marot à Monseigneur le Daulphin*—[Lyons, François Juste, 1536], in-8°.

The epitaph of the Dauphin (I 374, "Cy gist Françoys Daulphin de grand renom") was published in: *Recueil de vers latins et vulgaires [...] sur le trespas de feu Monsieur le Daulphin*—Lyons, François Juste, [1536], in-8.

The *blason* "du beau tétin" (II 241–242, "Tetin refect, plus blanc qu'ung œuf") was published in numerous editions of Alberti's *Hecatomphile* since 1536. See Magali Vène, "À propos d'une traduction retrouvée (*La Deiphire* de 1539): nouveaux éléments sur la diffusion française au XVIe siècle des écrits sur l'amour de Leon Battista Alberti," *Albertiana* 10 (2007): 95–123.

Table 5.1   Translation by Robert J. Hudson, "Prenatal poem celebrating the birth of the third child of My Lady Renée, Duchess of Ferrara, composed by Clément Marot, Secretary of the said Lady in July 1536 [sic], while in the same Ferrara"

Soissons, BM, ms. 202	
Little infant, whether daughter or son,	1
Til the destined nine months of growth are done,	
Gladly gestate: then leave the Royal womb,	
And your right place in this world's light assume.	
Without a cry, fearlessly to the light,	5
Come, and shun the common distressing plight	
For your Mother, meek soul whom God did choose.	
Then, with her bond, let your sweet laugh amuse.	
After you have begun her love to know,	
Take gently now some sustenance and grow:	10
Such that you might begin to speak somewhat,	
And all alone, you may toddle and strut	
On the tiles at your home, like no other,	
Delighting both your Father and Mother:	
Who, to see you, in this rich home do aim	15
With your Brother, and your Sister the same.	
Come in boldness, for when you bigger are,	
And you begin to grasp concepts afar,	
You then will find a century to learn	
In little time all a child can discern.	20
Come in boldness, for in time and with age,	
You will find more with which you can engage.	
You will find that the war has since begun	
Against darkness, by its raving troops run,	
At the same time, Virtue upheld before,	25
Which will make you a wise one even more,	
And, with fine arts, their meanings hard to seize,	
You'll by these means and with great books find ease.	
And I am sure, which will by all be sworn,	
That at your birth, with you will too be born	30
A docile soul, heart where no bile does hide,	
If anything comes from your Mother's side.	
Come in boldness, and Saturn never fear,	
His wordly cares never to you draw near:	
For you'll be born neither poor nor gaunt since	35
(Unlike me) you're the Child of a great Prince.	
Come safe and sound, let it surely be said	
That at your birth not a tear will be shed,	
In the manner of Thracians who mourn	

(*continued*)

8# 150 G. BERTHON

Table 5.1 (continued)

And sing laments when they meet a newborn:	40
All the sorrow, anguish, torment and strife	
That he'll surely make them endure in life.	
But you shall have (may God grant you this grace)	
The one true way to all sorrow erase,	
Through which on earth anguish loses its sting,	45
Along with death, though its knells ever ring.	
This one true way of such bounteous joy,	
It's the firm hope that we'll new life enjoy,	
Through JESUS CHRIST, our victor triumphant	
Of this world's death. So, come, little Infant:	50
Come listen to all the truths now revealed,	
Which for so long from our eyes remained sealed.	
Come listen to that which makes souls rejoice,	
So hypocrites wish to stifle their voice.	
Come see, come see that rash beast that does grouse,	55
Sworn enemy of your most noble house.	
Come soon and see how his triple cockscomb,	
Not fallen yet, but soon reaching its gloam.	
Come see this Christ, His reign on earth begun,	
And His honor by great agonies won.	60
O Golden Age, the finest we can find,	
Whose pureness was in the bright fire refined.	
O happiness of all those to Him sworn,	
And even more those who today are born.	
I would tell you yet a million things more,	65
Beneath heaven, that this world has in store,	
Fair to the eye, sweetest thoughts to transcend:	
But I would fear your Mother to offend:	
And then to see, and to think, overcome	
With great desire, that early you might come.	70
That's why (infant) whether daughter or son,	
Til the destined nine months of growth are done,	
Gladly gestate: then leave the Royal womb,	
And your right place in this world's light assume.	

Table 5.2 French variants of "Avant naissance du troiziesme enffant de madame Renee duchesse de Ferrare"

Soissons, BM, ms. 202, f. 169v–171r		*Chantilly, Musée Condé, ms. 524 (748), pp. 4–6*
Avant naissance du troiziesme enffant de madame Renee duchesse de Ferrare composé par Clement Marot secretere de ladicte dame en juillet vcxxxvi [sic] estant audict Ferrare[a]		*Avantnaissance du troiziesme enfant de Madame Madame la duchesse de Ferrare.*
Petit enffant quelle[b] [sic] sois fille ou filz	1	Petit enfant quel que soys fille ou filz
Parfais le temps de tes neuf mois prefix		
Heureusement puys sors du royal ventre		
Et de ce monde en la[c] grant lumiere entre		
Entre, sors, croy, viens sans peur en lumiere[d]	5	Entre sans cry, viens sans pleur en lumiere,
Viens sans donner destresse constumiere[e]		
A ta[f] mere humble et qui Dieu t'a fait naistre		A la mere humble, en qui Dieu t'a fait naistre
Puys d'un doulx ris commence à la congnoistre		
Apres que fait luy auras congnoissance		
Prens peu à peu norriture et[g] croissance	10	
Tant que à demy tu commence[h] à parler		Tant qu'à demy commances à parler
Et tout seullet en tripignant aller		
Sur les carreaulx de la maison prospere		
Au passe temps de ta mere et ton pere[i]		
Qui de te y veoir[j] ung de ces jours pretendent	15	
Avec ton frere et ta seur qui t'atendent		
Viens hardiment car quant grandet seras		
Et que à entendre ung peu commenceras		
Tu trouveras ung siecle pour aprendre		
En peu de temps ce que enffant peult comprendre	20	
Hardiment car ayant plus grant aage[k] [sic]		Vien hardyment: Car ayant plusgrant aage
Tu trouveras encores davantaige		
Tu trouveras la guerre commencee		
Contre ignorance et sa tourbe incensee		
Et au rebours vertu mise en avant	25	
Que[l] te rendra personnage sçavant		Qui te rendra personnaige sçavant
En tous beaulx artz tant soient ilz difficilles		
Tant par moyens que par livres faciles		Tant par moyens que par lettres faciles,
Puys je suys seur et on le congnoistra		
Qu'en[m] ta naissance avecques[n] naistra [sic]	30	Qu'à ta naissance, avecques toy naistra
Don de vertu et[o] [sic] ton ame logé		**Esprit docile, et cueur sans taiche amere**
Si tu tiens rien de ceulx qui t'ont forgé		**Si tu tiens rien, du costé de la mere**
Viens hardyment et ne crains que fortune		
En biens mondains te puisse estre importune		
Car tu naistras non ainsi pauvre et mynce	35	
Comme moy las mais enffant d'un grand prince		
Viens sain et sauf tu peulx estre asseuré[p]		
Que. à ta naissance il n'y aura pleuré[q]		
À la façon des Traces lamentans		À la façon des Thrauses lamentans

(continued)

Table 5.2 (continued)

Leurs nouveaulx nez et en grant dueil chantans	40	
L'ennuy le mal et la peyne asservye		
Qu'il leur failloit[r] souffrir en ceste vye		
Mais tu auras que dieu ce bien te face		
Le vray moyen qui tout ennuy efface		
Et fait que au monde angoisse on ne craint point	45	
Ne la mort mesme alors qu'elle nous point		
Le vray moien plain de joie feconde		Ce vray moien, plain de joye feconde,
C'est ferme espoir de la vie seconde		
Par Jesus Crist vaincqueur et tryumphant		
De ceste mort, viens dont petit enffant	50	
Viens escouter verité revellee		**Viens voir de terre et de mer le grant tour**
Qui tant de jours[s] nous a esté cellee		**Avec le ciel qui se courbe à l'entour**
Viens escouter pour ames[t] resjoir		**Viens voir, viens voir, maincte belle ornature**
Ce que caphards veullent garder d'oyr		**Que chascun d'eulx a receu de nature**
Viens veoir viens veoir la beste sans raison	55	**Viens veoir ce monde, et les peuples et princes**
Grande ennemye de ta noble maison		**Regnans sur luy en diverses provinces**
Viens tost la veoir à tout sa simple[u] [sic] creste		**Entre lesquelz est le plus apparent**
Non cheute encor mais de tomber bien preste		**Le roy Françoys, qui te sera parent,**
Viens veoir de Crist le regne commencé		**Soubz et par qui ont esté esclarciz**
Et son honneur par tourmens[v] avancé	60	**Tous les beaux artz paravant obscurciz.**
O siecle d'or le plus fin que l'on treuve		
Dont la bonté dedans le feu s'espreuve		Dont la bonté, soubz ung tel roy s'espreuve,
O bien heureulx tous ceulx qui le congnoissent[w]		O jours heureux à ceulx qui les congnoissent
Et encor plus ceulx que[x] aujourd'huy naissent		Et plus heureux ceulx qui aujourd'huy naissent.
Je te dirois encores bien d'autres[y] choses [sic]	65	Je te diroys encor cent mille choses
Qui sont sur terre autour du ciel encloses		Qui sont en terre autour du ciel encloses
Belles à l'œil et doulces à penser		
Mais j'aurois peur de ta mere offenser		
Et que de veoir et d'y penser tu prinsses		
Si grant desir que avant terme tu vinsses[z]	70	Si grant desir qu'avant le terme vinsses,
Parquoy enffant quelle[aa] sois [sic] fille ou filz		Parquoy enfant quel que soys fille ou filz
Parfaictz le temps de tes neuf mois prefix		
Heureusement puis sors du royal vendre[bb]		Heureusement, puis sors du royal ventre
Et de ce monde en la[cc] grant lumiere entre		

P: Paris, BnF, ms. fr. 2370, f. 48r–49r.

[a]P: Avant naissance du tiers enfant de madame la duchesse de Ferrare

[b]P: quel que

[c]P: sa

[d]P: *verse missing*

[e]P: accoustumiere

[f]P: la

[g]P: en

[h]P: demy commances

[i]P: ton pere et ta mere

[j]P: de te veoir

(*continued*)

Table 5.2 (continued)

[k]P: Viens hardiment car quant auras plus d'agge

[l]P: Qui

[m]P: Qu'à

[n]P: avecques toy

[o]P: en

[p]P: tu te peulx asseurer

[q]P: on n'y orra pleurer

[r]P: falloit

[s]P: jous

[t]P: l'ame

[u]P: triple

[v]P: torment

[w]P: O jours eureulx à ceulx qui les congnoissent

[x]P: plus à ceulx qui

[y]P: encores mille

[z]P: qu'avant le terme vinses

[aa]P: quel que

[bb]P: ventre

[cc]P: sa

Table 5.3   Translation by Robert J. Hudson, "Epistle sent from Venice to My Lady the Duchess of Ferrara by Clément Marot"

Paris, BnF, ms. fr. 4967

After having visited many days   1
In this city antique and of high praise
Where great honors and a dazzling display,
Homage to you, grand Princess, all did pay,
I discovered within the foundation   5
Of this city a strange fascination.
And moreover, what all things does surmount,
That far away one does best to recount,
It's far beyond her citizens to try
The body, eye to better satisfy.   10
Would to God that such great care were a goal,
Most good Lady, for their immortal soul.
Their actions make it easy to assess
An eternal soul they don't think to possess,
Or, if they do, their notions all enmesh,   15
Fancying that the soul's like mortal flesh.
So it follows, they never lift their eyes
To see beyond that which before them lies,
And in none do we find hope supernal
In the great feast that is life eternal.   20
It happens, too, that loving one's neighbor
In selfish hearts is foreign behavior,
And if someone should refrain from offense,
Fear of revenge is the only pretense.
But where can one find a place here abroad   25
To love others where none seem to love God?
And how could it ever take root and grow,
That love of God, which one first has to know?
I have, from youth, heard it affirmed thereof,
One needs to know, first, before one can love.   30
The signs are clear, distinct to those outside,
To witness that God does not here abide.
In the spirit, they do not Him adore,
Spirit He is, completely, nothing more,

(continued)

Table 5.3   (continued)

Thus, with loud chants, they process in robes dressed,	35
Their faces sullen (my God) all you detest.	
And still they are all poor citizens, heirs,	
Full of error like their pagan forebears.	
Marbled temples they both worship and build	
Painted icons at a great cost they guild;	40
While at their feet, moaning, huddle and wail	
The wretched nude, withered, hungry and pale.	
These are, these are images so intense	
That when apposed to excessive expense,	
These are the ones to bedeck and adorn,	45
Leaving the rest, far from us, all forlorn.	
The Eternal, after all, lifts His hand:	
Feed the living, leave the dead, His command.	
Will it not do to rebuke those so prone?	
Alas, Madame, they are far from alone;	50
Of this error, whose belief does abound,	
Christendom now is all empoisoned found.	
Not quite all, no, the Lord, looking down here	
In grace at this hypocritical sphere,	
Made himself known to a group quite steady,	55
Which to him is converted already.	
O Lord my God, let the remaining block	
Not see those who worship these gods of rock.	
It's an abuse of idolatrous sort,	
Which true Christians did so often abort,	60
And avarice always comes to restore	
For that great and abominable whore,	
With whom did lay, in lewd fornication,	
The kings of earth; rulers of each nation	
Drank public wine from her filthy chalice,	65
From which so long all were drunk in the palace.	
For all the rest, to make sure that this card	
Will not be found its main points to discard,	
I'll let you know, Princess, that at no date	

(*continued*)

Table 5.3   (continued)

No emperor in Rome ever set straight	70
Public order, and if closely we look,	
They the more great, more plain, more fair forsook.	
They are, indeed, great and wise worldly men,	
Keen in counsel, to execute sudden;	
Nothing I see in all their policies	75
As lavish as their fanfares, ecstasies.	
So plain they are that few works come to bear	
Worth the great name of Him to whom they swear.	
To claim the name of Christ they make a fuss,	
Living the law of gay Epicurus,	80
Letting the eyes, nose and ears revel in	
All that is to sight, touch and sound akin,	
To the delight of the senses, they treat	
The body like it is man's last retreat.	
Even among pleasures simple and plain,	85
More than elsewhere, Venus is found to reign.	
Venus is more revered in this era	
Than with the Greeks, on the isle Cythera;	
For the high rank of her reputation,	
Her liberty and esteemed adoration,	90
Upholds women all exposed on the street	
Equal to the chaste, honest and discreet.	
And they're inclined (so they say) to adore	
Venus, who's born from the sea, all the more,	
And to the sea they all trace their own birth.	95
They also say that Venice came to earth	
Built from the sea, Venus' legacy,	
And that, for this, they owe their loyalty.	
Now you see why all that's banned and unfit	
Here is widespread and they freely permit.	100
And I could write, Princess, more, even scores,	
Of Jews, of Turks, of Arabs and of Moors	
That one sees here, in excess, more each day;	
How things here seem, how pleasant is my stay;	

(*continued*)

Table 5.3   (continued)

Of their mansions, of each palace acclaimed,	105
Of their horses of bronze, antique and famed,	
Of their mighty arsenal, staid and good,	
Of their canals, of long mules made of wood,	
Of salted walls, which the city enclose,	
Of the great square, many things to expose,	110
But I would fear I might bore you, and then,	
You've seen it with eyes that surpass my pen.	
I'd also write, and more amply describe,	
Of the wise duke, and more broadly, his tribe	
Of prim old men. But, my Lady, mistress,	115
You know them all, and they know your highness.	
They know quite well that you are, it is true,	
Daughter of the king through whom they all knew	
The great power his proud arm did impart,	
Alongside his noble goodness of heart.	120
Thus, I'll close this note I poorly adorn,	
Begging you to, Princess, who's two times born,	
Remember that, while I here must remain,	
This same one does hope that you will retain	
Trust that it was, if his path did careen,	125
To flee vile foes of the most fair Christine.	

Table 5.4 French variants of "Epistre envoyee de Venize à Madame la duchesse de Ferrare"

Paris, BnF, ms. fr. 4967, f. 291v–293v		Chantilly, Musée Condé, ms. 524 (748), pp. 31–35.	
Epistre envoyee de Venize à Madame la duchesse de Ferrare par Clement Marot[a]		*Autres œuvres faictes à Venise* *À Madame de Ferrare*	
Apres avoir par mes[b] [sic] jours visité	1	Apres avoir par mainctz jours visité	1
Ceste fameuse et antique cité			
Où tant d'honneur et[c] pompe sumptueuse		Où tant d'honneur en pompe sumptueuse	
T'a esté faict, princesse vertueuse			
Je y ay trouvé que la[d] fondacion	5		5
Est chose estrange et d'admiracion[e]			
Quant au surplus[f] ce qui en est surmonte			
Ce que loing d'elle au myeulx on en[g] racompte			
Et n'est possible à Citadins myeux faire			
Pour à ce corps et à l'œil satisfaire	10		10
Que plust à Dieu, ma tresillustre dame,			
Qu'autant soigneux ilz fussent de leur ame,[h]			
Certes leurs faictz quasi font assavoir			
Qu'une ame[i] au corps ilz ne cuident avoir			
Ou s'ilz en ont[j] leur fantaisie est telle	15		15
Qu'elle est ainsi[k] comme le corps mortelle			
Dont il s'ensuit qu'ilz n'eslevent leurs yeulx			
Plus hault ne loing que les[l] terrestres [sic] lieux		Plus hault ne loing que ces terrestres lieux,	
Et que jamays espoir ne les convye			
Au grand festin de l'eternelle vie	20		20
Advient aussi que de l'amour du proche			
Jamays leur cueur partial ne s'aproche			
Et si quelcung de l'offencer se garde			
Crainte de peine et force l'en retarde			
Mays où pourra trouver[m] siege ne lieu	25		25
L'amour du proche où l'on n'ayme[n] poinct Dieu			
Et comment peult prendre racine et croistre[o]			
L'amour de Dieu sans premier le congnoistre[p]			
J'ay des enfance entendu affermer[q]			
Qu'il est besoing congnoistre avant qu'aymer	30		30
Les signes clers qui dehors apparoissent			
Font[r] tesmoigner que Dieu poinct ne congnoissent			
		C'est que par trop grans moyens et petitz	
		Laschent la bride à tous leurs appetitz	
		Si que d'iceulx certes peu d'oeuvres sortent	35
		Sentans celluy duquel le nom ilz portent	
		D'avoir le nom de chrestiens ont pris cure	
		Puis sont vivans à la loy d'Epicure	
		Faisant yeulx, nez, et oreilles jouyr	

(*continued*)

Table 5.4 (continued)

De ce qu'on peult veoyr, sentir et ouyr 40
Au gré des sens, et traictans ce corps, comme
Si là gisoit le dernier bien de l'homme.

C'est qu'en esprit n'adorent nullement
Luy est seul esprit totallement[s]
Ains par haulx chantz[t] par pompes et par mynes   35
Qui est (mon Dieu) ce que tu abhomines
Et sont encor[u] les pouvres citoyens
Pleins de l'erreur de leurs peres payans

D'or et d'azur de marbres blancs et noyrs
Sont enrichiz leurs temples et manoirs

Temples marbrins y font[v] et y adorent
D'art de paincture et medailles dorees   45
Images peinctz[w] qu'à grandz despens ilz dorent   40
Sont à grant coust leurs maisons decorees
Et à leurs piedz ullans[x] sont gemissans
Mais à leurs piedz (helas) sont gemissans
Les[y] pouvres nudz palles et languissans
Ce sont, ce sont telles ymaiges vives
Ce sont, ce sont, telles medailles vives
Qui de ces[z] grans despences excessives
50
Estre debvroient aornees et parees   45
Deussent avoir parade et Ornature
Ou pour le moins, qu'en recreant Nature
De leurs manoirs en ce point erigez
N'en fussent moins les povres soulagez

Et de noz yeulx les autres separees
Car l'Eternel les vives recommande
Et de fuir les mortes[aa] nous commande
Ne convient il en reprendre que iceulx
Helas Madame ilz ne sont pas tous seulz[bb]   50
De ceste erreur tant creue[cc] et foisonnee
La chestienté est toute enpoisonnee
Non toute non, le Seigneur regardant
D'œil de pitié ce monde caphardant
S'est[dd] faict congnoistre à une grand[ee] partie   55
Qui à luy seul est ores[ff] convertie
O[gg] seigneur Dieu faictz que le demourant
Ne voyse pas[hh] les pierres adorant
C'est ung abbus d'ydollastres sorty
Entre chestiens plusieurs foys amorty   60
Et remys sus tousjours pour[ii] l'avarice
De la paillarde et grande meretrice
Avec qui on[jj] [sic] faict fornicacion
Les roys de terre, et dont la potion
Du vin public de son calice immonde   65
A si[kk] longtemps enyvré tout le monde
Au residu afin que ceste carte
55
De son propos commancé ne s'escarte
Sçavoir te faictz princesse que deçà
Oncques romain empereur ne dressa   70
Ordre public s'il est bien regardé

(*continued*)

Table 5.4 (continued)

Plus grand plus rond plus beau[ll] ne myeux gardé			60
Ce sont pour vray grands et saiges mondains			
Meurs en conseil d'excuter[mm] [sic] soubdains		Meurs en conseils, d'executer soudains	
Et ne voy rien en toutes leurs poulices	75		
De superflu que pompes[nn] et delices		De superflu, que povres et delices.	
Tant en sont plains que d'eux peu d'œuvres[oo] sortent			
Sentans celuy duquel le nom ils portent			
D'avoir le nom de chestien ont prins cure			
Puis sont vivans à la loy d'Epicure[pp]	80		
Faisans yeulx, nez, et oreilles jouyr			
De ce qu'on peult veoir, sentir, et ouyr			
Au gré des sens[qq], et traictent ce corps comme			
Si là gisoit le dernier bien de l'homme			
Mesmes parmy tant de plaisirs[rr] menus	85		65
Trop plus qu'ailleurs y triumphe Venus.			
Venus y est certes plus reveree			
Qu'au temps des Grecz en l'isle citheree			
Car mesme renc de reputacion			
De liberté et d'estimation	90		70
Y tient la femme esventee et publicque			
Comme la chaste honnorable et pudicque			
Et sont enclins (ce[ss] disent) à aymer		Et sont enclins (se disent) à aymer	
Venuz d'autant qu'elle est nee[tt] de mer			
Et que sus mer ilz ont naissance prise	95		75
Disent aussi qu'ilz ont basty Venize			
Qui est de Venuz l'heritaige		En mer, qui est de Venus l'heritage.	
Et que pourtant ilz luy doivent hommaige			
Voilà commant ce qui est deffendu			
Est par deçà permys et espendu	100		80
Et t'escriproys, princesse bien encores		Si t'escriroys Princesse bien encores	
Des Juifz des Turcs des Arabes et Mores			
Qu'on veoit icy par trop[uu] ung chascun jour		Qu'on voit icy, par trouppes chascun jour	
Quel en est las[vv] [sic], quel en est le sejour		Quel en est l'air, quel en est le sejour	
De leurs palays et maisons[ww] autenticques	105	Du Grant canal, leur grant rue aquatique,	85
De leurs chevaulx de bronze tresantiques		Du monde rond bien la plus autentique	
De l'arcenal[xx] chose digne de poix		De l'arcenaf Chose digne de poix	
De leurs comaulx[yy] [sic], de leurs mules de boys		De leurs canaulx de leurs mulles de boys	
Des murs sallez dont leur[zz] cité est close			
De leur grand place et de mainte[aaa] autre chose	110		90
Mays j'auroys peur de t'ennuyer, et puis			
Tu l'as myeulx veu que escripre ne le puis			
Je t'escriproys aussi plus amplement			
Du saige duc, et generallement			

(continued)

Table 5.4 (continued)

Des beaulx vieillartz, mays[bbb] Madame et maistresse	115	95
Tu les congnoys si font il [sic] ta haultesse		
Ilz sçavent bien que tu es sans mentir		
Fille d'un roy qui leur a faict sentir		
Le grand pouvoir de son fort bras vinqueur		
Et la noblesse et bonté de son cueur	120	100
Parquoy clorray ma lettre mal aornee		
Te suppliant princesse deux foys nee		
Te souvenir tendys que icy me tiens		
De cestuy là que retiras pour tien		
Quant il fuyoit la fureur serpentine	125 Quant il fuyoit la fureur et les ruses	105
Des ennemys de la belle Christine.	Des ennemys d'Apollo, et des Nuses [sic].	

[H: De Venise ce xv Juillet 1536;
L: De Venize ce xve de julliet 1536]

H: Harvard University, Cambridge (Mass.), Houghton Library, ms. Fr. 337, f. 120v-123v.

L: Lausanne, Archives Cantonales Vaudoises (P SVG G 174 Variétés littéraires, Frédéric Chavannes, 1844–1881).

P: Paris, BnF, ms. fr. 22,558, f. 47r–48r. In this manuscript, verses 9–12, 17–20, 23–24, 31–38, 67-end are missing

[a]H: Marot A la tresillustre Dame Duchesse de Ferrare; L: A la tres illustre dame duchesse de Ferrare; P: S'ensuyt l'epitre que Marot envoya à madame de Ferrare au retour de Venise

[b]H L: mains

[c]H L: en

[d]L: sa

[e]P: Est choze digne de admiration

[f]P: Et tellement que

[g]P: a

[h]P: Mais j'ay congneu choze fascheuse à veoir

[i]L: Que. l'ame; P: Que. une

[j]P: Ou s'ilz la y ont

[k]P: aussi

[l]H L: ces

[m]P: Où peult trouver amour

[n]P: meme

[o]L: Et comme peult prendre racine et croistre; P: Où peult trouver prendre pasciensce ou croistre

[p]P: L'amour du proche sans premier l'acongnoistre

[q]P: ouy dire et affermer

(continued)

Table 5.4   (continued)

[r]H L: Pour

[s]H L: Luy seul quy est esprit totallement

[t]H: champs

[u]H L: encore

[v]H: ilx font; P: y sont

[w]H L: Pieces de bois

[x]H L P: helas

[y]P: Ces

[z]H L: ses; P: nos

[aa]P: autres

[bb]H P: ceulx

[cc]P: lont griefve

[dd]H L P: C'est

[ee]L: grande

[ff]H: c'est toute; L: est toute

[gg]L: Ou

[hh]H L: plus

[ii]H L P: par

[jj]H L P: ont

[kk]L: de

[ll]H: rond

[mm]H: Meur [sic] en conseil d'execution soudains

[nn]H: que pauvres; L: que en pompes

[oo]H: d'œuvres d'eux peu

[pp]H: de Picure

[qq]H: des sons; L: de ceulx

[rr]H: plairs

[ss]H: sons enclins ce; L: sont enclins, si

[tt]H: venue

[uu]H: Qu'on voit ycy par troupes; L: Que. ont veoit icy par trouppes

[vv]H L: l'air

[ww]L: De leurs maisons et pallais

[xx]H: arsenac

[yy]H L: canaulx

[zz]H: la

[aaa]L: et mainte

[bbb]H: de

BIBLIOGRAPHY

PRIMARY SOURCES

Le Laboureur, Jean, ed. 1659. *Mémoires de Messire Michel de Castelnau Seigneur de Mauvissière, Tome Premier.* Paris: P. Lamy.

Marot, Clément. 1547. *Epigramme faictz à l'imitation de Martial.* Poitiers: Jean and Enguilbert de Marnef, 27 September 1547.

———. 1958–1970. *Œuvres complètes.* 5 vols. Edited by Claude Albert Mayer. London: Athlone Press.

———. 1968. *Œuvres de Clément Marot de Cahors en Quercy, valet de chambre du roi, augmentées d'un grand nombre de ses compositions nouvelles par ci-devant non imprimées.* 5 vols. 1875–1931. Edited by Georges Guiffrey, with Robert-Charles Yve-Plessis and Jean Plattard. Reprint, Geneva: Slatkine.

———. 1980. *Les Traductions.* Vol. 6 of Œuvres complètes. Edited by Claude Albert Mayer. Geneva: Slatkine.

———. 1990–1993. *Œuvres poétiques complètes.* 2 vols. Edited by Gérard Defaux. Paris: Classiques Garnier.

———. 2007–2009. *Œuvres complètes.* 2 vols. Edited by François Rigolot. Paris: Flammarion.

———. 2010. *Recueil inédit offert au connétable de Montmorency en mars 1538 (Manuscrit de Chantilly).* Edited by François Rigolot. Geneva: Droz.

SECONDARY SOURCES

Belligni, Eleonora. 2011. *Renata di Francia (1510-1575). Un'eresia di corte.* Torino: UTET.

Berthon, Guillaume. 2014a. L'année politique et poétique 1538. De l'événement (la paix de Nice) aux recueils. In *La Muse de l'éphémère. Formes de la poésie de circonstance de l'Antiquité à la Renaissance,* ed. Aurélie Delattre and Adeline Lionetto, 359–373. Paris: Classiques Garnier.

———. 2014b. *L'Intention du Poète. Clément Marot "autheur."* Paris: Classiques Garnier.

———. 2018. L'invention du blason: retour sur la genèse d'un genre (Ferrare, 1535). In *Anatomie d'une anatomie. Nouvelles recherches sur les blasons anatomiques du corps féminin,* ed. Julien Goeury and Thomas Hunkeler, 135–156. Geneva: Droz.

———. 2019. *Bibliographie critique des éditions de Clément Marot (ca. 1521–1550).* Geneva: Droz.

Berthon, Guillaume, and Jérémie Bichüe. 2021. Le manuscrit poétique, de l'exercice à l'œuvre: le cas du manuscrit français 4967 de la BnF. In *Le Manuscrit littéraire à la Renaissance. Cahiers V.-L. Saulnier 37*, ed. Frank Lestringant and Olivier Millet, 147-162. Paris: Sorbonne Université Presses.

Berthon, Guillaume, and William Kemp. 2012. L'épître de Marot au dauphin (1536): le virage courtisan de François Juste. *Bulletin du bibliophile* 2: 367–373.

Berthoud, Gabrielle. 1963. Les ajournés du 25 janvier 1535. *Bibliothèque d'Humanisme et Renaissance* 25 (2): 307–324.

Bertoni, Giulio. 1933. Documenti sulla dimora di Clément Marot a Ferrara. In *Mélanges de philologie offerts à Jean-Jacques Salverda de Grave*, 9–11. Groningue, The Hague, and Batavia: J.B. Wolters.

Blaisdell, Charmarie Jenkins. 1975. Politics and Heresy in Ferrara, 1534–1559. *The Sixteenth-Century Journal* 6 (1): 67–93.

Catalogue général des manuscrits des bibliothèques publiques de France. 1885. Edited by Henry Martin. Paris: Plon.

Chatelain, Jean-Marc. 2003. *La Bibliothèque de l'honnête homme. Livres, lecture et collections en France à l'âge classique*. Paris: Bibliothèque nationale de France.

Gorris Camos, Rosanna. 1997. 'Un Franzese nominato Clemente': Marot à Ferrare. In *Clément Marot "Prince des poëtes François" 1496–1996. Actes du Colloque international de Cahors en Quercy, 1996*, ed. Gérard Defaux and Michel Simonin, 338–364. Paris: Champion.

———. 2005. 'Donne ornate di scienza e di virtù': donne e francesi alla corte de Renata di Francia. *Schifanoia* 28–29: 175–205.

———. 2011. L'insaisissable Protée: Ludovic Demoulin de Rochefort, médecin, poète et bibliophile entre Turin et Bâle. In *Pouvoir medical et fait du prince au début des temps modernes*, ed. Stéphane Velut and Jacqueline Vons, 147–209. Paris: De Boccard.

Herminjard, Aimé-Louis, ed. 1866–1897. *Correspondance des Réformateurs dans les pays de langue française*. Geneva, Basel, and Paris: H. Georg, M. Levy, and G. Fischbacher.

Jonas. Répertoire des textes et des manuscrits médiévaux d'oc et d'oïl, version. 2019. Institut de recherche et d'histoire des textes—CNRS. http://jonas.irht.cnrs.fr.

Knecht, Robert J. 1998. *Un Prince de la Renaissance. François Ier et son royaume*. Translated by Patrick Hersant. Paris: Fayard.

Leblanc, Paulette. 1955. *La Poésie religieuse de Clément Marot*. Paris: Nizet.

Mayer, Claude Albert. 1954. *Bibliographie des œuvres de Clément Marot*. 2 vols. Geneva: Droz.

———. 1972. *Clément Marot*. Paris: Nizet.

Mélançon, Robert. 1997. La personne de Marot. In *Clément Marot 'Prince des poëtes François' 1496–1996, Actes du Colloque international de Cahors en Quercy, 1996*, ed. Gérard Defaux and Michel Simonin, 515–529. Paris: Champion.

Peebles, Kelly D. 2018. Embodied Devotion: The Dynastic and Religious Loyalty of Renée de France (1510–1575). In *Royal Women and Dynastic Loyalty*, ed. Carolie Dunn and Elizabeth Carney, 123–137. Cham, Switzerland: Palgrave Macmillan.

Picot, Émile. 1969. *Querelle de Marot et Sagon*. Geneva: Slatkine Reprints.

Ritz-Guilbert, Anne. 2016. *La Collection Gaignières: Un inventaire du royaume au XVIIe siècle*. Paris: CNRS editions.

Rouget, François. 2006. Marguerite de Berry et sa cour en Savoie d'après un album de vers manuscrits. *Revue d'histoire littéraire de France* 106 (1): 3–16.

Screech, Michael Andrew. 1967. *Marot évangélique*. Geneva: Droz.

Speziari, Daniele. 2011. Clément Marot "ferrarese" nel ducato di Savoia e alla corte di Francia: l'esempio del ms. Fr. 337 della Houghton Library, Università di Harvard e del ms. di Chantilly. *Schifanoia* 40–41: 111–117.

Tinguely, Frédéric. 1997. Marot et le miroir vénitien. In *Clément Marot 'Prince des poëtes François' 1496–1996, Actes du Colloque international de Cahors en Quercy, 1996*, ed. Gérard Defaux and Michel Simonin, 365–377. Paris: Champion.

Webb, Charmarie Jenkins [Blaisdell]. *Royalty and Reform: the Predicament of Renée de France, 1510–1575*. PhD diss., Tufts University, 1969.

Wursten, Dick. 2010. *Clément Marot and Religion. A Reassessment in the Light of his Psalm Paraphrases*. Leiden-Boston: Brill.

Wursten, Dick, and Jetty Janssen. 2010. New Light on the Location of Clément Marot's Tomb and Epitaph in Turin. *Studi Francesi* 161 (LIV I II): 293–303.

CHAPTER 6

"C'est mon stile qui change": Clément Marot's Lyrical Turn in Renéc de France's *Pays Italique*

Robert J. Hudson

As something of a postscript to his epistle addressed to Marguerite de Navarre from Venice, imploring her to help vouchsafe his return to the French kingdom from his Italian exile, Clément Marot offered the following entreaty: "Si quelque mot s'y trouve inusité, / Pardonne moy: *c'est mon stile qui change* / Par trop oyr parler langage estrange" (If any uncommonly used word should there be found, / Forgive me: *It's my style that changed* / From having heard spoken this strange/foreign language).[1] From one of the final epistles composed before his eventual return to grace in Lyon in December 1536, where he would be triumphantly received by the *sodalitium lugdunense*, which would include his Neo-Latin *frères d'Apollon* alongside neoplatonist Petrarchists like Scève, all the while

[1] Clément Marot, *Œuvres poétiques*, 2 vols., ed. Gérard Defaux (Paris: Garnier, 1993), II, 123, vv. 192–94, italics added. All translations are my own.

R. J. Hudson (✉)
Brigham Young University, Provo, UT, USA
e-mail: bob_hudson@byu.edu

© The Author(s), under exclusive license to Springer Nature
Switzerland AG 2021
K. D. Peebles, G. Scarlatta (eds.), *Representing the Life and Legacy of Renée de France*, Queenship and Power,
https://doi.org/10.1007/978-3-030-69121-9_6

167

preferring the French vernacular to his Valois interlocutor, Marot appears to offer a retrospective accounting for a new Italic presence in his verse after Ferrara. Indeed, as C. A. Mayer demonstrates in the notes accompanying his 1977 edition of the *Epîtres*, Marot imitates in these verses the exiled Ovid, who dismisses the language of his *Tristia* as not being his fault but rather: *sed ista loci* (it's this place).[2] Nevertheless, Mayer would also suggest in his biographical study of Marot:

> [C']est précisément le séjour à Ferrare qui a détourné Marot du pétrarquisme. […] C'est en Italie, et en Italie seulement, qu'à cette époque Marot put se rendre compte que cette vogue [de pétrarquisme et d'imitation de poètes précieux du *quattrocento* italien] qu'il avait suivi naguère était méprisée par le public lettré. Dès la fin de son séjour à Ferrare, et surtout après son retour d'exil cette source est tarie. Marot ne pétrarquisera plus.[3]
>
> (It's precisely his stay in Ferrara that turned Marot away from Petrarchism. […] It's in Italy, and only in Italy, that Marot is able to realize at this time that the trend [of Petrarchism and imitation of the stilted poets of *quattrocento* Italy] that he had recently followed was now scorned by the lettered public. As soon as his sojourn in Ferrara had ended, and especially after his return from exile, that source had dried up. Marot would no longer petrarchize.)

Gérard Defaux, in his own critical biography traced in the introduction to his edition of Marot's *Œuvres poétiques*, would famously label the poet's exile of 1535–36 as "les années difficiles" (the difficult years).[4] In line with the interpretation of Defaux, both popular account (Déjean)[5] and critical

---

[2] Clément Marot, *Les Epîtres*, ed. Claude A. Mayer (Paris: Nizet, 1977), 250n1.

[3] Claude A. Mayer, *Clément Marot* (Paris: Nizet, 1972), 310–11. In all fairness, given the context of fifteenth-century precious poets mentioned in the same paragraph, Mayer could perhaps be limiting his use of the term "petrarchize" to those models, leaving Petrarch and Bembo as valid sources. Still, twice in this same paragraph he suggests Marot had turned from Petrarchism and had ceased to petrarchize, which certainly seems more definitive. The subsequent paragraphs in Mayer's biography likewise turn to Marot's studies and diplomatic hopes and away from lyric poetry. I offer my definition of the verb "petrarchize" at the beginning of the third section of the current essay.

[4] Marot, *Œuvres poétiques*, I, cxix.

[5] Jean-Luc Déjean, *Clément Marot* (Paris: Fayard, 1990), 247–81. Jean-Luc Déjean's trade paperback biography of Marot, written as narrative history for the general reader, aims to be far less critical than an erudite study and does a rather excellent job revealing and accounting for the traditional *idées reçues* surrounding the mythology of the poet.

attention (Berthon)[6] uphold the Ferrara exile as a time of great anguish and anxiety for Marot. However, this present collective reconsideration of the life and legacy of Renée de France begs that we reexamine the poetic effects of his reception into *her* Italian court, specifically: Does recent scholarship oversell the negative experience of Ferrara and Marot's apparent distaste for Italy? Did Marot really cease *all* Petrarchism after 1536? Did Italy, as well as Italian language and verse traditions, leave a perceptible trace on Marot's style, as he appears to suggest it did? Were things more nuanced? Could Ferrara actually be seen as a *locus amœnus* of lyrical development for Marot? To what degree is Renée responsible for Marot's lyrical turn and even the invention of the French sonnet?

HISTORIOGRAPHY BEFORE THE "PROTESTANT TURN": RELATIVIZING MAROT'S ITALIAN EXILE

Naturally, when Marot suggests "C'est mon stile qui change," one might astutely point out that in that particular missive, change in style is not necessarily perceived as a boon. And the purpose of that missive is stated explicitly in its concluding verse: "d'icy me retirer" (to withdraw myself from here [Italy]).[7] All the same, when reading Marot—even in his most autobiographical and personal works that are the *Epîtres*—one must always take into account his addressee. As I argue in my recent essay on "Marot vs. Sagon," for the former, questions of religion were always secondary to poetic creation.[8] Marot was always first and foremost a poet—a courtly poet, and a skillful one at that, one who certainly knew how to attune his verse to the tones and interests of his noble interlocutor, in this case, the reform-minded Marguerite. His other epistles from the Ferrara period, those addressed to his host and subject of this collection Renée de France (IV, XII), to Madame de Soubise (X), to her daughters Anne and Renée de Parthenay (IX, XI), to the two unidentified *sœurs savoisiennes* (V), and even to the king himself (VI, VIII), all likewise bear traces of code-

---

[6] Guillaume Berthon, *L'Intention du poète, Clément Marot "autheur"* (Paris: Garnier, 2014), 160. As a polar opposite to Déjean's biography, Berthon's immensely erudite and critical study is intended for specialists and may well be the most pointed study of Marot the academy has seen to date.

[7] Marot, *Œuvres poétiques*, II, 123, v. 196.

[8] See Robert J. Hudson, "Marot vs. Sagon: Heresy and the Gallic School, 1537," in *Representing Heresy in Early Modern France*, ed. Gabriella Scarlatta and Lidia Radi (Toronto: University of Toronto Press, 2017), 159–87.

switching, change in register, and other marks of the courtesan chameleon that Marot certainly was.[9] All things considered, while the verse epistles remain the most revelatory work of Marot's inner world, the gravity and nature of his religious commentaries from this time period must necessarily be contextualized and relativized against the ideas of the identified recipient of each composition.[10] The focus of the present analysis is recognizing that Marot's style indeed changed as result of the Ferrara experience in Renée's Italian court; it evolved, it became more lyrical, and he perceived it as such.

Later in his analysis of Marot's initial Italian exile, Defaux would move beyond his original categorical dismissal of the Ferrara period as a dreadful time and further nuance the question in the terms of the Gallic poet's creation:

> Le bilan de ces années difficiles entre toutes n'est malgré tout nullement négatif. S'il est arrivé à Marot d'avoir [...] à manipuler la vérité [...], (il) a par ailleurs connu à Ferrare des moments de plénitude heureuse, des moments où l'écriture n'était pas seulement pour lui une source de culpabilité, d'angoisse et de tourment.[11]
>
> (The overall assessment of these difficult years is nevertheless not entirely negative. If Marot was forced at times [...] to manipulate the truth, he experienced at the same time in Ferrara moments of complete happiness, moments when writing was not merely a source of guilt, anguish, and torment.)

In his pioneering 1923 study on Marot, Pierre Villey is even more positive in seeing the Italian sojourn as serving a distinct purpose in Marot's development, after which he would return to the king "mieux instruit dans les langues latine et italienne, en mesure, non pas seulement de faire de meilleurs vers, mais de remplir les missions diplomatiques" (better educated in both the Latin and Italian languages and now able not only to write better

[9] The numbering of these epistles corresponds to that adopted by Defaux in *Œuvres poétiques*, 77–101. The editorial grouping, while somewhat chronological, is certainly more generically thematic. For this reason, Mayer's strictly chronological progression is more contextually reflective of Marot's mental state at the time of the individual compositions.

[10] Indeed, one of the major issues with Déjean is a tendency to accept the epistles at face value. *Clément Marot*, 251–29. In his determinism to read Marot as a committed *réformateur*, Mayer does the same in his biography. *Clément Marot*, 276–301.

[11] Marot, *Œuvres poétiques*, I, cxlv. This same assessment of Ferrara is repeated in Gérard Defaux, *Le Poète en son jardin* (Paris: Champion, 2006), 144.

verses but also to fulfill diplomatic assignments).[12] While spent in exile, the Ferrara period, Villey argues, is one of development, growth, and overall happiness for Marot. A few years after Villey, in 1926, Henry Guy would concur, even speaking of a poetic flourishing in Ferrara:

> Marot n'a jamais été mieux inspiré que durant son séjour en Italie. Les vers qu'il écrivit à Ferrare sont nombreux et ont tous de la valeur. Et puis, quelle variété! On aurait tort de croire que, une fois entré dans le genre sérieux, le poète n'en soit plus sorti. Il y entre et il en sort à sa guise, selon son caprice, l'heure (et) le besoin.[13]
> (Marot had never been more inspired than during his Italian period. The verses he wrote in Ferrara are numerous and all have value. And then, what variety! We would be mistaken to believe that once he had undertaken to write in a sober mood, he never again abandoned it. He changes poetic mood as he pleases, according to his own fancies, the moment, and the need.)

As evidenced earlier, the consensus of Third Republic literary historians researching Marot and sixteenth-century France readily recognize the poetic and experiential variety evidenced from the Gallic poet's Italian exile. Why then does more contemporary criticism tend to focus almost exclusively on the verse epistles from this time period? Furthermore, why are we so quick to consider the famously playful and irreverent *Concours des blasons du corps féminin*, launched from Renée's court of Ferrara, out of context as a sort of a one-off in Marot's poetry from 1535? If Marot is the greatest poet from this period, *le prince des poëtes françois*, why not recognize his ability to vary tone, mood, and form at will?

The aftermath of WWII (i.e., the end of the Third Republic) and the ensuing interest in Marot outside of France may hold a plausible response to the questions posed above, as the year 1960 saw Mayer publish his French-language *La religion de Marot*. Likewise, M. A. Screech, who had published his Erasmian reading of Marot's contemporary and friend François Rabelais, *L'Evangélisme de Rabelais* in 1959, famously revisited the refrain "Il a mangé le lard" (i.e., Marot consumed flesh during the Lenten fast) in Evangelical terms in 1964 and followed this with his *Marot évangélique* in 1967.[14] While it would be difficult to overestimate the

---

[12] Pierre Villey, *Marot et Rabelais* (Paris: Champion, 1923), 80.
[13] Henry Guy, *Marot et son école* (Paris: Champion, 1926), 209.
[14] The religious-minded Screech would also later publish the English-language *Clément Marot, a Renaissance Poet Discovers the Gospel: Lutheranism, Fabrism and Calvinism in the*

importance of these twin monoliths of the 1960s–1990s, that is, of Mayer to Marot Studies and of Screech to the French Renaissance at large (as the latter's translations of and philological discoveries within the works of Rabelais and the *Essais* of Michel de Montaigne are considered among the very best, as are the Marot bibliographies and critical editions of the former), when it comes to the subject of Marot, both scholars brought a personal lens to the fore that colors their understanding of the poet. Each having fought for Great Britain in WWII and having made their careers in the English university system (Screech would even be ordained an Anglican clergyman in 1994), the excellent work of both scholars nonetheless wears its Evangelical leanings and determinism quite heavily, and both are rather definitive in establishing Marot as committed to Lutheran/Calvinist reform.[15] Still, as I have stated and continue to argue, Marot was foremost a poet and no procrustean bed can account for the mutable Protean character he was.[16]

Prior to this "Protestant turn" in Marot studies of the early 1960s, however, the consensus seems to be the following: in Renée's Ferrara, despite the political intrigue and his increasingly precarious situation, ever in full possession of his talents, Marot remained the genial, blithesome poet that had been his primary interest and occupation. Continuing on this point, Guy contends:

> [Q]uand on étudie les œuvres [que Marot] a composées pendant son exil, on remarque à l'instant qu'elles se laissent diviser en deux groupes: les unes, qui nous rappellent le Clément de l'*Adolescence*, l'Enfant sans souci, le bon vivant et le railleur, sont gaies, légères, crues et mordantes; les autres (sa seconde matière) prennent un ton austère, religieux, soucieux, et portent l'empreinte des chagrins qui l'obsède.[17]

Royal Courts of France and of Navarre and in the Ducal Court of Ferrara (Leiden: Brill, 1993).

[15] See the obituaries of each: "Obituary: C. A. Mayer," *The Independent*, June 1, 1998, and "The Rev. Professor Michael Screech," *The Times*, July 19, 2018.

[16] Hudson, "Marot vs. Sagon," 162–68. See also Florian Preisig's excellent study on Marot's metamorphoses as an author and his seemingly innate ability to transmutate as sacred and profane poet, socialite and courtesan, at will. *Clément Marot et les métamorphoses de l'auteur à l'aube de la Renaissance* (Geneva: Droz, 2004), especially 151–152. See also Mario Richter, "Considerazioni et proposte per una storia della poesia lirica francese nel secolo XVI." *Aevum* 44, no. 1/2 (Jan–April 1970): 72–112, 79.

[17] Henry Guy, *Marot et son école*, 209–10. Note also how Guy sees the austere, religious bent as the "secondary" tendency.

(When studying the works that Marot composed during his exile, one instantly notices that they are divisible into two groups: the first, which remind us of the Clément of the *Adolescence*, the carousing *enfant sans souci*, the vibrant and mocking epicurean, are cheerful, light, coarse, and scathing; the others (his secondary subject) take on another tone–stern, ascetic, worrisome–and are marked by his sorrows and preoccupations.)

When focusing almost entirely on this secondary group of texts (mostly verse epistles), as Marot scholarship has largely done for the past half-century, it is understandable that the view of Marot during this time period would be limited to the more apprehensive, dejected figure he presents himself as in expressing his desires to his reformist countrymen to return home.

Far more recently, Guillaume Berthon, in his exceptional work on Marot's authorship *L'Intention du poète*, documents this period briefly, referring to it as "la parenthèse ferraraise [...] un *excursus*, [...] une période transitoire" (the Ferraran parenthesis, an excursus, a transitory period).[18] As he nuances the period as not being entirely indicative of Marot's intellectual and poetic–not to mention religious–evolution, Berthon also calls into question Mayer's categorical "end of Petrarchism" claims cited at the beginning of the current essay:

L'arrivée à Ferrare devait-elle marquer la fin d'une époque et le commencement d'un nouveau service, ou constituer une retraite sûre en attendant que le vent tourne et qu'il puisse être restauré dans sa fonction?[19]

(Must we see Marot's arrival in Ferrara as marking the end of an era or the beginning of a new call of duty, or can we consider it a safe haven where he waited for the winds to change sufficiently to allow him to return to his commissions?)

In his analysis of this time apart, Berthon recognizes three types of verse produced by Marot during this *parenthesis*: "successivement, les pièces composées pour des occasions importantes de la vie de Renée, celles qui ont à cœur d'animer un divertissement courtisan, et enfin la traduction des *Psaumes*" (in succession, those pieces composed to commemorate important moments in Renée's life, those concerned with enlivening courtly

---

[18] Berthon, *L'Intention du poète*, 159–168.
[19] Berthon, *L'Intention du poète*, 159.

entertainment, and, finally, Marot's psalm translations).[20] Indeed, this idea of Marot's psalm translations taking root during the Ferrara period comes to us from the thesis of Rosanna Gorris in her comments from the 1996 Quincentennial celebration of Marot's birth in Cahors, in which she argues for a commissioned continuation of the psalm translations, under which Marot would accomplish another seven translations in a clandestine "chapelle réformée" in the Este palace.[21] In this prime example of scholarship written in the wake of the Protestant turn (in a volume edited by Defaux, no less), Gorris firmly proclaims Marot's "principal objectif, celui qui déjà oriente son existence et sa poétique: être le Poète, la voix, le truchement du Dieu qui s'est fait homme" (Marot's primary objective, to which his existence and poetics are now oriented: to be the Poet, the voice, the spokesman for God become man).[22] While Berthon convincingly argues against the conjecture of Marot having completed these psalm translations in Ferrara,[23] other elements of Gorris's excellently researched article on Marot in Ferrara establish the essay as the authoritative narrative of Marot's stay in the stronghold of the Court of Este.[24] In fact, she offers a superb segue into the second section of this essay, in recognizing 1535 Ferrara successively as "un havre 'sûr et paisible'" (a safe and peaceful refuge); "un Eden" (an Eden); "un milieu scientifique, académique et culturel" (a scientific, academic, and cultural setting); "un phare de la culture européenne" (a beacon of European culture), and "un centre d'élaboration philosophique et littéraire, un 'ouvroir' de poésie" (a center of philosophical and literary elaboration, a poetic "workshop").[25] What better setting to gratify an exiled Marot's humanist heart! As we press forward, it is not the

---

[20] Berthon, *L'Intention du poète*, 163.

[21] Rosanna Gorris, "'Un franzese nominato Clemente': Marot à Ferrare," in *Clément Marot "Prince des poëtes françois" 1496–1996, Actes du Colloque international de Cahors en Quercy, 1996*, edited by Gérard Defaux and Michel Simonin (Paris: Champion, 1997), 350–353.

[22] Gorris, "'Un franzese nominato Clemente,'" 347. It should be mentioned that Gorris's article on Marot's closest friend, Lyon Jamet, and his trip to Ferrara "'Va, lettre, va […] droict à Clément': Lyon Jamet, Sieur de Chambrun, du Poitou à la ville des Este, un itinéraire religieux et existentiel," also focuses fairly directly on reformist elements, seeing the trip as a "religious and existential itinerary," *Études rabelaisiennes* 43 (2006): 145–172. See especially, 144.

[23] Berthon, *L'Intention du poète*, 167–168.

[24] At this point in her career, Gorris (now in Verona) was teaching at the University of Ferrara.

[25] Gorris, "'Un franzese nominato Clemente,'" 339–346.

austere, sermonizing poet of the epistles that such a setting enlivens or brings to the fore; rather, Renée's Ferrara seems more conducive to the verse of the convivial Gallic Marot, the courtly poet at one with nature and his talents, one far more open to the lyrical flourishings of his Italian experience.

"MAROT, LE POËTE GALLIQUE (AU) PAYS ITALIQUE": RENÉE'S FERRARA BELVEDERE AS LOCUS AMŒNUS

As far as nature is concerned, Ferrara has no shortage of natural bounty to inspire our poet.[26] Indeed, nature and the beauty of Ferrara constitute central features of Marot's first epistle written in Ferrara and addressed to his protector Renée. Having narrowly escaped extradition to the Sorbonne at Bordeaux, when Marot leaves Marguerite's court at Nérac, traverses the Alps, and traces the River Po to Ferrara in April 1535 in order to "changer de dame" and be received and protected among other French intellectuals by Renée de France in the House of Este, he initially adopts the pose of little more than a lighthearted but grateful Gallic tourist:

> Salut à toy doncques très humblement;
> Humble salut, par ton humble Clement,
> Par ton Marot, le Poëte Gallique,
> Qui s'en vient veoir le pays italique
> Pour quelque temps [...].[27]

(Greetings to you, yea and most humbly so / Your humble Clement sends his humble hello / Gallic Marot, poet who came to see / The handsome sites of your fair Italy, For a short time [...].)

While this epistle begins innocently enough, with the wide-eyed poet describing and praising his pleasant passage across the duchies of northern Italy in organic terms, admiring both nature and subjects: "En traversant ton pays plantureux, / Fertile en biens, en dame bienheureux, / Et bien semé de peuple obeissant" (As I traverse all your lush countryside, / Fertile in goods, where gent ladies abide, / And sown throughout with just folks who obey), by his ninth verse, Marot already plants the seed of a

---

[26] For an examination of the role of bucolic nature in Marotic poetics, see my article "Bucolic Influence: Marot's Gallic Pastoral and Maurice Scève's *Arion*," *Romanic Review* 105, no. 3 (May-Nov 2014): 253–373.
[27] Marot, *Œuvres poétiques*, II, 78, vv. 36–39.

"vraye intention" (true intent) that eventually blossoms in the hemistich and verse immediately following those from the *salut* cited above, "si entre cy et là / Te peult servir ma plume [...]" (so if from now to then / [...] I may serve with my pen).[28] Of course, Marot is not arriving unannounced, his passage vouchsafed long before he set foot on Italian soil; all the same, the courtly game is *de rigueur*, especially for a first meeting. In this initial epistle to Renée, Marot acquits himself quite well, lavishing praise wherever he can, being ever benevolent and salutary. However, his intentions are very clear: the harried poet seeks a semi-permanent poetic position, a safe harbor from the fires of France following the infamous *Affaire des Placards* (October 17–18, 1534) (Fig. 6.1).

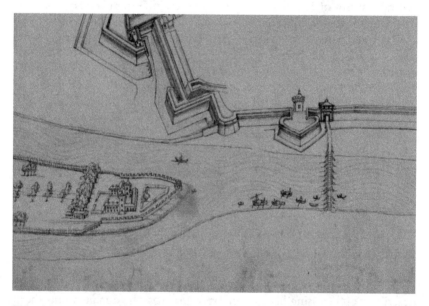

Fig. 6.1 Detail of the Belvedere island, south of Ferrara. Archivio di Stato di Modena, Mappario Estense—Topografie di città, n. 96. Su concessione del Ministero per I Beni et le Attività Culturali et per il Turismo—Archivio di Stato di Modeno, prot. no. 1625

---

[28] Marot, *Œuvres poétiques*, II, 77–78, vv. 1–3, 9, 39–40. For more on Renée and Marot's poetic/cultural exchange, see Kelly D. Peebles, "Renée de France and Clément Marot's Voyages: Political Exile to Spiritual Liberation," *Women in French Studies* Special Issue 7 (2018): 42–48.

Even if the imposingly massive Este palace would not prove to be the most welcoming of locations, with Ercole II d'Este growing increasingly wary and hostile to his wife Renée's seemingly endless throng of French intellectuals, refuge would nevertheless be found on the lush island retreat on the River Po left behind by the Duke of Ferrara's famous mother Lucrezia Borgia: *il Belvedere*.[29] In the sixteenth century and unlike today, the course of the Po ran to the south of the walled city of Ferrara (adjacent to the present day Canale di Burana), creating a sort of natural moat and, in 1513, the duke's father Alfonso II commissioned a bridge to be built from the south city gate to the sandy island *Boschetto* (grove) and for the *Belvedere* palace and gardens to be built. (While ruins of the fortifications to the immediate north end of the former island are visible today in patches on the north side of Ferrara's Via Darsena, satellite images of modern-day Ferrara offer a unique perspective of the size and position of the former 60-acre sixteenth-century *Boschetto*, which began a few hundred meters to the south of today's Stadio Paolo Mazza soccer arena in the area that is occupied by the new shopping mall/cinema Nuova Darsena and would have extended eastward roughly one kilometer from the municipal train station to just south of the still-existing sixth-century Mura di Ferrara which were the fortifications of the main city to the north).[30] As the Biagio Rossetti commemorative website explains, within a decade of its conceptualization "the site included new formal gardens, fountains, baths, enclosures for exotic animals, [...and] a complex system of buildings on the eastern end [...] richly decorated both inside and out."[31] Ariosto would enjoy the island for a decade, even writing about *il Belvedere* in his *Orlando Furioso* (1516/1532). All the same, poetically, Ariosto was far from the only luminary to frequent Ferrara in the *cinquecento*. Antonio Tebaldeo was born in Ferrara and had served as personal secretary to Lucrezia and tutor to her children until called to Rome in 1513. And, how could one forget the infamously torrid decades-long love affair between Pietro

[29] The author wishes to thank the Ministero per i Beni et le Attività Culturali et per il Turismo for permission to reproduce Fig. 6.1, Archivio di Stato di Modena, prot. n° 1625.
[30] An Italian website dedicated to commemorating the 500th anniversary of the death of Ferraran architect Biagio Rossetti (1447–1516), has excellent documentation and photographs, including sixteenth-century renderings of the island, related to *Il Boschetto*. See "Isola e palazzo di Belvedere scomparsi," Biagio Rossetti 500, https://biagiorossetti500.it/architettura/isola-e-palazzo-di-belvedere-scomparsi/.
[31] Biagio Rossetti 500. Translations to English from the website.

178   R. J. HUDSON

Bembo and Lucrezia begun in Ferrara in 1503?[32] Indeed, it was into this poetically haunted *locus amœnus* that Marot was received: "En ces lieux, où la bonté de la duchesse l'établit bientôt, Marot va se consoler et s'épanouir" (On these premises, where the duchess in her graciousness allowed him to take residence, Marot will find refuge and blossom).[33]

It is difficult to underestimate the role of Renée in Marot's lyrical evolution. Even if in other verse epistles, written for Madame de Soubise's two daughters, Marot would evoke Ferrara obliquely (and often in a melancholy tone), a holistic view of Marot's blossoming at the *Belvedere* is better seen when one looks beyond the epistles. Indeed, in two *dizain* epigrams addressed to these very same daughters of Soubise, entitled "A ma Dame de Pons" and "À Mademoiselle Renée de Partenay," Marot evokes the *Boschetto* directly as a *locus amœnus*. In the former, at the arrival of the Soubise daughter Anne, the newlywed Madame de Pons, the *Belvedere* is personified:

> Pour prendre en luy sejour, & reconfort,
> D'estre aggreable a mys tout son effort,
> Et a vestu sa verte robbe neufve.
>
> De ce sejour le Pau tout fier se treuve,
> Les Rossignolz s'en tiennent angelicques [...].[34]

(To find in her a comfortable abode, / For his delight, all efforts were bestowed, / And yea she shone, in vibrant green was gowned. / In this dwelling, the Po most proud was found, / The Nightingales like angels stood in watch.)

With imagery reminiscent of the medieval rhymes of Charles D'Orléans (e.g., the springtime rondeaux "Le temps a laissé son manteau [...] / Et s'est vestu de brouderie [...] / [Tous] Portent, en livrée jolie, / Gouttes d'argent d'orfaverie" (Nature left behind his frigit coat / and put on his brightest ebroidered cloak; / all others follow suit / and don their loveliest livery, / bedecked with drops of the silversmith's craftwork)).[35] Marot

---

[32] The affair between Bembo and Lucrezia is well documented by the latter in her letters to her lover held in the Milan Biblioteca Ambrosiana and published as *Lettere di Lucrezia Borgia a Messer Pietro Bembo*, ed. Bernardo Gatti (Milan: Ambrosiana, 1859).

[33] Déjean, *Clément Marot*, 251.

[34] Marot, *Œuvres poétiques*, II, 280–81, vv. 3–8.

[35] *Poètes et Romanciers du Moyen Âge* (Paris: Gallimard, 1952), ed. Albert Pauphilet, 1091–92.

transforms the *Belvedere* island retreat into a proudly adorned princess debuting a new dress and, so doing, enlivening flora, fauna, and natural setting alike. In the subsequent composition to Renée, the other Soubise daughter, the famous bucolic *locus amœnus* opening hemistich "En ce beau lieu" (In this lovely place) is adapted to the *Boschetto*: "Quand vous oyez, que ma Muse resonne / *En ce Bosquet*, qu'Oyseaulx font resonner" (And when you hear that my Muse does resound / In this green grove, where Birdsongs do abound).[36] Since both of these compositions appear, sequentially, for the first time in the Chantilly manuscript offered to Anne de Montmorency in March 1538, I feel justified in including the *huitain* epigram "Du Moys de May, & D'Anne" as part of a series of epigrams celebrating the *Belvedere*.[37] Even if my current allotted space does not allow a more extensive analysis of these Ferrara epigrams, allow me to quickly draw on the unifying presence of prairies, fields, and nightingales and the colors of Spring that adorn the *Bosquet* across the series (as well as the fact that the subsequent epigram in the Chantilly manuscript, "De son feu, & de celluy, qui se print au Bosquet de Ferrare," directly discusses the *Bosquet* as well). Suffice it to say that at Renée de France's *Belvedere*, we very much find ourselves in the realm of Marot's famous *élégant badinage* (or courtly diversion, as Berthon phrased it), one inspired by "ce beau lieu."

Concerning Marot's adoption of the epigram as a subjective, lyrically expressive form, Defaux appeals to the vogue in the 1530s inspired by Etienne Dolet—who would publish a volume of Marot's epigrams in July 1538—and Michel d'Amboise, who in 1533 published a volume of epigrams alongside vernacular translations of Marot's erstwhile model for bucolic verse Mantuan.[38] However, at the same time, Defaux affords the possibility of another source of discovery and distillation: "Marot a suivi à l'académie de Ferrare les cours de l'humaniste érasmien Celio Calcagnini, et [...] son séjour lui a permis d'affiner sa connaissance de la langue latine"

---

[36] Marot, *Œuvres poétiques*, II, 281, vv. 1–2. Italics added. While changed to "En ce Bosquet" in Marot's official *Œuvres* of 1538, Defaux notes that the original publication of this in the earlier 1538 Chantilly manuscript indeed read "En ce beau lieu," 1080, n2. See also Marot, *Recueil inédit*, 204–06.

[37] Marot, *Œuvres poétiques*, II, 281–82. Berthon comes to the exact same conclusion in *L'intention du poète*, 165.

[38] Baptista Spagnuoli (1477–1516), known by his demonym Mantuan, was a model for both the title of the *Adolescence clementine* and the Marotic eclogue. See Hudson, "Bucolic Influence," 254, and Scott Francis, *Advertising the Self in Renaissance France: Lemaire, Marot and Rabelais* (Newark: University of Delaware Press, 2019), 94.

(At the Academy of Ferrara, Marot had taken courses with the Erasmian humanist Celio Calcagnini, and these studies allowed him to refine his understanding of the Latin language).[39] In fact, Marot upholds this increase in ease of expression in Italian and Latin as a point of emphasis in his epistolary pleas to François to return to France, as they have made him a more apt and versatile poet and translator:

> Pour à l'estude ung temps m'entretenir
> Soubz Celius, de qui tant on aprent.
> Et si desir apres cela te prent
> De m'appeller en la terre gallique,
>
> Tu trouveras ceste langue italique
> Passablement dessus la mienne entée,
> Et la latine en moy plus augmentée [...].[40]

(For studying a while under the care / Of Celius, who has so much to teach. / And afterwards, should your desire me reach / That I return unto the Gallic land, / You then shall find new aptitudes at hand: / Italic speech onto my tongue I splice, / And Latin, too, increased and more precise.)

In his own contribution to the 1996 Cahors collection, François Rouget likewise upholds the epigram as the point of origin of a new lyrical verve in the poetry of Marot.[41] Accusations of Latin ignorance are a thing of the past; Marot's style has certainly changed and he has assumed his Protean mutability.

Remaining with the epigram form, Marot's most celebrated poetic undertaking of the Ferrara sojourn, the aforementioned *Concours des blasons anatomiques du corps féminin* are recognized by the poet himself as being epigrams. Whether or not all of the descriptive offerings would conform to the definition later established by Sébillet, it is most interesting that Marot's first printed mention of this term (two years prior to either the Chantilly manuscript or Dolet edition) was in February 1536 immediately after his return to France from Ferrara. Was the *blason* an Italian tradition? Absolutely. As Villey makes clear, Italian *strambottisti* of the

---

[39] Marot, *Œuvres poétiques*, II, 978–80. As Scott Francis has shown in his excellent new volume on self-fashioning in the French Renaissance, Marot's experience with Calcagnini affected his satirical verse in meaningful ways as well. *Advertising the Self*, 110.

[40] Marot, *Œuvres poétiques*, II, 93, vv. 40–46.

[41] François Rouget, "Marot poète lyrique," in *Clément Marot "Prince des poëtes françois" 1496–1996, Actes du Colloque international de Cahors en Quercy, 1996*, ed. Gérard Defaux and Michel Simonin, 582.

early sixteenth century preferred the descriptive genre and it is highly
probable that Olimpo da Sassoferato's image of *due capotoli* inspired
Marot in the first place to compose the "Blason du beau tétin."[42] This idea
was most recently expanded upon by Berthon who sees Olimpo's proto-
blason as a form with which Marot "récupère une forme ancienne qu'il
renouvelle par une idée originale" (recuperates an antiquated form that he
renews with an original idea).[43] More on the *strambotto* in a moment.
First, to continue with medieval and classical influences, Annwyl Williams
upholds Marot's "Le cler soleil," addressed "à Anne" as a perfect transi-
tional epigram from the Middle Ages to the Renaissance, a poem that
"trahit l'influence de Pétrarque, de Martial et des épigrammatistes néo-
latins" (betrays the influence of Petrarch, Martial, and the Neo-Latin epi-
grammatists). In other words, it is indicative of a changing style.[44] In the
latest work on the subject, *Anatomie d'une Anatomie: Nouvelles recherches
sur les blasons anatomiques du corps féminin*, several contributors (Marion
Uhlig, Laurence Boulègue, Andrea Torre, et al.) note the classical, medieval Italian and even Petrarchan sources into which Marot taps with his
"invention" of the French *blason*.[45] This new mastery of Latin and Italic
form would certainly impress the *sodalitium lugdunense*, and along with
them Maurice Scève, who would claim the laurels of the *Concours des blasons* and make his fame with his Petrarchan *durs epygrammes* of the *Délie* a
decade later.[46]

[42] Villey, *Marot et Rabelais*, 82. Florian Preisig recently discussed the transalpine intertext
present between Marot's *tetin* and Olimpo's *capitoli* in his presentation at the 2018 SCSC in
Albuquerque (1–4 November).

[43] See also Guillaume Berthon, "L'invention du blason: Retour sur la genèse d'un genre,"
in *Anatomie d'une Anatomie: Nouvelle recherches sur les blasons anatomiques du corps féminin*,
ed. Julien Goeury and Thomas Hunkeler (Geneva: Droz, 2018), 135–154. As the next section will demonstrate, Marot does the exact same thing with the sonnet, a form that embodies for him Renée's diplomatic mission in Ferrara.

[44] Annwyl Williams, "Clément Marot, 'Le cler soleil': Intertexte médiéval de l'épigramme
amoureuse," in *Clément Marot "Prince des poëtes françois" 1496–1996, Actes du Colloque
international de Cahors en Quercy, 1996*, ed. Gérard Defaux and Michel Simonin, 201–04.

[45] Goeury and Hunkeler, *Anatomie d'une Anatomie*, 41–109. While neither the central
focus nor the allotted space of this chapter allows me to flesh out the interesting points of
these contributions, I do highly recommend them to anyone researching the *blason* and its
origins.

[46] See also Rouget, "Marot poète lyrique," 582.

AN END OF PETRARCHISM?: MAROT AND LYRICISM AFTER 1536

Let us now return to Mayer's claims that Marot ceased his Petrarchan imitations after Ferrara. As a guiding definition, "to petrarchize" is to imitate the *trecento* Tuscan poet's pained, individualized lyrical pleas to a desired but pre-determinedly inaccessible beloved. Petrarch wrote his 317 sonnets to Laura, an already married then soon after deceased woman with whom, according to his own literary legend, he fell in love instantly—in a moment of *innamoramento* (love at first sight)—when he saw her outside of Sunday mass in Avignon. Like subsequent French Petrarchists (Scève and his eponymous Délie; Du Bellay and his Olive; Ronsard and Cassandre, Marie, and Hélène; Baïf and Méline), Marot christened his inaccessible, desired object of lyrical affection from this period "Anne," which Déjean points out "devient décidément le nom générique de la bien-aimée pétrar-quisée" (becomes decidedly the generic name of the Petrarchan beloved).[47] One certainly does not invent his Laura *after* one has finished with his Petrarchan imitation. Of course, Marot had petrarchized since the second half of the 1520s and even included Petrarch as a model in his "Temple de Cupido" as early as 1513–14. Not only was he first to translate a selection of Petrarch's *Canzoniere*—sonnets and visions—into French, he was also first to write an original sonnet in the vernacular, addressed to none other than "A Madame de Ferrare," Renée de France herself. Indeed, Marotic Petrarchism was just as alive and well in 1536, as it was certainly informed by the Gallic poet's lyrical turn in Renée's Italy.

Before examining this sonnet in more detail, the link should be empha-sized between this pioneering poetic effort and the marked increase of epigrammatic production that occurs in almost exact conjunction with Marot's arrival in Ferrara (when exposure to Martial becomes increasingly

---

[47] Déjean, *Clément Marot*, 261. See also Berthon, *L'Intention*, 165–66. Was this the same Anne de Beauregard, a young Frenchwoman from Renée's entourage who tragically died in Ferrara (hence the full name he gives her: *Beauregard* in French translates to *Belvedere* in Italian) and whom Marot includes in his *Cymetière* (Marot, *Œuvres poétiques*, I, 385)? Her tragic and untimely demise would certainly equate her with Petrarch's Laura. That Marot only includes the forename "Anne" in the poems from Ferrara after 1538, and perhaps as a smokescreen, only lends further credence to the idea that she, as muse or object of desire, is a Petrarchan invention.

available) and subsequent exchanges with the *sodalitium lugdunense*.[48] In his watershed article discussing this original sonnet, "Sonnet ou Quatorzain?," John McClelland demonstrates that the Italian marriage of a symmetrical eight-verse *ottavo* to a more musical, asymmetrical six-verse *strambotto* (originally accomplished by *duecento* Sicilian poet Giacomo da Lentini and standardized by Petrarch, who becomes the "father of the sonnet") is little more than another form of the epigram, a Gallic adaptation of an Italic form.[49] Sébillet had likewise stated as much in 1548: "*Qu'est Sonnet*—Le Sonnet suit l'épigramme de bien près, et de matière, et de mesure: Quand tout est dit, Sonnet n'est autre chose que le parfait épigramme de l'Italien, comme le dizain du Français" (What's a Sonnet? The sonnet aligns itself very closely with the epigram, in both matter and versification: When all is said, a sonnet is little more than the perfect epigram in Italian, much like the dizain for French).[50] In other words, not only is the original French Petrarchan sonnet an epigram, the sonnet itself—that poetic form most given to lyrical expression—was understood even half a decade after Marot's death (albeit prior to the Pléiade) as a nod to Italy, the Gallic poet's Italian forebears and Renée de France herself.[51]

Indeed, included in the Chantilly manuscript as the final of seven "Autres œuvres faites à Venise" (therefore, in Summer 1536) and beginning with an evocation of Renée's goodness toward the poet, the very first sonnet composed in French is quite evidently written in memory of and reference to the Duchess and Ferrara:

> Me souvenenant de tes bontez divines,
> Suis en douleur (Princesse) à ton absence ;
> Et si languy quant suis en ta presence,
> Voyant ce lys au milieu des espines.

[48] Marot, *Œuvres poétiques*, II, 978. See also Rouget, "Marot poètique lyrique," 574, and Marot, *Recueil inédit*, 175.

[49] John McClelland, "Sonnet ou quatorzain? Marot et le choix d'une forme poétique," *Revue d'Histoire littéraire de la France* 73, no. 4 (Jul-Aug 1973): 591–607, 607. See also François Rigolot, "The Sonnet," in *A New History of French Literature*, ed. Denis Hollier (Cambridge: Harvard University Press, 1989), 171–173, especially 171–172, and Walter Bullock, "The First French Sonnets," *Modern Language Notes* 39, no. 8 (1924): 475–478.

[50] Francis Goyet, ed. *Traités de poétique et de rhétorique de la Renaissance* (Paris: Poche, 1990), 107.

[51] My own article, "Clément Marot and the 'Invention' of the French Sonnet: Innovating the Lyrical Imperative in Renaissance France," *Anthropoetics* 14, no. 2 (Winter 2009), examines the anthropological potency of the Petrarchan sonnet, as well as Marot's adaptation of this form to the French vernacular.

O la doulceur des doulceurs femenines !
O cueur sans fiel, o race d'excellence !
O traictement remply de violance
Qui s'endurcist près des choses benignes.

Si seras tu de la main soustenue
De l'Eternel, comme sa cher tenue;
Et tes nuysans auront honte et reproche.

Courage, Dame : en l'air je voy la nue
Qui çà et là s'escarte et diminue,
Pour faire place au beau temps qui s'approche.[52]

(Remembering the kindnesses you've born, / I'm greatly pained, Princess, by your absence; / And languish too when I'm in your presence, / Seeing this *lys* alone midst nettled thorn. // O the goodness, feminine grace divine, / O guileless heart, o gent exquisite race! / O cruel sort, the crime you've had to face, / Whose hardened fist mocks all that is benign. // If you will be by His just hand upheld, / Eternal God will you with His flesh meld; / And those who harm will know shame and reproach. // Take heart, Lady: see now the gloomy cloud, / Both here and there has rent its dreary shroud, / And now gives way to bright days that approach.)

If, in addition to the modern expression of the individual poetic subject, lyricism is the literary genre of absence, this first sonnet is most certainly lyrical in its embodiment of its very lyrical turn at a meta level. Marot, who is often presented and believed to only feel homesickness and nostalgia for Valois France (and, in one famous example from his *L'Enfer*, for his native Cahors),[53] admits to being pained by an absence. However, in this case, this absence is not that of an inaccessible beloved but of Renée, who remains exiled in a hostile environment, while our poet returns to his long-regretted royal court. While he should ostensibly be able to enjoy his homecoming, Marot presents the paradox of having likewise languished while in her presence, perishing the thought of the cruelty of Ercole and his court toward her. Even if *Il Boschetto* was far from a realm of nettles and thorns for Marot, in the Este fortress, Renée would indeed be the one blossoming lily (or French fleur de lys), and, at the same time, as Kelly

---

[52] Here, I reproduce the original text from the Chantilly manuscript, for which I thank Guillaume Berthon for his invaluable paleographical assistance with the secretary hand. For Rigolot's transcription and notes: Marot, *Recueil*, 233, and for the Defaux reference with variants: Marot, *Œuvres poétiques*, II, 297–98 and 1099–1100.

[53] Marot, *Œuvres poétiques*, II, 19–33, especially vv. 395–406.

Peebles explains, the lone beatific figure of beauty and bounty for all in her entourage.[54] The pain of separation and the languishing at the thought of her mistreatment echoes across the apostrophic remembrances of the second quatrain stanza (vv. 5–7), as the inability to adequately express the overabundance of emotion the lyrical poet feels at this agonizingly paradoxical present absence renders the poem most remarkably Petrarchan through the quatrains.

At the *chute* or *volta* (the break in the 14-verse sonnet between the twinned quatrain *ottavo* pair ABBA and the concluding *strambotto* tercet pair, where symmetry gives way to asymmetry and the poem is ushered to its teleological end), the very lyricism of this sonnet is called into question. Make no mistake, his concern and indebted affection toward Renée is decidedly not the unrequited passion (*fol amour*) felt by Petrarch for Laura or even Marot himself for the Anne of other epigrams. No, as this sonnet is ushered to its prescribed ending in the tercet pair, the pain felt at the thought of Renée's present absence and mistreatment—as the amorous love of unrequited passion—is not mitigated and needs not to be. Rather, in a most unexpected *chute*, the mood shifts to one of prayerfulness and hope. At its anthropological origins, lyricism has been theorized to derive from a secularized supplication of a powerful paramour to end the suffering of the lyrical subject, in the same way prayer would call on an unseen divinity to make bare its almighty arm.[55] In this originary case of the sonnet in the French vernacular, Marot instigates a return to the human sources of lyricism by imploring the Eternal to bring an end to the suffering experienced by Renée and in so doing mitigates his own suffering in the face of this paradoxical present absence.

Not only is she the subject and addressee of the first French sonnet, Renée could even be seen as the physical embodiment of this amalgamation of French vernacular and Italian forms. As his protector and patron at the time of his Italian exile, when his verse took this lyrical turn, this new "invention" should also necessarily bear Renée's name as well as indications of her diplomatic objectives of unity between France and Italy, alongside her own domestic struggles. Marot had already lamented at great length (148 verses) the mistreatment of Renée at the hands of the duke in his "Complaincte à la Royne de Navarre du maltraitement de

---

[54] Peebles, "Renée de France's and Clément Marot's Voyages," 46–48.
[55] Eric Gans, "Naissance du Moi lyrique," *Poétique* 46 (1981), 129, and Nathalie Dauvois, *Le sujet lyrique à la Renaissance* (Paris: Presses universitaires de France, 2000), 21.

Madame de Ferrare par le Duc, son Mary."[56] That he would do so again in this initial sonnet should not be overlooked. As Berthon sees him doing with the blason form, in the sonnet, Marot again renews an essentially Italian form with a novel idea. Across his œuvre, Marot would only compose four original sonnets in addition to six translations of Petrarch; all ten of these compositions bear significant traces of his lyrical turn and, in turn, all are profoundly influenced by Renée.

During this same moment of "invention," in which he would adopt the Petrarchan form, Marot would likewise adapt it to French use with the inclusion of the *rime plate* rhyming couplet immediately following the *chute* in the ninth and tenth verse positions, which would become a staple of the French sonnet for centuries to follow and is noted for accentuating the rupture of symmetry and expectation (as Marot had done in the original French sonnet to Renée de France).[57] Not only would this lyrical set-up inform his sonnets, it would also appear in his epigrams, as well as in his psalm translations.[58] Even in the most reformist of undertakings, prior to his banishment from Geneva, ostensibly for drinking and gambling, Marot was still first and foremost a poet—and, thanks to Renée and her Italian court, a lyrical poet. Whether in Italy, France, or Switzerland, despite tendential claims to the contrary, Clément Marot never once alleged to have *oublié l'art de pétrarquiser.*

CONCLUSION

Marotic Petrarchism would continue throughout the remaining six years of his life, as Mia Cocco identifies Petrarchan intertext (most notably in the epigrams) all the way up to Marot's death in 1544.[59] However, Cocco is not alone in seeing Italianate inspiration in Marot's post-Ferrara production; neither is Petrarch alone as a subject of imitation for Marot. Even if Marot had petrarchized earlier, his links to Tebaldeo, Serafino, Cariteo,

---

[56] Marot, *Œuvres poétiques*, II, 183–87.

[57] André Gendre, *Évolution du sonnet français* (Paris: Presses universitaires de France, 1996), 32–34. See also my "Clément Marot and the 'Invention' of the French Sonnet."

[58] See Dauvois, *Le sujet lyrique*, 22, and Rouget, "Marot poète lyrique," 574. In his own book-length evangelical reevaluation of the psalm paraphrases, Dick Wursten reads past the poetics of the form in support of the protestant turn. *Clément Marot and Religion: A Reassessment in the Light of his Psalm Paraphrases* (Leiden: Brill, 2010), 357–370.

[59] Mia Cocco, *La Tradizione cortese et il petrarchismo nella poesia di Clément Marot* (Florence: Olschki, 1978).

and Olimpo (not to mention Ovid, Martial, and Virgil) could only have been strengthened and nuanced for the better after a time of apprenticeship in Renée's Italy and proximity to the printing hub that was sixteenth-century Venice.[60] And, the lyrical penchant of Ferrara sojourners Ariosto and Bembo, which would become all the rage for the Pléiade some 15 years later with the publication of the Giolito anthologies,[61] could not help but to have been palpable in the cultural hub that was 1535 Ferrara and to have found their way into Marot's verse.

In many ways, Renée's invitation of Marot to Ferrara marks a turning point in his poetic career. More than a mere parenthesis or inconvenience to wish away, it marks a moment of personal growth and professional development, as a poet much more than as a believer. Marot was no theologian. Marot was not a reformer. Marot was certainly no clergyman. He says as much upon his arrival in Ferrara, justifying his religious curiosity and dispelling claims of heresy in his lengthy but often anthologized "Epitre au roy":

> Bien il est vray, que livres de deffence
> On y trouva : mais cela n'est offence
> A ung Poëte, à qui on doibt lascher
> La bride longue, & rien ne luy cacher,
>
> Soit d'art magicq, nygromance, ou caballe;
> Et n'est doctrine escripte, ne verballe,
> Qu'un vray Poëte au chef ne deust avoir,
> Pour faire bien *d'escripre son debvoir.*[62]

(True though it is that volumes to defend / Are found all 'round, but none shall there offend / A Poet, no, but in their lore confide, / Leave bridles loose, and nothing from him hide, / Of darker arts, magic, kabbalic charm, / All doctrine writ and verbal rites to arm / A Poet true, so it's his right to ask, / To work his craft, *for writing is his task.*)

The duty of the poet is to render in verse the *zeitgeist* of his day, or at least as much as is practicable in a courtly setting. In an era constantly menaced

[60] See Berthon, "L'Invention," 142–44, and Gabriella Scarlatta, *The Disperata from Medieval Italy to Renaissance France* (Kalamazoo, MI: Medieval Institute Publications, 2017), 111.

[61] Joann DellaNeva, *Unlikely Exemplars: Reading and Imitating beyond the Italian Canon in French Renaissance Poetry* (Newark: University of Delaware Press, 2009), 59–62. See also Mayer, Clément Marot, 311.

[62] Marot, *Œuvres poétiques*, II, 84, vv. 135–42, italics added.

by the stake, the juggler of words had a far more daunting task with his quill than the jester and his clubs; it was impossible to be universally pleasing. Henry Guy states it quite well: "Trop luthérien pour Hercule, Marot ne l'était pas assez pour Renée" (Too Lutheran for Ercole, Marot was not quite Lutheran enough for Renée).[63] Too religiously tinged for some (Sagon, la Sorbonne) and not enough for others (Calvin): this summarizes quite well Marot's life after 1534—and even beyond if we account for the posthumous effacement of his funerary monument in Turin.[64] Taken for good or for evil, Marot remained ever a poet—and, yes, his style changed. It became more lyrical and more germane to the Renaissance ideals to be upheld by the Pléiade and generations of poets to follow. In other words, Marot's style changed for the better due to his brief and turbulent stay in Renée de France's *pays italique*.

BIBLIOGRAPHY

PRIMARY SOURCES

Borgia, Lucrezia. 1859. *Lettere di Lucrezia Borgia a Messer Pietro Bembo*. Edited by Bernardo Gatti. Milan: Ambrosiana.
Marot, Clément. 1977. *Les Epîtres*. Edited by Claude A. Mayer. Paris: Nizet.
———. 1990–1993. *Œuvres poétiques*. 2 vols. Edited by Gérard Defaux. Paris: Garnier.
———. 2010. *Recueil inédit offert au Connétable Anne de Montmorency en mars 1538*. Edited by François Rigolot. Geneva: Droz.

SECONDARY SOURCES

Berthon, Guillaume. 2014. *L'Intention du poète, Clément Marot 'autheur'*. Paris: Garnier.
———. 2018. L'invention du blason: Retour sur la genèse d'un genre. In *Anatomie d'une Anatomie: Nouvelles recherches sur les blasons anatomiques du corps féminin*, ed. Julien Goeury and Thomas Hunkeler, 135–154. Geneva: Droz.
Braun, Gabriel. 1988. Le marriage de Renée de France avec Hercule d'Esté: une inutile mésalliance, 28 juin 1528. *Histoire, économie & société* 7 (2): 147–168.

---

[63] Henry Guy, *Marot et son école*, 208.
[64] See Dick Wursten and Jetty Janssen, "New Light on the location of Clément Marot's tomb and epitaph in Turin," *Studi Francesi* 161 (2010): 293–303.

Bullock, Walter. 1924. The First French Sonnets. *Modern Language Notes* 39 (8): 475–478.

Cocco, Mia. 1978. *La Tradizione cortese et il petrarchismo nella poesia di Clément Marot*. Florence: Olschki.

Dauvois, Nathalie. 2000. *Le sujet lyrique à la Renaissance*. Paris: Presses universitaires de France.

Defaux, Gérard. 2006. *Le Poète en son jardin*. Paris: Champion.

Déjean, Jean-Luc. 1990. *Clément Marot*. Paris: Fayard.

DellaNeva, Joann. 2009. *Unlikely Exemplars: Reading and Imitating Beyond the Italian Canon in French Renaissance Poetry*. Newark: University of Delaware Press.

Francis, Scott. 2019. *Advertising the Self in Renaissance France: Lemaire, Marot and Rabelais*. Newark: University of Delaware Press.

Gans, Eric. 1981. Naissance du Moi lyrique. *Poétique* 46: 129–139.

Gendre, André. 1996. *Évolution du sonnet français*. Paris: Presses universitaires de France.

Goeury, Julien, and Thomas Hunkeler, eds. 2018. *Anatomie d'une Anatomie: Nouvelles recherches sur les blasons anatomiques du corps féminin*. Geneva: Droz.

Gorris, Rosanna. 1997. 'Un franzese nominato Clemente': Marot à Ferrare. In *Clément Marot 'Prince des poëtes françois' 1496–1996, Actes du Colloque international de Cahors en Quercy, 1996*, ed. Gérard Defaux and Michel Simonin, 339–364. Paris: Champion.

———. 2006. Va, lettre, va [...] droict à Clément': Lyon Jamet, Sieur de Chambrun, du Poitou à la ville des Este, un itinéraire religieux et existentiel. *Etudes rabelaisiennes* 43: 145–172.

Goyet, Francis, ed. 1990. *Traités de poétique et de rhétorique de la Renaissance*. Paris: Poche.

Guy, Henry. 1926. *Marot et son école*. Paris: Champion.

Hudson, Robert J. 2009. Clément Marot and the 'Invention' of the French Sonnet: Innovating the Lyrical Imperative in Renaissance France. *Anthropoetics* 14 (2) (Winter). http://anthropoetics.ucla.edu.

———. 2014. Bucolic Influence: Marot's Gallic Pastoral and Maurice Scève's *Arion*. *Romanic Review* 105 (3–4): 253–272.

———. 2017. Marot vs. Sagon: Heresy and the Gallic School, 1537. In *Representing Heresy in Early Modern France*, ed. Gabriella Scarlatta and Lidia Radi, 159–187. Toronto: University of Toronto Press.

"Isola e palazzo di Belvedere (scomparsi)." n.d. Biagio Rossetti 500. Accessed January 10, 2019. https://biagiorossetti500.it/architettura/isola-e-palazzo-di-belvedere-scomparsi/.

Mayer, Claude A. 1960. *La Religion de Marot*. Geneva: Droz.

———. 1972. *Clément Marot*. Paris: Nizet.

McClelland, John. 1973. Sonnet ou quatorzain? Marot et le choix d'une forme poétique. *Revue d'Histoire littéraire de la France* 73 (4): 591–607.

Pauphilet, Albert, ed. 1952. *Poètes et Romanciers du Moyen Âge.* Paris: Gallimard.

Peebles, Kelly Digby. 2018. Renée de France's and Clément Marot's Voyages: Political Exile to Spiritual Liberation. *Women in French* Special Issue 7: 33–60.

Preisig, Florian. 2004. *Clément Marot et les metamorphoses de l'auteur à l'aube de la Renaissance.* Geneva: Droz.

Richter, Mario. 1970. Considerazioni et proposte per una storia della poesia lirica francese nel secolo XVI. *Aevum* 44 (1/2): 72–112.

Rigolot, François. 1989. The Sonnet. In *A New History of French Literature*, ed. Denis Hollier, 171–173. Cambridge: Harvard University Press.

Rouget, François. 1997. Marot poète lyrique. In *Clément Marot 'Prince des poëtes françois' 1496–1996, Actes du Colloque international de Cahors en Quercy, 1996*, ed. Gérard Defaux and Michel Simonin, 573–591. Paris: Champion.

Scarlatta, Gabriella. 2017. *The Disperata from Medieval Italy to Renaissance France.* Kalamazoo, MI: Medieval Institute Publications.

Screech, Michael A. 1959. *L'Evangélisme de Rabelais.* Geneva: Droz.

———. 1964. *Il a mangé le lard* (What Marot Said and What Marot Meant). *BHR* 26 (2): 363–364.

———. 1967. *Marot évangélique.* Geneva: Droz.

———. 1993. *Clément Marot, A Renaissance Poet Discovers the Gospel: Lutheranism, Fabrism and Calvinism in the Royal Courts of France and of Navarre and in the Ducal Court of Ferrara.* Leiden: Brill.

The Independent. 1998. Obituary: C. A. Mayer. June 1, 1998.

The Times. 2018. The Rev Professor Michael Screech. July 19, 2018.

Villey, Pierre. 1923. *Marot et Rabelais.* Paris: Champion.

Williams, Annwyl. 1997. Clément Marot, 'Le cler soleil': Intertexte medieval de l'épigramme amoureuse. In *Clément Marot "Prince des poëtes françois" 1496–1996, Actes du Colloque international de Cahors en Quercy, 1996*, ed. Gérard Defaux and Michel Simonin, 201–212. Paris: Champion.

Wursten, Dick. 2010. *Clément Marot and Religion: A Reassessment in the Light of His Psalm Paraphrases.* Leiden: Brill.

Wursten, Dick, and Jetty Janssen. 2010. New Light on the Location of Clément Marot's Tomb and Epitath in Turin. *Studi Francesi* 161 (LIV–II): 293–303.

CHAPTER 7

Between Literature and Religion: Renata di Francia's Literary Network

Gabriella Scarlatta

In his *Discorso della virtù femminile e donnesca*, Torquato Tasso (1544–1599) debates the merits, virtues, and vices of women.[1] Dedicated to Eleonora of Austria, the Duchess of Mantova,[2] the *Discorso* offers Eleonora several examples of virtuous women, such as Mary of Austria, Margaret of Austria, Elizabeth I, and Catherine de Medici. The author also praises the women of the house of Este, "una casa da cui bellissime signore sono uscite e bellissime ci son maritate [...]." (A house from which came very beautiful ladies, and in which very beautiful ones married).[3] But

---

[1] "Discorso della virtù femminile e donnesca," (Venice: Bernardo Giunti, 1582). On Tasso's discourse, see Fabio Boni, "La riflessione di Torquato Tasso sulla donna nel 'Discorso della virtù femminile e donnesca,'" in *Annales Universitatis Paedagogicae Cracoviensis, Studia de Cultura* 9, no. 1 (2017): 215–222.

[2] Daughter of Ferdinand I, Holy Roman Emperor (House of Habsburg).

[3] And continues "nondimeno agguaglia con la sua bellezza non sole le quattro bellisime signore ch'ora in questa casa risplendono, ma la fama e la memoria ancora di tutte l'antiche, la virtù delle quali cosìbene adegua, che non può Alfonso invidiar felicità di moglie ad alcuno

---

G. Scarlatta (✉)
University of Michigan–Dearborn, Dearborn, MI, USA
e-mail: geschric@umich.edu

© The Author(s), under exclusive license to Springer Nature
Switzerland AG 2021
K. D. Peebles, G. Scarlatta (eds.), *Representing the Life and Legacy of Renée de France*, Queenship and Power,
https://doi.org/10.1007/978-3-030-69121-9_7

most importantly, he draws Eleonora's attention to her sister-in-law, Renée de France, to Renée's daughters Anna, Lucrezia, and Eleonora, and to her niece, Marguerite de France, Duchess of Savoie:[4]

> Chi vorrà anco nelle donne eroiche non sol la virtù dell'azione, ma quella della contemplazione, si rammenti di Renata di Ferrara e di Margherita di Savoia, dell'una e dell'altra delle quali mio padre mi soleva le meraviglie raccontare; e Anna e Lucrezia e Leonora, che di Renata sono nate, tali sono nell'intelligenza delle cose di Stato e nel giudizio delle lettere, che niuno che l'ode favellare si può da lor partire se non pieno di altissimo stupore.
>
> (In heroic women, who wants to find not only the virtue of actions but also that of contemplation, one must remember Renata of Ferrara and Marguerite of Savoia, whose wonders my father would describe to me; and of Anna, Lucrezia, and Eleonora, Renata's daughters, who are equally smart in matters of State and judgment in matters of letters, and no one who hears them speak can part from them without extreme amazement.)

In this passage, Tasso stresses two virtues in particular: acumen in matters of State and good judgment in matters of letters. Throughout her years in Italy, many would come to recognize and acknowledge these two important qualities not only in Renée de France herself, but also at her court in Ferrara. Between 1530 and 1570, amidst the dissent and controversial allegiances, the complex politico-religious negotiations caused by the Reformation and the Counter-Reformation in general and the French Wars of Religion in particular, the relationship between religion and literature became increasingly tangled. If spiritual questions were central to Medieval and Renaissance thought and preoccupations, including artistic and literary production, they were even more central to women's lives, whose worth was often measured according to their "religiosity" and their

suo antecessore" (and not only with her beauty she equals the other very beautiful ladies that brighten this House, but also her fame and memory equal those of all other ladies before her, whose virtue she also adapts, so that Alfonso cannot envy the wife of any of his ancestors). Referring to Alfonso II d'Este, son of Ercole II and Renée de France, Tasso wants to praise his wife, Margherita da Gonzaga, the Duchess of Ferrara, and daughter precisely of Eleonora and Guglielmo da Gonzaga. Translations throughout from both Italian and French are my own.

[4] To Anna, Lucrezia, and Eleonora, Tasso also dedicated poems, such as "Alle figlie di Renata."

Christian virtues, such as chastity and piety.[5] In the case of Renée de France and her sister, Claude de France, they learned early on the influence of the Church and its long-reaching religious and secular power. Their own mother, Anne, Duchesse de Bretagne, "bequeathed her pious regard for the Church and the understanding of its crucial social role" to her daughters, as Kathleen Wilson-Chevalier notes.[6] However, their conception of the Church as a spiritual and moral guide would significantly evolve during the adult life of the French princess and duchess.

This chapter focuses on the intersections of religion and literature at Renée's court in Ferrara, a space that was particularly receptive to debates over matters of faith and spirituality, both reformed opinions and traditional Church dogmas. These debates produced literary models whose consumption and circulation were constantly evolving and closely epitomized the literary production surrounding Renée and her court.[7] Writers sought to educate the young *fille de France-turned-Duchessa*, as well as to praise her position and virtues in order not only to secure her patronage, but also to influence and win over the loyalty of her female entourage. In fact, this chapter discusses four texts in which rhymes, faith, and the rhetoric of persuasion are closely interwoven.[8] Gianbattista Giraldi Cinzio's sonnet "Donna, che togli con gentil costume," Bernardo Zane's sonnet "Alla Signora Madama & Duchessa di Ferrara Reniera da Este," Suor Girolama Castellani's canzone "Pensier, che pur mi desti all'alta impresa," and Orazio Brunetto's dedication "Al'illustrissima et Eccellentissima Signora Renata di Francia Duchessa di Ferrara" in his *Lettere di Horatio Brunetto* represent an example of diverse textual production in which liter-

---

[5] See for example Renée de France's portrait in Giuseppe Betussi and Brantôme's works in Gabriella Scarlatta "Gender, Power, and Sexuality in Betussi's and Brantôme's *Illustrious Women*," *Royal Studies Journal* 6, no.2 (2019): 61–73, and Juan Luis Vives, *The Education of a Christian Woman: A Sixteenth-Century Manual*, ed. and trans. Charles Fantazzi (Chicago: The University of Chicago Press, 2000).

[6] "Claude de France: In her Mother's Likeness, a Queen with Symbolic Clout?," in *The Cultural and Political Legacy of Anne de Bretagne. Negotiating convention in Books and Documents*, ed. Cynthia J. Brown (Suffolk: Brewer, 2010), 123–144, 129. See also her Chap. 2 in this volume.

[7] See the introduction to *The Oxford Handbook of Early Modern English Literature and Religion*, ed. Helen Wilcox and Andrew Wilcox (Oxford: Oxford University Press, 2017), xxvii–xxx.

[8] For a background on the Reformation and its impact on women in power, see Nancy L. Roelker, "The Appeal of Calvinism to French Noblewomen in the Sixteenth Century," *The Journal of Interdisciplinary History* 2, no. 4 (1972): 391–481.

ary, religious, and political concerns intersect. It is not by chance that most of the writings dedicated to Renée, as well as those written explicitly about her, have a religious inflection. Indeed, following a well-established and long-standing tradition all the way up to the Reformation, most religious texts were available to well-born women. However, with the new wave of religious conflicts and ensuing political allegiances, the ground shifted and thus, most became not only taboo, but altogether censored by the Church as early as 1543,[9] thus rendering their reading problematic for learned women.

RENÉE'S ARRIVAL AND COURT IN FERRARA

When on June 28, 1528, Renée de France, the daughter of King Louis XII and Anne de Bretagne, married Ercole d'Este, the future Duke of Ferrara, Modena, and Reggio, it was her brother-in-law, King François I, who negotiated her marriage contract. François I, the husband of Claude de France, Renée's sister, was motivated by an alliance with the Dukes of Este in order to forge a strong coalition and secure a French presence south of the Alps. He was also motivated by a geo-political interest in securing for the crown the territories in Brittany bequeathed to Renée by her mother.[10] Indeed, as part of her dowry, Renée was assured the revenue from these territories, which would allow her to remain somewhat financially independent throughout her life.[11]

Upon her arrival in Ferrara in late 1528, Renée's personal secretary Bernardo Tasso, father of the aforementioned Torquato, was the only

---

[9] See Lodovica Braida, "Libri di lettere all'Indice. Censura, autocensura ed espurgazione delle raccolte epistolari nel XVI secolo," in *Cartas-Lettres-Lettere: discursos, practicas y representaciones epistolares (siglos XIV–XX)*, ed. Antonio Castillo Gómez and Véronica Sierra Blas (Alcalá de Henares: UAH, 2014), 331–348, 333. https://dialnet.unirioja.es/servlet/libro?codigo=561300.

[10] For more on Anne de Bretagne, see *The Cultural and Political Legacy of Anne de Bretagne, The Queen's Library. Image-Making at the Court of Anne of Brittany, 1477–1514*, ed. Cynthia J. Brown (Philadelphia: University of Pennsylvania Press, 2011), and Eleonora Belligni, *Renata di Francia (1510–1575) Un'eresia di corte* (Turin: UTET, 2011), 3–12.

[11] At the same time, though, this independence caused her additional hardships with the Kings of France. See Gabriel Braun, "Le mariage de Renée de France avec Hercule d'Esté: une inutile mésalliance. 28 juin 1528," *Histoire, économie et société* 7, no. 2 (1988): 147–168, and Caroline zum Kolk, "Les difficultés des mariages internationaux: Renée de France et Hercule d'Este," *Femmes et pouvoir politique. Les princesses d'Europe, XVe-XVIIIe siècle* (Rosny-sous-Bois, France: Bréal, 2007), 102–119.

Italian in her intimate circle. The new duchess was accompanied by a large and influential entourage of about 126 French nationals, including the reformed Michelle de Saubonne, Baronne de Soubise, who had been Anne de Bretagne's *dame d'honneur* and Renée's governess during her early childhood. Together with two of her daughters and son, Madame de Soubise settled in Ferrara and ensured that Renée maintained her French ties, manners, fashions, and even language, causing concerns as to whether the new duchess would ever learn to fit in and love her husband's country. Madame de Soubise remained an unfortunate "third wheel" between Renée and the duke, until he finally sent her back to France in 1536.[12] Most importantly, what followed Renée to Italy was a female legacy of power and intellectual affluence, what Nancy L. Roelker labels "the entourage factor," that is, a circle of noblewomen who believed in the supremacy of education and of reciprocal feminine support.[13] As Charmarie Blaisdell notes, "mature women at the French court had an extraordinary and powerful influence on the lives of the younger women in their circles."[14] Renée and her sister Claude came from a strong and powerful female environment, with a tradition born in the House of Bourbon with Anne de France de Beaujeu and her daughter, Suzanne de Bourbon, and in Anne de Bretagne's and Louise de Savoie's courts.[15] She had already forged a strong alliance with Marguerite de Navarre and Marguerite de Savoie, with whom she closely collaborated in sponsoring the arts and literature, and in protecting the religiously persecuted at their courts.[16]

---

[12] See Jules Bonnet, "Disgrâce de M et Mme de Pons à la cour de Ferrare 1544–1545," *Bulletin historique littéraire/Société de l'histoire du protestantisme français* 29, no. 1 (1880): 3–17. Her entourage also included the reformed family of Boussirons, Tanguy du Bouchet, Bejarry de la Guimeniere, and others but also German and Swiss scholars, such as Andreas Grünthler, Olimpia Morata's future husband, and Kilian Sinapius. See Belligni, *Renata di Francia*, 88–89, and Rosanna Gorris Camos, "'Donne ornate di scienza e di virtù': donne e francesi alla corte di Renata di Francia," *Schifanoia* 28–29 (2005): 175–205, 179.

[13] Blaisdell, "Marguerite de Navarre and her Circle (1492–1549)," *Female Scholars: A Tradition of Learned Women Before 1800*, ed. J.R. Brink (Montréal: Eden Press, 1980), 36–53, 37. See also Chap. 2 by Wilson-Chevalier.

[14] Roelker, "The Role of Noblewomen in the French Reformation,"*Archiv für Reformationsgeschichte*, 63 (1973): 168–195, 173.

[15] See Elodie Lequain, "La maison de Bourbon, 'escolle de vertu et de perfection': Anne de France, Suzanne de Bourbon, et Pierre Martin," *Médiévales*, 48 (2005): 1–15.

[16] Scholars have already noted the interesting parallels between the two French relatives-neighbors, Renata and Marguerite de Savoie, who had a similar background and tolerant nature. Blaisdell states, "the liberal atmosphere at court when they were growing up, Marguerite's influence as a second mother and their marriages to husbands who vigorously

Once in her duchy, Renée became an important evangelical figure upon whom many looked not only for protection, but also as a guide and as an ally to help spread the new reformed ideas.

RENATA'S CATHOLIC AND REFORMED NETWORK

Renata or Renea, as her circle of Italian intimates would call her, lived a courageous life amidst accusations of heresy and physical threats for protecting many interested in Church reform and exiled fellow citizens such as the poet Clément Marot, who arrived in Ferrara in April 1535, seeking asylum after the *Affaire des Placards*.[17] Jean Calvin himself[18] sojourned at Renata's palace sometime in 1536, and dedicated to her his *Christianae Religionis Institutio* (1536).[19]

In Ferrara and in her nearby palace in Consandolo, a present from Ercole in 1540, she succeeded in instituting a lively, mix-gendered, and tolerant court whose friendliness toward the religiously persecuted was perhaps one of its main strengths. After all, a climate of religious tolerance toward the Jews had already been present in Ferrara for centuries, nurtured by the dukes of Ferrara's tradition of liberality.[20] At the same time though, this collectivity demanded of the duchess her full patronage and discretion, thus, at times endangering her safety and damaging her reputation with the orthodox Catholic community and her husband, despite the privileged position deriving from her financial independence and presti-

---

persecuted heresy influenced their moderate stance toward the Reform." "Marguerite de Navarre and her Circle," 47.

[17] On the *Affaire des Placards*, see Mayer, *Clément Marot* (Paris: Nizet, 1972); on Marot and Ferrara, see Rosanna Gorris, "Un franzese nominato Clemente": Marot à Ferrare," in *Clément Marot "Prince des poëtes françois" 1496–1996, Actes du Colloque international de Cahors en Quercy 21–25 mai 1996*, ed. Gérard Defaux and Michel Simonin (Paris: Champion, 1997), and Kelly Digby Peebles, "Renée de France's and Clément Marot's Voyages: Political Exile to Spiritual Liberation," in *Women in French Studies* Special issue 7 (2018): 33–60.

[18] Supposedly under the pseudonym Charles d'Espeville.

[19] Renata and Calvin would also maintain a regular correspondence until his death in 1564. For Renée's relationship with Calvin, see Blaisdell, "Calvin's Letters to Women: The Courting of Ladies in High Places," in *Sixteenth Century Journal*, 13, no. 3 (1982): 67–84; Leonardo De Chirico and Daniel Walker, *Giovanni Calvino, Renata di Francia. Lealtà in tensione. Un carteggio protestante tra Ferrara e l'Europa (1537–1564)* (Caltanisetta, IT, Alfa & Omega, 2009); and Peebles's and Dick Wursten's chapters in this volume.

[20] See Marianna D. Birnbaum, "Jewish Patronage in Sixteenth-Century Ferrara," *Mediterranean Studies* 7 (1988): 135–141, and Luciano Chiappini, *La Corte Estense alla metà del Cinquecento. I compendi di Cristoforo di Messisbugo* (Ferrara: S.A.T.E., 1984), 17.

gious lineage, which undoubtedly gave her a privileged position. In turn, this independence allowed her to maintain a certain insularity and freedom to foster her own court which, as Chiara Franceschini has convincingly argued, was characterized by a remarkable patronage financed in part by the revenue from her French territories, but also by the expectations generated by her very presence in Italy which grew as her husband and the Genevan and Roman authorities tightened their control on the duchess and her circle.[21]

"THE LITERARY" AT RENATA'S COURT

Renata's financial independence and prestigious lineage thus offered both material support and social connections to her intimate entourage and her court, which had a reputation of being a true "scuola femminile" as Franceschini calls it,[22] particularly driven by women's interests and enlivened by her three daughters Anna, Lucrezia, and Eleonora, who learned and lived alongside women of great intellectual talents, such as Olimpia Morata, Margherita Brasavola, Françoise de Boussiron, Catherine de Panniers, and the Parthenay sisters, Madame de Soubise's daughters.[23] Furthermore, the Este duchesses that preceded Renata, including her mother-in-law, Lucrezia Borgia, and before her, Ercole II's grandmother, Eleonora d'Aragona, had already instituted powerful courts in which women exercised a considerable role and vast influence. I would argue that this Ferrarese tradition of strong matriarchs provided the new duchess with a "second entourage factor," to borrow Roelker's term.[24]

---

[21] Franceschini, "'*Literarum studia nobis communia*': Olimpia Morata e la corte di Renata di Francia," in *Schifanoia* 28–29 (2005); 207–232, 208.

[22] See Franceschini, "le aspettative suscitate dalla sua presenza in Italia, che crebbero di pari passo al progressivo controllo esercitato sulla vita della sua corte, del duca Ercole II, di Roma, di Ginevra." In "*Literarum studia nobis communia*," 208.

[23] A model of school for royal and elite women, with which Renée was already familiar, like Anne de France's. See Zita Rohr, "Rocking the Cradle and Ruling the World: Queens' Households in Late Medieval and Early Modern Aragon and France," in *Royal and Elite Households in Medieval and Early Modern Europe. More than Just a Castle*, ed. Theresa Earenfight (Boston: Brill, 2018), 309–337.

[24] See Werner L. Gundersheimer, "Women, Learning, and Power: Eleonora of Aragon and the Court of Ferrara," in *Beyond their Sex. Learned Women of the European Past*, ed. Patricia H. Labalme (New York: New York University Press, 1985), 43–65, and Diane Y. Ghirardo, "Lucrezia Borgia as Entrepreneur," *Renaissance Quarterly* 61 (2008): 53–91.

Renata's "school" was also praised by several literati, and it grew to be considered as a veritable academy by some of her Italian contemporaries thanks to the rigorous intellectual activities of creation and translation that took place therein.[25] It was at Renata's court that Clément Marot organized the famous *concours du beau tétin*, whose winning poet would be crowned by Renata herself. The *concours* invited French poets to write a *blason* in praise of the woman's body, in order to fashion a collection of *blasons du corps féminin*.[26] Rosanna Gorris argues that the *concours* made of Ferrara, "un vero e proprio centro di irradiazione poetica e di elaborazione di modelli letterari che vivacizzano la letteratura francese dell'epoca, un luogo dove avviene una felicissima 'rencontre des Muses', francesi e italiane" (A true center of poetic propagation and of elaboration of new literary models that vitalized French literature at the time; a place in which a fortunate French and Italian "meeting of the Muses" took place.)[27] The Franco-Ferrarese connection strengthened by Renata's presence was indeed an important phenomenon that greatly enriched the literary output of both countries during the sixteenth century. It also created a continuum in the two literatures, thereby sparking their mutual inspiration already well steeped in parallel traditions and cultural affinities.[28] The work of Ludovico Ariosto, one of the greatest Ferrarese authors of the time, for example, was vastly circulated and translated in France.[29] Several French

[25] Franceschini, "*Literarum studia nobis communia*," 211–212. See also Gorris, "Donne ornate di scienza e di virtù," as well as Belligni, *Renata di Francia*, in particular chapters 2–4.

[26] On this occasion, Marot wrote his "Blason du beau tétin," but it was actually Maurice Scève's blason "Le sourcil" that won the contest. See Mario Roffi, "Un concorso di poesia francese a Ferrara alla corte estense di Renata di Francia," *The Renaissance in Ferrara and its European Horizon*, ed. J. Salmon (Cardiff, UK: University of Wales Press, 1984), 263–269, and Guillaume Berthon, "L'Invention du blason: Retour sur la genèse d'un genre (Ferrare, 1535), in *Anatomie d'une anatomie, Nouvelles recherches sur les blasons anatomiques du corps féminin*, ed. Julien Goeury and Thomas Hunkeler (Geneva: Droz, 2018), 135–156. Furthermore, this *concours* and the stay in Ferrara overall marked important moments in Marot's career as he wrote his *épitres* and *blasons*, thereby launching "la mode des blasons," as François Rigolot notes in *Clément Marot Recueil inédit offert au Connétable de Montmorency en mars 1538*, ed. François Rigolot (Geneva: Droz, 2010), 158, and *Anatomie d'une anatomie* and Robert Hudson's and Guillaume Berthon's chapters in this volume.

[27] Gorris, "Donne ornate di scienza e di virtù," 182.

[28] See Enea Balmas, "Ferrara e la Francia nel XVI secolo: uno sguardo d'insieme," in *Alla corte degli Estensi, Filosofia, arte e cultura a Ferrara nei secoli XV e XVI*, ed. Marco Bertozzi (Ferrara: Università degli Studi, 1994), 355–364, 359.

[29] See Alessandro Cioranescu, *L'Arioste en France des origines à la fin du XVIIIe siècle* (Paris: Champion, 1939), and Gorris, "'Je veux chanter d'amour la tempeste e l'orage':

students also attended the university in Ferrara—*lo Studio*—where the local presence of a French princess loomed large and further fostered the intellectual and political exchanges between the two countries.[30]

DIVERSITY AT COURT

When considering the active intellectuals at Renata's court, what strikes the most is their religious diversity: from Catholics to Protestants, orthodox Catholics, Spirituals, and Nicodemites, her court was moved by a spirit of tolerance and openness to new ideas and doctrines, which went hand in hand with new literary tastes and initiatives, such as Gianbattista Giraldi Cinzio's experimentation with theater and Marot's poetry contest, to name but a few.[31]

From the 1530s to the 1550s in particular, Renata's cosmopolitan circle included several French poets, such as Marot and Lyon Jamet, while Italian literati included Lilio Gregorio Giraldi, Gianbattista Giraldi Cinzio, Olimpia Morata, Vittoria Colonna, Giulio Calcagnini, Nascimbene Nascimbeni, Antonio Brucioli, and Ercole Bentivoglio, who, in 1540, founded the Accademia degli Elevati, which was followed by the Accademia dei Filareti. This "shadow court"[32] sponsored as many as thirty literati from different backgrounds and beliefs, as Renata's account books testify,[33] constituting undoubtedly the court's very strength and vitality. As P. R. Horne has convincingly argued, all factions were tolerant because

---

Desportes et les *Imitations* de l'Arioste," in *Philippe Desportes (1546–1606) Un poète presque parfait entre Renaissance et Classicisme*, ed. Jean Balsamo (Paris: Klincksieck, 2000), 173–211.

[30] Balmas points to the correspondence of Dominique de Gabre, a military chief and later French ambassador to Venice, who provides many details about the Franco-Ferrarese connection. See *Correspondance politique de Dominique du Gabre, évêque de Lodève, trésorier des armées à Ferrare (1552–1554), ambassadeur de France à Venise (1554–1557)*, ed. Alexandre Vitalis (Paris: Champion, 1903).

[31] For more on the different religious affiliations, see Belligni, *Renata di Francia*, 150–239.

[32] Or "a court within the court," "Una corte nella corte," as Belligni calls it, *Renata di Francia*, 93.

[33] See Belligni, *Renata di Francia*, "Attorno a Ferrara e alla corte estense avevano scritto e insegnato tutti gli umanisti della generazione post-ariostea, che avevano avuto benefici o contatti con Renata in maniera indiretta," 315. For the literary and religious figures in Renata's circle in particular, see pages 315–319.

their humanistic ideas not only guided their pursuits, but also taught them compassion toward each other.[34]

Of this diverse and dynamic group, I will focus on four Italian writers to illustrate how Renata was regarded and praised by the literary elite, starting with Giraldi (1504–1573), Ercole II's official playwright.[35] His collection of poems, *Le Fiamme*, published in 1548, is dedicated to Ercole II and includes a sonnet in honor of Renata.[36] Giraldi was an orthodox Catholic and a regular presence at the duchess's court whose admiration toward her is clearly expressed in the following poem:

> Donna, che togli con gentil costume
> La luce a Phebo si, che col felice
> Vivo splendor, come di noi Beatrice,
> Par che di parte, in parte il mondo allume;
>
> Al tuo chiaro, sereno, eterno lume,
> Sotto lasciando'l mio stato infelice,
> (Per rinovarmi in te come Phenice)
> Spiego queste mie stanche, audaci piume.
>
> Non torcer da me dunque'l lume raro
> De tuoi be raggi, ma perfetta prova
> Mostra qui, che'l puoi far del tuo valore:
>
> Che se'n te'l mio pensier hor si rinova,
> Si dirà poi che non ha, od hebbe Amore
> Di te nel regno suo spirto piu chiaro.

(My lady, who, with gentle ways, steals / Phoebus's light, so that with a merry / Lively splendor, as did Beatrice for us, it appears that / From one side to the other, the world illuminates. / Toward your clear, serene, eternal light / Leaving behind my unfortunate state, / (So as to renew myself in

---

[34] P. R. Horne, "Reformation and Counter-Reformation at Ferrara: Antonio Musa Brasavola and Giambattista Cinthio Giraldi," *Italian Studies* 13, no. 1 (1958): 62–82, 78. Horne notes, for example, that Brasavola was an intellectual whose tolerance "springs also from his recognition that the Catholic Church is itself partly responsible, through the immorality of its ministers, for the Protestant revolt." 74. See also Chiappini, *La Corte Estense*, 24.

[35] Moreover, his first tragedy *Orbecche* includes a preface "La tragedia a chi legge" which he dedicated to Renata. Venice, Aldo, 1543. The tragedy was represented for the first time at court in 1541 and is considered "the prototype Italian horror-tragedy." See Horne, "Reformation and Counter-Reformation at Ferrara," 62 and Marzia Pieri's chapter in this volume.

[36] *Le Fiamme di M. Giovan-Battista Giraldi Cinthio Nobile Ferrarese*, Venice, Gabriel Giolito, 1548.

you as a Phoenix) / I spread these feathers of mine, tired and daring. / Do not deprive me of the rare light / Of your beautiful rays, / but show here the perfect proof / Of your valor, of which you are capable: / So that, if in you my thought is now renewed, / It will be said that Love does not have, nor ever had / A brighter spirit than you in its kingdom.)

Here, alluding to Dante's Beatrice, a spiritual guide who brightened the way for the lost poet, Giraldi depicts Renata as the most brilliant and lively lady of her husband's court, under whose protection the poet-persona can find comfort and renew his spirit. Just as the phoenix, symbol of renewal, he finds new and meaningful life in his muse, a symbolic play on her name Re-nata.[37] Begging her to continue to bestow upon him her beautiful light, as the "brightest star in Love's reign," a light that welcomes and convenes around her all tiresome and unhappy souls, he portrays her as the heart and life of those around her, a spotlight whose radiance is vital and restoring.[38] Renata is indeed featured as one of Giraldi's "fiamme" in his poetic celestial firmament, whose role is to give and renew life in those who surround her. The poet's role in praising his patron's wife is manifest, but this sonnet points as well to a sincere and respectful admiration for Renata who provides inspiration to the poet-playwright, further validating the importance of his function at the Este court. In likening her to Beatrice, who provides guidance and salvation to Dante, Renata provides re-birth, a renewed life as a phoenix, and light to the poet. Indeed, she bestows radiance to all who surround her. Thus, just as Dante who plays on Beatrice's name, Giraldi shows his dexterity by composing verses in which Re-nata's presence and role heighten the lyric tenor of his poem. As we shall soon see, Renata's portrayal as light and guide is a common theme to all four texts examined in this essay.

The second poem I examine by Cavalier Bernardo Zane, the Bishop of Spalatro, is a sonnet dedicated to the "Illustrissima Duchessa di Ferrara Reniera da Este." The opening quatrain crafts a compelling metaphor that

---

[37] The phoenix is a recurring figure in Giraldi's work, as Gorris has highlighted. See "Tragedia come apologo della crudeltà: il caso di *Orbecc-Oronte*," *Studi di letteratura francese* 18 (1992): 48–71. For more on Giraldi's theater, see Marzia Pieri's contribution in this volume. It is also a common theme in emblem books and in the poetry of other Renaissance poets.

[38] Renata was also portrayed in Giraldi's epic poem *Ercole* (1557) as the honest wife, "the chaste, and august Renata/whom the great king bestowed to you as wife." *Dell'Ercole canti ventisei* (Modena: Cornelio Gadaldini, 1557), 121 and 138.

stages the coupling of two fertile rivers, the Po and the Seine, and the coupling of the white eagle and the *fleur de lys*, the coat of arms of the Este and of the kings of France, respectively. As the waters of the two rivers meet and merge, so do the two powerful houses of Este and Valois, in order to produce a strong, crucial, geo-political alliance. Ercole appears as a valiant and strong hero who protects his bride from those who threaten her safety; indeed, the poet notes that he is responsible for a branch of the French king's *fleur de lys* as the father of the new Este-Valois progeniture. Furthermore, Zane addressed a sonnet to Ercole II as well, which precedes Renata's in his book of *Rime*, thus forging a textual alliance of the two spouses as an additional reminder that Renata was an integral part of the Este family.

Contrary to standard historical accounts,[39] the Estes are depicted as a tight, unwavering couple, rare in their happiness, "Felice coppia forse al mondo rara," which holds on to each other's emblem, "Hercole del Tuo Giglio intero ha un ramo / E tu il bianco Augello intero godi" (Ercole of your whole *Fleur de lys* holds a branch, / And you, you enjoy the whole white Bird). Ercole appears as a strong warrior, defending not only his bride, but also her entire family and interests. Moreover, the dynastic unity herein portrayed is crucial to the couple and the duchy and greatly emphasizes the importance of the alliance for each of the spouses.[40] The poet-persona seems particularly preoccupied with the success of their union and happiness as a central nexus not only for the two powerful dynasties, but also for Italy and the Church.

"Alla Signora Madama & Duchessa di Ferrara Reniera da Este"
Ben ti puoi gloriar superbo fiume
Poscia per sposa hai la gran Senna presa
Hor si che la Tua fama è al ciel' ascesa
& più chiaro del sole hor godi il lume
Ecco non men che le temute piume
Il bianco Augel dispiega alla diffesa
Di Te, del Gal, del Giglio e dell'offesa
Ti serba di chi'l danno suo prosume

---

[39] See Belligni, *Renata di Francia*, 132–149.

[40] As a princess, Renée was taught early on the importance of kinship and hierarchy, including the intricacies of the house of Este: see Tracy Adams, "Rivals or Friends? Anne de France and Anne de Bretagne," in *Women in French*, Special Issue (2010): 46–61.

Hercole del Tuo Giglio intero ha un ramo
E tu il bianco Augello intero godi
Felice coppia forse al mondo rara
Ambi vi prego poi ch'io tanto vi amo
E che'l Giglio e l'Augel in mille modi
Canto ch'abbiate la mia fede cara.

("To the illustrious Madame and Duchess of Ferrara Reniera da Este" You can glorify yourself well, superb river, / Since you have taken the great Seine in marriage. / Now Your fame has risen to the sky for sure, / And brighter than the sun, you enjoy the light. / Here, nothing less than its fearsome feathers, / The white Bird spreads them to defend / You, the Rooster, and the *Fleur de lys*, and from offense / It protects you from those who mean to harm you. / Ercole of your whole *Fleur de lys* holds a branch, / And you, you enjoy the whole white Bird. / Happy couple perhaps rare in the world / I pray you both, since I love you so, / Both the *Fleur de lys* and the Bird, in a thousand ways, / I sing that you hold my faith dear.)[41]

Here too, Renata is celebrated as a light, brighter than the sun, benefiting and nurturing the Po River and the surrounding duchy of Ferrara: "& più chiaro del sole hor godi il lume" (and brighter than the sun, you enjoy the light).

The poem concludes with a prayer that begs the couple to preserve its unity and the speaker's faith: "Canto ch'abbiate la mia fede cara" (I sing that you hold my faith dear). Clearly, the whole sonnet is pervaded by religious preoccupations that urge the Estes to remain a united safe keeper of the faith. We might conclude that Zane, the bishop of Spalatro, was referring to the Catholic faith, of which Ercole was a good representative and defender. However, Zane was very active in the Venetian literary scene and was close to *poligrafi* such as Gabriel Giolito, Antonio Brucioli, and Lodovico Domenichi, whom Renata knew as well, and who openly leaned toward reform. The poem and its writer's background leave the reader with thought-provoking questions regarding religious alliances and motives, underlining once again the close interweaving of literature and politics.

---

[41] *Rime volgari del Cavalier Zani nelle quali si contengono le lodi, nomi, cognomi, e titoli de grandi e grande d'Europa: a lingua dolosa* (Venice: n.p., 1555), no page numbers. Not much is known about Zane, but three of his poems were also printed in the fourth book *Delle rime di diversi nobilissimi et eccellentissimi autori*, ed. Andrea Arrivabene (Venice: n.p., 1550).

Ludovico Domenichi's 1559 groundbreaking anthology of women poets *Rime diverse d'alcune nobilissime, et virtuosissime donne* contains a poem by Suor Girolama Castellani dedicated to Renata, which is the third poem I examine.[42] A nun educated by her uncle Tommaso Castellani, also a writer, Suor Castellani penned her *canzone* "Pensier, che pur mi desti a l'alta impresa" within the walls of the convent of San Giovanni in Bologna, not too far from Ferrara. Suor Castellani, the only nun included in Domenichi's anthology, was able to pursue her studies and writing while looking to the nearby Este duchess for spiritual support and artistic patronage.[43] In a similar vein, Castellani also wrote a sonnet to Renata's sister-in-law, Eleonora d'Este (1515–1575), the Abbess of the nearby Corpus Domini convent, because, as Elisabetta Graziosi notes, Suor Castellani turned to Ferrara as a notable center of patronage fostered by strong female rulers, from Eleonora d'Aragona to Lucrezia Borgia and now to Renata, who inherited a well-established legacy of patronage and who championed monasteries throughout her duchy.[44] Renata continued this tradition by also becoming a patron for monasteries, which demonstrates her commitment on behalf of the Este dynasty and to its legacy.

One of the striking characteristics of Domenichi's anthology is the frequency with which women address women, or with which women dedicate poetry to other women. In fact, among the fifty-three women authors, thirty-five dedicate or address their compositions to another woman, including Castellani,[45] who seeks to construct her own female audience and community, and acknowledges and validates her female readership and friendship beyond the convent's seclusion. Castellani's *canzone* embodies her literary and spiritual journey from San Giovanni to Renata's

---

[42] Published in Lucca, by Busdrago, 1559. The *canzone* is on pages 64–66 of the anthology. See also Appendix A.

[43] See Elisabetta Graziosi, "Due domenicane poetesse, una nota, una ignota e molte sullo sfondo," in *Il velo, la penna, e la parola*, ed. Gabriella Zarri and Gianni Festa (Florence: Netbini, 2009), 163–177, 171–172. Graziosi notes that Bologna was an important city in the creation and dissemination of monastic poetry, as another anthology had already been published in 1525, the *Devotissime compositioni*, in which also appeared other poems by Suor Castellani, 164–165, "uno dei centri del protagonismo femminile," 169.

[44] For the sonnet, see Domenichi, *Rime diverse d'alcune nobilissime, et virtuosissime donne*, 62. Lucrezia Borgia is buried in the Corpus Domini monastery. See Gabriella Zarri, *La Religione di Lucrezia Borgia. Le lettere inedite del confessore* (Rome: Comitato nazionale incontri di studio per il centenario del pontificato di Alessandro VI, 2006).

[45] See Gabriella Scarlatta, "Women Writing Women in Lodovico Domenichi's Anthology of 1559," *Quaderni d'Italianistica* 30, no. 2 (2009): 67–85.

court, featuring a series of well-crafted images and metaphors that pay
tribute to "Renea Estense," whose "pregio alto, & gentile" (high and
noble merit) greatly moves and inspires her.[46] Starting with the first verse
and throughout the *canzone*, the poetic persona addresses her lady in distinct Petrarchan language and style, fully befitting the Italian lyric tradition, whereby the poet-lover portrays and worships the beloved, the object
of her desire, in this case a woman of much higher rank. As Konrad
Eisenbichler has shown, this type of same-sex expression was formulated
within the well-established Petrarchan lyric tradition, voicing feelings that
had by then become quite commonplace.[47] For example, the speaker
praises Renata's beautiful features, laments her physical absence, and sings
her unique virtues in humble verses:

> Et vuoi, che'n basso stile
> Canti, e in roze parole
> Le lodi al mondo sole
> Di Renea Estense, e il pregio alto, & gentile[48]

(You want that I, in simple style / And in coarse words, sing / To the world,
the praises of the one and only / Renata Estense, and of her high and
kind merit)

Moved by a "desire ardente" (ardent desire),[49] she pays tributes to her
cherished idol, "il caro Idolo mio," and laments painful feelings caused by
her distance.[50] Passion and emotions are clearly articulated by the poet-
nun throughout her *canzone*, as a spiritual longing for Renata, who is
portrayed as her intellectual soul mate. The duchess's approbation and
friendship are the object of a distinctly articulated desire.

However, in concluding her *canzone*, the poetic persona turns to preoccupations of faith, and urges her own thought to show Renata the truth,
"Scopri a Madonna intieramente il vero," at the culmination of its

---

[46] Domenichi, *Rime diverse*, 64.
[47] Konrad Eishenbichler, "Laudomia Forteguerri Loves Margaret of Austria," in *Same Sex Love and Desire among Women in the Middle Ages*, ed. Francesca Canadé Sautman and Pamela Sheingorn (New York: Palgrave, 2001), 277–304, 289.
[48] Domenichi, *Rime diverse*, 64.
[49] Domenichi, *Rime diverse*, 64.
[50] Domenichi, *Rime diverse*, 65.

journey.[51] Just as Zane, who asked Renata to protect his faith, here too, Suor Castellani interweaves in her poem the themes of dynasty and faith, and their inextricable connection by boldly reaching out of her convent walls to exhort an educated woman of a much higher rank and status than herself to recognize and acknowledge the only truth and faith. Furthermore, as in Giraldi's and in Zane's poems, here too Renata is a "fiamma," a guiding light near which the poet longs to be for spiritual sustenance and guidance: "Hor, se vicino a quella viva, E pura / Di virtu fiamma accesa."[52] The poet spiritually and emotionally joins Renata's family which appears to center around loyalty and faith, "honorata sua schiera gentile [...] di lealtade, & fede, / Anch'io con tuttol cor lieta m'aggiungo" (with loyalty and faith, / I, too, wholeheartedly want to join) a *topos* already employed by Zane.[53] Therefore, both nun and bishop seemed preoccupied with Renata's loyalty to the influential Este dynasty and to their faith, urging her to remain devoted both as a *fille de France* and as a literary and religious model. Amidst the highly disputed politico-religious debates over Renata's true devotion, and her fidelity to both her husband's Catholic faith and Italian dynasty, Zane and Castellani skillfully pledge to defend the duchess, but also urge her to stay the course as the loyal wife of Ercole d'Este from whom they expect guidance and patronage.[54]

In these last two poems, Renata's identity unfolds as an educated and irreproachable leader: she is no longer Ferrara's most controversial citizen, as she often appears in letters of diplomats or gossips,[55] rather, she is praiseworthy and faithful, a loyal community's beacon, as the whole world benefits from observing and admiring her, "Che mirandola gode il mondo, e ammira" as Castellani emphasizes.[56] Moreover, both poems are couched among *rime* dedicated to other noble and elite women, including Marguerite de Navarre, Vittoria Colonna, Margaret of Austria, Marguerite de Valois, and Veronica Gambara. Renata, therefore, found herself in good

---

[51] Domenichi, *Rime diverse*, 66.

[52] Domenichi, *Rime diverse*, 65.

[53] Domenichi, *Rime diverse*, 66.

[54] But, again, to which faith are the two poets referring? The Catholic or Reformed one? This is hard to gage in a period when many did not openly proclaim their own allegiance for fear of persecution, and many were suspected of heresy.

[55] See Fontana and Belligni.

[56] Domenichi, *Rime diverse*, 66.

company and in a virtual community,[57] where other notable women are praised, written into each other's lives, and immortalized in textual communities.[58]

Renata's library suffered several raids: first in 1554, when she was imprisoned, when about a hundred of her books were sequestered and subsequently burned, and then again in 1660, when two cases of her books were found and burned by order of the Inquisition. It is therefore difficult to establish how many books she had collected and how many literati had devoted their works to her,[59] but we do know that she received several book dedications from writers including Antonio Brucioli, Vittoria Colonna, Jakob Ziegler, and Horatio Brunetto (1521–1578),[60] the last writer to be addressed in this chapter. A physician and philosopher, he dedicated his *Lettere di Horatio Brunetto* to Renata in 1548,[61] an epistolary collection that features letters to and from known heretics, such as Domenichi, Ludovico Dolce, and Pietro Aretino,[62] and whose themes are a true justification of the free will and other reformed doctrines.[63]

In his long dedication, Brunetto praises the princess's spiritual qualities and divine virtues and portrays her as at once greeting and accepting all Christian souls: she is a "ricevitrice dè buoni christiani," or in other words, "one who welcomes good Christians." Brunetto's dedication clearly signals his desire to raise Renata's status as the protector and benefactor of intellectuals of reformist sympathies in Italy. Why else would he dedicate to her his book of letters written by openly reformed and controversial

---

[57] See Diana Robin, *Publishing Women. Salons, the Presses, and the Counter-Reformation in Sixteenth-Century Italy* (Chicago: University of Chicago Press, 2007), 62–71.

[58] Scarlatta, "Women Writing Women," 67–69.

[59] See Ugo Rozzo, "Il rogo postumo di due biblioteche cinquecentesche," in *Bibliografia e critica dantesca. Saggi dedicati a Enzo Esposito*, ed. Vincenzio de Gregorio (Ravenna: Longo, 1997), 136–166. Rozzo explains that Renata left behind two chests full of books that were sequestered by the local Inquisition, 164–166. See also Gorris, "La Bibliothèque de la duchesse. De la bibliothèque en feu de Renée de France à la bibliothèque éclatée de Marguerite de France, duchesse de Savoie," in *Poètes, Princes & Collectionneurs. Mélanges offerts à Jean Paul Barbier-Mueller*, ed. Jean Balsamo (Geneva: Droz, 2011), 473–525.

[60] See Rozzo, who notes that nonetheless between 1554 and 1560, Renata rebuilt her "biblioteca proibita," (forbidden library). "Il rogo postumo," 165.

[61] For Brunetto, see his biography in *Dizionario biografico dei Friulani*, http://www.dizionariobiograficodeifriulani.it/brunetto-orazio/.

[62] See Lodovica Braida, *Libri di lettere. Le raccolte epistolari del Cinquecento tra inquietudini religiose e "buon volgare"* (Roma-Bari: Laterza, 2009), 136–137.

[63] See Braida, *Libri di lettere*, 137.

individuals, a book which would be censored in 1574? Throughout his nineteen-page dedication, Brunetto refers to Renata as "principessa,"[64] a viewpoint shared also by other writers, including Giuseppe Betussi, François Rabelais, and Brantôme.[65]

Brunetto praises Renata's royal blood, "nata di **Re**, anzi **Re** nata" (born of a King, actually Re born), playing on the words Re (king) and re-, thus reminding her of her status and reiterating her own meaningful motto, *Di / Real / Sangue / Nata In / Christo / Sol / Renata*, which can be found on the binding of one of her extant books, *Cento giuochi liberali d'ingegno* by Vincenzo Ringhieri, underscoring the importance of her royal birth and her re-birth in Christ.[66] In fact, as Kelly Peebles notes, this motto "serves as a textual reminder of her physical person and of the abstract notion of dynastic loyalty and religious faith"[67] certainly two common themes echoed in the four texts here discussed. Moreover, I would like to argue that her own choice of the Italian language and of her identity textualized in her motto suggests Renata's acceptance of Italy as her new residence, her new life and renewed identity as *Re-nata*, a re-born Italian *Re-née*, the Duchess and Madame of Ferrara, as well as embracing her new family and dynasty, the Este, as Zane had so fervently desired.

Brunetto also wants to underscore Renata's Christian virtues, including piety, but most importantly, he means to elevate her as his spiritual guide because of her good judgment and the good people surrounding her. Echoing Giraldi's praise of Renata as spiritual and guiding light and patron, Brunetto too recognized Renata's prominent role in bringing together literati and in leading them along the right path. He also

---

[64] *Lettere di Messer Horatio Brunetto* (Venice: Andrea Arrivabene, 1548), A2r–A11r.

[65] See Betussi, *Libro di M. Gio. Boccaccio delle donne illustri tradotto per Messer Giuseppe Betussi con una additione fatta dal medesimo* (Venice: 1545); Rabelais, *Rabelais et l'Italie*, ed. Richard Cooper, *Etudes Rabelaisiennes* 24 (Geneva: Droz, 1991); and Brantôme, *Recueil des Dames, poésies, et tombeaux*, ed. Étienne Vaucheret (Paris: Gallimard, 1991).

[66] Ringhieri (Bologna, 1522), see Tammaro di Marinis, "Legatura artistica fatta per Renata di Francia, duchessa di Ferrara," *Gutenberg Jahrbuch* 39 (1964): 373–374, Rozzo, "Il rogo postumo di due biblioteche cinquecentesche," 166–167, and Gorris, "La Bibliothèque de la duchesse."

[67] It confirms as well her religious identity of being re-born into Christ alone, where, as Peebles explains, "Renée's persona, her name, and her motto collide into a mutually affirming construction that embodies, or enlivens, her internal devotion." "Embodied Devotion: The Dynastic and Religious Loyalty of Renée de France (1510–1575)," in *Royal Women and Dynastic Loyalty*, ed. Caroline Dunn and Elizabeth Carney (Cham, Switzerland: Palgrave Macmillan, 2018), 123–137, 126.

acknowledges Renata's reputation as a loving, charitable benefactor who surrounds herself with good people and shepherds their ideas:

> V.E. essendo grande di nobiltà di sangue, & di beni temporali, nata di **Re**, anzi **Re** nata, & prima Prencipessa d'Italia, ella non di meno è pietosissima christiana, molto lontana da le grandezze humane. Per questo ho eletto V.E. per mia guida in questo nuovo certame: nel quale entro per combattere col mondo […] ma perchè conoscendo il mondo la pietà di V.E. la quale non ama, se non gente buona, habbiamo rispetto di biasimare quelle cose, che sono lodate da lei, e sotto l'immaculato nome suo escono à la luce.[68]
>
> (Your Ladyship, being of great nobility of the blood, and of temporal goods, born from a **King**, rather **Re** born, and first Princess of Italy, she is not less a pitiful Christian, and not far from human greatness. This is why I chose Your Ladyship as my guide in this new certainty: in which I enter to fight with the world […] but because the world knowing Your Ladyship's piety, who only loves good people, we have respect to blame those things that are praised by you, and under whose immaculate name come to light.)

Brunetto highlights Renata's "singolar bellezze de l'animo suo" (her soul's unique beauty), whereby she is yet again presented as a spiritual and intellectual benefactor, carefully chosen to foster and endorse his own epistolary collection.[69] Renata is earnestly entrusted with the care of his book and with helping it to "come to light":

> Tra le quali, so che haverà luogo questo mio libretto, come cosa, che viene da una sincerità di core, assai risplendente per la presenza dello spirito: à cui è piacciuto di spargere alcuni di suoi raggi sopra di questo humile intelletto, come scorrendo per il libro.[70]
>
> (Among them, I know there will be room for my book, as a thing that comes from the sincerity of the heart, very much resplendent because of the spirit's presence: to whom it pleased to shed some of its rays on this humble intellect, as on my book.)

Brunetto gifts his book to Renata, as from near and far, her role is to inspire and to guide the reformers and the literati who humbly considered

---

[68] *Lettere di Messer Horatio Brunetto*, A7r.

[69] For an interesting history and analysis of the book's second edition of 1597, published in Venice by Giorgio Angelieri, see Braida, *Libri di lettere*, 280–281.

[70] *Lettere di Messer Horatio Brunetto*, A7v.

her their true leader, the protector of their beliefs and family, as well as the Este family's safekeeper, who should never forget her royal descent. Fittingly, she "spreads her rays on this humble intellect." Therefore, her role as enlightening those around her, including the writers and intellectuals, unmistakably resurfaces in this text during some of Renata's most challenging years, as in the preceding ones here discussed.

CONCLUSION

While it was not unusual for a French princess to be sent off to be married in a foreign land, Renée's innate "Frenchness" marked her difference in Ferrara, at once emphasizing her culture and mentality and allowing her to stand out as the engaged leader of a diverse, cosmopolitan court society. From her arrival in Ferrara in 1528, and an initial encounter with the plague, famine, and a bitter winter, to her departure in early 1560, after her husband's death, Renata emerged as the spiritual guide and soul mate of an intellectual and religious community that looked to her for direction and protection. Writers in and around Renata's court show that religion and literature innovatively intermingled and that they could flourish in spite of politico-religious anxieties and pressures. Their works creatively validate Renata's literary and religious community, while its members overtly embodied a powerful and appreciative group committed to immortalizing Renata's role and achievements in a space where the boundaries between religion and literature were nonexistent, although danger lurked.[71] The Catholic or Reformed ideals of the literati of her circle mattered less than Renata's capacity to protect and support their elite, openly and magnanimously, thus allowing them to continue their artistic and humanistic production.

The three poems and the dedication discussed in this study portray Renata di Francia as a nurturing "fiamma," a guiding light, and as a powerful, accomplished spiritual guide who must continue to provide assistance and lead her community. They are testimony to her crucial role, whatever their authors' faiths might have been. Renata's own beliefs must not falter and her allegiance to the Este dynasty and its traditions must endure. Zane makes it clear when exhorting Renata and Ercole to remain

---

[71] For similar circumstances at Anne de France's court, see Elodie Lequain, "Anne de France et les livres: la tradition et le pouvoir," in *Patronnes et mécènes en France à la Renaissance*, ed. Kathleen Wilson-Chevalier (Paris: Publications de l'Université de Saint-Etienne, 2007), 155–168.

loyal to each other and true to the *Fleur de lys* and the White Eagle, symbols of two of the most prominent dynasties which embodied both religious and secular power in all Europe:

> Happy couple perhaps rare in the world
> I pray you, since I love you so,
> Both the *Fleur de lys* and the Bird, in a thousand ways,
> I sing that you hold my faith dear.[72]

APPENDIX

Suor Girolama Castellani in *Rime diverse d'alcune nobilissime, et virtuosissime donne, raccolte per M. Lodovico Domenichi*, 64–66. Lucca: Busdrago, 1559.

> Pensier, che pur mi desti a l'alta impresa
> Cosi tacitamente,
> Et la mia voglia accesa
> Alletti, ove l'ingegno nol consente;
> Et vuoi, che'n basso stile
> Canti, e in roze parole
> Le lodi al mondo sole
> Di Renata Estense, e il pregio alto, & gentile:
> Tu sai, ch'Io mossa da cortesi affetti,
> Et da tuoi sproni ardenti,
> Piu volte ho in se ristretti
> Con le forze maggior gli spriti intenti;
> Et per far pago in parte
> Il mio desire ardente,
> Vergai carte sovente;
> E indarno ogn'hor tentai la penna, & l'arte.
> Pur mi ramenti il suo bel viso adorno,
> Mentre in quest'humil stanza
> Facea dolce soggiorno;
> Et verde anchor nodrisci la speranza,
> Ch'io ho di vederla: e intanto
> Nel cor mi stanno fisse

---

[72] *Rime volgari del Cavalier Zani.*

Le parole, che disse,
Quando al partir lascionne in doglia, e in pianto
Da indi in qua le feste, il gioco, e'l riso,
Et la gioia, e'l diletto,
E il nuovo paradiso,
Che si godea nel suo gradito aspetto,
Seco disparve; ond'Io
Di morte il viso impressa,
Vivo in odio a Me stessa,
Troppo lontana al caro Idolo mio.
Hor, se vicino a quella viva, & pura
Di virtu fiamma accesa,
Chel ghiaccio, & la paura
Spesso dal cor, che mi tenea sospesa,
Sgombro; quel che m'insegna
Amor, dir non potei;
Come lungi da Lei,
Dirò, di quante lodi Ella sia degna?
Pensier, dunque ti prego, homai quetarmi
Lascia; &, se brami in parte
Qualche soccorso darmi,
Vanne ove sempre vola in quella parte
Ogn'altro mio pensiero;
Et di quel, che nel core
Mi tien chiuso il timore,
Scopri a Madonna intieramente il vero.
Poscia al cortese suo Signor rivolto,
Fa riverenza humile;
E al bel numero accolto
De lhonorata sua schiera gentile,
Di; che al lor puro, & lungo
Servir, ch'ogni altro eccede.
Di lealtade, & fede,
Anch'Io con tuttol cor lieta m'aggiungo.
Canzon, s'ove s'aggira
Il mio pensier n'andrai,
Nuova beltà vedrai,
Che mirandola gode il mondo, e ammira.

Oh thought, which raises me to high achievements
So quietly,
And having ignited my desire
You go where my intellect doesn't allow;
You want that I, in simple style
And in coarse words, sing
To the world, the praises of the one and only
Renata Estense, and of her high and kind merit:
You know that, so moved by kind affections,
And by your ardent incitements,
Many times have I withheld
With great strength my determined spirit;
And to please in part,
My ardent desire
I often wrote;
And in vain I tried the pen and the art.
Still you remind me of her adorned face,
While here, in my humble room
I spent a sweet sojourn;
And I am still hopeful,
To see her. In the meantime,
In my heart, the words she said
Remain fixed,
When departing I left, mournful and crying
From then on the feasts, games, and laughs
And joy, and pleasures,
And the new paradise,
That one could enjoy in her pleasant demeanor,
It disappeared with her; of which I,
With death in my eyes,
I live in hate of myself
Too far from my dear Idol.
Now, if near that lively and pure
Of virtue burning flame,
I get rid of that ice, and fear
That often kept my heart suspended,
That which Love teaches me
I could not say;

How, so far from Her,
Will I say of how many praises She is worthy?
Oh thought, therefore, I beg you, let
Me now calm myself, & if you wish in part
To give me some relief,
Go to where all of my other thoughts
Always fly;
And that which fear keeps
Closed in my heart
Show Madonna the entire truth.
So that she can turn to her kind Lord,
And humbly bow
And to the hailed beautiful souls
Of his honored and kind array,
Tell them; that their pure and long service
Surpasses everybody else's.
With loyalty, & faith,
I, too, gladly join them with all of my heart.
Song, if you will go
Where my thought wanders
You will see new beauty,
Of which, from observing and admiring it, the whole world will benefit.

BIBLIOGRAPHY

PRIMARY SOURCES

Betussi, Giuseppe. 1545. *Libro di M. Gio. Boccaccio delle donne illustri tradotto per Messer Giuseppe Betussi con una additione fatta dal medesimo.* Venice: n.p.

Brantôme. 1991. *Recueil des Dames, poésies, et tombeaux.* Edited by Etienne Vaucheret. Paris: Gallimard.

Brunetto, Horatio. 1548. *Lettere di Messer Horatio Brunetto.* Venice: Andrea Arrivabene.

Correspondance politique de Dominique du Gabre, évêque de Lodève, trésorier des armées à Ferrare (1552–1554), ambassadeur de France à Venise (1554–1557). 1903. Edited by Alexandre Vitalis. Paris: Champion.

Delle rime di diversi nobilissimi et eccellentissimi autori. 1550. Edited by Andrea Arrivabene. Venice: Andrea Arrivabene.

Giraldi, Gianbattista Cintio. 1548. *Le Fiamme di M. Giovan-Battista Giraldi Cinthio Nobile Ferrarese*. Venice: Gabriel Giolito.

———. 1557. *Dell'Ercole canti ventisei*. Modena: Cornelio Gadaldini.

Marot, Clément. 2010. *Recueil inédit offert au Connétable de Montmorency en mars 153*. Edited by François Rigolot. Geneva: Droz.

Navarre, Marguerite de. 1984. *The Heptameron*. Edited and translated by P.A. Chilton. London: Penguin.

Rabelais, François. 1991. *Rabelais et l'Italie*. Edited by Richard Cooper. *Etudes Rabelaisiennes* 24. Geneva: Droz.

Rime diverse *d'alcune nobilissime, et virtuosissime donne*. 1559. Edited by Lodovico Domenichi. Lucca: Busdrago.

Tasso, Bernardo. 1582. Discorso della virtù femminile e donnesca. Venice: Bernardo Giunti.

Vives, Juan Luis. 2000. *The Education of a Christian Woman: A Sixteenth-Century Manual*. Edited and translated by Charles Fantazzi. Chicago: The University of Chicago Press.

Zane, Bernardo. 1555. *Rime volgari del Cavalier Zani nelle quali si contengono le lodi, nomi, cognomi, e titoli de grandi e grande d'Europa: a lingua dolosa*. Venice.

SECONDARY SOURCES

Adams, Tracy. 2010. Rivals or Friends? Anne de Bourbon and Anne de Bretagne. *Women in French Studies* Special Issue: 46–61.

Balmas, Enea. 1994. Ferrara e la Francia nel XVI secolo: uno sguardo d'insieme. In *Alla corte degli Estensi, Filosofia, arte e cultura a Ferrara nei secoli XV e XVI*, ed. Marco Bertozzi, 355–364. Ferrara: Università degli Studi.

Belligni, Eleonora. 2011. *Renata di Francia. Un'eresia di corte*. Turin: UTET.

Berthon, Guillaume. 2018. L'Invention du blason: Retour sur la genèse d'un genre (Ferrare, 1535). In *Anatomie d'une anatomie, Nouvelles recherches sur les blasons anatomiques du corps féminin*, ed. Julien Goeury and Thomas Hunkeler, 135–154. Geneva: Droz.

Birnbaum, Marianna D. 1988. Jewish Patronage in Sixteenth-Century Ferrara. *Mediterranean Studies* 7: 135–141.

Blaisdell, Charmarie J. 1980. Marguerite de Navarre and her Circle (1492–1549). In *Female Scholars A Tradition of Learned Women Before 1800*, ed. J.R. Brink, 36–53. Montréal: Eden Press.

———. 1982. Calvin's Letters to Women: The Courting of Ladies in High Places. *Sixteenth Century Journal* 13 (3): 67–84.

Boni, Fabio. 2017. La riflessione di Torquato Tasso sulla donna nel 'Discorso della virtù femminile e donnesca'. *Annales Universitatis Paedagogicae Cracoviensis, Studia de Cultura* 9 (1): 215–222.

Bonnet, Jules. 1880. Disgrâce de M et Mme de Pons à la cour de Ferrare 1544–1545. *Bulletin historique littéraire/Société de l'histoire du protestantisme français* 29: 3–17.

Braida, Lodovica. 2009. *Libri di lettere. Le raccolte epistolari del Cinquecento tra inquietudini religiose e "buon volgare"*. Roma-Bari: Laterza.

———. 2014. Libri di lettere all'Indice. Censura, autocensura ed espurgazione delle raccolte epistolari nel XVI secolo. In *Cartas-Lettres-Lettere: discursos, practicas y representaciones epistolares (siglos XIV–XX)*, ed. Antonio Castillo Gómez and Véronica Sierra Blas, 331–348. Alcalá de Henares: UAH.

Braun, Gabriel. 1988. Le mariage de Renée de France avec Hercule d'Esté: une inutile mésalliance. 28 juin 1528. *Histoire, économie et société* 7 (2): 147–168.

Brown, Cynthia J., ed. 2011. *The Cultural and Political Legacy of Anne de Bretagne, The Queen's Library. Image-Making at the Court of Anne of Brittany, 1477–1514*. Philadelphia: University of Pennsylvania Press.

Brunetto, Horatio. *Dizionario biografico dei Friulani*. http://www.dizionariobio-graficodeifriulani.it/brunetto-orazio/

Chiappini, Luciano. 1984. *La Corte Estense alla metà del Cinquecento. I compendi di Cristoforo di Messisbugo*. Ferrara: S.A.T.E.

Cioranescu, Alessandro. 1939. *L'Arioste en France des origines à la fin du XVIIIe siècle*. Paris: Champion.

Cooper, Richard. 1995. Marguerite de Navarre et la réforme italienne. In *Marguerite de Navarre 1492–1992, Actes du Colloque de Pau*, ed. Nicole Cazauran and James Dauphiné, 159–188. Mont de Marsan: Editions Interuniversitaires.

Cox, Virginia. 2008. *Women's Writing in Italy 1400–1650*. Baltimore: The Johns Hopkins University Press.

De Chirico, Leonardo, and Daniel Walker, eds. 2009. *Giovanni Calvino, Renata di Francia. Lealtà in tensione. Un carteggio protestante tra Ferrara e l'Europa (1537–1564)*. Caltanisetta: Alfa & Omega.

Eishenbichler, Konrad. 2001. Laudomia Forteguerri Loves Margaret of Austria. In *Same Sex Love and Desire among Women in the Middle Ages*, ed. Francesca Canadé Sautman and Pamela Sheingorn, 277–230. New York: Palgrave.

Ferguson, Gary, and Mary McKinley, eds. 2013. *A Companion to Marguerite de Navarre*. Boston: Brill Luden.

Franceschini, Chiara. 2005. '*Literarum studia nobis communia*': Olimpia Morata e la corte di Renata di Francia. *Schifanoia* 28–29: 207–232.

Ghirardo, Diane Y. 2008. Lucrezia Borgia as Entrepreneur. *Renaissance Quarterly* 61: 53–91.

Gorris, Rosanna. 1992. Tragedia come apologo della crudeltà: il caso di *Orbecc-Oronte*. *Studi di letteratura francese* 18: 48–71.

———. 1997. "Un franzese nominato Clemente": Marot à Ferrare. In *Clément Marot "Prince des poëtes françois" 1496–1996, Actes du Colloque international de Cahors en Quercy 21–25 mai 1996*, ed. Gérard Defaux and Michel Simonin, 339–364. Paris: Champion.

———. 2000. 'Je veux chanter d'amour la tempeste e l'orage': Desportes et les *Imitations* de l'Arioste. In *Philippe Desportes (1546–1606) Un poète presque parfait entre Renaissance et Classicisme*, ed. Jean Balsamo, 173–211. Paris: Klincksieck.

———. 2005. 'Donne ornate di scienza e di virtù': donne e francesi alla corte di Renata di Francia. *Schifanoia* 28–29: 175–205.

———. 2011. La Bibliothèque de la duchesse. De la bibliothèque en feu de Renée de France à la bibliothèque éclatée de Marguerite de France, duchesse de Savoie. In *Poètes, Princes & Collectionneurs. Mélanges offerts à Jean Paul Barbier-Mueller*, ed. Jean Balsamo, 473–535. Geneva: Droz.

Graziosi, Elisabetta. 2009. Due domenicane poetesse, una nota, una ignota e molte sullo sfondo. In *Il velo, la penna, e la parola*, ed. Gabriella Zarri and Gianni Festa, 163–177. Florence: Netbini.

Gundersheimer, Werner L. 1985. Women, Learning, and Power: Eleonora of Aragon and the Court of Ferrara. In *Beyond their Sex. Learned Women of the European Past*, ed. Patricia H. Labalme, 43–65. New York: New York University Press.

Heckel, Waldemar. 2018. King's Daughters, Sisters and Wives: Fonts and Conduits of Power and Legitimacy. In *Royal Women and Dynastic Loyalty*, ed. Caroline Dunn and Elizabeth Carney, 19–30. New York: Palgrave Macmillan.

Horne, P.R. 1958. Reformation and Counter-Reformation at Ferrara: Antonio Musa Brasavola and Giambattista Cinthio Giraldi. *Italian Studies* 13 (1): 62–82.

Jordan, Constance. 1990. *Renaissance Feminism. Literary Texts and Political Models.* Ithaca and London: Cornell University Press.

Lequain, Élodie. 2005. La Maison de Bourbon 'escolle de vertu et de perfection': Anne de France, Suzanne de Bourbon, et Pierre Martin. *Médiévales* 48: 1–15.

———. 2007. Anne de France et les livres: la tradition et le pouvoir. In *Patronnes et mécènes en France à la Renaissance*, ed. Kathleen Wilson-Chevalier, 155–168. Paris: Publications de l'Université de Saint-Etienne.

Marinis, Tammaro di. 1964. Legatura artistica fatta per Renata di Francia, duchessa di Ferrara. *Gutenberg Jahrbuch* 39: 373–374.

Mayer, Claude A. 1972. *Clément Marot.* Paris: Nizet.

Peebles, Kelly D. 2018a. Embodied Devotion: The Dynastic and Religious Loyalty of Renée de France (1510–1575). In *Royal Women and Dynastic Loyalty*, ed. Caroline Dunn and Elizabeth Carney, 123–137. New York: Palgrave Macmillan.

———. 2018b. Renée de France's and Clément Marot's Voyages: From Political Exile to Spiritual Liberation. *Women in French Studies* Special Issue 7: 33–60.

Robin, Diana. 1997. Woman, Space, and Renaissance Discourse. In *Sex and Gender in Medieval and Renaissance Texts. The Latin Tradition*, ed. Barbara Gold, Paul Allen Miller, and Charles Platter, 165–187. New York: SUNY Series in Medieval Studies.

———. 2007. *Publishing Women. Salons, the Presses, and the Counter-Reformation in Sixteenth-Century Italy*. Chicago: University of Chicago Press.

Roelker, Nancy L. 1972. The Appeal of Calvinism to French Noblewomen in the Sixteenth Century. *The Journal of Interdisciplinary History* 2 (4): 391–481.

———. 1973. The Role of Noblewomen in the French Reformation. *Archiv für Reformationsgeschichte* 63: 168–195.

Roffi, Mario. 1984. Un concorso di poesia francese a Ferrara alla corte estense di Renata di Francia. In *The Renaissance in Ferrara and its European Horizon*, ed. J. Salmon, 263–269. Cardiff, UK: University of Wales Press.

Rohr, Zita. 2018. Rocking the Cradle and Ruling the World: Queens' Households in Late Medieval and Early Modern Aragon and France. In *Royal and Elite Households in Medieval and Early Modern Europe: More than Just a Castle*, ed. Theresa Earenfight, 309–337. Boston: Brill.

Ross, Sarah Gwyneth. 2009. *The Birth of Feminism: Woman as Intellect in Renaissance Italy and England*. Cambridge: Harvard University Press.

Rozzo, Ugo. 1997. Il rogo postumo di due biblioteche cinquecentesche. In *Bibliografia e critica dantesca. Saggi dedicati a Enzo Esposito*, ed. Vincenzo de Gregorio, 159–186. Ravenna: Longo.

Scarlatta, Gabriella. 2009. Women Writing Women in Lodovico Domenichi's Anthology of 1559. *Quaderni d'Italianistica* 30 (2): 67–85.

———. 2019. Gender, Power, and Sexuality in Betussi's and Brantôme's *Illustrious Women*. *Royal Studies Journal* 6 (2): 61–73.

Stephenson, Barbara. 2004. *The Power and Patronage of Marguerite de Navarre*. Aldershot: Ashgate.

Stevenson, Joseph, ed. 1853. *The Church Historians of England, The Historical Works of the Venerable Beda*. Vol. I, Part II. London: Seeleys.

Wilcox, Helen, and Andrew Wilcox, eds. 2017. *The Oxford Handbook of Early Modern English Literature and Religion*. Oxford: Oxford University Press.

Wilson-Chevalier, Kathleen. 2010. Claude de France: In her Mother's Likeness, a Queen with Symbolic Clout? In *The Cultural and Political Legacy of Anne de Bretagne. Negotiating Convention in Books and Documents*, ed. Cynthia J. Brown, 123–144. Suffolk: Brewer.

Winn, Colette, ed. and trans. with Nicholas Van Handel. 2017. *Sin and Salvation in Early Modern France: Three Women's Stories*. The Other Voice in Early Modern Europe: The Toronto Series. Toronto: CRRS and Iter.

Zarri, Gabriella. 2006. *La Religione di Lucrezia Borgia. Le lettere inedite del confessore*. Rome: Comitato nazionale incontri di studio per il centenario del pontificato di Alessandro VI.

Zum-Kolk, Caroline. 2007. Les difficultés des mariages inernationaux: Renée de France et Hercule d'Este. In *Femmes et pouvoir politique. Les princesses d'Europe, XVe–XVIIIe siècle*, ed. Isabelle Poutrin and Marie-Karine Schaub, 102–119. Ronsy-sous-Bois, France: Bréal.

CHAPTER 8

Renata di Francia and the Theater: Some Hypotheses

Marzia Pieri

Translated by Gabriella Scarlatta

Renata di Francia remains an elusive character, whose many legends, often conflicting, have excessive nuances, mainly the fault of *damnatio memoriae* imposed by the Holy See in 1600, an effort to remove her from public memory, but also due to her strategy of acting as a "nicodemita chiassosa ed eclatante" (a noisy and conspicuous Nicodemite) at the center of a game of chess larger than herself, as a French woman in Italy and a foreigner in her homeland, one who was always wary of igniting open conflict.[1] Her marriage with Ercole II was a strategically arranged union, the result of political ambitions in unfortunate circumstances. She arrived in

---

[1] Eleonora Belligni, *Renata di Francia (1510–1575). Un'eresia di corte* (Turin: UTET, 2011), 200.

M. Pieri (✉)
University of Siena, Siena, Italy
e-mail: marzia.pieri@unisi.it

Ferrara in 1528 as *fille de France*, daughter of King Louis XII. Hers was indeed an inconvenient and contested prestige, which generated deep devotions and suspicions, a problem that other duchesses before her experienced as well, due to the fact that their husbands were of inferior rank, from Eleonora d'Aragona to Lucrezia Borgia.[2] Renata also knew two skillful women from her own country who were both well versed in the game of power and in exercising a superb patronage and whom she would never forget: her mother, Anne de Bretagne, and her godmother, Anne de France.[3] Furthermore, young Renata shared a discreet and constant strategy of resistance with Marguerite de Navarre who acted as an elder sister. Marguerite possessed an individual faith and culture that would sustain the Duchess of Ferrara through an intimate correspondence and circle of friends. When in 1528 Renata arrived in Ferrara with her following of 126 courtiers, she shaped for herself a cultural, political, and religious Franco-Ferrarese enclave, over which her husband soon realized he could only exercise partial and intermittent control. For 30 years, she held a court parallel to his, a lavish and expensive one.[4] She corresponded with

[2] These courts' influence was due to the prestige of the bride's family, but the true distinction was economic, as it had to do with the presence of salaried employees. Eleonora, as the first lady of Ferrara after Borso d'Este's long celibate, started the tradition by relocating in a separate wing in Castelvecchio, where she kept only few Neapolitan courtiers, chosen by her husband and assimilated. Lucrezia's following, on the other hand, seemed to many to be too Spanish and expensive. Renata's entourage was chosen by François I, to whom reported the Soubise family, and included a fixed number of salaried employees, as well as a guaranteed welcome and support to her dowry lands' countrymen and women. Renata's account books were hidden from her husband, according to French chancery rules, and his attempts to insert one of his trusted employees and interrupt the flux of resources and people that surrounded his wife failed continuously. See Chiara Franceschini, "La corte di Renata di Francia (1528–1560)," *Storia di Ferrara, Il Rinascimento. Situazioni e personaggi*, Vol. 6, ed. Adriano Prosperi (Ferrara: Corbo, 2000), 186–214.

[3] For Anne de Bretagne and Anne de France's complex relationship and their specific feminine pedagogy which they created, see Elodie Lequain, "Anne de France et les livres: la tradition et le pouvoir," in *Patronnes et mécènes en France à la Renaissance*, ed. Kathleen Wilson-Chevalier (Paris: Publications de l'Université de Saint-Etienne, 2007), 155–168, Tracy Adams, "Rivals or Friends? Anne de France and Anne de Bretagne," in *Women in French*, Special Issue (2010): 46–61, and Zita Rohr, "Rocking the Cradle and Ruling the World: Queens' Households in Late Medieval and Early Modern Aragon and France," in *Royal and Elite Households in Medieval and Early Modern Europe. More than Just a Castle*, ed. Theresa Earenfight (Boston: Brill, 2018), 309–337.

[4] Many studies have analyzed, from various perspectives, the presence and influence of women in power during the Middle Ages and the Renaissance focusing on juridical, gender, and anthropological questions. See in particular Craig Taylor, "The Salic Law, French

many personalities in Europe and managed to maintain her restless religious pursuits, shielded by her rank as *fille de France* and by her dowry, which allowed her a substantial autonomy, without, nevertheless, ever breaking with Ercole nor with the Pope or with the pressing requests which came from Geneva and from her mentor, Calvin.[5]

Despite being constantly spied on and controlled by the Italian and French inquisitors that haunted her every move, she continued to welcome and protect suspected heretical exiles. She ably coped on all fronts, staying truthful to the Catholic liberalism of her youth.[6] Thanks to the fascinating renewed scholarly interest in her life in Italy and in her vast network, we can gauge a better understanding of the theater activities in Ferrara. Indeed, fragments of news, correspondence, exchanges, and movements of books and men allow us to reconstruct Renata's role as a spectator and eventually, her role as an authoritative influencer of ritual events full of meaning. By unveiling a thick plot of clues that deserve patience and attention, this essay will outline Renata's role and involvement in the promotion and growth of theater activities at the Este court, as well as her deep-rooted enthusiasm for dramatic texts and arts and for the theater life of Ferrara, which for her, a stranger in Italy, represented an entirely new experience. Renata offered both an authoritative patronage and the assistance of her ladies-in-waiting in staging scenes of the plays, and possibly even some concrete suggestions for their iteration, as well. The main court playwright, Gianbattista Giraldi Cinzio, was very attached to the duchess, and ultimately, thanks to Renata, the novelties of Ferrara's theater arrived in France via her entourage's ladies and gentlemen, who brought books and memories of lived experiences back with them. Her specific role in theater renewal has been underestimated up to now,

---

Queenship and the Defense of Women," *French Historical Studies*, 29, no. 4 (2004): 543–564, Fanny Cosandey, "De Lance en quenouille. La place de la reine dans l'état moderne, XVIe-XVIIe siècles," *Annales, Histoire, Sciences Sociales*, 52, no. 4 (1997): 799–820, and Theresa Earenfight, "A Lifetime of Power: Beyond Binaries of Gender," in *Medieval Elite Women and the Exercise of Power, 1100–1400. The New Middle Ages*, ed. Heather J. Tanner (London: Palgrave Macmillan, 2019), 543–564. See also the editor's introduction to the volume *Medieval Elite Women and the Exercise of Power*, 1–18, for a compelling methodological frame to these questions.

[5] On Calvin's relationship with Renée, see also Dick Wursten, Robert Hudson's, and Kelly Peebles's contributions to this volume.

[6] On the religious influences of Renée's youth, see Kathleen Wilson-Chevalier's first contribution to this volume.

especially where it pertains to the Italian models that contributed to the birth of modern theater in France.

Among her numerous protected men and women, many were linked to Ferrara's theater in various ways, from Clément Marot, that restless poet with an air of heresy, who was so dear to Marguerite de Navarre and caught up in the *Affaire des Placards* of 1534, to François Rabelais, from Francesco Negri da Bassano, author of the bizarre *Tragedia del libero arbitrio* (1546), a theological and allegorical tragedy, to Michelangelo Florio, the heterodox Franciscan friar exiled in England, to whom we might owe the great Elizabethan fortune of Giraldi, through his son Giovanni, who would be the most important popularizer of Italian culture in England. Her correspondents were authors of comedy and tragedy, translators, and editors, and were linked to the Venetian intellectual networks in which dramaturgy and religious heterodoxy were traditionally intertwined. Indeed, we must not forget that the reinvention of modern theater in Cinquecento Italy closely intersects with political history, especially in Ferrara, where spectacles, festivities, and ceremonies were closely scrutinized and coveted by princes. The duke's family, following a long antique tradition centered around the need to control rather than to bestow patronage, was invested in crucial representative roles. Renata, thus, could not evade this tradition. On the contrary, she embraced it in her own way.

The Theater Scene in Ferrara

The history of the stage, therefore, and that of the court go hand in hand and can be divided into dynastic phases. Ercole I had the time and will to found a solid and recognizable tradition in his long principality, a true theatrical era comparable to that of Elizabeth I or Louis XIV. After him, his successor—Alfonso I, and the other children with their respective satellite courts—also cultivated this family passion and, therefore, the productions intermingled and renewed themselves. Alfonso I, after a forced pause due to political conflicts, resumed theatrical performances beginning, in fact, with the sumptuous wedding of his son to the French princess, while his brothers emulated him by cultivating their own strategic theatrical plans. Isabella d'Este founded the vulgar comedy in Mantua in competition with her illustrious father, Ercole I. Her sister, Beatrice d'Este, did the same in Milan with her husband, Ludovico il Moro, while Cardinal Ippolito d'Este became a link between the Este family and Pope Leo X in Rome. There, Ludovico Ariosto oversaw the recitals of the *Mandragola* by

Niccolò Machiavelli and of the *Calandra* by Bernardo Dovizi, which deeply renewed his playwright talents after his 1525 return to Ferrara. With the next generation of Este dukes, Ercole II revitalized theatrical representations focusing on the tragic and pastoral genres, while his brother, Cardinal Ippolito, a great passionate spectator and advocate of entertainments and performances, carried to France books and theatrical memories as Italianate novelties, which were met with much success.[7] Furthermore, during his years in Siena as François I's lieutenant, he enthusiastically attended performances of the *Rozzi* and the *Intronati*, the city academies around which revolved the vivacious, festive life of the Republic. On the stage, Ercole I, a *praefectus ad voluptates* (lord of the festival), promoted the idealized image of power, both sacred and profane, and firmly enjoined the intellectuals from the *Studio* to produce translations of Latin comedies. His successors would continue this cumbersome practice with the court literati,[8] whose humanistic utopia was to control the public sphere through poetic and theatrical productions. This utopia drove them also to write texts and to direct representations: playwrights like Matteo Boiardo and Ariosto secured the duke's full patronage, and Pellegrino Prisciani exerted on him a distinct ideological influence. Later on, Giraldi would demonstrate his passion for Ercole II, as he was less fortunate in working for Alfonso II. Giraldi's rushed departure in 1563 coincided with an evasive and spectacular change in the Este performances, where the literary theater performed by gentlemen was supplanted by the

---

[7] See Luigi Suttina, "Commedie, feste e giuochi a Roma e Ferrara presso il cardinale Ippolito d'Este nel carnevale degli anni 1540 e 1547," *Giornale Storico della Letteratura Italiana* 99 (1932): 279–284 and *Ippolito II d'Este cardinale, principe, mecenate*, ed. Marina Cogotti and Francesco Paolo Fiore, (Rome: De Luca, 2013).

[8] Unfortunately, though, not a line was found from Boiardo's vulgarizations, and not even from the *Menaechmi*, the *Aulularia*, the *Andria*, the *Eunuco*, nor the *Formio* translated by Ludovico Ariosto. Giovan Battista Giraldi, also known as Cinzio, notes that, in order to finish the *Andria* and the *Eunuco*, "su quella meravigliosa scena che per simili rappresentazioni già avea fatto apparecchiare sua Eccellenza per la rappresentazione della *Cassaria*," "non gli bastò nondimeno il poco tempo che gli fu dato a tradurre quelle favole in verso. Perché i versi non si sputano né si gittano a stampa ma vogliono in lunghezza di tempo molta considerazione" (on that marvelous scene, which for similar shows had already convened His Excellency for the representation of *Cassaria*. The little time that was given to him to translate the fables into verses was nonetheless not enough. Because verses are not to be spit out nor thrown into the press, but need much time and consideration). G. B. Giraldi, *Lettera sulla tragedia*, in *Trattati di poetica e retorica del Cinquecento*, vol. 1, ed. Bernard Weinberg (Bari: Laterza, 1970), 4. Also, Celio Calcagnini, when writing his *Miles gloriosus*, was forced by Alfonso to assign the parts one by one as he was translating them.

monumental apparatus of the Cavalry and by the successful competition by the artists of the *Commedia dell'Arte.*[9] Giovanni Battista Guarini and Torquato Tasso would not fare well in this new context, which was less and less dialectic and dialogic, where the poets' words stayed in the background, the scripts continued to be exploited and lost, and the court dialectic became more and more insidious.[10]

Renata shared the main part of this story: it is indeed revealing that her wedding, the result of political negotiations for which her father-in-law had great expectations, coincides in fact with the "revival" of the urban stage after a long theatrical stagnation following Ercole I's death. The wedding, as is well known, was supposed to establish an important alliance with François I,

> il quale era di continuo stato in amicitia, et in fede con la casa da Este, e che da quella in ogni impresa, ch'egli havea fatto in Italia era stato aiutato con facultà, con consiglio et con fortezza, e che sapeva benissimo come il nobilissimo sangue di questi principi haveva havuto origine dalla nobiltà di Francia, per ritornare nell'esser di prima il parentado interrotto per lungo spatio di tempo, e per confermare anchora con nodo di parentela l'amicitia e la benivolenza la quale era sempre stata fra i re di Francia e i signori da Este, mosso dalla fama di questo nobilissimo, e chiarissimo giovanetto, deliberò dargli per moglie Renata con reciproco accrescimento di splendore.[11]

> (who was still in friendship with, and of the same faith, as the House of Este, and who had helped him with ability, advice, and fortitude in all that he had undertaken in Italy, and who knew very well how the noble blood of these princes had originated from the nobility of France, and to return them

---

[9] In 1570, for example, Zan Ganassa is the star at the wedding of Renée and Ercole's daughter, Lucrezia d'Este, and Francesco Maria II, duke of Urbino. See Sergio Monaldini, "Visioni di comico: Alfonso II, la corte estense e la Commedia dell'arte," *Maske und Kothurn* 50, no. 3 (2004): 45–64.

[10] See the example of Gabriele Bombace's tragedy, *Alidoro*, which was sumptuously performed in Reggio in 1568, and of which remains a print copy of its success, thoroughly recounted, but not the text itself. Guarini, in particular, defends the survival of his *Idropica* and *Pastor Fido*, among lost copies and deferred performances. See Marzia Pieri, "Idropiche fra corte, accademia e tipografie: il nuovo pubblico di Guarini," in *'Rime' e 'Lettere' di Battista Guarini*, Atti del Convegno di Studi, Padova, 5–6 dicembre 2003, ed. Maria Da Rif, (Alessandria: Edizioni dell'Orso, 2008), 475–504.

[11] Giraldi Cinzio, *Commentario delle cose di Ferrara et de' principi da Este di M. Giovambattista Giraldi Gentilhuomo ferrarese eccc, tratto dall'epitome di M Gregorio Giraldi tradotto da Lodovico Domenichi* (Venice: Giovanni de' Rossi, 1556), 162.

to the original parents from whom they had been separated for a long period of time, and to confirm again the friendship and benevolence with a kinship bond which had always existed between the kings of France and the lords of Este, moved by the fame of this most noble duke, and very good young man, he decided to give him Renata as wife so that they could both continue to grow their splendor.)

This is how, in the 1540s, Giraldi celebrated the event in his *Commentario*, written on commission and translated into Italian by Ludovico Domenichi in 1556, neglecting to say that, at the time, such "splendor" was not so obvious.[12] Ercole I was not a connoisseur of Latin texts, but he understood well the importance of cultural politics, and in particular of the theater, and utilized it therefore to found the prominence of Italian-language comedy on the Ferrara stage, which stood in competition with its eternal rival, Florence.[13] His death, however, had left a void that his son Alfonso I—who was little cultivated and afflicted by long-standing wars—was unable to fill, and "si pentiva talmente di non havere imparato lettere, ch'essendo hoggi mai vecchio desiderava per qualche dono di Dio di poter ritornare fanciullo, e guaire un'altra volta in culla per impararle" (was sorry not to have learned the letters, because now that he was old, he wished to receive his youth through a gift from God, and lay in his crib so that he could learn them).[14] In the meantime, the splendors of the Ferrara performances had faded, while in Urbino, Florence, and Rome, the scenographic and dramatic experimentations by Tuscan authors were numerous and met significant fortune while instead diminishing the eternal representations of Plautus and Terence in Ferrara, which in turn were criticized by Machiavelli as being void of "sali che ricerca una

---

[12] Giraldi, *Commentario delle cose di Ferrara*, 162.

[13] "Non haveva il Duca Hercole lettere latine, perciochè essendo egli stato travagliato troppo dalla fortuna, non ci havea potuto metter l'animo. Ma sapendo benissimo come la cognitione delle lettere è di grandissima utilità a' principi grandi, per governare se stessi e i popoli loro, stimò sempre molto i professori delle buone lettere, e da loro con animo ingordissimo cercava d'imparare i modi di signoreggiare giustamente le cagioni delle cose, e la cognitione di tutte l'historie antiche" (the Duke Hercole did not have Latin letters, therefore, being occupied with bad luck, he couldn't put his mind to it. But knowing very well how being educated is of great importance to princes, in order to govern themselves and their people, he had always esteemed very much the professors of letters, and from them, with an eager soul, he sought to learn the ways to govern in a just way the ways of things, and the knowledge of all ancient things), Giraldi Cinzio, *Commentario delle cose*, 110.

[14] Giraldi Cinzio, *Commentario delle cose*, 155.

commedia" (the salt that a comedy demands) and of the resourceful "motti fiorentini" (Florentine achievements).[15]

The stability of the theater foreseen by Ercole was not realized,[16] and the courtiers nurtured only the aristocratic diversions from the Quattrocento tradition that did not have a solid potential for continuity, including chess and board games, music, equestrian prowess, and reading of romances and dramas.[17] The recited dramaturgy destined to the courtiers in palaces, *delizie*, and private residences was used more as a reference, as it was less entertaining and tempting than the Carnival games performed by the court jesters. Furthermore, it was for the most part constituted by hasty translations of classical texts extorted from the literati of the *Studio*. Unlike the texts written to be represented, these translations could rarely be used quickly. However, in the 1520s something started to change:

> passato l'anno della peste grande, che fu del 1528 si comenciò a recitare qualche comedia dell'Areosto, sendosi posto a dormire quelle che si costumavano tradurre di Plauto in volgare, e massimamente farle in versi, cosa non molto laudabile, che per vecchie e belle che fossino divenivano storpiate, come dico cominciorono a comparire in scena quelle dell'Areosto, che riconcie in versi sciolti ch'esso poeta chiamava jambi volgari, eccitorno molti ingegni, che composero e Comedie e Tragedie, che sebbene non tutte sono state eccellentissime, non erano però goffi affatto.[18]

---

[15] In *Discorso intorno alla lingua*, this judgment also pertains to the Ferrara comedies, including Ariosto's. See the edition by Paolo Trovato (Padua: Antenore, 1982), 63.

[16] "Né solamente il Duca Hercole si dilettò di così fatte lettere, ma talmente favorì la commedia, che con grandissime spese, e reale apparato rinovò i giuochi delle scene, il cui uso s'era dismesso affatto al suo tempo. Et già havea cominciata a provedere un bellissimo luogo a' posteri per recitare quelle favole, et lo avrebbe fornito, se la crudel morte non havesse rotto i suoi disegni. Percioché l'anno 1504 e del suo principato 33 a 16 di gennaio, quel giorno ch'egli haveva apparecchiato di far recitare una comedia al popolo, che passava settanta anni della sua vita, venne a morte" (not only did the Duke Hercole enjoy learning about letters, but he so much favored comedy, that with great expenses and real apparatus renewed the acts on stage, whose usage had ended for a while. And he had already started to provide a beautiful place for those stories to be rehearsed, and he would have completed this, had not cruel death broken his design. Therefore, in the year 1504 and 33 in his dukedom, on January 13, that day in which he had prepared to have a comedy played in front of his people, when he was 70, he died), Giraldi, *Commentario delle cose*, 112.

[17] See Angelo Solerti, "La vita ferrarese nella prima metà del secolo decimosesto descritta da Agostino Mosti," *Atti e Memorie delle Province di Romagna*, series III, vol. 10 (Bologna: s.n., 1891–1892), 171.

[18] See Solerti, *La vita ferrarese nella prima metà del secolo decimosesto*, 180.

(when the year of the big plague passed, which was 1528, some of Ariosto's comedies began to be played, since those translated into Italian written by Plautus were put aside, and put them in large part into verse, which was not very praiseworthy, as even if they were antique and beautiful they became spoiled, as I say, Ariosto's plays were starting to be played, and put into free verse, which this same poet called vulgar iambic verses, they excited many ingenious writers who composed both Comedies and Tragedies, which, although they were not all very excellent, they were not bad either.)

The arrival of the foreign princess was solemnized by a sumptuous feast, and to the usual wedding celebrations of the Italian courts, modern comedy was renovated for the occasion. The wedding was celebrated on June 28, in Paris, but the plague delayed the bride's arrival until fall. On November 12, in Modena, she was celebrated with shots of jubilation and fireworks; after a long trip along the Panaro, Renata arrived at Belvedere a few days later among more shots of jubilation, and the day after, she entered Ferrara on a stretcher under a canopy, dressed in French fashion[19] and proudly wearing a crown, which raised some critical whispers.[20] The parade of clerics and knights that accompanied her was preceded by the Spanish jester Diego, riding a dromedary, and at the palace she was welcomed by her sister-in-law Isabella. The handling of the keys, the solemn blessing in the Duomo,[21] and the music and dances along the city route represented a public prelude to the private celebration that continued at the palace under Ariosto's direction. Indeed, together with the actor Ruzante, the playwright offered the staging of his *Lena* to the French

---

[19] Strabellino described to Isabella d'Este the ladies' "scuffiotti d'oro in testa" (gold embellishments in their hair), as well as the garb and ornaments of the foreigners. It was the first mark of the desire to Italianize the duchess which would also become a source of conflict between the duke and Madame de Soubise. See Rosanna Gorris, "'D'un château l'autre': la corte di Renata di Francia a Ferrara (1528–1560)," *Il palazzo di Renata di Francia*, ed. Loredana Olivato Puppi (Ferrara: Cassa di Risparmio di Ferrara, 1997), 150 and Benedetto Fontana, *Renata di Francia, duchessa di Ferrara: sui documenti dell'archivio Estense, del Mediceo, del Gonzaga e dell'archivio segreto Vaticano*, vol. 1 (Rome: Forzani, 1889), 75.

[20] Fontana, *Renata di Francia*, vol. 1, 69.

[21] Fontana, *Renata di Francia*, vol. 1, 69.

guests,[22] with a moralizing prologue written for the occasion and performed by the Prince Francesco d'Este.[23]

At the end of January, the new groom organized another reception for his parents, his aunt Isabella, and the French ambassadors, inaugurated this time by Ariosto's *Cassaria*. The banquet took place in the grand hall, with 15 sugar statues symbolizing Ercole's struggles, and with dances and music by Alfonso della Viola, and scenes acted by Ruzante and his colleagues. However, the *Menaechmi*, a representation to be performed in French, did not occur,[24] and it is important to note that the participants had to "endure" four hours of performances threatened by a ducal ban issued against eventual disruptors.[25] The amalgam of the new arrivals, who were not used to this type of entertainment, was slow and grueling, but a subsequent festivity on May 20, organized by Ippolito d'Este in the Belfiore gardens, with the indoor recital of a farce followed by an outdoor banquet, with music, dances, and jesters, encountered the active participation of the foreign ladies-in-waiting.[26]

In Baldassare Castiglione's *Cortegiano*, the French are portrayed as appreciating only the "nobiltà delle arme," (the nobility of arms) and as somewhat unrefined.[27] For Renata and her entourage, the dramatic theater, of which the Este court was extremely proud, was a complete novelty. During her youth in France, modern profane entertainment had yet to flourish, as she had only experienced lyrical and allegorical *comédies* of a gnomic and sacred nature, including those performed at the court of Marguerite de Navarre.[28] In order to evaluate the difficulty, not only

---

[22] The festivities and efforts did not go unnoticed and on January 13, François I wrote Alfonso a letter in which he expressed his satisfaction regarding the wonderful welcome that his sister-in-law received, which was promptly referred to him. Fontana, *Renata di Francia*, 90.

[23] Fontana, *Renata di Francia*, 83.

[24] Fontana, *Renata di Francia*, 99. We know little of the foreign translations of some of the Italian plays prepared for a foreign public, such as *Orbecche* in French, commissioned by François I, *Altile* in Spanish performed in Parma, or *Sofonisba* by Trissino, performed in Blois in 1556.

[25] See Michele Catalano, *Vita di Ludovico Ariosto ricostruita su nuovi documenti*, Vol. 1 (Geneva: Olschki, 1931), 584.

[26] Fontana, *Renata di Francia*, vol. 1, 154.

[27] See *Il libro del Cortegiano*, ed. Ettore Bonora (Milan: Mursia, 1976), book 1, chapter 42, 84.

[28] See Marguerite de Navarre, *Les comédies bibliques*, ed. Barbara Marczuk (Geneva: Droz, 2000). The representations started in the 1540s at the small court of Nérac, but the tradition

linguistic, of this new experience for the duchess, we can recall that, 20 years after her arrival in Italy, the famous recital of Dovizi's *Calandra* offered in Lyon by the Florentines at the French court in honor of the new Queen Catherine de Medici, with a rich musical apparatus comprised also of allegorical interludes, left the public completely perplexed and confused:

> ora, se bene in cotal modo la Notte dimostrò aver dato l'ultimo fine alla commedia, niuno però degli spettatori fu che per allora si movesse: ma stetteno tutti fermi a rimirare buon pezzo di poi lo apparato, il quale nel vero faceva un bellissimo et suntuosissimo vedere. Circa alla soddisfazione della comedia, non pur Sua Maestà, che lo disse più d'una volta, ma ancora i Signori e Gentiluomini di Corte per una voce tutti affermavano non aver mai veduto il più bello spettacolo.[29]
>
> (now, even if in that way the Night demonstrated to have ended the comedy, none of the spectators moved right then: but they all stayed where they were and kept on looking at the apparatus, which in truth made a very beautiful and sumptuous sight. As far as the success of the comedy, not even His Majesty, who repeated it more than once, but even more the Gentlemen and Lords of the Court in one voice all affirmed to have never seen a more beautiful show than this one.)

The inability to understand that the performance was over after the last interlude, apart from the expressions of praise, reflects the total naïveté of a public that was not used to performances, which, however, was followed by a more successful one.[30] Later on, the fortune of Italian theater in

to dramatize sacred texts in the form of *jeus* or *ludi* with a joyful ending started in the convents. This tradition did not intersect with the humanistic discovery of classical theater. Brantôme writes that Marguerite would compose comedies and moral and pastoral novels: "qu'elle faisoit jouer et représenter par des filles de sa court" (that she would have performed and interpreted by the girls at her court) and that she had staged a comedy for her husband: "une traduction tragicomique" (a translated tragi-comedy) of almost the entire Testament. See *Les Comédies bibliques*, 19. This type of short and lyric private *mysthères*, with few characters and numerous monologues, show an aristocratic theatrical background destined to be inexorably included in the arrival of classical dramaturgy, which would survive in the tradition of the northern Protestant rhetoric. In some of Giraldi's scenes, Renata could have found some of these same characteristics.

[29] See Bernardo Dovizi il Bibbiena, *Calandra*, ed. G. Padoan (Padua: Antenore, 1985), 235.

[30] This detail was noted in a document edited in March 1549 which is no longer available, and which contained *Particolare descrizione della Comedia che fece recitare la Nazione*

France, in particular Tuscan plays, would be unrelenting and fruitful thanks to Catherine de Medici and her successors' mediation. However, there is also another side to this story, less known and more bookish, that has its origins in Ferrara, with the socialite Cardinal Ippolito and with his faithful companion Luigi Alamanni,[31] and with Renata's numerous guests and courtiers who brought back to France the memories of the Este's festivities. For example, in 1537, Sebastiano Serlio, the future painter and architect of Fontainebleau, dedicated to Ercole II his *Regole generali di architettura*.[32] Also, Renata's former almoner, Jean de Boghlat, translated and published an elegant edition of the work of the Este steward Christoforo di Messisbugo, *Banchetti, compositioni di vivande et apparecchio generale*, which would become the bible of gastronomy at the European courts.[33] Finally, using the techniques he had learned in Italy, Maurice Scève organized the luxurious festivities in Lyon for the 1536 arrival of Ippolito, who had just been named archbishop.

PERFORMANCE AT THE FERRARA COURT

During the first years in Italy, Duchess Renata became acquainted with court performances consisting mostly of classic and moralistic comedies, encomiastic in nature, and performed in Latin and Italian. Ariosto's and Ruzante's performances alternated with those written by Celio Calcagnini.

Fiorentina a richiesta di Sua Maestà Cristianissima, according to Italian nuptial pamphlets which published the notice of marriage. See Dovizi il Bibbiena, *Calandra*, 214.

[31] See Gorris, "*'Jean Baptiste Giraldy Cynthien gentilhomme ferrarois': il Cinthio in Francia*," *Giovan Battista Giraldi Cinzio gentiluomo ferrarese*, ed. Paolo Cherchi, Micaela Rinaldi and Mariangela Tempera (Florence: Olschki, 2008), 77–129, who sees Renata's influence on Giraldi's earlier fortune in France.

[32] The architect Sebastiano Serlio, a pupil of Baldassarre Peruzzi, settled in France in the 1540s, invited by François I to work on the construction of the château de Fontainebleau; after the king's death, in 1547 he moved from Paris to Lyon in the service of Ippolito d'Este and devoted himself to intense theoretical work; his *Secondo libro di Perspectiva*, published in Paris in 1545, is a fundamental treatise on scenography, enriched by three famous engravings related to the comic, tragic, and satirical scene, that summarizes and disseminates the models of the Italian spectacle. The text can be read in *Lo spettacolo dall'Umanesimo al Manierismo. Teoria e tecnica*, ed. Ferruccio Marotti (Milan: Feltrinelli, 1974), 190–205.

[33] The works of Christoforo di Messisbugo, Ercole II's superintendent of feasts, were printed a year after his death in 1549, by Giovanni de Buglhat and Antonio Hucher, and describe his vast experience in the matter of *scalcheria*, that is, cutting of meat, culinary recipes, and the organization of court banquets. A modern edition by Ferdinando Bandini was printed in Venice by Neri Pozza in 1992.

And Ariosto's death in 1533, after the tragic fire of the Sala Grande stage of the previous year, marked a new interruption. The performances started only two years later in Schifanoia, but playwrights were scarce. While Ercole II, who became duke in 1534, preoccupied himself with politics in the ever changing international arena, his duchess organized her own circle's entertainment, enlivened by the courtly games of Clément Marot, who arrived in Ferrara in 1535, and who quickly became Renata's *valet de chambre* and secretary.[34] He was a cumbersome guest, who was intellectually connected to Calcagnini, Alamanni, and Niccolò Zoppino during the dark times of restless humanism, which was nonetheless modern, autonomous, and vibrant. Zoppino, in particular, was an eclectic printer and singer who took a primary role in Renata's early theater interests. From being an actor to a Roman *pasquinate* companion to Pietro Aretino and Campani, also known as Strascino, a famous actor and storyteller active between Rome and the northern courts, Zoppino became an editor of anthologies of *rime*. Furthermore, he was one of the first literati to understand the potential of transferring orally performed ephemeral dialogues to the page, and to found a specialized editorial division, after the actor Francesco de' Nobili, also known as Cherea, had failed to print in Venice some of the plays that had been performed in Ferrara during Ercole I's times.[35]

Under Marot's direction, Renata's court became a sophisticated lyrical and theatrical laboratory, one free from prejudice and where the educated ladies, according to eyewitnesses, "menent joyeuse existence" (lead a joyful existence).[36] The famous poetry contest, the *concours du beau tétin*, organized by Marot in 1535 drew significant attention, even from the solemn Calcagnini who participated as well, and the award was offered by the duchess herself.[37] As a duchess, Renata fulfilled her duties as a landlady and good wife in her new country, and became "Italianized" little by little: in 1532, for example, she undertook an official trip to Venice, where she arrived in the city in an official Este boat as the honored guest of the Compagnia dei Cortesi, hired by the authorities for 100 ducats.[38] Her

---

[34] See also Guillaume Berthon's and Robert J. Hudson's contributions to this volume.

[35] See Severi, *Sitibondo nel stampar de' libri. Niccolò Zoppino tra libro volgare, letteratura cortigiana e questione della lingua.* Rome: Vecchiarelli.

[36] See Gorris, "D'un château l'autre," 145, and "'Donne ornate di scienza e di virtù': donne e francesi alla corte di Renata di Francia," *Schifanoia*, 28–29 (2005), 175–205.

[37] See Gorris, "D'un château l'autre," 146.

[38] Ernesto Masi, *I Burlamacchi e di alcuni documenti intorno a Renata d'Este duchessa di Ferrara* (Bologna: Zanichelli, 1876), 232.

presence at court performances is well documented in the records that survived the inquisitional burnings. For example, she was present at the premiere of Giraldi's *Orbecche* in 1541, at the festivities in honor of Pope Paul II in 1543, and at the premiere of Giraldi's *Cleopatra*, staged at night, in 1555.[39] We also have documents testifying to representations dedicated explicitly to her court, including the representation of Agostino Beccari's *Sacrificio* on March 4, 1554, and the love eclogue in act written and directed by Sebastiano Clavignano da Montefalco, Ercole II's most famous actor:

> Vero è che il nostro Montefalco, che tutto era nato alla scena, già in casa nostra indusse una egloga a servizio dell'università degli scolari delle arti, la quale era divisa in atti e in iscene, della quale egli fu [...] autore e rappresentatore, la quale poscia anco fu dal medesimo rappresentata in corte della serenissima madama Renea, allora degnissima duchessa di Ferrara, con molta soddisfazione degli spettatori. La quale egloga conteneva un maneggio di pastorale amore, e vi s'introduceva la ninfa amata a ragionare.[40]
>
> (It is true that our Montefalco, who was born completely on stage, already at our house he had recited an eclogue for the university students of the arts, which was divided into acts and scenes, of which he was [...] author and actor, and which was also represented at court by himself in front of madama Renea, who was then the illustrious duchess of Ferrara, with much of the audience satisfaction. The eclogue included a combination of pastoral love, and introduced the nymph who loved to reason.)

Renata also continued her more serious occupations, as up to 1550 she participated, together with her daughters and ladies-in-waiting, in the Holy Week ceremonies. On this occasion, she offered a dinner for 13 poor citizens, dressed in new clothes, and carried out, in private and inside her *maison* in a reformed manner, the penitential ceremony of the washing of the feet, which, since Ercole I's times was exclusively performed in public by the male members of the Este family. Renata's charitable deeds took place in her chapel, which allowed her to entertain more freely the religious dissidents, as well as conduct necessary financial operations more privately.[41]

---

[39] See G. B. Giraldi Cinzio, *Scritti critici*, ed. Camillo Guerrieri Crocetti (Milan: Marzorati, 1973), 278.

[40] G. B. Giraldi, *Lettera sulla tragedia*, 241–242.

[41] See Franceschini, *La corte di Renata di Francia*, 197.

Renata entertained in five separate palaces, away from her husband, and in particular in Consandolo, in nearby Argenta, a 1540 gift from her husband, where she would seek shelter, surrounded by rich paintings and a "reformed" chapel decorated by Girolamo da Carpi, the official stage designer of court entertainments, who was very loyal to the duchess and who also painted a portrait of Anne de Parthenay, Madame de Soubise's daughter.[42] Here, Renata educated her children with much thought and supervision, paying particular attention to memorization and translation of classical texts, including Terence, who had always had a privileged place in Ferrara's intellectual circles. The public display of the Este children's scholastic prowess occupied a favored place within the cultural Renaissance manner of representations throughout Italy, where these scholastic recitals were accompanied by musicians, dancers, and jesters.[43]

Furthermore, the young Este progeny played in the official ceremonies of the court. We know that Anna, for example, performed *Andria* in Latin during the St. George festivities in 1539, as Ercole II recounts in a letter to his father, very proud of the quality of his own seed:

> Vorei che fusti contento venire a questa giostra ch'io faccio fare a Santo Georgio, affine che se possiamo goder un poco insieme: et oltre la giostra et altri passatempi che mi forciarò di farvi havere, voglio che vediate recitare, in secreto però, una comedia, nella quale la mia primogenita Anna recita anchor lei: et anchor che sii latina per essere la Andria di Terenzio son sicuro che non vi spiacerà una puta di 7 anni servir nella persona di Panfilo. Voi direte forsi ch'io sono patre et come la cornacchia: questo non mi dà noia, bastami ch'io spero farvi vedere ch'el mio sperma è pieno di bon spirito.[44]
>
> (I would love for you to come happily to this festivity which I will organize in Santo Giorgio, so that we can enjoy some time together; and with the festivity and other events which I will have for you, I want you to watch, in secret however, a comedy in which my first born, Anna, will act: and it will even be in Latin as Terence's *Andria*, and I am sure you will not mind that

---

[42] For Carpi and his paintings, see Wilson-Chevalier's contribution in this volume. See also Alessandra Pattanaro, *Girolamo da Carpi. Ritratti* (Padua: Bertoncelli Arti Grafiche, 2000). To the painting's *ekphrasis*, whose location remains unknown, Giraldi dedicates his composition *Poematia* entitled *Renata Parthenia*. See Gorris, "*J.B. Giraldy Cinthien gentilhomme Ferrarois*," 83.

[43] A famous example is that of the recitals in the 1513 carnival at the court of Urbino, which alternated Bibbiena's *Calandra* and Nicola Grasso's *Eutychia* recited by gentlemen, and a lost comedy by 14-year-old Guidubaldo Rugiero recited by children.

[44] The letter is addressed to Cardinal Gonzaga. See Fontana, *Renata di Francia*, vol. 2, 90.

a girl of seven will play Panfilo. You will probably say I am the father and like the crow who likes to brag: this does not bother me, as long as I can show you that my sperm is full of good spirit.)

In 1543, all of the duke's five children performed Terence's *Adelphoi* in Latin in front of Pope Paul II during his official visit.[45] The performance's director was their tutor and court doctor, Giovanni Sinapio.[46] The duchess was still the honored and authoritative hostess, to whom the pope owed respect, and who, in a letter of July 5 of that year, saved her from the Ferrara inquisitors, threatening excommunication to whoever would accuse her of heresy. At her besieged court, yet with relative ability of movement, Renata received literati and poets, rigorously supervised her daughters' and her *dame de chambres*' education, and participated as honored guest to the many theater representations across town.

GIANBATTISTA GIRALDI CINZIO

As Curione defines her court during his journey through Ferrara in 1542, the "private reginae ferrarensis academia" (the privatae academy of the queen of Ferrara)[47] was a space of vibrant sociability which, at least up to the crisis of 1554, was in dialogue with her husband's court, and in particular with one of its most active members, Giraldi, who became Ercole's private secretary in 1541. In this role, he not only fulfilled his diplomatic and political routine tasks, but he also personally carried out the strict implementation of vulgar Italian (lyric, poetry, treatise, and novels). However, his most ambitious objective was to focus on theater production and its ongoing organic extension of ducal politics. In the 1540s through 1560s, Giraldi embarked on a copious writing effort, *mise-en-scène*, and exegesis of drama which resulted in the fairly original composition and production of nine tragedies, one pastoral, one comedy, and numerous poetic texts and treatises. During this time, the notion of tragedy was still

---

[45] Ercole II wrote that, after dinner, the pope was invited to attend a comedy in which Anna (13) played the lover, Alfonso (10) another lover, Lucrezia (8) the choir, Eleonora (6) a young lady, and Luigi (5) a servant. Fontana, *Renata di Francia*, vol. 2, 182–183.

[46] For more on Sinapio, also known as Johannes Sinapius, or Senff, and his connection to Renée's court and to Jean Calvin, see Dick Wursten's contribution to this volume.

[47] See Federica Ambrosini, "Literarum studia nobis communia": Olimpia Morata e la corte di Renata di Francia," *Olimpia Morata: cultura umanistica e Riforma protestante tra Ferrara e l'Europa, Schifanoia* 28–29 (2005): 207–232, especially 212.

vague, but Giraldi, in his new, experimental impetus defined it as an expressive language of entertainment, susceptible to various types of consumption, including the viewing of the performance, the listening of the "dramatized" text, and its silent reading, all the while fully embracing its emotional and educational function. Offered to the duke as a prestigious encomiastic and propagandistic gift, the tragedy probed into the contradictions of power, prodded into the characters' anxieties, who were fragile and lost, and expressed the hardships of a society absorbed by the Counter-Reformation crisis. At least at the *Orbecche* (1541) premiere, it also staged the agonizing hypothesis of the triumph of an irrational and never-ending horror. *Orbecche* is the first Italian tragedy performed and not only written[48]: it met an extraordinary editorial and performance success, but remained unique in Giraldi's *œuvre*, which turned almost immediately to the dramatic alternative of tragi-comedies. Though distressing, they end happily and interweave joyful and tearful moments in which kings, fathers, or lovers are always morally just, while the responsibility of evil falls on wicked courtiers who anticipate Iago from Shakespeare's *Othello*, a character prototype that would liberate the misled princes from embarrassing predicaments.

These types of severe and decorous entertainments were bound to please the duchess. Even before his promotion as Ercole's secretary, Giraldi had paid tribute to Renata and to her guests on several occasions, celebrating, for example, her ladies-in-waiting in the 1537 Latin play *Silva*, or dedicating to her some of his *Poematia* on nuptial occasions in which she was involved.[49] This was a deference on his part, and maybe even, at first at least, a courtier's calculation,[50] which would however grow

[48] *Orbecche*'s tragic realism quickly became popular in France through Renata's circle, thus nourishing a mystic and millenarian current of "cruelty tragedies" continuous with the years of civil wars and inaugurated by Edouard du Monin's *Orbec-Oronte*. See Rosanna Gorris, "La tragedia della crudeltà," *Dalla tragedia rinascimentale alla tragicommedia barocca*, ed. Elio Mosele (Fasano: Schena Editore,1993), 294–309.

[49] It was Anne de Parthenay's wedding to Anthoine de Pons in 1533, and Sinapio's wedding to Françoise de Boussiron in 1539 that Giraldi celebrated, although the de Pons would be sent back to France by Ercole in 1544. See Gorris, "J.B. Giraldy Cinthien gentilhomme Ferrarois," 182.

[50] Guy Lébatteux notes Giraldi's rise as a member of the lower nobility, who arrives to the Este court from the Studio as a philosopher and scientist, and then becomes a literato. In his social and economic climbing are involved a series of individuals who were loyal to Renata in not only mundane and political ways, but also in ethical and idealistic ways, including Celio Calcagnini, Anton Musa Brasavola, Bernardo Tasso, Renata's secretary until 1531, Francesco

into a sincere kinship with the duchess as time went by, and which remained
unwavering even during the difficult years. His encomiastic verses, written
in honor of Renata's education and high morals, resonate with ethical kinship, and echo as well in his homage in the 1543 *Orbecche*'s princeps, titled
Tragedia a chi legge:

> Né stran ti paia che le donne ch'io
> ho meco in compagnia sian via più saggie
> che paia altrui che si convenga a donne.
>
> Ch'oltre il lume, qual ha de la ragione
> come l'uomo la donna, il gran sapere
> che chiude in sé quella sublime e rara
>
> donna, il nome di cui alto e reale
> con somma riverenza e sommo onore
> oscuramente entro a me chiaro serbo,
>
> far può palese a ogni giudicio intiero
> non pur quanto di pregio in sé aver possa
> donna gentil, ma che 'n prudenzia e senno
>
> (rimossa che ne sia la invidia altrui)
> agguagliar puote ogni saggio uom del mondo.[51]

(And it should not seem odd to you / that the women in my company are
wiser / which may not seem to befit women. / And apart from the light,
which comes from / reason that both men and women have, the / great
knowledge enclosed in that sublime / and rare woman, whose high and
regal name / with lofty reverence and lofty / honor I withhold obscurely in
myself, / can make obvious to any intact judgment / not in how much
praise a *gentildonna* / can possess, but in how much prudence and sense /
(once other people's envy is removed) / she can equal any wise man in
the world.)

The same tone pervades the various verses in the 1554 *Ercole*, written
in honor of "Renata the great," "saggia, gentile, honesta donna / in cui,
quanta esser può, virtù s'indonna" (wise, kind, honest woman / in whom,

Porto and his uncle, Lilio Gregorio Giraldi, Diana Ariosti, who was Antoine de Pons's tutor.
See Lébatteux, "Idéologie monarchique et propagande dynastique dans l'oeuvre de
Giambattista Giraldi Cinthio," *Les écrivains et le pouvoir en Italie à l'époque de la Renaissance
(deuxième série)*, ed. André Rochon (Paris: CNRS, 1974), 243–312.
[51] See *Teatro del Cinquecento. La tragedia*, ed. R. Cremante, vol. 1 (Milan-Naples:
Ricciardi, 1997), 438–439.

as much as there can be, virtue becomes female), and "casta e augustissima" (chaste and dignified)[52] or again in the dedication to her in his 1555 *Epitome* as "lectissimam foeminam, regio splendori moribus ac virtutibus parem" (excellent woman, with regal magnificence, equally good morals and virtue).[53]

Giraldi's official patron remained Ercole II, who, unlike his father, had received a refined and modern education, was very passionate for music and poetry, and promoted a deep urban renewal of the Italian culture, assisted also by an army of gentlemen from the Academy of the Elevati, which then became the Academy of the Filareti. This army was also engaged in an effort to renew the antique institution of classical Latin, while also remaining faithful to Guarini's utopia to support the duke for the common good. The passage from Latin to vulgar Italian was symbolically embodied by Giraldi, who inherited the professorship from Calcagnini and who enthusiastically concentrated his efforts to realize his duke's ambitious cultural strategy, founded on the theoretical and practical reinvention of the Italian tragedy, followed by the satiric tale, and the tragicomedy. It would become a strenuous "euristica teatrale per via filologica" (theatrical heuristic through philology).[54]

Giraldi's efforts would become an adventurous experiment undertaken without continuity with the previous Ferrarese tradition, but with norms and orders based on a more formal than substantial Aristotelianism. The barriers between comedy and tragedy, which had always been uncertain in Ferrara, began to almost fall; the custom of acting on bi-dimensional stages continued, realized with expenses and labor in "ambienti da camera" (private rooms), with fixed scenes on painted backgrounds and buildings in perspective, offered to the public at the lowering of the "coltrina" (the curtain), and onto which appeared sumptuous costumes, another element of the Este scene.[55] The texts acquired a new dignity but remained

---

[52] *Dell'Hercole di M. Giovanbattista Giraldi Nobile Ferrarese* (Modena: Gadaldini, 1557), 121, 138.

[53] See Giovan Battista Giraldi Cinzio, *De Ferraria et Atestinis principibus commentariolum ex Lilii Gregorii Gyraldi epitome deductum* (Ferrara: per Franciscum Rubeum, 1556), 70v. See also Giraldi's sonnet in Gabriella Scarlatta's chapter in this volume.

[54] See Riccardo Bruscagli, *G. B. Giraldi: comico, satirico, tragico, Stagioni della civiltà estense* (Pisa: Nistri-Lischi, 1983), 167.

[55] See "Discorso over lettera di messer Giovambattista Giraldi Cinthio, nobile ferrarese et segretario dell'illustrissimo Duca di Ferrara, a messer Giulio Pontio Ponzoni, intorno al comporre delle comedie et delle tragedie," in *G. B. Giraldi Cinthio, Discorsi intorno al comporre rivisti dall'autore nell'esemplare ferrarese Cl. I 90*, ed. Susanna Villari (Messina: Centro Interdipartimentale di Studi Umanistici, 2002), 306.

almost always only occasional and in manuscript form. Their style is bare and clear, devoid of any Spanish *préciosismes*, judgmental and filled with rhetorical figures.[56] The actors, called "dicitori" (speakers), were trained by the writer-director to speak in an animated way, more than to act. Thus, the dialogues were without embellishment, the monologues were numerous, and the action was slow and filled with music and choirs in the interlude. Even the Senecan characteristics, which were regularly discussed in these compositions, were often used to amplify the majestic *gravitas* of the monologues. The duke often provided feedback on his secretary's work, with intermissions that constituted its worth. He also commissioned some plays, such as *Cleopatra* and *Didone*, and maybe even later *Arrenopia* for the wedding of his daughter Anna with François de Lorraine, who became Duc de Guise. He set as well the modality and the standard length of the performances, insisted on the dates of completion, financed the scenery, often mounted on private palaces, provided the music, and when needed, intervened to call the actors to order when they would lose concentration during the long recitals.[57]

The recitals' impressive effectiveness and the success they encountered with the public derived from their inventive intertwining of emotions and from the strength of their distressing moments, which the tragi-comedies created in the heart's meanders. It certainly did not derive from the illusion that the production, which was founded on an idealized elementary mimesis, mimicking great distances and the proximity between the characters in very small spaces, nor from the verisimilar façade, which, on the other hand, explains in part their fortune with the comics of the *Commedia dell'Arte* and their relative misfortune with the literati.[58] All that rendered the comedy slow and strenuous was enacted on the tragic scene in Ferrara, which was not abandoned, but rather was dissipated with less quality than

---

[56] "Discorso over lettera," 300.

[57] See for example the letter of November 3, 1549, where Giraldi reassures the duke about the preparations for the staging of *Antivalomeni*. See G.B Giraldi, *Carteggio*, ed. Susanna Villari (Messina: Sicania, 1966), 237. For Giraldi's staging, see Pieri, "Mettere in scena la tragedia. Le prove del Giraldi," *Schifanoia* 12 (1992): 129–142, and *Scenery, Set and Staging in the Italian Renaissance Studies in the Practice of Theatre*, ed. Christopher Cairns (New York: Edwin Mellen Press, 1996).

[58] In fact, *Zibaldone*'s actor Stefanelo Botarga filled with Giraldi material. See Maria del Valle Ojeda Calvo, *Stefanelo Botarga e Zan Ganassa. Scenari e zibaldoni di comici italiani nella Spagna del Cinquecento* (Rome: Bulzoni, 2007). Furthermore, Angelo Ingegneri "erases" Giraldi from the dramaturgical canon in his 1598 treaty *Della poesia rappresentativa e del modo di rappresentare le favole sceniche*.

the successful comedies in Siena, Florence, and Venice. Ferrara remained stubbornly reticent in accepting the comical, which it found hard to handle.[59] Giraldi theorized a measured and moralistic version, which was definitely weak: his only example of the genre, *Gli Eudemoni*, almost similar to his more bourgeois tragedy, *Antivalomnei*, remains unpublished, while the more fortunate examples of his friend Ercole Bentivoglio, to whom he dedicated his *Discorso sulle commedie e le tragedie* for his "grande cognizione delle materie sceniche," (his great knowledge of the scene subjects)[60] are unique with some Aristotelian notoriety, which Giraldi deemed to be the only possible paradigm of the genre: "tra le lodevoli [commedie] oggidì sono di una sola maniera, et sono quelle che imitano quelle dell'Ariosto" (among the acclaimed comedies nowadays they are one way only, and those that imitate Ariosto's comedies).[61]

With strenuous commitment, particularly during the 1540–1550s,[62] Giraldi, "conformista e ingegnoso" (conformist and ingenious),[63] renewed the Este stage with high and gnomic style, pairing as well a series of rehearsal experiments and a systematic and very modern poetic exegesis. Giraldi was an intellectual, certainly less orthodox than what has been believed up to now, who supported and shared his duchess's severe

[59] Giraldi himself, in his long revision of his *Discorso sulle commedie* hesitates to enter the critical analysis of the comic *vis* of the classical writers, adding and deleting in indecisive terms his notes. See Villari, "Premessa" to *G. B. Giraldi Cinthio, Discorsi intorno al comporre*, XC–XCI.

[60] G. B. Giraldi, *Discorso*, 205. The gentleman, who was already one of Ariosto's friends and an illustrious member of the *Elevati* academy, had written a tragedy, *Arianna*, and various "gentili et molto giudiciose comedie" (refined and very serious comedies), among them *Il Geloso* and *I fantasmi* (a rewriting of Plautus's *Mostellaria*), which dated from the 1530s, were edited in Venice in 1544 by Domenichi, with a dedication to Alberto Lollio.

[61] See Giraldi, *Discorso*, 234.

[62] The chronology of his compositions has not always been determined for sure, also because the author comes back to his writings at various stages, with several rehearsals and preliminary tests of public readings. *Orbecche* was composed and rehearsed at various stages, in 1541, then published in 1543. *Didone* was read in 1541, *Altile's* announced representation in 1543 was compromised by the murder of the main actor, and therefore did not materialize until 1545. *Cleopatra*, composed in 1543, was not represented until 1555 (or maybe before), and *Egle* was prepared in 1545 and edited a bit later. In 1548, after a short pause, *Antivalomeni* was represented and *Eudemoni* was written. *Selene* and *Eufimia* were represented several times in 1547 and 1560; *Arrenopia* was represented in front of Alfonso II in 1563 and *Epitia*, which was never represented, was written between 1543 and 1554.

[63] This is the dazzling judgment by Cesare Garboli in Volume 5 of *Enciclopedia dello Spettacolo*, Florence (Rome: Sansoni, 1958).

spirituality. To a certain extent, he shared her destiny as well: in 1564, he was brutally fired by Alfonso II for his "incompatibilità ambientale" (incompatibility with the environment) of the new duke's court. Sincerely irenic and lost in the face of the harshness of his times, he moved in the dangerous labyrinth of the court, as maybe not so much a Nicodemite in strict terms, with prudence and ruthlessness, at least until his exile to Mondovì, where he fell to old age's harshness and threats in the shadows of the Jesuits. His continuous professions of religious orthodoxy and his sincere devotion to the court exorcize only partially his deep artistic restlessness, nourished by his former acquaintance with people as worried as himself, close to Renata, or heterodox like the heretic Ludovico Castelvetro, whose friendship he would never disown.

Giraldi's dramaturgy, so rigorously measured and planned in both form and content, always deals with political and moral themes which remain close to the religious debates of his times, and which is also characterized by the overcrowding of virtuous and unhappy queens, living distressing marital conflicts, which seem to allude transparently to the Este's laborious *ménage*, and always from their point of view.[64] After all, the theme of matrimony was very much in fashion in Ferrara and was the cause for many theoretical reflections of ethical, philosophical, and theological nature surrounding the debate of the Council of Trent, which would conclude with the 1563 decree *Tametsi*.[65] The profile of a troubled duchess can be recognized behind Giraldi's unhappy heroines, at times disobedient

---

[64] This is also the hypothesis of Paola Cosentino, "Tragiche eroine," *Italique. Poésie italienne de la Renaissance* 9 (2006): 69–99, and Corinne Lucas, "Le personnage de la reine dans le théâtre de Giraldi Cinzio," in *La corte di Ferrara e il suo mecenatismo, 1441–1598*, ed. Marianne Pade, Lene Waage Petersen, and Daniela Quarta (Modena: Panini: 1990), 283–300. See also the more recent contributions by Irene Romera Pintor, "Las heroinas tràgicas del teatro de Giraldi Cinthio," and by Villari, "Le eroine 'tragiche' delle novelle giraldiane," *Eroine tragiche nel Rinascimento*, ed. Sandra Clerc and Umberto Motta (Bologna: EMIL, 2019), 175–200 and 201–220.

[65] The decree gave authority to the priest and no longer to the spouses' agreement the *potestas* to officially ratify the validity of the wedding, thus annulling almost completely the lawfulness of the clandestine weddings. Several years ago, I discussed this topic in an essay, "La strategia edificante degli *Ecatommiti*" *Esperienze letterarie* 3 (1978): 43–74. Riccardo Bruscagli, however, has persuasively debunked my theory, showing that, on the contrary, Giraldi still lives in a rigorous and pre-tridentine regime. "Il racconto del matrimonio negli *Ecatommiti* di Giraldi Cinzio," *Studi di Letteratura Italiana per Vitilio Masiello*, ed. Pasquale Guaragnella and Marco Santagata (Bari: Laterza 2006), 553–575. This is an additional confirmation of how recently the documents and historiography about Giraldi's context have been enriched, but also muddled.

by necessity to the male authority. They live unfortunate love stories, they witness heroic abnegations, they are patient and vilified brides, or victims of political maneuverings, and they fight between destiny and free will. In Giraldi's cast, there are numerous handmaids, wet nurses, and female relatives impersonated perhaps by Renata's educated ladies of Consandolo, who impress the many witnesses, including Aonio Paleario, who writes:

> le [...] donne sono più sagge dei re. Le figlie di Renata, Anna e Lucrezia, sono dotte in greco e in latino, e la madre loro, nata da un potentissimo re, moglie di un duca illustre, benché colta nelle letterature classiche, non è stata paga della scienza nuova, ma per il suo grande ingegno e per amore della santità, si è dedicata in età matura alla teologia e allo studio delle Sacre Scritture.[66]
>
> (women [...] are wiser than kings. Renata's daughters, Anna and Lucrezia, are knowledgeable in Greek and Latin, and their mother, born from a very powerful king, and wife of an illustrious duke, although educated in the classic literatures, had not been taught about the new science, but because of her great intellect and love of sanctity, at a mature age, she dedicated herself to theology and to the study of the Holy Scriptures.)

Although there is no space to deepen this discussion, we can imagine the destination for these tragedies—often preceded by public readings, adorned with relatively simple backgrounds, and all to be recited on the scene—a theater that took place in a private room with the active participation of Renata's ladies-in-waiting. In nine out of ten cases, the singing choirs were female, with one exception only, that is, the chivalric *Arrenopia*, written and represented in 1563, before Giraldi's exile in Mondovì. By then, the duchess had already returned to France, and her court had been dissolved. The dates of the compositions and representations are often intertwined with the moments of conjugal and political conflicts, which time after time forced the duchess to recede, to submit herself, or to respond strategically to threats by calling on her powerful family back in France, which opportunistically sided with the husband or with the Church when it was absolutely necessary, but was just as much ready to intervene against Ercole's harshness when it was time to defend the dowry revenues from her French territories.

---

[66] This enthusiastic judgment is expressed in a 1552 letter to Bartolomeo Ricci. See Gorris, "D'un château l'autre," 145.

Giraldi's texts presuppose a rhetorical and elevated acting, entirely
founded on empathy and effusion in line with the aristocratic *status* and
intellectual profile of Renata's ladies, which is confirmed by an eloquent
report offered in *Eufimia*'s tenth scene, act four, a tragedy written almost
certainly in 1560, immediately before Renata's departure for France in
August. The protagonist of the plot is a particularly miserable queen, ill
married for the love of an inferior and cruel man, who, tired of her, plots
to have her killed under the false accusations of adultery. But Juno inter-
venes and saves her, thus unleashing a complex military and political
machine. The unfaithful Acaristo, whom Eufimia would continue to love
despite everything, would be killed in a duel, and the queen, for the good
of the kingdom, would obediently marry the good knight who won the
duel. Among the 24 characters who animate the plot there is the *nana*
Pomilla, who, at the center of a solitary cameo, laments the hopeless destiny of her queen and wishes to be soon reunited with her: "patria antica
/ et vita privata" (my homeland / and private life).[67] In the dwarf character, who only appears in this scene, we can recognize the noble *nana*
Agnes, the duchess's favorite and influential counselor,[68] to whom the
playwright dedicates such an allusive scenic affliction as a farewell homage.

[67] This lamentation, 33 verses long, appears as an appendix of elevated oration when compared to the main plot: "Che serà più di me, poi che perduta / ho la reina mia? Misera, dove
/ porò girar la mente perch' io possa / trovar conforto a questo grave affanno? / Non è per
me più questa corte, poi / che non vi è chi era la mia certa speme. / [....] Che debbo far io,
che mi nacqui nana? / Io son sì in dubbio di me stessa ch'io / esser non vorrei nata; o non
vorrei, / poi che pur nacqui, esser venuta a questa / corte infelice, poi che non ci è quella /
alma gentil che noi faceva liete, / e tutte siamo in preda a questo cane. / [...] ritornar voglio
alla mia patria antica / et in vita privata, col mio padre / e con la madre mia, starmi più tosto
/ che star qui in corte, ove mi tremi sempre / nel petto il cor per la continua tema / che
debbiam tutte aver di questa fiera." (What will become of me, since I have lost / my queen.
Wretched, where / can I turn to find comfort / for this grave sorrow? / This court is no
longer for me, since / there is no longer what was my true hope. / [...] What should I do,
I, who was born a dwarf? / I am in such doubt of myself that / I wish I hadn't been born;
or do not want, since I was born, to have come to this / unhappy court, since that kind soul
/ is no longer here, she, who made us happy, / and we are all at the mercy of this dog. / [...]
I want to go back to my homeland / and in private life, with my father / and with my
mother, feel more at home / than staying here at court, where my heart constantly / shivers
in my chest for the continuous fear / that we all should have of this situation.) See Giraldi,
Eufimia. An Italian Renaissance Tragedy, ed. Philip Horne (New York: Edwin Mellen Press,
2003), 154.
[68] See Belligni, *Renata di Francia*, 96.

The events and circumstances that we have discussed are only hypothetical. However, they are coherent with Renata's most recent historiographic portrait, that of a duchess who was neither a prisoner nor submissive, nor particularly estranged from her life in Ferrara and its culture and history. On the other hand, she was able to show herself with self-assurance in order to defend the people she wished to protect and to emerge almost unscathed from the 1554 events, when she was isolated and threatened. During her 30 years in Italy, which started in a very Burgundian fashion where the jester Diego preceded her nuptial procession, ending with a tragicomic play *a chiave*, much as a *roman à clé*, it symbolized the people and the events that were occurring around her. None of her five children shared in her beliefs, and her return to France, certainly planned for a while, took place against dramatic events, through which, however, she moved with astuteness, ruthlessness, and generosity, nested between the Guises and the Huguenots. Giraldi, a truncated and beaten innovator, was less fortunate in his exile in the Piedmont region in Mondovì, where he responded to Counter-Reformation demands, and continued to give his duchess a veiled homage of loyalty, translating in the novels by the *Ecatommiti* the marital imaginary and wifely heroism that had been tested on the Ferrara stage during his more fortunate years.

BIBLIOGRAPHY

PRIMARY SOURCES

Castiglione, Baldassarre. 1976. *Il libro del Cortegiano*. Edited by Ettore Bonora. Milan: Mursia.

Catalano, Michele. 1930. *Vita di Ludovico Ariosto ricostruita su nuovi documenti*. 2 Vols. Geneva: Olschki.

Cremante, Renzo, ed. 2007. *Teatro del Cinquecento. Volume 1, La tragedia*. Milano: Napoli.

Dovizi, Bernardo Il Bibbiena. 1985. *Calandra*. Edited by Giorgio Padoan. Padua: Antenore.

Giraldi, Giovan Battista il Cinzio. 1556a. *Commentario delle cose di Ferrara et de' principi da Este di M. Giovambattista Giraldi Gentilhuomo ferrarese eccc, tratto dall'epitome di M Gregorio Giraldi tradotto da Lodovico Domenichi*. Venice: Giovanni de' Rossi.

———. 1556b. *De Ferraria et Atestinis Principibus commentariolum ex Lilii Gregorii Gyraldi epitome deductum*. Ferrara: per Franciscum Rubeum.

————. 1557. *Dell'Hercole di M. Giovanbattista Giraldi Nobile Ferrarese.* Modena: Gadaldini.

————. 1966. *Carteggio.* Edited by Susanna Villari. Messina: Sicania.

————. 1970. *Lettera sulla tragedia.* In *Trattati di poetica e retorica del Cinquecento.* Edited by Bernard Weinberg, Vol. I, 471–486. Bari: Laterza.

————. 1973. *Scritti critici.* Edited by Camillo Guerrieri Crocetti. Milan: Marzorati.

————. 2002. *Discorsi intorno al comporre rivisti dall'autore nell'esemplare ferrarese Cl. I 90.* Edited by Susanna Villari. Messina: Centro Interdipartimentale di Studi Umanistici.

————. 2003. *Eufimia. An Italian Renaissance Tragedy.* Edited by Philip Horne. New York: Edwin Mellen Press.

Ingegneri, Angelo. 1974. Della poesia rappresentativa e del modo di rappresentare le favole sceniche. In *Lo spettacolo dall'Umanesimo al Manierismo. Teoria e tecnica*, ed. Ferruccio Marotti, 271–308. Milano: Feltrinelli.

Machiavelli, Niccolò. 1982. *Discorso intorno alla nostra lingua.* Edited by Paolo Trovato. Padua: Antenore.

Masi, Ernesto. 1876. *I Burlamacchi e di alcuni documenti intorno a Renata d'Este duchessa di Ferrara.* Bologna: Zanichelli.

Messisburgo, Christoforo di. 1992. *Banchetti, compositioni di vivande et apparecchio generale.* Edited by Fernando Bandini. Venezia: Neri Pozza.

Navarre, Marguerite de. 2000. *Les Comédies bibliques.* Edited by Barbara Marczuk. Geneva: Droz.

Solerti, Angelo, ed. 1892. *La vita ferrarese nella prima metà del secolo decimosesto descritta da Agostino Mosti.* Atti e Memorie delle Province di Romagna, Series III, Vol. 10. Bologna: n.p.

SECONDARY SOURCES

Adams, Tracy. 2010. Rivals or Friends? Anne de Bourbon and Anne de Bretagne. *Women in French Studies* (Special Issue): 46–61.

Ambrosini, Federica. 2005. 'Literarum studia nobis communia': Olimpia Morata e la corte di Renata di Francia. In *Olimpia Morata: cultura umanistica e Riforma protestante tra Ferrara e l'Europa*, ed. Azzura Aiello. *Schifanoia* 28–29: 207–32.

Belligni, Eleonora. 2011. *Renata di Francia (1510–1575). Un'eresia di corte.* Turin: UTET.

Bruscagli, Riccardo. 1983. G. B. Giraldi: comico, satirico, tragico. In *Stagioni della civiltà estense*, ed. Riccardo Bruscagli, 158–171. Pisa: Nistri-Lischi.

————. 2006. Il racconto del matrimonio negli *Ecatommiti* di Giraldi Cinzio. In *Studi di Letteratura Italiana per Vitilio Masiello*, ed. Pasquale Guaragnella and Marco Santagata, 553–575. Bari: Laterza.

Cairns, Christopher, ed. 1996. *Scenery, Set and Staging in the Italian Renaissance Studies in the Practice of Theatre*. New York: Edwin Mellen Press.

Cogotti, Marina, and Fiore Francesco Paolo, eds. 2013. *Ippolito II d'Este cardinale principe mecenate*. Rome: De Luca.

Cosandey, Fanny. 1997. De Lance en quenouille. La place de la reine dans l'état moderne (XVIe–XVIIe siècles). *Annales, Histoire, Sciences Sociales* 52 (4): 799–820.

Cosentino, Paola. 2006. Tragiche eroine. *Italique. Poésie italienne de la Renaissance* 9: 69–99.

Earenfight, Theresa. 2019. A Lifetime of Power: Beyond Binaries of Gender. In *Medieval Elite: Women and the Exercise of Power 1100–1400. The New Middle Ages*, ed. Heather J. Tanner, 271–293. London: Palgrave Macmillan.

Fontana, Bartolomeo. 1889. *Renata di Francia, duchessa di Ferrara: sui documenti dell'archivio Estense, del Mediceo, del Gonzaga e dell'archivio segreto Vaticano*. 3 Vols. Rome: Forzani.

Franceschini, Chiara. 2000. La corte di Renata di Francia (1528-1560). In *Storia di Ferrara, Vol. 6, Il Rinascimento. Situazioni e personaggi*, ed. Adriano Prosperi, 186–214. Ferrara: Corbo.

Gorris, Rosanna. 1993. La tragedia della crudeltà. In *Dalla tragedia rinascimentale alla tragicommedia barocca*, ed. Elio Mosele, 294–309. Fassano: Schena.

———. 1997. 'D'un château l'autre': la corte di Renata di Francia a Ferrara (1528–1560). In *Il palazzo di Renata di Francia*, ed. Loredana Olivato Puppi, 137–173. Ferrara: Cassa di Risparmio di Ferrara.

———. 2005. 'Donne ornate di scienza e di virtù:' donne e francesi alla corte di Renata di Francia. In *Olimpia Morata: cultura umanistica e Riforma protestante tra Ferrara e l'Europa*, Edited by Azzura Aiello. *Schifanoia* 28–29: 175–205.

———. 2008. 'Jean Baptiste Giraldy Cynthien gentilhomme ferrarois': Il Cinthio in Francia. In *Giovan Battista Giraldi Cinzio gentiluomo ferrarese*, ed. Paolo Cherchi, Micaela Rinaldi, and Mariangela Tempera, 77–129. Florence: Olschki.

Lébatteux, Guy. 1974. Idéologie monarchique et propagande dynastique dans l'oeuvre de Giambattista Giraldi Cinthio. In *Les écrivains et le pouvoir en Italie à l'époque de la Renaissance (deuxième série)*, ed. André Rochon, 243–312. Paris: CNRS.

Lequain, Élodie. 2007. Anne de France et les livres: la tradition et le pouvoir. In *Patronnes et mécènes en France à la Renaissance*, ed. Kathleen Wilson-Chevalier, 155–168. Paris: Publications de l'Université de Saint-Etienne.

Lucas, Corinne. 1990. Le personnage de la reine dans le théâtre de Giraldi Cinzio. In *La corte di Ferrara e il suo mecenatismo, 1441–1598*, ed. Marianne Pade, Lene Waage Petersen, and Daniela Quarta, 283–300. Copenhagen: Museum Tusculanum Press.

Marotti, Ferruccio, ed. 1974. *Lo spettacolo dall'Umanesimo al Manierismo. Teoria e tecnica*. Milan: Feltrinelli.

Monaldini, Sergio. 2005. Visioni del comico: Alfonso II, la corte estense e la Commedia dell'arte. *Maske und Kothurn* 50 (3): 45–64.

Ojeda Calvo, Maria del Valle. 2007. *Stefanelo Botarga e Zan Ganassa. Scenari e zibaldoni di comici italiani nella Spagna del Cinquecento*. Rome: Bulzoni.

Pattanaro, Alessandra. 2000. *Girolamo da Carpi. Ritratti*. Padua: Bertoncelli Arti Grafiche.

Pieri, Marzia. 1978. La strategia edificante degli *Ecatommiti. Esperienze letterarie* 3: 43–74.

———. 1992. Mettere in scena la tragedia. Le prove del Giraldi. *Schifanoia* 12: 129–142.

———. 2008. 'Idropiche' fra corte, accademia e tipografie: il nuovo pubblico di Guarini. In *Rime e Lettere di Battista Guarini. Atti del Convegno di Studi, Padova 5–6 dicembre 2003*, ed. Bianca Maria Da Rif, 475–504. Alessandria: Edizioni dell'Orso.

Rohr, Zita. 2018. Rocking the Cradle and Ruling the World: Queens' Households in Late Medieval and Early Modern Aragon and France. In *Royal and Elite Households in Medieval and Early Modern Europe. More than Just a Castle*, ed. Theresa Earenfight, 309–337. Boston: Brill.

Romera Pintor, Irene. 2019. Las heroinas tràgicas del teatro de Giraldi Cinthio. In *Eroine tragiche nel Rinascimento*, ed. Sandra Clerc e Uberto Motta, 175–200. Bologna: EMIL.

Severi, Luigi. 2009. *Sitibondo nel stampar de' libri. Niccolò Zoppino tra libro volgare, letteratura cortigiana e questione della lingua*. Rome: Vecchiarelli.

Suttina, Luigi, ed. 1932. Commedie, feste e giuochi a Roma e a Ferrara presso il cardinale Ippolito II d'Este nel carnevale degli anni 1540 e 1547. *Giornale Storico della Letteratura Italiana* 99: 279–284.

Tanner, Heather. 2019. Introduction. In *Medieval Elite: Women and the Exercise of Power 1100–1400. The New Middle Ages*, ed. Heather J. Tanner, 271–293. London: Palgrave Macmillan.

Taylor, Craig. 2004. The Salic Law, French Queenship and the Defense of Women. *French Historical Studies* 29 (4): 543–564.

Villari, Susanna. 2019. Le eroine "tragiche" delle novelle giraldiane. In *Eroine tragiche nel Rinascimento*, ed. Sandra Clerc and Uberto Motta, 201–220. Bologna: EMIL.

CHAPTER 9

A Challenging Wife: Renée de France and Simulated Celibacy

Eleonora Belligni

Since the early 1540s, the Roman Inquisition had been aware that the Duchess of Ferrara, Renée de France, was leading a heterodox community. It was only in the late 1540s, though, that direct complaints about her behavior reached her husband, Duke Ercole II d'Este, as his ambassadors in Rome were tipped off by Cardinal Inquisitors Giovanni Andrea Cortese, Marcello Cervini, Juan Alvarez de Toledo, and most of all, Giampietro Carafa. In 1550, after a sharp conversation with the latter, Giulio Grandi, the duke's man in Rome, reported to his master that the Inquisition was perfectly aware that "in casa della signora Duchessa illustrissima ve siano de male spine infette de questa falsa opinione lutherana et che anche nel Stato suo si admettano et tolerano de ladri simili" (some infected thorns belonging to this mendacious Lutheran belief are currently living in the *Duchessa illustrissima*'s household and that in the duke's own State such

E. Belligni (✉)
University of Turin, Turin, Italy
e-mail: eleonora.belligni@unito.it

© The Author(s), under exclusive license to Springer Nature
Switzerland AG 2021
K. D. Peebles, G. Scarlatta (eds.), *Representing the Life and Legacy
of Renée de France*, Queenship and Power,
https://doi.org/10.1007/978-3-030-69121-9_9

thieves were allowed and tolerated).[1] Ercole replied that he was really grateful for this informal warning, as the news, totally unheard-of and shocking, had left him astonished and worried.

Of course, it was no news at all to him, as he had known about his wife's religious activities since the mid-1530s. But it was only after a few years, in the summer of 1553, claiming his firm intention of reducing his injudicious wife to reason, that he added that they should be aware of his lack of power toward his wife: a weakness partially due to the previous pope's measure in favor of Renée, but most of all to his fear of the French crown. "Quanto alle parole che vi disse della Duchessa nostra consorte" (As for the words he [the Pope] told you about our wife, the duchess), he asked to explain to Julius III "che noi non siamo tale che ci lasciamo governare da donne" (that we are not such that we let ourselves be governed by women); he admitted, however, that he would not mind being helped by the Pope himself:

> per via di qualche ammonitione [...] di provedere a qualche strana fantasia che in questa materia ha predetta Duchessa, il che confermamo di nuovo, certificandola che ci sarà oltre modo grato ch'ella vedesse di fare tale ufficio o per via dell'ambasciatore francese o da cardinali o da altri di quella natione, non potendo noi farvi quella provvisione per li rispetti che può ben sua prudenza imaginarsi, sì come non saressimo stato da noi medesimo s'ella fosse di altro sangue di che è.
>
> (through some admonition [...] to take care of some strange fantasy that the duchess has shown in this matter [...] either through the French ambassador or through cardinals or others of that [French] nation, as we are not able to do such a thing [i.e., to stem Renée] for reasons of prudence, which His Holiness's sensitivity could easily figure out, reasons that would not stand if she [the duchess] were of other blood than she is.)[2]

In these letters, Ercole II d'Este was being nothing but sincere about his marriage. His deep sense of powerlessness, which had been constantly growing since their wedding in 1528, was the result of a combination of factors that were making his wife act as if she were not simply the Duchess of Ferrara, but the indisputable lady of her own household, the owner of

[1] Archivio di Stato di Modena (ASMo); *Ambasciatori Roma*, b. 40, Giulio Grandi to Ercole II, Roma July 18, 1550; see also *Ambasciatori Venezia*, b. 40, Ercole II to Girolamo Feruffini, Ferrara July 22, 1550.
[2] ASMo, *Ambasciatori Roma*, b. 57, Ercole II to Giulio Grandi, August 4, 155.

her own dowry, and last but not least, the absolute master of her soul. He was not alone in feeling this way. In the same decades, other husbands of ladies in high places were experiencing a similar situation: a lack of power over their wives, who were behaving in some respects as if they were not married at all, often resulting in conflicts related, for instance, to politics and religion.

The following contributes to an understanding of the relationship between marriage and power in early modern Europe (from the end of the fifteenth to the end of the sixteenth century) from a niche perspective: the social, religious, and cultural behaviors of a group of women who were practicing a way of being I would like to call "simulated celibacy." First, I demonstrate that this set of behaviors was actually a result of a combination of many factors, including above all a challenging attitude that these women displayed before their husbands and male relatives, as well as their high status, and the deep changes in the historical context in which they lived. Then, I examine this group of elite women by focusing on Renée de France. Among those who have been recently studied, the case of the Duchess of Ferrara—and especially her cultural and religious agency that spanned many decades—supports my hypothesis, though she is not an exemplary case. Nevertheless, what makes Renée interesting from a historical perspective are both her adherence to a persistent French pattern, a female legacy whereby she represented the group by taking on the role of a religious and cultural patron, and the set of circumstances in which she acted.

SIMULATED CELIBACY

As a premise, I would like to clarify that I have not borrowed the expression "simulated celibacy" from historiographic literature. Rather, it is a concept that I have coined by merging the early modern notion of simulation and dissimulation,[3] typical of many political treatises of that time, with the religious notion of celibacy, a state of being unmarried as a result of a vow, or an explicit act of renunciation. Using "simulated celibacy" I do not refer directly to a proper status, such as marital status. Instead, I aim to define a set of habits and bearings that made some high-ranking

[3] For the early modern concept of dissimulation and simulation, see *Dissimulation and Deceit in Early Modern Europe*, ed. Miriam Eliav-Feldon and Tamar Herzig (London: Palgrave Macmillan, 2015).

married women act purposely as if they were unmarried (according to standards of their times), often taking advantage of the transformations that European society experienced between the fifteenth and the sixteenth centuries. As a matter of fact, "simulated celibacy" was typically adopted by women of high nobility, who have recently attracted the scrutiny of many historians,[4] but we can also find examples among members of the urban political aristocracy and the wealthy patriciate (as in Italy), the merchant class, and landed gentry.[5] The focus is not on wealth or status per se, but on the chance of gaining access to ample resources—both material and relational—outside of the family's control.

In a nutshell, to discuss simulated celibacy is to recognize that certain early modern women learned how to exploit marriage as an opportunity to gain autonomy and power for themselves, even if it implied being challenged by their husbands, or defying their husbands explicitly. More than this, their challenge was mainly individual, not part of a family network or familial strategy—as was the case from late antiquity to the Middle Ages—and therefore, it was somehow a new expression of consciousness about female power and leadership, and about its bounds and borders.

Simulated celibacy can be used as a key to understand what happened to the exercise of power and agency by married women in high places, especially through the sixteenth and seventeenth centuries, for at that time, Europe was encountering significant cultural, political, and religious transformations, as well as the concurrent—though perhaps fainter—cultural stream sparked by the works of Christine de Pisan, known as the *querelle des femmes*.[6] Nevertheless, it was not a complete novelty in early modern Europe, but mainly a symptom of a long-established western tradition: a legacy of government and governance practices (which often outclassed theories), where women had been considered as a substantial part of familial groups and network strategies and sometimes had been developing strategies on their own (either to increase their own influence, or to

[4] See, for instance, *Queenship, Gender, and Reputation in the Medieval and Early Modern West, 1060–1600*, ed. Zita Rohr and Lisa Benz (London: Palgrave Macmillan, 2016).
[5] See Evelyn Welch, "Women in Debt: Financing Female Authority in Renaissance Italy," In *Donne di potere nel Rinascimento*, ed. Letizia Arcangeli and Susanna Peyronel (Rambaldi, Rome: Viella, 2008), 45–66.
[6] Joan Kelly, "Early Feminist Theory and the 'Querelle des Femmes' 1400–1789," *Signs* 8, no. 1 (1982): 4–28.

create their own network, or to escape some of their constraints and limitations).[7]

It is somehow misleading to contemplate this topic—that is, that of female power through and against marriage—as if we were watching a chess game being played between continuity and change (the opponents being the long-lasting Middle Ages or the game-changing Renaissance), or even a zero-sum game (resulting in either a significant loss of power or a growing realm of female leadership and independence).[8] Of course, acting according to simulated celibacy does not entirely explain how in the fifteenth century, certain high-ranking early modern ladies were able to establish successful cultural enterprises, parallel courts and circles, along with sophisticated systems of religious patronage, as these achievements had been natural expressions of feminine power throughout history, as recently demonstrated throughout the European Middle Ages.[9] Premodern queens, princesses, and other elite women routinely maintained independent households and courts, and this cannot be read as a symptom of emancipation from their husbands or native families, but rather, as a socially approved means of exercising power in its soft form,

---

[7] For the "unexceptionalist" paradigm, see *Medieval Elite Women and the Exercise of Power, 1100–1400: Moving Beyond the Exceptionalist Debate*, ed. Heather J. Tanner (London: Palgrave Macmillan, 2019), especially the introduction by Heather J. Tanner, Laura L. Gathagan, and Lois L. Hunneycutt, 1–18, and Theresa Earenfight's chapter, "A Lifetime of Power: Beyond the Binaries of Gender," 543–564, and Zita Rohr's interesting essay, which concentrates on the continuity and change of women's power, "Rocking the Cradle and Ruling the World: Queens' Households in Late Medieval and Early Modern Aragon and France," in *Royal and Elite Households in Medieval and Early Modern Europe. More than Just a Castle*, ed. Theresa Earenfight (Boston: Brill, 2018), 309–337. See also Tracy Adams, "Anne de France and Gift-Giving: The Exercise of Female Power" in *Women and Power at the French Court, 1483–1563*, ed. Susan Broomhall (Amsterdam: Amsterdam University Press, 2018), 65–84; *Femmes de pouvoir, femmes politiques durant les derniers siècles du Moyen Âge et au cours de la première Renaissance*, ed. Eric Bousmar, Jonathan Dumont, Alain Marchandisse, and Bertrand Schnerb (Brussels: de Boeck, 2012).

[8] The loss of female power during the Renaissance is the core of the most famous thesis of Joan Kelly, "Did Women Have a Renaissance?" in *Becoming Visible: Women in European History*, ed. Renate Bridenthal, Claudia Koonz, and Susan Mosher Stuard (Boston: Houghton Mifflin, 1977). On Kelly's thesis, see David Herlihy, "Did Women Have a Renaissance? A Reconsideration," *Medievalia et Humanistica* 13 (1985): 1–22. A further discussion can be found in Sophie Cassagnes-Brouquet, Christiane Klapisch-Zuber, and Sylvie Steinberg, "Sur les traces de Joan Kelly," *Clio. Femmes, Genre, Histoire* 32 (2010): 17–52.

[9] See, for example, the studies listed in note 7.

through influence and agency.[10] Indeed, the highest-ranked women, as queens-regnant, but also as queens-consort and queens-dowager, regents, and feudal châtelaines, could hold power in various degrees, shapes, and shades over the course of their life and depending on the context, at times, even in its hard, normative, or military form.[11] Most of the time, by simply following the rules of a patriarchal and misogynistic society, they did not need to defy their own husbands in order to govern, to be influential, or to gain control and autonomy over people, networks, and institutions. Power, authority, and agency were not an exceptional attribute for individual women. In its myriad forms—even if mostly in its soft form—it was routine.[12]

Nevertheless, as historians have recently reaffirmed, elite women's direct wielding of power, being mostly a part of a familial network group strategy from late Christianity, had been threatened and increasingly curtailed by "centralized governance and bureaucracy, and primogeniture and monogamous marriage in the twelfth through fifteenth century."[13] Something changed again at the beginning of the early modern age, when certain women in high places started to deal with their power by negotiating it with their families and their male counterparts in a way somehow different from before. In a perspective that emphasizes historical continuity, of course, we could see these women as heirs of a well-established and centuries-long Medieval tradition of women's exercise of power and authority. However, by stretching this argument to the point of taking early modern powerful women as a mere projection of Medieval customs and practices of authority and government, we risk missing how political institutions, theories, praxis, and customary practices were changing in Europe between the fifteenth and sixteenth centuries and how powerful, influential, and very well-connected women were bound to face, recognize, fight, or accommodate the same transformations that were somehow

---

[10] See Earenfight, "A Lifetime of Power," 274–275.

[11] See Earenfight, "A Lifetime of Power."

[12] See Earenfight, "A Lifetime of Power."

[13] Earenfight's thesis reaffirms McNamara-Wemple's thesis that elite women's direct wielding of power was curtailed by these factors: "The Power of Women through the Family in Medieval Europe: 500–1100," *Feminist Studies* 1, no. 3/4 (1973): 126–141.

upsetting the social, cultural, and political world of their male counterparts, or partners-in-power.[14]

Not so far from Catherine in space and time, during the so-called French Renaissance and the beginning of the *querelle des femmes*, certain high-ranking women challenged cultural and political norms, thereby starting a long-standing pattern of securing autonomy and influence—even more autonomy and more influence than had been seen previously—sometimes by manipulating or defying their husbands, sometimes by overshadowing them in the exercise of power. This all started, however, with a wife who did not publicly challenge her husband. Queen-regent Anne de Beaujeu (1441–1522), also known as Anne de France, or as Anne de Bourbon, dared to explicitly defy her husband Pierre de Bourbon's will only after he died.[15] But then again, she did not need to fight him before, as their marriage constituted an effective political cooperation, able to lead post-war France toward a more stable monarchy. Nevertheless, Anne was probably the first French queen (regent) to demonstrate the importance of building women-only networks, following paths in politics and diplomacy unknown to men, acting and thinking explicitly outside a box built by a misogynistic society.[16] Her legacy reached, a few decades later, her god-daughter, Renée de France. The Duchess of Ferrara exported to Renaissance Ferrara this French pattern, in a version that had been sharpened by the religious and political events of the first decades of the fifteenth century: a version that we can call simulated celibacy, and one that was very far from Anne's cooperative manipulation of her husband and her brother's will and her silent diplomatic word.[17]

---

[14] See, for example, Catherine of Aragon, who, while she cannot be taken as an example of simulated celibacy, is a great example of how the first decades of the sixteenth century required from queens and high-ranking ladies a life-long renegotiation and a constant reconfiguration of their role in order to adapt to changing times, which could result in strong conflicts with their family of origin or their husbands.

[15] It was mainly about the marriage of her brother Charles with Anne de Bretagne. See Tracy Adams, "Rivals or Friends? Anne de France and Anne de Bretagne," in *Women in French*, Special Issue 3 (2010): 46–61.

[16] Tracy Adams, "Fostering Girls in Early Modern France," in *Emotions in the Household, 1200–1900*, ed. Susan Broomhall (New York: Palgrave Macmillan, 2008), 103–118.

[17] Adams, "Rivals or Friends."

Early Modern Challenges and the French Pattern

Despite the great variety of situations, the status of lay, single women—both unmarried women, which in Protestant countries included divorcées, and widows—was considered an exception to, if not a true violation of, societal norms.[18] Many centuries of European culture have claimed the benefits of marriage. Catholicism had reaffirmed its sacramental value, which the Eastern Orthodox Church had always strongly advocated.[19] In Northern countries, especially in Germany, Lutheranism had considered marriage as the foundation of the whole Christian society: a conviction that religious and sectarian minorities had largely shared, except for some radical sects with their rather creative experiments on coupling.[20] Nevertheless, in early modern Christian Europe, widowhood and religious celibacy could generate a wide range of experiences for women, which differed according to quality of life, reputation, social status, and socioeconomic components (as inheritance systems, relations of production, marriage market trends, and property rights).

Nonetheless, certain widows benefited from their status more than others.[21] For instance, only after her husband's death in 1560, was Renée de France allowed to return to France and regain her status as chatelaine of Montargis (or to what was left of it), feeling important and "royal" again. She no longer needed to be afraid of her husband's sudden decisions against either her people or her customs, nor constantly annoyed by his complaints over the way she was spending her dowry. She did not have to

---

[18] Sandra Cavallo and Lyndan Warner, *Widowhood in Medieval and Early Modern Europe* (London and New York: Routledge, 2014), 3–22, 57–107, 240–265. On widowhood in sixteenth-century France see also Eliane Viennot, "Veuves de mère en fille au XVIᵉ siècle: le cas du clan Guise," in *Veufs, veuves et veuvage dans la France d'Ancien Régime. Actes du colloque de Poitiers, 11–12 juin 1998*, ed. Nicole Pellegrin and Colette Winn (Paris: Champion, 2003), 187–198. See also Catherine King, *Renaissance Women Patrons: Wives and Widows in Italy, c. 1300–1500* (Manchester: Manchester University Press, 1998).

[19] See the bibliography provided in David Heith-Stade, "Den ortodoxa kyrkans äktenskapsrätt," *Signum* 7 (2012): 17–21.

[20] John Witte, Jr., "The Mother of All Earthly Laws: The Lutheran Reformation of Marriage," *Gettysburg Seminary Ridge Review* 15, no. 2 (2013): 26–43.

[21] Beatrice Moring and Richard Wall, *Widows in European Economy and Society, 1600–1920* (Woodbridge: Boydell Press, 2017), 131, 137–8, 212–15; ed. Antoinette Fauve-Chamouz and Emiko Ochiai, *The Stem Family in Eurasian Perspective: Revisiting House Societies, Seventeenth to Twentieth Centuries* (Bern: Peter Lang, 2009) and *Singlewomen in the European Past, 1250–1800*, ed. J. Bennett and A. M. Froide (Philadelphia, PA: University of Pennsylvania Press, 1998).

bear her son Alfonso's attempts to restrain her in every possible way, nor to tend to her other son Luigi's constant bad health. Above all, she was mistress of her own religious life, free to patronize and protect her fellow believers openly and to associate again with any kind of believer whatsoever. As her marriage had been a worry for more than three decades, Paris and Montargis offered a shelter despite being disrupted by the Wars of Religion.[22]

Simulated celibacy was a creative synthesis between widowhood and spinsterhood. The concept evokes a secular path to a religious-like vocation for celibacy, but in fact is a manner of feigning a happy and wealthy widowhood, as was Renée's, rather than feigning spinsterhood. In a way, with Ercole II's death, Renée de France formally reached a status that she had long been practicing. Of course, challenging wives were often charged with madness, perversion, or corruption (whether active or passive).[23] At times, as was the case with Anne de France, their agency and political strategies were mistaken for "greed" for power and goods (luxury items more so than money) according to a long-standing, misogynistic tradition of biographers and historians.[24] Allegations of corruption and greed were a natural consequence of the fact that these women—just as financially independent widows—often decided to invest economic capital in tangible or intangible goods to increase their own reputation, boost their patronage, or enhance social relations (namely to build a long-lasting network). Undoubtedly, it was a way to extend the usual limits of a marriage, turning it into an opportunity to establish an autonomous space for spending, practicing, and voicing political or religious beliefs. Not every husband, though, was happy to watch his wife behaving as a woman with strong agency and sufficient financial and human resources to achieve her own purposes. Gender-role biases apart, men knew perfectly well that the chances to share the same goals or strategy with the other half of the couple were inversely proportional to their wives' resources, intelligence, and power of negotiation.

---

[22] For Renée's French last years, see the bibliography quoted in Belligni, *Renata di Francia*, 367–390.

[23] See Zita Rohr, "Playing the Catalan: The Rise of the Chess-Queen; Queenship and Political Motherhood in Late Medieval Aragon and France", in *Virtuous or Villainess? The Image of the Royal Mother from the Early Medieval to the Early Modern Era*, ed. C. Fleiner and E. Woodacre (New York: Palgrave MacMillan, 2016), 173–97.

[24] See Adams, "Fostering Girls in Early Modern France," 65–76.

But, even if many women shared a propensity to simulate celibacy, this was done so unconsciously and the goals for these practices were individual. More women gained access to different ways of being influential and powerful, but they did not become collective actors. When some of them, as the Protestant noblewomen in sixteenth-century France, shared a common end, their action was neither systematic nor continuous. Normally, their intentions were different, even if they tended to combine religious, cultural, artistic, or political interests.

These women can be easily identified as a group only ex post, even if the French princesses (from Anne de France to Renée de France) were well aware that they were a part of an established tradition.[25] The *querelle des femmes* itself ignited a spark of identity awareness that was, of course, very far from a systematic interaction. Emancipation from the marital yoke was just one of the resources they put in place to acquire autonomy or authority over a certain milieu, but certainly not the only one. There was no common emancipation strategy: if anything, it became an emerging effect of simulated celibacy, slowly growing over time.

Contextual changes such as the Reformation, the modern State, the invention of movable type, and the printing press reduced the disincentives for behaviors that dared to be transgressive or heterodox, namely not in line with the patriarchal model, but these were just signals, tenuous expressions of how the man-woman relationship was transforming. Simulated celibacy does not represent an *ante litteram* feminism, but a fragment of women's history that cannot be merely defined by idiosyncratic characteristics of individual noblewomen. In this limited and circumscribed phenomenon, Renée de France had a place: perhaps not emblematic or exceptional, but still significant.

RAISING CHILDREN, CROSSING BORDERS: THE FRENCH MODEL

At the beginning of the early modern age, new cultural and religious conditions allowed women to qualify as worthy interlocutors for humanists and theologians. Their freedom to take part in cultural activities grew faster, helped by many exogenous factors, such as the printing press

---

[25] See, for instance, Craig Taylor, "The Salic Law, French Queenship and the Defense of Women in the Late Middle Ages," in *French Historical Studies* 29, no. 4 (2006): 543–564, and Fanny Cosandey, "De lance en quenouille: la place de la reine dans l'Etat moderne," *Annales. Histoire, Sciences Sociales* 52, no. 4 (1997): 799–820.

revolution, or the fact that humanism promoted the inclusion of women in the world of learning and classical academia. Just a few decades later, these conditions acted as a trigger for female religious patronage.

But first came literacy and culture, so to speak. From the fifteenth century onward, some high-ranking politically talented female individuals started to lead intellectual networks,[26] and at the same time, cultivated "schools" for female education and smaller courts inside the larger European courts.[27] Alongside these schools, other women of lower status used their education and intellectual gifts not only to earn a living, but to write, speaking against prevailing misogyny and appealing to common sense and humanity. The *querelle des femmes* officially opened the debate on women's dignity in the mid-fifteenth century, 50 years after *The City of Women* that the young widow, Christine de Pisan, had written while supporting her family with her writing.[28]

The precursor of the humanist conception of women was the *virago*, depicted in Giovanni Boccaccio's *De claris mulieribus*, where the author imagined that only very talented women experienced a kind of metamorphosis, leading them from being a female in substance and qualities to becoming a male in substance, but with female qualities in exterior appearance, voice, and temper. Along with the evolvement of new theories about the female gender, some women started to lay the foundation for a new feminine relationship between *oikos* and *polis*, private *and* public.[29] Anne de France, who was King Louis XI's daughter and Charles VIII's sister,

---

[26] See Thomas Tolley, "States of Independence: Women Regents as Patrons of the Visual Arts in Renaissance France," *Renaissance Studies* 10 (1996): 237–258; Pauline Matarasso, *Queen's Mate. Three Women of Power on the Eve of the Renaissance* (Farnham: Ashgate, 2001) and *Patronnes et mécènes en France à la Renaissance*, ed. Kathleen Wilson-Chevalier and Eugénie Pascal (Saint-Etienne: Publications de l'Université de Saint-Étienne, 2007).

[27] On the House of Bourbon's educational tradition, see *Anne of France: Lessons for My Daughter*, ed. and trans. Sharon Jansen (Cambridge: D. S. Brewer, 2004), 69–89; Elodie Lequain, "La Maison de Bourbon, 'escolle de vertu et de perfection'. Anne de France, Suzanne de Bourbon et Pierre Martin," *Médiévales* 48 (2005): 1–15, and "Anne de France et les livres: la tradition et le pouvoir," in *Patronnes et mécènes*, 155–168.

[28] On Christine de Pisan, see Françoise Autrand, "Christine de Pisan et les dames à la cour," in *Autour de Marguerite d'Écosse. Reines, princesses et dames du xvᵉ siècles. Actes du colloque de Thouars, 23 et 24 mai 1997*, ed. Geneviève Contamine and Pierre Contamine (Paris: Champion, 1999), 19–31.

[29] See the study on Louise de Savoie's power-building by Aubrée David-Chapy, *Anne de France, Louise de Savoie, inventions d'un pouvoir au féminin* (Paris: Champion, 2017), and "La 'Cour des Dames' d'Anne de France à Louise de Savoie: Un espace de pouvoir à la rencontre de l'étique e du politique," in *Femmes à la cour de France, charges et fonctions (XV–*

was the unofficial regent until the adulthood of her brother. We know that, instead of breaking the rules of a misogynist and patriarchal society, she made new ones, drawn up by adapting powerful women patrons or brokers' standards to a traditional way to exercise the king's power in order to accomplish goals that would have eluded men. The outcome of her experience—a king with queen's ways and vice versa—was basically described by the series of rules and precepts which she later passed on to her own daughter, Suzanne de Bourbon, in a treatise titled *Les Enseignements à sa fille*.[30] Apart from this cultural and political legacy, she firmly believed in educating high-ranking young women in agency and influence. In her own circle, she was the ancestor of other French female patrons.[31]

Although in the Middle Ages, some great feudal ladies had fed numerous and notable courts of followers,[32] it was only when humanism spread rapidly throughout Europe that women's circles and networks were pervaded by an increased awareness, involving issues such as education, the spread of knowledge and values, and intangible cultural heritage,[33] in which religion grew increasingly important through the decades. Anne de France[34] had passed on the torch to her sister-in-law, Anne de Bretagne, a woman of exceptional temperament, gifted with the extraordinary ability to place her daughters, and a political awareness above the will of her husband and king, Louis XII of France. In the early sixteenth century, during a long series of difficult pregnancies and miscarriages, the duchess turned her small court into a cultural laboratory, choosing to settle down in her

---

XIXe siècles), ed. Caroline zum Kolk and Kathleen Wilson-Chevalier (Lille: Presse Universitaire du Septentrion, 2018), 49–65.

[30] On the transmission of cultural and political knowledge from mother to daughter, see Éliane Viennot, "La transmission du savoir-faire politique entre femmes, d'Anne de France à Marguerite de Valois," in *La Transmission du savoir dans l'Europe des XVIe et XVIIe siècles*, ed. Marie Roig Miranda (Paris: Champion, 2000), 87–98, and Sharon Jansen, *The Monstrous Regiment of Women: Female Rulers in Early Modern Europe* (New York: Palgrave Macmillan, 2002), 181–222.

[31] Jansen, *The Monstrous Regiment*, 181–222.

[32] Kathy M. Krause, "From Mothers to Daughters: Literary Patronage as Political Work in Ponthieu," in *Medieval Elite Women and the Exercise of Power*, 271–293.

[33] Sharon Kettering, "The Patronage Power of Early Modern French Noblewomen," *The Historical Journal* 32, no. 4 (1989): 817–841.

[34] Lequain, "La Maison de Bourbon," Adams, "Rivals or Friends," and Kettering, "The Patronage Power."

beloved Blois.[35] There was a proper female government that supported a library of nearly 50 books (some books of hours, but also historical, political, and moral treatises) where women acted as patrons and chose learned protégés.[36] They also organized cultural events and denounced the misogyny of popular writers, while promoting others more inclined to extol feminine virtues. The first gentlemen of the court honored and respected women.[37] This was seen through their actions by not only avoiding to urinate in their presence, as was fairly common in parts of Europe, but by mostly recognizing female authority in politics, culture, and morals, even though all around Blois the misogynous views of the famous *Roman de la Rose* were gaining in popularity thanks to the printing press.[38] A group of poets and men of letters stand out among the rest, the so-called *Grands Réthoriqueurs*, including Jean Bouchet, André de La Vigne, Jean d'Auton, Octovien de Saint-Gelais, Jean Marot, and Jean Lemaire de Belges, who were almost all mentored and protected by Queen Anne. It is not clear if Anne's protection and patronage involved the great humanists, such as Erasmus of Rotterdam, who spent some time in Paris, or the humanist and jurist Guillaume Budé, who was also employed by the king on several diplomatic missions, or the classical scholar Jacques Lefèvre d'Étaples. The *Grands Réthoriqueurs* were connoisseurs of classical languages and history, and their works contributed greatly to the spread of Latin, as well as the French vernacular, throughout France. Even if they were the queen's men—and not his own courtiers—the king viewed their works with

[35] See the following contributions in *The Cultural and Political Legacy of Anne de Bretagne: Negotiating Convention in Books and Documents*, ed. Cynthia J. Brown (Cambridge: D.S. Brewer, 2010); Diane Booton, "The Book Trade in and beyond the Duchy of Brittany during the Reign of Anne de Bretagne," 11–28; Malcolm Walsby, "The Printed Book in Brittany during the Reign of Anne De Bretagne," 29–44; Lori J. Walters, "Anthoine Vérard's Reframing of Christine de Pizan's Doctrine for Anne de Bretagne," 47–64, and Michelle Szkilnik, "Mentoring Noble Ladies: Antoine Dufour's Vies des femmes célèbres," 65–80.

[36] Cynthia J. Brown, *The Cultural and Political Legacy* and *The Queen's Library: Image-Making at the Court of Anne of Brittany, 1477–1514* (Philadelphia: University of Pennsylvania Press, 2011).

[37] A parallel with Italian courts can be found in Androniki Dialeti, "Defending Women, Negotiating Masculinity in Early Modern Italy," *The Historical Journal* 54, no. 1 (2011): 1–23.

[38] About Guillaume de Lorris and Jean de Meun's most famous *Le Roman de la Rose*, see, for example, *Debating the Roman de la Rose: A Critical Anthology*, ed. Christine McWebb (London and New York: Routledge, 2007). See also Kelly, "Early Feminist Theory."

approval, especially where history and apologetics were used to serve the cause for France in the Italian Wars and against Gallican Church claims.[39]

The queen's ladies, meanwhile, were chosen not only for their wit and knowledge of ancient languages, but also for their ability to attract *novatores*, *avant-garde* intellectuals, and groundbreaking scholars. Michelle de Saubonne, or "the mieux aimée," was the highest rated among Anne's circle. She recruited poet Jean Marot, father of Clément, and historian and poet Jean Lemaire. Saubonne, who married Baron Jean de Parthenay-l'Archeveque in 1507, becoming then Baronne de Soubise, was assigned the task of looking after and educating Queen Anne and King Louis's two daughters, Claude and Renée de France.[40] Saubonne took her educational mission to the extreme; she was one of the first Huguenots, converting to heterodoxy Renée de France's whole entourage when the king's daughter became Duchess of Ferrara.[41] One can say that she was so precociously convinced of her religious beliefs that she was the first to convert Calvin himself to Calvinism, after his escape from France.

In turn, Anne de Bretagne passed on the baton to an exceptional female milieu, led by Louise de Savoie (one of Anne de France's pupils), mother-demiurge of the Valois-Angoulême rise to the throne. She was responsible for turning her teenage son into the powerful François I, King of France, and unpredictably became an ancestor of a dynasty of exceptional female paladins of the Reformation. Followed by Catherine de Medici, Henri II's wife,[42] Louise created the first "courtly schools,"[43] small circles for women and young girls with the goal of providing access to culture and *humane litterae*.[44] The courtly schools were proper educational projects that suc-

---

[39] Frederic J. Baumgartner, *Louis XII* (New York: St. Martin's Press, 1996), 153–168.

[40] About the transmission of immaterial heritage from Anne to Claude, see Kathleen Wilson-Chevalier (2010: 123–144), and her chapter two in this volume.

[41] Belligni, *Renata di Francia*, 3–62, 69–96, and 146–147.

[42] Katherine Crawford, "Catherine de Medicis and the Performance of Political Motherhood," *The Sixteenth-Century Journal* 31, no. 3 (2000): 643–673. Sheila Ffolliott, "La reine mécène idéale de la Renaissance: Catherine de Médicis définie par elle-même ou définie par les autres," 455–466, and Kerrie-rue Michahelles, "Apprentissage du mécénat et transmission matrilinéaire du pouvoir. Les enseignements de Catherine de Médicis à sa petite-fille Christine de Lorraine," 557–576, in *Patronnes et mécènes en France à la Renaissance*.

[43] Louise's courtly school was in fact a development of the "cours des dames" stated by Anne de Beaujeu and especially Anne de Bretagne as described in David-Chapy, "La 'Cour des Dames,'" 27–36.

[44] See Myra Dickman Orth, "Louise de Savoie et le pouvoir du livre," in *Royaume de fémynie. Pouvoirs, contraintes, espaces de liberté des femmes de la Renaissance à la Fronde*, ed.

ceeded to carry on despite many wars, hardships, and hostility from men and children.

Furthermore, far beyond Louise's intentions, her descendants proved to be challengers to the French Catholic crown, from her daughter Marguerite to her grandchildren, Jeanne d'Albret and Marguerite de Savoie, as well as her great-granddaughter Catherine de Bourbon.[45] In fact, while her patronage was more cultural than religious, and therefore seen as innocuous in the court's eyes, her daughter Marguerite started a tradition of female religious (heterodox) leadership. If Catherine de Medici's widowhood, and the resultant power vacuum, proved to be the hardest time for France (the French Wars of Religion)—and not the greatest period for her, as well[46]—it was the opposite for Louise and Marguerite, as their husbands' passing was the happiest of times for them, granting a high level of freedom and autonomy. As it often happened, Marguerite was pushed to marry again, this time with Henri II of Navarre after Charles d'Alençon's death. Since that moment, she struggled deeply to keep the independence she experienced in her widowhood.[47] Her new husband, Henri II de Navarre, demonstrated over the years, sometimes violently, his acute sense of inferiority toward his royal wife who, having shaped French politics and written groundbreaking literature, outshined his power since their wedding day.

For Marguerite, the new Queen of Navarre, Henri d'Albret was not easy to fool or to elude. Sometimes he proved to be an uncompromising partner, even if the couple shared support for the Huguenots' cause. Most of the 72 stories of Marguerite's literary masterpiece, the *Heptameron*, represented not only the "feminist" party of the *querelle des femmes*, praising feminine virtues against misogynists, but they were also the first

Wilson-Chevalier and Eliane Viennot (Paris: Honoré Champion, 2000), 71–90 and Mary Beth Winn, "Louise de Savoie, ses enfants et ses livres: du pouvoir familial au pouvoir d'État," in *Patronnes et mécènes*, 251–281.

[45] Marie-Hélène Grintchenko, *Catherine de Bourbon (1559–1604): influence politique, religieuse et culturelle d'une princesse calviniste* (Paris: Champion, 2009).

[46] About the regency time, see above all Thierry Wanegffelen, *Catherine de Médecis. Le pouvoir au féminin* (Paris: Payot, 2005). See also Denis Crouzet, *Le Haut Coeur de Catherine de Médicis* (Paris: Albin Michel, 2005).

[47] See in particular Nouvelles 2, 15, 49 as suggested in Miho Suzuki, "Gender, Power, and the Female Reader: Boccaccio's *Decameron* and Marguerite de Navarre's *Heptameron*," *Comparative Literature Studies* 30, no. 3 (1993): 231–52. See also Nancy Frelick, "Female Infidelity: Ideology, Subversion, and Feminist Practice in Marguerite de Navarre's *Heptaméron*," *Dalhousie French Studies* 56 (2001): 17–26.

psychological interpretation of gender inequality from a female perspective.[48] In those lines, you can clearly hear Marguerite's voice: the voice of a woman who, despite her highest rank (sister to a king, wife to another one, and lady of one of the biggest fiefdoms in France), happened to experience directly how much energy is needed for a woman to fight a domineering man.[49]

The costs of self-determination for women were literally and metaphorically very high. Being cultural and religious patrons of intellectuals required large sums of money from these committed wealthy women.[50] A large annual budget supported the inner-court circles with ladies-in-waiting and secretaries, pupils and tutors, pages, waiters, and officers, all of whom directly or indirectly helped create a safe and stimulating environment.[51] Money proved to be fundamental in helping high-ranking noblewomen and rich women of lower rank, turning them into patrons and mentors and, in the case during the French Wars of Religion, financial backers of a political party. Women did not take part in combat in the battlefields or supervise sieges and city defenses. However, they could be dangerous opponents because they were guaranteed greater immunity than their spouses, co-religionists, and party-fellows.[52] They were also

---

[48] Evelyn Welch, "Women as Patrons and Clients in the Courts of Quattrocento Italy," *Women in Italian Renaissance Culture and Society,* ed. Letizia Panizza (Oxford: European Humanities Research Centre, 2000), 18–34.

[49] See the bibliography in Carla Freccero, "Queer Nation, Female Nation: Marguerite de Navarre, Incest, and the State in Early Modern France," *Modern Language Quarterly* 65, no. 1 (2004): 29–47, "Marguerite de Navarre and the Politics of Maternal Sovereignty," *Cosmos* 7 (1992): 132–49 and "Archives in the Fiction: Marguerite de Navarre's Heptaméron," in *Rhetoric and Law in Early Modern Europe,* ed. V. Kahn, L. Hutson (New Haven: Yale University Press, 2001), 73–94. See also the debate in Reinier Leushuis, "Mariage et "honnête amitié" dans l'Heptaméron de Marguerite de Navarre: des idéaux ecclésiastique et aristocratique à l'agapè du dialogue humaniste," *French Forum* 28, no. 1 (2003): 29–56.

[50] Caroline zum Kolk, "The Household of the Queen of France in the Sixteenth Century," *The Court Historian* (2009): 3–22. See also the online database "Les membres des maisons royales de la cour de France," ed. zum Kolk: https://cour-de-france.fr/bases-de-donnees/bases-de-donnees-publiees-par-cour-de-france-fr/les-membres-des-maisons-royales-de-la-cour-de-france/?lang=fr.

[51] On French women and warfare, see, for instance, Nancy L. Roelker, "Les femmes de la noblesse huguenote au XVIe siècle," *Bulletin de la Société de l'Histoire du Protestantisme français* (1974): 227–250. See also Sylvie Steinberg, "Le mythe des Amazones et son utilisation politique de la Renaissance à la Fronde," *Royaume de fémynie,* 261–273.

[52] Evelyn Welch, "Women as Patrons and Clients in the Courts of Quattrocento Italy," *Women in Italian Renaissance Culture and Society,* ed. Letizia Panizza (Oxford: European Humanities Research Centre, 2000), 18–34.

normally seen, and often mistakenly, as political and religious mediators. In fact, while some women played a leading role in the establishment of agreements and peace treaties, others were not at all willing to mediate (as was the case with Princesse de Condé in Troyes in 1564[53] and Jeanne d'Albret in her dominions throughout the duration of the wars), as convinced of being personally called to defend the true religion. They were mostly Protestants, although one could find an example of female leadership within the Catholics, namely through Catherine de Lorraine, Duchesse de Montpensier, sister of the duke, and the Cardinal de Guise.

Fighters or not, married women played a key role in the Wars of Religion, especially when they succeeded to circumvent their husbands and win over their resistance, or ultimately convert them. This was accomplished by brave wives through either waiting for their spouses to leave for war (and perchance to die) or, if their husbands remained around, to drag them on their side. Since the early decades of the sixteenth century, certain French noblewomen, such as Louise de Montmorency, had been passing on their heterodox religious convictions to their daughters and younger mentees as a legacy. It was only at the beginning of the 1560s, as the political and religious climate deteriorated, that they felt the urge to convert sons and husbands. That happened to Marguerite de Navarre's daughter, Jeanne d'Albret, mother of Henri IV and wife of Antoine de Bourbon, after having annoyed her during their marriage, the latter eventually died, turning his wife into a merry widow.[54] In fact, some leaders of the French Reformation only converted after their wives had embraced Protestantism. Eleonore de Roye converted her husband, Louis I de Bourbon, Prince de Condé.

Undoubtedly, it was easier for women to address their leadership skills in religion, where it was easier for the talented, the unconventional, and the inquisitive ones crossing boundaries and acting as outsiders. During the sixteenth century, many steps had been taken to acknowledge the role of the female factor in religious dissent and to encourage women to voice disagreement against the Catholic Church and its corruption. For instance, in 1541, the German reformer Philipp Melanchthon seemed to consider

---

[53] Jane Couchman, Colette Winn, and François Rouget, *Autour d'Éléonore de Roye, Princesse de Condé. Étude du milieu protestant dans les années 1550–1565 à partir de documents authentiques nouvellement édités* (Paris: Champion, 2012), 257–269.

[54] On Jeanne d'Albret, see David Bryson, *Queen Jeanne and the Promised Land: Dynasty, Homeland, Religion and Violence in Sixteenth-Century France* (Leiden: Brill, 1999).

women as believers equally with men. According to Melanchthon, who was Martin Luther's closest associate and a major Protestant theologian, what was called Eve's legacy—namely women's inferiority and the need to exhibit their submission—was an "*adiafora*," that is, a matter not regarded as essential to faith. Before that, the principle of *Sola Scriptura* had encouraged female readers and interpreters; Luther had given credit to women in his apology of marriage, and in the 1540s, Calvin suggested that no interpretation of the Pauline writings could really lead to misogyny.[55] This latter assertion was perhaps intended, at least in Swiss and French intellectual circles, as an incentive to set up a principle of equality in the community of believers. Indeed, contrary to further evolutions of Calvinism and some radical religious experiences, we know that Jean Calvin was not really oriented to recognize male and female human beings as equivalent. But he (and his pupil Théodore de Bèze after him) knew how to recognize an alternative and, if necessary, to derogate from their fundamentally misogynist principles. In those days, if women of faith wanted to be equal to men, it was better to take them seriously, and possibly to identify those perceived as more equal than others, as ideal targets of Protestant propaganda, founders, backers, and sponsors.

In the 1560s, Calvin and a small group of Swiss followers became good friends with some French women of high social status devoted to the Protestant cause. Renée de France, former Duchess of Ferrara, had already been involved for many years in his strategy for exploitation of noblewomen as possible hubs of religious networks.[56] This was a strategy similarly pursued by Ignatius of Loyola during the same time. Renée de France was somehow special in Calvin's eyes, as his relationship with Ferrara's heterodox circle, established in the mid-1530s, was the first sample of what became later his specific *modus operandi*.

---

[55] John Lee Thompson, *John Calvin and the Daughters of Sarah: Women in Regular and Exceptional Roles in the Exegesis of Calvin, His Predecessors and His Contemporaries* (Geneva: Droz, 1992), 1–64.

[56] Charmarie Jenkins Blaisdell, "Calvin's Letters to Women: The Courting of Ladies in High Places," *Sixteenth-Century Journal* 13, no. 3 (1982): 67–84. See also Dick Wursten's and Kelly Peebles's contributions to this volume.

MARRIAGE ITALIAN STYLE: THE CASE OF RENÉE DE FRANCE

The only surviving daughter of Louis XII of France used to remember bitterly that, if she had had a beard, the ungrateful Salic law would not have denied her the kingdom.[57] Furthermore, she could not ignore the fact that as a foreign princess with an appropriate dowry to spend for herself, she was not a common, high-ranking Italian bride. Her biographers, from Bartolommeo Fontana to Charmarie Blaisdell, suggest that if a better marriage arrangement had been found during her childhood, her restless spirituality would have been appeased rather than triggered by a frustrated ambition and her name inextricably linked to the fate of the European Reformation.[58] Then again, we could shift the perspective: perhaps she engaged in religious patronage not because she was frustrated about her mésalliance,[59] but rather as a means of taking advantage of an undesirable marriage.

Arriving in Ferrara in 1528 to seal a fluctuating and fragile alliance between the Este dukes and the crown of France, Renée brought the seeds of a highly contagious heresy with her from her family's Valois court.[60] Moving with a large group of French servants, gentlemen, and ladies numbering over 150 people, her largely frustrated attempt to recreate a

[57] Pierre de Bourdeille, seigneur de Brantôme, in *Recueil des Dames, poésies et tombeaux*, ed. Étienne Vaucheret (Paris: Gallimard, 1991), 174.

[58] See Fontana, *Renata di Francia Duchessa di Ferrara sui documenti dell'archivio Estense, del Mediceo, del Gonzaga (1537–1560)*, vol. III (Roma: Forzani, 1889–99). See also Charmarie Jenkins Webb [Blaisdell], *Royalty and Reform: the Predicament of Renée de France 1510–1575*, Unpublished PhD Dissertation, Tufts, 1970; "Politics and Heresy in Ferrara, 1534–1559," *The Sixteenth Century Journal* 6, no. 1 (1975): 67–93, "Calvin's Letters to Women: The Courting of Ladies in High Places," and "Renée de France between Reform and Counter-Reform," *Archiv für Reformationsgeschichte-Archive for Reformation History* 63 (1972): 196–226. See also *Alla corte degli Estensi. Filosofia, arte e cultura a Ferrara nei secoli XV e XVI, Ferrara 5–7 marzo 1992*, ed. Marco Bertozzi (Ferrara: Università degli Studi, 1994) and more recent works such as Florence Whitfield Barton, *Calvin and the Duchess* (Louisville, KY: John Knox Press, 1989), Wilson-Chevalier, "Claude de France: In her Mother's Likeness, A Queen with Symbolic Clout?" 123–144, and Elena Taddei, *Zwischen Katholizismus und Calvinismus: Herzogin Renata d'Este. Eine Eklektikerin der Reformationszeit* (Hamburg: Verlag Dr. Kovač, 2004).

[59] On her mésalliance, Gabriel Braun, "Le mariage de Renée de France avec Hercule d'Este: une inutile mésalliance, 28 juin 1528," *Histoire, Économie, Société* 7, no. 2 (1988): 145–168, in particular page 150.

[60] Belligni, "Renata di Francia fra Ferrara e Montargis," in *La Réforme en France et en Italie. Contacts, comparaisons et contrastes*, ed. Phillip Benedict, Silvana Seidel Menchi, and Alain Tallon (Rome: Publications françaises de l'Ecole de Rome, 2005), 363–379.

suitable habitat in Italy in order to survive her homesickness turned in a lasting experiment of artificial explantation of a heterodox religious breed. But while the original environment, that is, the court of François I, Louise, and Marguerite in the early decades of the sixteenth century, was partially favorable to religious reforms, Italy, from Pope Paul III Farnese to Pope Pius IV de Medici was definitely another story. Undoubtedly, during her many years in Ferrara, Renée witnessed the parable toward the dissolution of the Reformation in Italy.

In many ways, the duke's marital life was so much worse than his wife's. Left to her own devices, and to her own people and religious inclinations, she was quite happy. She enjoyed being married as long as she did not have to lead a proper married life, or an Italian lifestyle for that matter.[61] She did not learn her husband's language for years.[62] The very structure of her *maison*, as court records indicate, reproduced the Valois court (la *chambre*, la *chapelle*, and six offices: *paneterie, echansonnerie, cuisine, fruiterie, escuyrie, fourriere*), despite Ercole II's repeated attempts to resize it. The duchess's entourage revealed marked heterodox tendencies since the early 1530s, under the leadership of Renée's former governess Madame de Soubise, who had returned to her side.[63] Soubise came with an uncompromising family clan, whose attitude and unorthodox religious inclinations were bound to annoy the duke for more or less two decades. According to him, for instance, Anne de Parthenay, Madame de Soubise's daughter, was "the one who already persuaded the aforementioned consort to her servants, and thus she took Clemente Marotta and others who fled from France because they were Lutherans."[64] Meanwhile, in the land of Emilia and Romagna, the spread of heterodox doctrines had begun to show up with the arrival of Renée's court, and in early 1535, following the *affaire des placards*, other "evangelic" Frenchmen settled in Ferrara, an event that

---

[61] Gorris, *Alla corte del principe. Traduzione, romanzo, alchimia, scienza e politica tra Italia e Francia nel Rinascimento* (Ferrara: Università degli studi, 1996), and "'D'un chateau l'autre,'" 139–173.

[62] By 1534, as written in Antonio Romeo's letters to the duke, Renée was still using an interpreter to speak to her husband: see ASMo, *Ambasciatori Venezia*, b. 32.

[63] Chiara Franceschini, "La corte di Renata di Francia (1528–1560)," in *Storia di Ferrara*, VI, *Il Rinascimento: situazioni e personaggi*, ed. Adriano Prosperi (Ferrara: Corbo, 2000), 185–216.

[64] ASMo, Ambasciatori Francia, b.13, Ercole II to Girolamo Feruffini, Ferrara June 20, 1536, complained that it was Anne de Pons who made him "stimular [...] a prender Gianetto."

sanctioned a profound change in the prospects of the heterodox communities across the Alps, including the duchess's entourage.

In the 1530s, Renata's existence was marked by continuous pregnancies. Despite her precarious health and terrible migraines, the duchess wanted to keep her three daughters close to her, and the duke seemed not to care, even if he clearly knew they were going to be raised in his wife's ambiguous circle, and according to her religious convictions. So, Anna, Lucrezia, and Eleonora became part of a highly reputable female group and enjoyed a remarkable intellectual and religious freedom, growing up surrounded, and sometimes lectured by, female intellectuals.[65] This was nothing other than a court school following the models of Anne de France, Anne de Bretagne, Louise de Savoie, and Marguerite d'Angoulême's exercise of patronage.[66]

Why didn't the duke react to his wife's brazen lifestyle? In some respects, he did not want to give up his own. The Este court was still exercising its Ferrarese Renaissance ways: new ideas (including religious inclinations) found fertile ground and, not surprisingly, a relatively complacent patron.[67] Ferrara was still breeding humanists and intellectuals, polymaths, writers, geographers, excellent philologists, doctors with encyclopedic knowledge, and avant-garde musicians.[68] Religious issues arose as a symptom of constantly increasing collective inclinations. It was the time to experiment and enjoy tolerance. For that matter, since the middle of the 1530s the dukedom's heretical inclinations were already known to the future head of the Inquisition, Gian Pietro Carafa. Everyone knew that in Ferrara, unorthodox individuals were tolerated, for Jews were able to

[65] These women included Olimpia Morata, Françoise de Boussiron, and Anne de Beauregard; Anna, Charlotte, and Renée Parthenay-l'Archevêque, Madame de Soubise's daughters; Renée de Thunes, Marie Teronneau, and her sister Marguerite, with her five daughters; as well as the dwarf Agnes and her servant Lucrezia, also a dwarf.

[66] Gorris Camos, "'Donne ornate di scienza e di virtù.' Donne e francesi alla corte di Renata di Francia," *Schifanoia* 28/29 (2005): 185–186.

[67] Marco Folin, *Rinascimento estense: politica, cultura, istituzioni di un antico Stato italiano* (Roma-Bari: Laterza, 2001).

[68] Intellectuals at Ercole's court included writers Celio Calcagnini, Fulvio Pellegrino Morato, and Antonio Brucioli; Lilio Gregorio Giraldi and Giraldi Cinthio, Ortensio Lando, and Bartolomeo Ricci; Charles Fontaine, Bartolomeo Ferino and Molza; geographer Jacob Ziegler, philologists Francesco Porto and Ludovico Castelvetro, doctors Johannes Senft (Sinapius), Johannes Fichard, and Antonio Musa Brasavola; and musicians Adrian Willaert and the Viola family.

prosper under the duke's protection.[69] Apparently Ercole could be a great accomplice, if not a charming husband. Somehow, the ducal couple was competing to seduce and retain the most beautiful minds, and that was undoubtedly the best part of their relationship.[70]

Jean Calvin's passage to Ferrara dates to the spring of 1536, when his *Institutio christianae religionis* had just been released in Basel. His visit is attested by his first biographers, such as Théodore de Bèze and Nicolas Collodon, and by the letters Calvin received from the Sinapi (Giovanni and Françoise de Boussiron). We do not know his real aim, nor his immediate destination when he left Ferrara, only that he arrived there under the name of Charles d'Espeville, had a partner, probably Louis du Tillet, and became part of Renée's small community life, proposing (sometimes imposing) himself as a spiritual guide for years to come. His arrival roughly coincided with the expulsion of Madame de Soubise from Ferrara and with the first trial against Renée's group.[71]

For the first time, the duchess had to move her powerful relational resources to renegotiate her marriage conditions. She wanted mainly to be left alone with her people, free to spend and to believe whatever pleased her, without interferences. But she had to prove a point: her husband had married a princess of France, and that was all he could boast about. In her opinion, she did not need to be married to him. Furthermore, she could be an enemy, capable of unleashing allied forces, including those of the King of France or the Pope. On Good Friday of 1536, the cantor Jehannet Bouchefort, exiled in Ferrara since 1535, ostentatiously refused to adore the cross. Upon hearing of the news, the Inquisitor of Ferrara, Pietro Martire da Brescia, asked for the arrest of the musician and other impious French natives living at Madame's court, whose names jumped out on the first investigations of April 29 and 30 and thereby started a complicated jurisdictional battle.[72] While the duke supported the local Inquisition and

---

[69] Belligni, *Renata di Francia*, 63–150.

[70] Stefano Jossa, "All'ombra di Renata. Giraldi e Castelvetro tra Umanesimo ed eresia," *Schifanoia* 28/29 (2005): 248–276.

[71] For a new interpretation of Calvin's relationship with Renée, as well as the expulsion of Madame de Soubise from Ferrara, see Dick Wursten's chapter.

[72] *La nunziatura in Francia di Rodolfo Pio di Carpi, 1535–1537*, ed. Pier Giovanni Baroni (Bologna: Tamari, 1962), 454–461. A French Franciscan friar, followed by an Italian brother, had explicitly denounced to the inquisitor at Renée's court, where apparently even women were allowed to argue about doctrine. Some people were discovered and identified as heretics: Jehannet himself, who had escaped the placards; the poet Clément Marot, a "Lutheran"

held the French courtiers prisoner, they requested to be extradited to Rome. Renée turned to the French king and her highest acquaintances to obtain their immunity through the pope.[73]

In other words, the ducal couple got even. Some French, including Soubise and Marot, left forever, but their exile was followed by others' arrival.[74] Far from being intimidated, the duchess moved her whole court to the small village of Consandolo, acting out a stronger kind of celibacy by giving up her official duties for all practical purposes and often refusing to show up at the main court in Ferrara.

Meanwhile, Renée's community became part of an intricate network of relations with the heterodox European movement. While Italy was wit nessing the rapid rise of the inquisitorial party, Consandolo was meeting different realities: the Italian Calvinists, refugees or clandestines, the so-called spirituals, that is, followers of Juan de Valdés, and the most radical sects.[75] In the meantime, Calvin used to consider Renée's entourage as his own enclave, although not completely reliable: at the end of the 1540s, the eucharist was celebrated in the "sacramental" manner, according to the model of Zwingli and then of Bullinger. Yet the irenic example of Marguerite de Navarre and her circle stayed strong. If Renée was simulat-ing celibacy with her husband, making unequivocal statements, and build-ing her own household far from Ferrara, she did not intend to become Calvin's puppet. In short, despite the direct interest of Geneva, Consandolo Calvinism was more anomalous and corrupt than other Italian communities.[76]

But Ercole probably was aware of all of this, namely what was really going on in Consandolo. The duke's effective inability to force the com-munity of Consandolo to disperse is not easy to read. With his deep con-science about the State and his own business, he had even been trying for

---

persecuted by the French authorities; Jean Cornillau; Guiges de Guiffrey, lord of Boutières; a preacher, identified as Agostino Foliati from Cremona; Madame's perfumer, Niccolò "Speziale," and another unknown Augustinian hermit.

[73] Paul III reacted with the brief of May 10, 1536, addressed to the Inquisitor of Ferrara, requiring the extradition of the bearers of the "noviter detecta pestis." Fontana, *Renata di Francia, Duchessa di Ferrara*, 501–503.

[74] Leon Jamet, Ambroise de Charcigny, the same Bouchefort, remained in Ferrara or started to work on her behalf in France until the 1550s.

[75] The Anabaptists, the anti-Trinitarians, the "Georgians," who were followers of the cre-ative heretic Giorgio Siculo, as well as the libertine atheists.

[76] On Calvin's later interest in Renée's faith, see Kelly Peebles's chapter.

a long time to take some marginal advantage from the presence of his wife's dangerous friend. For instance, the trust he granted to Leon Jamet, Lord of Chambrun and great friend—"second toy"—of Clément Marot, is in many ways inexplicable: notorious heretic, "more infected than Cornilao," he was nevertheless treated on several occasions as a man of the duke.

But his wife's blackmail strictly depended on the international situation, namely the long-lasting wars in Italy and in Siena.[77] In the 1550s the duke started to feel that, while his link with the French crown was loosening, his marital bond needed to be tightened up, just to remind the duchess she was actually married. In September 1554, a new repression orchestrated by the duke struck Renée's close circle. After numerous warnings from the Roman Inquisition, from 1551, he had invoked the help of two people, the Jesuit Jean Pellettier and Dominique du Gabre, Bishop of Lodève; these were joined in 1554 by the local inquisitor Girolamo Papino, and by Mathieu Ory, prior to the Dominicans of Paris.[78]

It was a concerted action against Renée. The duke and King Henri II of France, for once together, took action to avoid the outbreak of an international scandal that seemed imminent. The duchess was imprisoned in three rooms in Ferrara and 100 books from her library were confiscated. After a few days, she was persuaded to attend Mass, as a formal pledge of conversion and repentance. This was followed by a series of convictions, such as that of the Milanese Ambrogio Cavalli, the duchess's almsgiver, and by the exile of some of her followers, such as the Greek scholar Francesco Porto.[79] Then, the complexity of Renée's network came to light.

---

[77] See Clizia Magoni, *I gigli d'oro e l'aquila bianca. Gli Estensi e la corte francese tra '400 e '500: un secolo di rapporti* (Ferrara: Deputazione Provinciale Ferrarese di storia Patria, 2001), 15–40, Giovanni Maria Zerbinati, *Croniche di Ferrara. Quali comenzano del anno 1500 sino al 1527*, ed. Maria Giuseppina Muzzarelli (Ferrara: Deputazione Provinciale Ferrarese di storia Patria 1989), 53; Giovanni Ricci, *Il principe e la morte. Corpo, cuore, effigie nel Rinascimento* (Bologna: Il Mulino, 1998); Paolo Prodi, *Diplomazia del Cinquecento. Istituzioni e prassi* (Bologna: Patron, 1963); Thierry Wanegffelen, *Le Pouvoir contesté. Souveraines d'Europe à la Renaissance* (Paris: Payot, 2008), 33.

[78] ASF (Archivio di Stato di Firenze), *Mediceo*, 2886, Francesco Babbi to Cosimo I, 3 settembre 1554. Bartolommeo Fontana, vol. 2, 372. See also Francesco Bonaini, "Dell'imprigionamento per opinioni religiose di Renata d'Este e di Lodovico Domenichi," *Giornale storico degli archivi toscani*, III (1859): 268–287.

[79] Fontana, *Documenti dell'Archivio vaticano e dell'Estense sull'imprigionamento di Renata di Francia Duchessa di Ferrara*, *Archivio della Reale Società Romana di Storia Patria*, IX (1886), 3–67, Blaisdell (1970: 257–278).

The trials made it known that, between the 1540s and 1550s, very varied doctrinal positions had manifested in Renata's group.[80] Some had been drawn into Calvin's orbit; others, instead, had been keeping their aversion to dogmatism over the years. Many famous preachers, sometimes clandestinely, had been to Ferrara and Consandolo. Even many of Juan de Valdés's followers had not missed the chance to see what was happening there.[81] We are talking about hundreds of heretics. Apparently, the duke had not found a good reason or a decent occasion to boycott all this traffic.[82]

The duke's wrath had few meaningful consequences to his marital life. The overwhelming evidence about Renée's sponsoring heretics of every possible kind and convictions did not lead to very strict measures. After the first period, interventions were mild, left to the good will of Ercole, who, after a few months, got back to his usual mode of turning a blind eye to the habits and acquaintances of his wife. The wife herself started again with her mostly happy, mostly unmarried life. After her husband died on October 3, 1559, and after bitter arguments with her son Alfonso II, the new duke, Renée decided to leave Ferrara forever. Apparently, it was easier to simulate celibacy than to be childless.[83]

For all their marriage, Ercole kept what was likely to seem a reasonable behavior to most high-ranking husbands. Most of the time, it was better to cover his eyes and ears from his wife's habits and deeds, unless they caused him terrible trouble in foreign policy. Even in his last days, he unleashed his anger against the duchess and some French members of her entourage only when the Great Wars of Italy were coming to an end, and that was just because the results of the war in Siena and the treaty of Cateau-Cambresis had shown him that the French crown had been making fun again of his loyalty and of his financial and economic commitment.[84] That time, Renée had complained just feebly, knowing his marital

---

[80] *Eretici che erano in Ferrara al tempo di madama Renea*, ASMo, *Archivio Fiaschi*, b. 42 quoted in Fontana, vol. 3, XXXI–XLIV.

[81] Federica Ambrosini, "I reticolati del dissenso e la loro organizzazione in Italia," in *La Réforme en France et en Italie*, 87–103.

[82] Belligni, "Renata di Francia fra Ferrara e Montargis."

[83] Belligni, *Renata di Francia*, 355–390.

[84] For Ferrara's involvement in the War of Siena, see Guy Baguenault de Puchesse, "Négociations de Henri II avec le duc de Ferrare," *Revue des Questions Historiques* 5 (1868): 484–516.

consciousness was bound to weaken in a few weeks: in fact, it was not stronger than hers. Most of the time, Ercole himself liked to feign celibacy.

RELIGIOUS PATRONAGE AND SIMULATED CELIBACY

Even if she was surrounded by independent and powerful wives, in Italy, Renée's religious patronage was unique. As written in the *Compendium* of the proceedings of Cardinal Giovanni Morone's trial, the duchess was called a "subventrix hereticorum"[85] by Giulio Antonio Santoro, Secretary of the Holy Office, a term namely referring to heretics' main funding source or sponsor. In her role of *subventrix* of the Reformation in Italy, Renée adopted a much broader perspective than what would have implied a rigid adherence to Calvin's teachings. She was the main supporter of heretics coming from every part and every level of society, regardless of gender, age, profession, social role, and, most of all, religious belief. Her protégés almost covered the full spectrum of unorthodox creeds in Europe. Her help could range from eight ducats to complete support, as shown in her account books and in the letters sequestered by her husband, which both revealed a secret special fund meant to give money to Grisons communities and Protestant refugees. From the 1530s to the 1560s (and later, when she moved to France), Renée granted many people a job, lodging, political protection, and often money for their living expenses or for their religious cause, according to their needs.

Renée's heretical network was a heterodox heterogeneous environment and was undoubtedly shaped by a pattern she had known and experienced in France when she was a young girl. This pattern was her cousin Marguerite de Navarre's ultimate legacy,[86] drawn from the glorious French genealogy

---

[85] On October 12, 1557, in Rome, the Burgundian Dominican "penitentiario" (Father Confessor of the Apostolic Penitentiary), Gabriel Martinet, had reported the recantation of a certain "heretic" brother, "in qua abiuratione nominabat multas graves personas, inter quas [...] ducissam Ferrariae, cuius verba addebat videlicet 'Ego potius venderem camiciam quam deesse necessitati fratrum nostrorum,' per fratres intelligens lutheranos" (In that recantation he named lots of people in high places, and among those the Duchess of Ferrara, and then he added her words, such as "I would rather sell my shirt than fail to help my needing brothers"), *Deposizione di Gabriel Martinet di Borgogna* in *Processo Morone*, vol. 6, 288.

[86] Patricia Cholakian and Rouben Cholakian, *Marguerite de Navarre. Mother of the Renaissance* (New York: Columbia University Press, 2005), 143, and Barbara Stephenson, "La protection de vostre faveur. Le patronage humaniste de Marguerite de Navarre," in *Patronnes et mécènes en France à la Renaissance*, ed. K. Wilson-Chevalier and E. Pascal (Saint-Étienne: Publications de l'Université de Saint-Étienne, 2007), 303–319. See also

of female cultural entrepreneurs and patron-queens mentioned earlier. Marguerite's intellectual and spiritual charisma, which Renée couldn't match during her long-term religious patronage, were replaced by her determination and ability to develop, foster, and preserve her network even in its darkest hour.[87]

Like her French role models and predecessors, Renée was in many respects the ideal leader of a heretical community. Her cultural skills were maybe limited, as Pellettier said, but she compensated for this lack of sophistication with other qualities: she held money, she could dispose of her dowry jewelry, and of her French feuds' revenues and, unfortunately for Ercole II d'Este, she was perfectly aware that she had married far below her condition, not with a king, but with a powerless duke. She could count on a large group of *clientes* and family members who had been raised and educated at the court of François Ier in the first decades of the sixteenth century, providing an atmosphere of cultural and religious awakening. Some of her protégés behaved as cultural and religious brokers, connecting Ferrara and Reformed areas, normally with the duchess's financial help. In order to keep her entourage and support her followers' travels across Europe, Renée could freely provide with her nuptial dowry, drawing on incomes from her French assets and properties.[88] Her money and the promise of a shelter, free from censorship and prosecutions, acted as enticement to attract intellectuals, spiritual leaders and preachers, humanists, and divine teachers. Being at the top of the social hierarchy,

---

Barbara Stephenson, *The Power and Patronage of Marguerite de Navarre* (Aldershot: Ashgate, 2004). See more recently Jonathan A. Reid. *King's Sister. Queen of Dissent Marguerite of Navarre (1492–1549) and Her Evangelical Network* (Leiden and Boston: Brill, 2009).

[87] On Renée's limited cultural skills, see Blaisdell, *Royalty and Reform*, and the analysis of her letters by Odette Turias, *Renée de France, Duchesse de Ferrare, témoin de son temps: 1510–1575* (PhD diss., Université de Tours, 2005). In the early 1550s, people who talked to Renée during her husband's attempts to take her back to Catholicism expressed the same opinion (especially the preacher Francesco Visdomini and the Jesuit Jean Pellettier); see Belligni, *Renata di Francia*, 288–289.

[88] On Renée's followers and her way to support them, see Belligni, *Renata di Francia*, 83–114, 240–354. See in particular the declarations of Ambrogio Cavalli da Milano reported in the *constituti* of his trial, about the duchess's protégés and their escape after being prosecuted by the Inquisition, 286–340. See also Ugo Rozzo, "Gli anni ferraresi e la morte sul rogo dell'eremitano Ambrogio da Milano (1547–1555)," in *Alla corte degli Estensi*, ed. Marco Bertozzi (Ferrara: Università degli Studi, 1994), 299–322, and Cavalli Ambrogio, *Dizionario Biografico degli Italiani* (DBI).

Renée was a duchess, but first she was a king's daughter, making her an ideal mentor, and at the same time, a unique and privileged interlocutor for spiritual leaders, including Calvin, Bullinger, and Ignatius of Loyola.[89]

It was not any less important that her husband, Duke Ercole II, happened to be not only a victim of the greatest political instability, but also a pawn in a chess game whose players (France, the Papacy, the Duchy of Tuscany, the Emperor) seemed to constantly change strategies and alliances. The duchess was at the very core of a web of blackmail scandals and sometimes vulnerable actors, who shared the desire to maintain power, lands, or at the very least, some influence in Italy.[90] She was in the ideal position to be blackmailed from time to time, both by her spouse and by her household of origin—her cousins, the kings of France—confronting them either with her unreachably high status or with her scandalous religious behavior.[91] Her notable talent in keeping her royal relatives and her husband away from what really mattered to her—money, assets, protégés, and religion—classifies her as one of the women most successful at simulating celibacy in the European Renaissance.

Renée was actually part of a small number of Italian noblewomen who, during the same decades, were successful at exploiting either widowhood or simulated celibacy in order to take a lead role in religious dissent. It is important to note, though, that even in Italy, being a woman was not the main obstacle to religious community leadership. If high in social status and reasonably wealthy, both Italian widows and those feigning to be spinsters happened to be courted by masters of the Reformation, for example, by Juan de Valdés and his followers, or Northern Calvinist communities, or religious radicals, and also individual thinkers, free riders, and sometimes even free loaders. These groups of people were trying to get a hold of wealthy women in order to convert them into religious followers and eventually to reap the benefits of their support: shelter, protection, and perhaps some money to get by.[92] The Valdesian noblewomen who were close to Renée de France, such as Vittoria Colonna, Isabella Villamarina, Giulia Gonzaga, Caterina Cybo, Caterina Sauli, and Isabella della Frattina,

---

[89] On Loyola and Ferrara, see Belligni, *Renata di Francia*, 251–255.

[90] Blaisdell, "Politics and Heresy in Ferrara," 67–93. See also the bibliography in Belligni, *Renata di Francia*, 69–82.

[91] Blaisdell, "Politics and Heresy in Ferrara," 67–93.

[92] Prosperi, *L'Inquisizione romana. Letture e ricerche* (Rome: Storia e Letteratura), and Massimo Firpo *Juan de Valdés e la Riforma nell'Italia del Cinquecento* (Rome-Bari: Laterza, 2016).

proved to be great cultural and political agents and effective trojan horses for heterodox doctrines in Italy. After the 1550s, the most important trials of heretics made clear what the Roman Inquisition had been suspecting for a long time: that these distinguished women, widows, and supposed spinsters had been acting as patrons and brokers for Italian religious dissenters. A decade later, after the 1560s, their activities as religious leaders, patrons, and sponsors were swept away with the Inquisition's systematic attack on heterodox networks.

Due to the Wars of Religion in France, women's religious patronage survived Henri de Bourbon's abjuration, as witnessed by the story of Catherine de Parthenay, granddaughter of Renée's lady-in-waiting and religious tutor, Madame de Soubise. Catherine was the heiress to the Huguenot Parthenay-L'Archeveque family and to a lineage of outstanding women, raised by her mother, Antoinette d'Aubeterre, to be a playwright, author, and mathematician. After the death of her second husband, Catherine had the chance to educate her six children with no one to interfere and distinguish herself as a heroine during the siege of La Rochelle, in 1628. Meanwhile, the Third Estate was also increasing the number of women who dedicated themselves to professions often considered masculine and also reflected in writing on the condition of the fairer sex. By the end of the sixteenth century, many writers—and many female writers— showed their support of the anti-misogynist groups in Italy, France, and England.[93] But it was only after the beginning of the eighteenth century that authors, such as Gabrielle Suchon in *Du célibat volontaire ou la vie sans engagements* (Paris, 1700) and Mary Astell in *Some Reflections upon Marriage* (London, 1730), dared to recommend women to stay unmarried, providing a much better option than waiting for widowhood or trying for many years to manipulate a hindering *pater familias*.[94] It was time for a new challenge: simulated celibacy, a socially tolerated expedient to

[93] Stephen Kolsky, "Moderata Fonte, Lucrezia Marinella, Giuseppe Passi: An Early Seventeenth-Century Feminist Controversy," *Modern Language Review* 96 (2001): 973–989.

[94] See *Perspectives on Feminist Political Thought in European History: from the Middle Ages through the Present*, ed. Tjitske Akkerman and Siep Stuurman (London and New York: Routledge, 2003), in particular their "Introduction: Feminism in European History," 1–34; Miri Rubin, "The Languages of Late-Medieval Feminism," 34–49; Brita Rang, "A 'learned wave': Women of Letters and Science from the Renaissance to the Enlightenment," 50–66, and Stuurman, "L'égalité des sexes qui ne se conteste plus en France: Feminism in the Seventeenth Century," 67–84.

gain autonomy from marriage, gave place to the idea that being single and independent could be an ideal condition for launching cultural and religious enterprises.

BIBLIOGRAPHY

PRIMARY SOURCES

Anne de France. 2004. *Anne of France: Lessons for My Daughter*. Edited and translated by Sharon Jansen. Cambridge: D. S. Brewer.

Archivio di Stato di Modena (ASMo); Ambasciatori Francia, b.13; Ambasciatori Roma, b. 40, b. 57; Ambasciatori Venezia, b. 32, b. 40; Archivio Fiaschi, b. 42.

"Les membres des maisons royales de la cour de France." Edited by Caroline zum Kolk. https://cour-de-france.fr/bases-de-donnees/bases-de-donnees-publiees-par-cour-de-france-fr/les-membres-des-maisons-royales-de-la-cour-de-france/?lang=fr.

SECONDARY SOURCES

Adams, Tracy. 2008. Fostering Girls in Early Modern France. In *Emotions in the Household, 1200–1900*, ed. Susan Broomhall, 103–118. London: Palgrave Macmillan.

———. 2010. Rivals Or Friends? Anne de Bourbon and Anne de Bretagne. *Women in French Studies* Special Issue 3: 46–61.

———. 2018. Anne de France and Gift-Giving: The Exercise of Female Power. In *Women and Power at the French Court, 1483–1563*, ed. Susan Broomhall, 65–84. Amsterdam: Amsterdam University Press.

Akkerman, Tjitske, and Siep Stuurman. 1998. Introduction: Feminism in European History. In *Perspectives on Feminist Political Thought in European History: From the Middle Ages Through the Present*, ed. Tjitske Akkerman and Siep Stuurman, 1–34. London and New York: Routledge.

Ambrosini, Federica. 2007. I reticolati del dissenso e la loro organizzazione in Italia. In *Réforme en France et en Italie: contacts, comparaisons et contrastes*, ed. Philip Benedict, Alain Tallon, and Silvana Seidel Menchi, 87–103. Rome: École française de Rome.

Autrand, Françoise. 1999. Christine de Pisan et les dames à la cour. In *Autour de Marguerite d'Écosse. Reines, princesses et dames du xv* siècle. Actes du colloque de Thouars, 23 et 24 mai 1997*, ed. Geneviève Contamine and Pierre Contamine, 19–31. Paris: Champion.

Baguenault de Puchesse, Guy. 1868. Négociations de Henri II avec le duc de Ferrare. *Revue des Questions Historiques* 5: 484–516.

Baroni, Pier Giovanni, ed. 1962. *La nunziatura in Francia di Rodolfo Pio di Carpi, 1535–1537.* Bologna: Tamari.

Barton, Florence Whitfield. 1989. *Calvin and the Duchess.* Louisville, KY: John Knox Press.

Baumgartner, Frederic J. 1996. *Louis XII.* New York: St. Martin's Press.

Belligni, Eleonora. 2005. Renata di Francia fra Ferrara e Montargis. In *La Réforme en France et en Italie. Contacts, comparaisons et contrastes,* ed. Phillip Benedict, Silvana Seidel Menchi, and Alain Tallon, 363–379. Rome: Publications françaises de l'Ecole de Rome.

———. 2011. *Renata di Francia (1510–1575). Un'eresia di corte.* Turin: UTET.

Bennett, Judith M., and Amy M. Froide, eds. 1998. *Singlewomen in the European Past, 1250–1800.* Philadelphia, Pennsylvania: University of Pennsylvania Press.

Bertozzi, Marco, ed. 1994. *Alla corte degli estensi : filosofia, arte e cultura a Ferrara nei secoli XV e XVI : atti del convegno internazionale di studi, Ferrara, 5–7 marzo 1992.* Ferrara: Università degli studi.

Blaisdell, Charmarie Jenkins. 1975. Politics and Heresy in Ferrara, 1534–1559. *The Sixteenth-Century Journal* 6 (1): 67–93.

———. 1982. Calvin's Letters to Women: The Courting of Ladies in High Places. *Sixteenth-Century Journal* 13 (3): 67–84.

Bonaini, Francesco. 1859. Dell'imprigionamento per opinioni religiose di Renata d'Este e di Lodovico Domenichi. *Giornale storico degli archivi toscani* III: 268–287.

Booton, Diane. 2010. The Book Trade in and beyond the Duchy of Brittany during the Reign of Anne de Bretagne. In *The Cultural and Political Legacy of Anne de Bretagne: Negotiating Convention in Books and Documents,* ed. Cynthia J. Brown, 11–28. Cambridge: D. S. Brewer.

Bousmar, Eric, Jonathan Dumont, Alain Marchandisse, and Bertrand Schnerb, eds. 2012. *Femmes de pouvoir, femmes politiques durant les derniers siècles du Moyen Age et au cours de la première Renaissance.* Brussels: de Boeck.

Brantôme, Pierre de Bourdeille, sieur de. 1991. *Recueil des Dames, poésies et tombeaux.* Edited by Étienne Vaucheret. Paris: Gallimard.

Braun, Gabriel. 1988. Le mariage de Renée de France avec Hercule d'Este: une inutile mésalliance, 28 juin 1528. *Histoire, Économie, Société* 7 (2): 145–168.

Brown, Cynthia J. 2010. *The Cultural and Political Legacy of Anne de Bretagne. Negotiating Convention in Books and Documents.* Cambridge: D. S. Brewer.

———., ed. 2011. *The Queen's Library. Image-Making at the Court of Anne of Brittany, 1477–1514.* Philadelphia: University of Pennsylvania Press.

Bryson, David. 1999. *Queen Jeanne and the Promised Land: Dynasty, Homeland, Religion and Violence in Sixteenth-Century France.* Leiden: Brill.

Cassagnes-Brouquet, Sophie, Christiane Klapisch-Zuber, and Sylvie Steinberg. 2010. Sur les traces de Joan Kelly. *Clio. Femmes, Genre, Histoire* 32: 17–52.

Cavallo, Sandra, and Lyndan Warner. 2014. *Widowhood in Medieval and Early Modern Europe.* London and York: Routledge.

Cholakian, Patricia, and Rouben C. Cholakian, eds. 2005. *Marguerite de Navarre. Mother of the Renaissance.* New York: Columbia University Press.

Cosandey, Fanny. 1997. De Lance en quenouille. La place de la reine dans l'État moderne (XIVe–XVIIe siècles). *Annales. Histoire, Sciences Sociales* 52 (4): 799–820.

Couchman, Jane, Colette Winn, and François Rouget, eds. 2012. *Autour d'Eléonore de Roye, Princess of Condé. Etude du milieu protestant dans les années 1550–1565 à partir de documents authentiques nouvellement édités.* Paris: Honoré Champion.

Crawford, Katherine. 2000. Catherine de Medicis and the Performance of Political Motherhood. *The Sixteenth-Century Journal* 31 (3): 643–673.

Crouzet, Denis. 2005. *Le Haut Cœur de Catherine de Médicis.* Paris: Albin Michel.

David-Chapy, Aubrée. 2017a. *Anne de France, Louise de Savoie, inventions d'un pouvoir au féminin.* Paris: Classiques Garnier.

———. 2017b. La 'Cour des Dames' d'Anne de France et de Louise de Savoie: un espace de pouvoir à la rencontre de l'éthique et du politique. In *Femmes à la cour de France. Statuts et fonctions*, ed. Kathleen Wilson-Chevalier and Caroline zum Kolk, 49–65. Villeneuve-d'Ascq: Presses universitaires du Septentrion.

Dialeti, Androniki. 2011. Defending Women, Negotiating Masculinity in Early Modern Italy. *The Historical Journal* 54 (1): 1–23.

Earenfight, Theresa. 2019. A Lifetime of Power: Beyond the Binaries of Gender. In *Medieval Elite Women and the Exercise of Power, 1100–1400: Moving Beyond the Exceptionalist Debate*, ed. J. Tanner Heather, 271–293. London: Palgrave Macmillan.

Eliav-Felton, Miriam, and Herzig, Tamar, eds. 2015. *Dissimulation and Deceit in Early Modern Europe.* London: Palgrave Macmillan.

Fauve-Chamoux, Antoinette, and Emiko Ochiai, eds. 2009. *The Stem Family in Eurasian Perspective.* Revisiting House Societies, 17th–20th Centuries. New York: Peter Lang.

Ffolliott, Sheila. 2007. La reine mécène idéale de la Renaissance: Catherine de Médicis définie par elle-même ou définie par les autres. In *Patronnes et mécènes en France à la Renaissance*, ed. Kathleen Wilson-Chevalier and Eugénie Pascal, 455–466. Saint-Étienne: Publications de l'Université de Saint-Étienne.

Firpo, Massimo. 2016. *Juan de Valdés e la Riforma nell'Italia del Cinquecento.* Rome and Bari: Laterza.

Folin, Marco. 2001. *Rinascimento estense: politica, cultura, istituzioni di un antico Stato italiano.* Roma-Bari: Laterzam.

Fontana, Bartolommeo. 1886. Documenti dell'Archivio vaticano e dell'Estense sull'imprigionamento di Renata di Francia Duchessa di Ferrara. *Archivio della Reale Società Romana di Storia Patria* 9: 3–67.

———. 1889–1899. *Renata di Francia Duchessa di Ferrara sui documenti dell'archivio Estense, del Mediceo, del Gonzaga (1537–1560), III voll.* Forzani: Roma.

Franceschini, Chiara. 2000. *La corte di Renata di Francia (1528–1560).* In *Storia di Ferrara, VI, Il Rinascimento: situazioni e personaggi,* ed. Adriano Prosperi, 185–214. Ferrara: Corbo.

Freccero, Carla. 1992. Marguerite de Navarre and the Politics of Maternal Sovereignty. *Cosmos* 7: 132–149.

———. 2001. Archives in the Fiction: Marguerite de Navarre's *Heptaméron.* In *Rhetoric and Law in Early Modern Europe,* ed. Victoria Kahn and Lorna Hutson, 73–79. New Haven: Yale University Press.

———. 2004. Queer Nation, Female Nation: Marguerite de Navarre, Incest, and the State in Early Modern France. *Modern Language Quarterly* 65 (1): 29–47.

Frelick, Nancy. 2001. Female Infidelity: Ideology, Subversion, and Feminist Practice in Marguerite de Navarre's Heptaméron. *Dalhousie French Studies* 56: 17–26.

Gorris, Rosanna. 1996. *Alla corte del principe. Traduzione, romanzo, alchimia, scienza e politica tra Italia e Francia nel Rinascimento.* Ferrara: Università degli studi.

———. 1997. *'D'un château l'autre': la corte di Renata di Francia a Ferrara (1528–1560).* In *Il palazzo di Renata di Francia,* ed. Loredana Olivato Puppi, 139–173. Ferrara: Corbo Editore.

———. 2005. *'Donne ornate di scienza e di virtù'. Donne e francesi alla corte di Renata di Francia. Schifanoia* 28/29: 175–205.

Grintchenko, Marie-Hélène. 2009. *Catherine de Bourbon (1559–1604): influence politique, religieuse et culturelle d'une princesse calviniste.* Paris: Champion.

Heith-Stade, David. 2012. Den ortodoxa kyrkans äktenskapsrätt. *Signum* 7: 17–21.

Herlihy, David. 1985. Did Women Have a Renaissance? A Reconsideration. *Medievalia et Humanistica* 13: 1–22.

Jansen, Sharon. 2002. *The Monstrous Regiment of Women: Female Rulers in Early Modern Europe.* New York: Palgrave Macmillan.

Jossa, Stefano. 2005. All'ombra di Renata. Giraldi e Castelvetro tra Umanesimo ed eresia. *Schifanoia* 28/29: 248–276.

Kelly, Joan. 1977. Did Women Have a Renaissance? In *Becoming Visible: Women in European History,* ed. Renate Bridenthal, Claudia Koonz, and Susan Mosher Stuard, 174–201. Boston: Houghton Mifflin.

———. 1982. Early Feminist Theory and the 'Querelle des Femmes' 1400–1789. *Signs* 8 (1): 4–28.

Kettering, Sharon. 1989. The Patronage Power of Early Modern French Noblewomen. *The Historical Journal* 32 (4): 817–841.

King, Catherine E. 1998. *Renaissance Women Patrons: Wives and Widows in Italy, c. 1300–1500*. Manchester: Manchester University Press.

Kolsky, Stephen. 2001. Moderata Fonte, Lucrezia Marinella, Giuseppe Passi: An Early Seventeenth-Century Feminist Controversy. *Modern Language Review* 96: 973–989.

Krause, Kathy. 2019. From Mothers to Daughters: Literary Patronage as Political Work in Ponthieu. In *Medieval Elite Women and the Exercise of Power, 1100–1400: Moving Beyond the Exceptionalist Debate*, ed. Heather J. Tanner, 271–293. London: Palgrave Macmillan.

Lequain, Élodie. 2005. La Maison de Bourbon 'escolle de vertu et de perfection'. Anne de France, Suzanne de Bourbon et Pierre Martin. *Médiévales 48*: 39–54.

Leushuis, Reiner. 2003. Mariage et 'honnête amitié' dans *l'Heptaméron* de Marguerite de Navarre: des idéaux ecclésiastiques et aristocratiques à l'agapè du dialogue humaniste. *French Forum* 28 (1): 29–56.

Magoni, Clizia. 2001. *I gigli d'oro e l'aquila bianca. Gli Estensi e la corte francese tra '400 e '500: un secolo di rapporti*. Ferrara: Deputazione Provinciale Ferrarese di storia Patria.

Matarasso, Pauline. 2001. *Queen's Mate. Three Women of Power in France on the Eve of the Renaissance*. Aldershot: Ashgate.

McNamara, Jo Anne, and Suzanne Wemple. 1973. The Power of Women Through the Family in Medieval Europe: 500–1100. *Feminist Studies* 1 (3/4): 126–141.

McWebb, Christine, ed. 2007. *Debating the Roman de la Rose: A Critical Anthology*. London and New York: Routledge.

Michahelles, Kerrie-rue. 2007. Apprentissage du mécénat et transmission matrilinéaire du pouvoir. Les enseignements de Catherine de Médicis à sa petite-fille Christine de Lorraine. In *Patronnes et mécènes en France à la Renaissance*, ed. Kathleen Wilson-Chevalier and Eugénie Pascal, 557–576. Saint-Étienne: Publications de l'Université de Saint-Étienne.

Moring, Beatrice, and Richard Wall. 2017. *Widows in European Economy and Society, 1600–1920*. Woodbridge: Boydell Press.

Orth, Myra Dickman. 1999. Louise de Savoie et le pouvoir du livre. In *Royaume de fémynie. Pouvoirs, contraintes, espaces de liberté des femmes de la Renaissance à la Fronde*, ed. Kathleen Wilson-Chevalier and Éliane Viennot, 71–90. Paris: Honoré Champion.

Prodi, Paolo. 1963. *Diplomazia del Cinquecento. Istituzioni e prassi*. Bologna: Patron.

Prosperi, Adriano. 2003. *L'Inquisizione romana. Letture e ricerche*. Rome: Storia e letteratura.

Rang, Brita. 2003. A 'learned wave': Women of Letters and Science from the Renaissance to the Enlightenment. In *Perspectives on Feminist Political Thought in European History: 1400–2000*, ed. Tjitske Akkerman and Siep Stuurman, 50–66. London and New York: Routledge.

Reid, Jonathan A. 2009. *King's Sister. Queen of Dissent Marguerite of Navarre (1492–1549) and Her Evangelical Network.* Leiden and Boston: Brill.

Ricci, Giovanni. 1998. *Il principe e la morte. Corpo, cuore, effigie nel Rinascimento.* Bologna: Il Mulino.

Roelker, Nancy L. 1974. Les femmes de la noblesse huguenote au XVIᵉ siècle. *Bulletin de la Société de l'Histoire du Protestantisme français.* 227–250.

Rohr, Zita. 2016. Playing the Catalan: The Rise of the Chess-Queen; Queenship and Political Motherhood in Late Medieval Aragon and France. In *Virtuous or Villainess? The Image of the Royal Mother from the Early Medieval to the Early Modern Era,* ed. Carey Fleiner and Elena Woodacre, 173–197. New York: Palgrave Macmillan.

———. 2018. Rocking the Cradle and Ruling the World: Queens' Households in Late Medieval and early Modern Aragon and France. In *Royal and Elite Households in Medieval and Early Modern Europe: More than Just a Castle,* ed. Theresa Earenfight, 309–337. Leyden: Brill.

Rohr, Zita, and Lisa Benz, eds. 2016. *Queenship, Gender, and Reputation in the Medieval and Early Modern West, 1060–1600.* London: Palgrave Macmillan.

Rozzo, Ugo. 1994. Gli anni ferraresi e la morte sul rogo dell'eremitano Ambrogio da Milano (1547–1555). In *Alla corte degli Estensi,* ed. Marco Bertozzi, 299–322. Ferrara: Università degli Studi.

Rubin, Miri. 2003. The Languages of Late-Medieval Feminism. In *Perspectives on Feminist Political Thought in European History: 1400–2000,* ed. Tjitske Akkerman and Siep Stuurman, 34–49. London and New York: Routledge.

Steinberg, Sylvie. 1999. Le mythe des Amazones et son utilisation politique de la Renaissance à la Fronde. In *Royaume de fémynie. Pouvoirs, contraintes, espaces de liberté des femmes, de la Renaissance à la Fronde,* ed. Kathleen Wilson-Chevalier and Éliane Viennot, 261–273. Paris: Champion.

Stephenson, Barbara. 2004. *The Power and Patronage of Marguerite de Navarre.* Aldershot: Ashgate.

———. 2007. La protection de vostre faveur. Le patronage humaniste de Marguerite de Navarre. In *Patronnes et mécènes en France à la Renaissance,* ed. Kathleen Wilson-Chevalier and Eugénie Pascal, 303–319. Saint-Étienne: Publications de l'Université de Saint-Étienne.

Stuurman, Siep. 2003. L'égalité des sexes qui ne se conteste plus en France: Feminism in the Seventeenth Century. In *Perspectives on Feminist Political Thought in European History: 1400–2000,* ed. Tjitske Akkerman and Siep Stuurman, 67–84. London and New York: Routledge.

Suzuki, Miho. 1993. Gender, Power, and the Female Reader: Boccaccio's 'Decameron' and Marguerite de Navarre's 'Heptameron'. *Comparative Literature Studies* 30 (3): 231–252.

Szkilnik, Michelle. 2010. Mentoring Noble Ladies: Antoine Dufour's Vies des femmes célèbres. In *The Cultural and Political Legacy of Anne de Bretagne: Negotiating Convention in Books and Documents*, ed. Cynthia J. Brown, 65–80. Cambridge: D. S. Brewer.

Taddei, Elena. 2004. *Zwischen Katholizismus und Calvinismus: Herzogin Renata d'Este. Eine Eklektikerin der Reformationszeit*. Hamburg: Verlag Dr. Kovač.

Tanner, Heather J., ed. 2019. *Medieval Elite Women and the Exercise of Power, 1100–1400: Moving Beyond the Exceptionalist Debate*. London: Palgrave Macmillan.

Taylor, Craig. 2006. The Salic Law, French Queenship and the Defense of Women. *French Historical Studies* 29 (4): 543–564.

Thompson, John Lee. 1992. *John Calvin and the Daughters of Sarah: Women in Regular and Exceptional Roles in the Exegesis of Calvin, His Predecessors and His Contemporaries*. Geneva: Librairie Droz.

Tolley, Thomas. 1996. States of Independence: Women Regents as Patrons of the Visual Arts in Renaissance France. *Renaissance Studies* 10: 237–258.

Turias, Odette, 2004. *Renée de France, Duchesse de Ferrare, témoin de son temps: 1510–1575*. Ph.D. diss., Université de Tours.

Viennot, Eliane. 2000. La transmission du savoir-faire politique entre femmes, d'Anne de France à Marguerite de Valois. In *La Transmission du savoir dans l'Europe des XVIᵉ et XVIIᵉ siècles*, ed. Marie Roig Miranda, 87–98. Paris: Payot.

———. 2003. Veuves de mère en fille au XVIᵉ siècle: le cas du clan Guise. In *Veufs, veuves et veuvage dans la France d'Ancien Régime. Actes du colloque de Poitiers, 11–12 juin 1998*, ed. Nicole Pellegrin and Colette Winn, 187–198. Paris: Champion.

Walsby, Malcolm. 2010. The Printed Book in Brittany during the Reign of Anne De Bretagne. In *The Cultural and Political Legacy of Anne De Bretagne: Negotiating Convention in Books and Documents*, ed. Cynthia J. Brown, 29–44. Cambridge: D. S. Brewer.

Walters, Lori J. 2010. Anthoine Vérard's Reframing of Christine de Pizan's Doctrine for Anne de Bretagne. In *The Cultural and Political Legacy of Anne De Bretagne: Negotiating Convention in Books and Documents*, ed. Cynthia J. Brown, 47–64. Cambridge: D. S. Brewer.

Wanegffelen, Thierry. 2005. *Catherine de Médicis. Le pouvoir au féminin*. Paris: Payot.

———. 2008. *Le Pouvoir contesté. Souveraines d'Europe à la Renaissance*. Paris: Payot.

Webb, Charmarie Jenkins [Blaisdell]. 1970. *Royalty and Reform: the Predicament of Renée de France 1510–1575*. Ph.D. diss. Tufts.

Welch, Evelyn. 2000. Women as Patrons and Clients in the Courts of Quattrocento Italy. In *Women in Italian Renaissance Culture and Society*, ed. Letizia Panizza, 18–34. Oxford: European Humanities Research Centre.

———. 2008. Women in Debt: Financing Female Authority in Renaissance Italy. In *Donne di potere nel Rinascimento*, ed. Letizia Arcangeli and Susanna Peyronel Rambaldi, 45–66. Rome: Viella.

Wilson-Chevalier, Kathleen. 2010. Claude de France: In her Mother's Likeness, A Queen with Symbolic Clout? In *The Cultural and Political Legacy of Anne de Bretagne: Negotiating Convention in Books and Documents*, ed. Cynthia J. Brown, 123–144. Cambridge: D. S. Brewer.

Wilson-Chevalier, Kathleen, and Eugénie Pascal, eds. 2007. *Patronnes et mécènes en France à la Renaissance*. Saint-Étienne: Publications de l'Université de Saint-Étienne.

Wilson-Chevalier, Kathleen, and Éliane Viennot, eds. 1999. *Royaume de fémynie. Pouvoirs, contraintes, espaces de liberté des femmes, de la Renaissance à la Fronde*. Paris: Champion.

Winn, Mary Beth. 2007. Louise de Savoie, ses enfants et ses livres: du pouvoir familial au pouvoir d'État. In *Patronnes et mécènes en France à la Renaissance*, ed. Kathleen Wilson-Chevalier and Eugénie Pascal, 251–281. Saint-Étienne: Publications de l'Université de Saint-Étienne.

Witte, John, Jr. 2013. The Mother of All Earthly Laws: The Lutheran Reformation of Marriage. *Gettysburg Seminary Ridge Review* 15 (2): 26–43.

Zerbinati, Giovanni Maria. 1989. *Croniche di Ferrara. Quali comenzano del anno 1500 sino al 1527*. Edited by Maria Giuseppina Muzaarelli. Ferrara: Deputazione Provinciale Ferrarese di storia Patria.

Zum Kolk, Caroline. 2009. The Household of the Queen of France in the Sixteenth Century. *The Court Historian* 14: 3–22.

CHAPTER 10

Under the Rubble: Renée de France and Fragments of Art from Her Italian Years

Kathleen Wilson-Chevalier

The power of art is indisputable. Many Renaissance princes and princesses understood it as a means of ensuring their immortality, and Alfonso I d'Este, Duke of Ferrara, like many of his predecessors and contemporaries, invested an impressive part of his income therein.[1] Alfonso chose to marry his son Ercole up the social ladder to Renée de France who, no less than her consort, at the castle of Blois, had been born into art. A plethora of documents, including account books, epistles of many types, book dedications, and prints, proves that Renée went on to wield this indispensable tool of strong rulers over the course of her sixty-five-year-long life,[2] while

---

[1] Diane Yvonne Ghirardo discusses Alfonso and his second wife Lucrezia Borgia's differing attitudes to patronage and spending in "Lucrezia Borgia as Entrepreneur," *Renaissance Quarterly* 61, no. 1 (Spring 2008): 53–91.

[2] For detailed studies of her account books in the Turin archives, see Chiara Franceschini, "La corte di Renata di Francia (1528–1560)," in *Storia di Ferrara*, ed. Adriano Prosperi (Ferrara: Corbo Editore, 2000), 185–214, and "Tra Ferrara e la Francia: notizie su orefici e

---

K. Wilson-Chevalier (✉)
The American University of Paris, Paris, France
e-mail: kchevalier@aup.edu

K. D. Peebles, G. Scarlatta (eds.), *Representing the Life and Legacy of Renée de France*, Queenship and Power,
https://doi.org/10.1007/978-3-030-69121-9_10

a case study of the artworks associated with this unique French Duchess of
Ferrara highlights—unfortunately—their ephemeral nature. The motto
adorning her only surviving book cover, DI/REAL SANGUE NATA/IN
CHRISTO/SOL/RENA/TA, affirms, wisely, that this princess of royal
blood placed her trust in Christ alone.[3] Her library was burned.[4] The
exquisite prayer book gifted to her during her childhood by her sister,
Queen Claude de France, was stolen in modern times.[5] Remains are perhaps extant of the grand tapestries that traveled with her to Italy in 1528
and formed a sumptuous backdrop to the first of her many encounters
with Isabella d'Este, her spouse's aunt.[6] Renée's interest in portraiture is
amply documented, and consummate artists like Girolamo da Carpi and
Francesco Primaticcio produced dynastic images financed by her consort,
but also by her.[7] Sebastiano del Piombo, whose *Visitation* adorned her

pittori al servizio di Renée de France," *Franco-Italico* 19–20 (2001): 65–104, in the latter of
which only 1536–1537 and 1550–1551 are transcribed, 84–99. Portraits, tapestries, decorated litters, carriages, book bindings, furniture, and jewels are discussed. See Peter Führing
in *Jacques Androuet du Cerceau* "un des plus grands architectes qui se soient jamais trouvés
en France," ed. Jean Guillaume (Paris: Picard, 2010), 117, for the *Livre de grotesques* dedicated to her. Further sources, including work for Renée financed by others, will be
cited herein.

[3] Tammaro De Marinis, *La legatura artistica in Italia nei secoli 15. e 16. 2, Bologna, Cesena,
Ferrara, Venezia* (Florence: Flli. Alinari, 1960), 373.

[4] Rosanna Gorris Camos, "La bibliothèque de la duchesse. De la bibliothèque en feu de
Renée de France à la bibliothèque éclatée de Marguerite de France, duchesse de Savoie," in
Poètes, princes & collectionneurs. Mélanges offerts à Jean Paul Barbier-Mueller, ed. Nicolas
Ducimetière, Michel Jeanneret, and Jean Balsamo (Geneva: Droz, 2011), 473–476.

[5] Roger Wieck and Cynthia J. Brown, *The Prayer Book of Claude de France MS M.1166. The
Pierpont Morgan Library, New York* (Lucerne: Quadernio Verlag, 2010). See also Wieck's
contribution to this volume.

[6] Bartolommeo Fontana, *Renata di Francia duchessa di Ferrara sui documenti dell'Archivio
Estense, del Mediceo, del Gonzaga e dell'Archivio Secreto Vaticano (1510–1536)* (Rome:
Forzani e C., 1888–1899), I, 76–77. The tapestries are addressed below.

[7] Amalia Mezzetti, *Girolamo da Ferrara detta da Carpi* (Milano: Silvana, 1977), 61
(1548); Alessandra Pattanaro, *Girolamo da Carpi Ritratti* (Cittadella: Bertoncello
Artigrafiche, 2000), 13; Ian Wardropper, "Le voyage italien de Primatice en 1550," *Bulletin
de la Société de l'histoire de l'Art français* 30, no. 73, 1981 (1983): 27–29; Franceschini, "Tra
Ferrara," 67, 74–80, including a gift in 1542 to Marguerite of Navarre and the French court
of effigies of the first two ducal children, 75. Renée gave Primaticcio a gold chain in exchange
for portraits of her younger daughters, but also for unspecified paintings he gifted to her:
"faict present de painctures a madame," Franceschini, "Tra Ferrara," 77–79. These were
perhaps but not necessarily portraits, since he conceived the *Combat d'un chien* for Renée's
audience hall chimneypiece in Montargis in 1572. See J.T.D. Hall, "Three letters of
Primaticcio," *Burlington Magazine* 115 (January 1973): 35–37, and 37–38 for a commen-

sister's chamber in Blois, figures among the Italians documented as having painted the duchess's likeness, for which the noble poetess Vittoria Colonna, in Ferrara in 1537–1538, is a potential link.[8] Yet the only somewhat convincing courtly depictions from her adult years are minor works:[9] a woodcut published by Guillaume Rouillé in Lyon in 1553 (Fig. 10.1),[10]

tary by Anthony Blunt citing BnF, ms. fr. 3809, f. 25r, then in contact with a painter who had come from Ferrara. See also Sylvie Béguin, "Primaticcio's 'Chien de Macaire,'" *Burlington Magazine* 115 (October 1973): 676–680; Führing, in Guillaume, *Androuet du Cerceau*, 319.

[8] Cécile Scailliérez, *François Iᵉʳ et ses artistes dans les collections du Louvre* (Paris: Réunion des musées nationaux, 1992), 117, fig. 47; Roberto Contini, in *Sebastiano del Piombo 1485–1547*, ed. Claudio Strinati and Bernd Wolfgang Lindemann (Rome: Federico Motta Editore, 2008), 192–195, figs. 39 and 40; Rosanna Gorris, "'D'un château l'autre': la corte di Renata di Francia a Ferrara (1528–1560)," in *Il Palazzo di Renata di Francia*, ed. Loredana Olivato Puppi (Ferrara: Il Corbo Editore, 1997), 152; Richard Cooper, *Litterae in tempore belli. Études sur les relations littéraires italo-françaises pendant les guerres d'Italie* (Geneva: Droz, 1997), 167–169; Massimo Firpo, *Artisti gioiellieri eretici: il mondo di Lorenzo Lotto tra riforma e controriforma* (Roma: Laterza. 2001), 333–335 and Adriano Prosperi, "Zwischen Mystikern und Malern: Überlegungen zur Bilderfrage in Italien zur Zeit Vittoria Colonnas," in *Vittoria Colonna Dichterin und Muse Michelangelos*, ed. Sylvia Ferino-Pagden (Milan: Skira editore, 1997), 283–295 on Sebastiano and religion.

[9] Neither of the two most-often reproduced portraits of the adult Renée present credible likenesses. These are located in Paris at the Bibliothèque de la Société de l'Histoire du Protestantisme Français, and in Frankfurt, at the Städelsches Kunstinstitut, Inv. Nr. 946. Anne Dubois de Groër, *Corneille de La Haye dit Corneille de Lyon* (Paris: Arthena, 1996), retains no portrait of Renée. Despite Alessandra Pattanaro's valiant defense of the Frankfurt painting (*Ritratti* 74–75, fig. 6, 142, and "Per la *Dama in verde* dello Städelsches Kunstinstitut di Francoforte. Un problema di rapporti nord-sud," in *Culture figurative a confronto tra Fiandre e Italia dal XV al XVII secolo Nord/Sud*, ed. Anna De Floriani and Maria Clelia Galassi [Cinisello Balsamo: Silvana Editore, 2008], 136–145), this unlikely portrayal continues to oscillate uncomfortably between Girolamo da Carpi and Peter de Kempeneer.

[10] *La Seconde partie du promptuaire des medalles, commençant à la nativité de nostre Sauveur Jesus Christ, & continuant jusques au Treschrestien Roy de France Henri II, à present eureusement regnant* (Lyon: G. Rouillé, 1553), 230 (published in Latin, French, and Italian). Pattanaro, *Ritratti* 76 (from a later edition); Ilaria Andreoli, "La storia in soldoni: il *Promptuaire des medailles* di Guillaume Rouillé," in *Storia per parole e per immagini. Proceedings of the symposium at Cividale del Friuli*, ed. Mino Gabriele et Ugo Rozzo (Udine: Forum, 2006), 235–266; Élise Rajchenbach-Teller, "De 'ceux qui de leur pouvoir aydent et favorisent au publiq' Guillaume Rouillé, libraire à Lyon," in *Passeurs de textes Imprimeurs et libraires à l'âge de l'humanisme*, ed. Christine Bénévent, Anne Charon, Isabelle Diu and Magali Vène (Paris: Publications de l'École nationale des chartes, 2012), 99–116. The credibility of the image is high, as Rouillé published Clément Marot, Ariosto, and a New Testament in Italian dedicated to Ippolito d'Este (1547), and his contacts included Ludovico

Fig. 10.1 *Renée de France.* Woodcut from Guillaume Rouillé, *La seconde partie du proptuaire des medalles* (Lyon: Guillaume Rouillé 1553), 230. © Typ 515.53.753 Houghton Library, Harvard University

wherein her three-quarters portrait faces her medallion-like consort in profile, and a watercolor in Filippo Rodi's *Annali* post-dating her life (Fig. 10.2).[11] Virtually nothing subsists of Renée's contributions to her personal residences—the Palace of San Francesco in Ferrara to which her name has accrued,[12] the *delizia* of Consandolo,[13] then later the castle of Montargis—although one of the most important French publications on

Domenichi, whose life Renée helped save in 1552. See Fontana, *Renata*, II, 280–281; Natalie Zemon Davis, "Publisher Guillaume Rouillé, businessman and humanist," in *Editing Sixteenth Century Texts,* ed. Richard J. Schoeck (Toronto: University of Toronto, 1966), 91, 95, 99.

[11] Biblioteca Ariostea, Cl. I 645, t. II, fol. 547v; completed after 1598 (replicating an earlier image?). My thanks to Mirna Bonazza.

[12] *Il Palazzo di Renata di Francia,* ed. Loredana Olivato (Ferrara: Il Corbo Editore, 1997). Francesco Guidoboni attributes the extant chapel to Renée in "Gli edifici di Ippolito II d'Este a Ferrara e gli interventi dopo il terremoto del 1570," in *Ippolito II d'Este cardinale principe mecenate,* ed. Marina Cogotti and Francesco Paolo Fiore (Roma: De Luca Editori d'Arte, 2013), 24.

[13] *Gli Estensi a Consandolo. La Delizia ritrovata,* ed. Elena Marescotti et. al. (Consandolo: Associazione Ricerche Storiche di Consandolo, 2008); *La vita di Renata di Francia a Consandolo dal 1540 a 1560* (Consandolo: Associazione Ricerche Storiche Consandolo, 2013–2017).

Fig. 10.2 *Renée de France, duchesse of Ferrara*. Watercolor from Filippo Rodi, *Annali*, manuscript. Ferrara, Biblioteca Ariostea I 645, t. II, fol. 547v. © Biblioteca Ariostea

RENEA F DI LOD.ˣII RE DI FRANCIA MOG. DI ERCOLE II D DI FERR.

sixteenth-century architecture, Androuet du Cerceau's *Les plus excellents bâtiments de France*, was initially conceived for her.[14]

This chapter examines a tiny sampling of Ferrarese art connected with Renée and Ercole, but also with other female and male ruling kin. Artworks can help break down prevailing oversimplified binary oppositions and contribute to an on-going revision of our image of Renea, the name by which she was often known to the inhabitants of their duchy. My goal is to hone Renée's profile as a formidably resilient French princess whose commanding rank and particularly fine education (the latter one of a number of traits she shared with her spouse) allowed her to assume a more important place in Ferrara's tendentially tolerant mainstream culture than is generally acknowledged, during an uncomfortably complex age of religious and political change.

---

[14] Jean Guillaume, in Guillaume, *Androuet du Cerceau*, 25–29; Françoise Boudon and Claude Mignot, *Jacques Androuet du Cerceau. Les dessins des Plus excellents bâtiments de France* (Paris: Picard, 2010), 19–30, 241–243.

Bastardy and Art at the Ferrarese Court

The power of dynastic art to assert legitimacy was at the very core of the June 28, 1528 wedding of the ducal heir, Ercole d'Este, and Renée de France. The French matchmakers were King François I and his mother, Louise de Savoie, a key member of the king's Privy Council,[15] and the celebration was staged in the Parisian Sainte-Chapelle. Louis IX's Gothic artistic gem foregrounded the long-established and hierarchically superior royalty of Ercole's young spouse, whom ambassador Malatesta described in regal dress, a crown on her head ("vestita con habito regale e con la corona in testa"). What has come to be the standard historical trope had already been penned by the loquacious groom, who had informed his father on May 23 that this daughter of King Louis XII and Queen Anne de Bretagne was not beautiful ("Ma Madama Renea non è bella"), while praising other facets of her persona nonetheless ("pure se compensara con le altre bone conditioni").[16] Historians have paid less attention to the bride's own plight. The pawn of her royal brother-in-law and his willful mother after her sister's death, Renée was catapulted into a ducal family that had consolidated its rule by uniting bastardy and first-class Renaissance art.[17]

Of the three highly renowned art patrons sired by Niccolò III d'Este (1383–1441), the first two, Leonello (1407–1450) and Borso (1413–1471), were illegitimate.[18] The Este line was ultimately assured by their legitimate half-brother Ercole I (1431–1505), who in 1502, none-theless married his heir Alfonso I (1476–1534) to the illegitimate daughter of Pope Alexander VI. Yet while Ercole II (1508–1559) was the legitimate son of Alfonso and the illegitimate Lucrezia Borgia (1480–1519),[19] two of Ercole's legitimized brothers, Alfonso (1527–1587)

---

[15] Cédric Michon, *Les Conseillers de François Ier* (Rennes: Presses universitaires de Rennes, 2011): "*Première partie*: L'époque Louise de Savoie."

[16] See Fontana, *Renata*, I, 42–46 for a general account and these citations, 43 and 28; Emmanuel Rodocanachi, *Renée de France, une protectrice de la réforme en France et en Italie* (Paris: P. Ollendorf, 1895), 29–42.

[17] Marco Folin draws a direct link between the bastardy of rulers and the influence of their higher-ranking foreign consorts and courts in "Bastardi e principesse nelle corti del Rinascimento: spunti di ricerca," *Schifanoia* 28/29 (2005): 167–174.

[18] Filippo Rodi, *Annali*, Biblioteca Ariostea (Sala dei manoscritti), Cl. I 645, t. 1 includes portraits of a truly impressive number of illegitimate offspring.

[19] For a finely revised vision of Borgia, see Gabriella Zarri, *La religione di Lucrezia Borgia. Le lettere inedite del confessore* (Rome: Roma nel Rinascimento, 2006) and the articles of Diane Yvonne Ghirardo listed in this chapter's bibliography.

and Alfonsino (1530–1547), descended from his father's highly visible non-noble mistress, Laura Dianti (†1573), who had been magnificently, if equivocally, portrayed by Titian a few years prior to Renée's arrival in Ferrara on December 1, 1528.[20] Alfonso I destabilized traditional male definitions of female honor by renaming his "lowly" mistress "Eustochia" (a follower of Saint Jerome), by having her cast as the chaste Daphne, and by marrying her just prior to his death no doubt.[21] Laura went a step further when she had the Dossi brothers paint her as the rare and learned *Santa Paola*, Eustochia's mother, responding to the defunct duchess's identification with an equally rare and learned *Santa Lucrezia*.[22]

If Ercole's relationship with his last-minute stepmother Laura has been considered tortuous, Renée's has been judged cordial instead.[23] Duke Alfonso, in one of his testaments, prompted her mercy by leaving her a precious stone, to be chosen worthy of a descendent of King Louis XII. He praises his beloved daughter-in-law ("Nora Dilettissima") for her exceptional goodness, kindness, and fine manners ("inaudita bontà et summa gentilezza, et optima creanza"), while asking her to extend "her just and loving help" to *all* of his children, clearly with Laura Eustochia's sons in mind ("raccomanda ad essa Illma Madama *li figlioli tutti di esso S^or testatore. Pregandola in ogni occorrenza ad havere la loro protetione, et prestarli sempre il suo Justo et amorevole aiuto*").[24] Alfonso endowed his mistress with possessions in Ferrara and other ducal territories; thirteen years after Renata's return to France, Laura continued to maintain a small but brilliant court of her own.[25] In an exceptionally long, chatty epistle penned in July 1539 for her trustworthy knight of honor Antoine de Pons, Renée

[20] Joanna Woods-Marsden, "The Mistress as 'Virtuous': Titian's Portrait of Laura Dianti," in *Titian: Materiality, Likeness, Istoria*, ed. Joanna Woods-Marsden (Turnhout: Brepols, 2007), 53–69.

[21] Ludovico Antonio Muratori, *Delle Antichità estensi continuazione, o sia Parte Seconda* (Modena: Stamperia ducale, 1740), 363; Andrea Bayer in *Dosso Dossi. Pittore di corte a Ferrara nel Rinascimento*, ed. Andrea Bayer (Ferrara: Ferrara Arte, 1998), 45–46.

[22] Peter Humfrey, in *Dosso Dossi*, 181–184; Zarri, "*La* religione," 199–202.

[23] Giulio Righini, *Due donne nel destino di casa d'Este: Marchesella degli Adelardi, Laura Dianti* (Ferrara: Deputazione Provinciale Ferrarese di Storia Patria, 1964), 87–88.

[24] Fontana, *Renata*, I, 202 (1533).

[25] Muratori, *Delle Antichità*; Righini, *Due donne*, 74–165; Andrea Marchesi, *Delizie d'archivio. Regesti e documenti per la storia delle residenze estensi nella Ferrara del Cinquecento*. Tomi I–II: dimore urbane (Ferrara: Le Immagini edizioni, 2015), 618–628, for her *delizia del Verginese*.

describes going to see "Madone Laure" at the *delizia* del Barco. From there they returned in a carriage surrounded by Renée's ladies on horseback ("Une aultre feus au barc trouver Madone laure en coche ou Jentre avecques elle et mes fames demourerent a cheval").[26] On another occasion, she foresaw dining with her ("Voullons aler bien tost diner cheulx madone laure") with Pons's wife Anne de Parthenay/Soubise.[27] Her exceptionally learned lady-in-waiting Anne—one of the daughters of her lady of honor and protector since childhood Michelle de Saubonne, Baronne de Soubise—had recently given birth to a son.[28]

Between the two encounters, the famed court doctor Antonio Musa Brasavola ("le bresaule"), whose daughter Margherita had assisted the duchess in childbirth, paid a post-partum medical visit to Anne.[29] In 1536, Brasavola, whose "dangerous" religious heterodoxy is often invoked alongside Renée's, had dedicated a medical text in Latin to both Ercole and Renée.[30] He also dedicated to Laura a chapter of his *Vita di Jesu Christo*, written at the request of Renée's sister-in-law, Eleonora d'Este. The latter, a strong woman who had taken vows following her mother's but not her father's will,[31] was abbess of the convent of Corpus Domini, an Este preserve near which Renée came to reside. The two Este princesses shared not only a close relationship with Ercole's brother Archibishop (later Cardinal) Ippolito II, but also an interest in music, in reading the Holy Scriptures differently, and in Church reform. In 1544, Renée gifted to Eleonora portraits by Girolamo da Carpi, an artist who also portrayed Anne de Parthenay, whose musical voice was acclaimed.[32]

Despite differing social origins and religious practices, Renée and Laura (and Ercole and Eleonora) employed the same scholars and artists a number of times. The two humanists that Laura chose as tutors for her sons were the future Protestant Pellegrino Morato, whom Renée protected and

[26] Fontana, *Renata*, II, 110,

[27] Fontana, *Renata*, II, 115.

[28] On the Parthenay/Soubise, see my and Berthon's contributions in this volume.

[29] Fontana, *Renata*, II, 101, 106–117, 113.

[30] Rosanna Gorris, "'Un franzese nominato Clemente': Marot à Ferrare," in *Clément Marot, "Prince des Poëtes françois," 1496–1996*, ed. Gérard Defaux and Michel Simonin (Paris: Honoré Champion, 1997), 355–357.

[31] Eleonora Belligni, *Renata di Francia (1510–1575). Un eresia di corte* (Turin: UTET Libreria, 2011), 114, 155–157.

[32] Zarri, *La religione*, 72, 114–116, 131; Laurie Stras, *Women and Music in Sixteenth-Century Ferrara* (Cambridge: Cambridge University Press, 2018), 30–74; Franceschini, "Tra Ferrara," 75.

whose remarkable scholarly daughter Olimpia contributed to the superior education of Anna d'Este, the ducal couple's firstborn, and Cinzio Giraldi. In 1547, the latter was charged with a "royal" funeral oration in honor of Renée's brother-in-law François I ("un solenissimo funerale con apparato Regio"), as well as, five months later, that of Alfonsino, Laura's younger son.[33] Even more tellingly, although he expired at the tender age of seventeen, Alfonsino had sired a daughter who bore Renea's name. Her appreciative grandmother Laura, by whose side Renea was raised, endowed her in her 1564 will for her reverence and obedience ("per la riverenza ed obbedienza sempre avuta e dimostrata verso [di lei] dai suoi anni più teneri fino al matrimonio").[34] The writer Vincenzo Brusantini proffered another sign of their peaceful coexistence in his *Angelica inamorata* (dedicated to Ercole in 1550) when, in close succession, he praised Renée, her three daughters, and "Laura Eustochia d'Este."[35]

The legitimate and illegitimate Este lines were not only culturally, but also politically intertwined. When Renée assumed the regency at Ercole's death, it was "Laura's" Alfonso whom she dispatched to Modena to maintain control over the town while she ruled over the State until "her" Alfonso returned from France. The absence of an heir at the latter's death in 1597 enabled a papal takeover grounded in the politically motivated claim that Laura's grandson Cesare d'Este descended from "an infected line."[36] Bastardy was nonetheless a structural component of Italian city-states, and of their ecclesiastical dignitaries, during Renée's Italian sojourn and beyond.

Renée's strong moral upbringing, inflected by the reformers Guillaume and Denis Briçonnet and Jacques Lefèvre d'Étaples,[37] did not however make her a prude. Her youth in France had been marked by the presence of not only her sister, Madame de Soubise, and Marguerite, but also two

---

[33] Muratori, *Delle Antiquità*, 370. On Giraldi, see also Gabriella Scarlatta's and Marzia Pieri's chapters.

[34] Cited by Righini, *Due donne*, 94. Andrea Marchesi, *Delizie d'archivio. Regesti e documenti per la storia delle residenze estensi nella Ferrara del Cinquecento. I. Dimore suburbane e extraurbane* (Ferrara: Le Immagini edizioni, 2011), Doc. 6 for Alfonso d'Este's expenditures regarding Renea, Duke Alfonso, and Ippolito.

[35] Muratori, *Delle Antiquità*, 467; other examples 453, 463, 466.

[36] Muratori, *Delle Antiquità*, 427.

[37] See chapter two in this volume.

mistresses of her brother-in-law, François I.[38] The first, Françoise de Châteaubriant, was her sister's lady of honor in 1523, whereas the future Duchesse d'Étampes—surely Louise de Savoie's maiden whom Malatesta sighted at the king's side in the Sainte-Chapelle ("una delle donzelle di sua matre")[39]—surfaced after Claude's death. Historians present Renée's consort Ercole as a princely womanizer, too. He had an upper-class lover, Diana Trotti, at least two illegitimate children,[40] and in 1537, a messy affair with one of Renée's French ladies-in-waiting, Madame de Noyant.[41] "Lucrezia naturale" (†1572), distinguished from "Lucrezia legitima" (1535–1598), entered Corpus Domini in 1538,[42] while Renée's and Ercole's fifth child, Luigi, was born at the end of the same year. Renée visited the duke and his French mistress at the *delizia* of the *Montagna* in 1539.[43]

Renée's Francophile brother-in-law Ippolito II d'Este offers another case in point. In 1531, he was charged with baptizing Ercole's and Renée's first child, Anna,[44] honored with Anne de Bretagne's name. Three years later, upon his father's death, the archbishop inherited the Palazzo San Francesco, taking over a building occupied until 1533 by Lucrezia Borgia's friend, Isabella d'Aragona del Balzo, an exiled Neapolitan queen with whose daughters Renée banqueted, danced, and rode about town in the early 1530s.[45] In 1534–1535, Ippolito oversaw a grandiose remodeling of

---

[38] Véronique Garrigues, "Les clairs-obscurs de Françoise de Foix, dame de Châteaubriant (1494?–1537): revisiter l'historiographie d'une favorite royale," in *Femmes à la cour de France. Charges et fonctions XVᵉ–XIXᵉ siècle*, ed. Caroline zum Kolk and Kathleen Wilson-Chevalier (Villeneuve-d'Ascq: Presses Universitaires du Septentrion, 2018), 321–337; David Potter, "The Life and After-Life of a Royal Mistress Anne de Pisseleu, Duchess of Étampes," in *Women and Power at the French Court, 1483–1563*, ed. Susan Broomhall (Amsterdam: Amsterdam University Press, 2018), 309–334.

[39] Fontana, *Renata di Francia*, I, 44.

[40] Gino Benzoni, "Ercole II d'Este," in *Dizionario Biografico degli Italiani*, Vol. 43 (1993).   http://www.treccani.it/enciclopedia/ercole-ii-d-este_%28Dizionario-Biografico%29/.

[41] Fontana, *Renata di Francia*, I, 214, and II, 72–74, 110; Rodocanachi, *Renée de France*, 138–139.

[42] Muratori, *Delle Antiquità*, 471–472, citing Gasparo Sardi; Fontana, *Renata di Francia*, I, 87. See Marchesi, *Delizie d'archivio I*, for work on her palatial conventual lodging.

[43] Fontana, *Renata*, II, 109–110: "Je le mene apres souper a la montagne ou monsieur soupoit avecques la calcagnine [la Noyant]."

[44] Lucy Byatt, "Este, Ippolito d'," in *Dizionario Biografico degli Italiani*, Vol. 43 (1993). http://www.treccani.it/enciclopedia/ippolito-d-este_%28Dizionario-Biografico%29/.

[45] Fontana, *Renata*, I, 143–144, 154, 156.

Biagio Rossetti's fifteenth-century palace,[46] spawning a magnificent self-sufficient center of governance, replete with marble, frescoed decorations, and newly planted gardens, and uniting on the coffered ceiling of the main audience hall his own arms with those of his brother Ercole and Renée ("uno armone intaiado larma duchale de Madama").[47] No more than a year after his departure for France in 1536, Renée moved into this state-of-the-art Renaissance palace, worthy of the queen she had frequented ("la Serenissima Regina Isabella"),[48] and worthy of her worldly ecclesiastical brother-in-law, who continued to finance transformations for her. As late as 1554–1555, before and after her house arrest, he paid for work on Renée's rooms, those of her daughters, the courtyard, and the façade.[49]

Surely a sign of their deep dynastic and political alliance, Ippolito christened his illegitimate daughter Renea, echoing the name of Laura Eustochia's granddaughter. "Renea d'Este" bore her father's household patronym, as was the custom in France. Anne de Bretagne's master of the household was her bastard brother, François de Bretagne, sire d'Avaugour, while her bastard sister, Françoise de Bretagne, was one of her ladies-in-waiting.[50] François I's half-sisters, Jeanne and Souveraine, were integrated into the Angoulême line, while Henri II's first (illegitimate) child was "Diane de France"; all three served as marriage pawns at the French court.[51] Renea d'Este was likely raised by Renée prior to her betrothal to Ludovico Pico della Mirandola in 1553. The territory of Mirandola,

---

[46] Thomas Tuohy, *Herculean Ferrara. Ercole d'Este (1471–1505) and the invention of a ducal capital* (Cambridge: Cambridge University Press, 1996), 328–332; Losito, "Il palazzo," 99–105; Guidoboni, "Gli edifici," 17–26.

[47] Maria Losito, "Il palazzo tra definizioni e manomissioni," in *Il Palazzo*, 105–109; Alessandra Farinelli Toselli, "Il palazzo attraverso i documenti," in *Il Palazzo*, 35–58; Gorris, "'D'un château l'autre,'" 156–159 (157 for the citation).

[48] Marchesi, *Delizie d'archivio II–III*: 1508, Doc. 1.

[49] *Delizie d'archivio II–III*, 633–653 [1533–1560].

[50] Jacques Santrot, *Les Doubles funérailles d'Anne de Bretagne. Le corps et le cœur (janvier-mars 1514)* (Geneva: Droz, 2017), 515 and 524–525. See chapter two in this volume for the family's enduring presence in Renée's lifetime.

[51] Louis Chasot de Nantigny, *Généalogie historique de la Maison Royale de France* (Paris: Le Gras etc., 1738), 253–254; R. J. Knecht, *Renaissance Warrior and Patron. The Reign of Francis I* (Cambridge: Cambridge University Press, 1994), 2; Aubrée David-Chapy, *Anne de France, Louise de Savoie, inventions d'un pouvoir au féminin* (Paris: Classiques Garnier, 2016), 564; Kathleen Wilson-Chevalier in *Patronnes et mécènes en France à la Renaissance*, 24–26.

Francophile like Renea's father Ippolito, was viewed by the Church as a
site of heresy and linked by the Inquisition to Renée.[52]

In September 1553, the duchess, an important patron of French and
Italian goldsmiths, ordered a payment to Jacques Vignon and Domenico
Pomatelli for a gold chain, a choker ("carcan"), and a headband ("fron-
tail") with rubies, diamonds, and pearls which she gifted to "seigneure
Renee de Est, fille de Monseigneur le Cardinal de Ferrare" shortly before
her wedding.[53] Renea d'Este died in 1555, having given birth to at least
one daughter, Ippolita.[54] The preceding year, Ercole had brought the
medallist Pastorino de' Pastorini to Ferrara,[55] and one of his works com-
memorates Ippolito's daughter (Fig. 10.3).[56] Pastorino's Este family gallery, indifferent to issues of legitimacy, includes Laura Eustochia's
legitimized sons and Niccolò d'Este, an illegitimate son of Ercole's brother
Francesco, too.[57] Did political considerations instead come into play?
Anna d'Este, married to the future Duc de Guise in 1548, hence an ally of
the French, does not figure among the extant medals of the ducal progeny,
and even more remarkably, Duchess Renée is absent as well. Pastorino
began working for the duke around the time of her house arrest, and his
consort's invisibility coincides with a moment of bitter complaint. On
March 6, 1555, Ercole lamented that Renée had hoarded her dowry,
never sharing a "scudo" with him or his children ("prefata Duchessa nostra consorte ha sempre goduti et la dote et la sopradote senza che noi ne
alcuni dei nostri figliuoli ne habbia sentito mai un minimo utile ne havu-
tone pur un scudo"). On April 10, 1555, he admonished that love and
obedience alone could improve his consort's lot ("Amorevole e obbedi-
ente consorte otterrà ogni cosa ragionevole").[58] However, Renée's medal,
like her library, could also have been suppressed at the instigation of
the Church.

[52] Fontana, *Renata di Francia*, II, 241–245.
[53] Franceschini, "Tra Ferrara," 71 and n27.
[54] Girolamo Tiraboschi, *Memorie storiche modenesi*, Tome IV (Modena: la Società tipografica, 1794), 205; Ippolito commissioned a painting from Bastianino for his granddaughter in 1569 (Marchesi, *Delizie d'archivio II–III*, 716, 1569, Doc. 9).
[55] Philip Attwood, in *The Currency of Fame: Portrait Medals of the Renaissance*, ed. Stephen
K. Scher (New York: Harry N. Abrams, Inc. & The Frick Collection, 1994), 177–180.
[56] Giorgio Boccolari, *Le medaglie di casa d'Este* (Modena: Aedes Muratoriana, 1987),
91–92, 114, fig. 90: RENEA.EST.PIC.MIRAN.DNA P.1555. Alfred Armand, *Les médailleurs italiens des quinzième et seizième siècles* (Paris: Plon, 1883–1887), I, 204, fig. 99.
[57] Boccolari, *Medaglie*, 92–93; 118 & 120, figs. 95, 96, and 98; 122, fig. 100.
[58] Fontana, *Renata di Francia*, II, 405–408.

Fig. 10.3 Pastorino de' Pastorini, *Renea d'Este*, medal, 1555. Paris, Bibliothèque nationale de France, Cabinet des médailles, It.Princ. 149. Source: BnF

Initially, match-maker Alfonso I had promised Renée that she would be "the Lady commanding over everything" ("sara Signora de tutto"), but within a year he was expecting the French royal milieu to understand that he, the duke, was best positioned to "govern her" ("potevano pur ancho confidare che noi fussimo apto a saperla governare").[59] In 1553, Ercole rearticulated his father's opposition to being governed by women ("noi non siamo tale che ci lasciamo governare da donne").[60] Yet while the Este princes insisted on female obedience, they had put themselves in a bind: by marrying up the social scale, they found themselves with unconstrained wives.

A Trilogy of Independent Duchesses

Renée was the third legitimately married Ferrarese duchess in a row to prove herself grandly able to hold her own. Neither Alfonso's mother, Eleonora d'Aragona, of regal status and owner of a text devoted to the

---

[59] Fontana, *Renata di Francia,* I, 68 and 124.
[60] Fontana, *Renata di Francia,* II, 340.

(first) coronation of Renée's queenly mother,[61] nor his spouse, Lucrezia Borgia, had reinforced traditional gender stereotypes. On a medal by Sperandio celebrating Eleonora's marriage to Ercole I, standard patterns are broken when the duchess assumes precedence on her consort's heraldic right.[62] In 1477, pioneering a major shift from the Ducal Palace (Palazzo del Corte) to the formidable fourteenth-century Este Castle, Eleonora began devising lodgings worthy of her rank, in part financed by her own dowry and apanage, from whence her imposing household operated and her children were safe. Views of Naples highlighted her origins and those of her Neapolitan ladies, as did the gardens devised by her Neapolitan gardeners, including a hanging court garden in the west wing of the Castello and the "Zardino de Madama" on the other side of the moat.[63] Her spouse, Ercole I, who begot his second illegitimate child five years into their marriage,[64] was housed in the nearby Corte. The fact that Renée and Ercole II resided in different locations has been read as a sign of their estrangement, but Eleonora d'Aragona had consolidated the practice of consorts living in separate spaces.[65]

[61] Marco Folin, "La corte della duchessa: Eleonora d'Aragona a Ferrara," in *Donne di potere nel Rinascimento*, ed. Letizia Arcangeli and Susanna Peyronel (Rome: Viella, 2008), 486.

[62] Marco Folin, "Spazi femminili nelle dimore signorili italiane del quattrocento: il caso di Ferrara," *Viglevanum. Rivista della Società Storica Viganese* 25 (2015): fig. 7 (this is not the case on another medal cast in the same year, fig. 8); John Graham Pollard, *Renaissance Medals. The Collections of the National Gallery of Art Systematic Catalogue* (Washington: National Gallery, 2007), I, fig. 85. On Sperandio in Ferrara, see Luke Syson in Scher, *The Currency of Fame*, 91–94.

[63] Tuohy, *Herculean Ferrara*, 40–41, 70–71, 95–103; Marco Borella, in *Il trionfo di Bacco. Capolavori della scuola ferrarese a Dresda 1480-1620*, ed. Gregor J. M. Weber (Torino, London, Venice: Umberto Allemandi & Co., 2002), 21–22; Folin, "La corte," 492–511; Marco Folin, "Studioli, vie coperte, gallerie: genealogia di uno spazio del potere," in *Il Regno e l'arte: I camerini di Alfonso I d'Este, terzo duca di Ferrara*, ed. Charles Hope (Florence: Leo S. Olschki, 2012), 240–243, and Folin, "Spazi femminili," 108–118. Franceschini, "La corte," 188–189, notes the control maintained over Eleonora's court.

[64] Trevor Dean, "Ercole I d'Este, duca di Ferrara Modena e Reggio," in *Dizionario Biografico degli Italiani*, Vol. 43 (1993) http://www.treccani.it/enciclopedia/ercole-i-d-este-duca-di-ferrara-modena-e-reggio_%28Dizionario-Biografico%29/; Rodi, *Annali*, II, 42r, 42v.

[65] Tuohy, *Herculean Ferrara*, 53–79; Borella, in *Il trionfo*, 21; Folin, "Studioli," 236–243.

Eleonora and Renée had more in common than high status, imposing and independent households, and a love for gardens, though:[66] they also shared an interest in the *querelle des femmes*. As a child in Blois, Renée had access to her mother's library, with (for instance) its *Nobles et cleres dames* and the abundantly illustrated *Vies des femmes célèbres* by Antoine Dufour.[67] The Estense library in Ferrara contained Eleonora's *De laudibus mulierum* by Bartolommeo Goggio (British Library, Add. MS 17 415), and Antonio da Cornazzano's famed *Del modo di regere e di regnare* (New York, The Morgan Library and Museum, MS M. 732, fol. 2v),[68] in which Eleonora appears receiving the regent's scepter she first wielded in 1478–1479.[69] Renée was familiar with female regents, having observed Louise de Savoie's governance of France in 1515 and 1525–1526. Eleonora was, however, modeling the specific role that Renée would adopt: first in 1535, with, yet above, Ercole's brothers—something unusual Ercole argued ("habbiamo lassato a lei e a lj Ill^mi nostri fratelli, havemo pero lassato il Principal Governo a sua signoria il che non si suole gia fare da lj altrj principi in Italia")—and second alone, but not isolated, in 1559.[70]

Lucrezia Borgia, Ercole's mother, was known to Renée well before her marriage was arranged. Her sister Claude exchanged epistles with both of Ercole's parents shortly after her rise to the throne in early 1515.[71] Then three years later, about a month after the dauphin's birth, Lucrezia had a

---

[66] Du Cerceau reproduces her parents' Italianate gardens at Blois and her own at Montargis (Boudon and Mignot, *Du Cerceau*, 140–149 and 76–85).

[67] Cynthia J. Brown, *The Queen's Library: Image-making at the Court of Anne of Brittany, 1477–1514* (Philadelphia: University of Pennsylvania Press, 2011), 166–180, with additional examples, and chapter two in this volume.

[68] Maria Francesca Saffiotti and Daniele Benati in *La miniatura a Ferrara dal tempo di Cosmè Tura all'eredità di Ercole de' Roberti*, ed. Anna Maria Visser Travagli et al. (Modena: Franco Cosimo Panini, 1998), fig. 44, 232–234. On Eleonora's *studiolo*, art (including Ercole de' Roberti's *Famous Women*) and library, see Leah R. Clark, *Collecting Art in the Italian Renaissance Court. Objects and Exchanges* (Cambridge: Cambridge University Press, 2018), 122–157, 198–206, 217–233. Folin, "La corte," 491, cites Diomede Carafa's *De regentis et boni principis officis* too.

[69] Folin, "La corte," 487–492, 511–512.

[70] Fontana, *Renata di Francia*, I, 231, and II, 441–444 ("We have left [the government] to her and our Illustrious brothers, yet we have left the Main Government to her, something which is not usually done by other princes in Italy").

[71] Diane Ghirardo (whom I thank profusely for this and the information in the following note) uncovered a letter from Claude to Alfonso (February 7, 1515), misfiled under Louise Borgia (ASMo, Particolari, b. 209). Claude alludes to recent "letters" to her, regarding the death of her father and the raising ("augmentation") of her husband to the throne, promis-

piece of her jewelry reassembled for Claude.[72] Louise de Savoie inquired about the deceased Lucrezia, too, just before the newly wed ducal couple left France for Ferrara in 1528 ("Et Madama in especie me interrogo, come era tenuta la Signora mia madre de bona memoria, et che vita la faceva").[73] An informed and positive light has finally been shed on Lucrezia's wildly mythical persona.[74] As Duchess of Ferrara, she was an astute businesswoman (Eleonora d'Aragona had already owned live-stock[75]) and one of the first Italians of her age to invest in land reclama-tion, including land acquisition, hydraulic works, canal construction, and wetlands drainage, on "a staggeringly large scale."[76] Like Eleonora, she was a proactive woman of piety and Church reform, and she funded the neediest monasteries of Ferrara, particularly those of the Poor Clares.[77] Both traits led her to build. From 1509, she erected the convent of San Bernardino for her illegitimate niece Camilla Borgia, at which reforms were introduced in 1516, "for pious women living honestly." From 1515, she undertook her own suburban palace, which served as her business headquarters.[78] When Renée moved into the Palazzo San Francesco, Lucrezia's former Palazzo Borgia was also nearby.[79]

The deep interlocking of Eleonora's and Lucrezia's patronage with the Catholic churches of Ferrara could not provide a viable role model for Renée. Yet religious art involved much more than religion per se. From

ing future mediation. My thanks to Kelly Peebles, Elizabeth L'Estrange, and David Potter (who commented on the letter's rarity) for their help interpreting this missive.

[72] An addition to n° 78 of Lucrezia's registry of jewelry (ASMo, Archivio Estense, Amministrazione dei Principi, b. 1139) explains that a gold chain by Maestro Hercole was dismantled and 14 of its 19 medallions ("19 botteselle grande belle lavorate di oro cum smalti di più coloro piene di compositione et fatta novamente") were transformed into two "manille cum li ligamenti" to be sent to Claude (April 27, 1518).

[73] Ercole writing to his father; Fontana, *Renata di Francia*, I, 66 (September 21, 1528).

[74] Laura Laureati, "Da Borgia a Este: due vite in quarant'anni," in *Lucrezia Borgia*, ed. Laura Laureati (Ferrara: Ferrara Arte, 2002), 21–75; Zarri, *La* religione, and Ghirardo's articles; Andrea Vitale, "Lucrezia, il mestiere di principessa," in *I Borgia*, ed. Alfano Carla and Felipe V. Farin Llombart (Milan: Mondadori Electa, 2002), 241–247.

[75] Folin, "Spazi femminili," 116.

[76] See Ghirardo's articles in the bibliography.

[77] Zarri, "*La* religione," 71–72, 78, 103–104, 106–108, 113–114, 130–133, and following.

[78] Diane Yvonne Ghirardo, "Lucrezia Borgia's Palace in Renaissance Ferrara," *The Journal of the Society of Architectural Historians* 64, no. 4 (December 2005): 474–497; Marchesi, *Delizie d'archivio II–III*, 615–620.

[79] Marchesi, *Delizie d'archivio II–III*, 3, for a map.

the early 1480s, Eleonora d'Aragona developed tight connections with the sculptor Guido Mazzoni; Renée surely scrutinized the extant life-size *Lamentation*, then in Santa Maria della Rosa, where Eleonora figured as Mary Salome alongside her consort as Joseph of Arimathea.[80] While such theatrical piety may not have been consonant with Renée's sensitivities, the artist Mazzoni surely caught her eye. Eleonora's connection to Naples had facilitated the sculptor's employment at her brother Alfonso II's court. From there, knighted, Mazzoni departed in 1495 for France in the wake of the army of Renée's mother's first husband, Charles VIII. About fifteen years after producing Eleonora's *Lamentation*, Mazzoni went on to create the tomb that Anne de Bretagne commissioned for her deceased royal spouse.[81] Renée's sister Claude's primer, another volume she surely perused in her formative years, has been tentatively attributed to Mazzoni's workshop as well.[82] The active presence of his wife and daughter by his side might explain why it has been difficult to recognize Mazzoni's hand. Anne is known to have employed "peinteresses" at Amboise in 1495, while around 1520, a female author, Anne de Graville, penned works for Claude.[83] In the same vein, when Sofonisba Anguissola's self-portrait was

[80] Today in the Chiesa del Gesù; Mario Scalini, in *Emozioni in terracotta. Guido Mazzoni / Antonio Begarelli. Sculture del Rinascimento emiliano*, ed. Giorgio Bonsanti and Francesca Piccinini (Modena: Franco Cosimo Panini, 2009), fig. 20, 131–132; also fig. 19, 129–130.

[81] Timothy Verdon, "Guido Mazzoni in Francia: nuovi contributi," *Mitteilungen des Kunsthistorischen Institutes in Florenz* 34, no. 1–2 (1990): 139–141; Jens Burk, "'A l'antique' à Nantes et 'à la moderne' à Brou: styles architecturaux et conception de la statuaire funéraire au moment du passage du gothique tardif à la Renaissance," in *Patronnes et mécènes*, 230–231.

[82] Eberhard König, in *The Primer of Claude de France. MS 159, The Fitzwilliam Museum, Cambridge*, ed. Roger S. Wieck, Cynthia J. Brown and Eberhard König (Lucerne: Quadernio Verlag, 2012), 139–149.

[83] *Pomponius Gauricus. De Sculptura (1504)*, ed. André Chastel and Robert Klein (Geneva: Droz, 1969), 9; *Royaume de fémynie. Pouvoirs, contraintes, espaces de liberté des femmes, de la Renaissance à la Fronde*, ed. Éliane Viennot and Kathleen Wilson-Chevalier (Paris: Honoré Champion, 1999), 11n7. For bibliography on Graville: Mawy Bouchard, "The Power of Reputation and Skills according to Anne de Graville. The *Rondeaux* and the Denunciation of Slander," in *Women and Power at the French Court, 1483–1563*, ed. Susan Broomhall (Amsterdam: Amsterdam University Press, 2018), 241–262. Kathleen Wilson-Chevalier, "Claude de France and the Spaces of Agency of a Marginalized Queen," also in Broomhall, *Women and Power*, 139–172.

sent to the duke in 1556, the artist had Ercole's and Renée's daughter, Lucrezia, in mind.[84]

Renée came to question the cult of relics underlying a set of three finely incised silver plaques for the reliquary of the bishop patron saint of Ferrara San Maurelio.[85] The local saint's renunciation of wealth and worldly pomp might have appealed to her charitable soul nonetheless, while the gendered presentation of these artworks, attributed to Gianantonio Leli da Foligno and thought to commemorate Alfonso d'Este's resounding Ferrarese military victory over Venice in 1512, surely did. One of the plaques (Fig. 10.4) underscores the commanding role of a princess in the grooming of her progeny—Renée's husband Ercole, shown as Lucrezia Borgia's four-year-old son.[86] In contrast to the accompanying plaques, the staging of the duchess and five of her ladies-in-waiting in all their finery almost steal the show from San Maurelio, pictured giving his blessing to

Fig. 10.4 Gianantonio Leli da Foligno (attributed to), *Lucrezia Borgia Presenting Ercole d'Este to San Maurelio*, silver plaque. Ferrara, San Giorgio fuori le mura. © San Giorgio fuori le mura

[84] Rossana Sacchi, in *Sofonisba Anguissola e le sue sorelle,* ed. Paolo Buffa (Milan: Leonardo Arte, 1994), 188, 364.

[85] Maria Teresa Gulinelli, in Laureati, *Lucrezia Borgia,* 200–203, figs. 41b and c; Zarri, "*La* religione," 196–199.

[86] Sincere thanks to Diacono Emanuele Maria Pirani for this image.

the future duke. Fashion and hairstyles played into the politics of Renaissance courts, and Alfonso's sisters, Beatrice and Isabella d'Este, were particularly apt at using style with intent. Lucrezia and two of her ladies are depicted with a *coazzone*, a Spanish hairdo that Beatrice had introduced at the court of Milan in 1493, as a sign of resistance to Lombard power.[87] Beatrice's insistence on her mother's Spanish ascendancy is here paralleled by Lucrezia's nod to her own Spanish roots.

The French were experts at the style game, too. Anne de Bretagne commissioned fashion dolls; and when her daughter Renée was five, her brother-in-law, François I, requested one from Isabella d'Este that would show how Mantuan ladies wore shirts, undergarments, outer garments, dresses, headdresses, and hairstyles.[88] A few days before Renée's and Ercole's wedding, around the festivities of the bonfires of St. John, the City of Paris offered the king's children, Renée's childhood companions, a horse-driven carriage with two female dolls, the smaller of which was dressed "à la mode d'Italie," replete with a page in the king's livery, dogs and a monkey.[89] Having formerly interacted with Anne de Bretagne,[90] Isabella d'Este was cognizant that Renée had been perfectly groomed in the use of fashion for political ends, and until her death in 1539, she closely monitored the French princess's every stylistic move.[91]

---

[87] Evelyn Welch, "Art on the edge: hair and hands in Renaissance Italy," *Renaissance Studies* 23, no. 3 (June 2009): 247–254 (this image seems to contradict her assertion that "the coazzone never made it beyond Milan's borders," 254).

[88] Yassana C. Croizat, "'Living Dolls': François Ier Dresses His Women," *Renaissance Quarterly* 60 (2007): 98–102, 106–107.

[89] Michel Manson, "Diverses approches sur l'histoire de la poupée du XVe au XVIIe siècle," in *Les Jeux à la Renaissance. Actes du XXIIIe colloque international d'études humanistes (Tours–juillet 1980)*, ed. Philippe Ariès and Jean-Claude Margolin (Paris: Vrin, 1982), 530 for the municipal text.

[90] Including via her sister-in-law Clara da Gonzaga: Nicole Dupont-Pierrart, *Claire de Gonzague, Comtesse de Bourbon-Montpensier (1464–1503). Une princesse italienne à la cour de France* (Villeneuve-d'Ascq, Presses Universitaires du Septentrion, 2017), 104–105, 262–263.

[91] As noted by Anna Maria Fioravanti Baraldi, "Vita artistica e dibattito religioso a Ferrara nella prima metà del Cinquecento," in *La pittura in Emilia e in Romagna Il Cinquecento. Un romanzo polifonico tra Riforma e Controriforma*, ed. Vera Fortunati (Ferrara: Nuova Alfa Editoriale, Elemond Editori Associati, 1995), 120.

RENÉE ON THE COURTLY STAGE

The size and cost of Lucrezia Borgia's retinue became a subject of dispute shortly after her Ferrarese wedding festivities came to an end.[92] Controversy re-erupted after Renée arrived with a still larger court, which Ercole down-sized doggedly: by 1554, her household of (probably well more than the listed) 157 had been cut back to (at the very least) 107.[93] Pageantry was nonetheless an integral part of the power ploy. Four days out of Paris, when the newlyweds presented themselves to their subjects in Montargis, Isabella d'Este received a detailed epistolary account.[94] When they arrived in Ferrara, just as Isabella had formerly awaited Lucrezia and her ladies in 1502,[95] she and a select group of Ferrarese ladies greeted Renée and her suite at the bottom of the Corte staircase,[96] which Ercole I had conceived for the grand reception of his spouse.[97] The company then escorted Renée, dressed in her queenly wedding gown and boldly crowned, to "her regally prepared lodgings" ("et così fu accompagnata a li sui alloggiamenti appa-rati regiamente") where, in the audience hall, the memorable "gold and silk" tapestries she had brought with her adorned the walls ("et maxime la sala grande cum quelle belle tapezarie franzese d'oro e di seta che deve haver viste V. Ex. quale pasceno l'ochio mirabilmente").[98]

François I's wedding gift of costly narrative hangings depicting the tale of Lerian and Laureolle, taken from Diego de San Pedro's *Cárcel de amor*, constituted a consummate example of meaningful courtly cultural exchange. While the Ferrarese Lelio Manfredi had undertaken an Italian translation for Isabella d'Este, Ercole's mother, Lucrezia Borgia, was

---

[92] Laureati, "Da Borgia," 45.

[93] Caroline Zum Kolk, "Les difficultés des mariages internationaux: Renée de France et Hercule d'Este," in *Femmes et pouvoir politique. Les princesses d'Europe XVe–XVIIIe siècle,* ed. Isabelle Poutrin and Marie-Karine Schaub (Rosny-sous-Bois: Éditions Bréal, 2007), 108–109, citing her *états de maison* for 1528–1529 (BnF ms. fr. 3002, fol. 41), 1532–1533 (BnF coll. Clairambault 816, fol. 9), and 1553–1554 (BnF ms. fr. 21478, fol. 75 and ms. fr. 3230, fol. 78).

[94] Fontana, *Renata di Francia,* I, 64.

[95] Laureati, "Da Borgia," 42.

[96] Fontana, *Renata di Francia,* I, 76–78 for Luigi Gonzaga's account.

[97] Tuohy, *Herculean Ferrara,* 65, 73–75; Marco Folin, "La committenza estense, l'Alberti e il Palazzo di Corte di Ferrara," in *Leon Battista Alberti Architettura e committenti,* ed. Arturo Calzona, Vol. I (Florence: Leo S. Olschki, 2009), 284–296, for Ercole I's renovation of the Corte prior to his marriage.

[98] Fontana, *Renata di Francia,* I, 77.

surely the initial link to the Spanish court.[99] In France, signs that the text appealed to courtly women appeared during the reign of Claude de France, who seems to have received the first French manuscript translation, possibly as early as 1518.[100] Other manuscripts include a finely illuminated version for Jacquette de Lansac,[101] whose second marriage, interestingly, was to Jacques de Pons, a member of Renée's knight of honor's clan.[102] Another entitled *Carcer Damour* has been linked to the marriage of Marguerite d'Angoulême/Navarre in 1527.[103] The author François Dassy, by 1526 secretary to Marguerite de Navarre's spouse, was already in the service of Cesare Borgia's daughter Louise de Valentinois. Louise is the probable dedicatee of Dassy's translation of Giacomo Caviceo's *Libro del Peregrino*, dedicated to her aunt Lucrezia in 1508, of which Galliot du Pré's *princeps* edition appeared in Paris in 1527. When Ercole, Renée, and the tapestries left Montargis for Italy in September 1528, Louise ("Madama de la Tramoglia") rode to Grenoble by her cousin's and his spouse's side. In Ferrara, once Renée and Isabella had proceeded to the Corte hall and viewed the *Forgiveness of the King* (Fig. 10.5), they could literally imagine themselves mirroring the encounter of Laureolle and her mother, the queen.[104]

For Renée, an eighteen-year-old envoy shipped off to a foreign land, the gift had to be comforting, giving expression to her superior rank and the appeal of French chivalric culture, made tangible by the Gothic text of

[99] Myra Dickman Orth, "'The Prison of Love': A Medieval Romance in the French Renaissance and Its Illustration (B.N. MS fr. 2150)," *Journal of the Warburg and Courtauld Institutes* 46 (1983): 212; Emily C. Francomano, "Reversing the Tapestry: *Prison of Love* in Text, Image, and Textile," *Renaissance Quarterly* 64, no. 4 (Winter 2011): 1075.

[100] Hispanic Society of America, MS HC 380/636, fols. 21–276, followed by texts concerning the Dauphin François, fols. 277–285; Irene Finotti, "Pour une classification des témoins de 'La Prison d'amour' de François Dassy: paratexte et macrostructure," *Studi Francesi* 166, no. 1 (2012): 71n17, n18.

[101] Myra D. Orth, *Renaissance Manuscripts. The Sixteenth Century* (London, Turnhout: Harvey Miller, 2015), II, n30, 116–121; she situates Jacquette in the service of Claude.

[102] BnF ms. n. a. fr. 7552. Gaspard Thaumas de la Thaumassière, *Histoire du Berry* (Bourges: François Toubeau, 1689), 970. Francomano, "Reversing the Tapestry," relays the belief that Jacquette de Lansac produced an illegitimate son with François I.

[103] BnF ms. fr. 2150. Orth, "Manuscrits pour Marguerite," 90–91; Mathilde Thorel, "La première réception du *Peregrin* en France: lecture éditoriale et recontextualisation culturelle," *Réforme, Humanisme, Renaissance* 75 (2012): 90.

[104] On the possible relationship between this Cluny tapestry (Inv. Cl. 22742) and Renée's original set, see Fabienne Joubert, *La Tapisserie médiévale au musée de Cluny* (Paris: RMN, 1987), X, 127–134.

Fig. 10.5 *The Forgiveness of the King (Lerian and Laureolle)*, tapestry. Paris, musée de Cluny—musée national du Moyen-Âge, Inv. Cl. 22742. © RMN-Grand Palais / Art Resource, NY. (Photo: Jean-Gilles Berizzi)

the scroll above. Isabella was then fifty-four, but unnatural age inversions aside, Renée would have identified with Laureolle's mother (her mother) the queen, donning her crown as she and her daughter embrace. Shared codes rendered the image accessible to the intermixed French and Italian courtiers in Ferrara:[105] recognizable literary tropes; the pageantry of princely travel with mules, chests, coats-of-arms, and emblematic display;

[105] Francomano, "Reversing the Tapestry."

discrete yet portentous military might; parallel private and public spheres...
Laureolle and her mother meet in an enclosed garden, symbolizing the
chastity upon which Isabella and Renée's very honor depended, from
which their masculine counterparts were exempt. Yet the female protagonists commandeer the heraldic right of the tapestry's luxurious display
while, in the distance, the epistolary exchange between Laureolle and the
viateur (traveler) conjures up the incessant diplomatic roles both princesses would play when off stage.

Renée's religious leanings and political entanglements with her consort
have overshadowed her role as an extremely effective head of court.[106]
From her arrival in Ferrara, her aptitude for public performance was clear.
Isabella was present in early 1529, when Ariosto projected Renée into his
theatrical performance of *La Cassaria*. If the Marchesa was elsewhere,
then her informants kept her abreast, signaling Renée's lodging at the
Palazzo Schifanoia from May 1529 ("La Signora Duchessa andò a stanziar
a Schifanoia").[107] In September 1530, Renée staged therein grand festivities celebrating the end of the captivity of her French royal nephews and
the remarriage of her brother-in-law to Éleonore d'Autriche, formerly a
Portuguese queen. Isabella's learned and fashion-sensitive emissary,
Battista Stabellino, penned three letters describing the dress and coifs of
the intermingling courts.[108] Madame de Soubise resided above Renée; and
as Ercole (housed on the ground floor) danced with a Soubise daughter
("una de le figlie de Madama Sebis"), Renée, in a "novel costume" conceived for the event, kept step with a daughter of the dethroned Neapolitan
queen.[109] The images of sexual license and adultery in Borso d'Este's sixty-
year-old Hall of the Months fresco cycle (*April, September*)[110] formed an
unproblematic backdrop to Renée's "honest" Portuguese dress ("molto
galante et honesto, et da gran madonne, et lo chiamano vestire alla
Portogallese").[111] Stabellino's third letter debates the political meaning of
a reversion from Portuguese to French costume, attributed to the

[106] As noted by Franceschini, "La corte," 185. Gorris, "'D'un château l'autre,'" 139–143.
[107] Marchesi, *Delizie d'archivio II–III*, 689, Doc. 5.
[108] Gorris, "La corte," 150–151.
[109] Fontana, *Renata di Francia*, I, 144.
[110] Defined by Alison Cole, *Virtue and Magnificence: Art of Italian Renaissance Courts*
(New York, Harry N. Abrams, 1995), 126, as "a suburban administration-cum-pleasure
complex;" Marco Bertozzi, in *Este a Ferrara. Una corte nel Rinascimento*, ed. Jadranka
Bentini (Milan: Silvana Editoriale, 2004), 108–115.
[111] Fontana, *Renata di Francia*, I, 145.

politically astute Madame de Soubise.[112] In February 1531, after Queen Eleonora's brother Charles V had confirmed Duke Alfonso's control over Modena and Reggio, Renée and her ladies again donned Portuguese fashion, with an Italian touch, alongside local women ("le done de la tera") for another Ariostean performance. A month later, Ercole enacted a knight errant at a Franco-Italian banquet organized by his brother, Ippolito, at Belfiore in honor of Renée ("Illma Sig^ra Renea con tutte le sue francese, et a molte nostre gentil donne de la terra"). The event ended with Renée heading off in a carriage with the daughters of the former Neapolitan queen, followed by women on horseback and others in carts.[113] By this point, Renée was pregnant with Anna d'Este, and she spent the summer with the court at Belriguardo—an alternative seat of government, the grand and regal Estense *delizia* par excellence.[114]

BELRIGUARDO AND THE SALA DELLA VIGNA

Belriguardo sported a "courtyard of women" ("cortile delle donne") and a "room of women" ("sala delle donne") as early as 1458,[115] and Lucrezia Borgia died there in childbirth in 1519. After examining Renée's account books and populating the site with Brasavola's wild animals, a dwarf, and parrots, Rodocanachi identified the *delizia* as her favorite early country retreat.[116] In May 1529, she is associated with its fresh air and courtly entertainment in a letter Duke Alfonso wrote to reassure the French court after a worrisome illness: "Madama la Duchessa nostra è stata alcuni giorni a prendere spasso et aere al nostro Belriguardo et seco il Duca suo consorte, et l'archivescovo di Milano [Ippolito], et se è pensato di darle tutti

---

[112]Fontana, *Renata di Francia*, I, 148–149. Marchesi, *Delizie d'Archivio II–III*, 690, Doc. 10.

[113]Fontana, *Renata di Francia*, I, 154–157. Renée's festive association with Schifanoia continued through 1532 (Marchesi, *Delizie d'Archivio II–III*, 691, 1531, Doc. 1; 1532, Docs. 2 & 3).

[114]Folin, "Le residenze di corte," Maria Teresa Sambin de Norcen, "I miti di Belriguardo," in *Nuovi antichi. Committenti, cantieri, architetti, 1400–1600*, ed. R. Schofield (Milan: Electa, 2004), 17–66, "'Ut apud plinium': giardino e paesaggio a Belriguardo nel Quattrocento," in *Delizie in Villa. Il giardino nel Rinascimento e i suoi committenti*, ed. Gianni Venturoli and Francesco Ceccarelli (Florence: Leo S. Olschki, 2006), 65–89, and "Nuove indagini su Belriguardo e la committenza di villa nel primo Rinascimento," in *Delizie Estensi Architetture di villa nel Rinascimento italiano ed europeo*, ed. Francesco Ceccarelli and Marco Folin (Florence: Leo S. Olschki, 2009), 145–180.

[115]Folin, "Spazi femminili," 110.

[116]Rodocanachi, *Renée*, 69–70.

quelli piacevoli intertenimenti, che si è creduto che la aggradino" (Madame our Duchess was at Belriguardo to spend time in open air with the Duke her consort, and the archbishop of Milan, and they thought of giving her all of those entertainments that they believed would please her).[117] The first extant archival document of the 1530s concerns Renée's rooms ("le stantie per Madama"), the second a Frenchman who in 1534 fell into a well.[118] In September 1535, when she was in the sixth month of a difficult pregnancy, Madame de Soubise was on the verge of being removed, and Ercole was gearing up to forbid Renée's reuniting with the French court in Lyon, it was here that Ippolito attempted an unsuccessful heart-to-heart talk with her one night.[119] In August 1536, one of Isabella d'Este's informants locates Renée at Belriguardo, as the duke came and went. Here, Renée learned of the death of the Dauphin of France at the end of the month; from here she expedited her condolences to the King and the Queen of Navarre (Marguerite).[120]

The famed artist Giulio Romano probably visited Belriguardo in early 1535. He subsequently produced sketches for the decoration of a ground-floor reception hall/banqueting room set between the main court and a secret [private] garden (one of Belriguardo's famed).[121] Then in July and August 1537, a vast team including the finest Ferrarese artists, Garofalo, the Dossi brothers, and Girolamo da Carpi, frescoed the now badly damaged, yet still impressive, Sala della Vigna. A number of historians have reflected on the artistic hands at play, caryatid-cycle precedents, and the majestically foreshortened architectural stage opening onto landscapes beyond (Fig. 10.6).[122] Jadranka Bentini underlined the "domestic and

---

[117] Fontana, *Renata di Francia*, I, 126.

[118] Marchesi, *Delizie d'Archivio I*, 30–31, Belriguardo, 1531, Doc. 1, 1534, Doc. 1.

[119] Fontana, *Renata di Francia*, I, 228–229.

[120] Fontana, *Renata di Francia*, I, 408–409.

[121] Denis Ribouillault, "Le ville dipinte del cardinale Ippolito d'Este a Tivoli: l'architettura di fronte all'antico, la tradizione ferrarese, e un nuovo documento su Belriguardo," in *Delizie estensi*, ed. Ceccarelli and Folin, 362–365.

[122] Jadranka Bentini, "La Sala delle Vigne nella 'delizia' di Belriguardo," *Atti e Memorie Accademia Clementina Bologna* 35–36 (1995–1996), 9–37; Gudrun Dauner, "Girolamo da Carpi e le belle donne di Belriguardo," *Pittura antica* 1, no. 4 (2005): 18–37; Carla Di Francesco, Jadranka Bentini and Adriano Cavicchi, *Arte e storia a Belriguardo. "La Sala delle Vigne"* (Ferrara: Belriguardo, 1997); Alessandra Pattanaro, "I pittori di Ercole II a Belriguardo: modelli giulieschi e tradizione vitruviana," *Prospettiva* 141–142 (Gennaio–Aprile 2011): 100–123; Enrico Benetti, *al Belriguardo. Piccola storia del rapporto tra la famiglia d'Este e la Delizia di Voghiera* (Voghiera: Edizioni arstudio C, 2007), 34–54; Sergio Cariani, *La Sala della Vigna al Belriguardo "Una polifonia di proporzioni che la mente rinascimentale intendeva e l'occhio rinascimentale sapeva vedere"* (Città di Castello: Edit Art,

Fig. 10.6 *Caryatid Herms* (attributed to the Dossi brothers), fresco. Voghiera, Delizia di Belriguardo, Sala della Vigna, southeast wall. (Photo: Filippo Greselin)

captivating tone" of its particularly numerous and unusually lively gallery of female types—Gudrun Dauner's "beautiful women of Belriguardo," whose fictive stage she links to the periodic transformation of the room into a real stage[123]—suggesting a link between its "fantastic universe of ambiguous female metaphors" and Ludovico Ariosto's "rhetoric and strategy of irony."[124] Courtesans and/or prostitutes[125] cast suggestive sidelong gazes (Fig. 10.7), wet nurses and pregnant women (Figs. 10.8

Fig. 10.7 *Two Caryatid Herms* (attributed to the Dossi brothers), fresco. Voghiera, Delizia di Belriguardo, Sala della Vigna, southeast wall. (Photo: Filippo Greselin)

2016); Marchesi, *Delizie d'archivio I*, 31–41 for the many related archival documents. My thanks to Alessandro Boninsegna for on-site discussions and follow-up.

[123] Dauner, "Girolamo da Carpi," 30.

[124] Bentini, "La Sala delle Vigne," 21, 23, 28, 30.

[125] On prostitution in Ferrara, see Diane Yvonne Ghirardo, "The Topography of Prostitution in Renaissance Ferrara," *The Journal of the Society of Architectural Historians* 60, no. 4 (December 2001): 402–431.

Fig. 10.8 *Caryatid Herm* (attributed to the Dossi brothers), fresco. Voghiera, Delizia di Belriguardo, Sala della Vigna, southeast wall. (Photo: Filippo Greselin)

and 10.9) surround its spectators. Although Renée plausibly figured on the short wall opposite (today's ruins of) her spouse,[126] the almost monopolistic presence of women has not led historians to envision a commission conceived not for Ercole alone (the financier of the duchess's rooms and

---

[126] Benetti, *al Belriguardo*, 45. Pattanaro, "I pittori di Ercole II," 116n25, hypothesizes a *damnatio memoriae* after the devolution of the duchy to the papacy; hence the near-total censorship of Renée's wall?

Fig. 10.9 *Three Caryatid Herms* (attributed to Girolamo da Carpi), fresco. Voghiera, Delizia di Belriguardo, Sala della Vigna, northwest wall. (Photo: Filippo Greselin)

the Sala della Vigna), but as the product of conjugal patronage instead. The ensemble may actually be tied to Clément Marot's "Blason du beau Tétin envoyé de Ferrare à la court de France," which launched the "blason anatomique" competition from Ferrara in 1535–1536, concluding with a prize distributed by Renée. As in the Belriguardo frescoes, the female breast is foregrounded in a literary topos that Marot shared with "Olimpo da Sassoferrato," and that plays on the revealed and the unrevealed, the body and the mind.[127]

On another plane, Alessandra Pattanaro, examining Renaissance prints and treatises including those of Fra Giocondo and Sebastiano Serlio, has convincingly read this architecturally savvy ensemble as a reflection on Vitruvius and the Orders.[128] Italian architects entered Renée's life at the cradle. Her baptismal furniture was designed by Anne de Bretagne's woodworker, Domenico da Cortona, like Mazzoni one of the Italians who had followed her first husband back to France.[129] Fra Giocondo also arrived with King Charles VIII; and Jacques Lefèvre d'Étaples, who became the royal children's evangelical religious mentor in the 1520s, had attended the friar/theoretician's lessons on Vitruvius in Paris eight years before Renée's birth. During her parent's reign, Giocondo had engineered fountains at Blois and designed Paris's Pont Notre-Dame, the first official royal crossing of which was her mother's funeral procession (1514). In 1537, the very year the Belriguardo frescoes were executed, Sebastiano Serlio, a Bolognese architect/theoretician who had resided and taught in Venice from 1528, dedicated his *Regole generali di architettura* to Ercole II. Scholars have laid bare Serlio's heterodox religious penchant,[130] which opens a door onto a possible connection to Renée, especially in light of his move from Venice to France in 1541. There, with Androuet du Cerceau (who honored Giocondo's bridge in his *Plus excellents bâtiments*),[131] Serlio

[127] Guillaume Berthon, "L'invention du blason: retour sur la genèse d'un genre (Ferrare, 1535)," in *Anatomie d'une anatomie*, ed. Julien Goeury and Thomas Hunkeler (Geneva: Droz, 2018), 135–156 for the genesis of the poem in Ferrara and its probable link to Caio Baldassare Olimpo Alessandri's "Capitolo delle poppe, tette de Pegasea," 140 for Renée as distributor of the prize to Maurice Scève. My thanks to Kelly Peebles for this bibliographical reference.

[128] In a very detailed manner in Pattanaro, "I pittori di Ercole II," 105–110.

[129] Pauline Matarasso, *Le Baptême de Renée de France en 1510. Compte des frais et préparatifs* (Paris: CNRS Éditions, 2011), 14, 103–109; Flaminia Bardati, "Anne de Bretagne bâtisseuse: identité et mémoire," in *Bâtir au féminin? Traditions et stratégies en Europe et dans l'Empire ottoman*, ed. Sabine Frommel and Juliette Dumas (Paris: Picard, 2013), 99–100.

[130] Beginning with Manfredo Tafuri, "Ipotesi sulla religiosità di Sebastiano Serlio," in *Bâtir au féminin? Traditions et stratégies en Europe et dans l'Empire ottoman*, ed. Christof Thoenes (Milan: Electa, 1989), 57–66 and Mario Carpo, *La Maschera e il modello. Teoria architettonica ed evangelismo nell'Extraordinario Libro di Sebastiano Serlio (1551)* (Milan: Jaca Book, 1993).

[131] Jean-Pierre Babelon, *Paris au XVIe siècle* (Paris: Diffusion Hachette, 1986), 93, 114, 116; Étienne Hamon, *Une capitale flamboyante la création monumentale à Paris autour de 1500* (Paris: Picard, 2011), 115–117.

would benefit from the financial support of her brother-in-law's sister, her youthful protectress, and close political and religious ally Marguerite de Navarre.[132]

In May 1534, as the future duke held down the fort with their children in Ferrara, Renée traveled to Venice at the head of a delegation charged with reclaiming the Este palace on the Grand Canal.[133] Doge Andrea Gritti ceremoniously received her and her household, Italian courtiers and ladies and her Ferrarese brothers-in-law, including Ippolito—after 1541, the other great defender of Serlio (and his wife) in France.[134] Gritti appears amid the *Regole generali* dedications, and the volume contains a ceiling Serlio devised for his Ducal Palace library.[135] The French ambassador to Venice was then Georges de Selve. Like his successor Georges d'Armagnac (another protégé of Marguerite), both corresponded actively with Renée, and both were then evangelically inclined. On July 21, 1536, d'Armagnac wrote from Venice that he had spent six days in Ferrara trying to convince Ercole to release his French religious prisoners (Bouchefort, Cornillau, Jamet...).[136] His humanist secretary and Greek and Latin tutor, Guillaume Philandrier, assiduously attended Serlio's Venetian lessons, and Serlio's friend Titian painted the erudite pair.[137] D'Armagnac encouraged Serlio to publish his treatise, while Philandrier, a budding Vitruvian scholar, was

[132] Sylvie Deswarte-Rosa, "Serlio et Jacques Androuet du Cerceau, dans le *Recueil de dessins de Camille de Neuville* à Lyon," in *Sebastiano Serlio à Lyon Architecture et imprimerie*. Volume 1: *Le traité d'architecture de Sebastiano Serlio une grande entreprise éditoriale à Lyon au XVI᷈ siècle*, ed. Sylvie Deswarte-Rosa (Lyon: Mémoire active, 2004), 454–461.

[133] Fontana, *Renata di Francia*, I, 138 & 187–197; Marchesi, *Delizie d'archivio I*, 586–599.

[134] Carmelo Occhipinti, "La Villa d'Este a Fontainebleau e le sue stufette. Documenti su Serlio e il Cardinale di Ferrara," *Prospettiva* 89–90 (Gennaio–Aprile 1998): 169–170.

[135] Loredana Olivato, "Per il Serlio a Venezia: documenti nuovi e documenti rivisitati," *Arte Veneta* 25 (1971): 286; Sabine Frommel, *Sebastiano Serlio architetto* (Milan: Electa, 1998), 190; Francesca Maffei, *Eterodossia e vitruvianesimo: Palazzo Naselli a Ferrara 1527–1538* (Rome: Campisano, 2013), 181.

[136] Rodocanachi, *Renée de France*, 111–126; Gorris, "Un franzese," 362–364; Belligni, *Renata di Francia*, 135–144. On this incident, see also Dick Wursten's contribution to this volume.

[137] Michael Jaffé, "The Picture of the Secretary of Titian," *The Burlington Magazine* 108 (March 1966): 114–127; Charles Samaran, "Georges d'Armagnac, ambassadeur de François Ier à Venise, peint par le Titien en compagnie de son secrétaire Guillaume Philandrier," *Comptes rendus des séances de l'Académie des Inscriptions et Belles-Lettres* 110e année, no. 1 (1966): 38–44.

disappointed that the Italian failed to take one of his suggestions into account.[138]

Serlio's *Regole generali* sheds light on the heterodox Vitruvian milieu of Ferrara, with references to (Ercole's and) Celio Calcagnini's knowledge of architecture, and the Palazzo Naselli, adorned with Erasmian inscriptions that Calcagnini helped select.[139] Church canon, secretary to the duke, teacher of Latin and Greek, and like Erasmus a bastard son, Calcagnini (†1541) was the official historian of the Este dukes from 1517. He has been labeled a "Nicodemite," and in 1537, his religiously suspect friends included Brasavola and Pellegrino Morato. The multivalent humanist pursued an epistolary exchange concerning Vitruvius with the heretical cartographer Jacob Ziegler, who, in 1532, had dedicated his remarkable *Terrae Sanctae* to Renée.[140] Rabelais testified to Calcagnini's affinities with the religious refugees around the duchess as these frescoes were being conceived.[141] In 1536, Calcagnini lauded Giulio Romano as a very talented man ("uomo di eccellente ingegno").[142] Did he help ideate the humanist program underlying the Sala della Vigna?

As seats of government, courts were minefields where the survival of princes, princesses, and courtiers required consummate skill. Calcagnini had addressed the art of dissimulation and forbearance in his unpublished "Simultatae virtutis defensio,"[143] akin to French anti-courtier satire.[144] Both Ercole and Renée were masters of dissimulation, opening epistles entering and leaving their households, as rulers of their age were wont to do.[145] A pervasive atmosphere of distrust helps comprehend why the Sala della Vigna

---

[138] Frommel, *Serlio*, 25; Frédérique Lemerle, *Les Annotations de Guillaume Philandrier sur le De Architectura de Vitruve Livres I à IV* (Paris: Picard, 2000), 13–14, and *Les Annotations sur L'Architecture de Vitruve Livres V à VII* (Paris: Classiques Garnier, 2011), 12; Maria Beltramini, "Un equivoco vitruviano di Sebastiano Serlio: la 'corona lisis'," *Annali della Scuola Normale Superiore di Pisa. Classe di Lettere e Filosofia* Serie IV. Vol. 5–1 (2000): 290–292.

[139] Francesca Maffei, "Celio Calcagnini, Terzo Terzi e la cultura architettonica a Ferrara nel primo Cinquecento (1513–1539)," *Arte lombarda* 166, no. 3 (2012): 40–61, and *Eterodossia*, 118.

[140] Belligni, *Renata di Francia*, 105–110; John R. Bartlett, *Mapping Jordan Through Two Millenia* (Routledge: Abingdon and New York, 2017), 43–48.

[141] Gorris, "Un franzese," 354–357.

[142] Maffei, *Eterodossia*, 78–79.

[143] Belligni, *Renata di Francia*, 105–106; Jon R. Snyder, *Dissimulation and the Culture of Secrecy in Early Modern Europe* (Berkeley: University of California Press, 2009), 50–52.

[144] Pauline M. Smith, *The Anti-courtier Trend in French Literature* (Geneva: Droz, 1966). On these themes related to Renée's evangelical upbringing, see chapter two in this volume.

[145] Fontana, *Renata di Francia*, II, 105, for instance.

caryatid/herms are cast as vigilant female figures with alert minds, chaste or unchaste prisoners of an ever-present controlling gaze. If Mario Carpo is correct in arguing that Serlio's architectural vision hinges on the conflict between Vitruvian "modesty" and architectural "license,"[146] then these women from all walks of life become bearers of a proper ("modest") illusionistic Vitruvian frame, which is charged with governing an ungainly whole. The often improper "belle donne" of Belriguardo then take on metaphorical roles.

The masters of Belriguardo commanded over their frescoes and choreographed their courtly show from the center of the N/NW wall that opened onto the secret garden. If Ercole's seating was consonant with his portrayal on the wall to their left, then the heraldic right would have accrued to Renée, positioned below the lovely matron depicted in Fig. 10.10. Real windows, once topped by allegories of the seasons, are separated by landscapes that pierce the frescoed stage. The tentative identification of their geographical siting as the region of Trent surely signifies more than a simple stylistic link to landscapes that the Ferrarese Dossi

Fig. 10.10 *Winter and Hermathena* (attributed to Garofalo), fresco. Voghiera, Delizia di Belriguardo, Sala della Vigna, northwest wall. (Photo: Filippo Greselin)

---

[146] Carpo, *La maschera*, 13, on the conflict between "modestia" and "licenza."

brothers had recently executed at the Palazzo del Buonconsiglio for Bernardo Cles, Cardinal of Trent.[147] In February 1536, Rabelais witnessed an encounter in Rome between two champions of a church council in the name of religious peace: the imperially inclined Cles and Cardinal Jean du Bellay, one more ecclesiastical ally of Marguerite and Renée.[148] Convoked in 1545, the Council of Trent was transferred to Bologna in 1547–1548, and the French emissaries included du Bellay and the future evangelical chancellor of France, Michel de l'Hospital, part of a delegation that frequented the Duchess of Ferrara (and whose sepulcher would be impelled by Renée and her like-minded niece Marguerite de Savoie in 1573).[149] De l'Hospital addressed an epistle to a close friend of (the then-deceased) Calcagnini, the Bolognese scholar Achille Bocchi,[150] whose 1555 *Symbolicae quaestiones* contains an emblem dedicated to Renée (LXI, *Proteus bound*), interpreted as "crypted praise of dissimulation."[151] Another emblem (CII) glorifies Hermathena, who unites eloquence and the arts. The name accrued to Bocchi's academy, its image adorned his palace; and this double-figure, conjoined by Love, is seen as embodying the evangelical program he (like Calcagnini) shared with Renée.[152]

Two caryatids in the Sala della Vigna stand out as "kingpins." The first, to the right of *Winter* (Fig. 10.11), the only extant season, reads as an athletic Pallas/Minerva herm—an early incarnation of the Hermathena, it would seem.[153] A nearby Janus-like corner figure looks on the one hand

---

[147] Humfrey and Lucco, in *Dosso Dossi*, 47–48; Benetti, *al Belriguardo*, 44; for a different reading, Pattanaro, "I pittori di Ercole," 110–111.

[148] Alain Tallon, *La France et le concile de Trente (1518–1563)* (Rome: École française de Rome, 2017), 501n38.

[149] Denis Crouzet, *La Sagesse et le malheur. Michel de l'Hospital, chancelier de France* (Seyssel: Champ Vallon, 1998), 75–77; Loris Petris, *La Plume et la tribune. Michel de l'Hospital et ses discours (1559–1562)* (Geneva: Droz, 2002), 68n529; Gorris, "La bibliothèque," on the relationship between Renée and Marguerite.

[150] See Elizabeth Watson, *Achille Bocchi and the Emblem Book as Symbolic Form* (Cambridge: Cambridge University Press, 1993), 74; Crouzet, *La Sagesse*, 75–76.

[151] Anne Rolet, *Les Questions symboliques d'Achille Bocchi. Symbolicae quaestiones, 1555* (Rennes: Presses universitaires François-Rabelais de Tours, Presses universitaires de Rennes, 2015), I, 139, 219, 376–378; II, 323–342; Watson, *Bocchi*, 24, 132. On Renée and emblematic exemplarity, see Kelly D. Peebles, "Embodied Devotion: The Dynastic and Religious Loyalty of Renée de France (1510–1575)," in *Royal Women and Dynastic Loyalty*, ed. Caroline Dunn and Elizabeth Carney (Switzerland: Palgrave MacMillan, 2018), 123–137.

[152] Rolet, *Les Questions*, 521–532.

[153] Vincenzo Cartari's Hermathena, with "an almost virile face," is both eloquent and prudent; Vincenzo Cartari, *Imagini delli dei de gl'antichi* (Venice: Nicolò Pezzana, 1624), 176.

Fig. 10.11 *Caryatid Herms with Landscape*, fresco. Voghiera, Delizia di Belriguardo, Sala della Vigna, northwest wall. (Photo: Filippo Greselin)

toward the (unchaste) duke, on the other toward this strong chaste female figure, aligned with the bitter season. The Pallas-herm casts a moderate and virtuous though direct gaze, her aegis signaling the just causes she defends, among which, surely, the ability to rule oneself.[154] Since infancy, Renée had been familiar with Minerva, associated with Janus and Prudence.[155] Christian humanists like Erasmus linked Pallas/Minerva to "women's intellectual, spiritual and moral capacities"; and in France, debates on reciprocal love, enriched by Leone Ebreo's neo-Platonic *Dialoghi d'amore*, invoked "Madame Minerve."[156] The Sala della Vigna's Hermathena, in perfect synchrony with its "governing" fictive Vitruvian frame, embodies a model of steadfast rectitude in a universe subject to political and religious turmoil and unruly love. Unlike some of her voluble companions (Fig. 10.9), Hermathena's mouth is prudently, stoically,

[154] The inscription over the door to the Temple of Janus, Bocchi's final emblem, CLI, reads "The mind watches all things; it acts with prudence and skill;" Watson, *Bocchi*, 147–148, Rolet, *Les Questions*, I, 604–606, II, 879–892.
[155] See chapter two in this volume.
[156] Kelly D. Peebles, *Jeanne Flore. Tales and Trials of Love* (Toronto: Centre for Reformation and Renaissance Studies, 2014), 18–19, 23–31; discussing a "rhétorique paradoxale" which is pertinent here.

closed.[157] Both Calcagnini and Bocchi propounded Nicodemism as the best response to the "bitter season" that had recently forced refugees under Renée's protection to flee, among whom the Erasmian Marot.[158] Following the St. Bartholomew's day massacre—so in even harsher times—Michel de l'Hospital invoked the "noble and pure soul" of Renée's daughter Anna d'Este, whose marriage thrust her into a hostile religious environment in France that forced her to "dissimulate and pretend." His comparison of Anne to a ship trying to remain steady in a tempest prolongs the spirit of Belriguardo's Hermathena, resisting in an "agitated sea."[159]

The second "kingpin" caryatid/herm, set opposite the princess and the prince (Fig. 10.12), marks the program's crux. Associated by Pattanaro with the prisoners of Raphael/Marcantonio Raimondi's Persian Portico (its male figures excised though),[160] even more importantly she reads it as the polar opposite of another engraving by Raimondi, *Woman Tearing Her Hair* (becoming, in Bocchi's emblem XVII, Lust).[161] Calmly wrapping her hands around ordered symmetrical braids, like Bocchi's "cosmic" Pan (emblem XLV), she points to her superior seat, her head.[162] The latter merges with an Ionic capital—the feminine order invoked in the secret garden of Isabella d'Este, but also linked by Serlio (and the Palazzo Naselli) to men of learning and peaceful lives ("huomini litterati et di vita quieta").[163] Casting a knowing smirk toward today's blank wall (Renée's), she proffers an ideal of balance worthy of duke and duchess alike, silently tying together the erudite yet down-to-earth, tension-ridden yet harmony-seeking (heterodox) whole.

[157] Rolet, *Les Questions*, 332–333, interprets Bocchi's *Proteus* emblem dedicated to Renée as "crypted praise of dissimulation."

[158] Berthon, *L'Intention*, 464 on the Erasmian inflection of Marot's "Chant nuptial de Renée de Ferrare." Rémi Jimenes, *Charlotte Guillard. Une femme imprimeur à la Renaissance* (Tours: Presses universitaires François-Rabelais and Rennes: Presses universitaires de Rennes, 2017), 256, 257, 262, for Marot's translations of Erasmus's *Apophtegemes*, published in 1539 and 1540 by Charlotte Guillard, linked by Jimenes to the Navarrian network.

[159] Crouzet, *La Sagesse*, 76–77.

[160] Pattanaro, 'I pittori di Ercole," 106–110, fig. 24, 122n21.

[161] Rolet, *Les Questions*, I, 280–281, II, 130–133; reproduced 132 (Bartsch XIV.329.437).

[162] Rolet, *Les Questions*, 247–261.

[163] Maffei, *Eterodossia*, 94 and 218.

Fig. 10.12   *Caryatid Herm with Braids*, fresco. Voghiera, Delizia di Belriguardo, Sala della Vigna, southeast wall. (Photo: Filippo Greselin)

CONCLUSION

Studies of Renée's interactions with mainstream art in "Erasmian" Ferrara are in their infancy. Micaela Torboli has linked to the duchess Girolamo da Carpi's exquisite *Opportunity (or Chance) and Patience (or Penitence)* in Dresden, seemingly painted in 1541, and inspired by Lilio Gregorio Giraldi, a tutor of her daughters, who were diligently schooled in Erasmus's texts.[164] In 1545, Pietro Lauro dedicated to Renée his translation of Erasmus's *Colloqui famigliari* published in Venice, "al segno di Erasmo," by the naturalized French printer Vincenzo Valgrisi.[165] In the difficult mid-1550s, the long-term survival of the duchy was increasingly at stake. Forbearance remained such a crucial value that Ercole dedicated an entire apartment in the Este Castle to the theme of Patience,[166] where the now lost portraits painted by Giacomo Vighi definitely included Renée ("i retratti dello illustrissimo signor Duca nostro e della illustrissima Madama, figioli e fratelli").[167] *Patience* also adorns the magnificent pedestal of Ercole's marble bust in the Galleria Estense, Modena.[168] That the duke sports the French collar of the Order of Saint-Michel around his neck in this late 1554 representation is fascinating, since Renée had just come under violent attack. Ercole, too, took risks in the name of tolerance, for instance allowing the publishing of a Jewish Bible in Ferrara in 1553, shortly before Julius III burned the Talmud in Rome; and still in 1558,

---

[164] Kirsten Faber, in Gregor, ed., *Il trionfo*, "Kairos e Penitentia," fig. 21, 125–128; Micaela Torboli, "Erasmo da Rotterdam alla corte di Ferrara," *Ferrara. Voce di una città* 32 (Giugno 2010). https://rivista.fondazionecarife.it/it/2010/2010; Belligni, *Renata di Francia*, 110–111, 217 on Gregorio Giraldo.

[165] "Alla illustrisima et virtuosissima principessa Madama Renee di Francia, Duchessa di Ferrara, Pietro Lauro Modonese humilissimo servitor," *Colloqui famigliari di Erasmo Roterodamo ad ogni qualità di parlare & spetiamente a cose pietose accomodati. Tradotti di latino in italiano, per m. Pietro Lauro modonese* (Venice: Vicenzo Valgrisi, 1545), 2r–3r, https://books.google.be/books?vid=GENT900000080792.

[166] Costanza Cavicchi, "Nuove acquisizioni documentarie sulla trasformazione del Castello Estense di Ferrara ad opera di Girolamo da Carpi," *Schifanoia* 13/14 (1992): 41–70; Anna Bisceglia, *Giorgio Vasari e l'Allegoria della Pazienza* (Livorno: sillabe, 2013), figs. 6–8, 69–81 and [Simona Mammana] "La Pazienza antologica," in Bisceglia, *Giorgio Vasari*, 101–105.

[167] Jadranka Bentini and Marco Borella, *Il Castello Estense* (Viterbo: BetaGamma editrice, 2002), 204. Marchesi, *Delizie d'archivio II–III*, 718–721, for Renée's and Ercole's other commissions from Vighi (1553–1558).

[168] Andrea Marchesi, "Il busto di Ercole II d'Este dello Spani," *Ferrara. Voci di una città* 32 (giugno 2010): 64–66.

Pastorino de' Pastorini was able to cast a medal of the Jewish Grazia Nasi (Gracia Mendes).[169] Patience, the subject of Bocchi's emblem XLIX, was in fact a key Erasmian virtue for the aging ducal pair. Under the rubble of history, the reframing of Renée's impact on the Ferrarese art scene, above and beyond jewels, portraits, and furniture, is slowly underway.

BIBLIOGRAPHY

PRIMARY SOURCES

Cartari, Vincenzo. 1624. *Imagini delli dei de gl'antichi.* Venice: Nicolò Pezzana.
Lauro, Pietro. 1545. Alla illustrisima et virtuosissima principessa Madama Renee di Francia, Duchessa di Ferrara, Pietro Lauro Modonese humilissimo servitor. In *Colloqui famigliari di Erasmo Roterodamo ad ogni qualità di parlare & spetiamente a cose pietose accomodati. Tradotti di latino in italiano, per m. Pietro Lauro modonese,* 2r–3r. Venice: Vicenzo Valgrisi. https://books.google.be/books?vid=GENT900000080792.
Muratori, Ludovico Antonio. 1740. *Delle Antichità estensi continuazione, o sia Parte Seconda.* Modena: Stamperia ducale.
Rodi, Filippo. Annali. Biblioteca Ariostea (Sala dei manoscritti), Cl. I 645. 3 vols.
Rouillé, Guillaume. 1553. *La Seconde partie du promptuaire des medalles, commençant à la nativité de nostre Sauveur Jesus Christ, & continuant jusques au Treschrestien Roy de France Henri II, à present eureusement regnant.* Lyon: G. Rouillé.
Thaumas de la Thaumassière, Gaspard. 1689. *Histoire du Berry.* Bourges: François Toubeau.
Tiraboschi, Girolamo. 1794. *Memorie storiche modenesi.* Tome IV. Modena: la Società tipografica.

SECONDARY SOURCES

Andreoli, Ilaria. 2006. La storia in soldoni: il *Promptuaire des medailles* di Guillaume Rouillé. In *Storia per parole e per immagini. Proceedings of the symposium at Cividale del Friuli, 2003,* ed. Mino Gabriele and Ugo Rozzo, 235–266. Udine: Forum.
Armand, Alfred. 1883–1887. *Les médailleurs italiens des quinzième et seizième siècles.* 3 vols. Paris: Plon.

---

[169] Attwood, in Scher, *Currency of Fame,* 178; Marianna D. Birnbaum, *The Long Journey of Gracia Mendes* (Budapest: Central European University Press, 2003), chapter five, http://books.openedition.org/ceup/2137.

Babelon, Jean-Pierre. 1986. *Nouvelle Histoire de Paris. Paris au XVIe siècle.* Paris: Diffusion Hachette.

Bardati, Flaminia. 2013. Anne de Bretagne bâtisseuse: identité et mémoire. In *Bâtir au féminin? Traditions et stratégies en Europe et dans l'Empire ottoman,* ed. Sabine Frommel and Juliette Dumas, 91–114. Paris: Picard.

Bartlett, John R. 2017. *Mapping Jordan Through Two Millenia.* Abingdon, UK and New York: Routledge.

Bayer, Andrea, ed. 1998. *Dosso Dossi. Pittore di corte a Ferrara nel Rinascimento.* Ferrara, Civiche Gallerie d'Arte Moderna e Contemporanea di Ferrara. Ferrara: Ferrara Arte. Exhibition catalog.

Béguin, Sylvie. 1973. Primaticcio's 'Chien de Macaire.' *Burlington Magazine* 115: 676–680.

Belligni, Eleonora. 2011. *Renata di Francia (1510–1575). Un eresia di corte.* Turin: UTET.

Beltramini, Maria. 2000. Un equivoco vitruviano di Sebastiano Serlio: la 'corona lisis.' *Annali della Scuola Normale Superiore di Pisa. Classe di Lettere e Filosofia* Serie IV 5-1: 275–316.

Benetti, Enrico. 2007. *Al Belriguardo. Piccola storia del rapporto tra la famiglia d'Este e la Delizia di Voghiera.* Voghiera: Edizioni arstudio C.

Bentini, Jadranka. 1995–1996. La Sala delle Vigne nella 'delizia' di Belriguardo. *Atti e Memorie Accademia Clementina Bologna* 35–36: 9–37.

Bentini, Jadranka, ed. 2004. *Este a Ferrara. Una corte nel Rinascimento.* Milan: Silvana Editoriale. Exhibition catalog.

Bentini, Jadranka, and Marco Borella. 2002. *Il Castello Estense.* Viterbo: BetaGamma editrice.

Benzoni, Gino. 1993. Ercole II d'Este. In *Dizionario Biografico degli Italiani,* ed. Fiorella Bartoccini and Mario Caravale, vol. 43. Instituto della Enciclopedia Italiana. http://www.treccani.it/enciclopedia/ercole-ii-d-este_%28Dizionario-Biografico%29/.

Birnbaum, Marianna D. 2003. *The Long Journey of Gracia Mendes.* Budapest: Central European University Press. http://books.openedition.org/ceup/2137.

Bisceglia, Anna. 2013. *Giorgio Vasari e l'Allegoria della Pazienza.* Livorno: Sillabe. Exhibition catalog.

Boccolari, Giorgio. 1987. *Le medaglie di casa d'Este.* Modena: Aedes Muratoriana.

Bonsanti, Giorgio, and Francesca Piccinini, eds. 2009. *Emozioni in terracotta. Guido Mazzoni / Antonio Begarelli. Sculture del Rinascimento emiliano.* Modena: Franco Cosimo Panini. Exhibition catalog.

Bouchard, Mawy. 2018. The Power of Reputation and Skills according to Anne de Graville. The *Rondeaux* and the Denunciation of Slander. In *Women and Power at the French Court, 1483–1563,* ed. Susan Broomhall, 241–262. Amsterdam: Amsterdam University Press.

Boudon, Françoise, and Claude Mignot. 2010. *Jacques Androuet du Cerceau. Les dessins des Plus excellents bâtiments de France*. Paris: Picard.

Brown, Cynthia J. 2011. *The Queen's Library: Image-Making at the court of Anne of Brittany, 1477–1514*. Philadelphia: University of Pennsylvania Press.

Buffa, Paolo, ed. 1994. *Sofonisba Anguissola e le sue sorelle*. Milan: Leonardo Arte. Exhibition catalog.

Burk, Jens. 2007. 'A l'antique' à Nantes et 'à la moderne' à Brou: styles architecturaux et conception de la statuaire funéraire au moment du passage du gothique tardif à la Renaissance. In *Patronnes et mécènes en France à la Renaissance*, ed. Kathleen Wilson-Chevalier, 225–250. Saint-Étienne: Publications de l'Université de Saint-Étienne.

Byatt, Lucy. 1993. Este, Ippolito d'. In *Dizionario Biografico degli Italiani*, ed. Fiorella Bartoccini and Mario Caravale, vol. 43. Instituto della Enciclopedia Italiana. http://www.treccani.it/enciclopedia/ippolito-d-este_%28Dizionario-Biografico%29/.

Cariani, Sergio. 2016. *La Sala della Vigna al Belriguardo "Una polifonia di proporzioni che la mente rinascimentale intendeva e l'occhio rinascimentale sapeva vedere."* Città di Castello: Edit Art.

Carpo, Mario. 1993. *La Maschera e il modello. Teoria architettonica ed evangelismo nell' Extraordinario Libro di Sebastiano Serlio (1551)*. Milan: Jaca Book.

Cavicchi, Costanza. 1992. Nuove acquisizioni documentarie sulla trasformazione del Castello Estense di Ferrara ad opera di Girolamo da Carpi. *Schifanoia* 13 (14): 41–70.

Chasot de Nantigny, Louis. 1738. *Généalogie historique de la Maison Royale de France*. Paris: Le Gras etc.

Chastel, André, and Robert Klein, eds. 1969. *Pomponius Gauricus. De Sculptura (1504)*. Geneva: Droz.

Clark, Leah R. 2018. *Collecting Art in the Italian Renaissance Court. Objects and Exchanges*. Cambridge: Cambridge University Press.

Cole, Alison. 1995. *Virtue and Magnificence: Art of Italian Renaissance Courts*. New York: Harry N. Abrams.

Cooper, Richard. 1997. *Litterae in tempore belli. Études sur les relations littéraires italo-françaises pendant les guerres d'Italie*. Geneva: Droz.

Croizat, Yassana C. 2007. 'Living Dolls': François Ier Dresses His Women. *Renaissance Quarterly* 60: 94–130.

Crouzet, Denis. 1998. *La Sagesse et le malheur. Michel de l'Hospital, chancelier de France*. Seyssel: Champ Vallon.

Dauner, Gudrun. 2005. Girolamo da Carpi e le belle donne di Belriguardo. *Pittura antica* 1 (4): 18–37.

David-Chapy, Aubrée. 2016. *Anne de France, Louise de Savoie, inventions d'un pouvoir au féminin*. Paris: Classiques Garnier.

Davis, Natalie Zemon. 1966. Publisher Guillaume Rouillé, businessman and humanis. In *Editing Sixteenth Century Texts. Papers Given at the Editorial Conference University of Toronto, October 1965*, ed. Richard J. Schoeck, 72–112. Toronto: University of Toronto.

De Marinis, Tammaro. 1960. *La legatura artistica in Italia nei secoli 15. e 16. 2, Bologna, Cesena, Ferrara, Venezia.* Florence: Flli. Alinari.

Dean, Trevor. 1993. Ercole I d'Este, duca di Ferrara Modena e Reggio. In *Dizionario Biografico degli Italiani.* Vol. 43. http://www.treccani.it/enciclopedia/ercole-i-d-este-duca-di-ferrara-modena-e-reggio_%28Dizionario-Biografico%29/.

Deswarte-Rosa, Sylvie. 2004. Serlio et Jacques Androuet du Cerceau, dans le *Recueil de dessins de Camille de Neuville* à Lyon. In *Sebastiano Serlio à Lyon Architecture et imprimerie.* 2 vols. Volume 1: *Le traité d'architecture de Sebastiano Serlio une grande entreprise éditoriale à Lyon au XVIᵉ siècle*, ed. Sylvie Deswarte-Rosa, 454–461. Lyon: Mémoire active.

Di Francesco, Carla, Jadranka Bentini, and Adriano Cavicchi. 1997. *Arte e storia a Belriguardo. "La Sala delle Vigne."* Ferrara: Belriguardo. Exhibition catalog.

Dubois de Groër, Anne. 1996. *Corneille de La Haye dit Corneille de Lyon.* Paris: Arthena.

Dupont-Pierrart, Nicole. 2017. *Claire de Gonzague, Comtesse de Bourbon-Montpensier (1464–1503). Une princesse italienne à la cour de France.* Villeneuve-d'Ascq: Presses Universitaires du Septentrion.

Farinelli Toselli, Alessandra. 1997. Il palazzo attraverso i documenti. In *Il Palazzo di Renata di Francia*, ed. Loredana Olivato Puppi, 35–95. Ferrara: Il Corbo Editore.

Ferino-Pagden, Sylvia, ed. 1997. *Vittoria Colonna Dichterin und Muse Michelangelos.* Milan: Skira editore. Exhibition catalog.

Finotti, Irene. 2012. Pour une classification des témoins de 'La Prison d'amour' de François Dassy: paratexte et macrostructure. *Studi Francesi* 166 (1): 69–78.

Fioravanti Baraldi, Anna Maria. 1995. Vita artistica e dibattito religioso a Ferrara nella prima metà del Cinquecento. In *La pittura in Emilia e in Romagna Il Cinquecento. Un romanzo polifonico tra Riforma e Controriforma*, ed. Vera Fortunati, 105–125. Ferrara: Nuova Alfa Editoriale, Elemond Editori Associati.

Firpo, Massimo. 2001. *Artisti gioiellieri eretici: il mondo di Lorenzo Lotto tra riforma e controriforma.* Rome: Laterza.

Folin, Marco. 2005. Bastardi e principesse nelle corti del Rinascimento: spunti di ricerca. *Schifanoia* 28–29: 167–174.

———. 2008. La corte della duchessa: Eleonora d'Aragona a Ferrara. In *Donne di potere nel Rinascimento*, ed. Letizia Arcangeli and Susanna Peyronel, 481–512. Rome: Viella.

———. 2009a. La committenza estense, l'Alberti e il Palazzo di Corte di Ferrara. In *Leon Battista Alberti Architettura e committenti. Atti dei convegni internazionali del Comitato nazionale 6. centenario della nascita di Leon Battista Alberti: Firenze, Rimini, Mantova, 2004.* Vol. I, ed. Arturo Calzona, Joseph Connors, Francesco Paolo Fiore, and Cesare Vasoli, 257–304. Florence: Leo S. Olschki.

———. 2009b. Le residenze di corte e il sistema delle Delizie fra Medioevo ed età moderna. In *Delizie Estensi. Architetture di villa del Rinascimento italiano ed europeo Ferrara Paesaggio Estense 4*, ed. Francesco Ceccarelli and Marco Folin, 79–135. Florence: Leo S. Olschki.

———. 2012. Studioli, vie coperte, gallerie: genealogia di uno spazio del potere. In *Il Regno e l'arte: I camerini di Alfonso I d'Este, terzo duca di Ferrara*, ed. Charles Hope, 234–257. Florence: Leo S. Olschki.

———. 2015. Spazi femminili nelle dimore signorili italiane del quattrocento: il caso di Ferrara. *Viglevanum. Rivista della Società Storica Vigevanese* 25: 26–39.

Fontana, Bartolommeo. 1888–1899. *Renata di Francia duchessa di Ferrara sui documenti dell'Archivio Estense, del Mediceo, del Gonzaga e dell'Archivio Secreto Vaticano (1510–1536)*. Vol. 3 vols. Rome: Forzani e C.

Franceschini, Chiara. 2000. La corte di Renata di Francia (1528–1560). In *Storia di Ferrara*, ed. Adriano Prosperi, 185–214. Ferrara: Corbo Editore.

———. 2001. Tra Ferrara e la Francia: notizie su orefici e pittori al servizio di Renée de France. *Franco-Italico* 19–20: 65–104.

Francomano, Emily C. 2011. Reversing the Tapestry: *Prison of Love* in Text, Image, and Textile. *Renaissance Quarterly* 64 (4, Winter): 1059–1105.

Frommel, Sabine. 1998. *Sebastiano Serlio architetto*. Milan: Electa.

Garrigues, Véronique. 2018. Les clairs-obscurs de Françoise de Foix, dame de Châteaubriant (1494?–1537): revisiter l'historiographie d'une favorite royale. In *Femmes à la cour de France. Charges et fonctions XVᵉ–XIXᵉ siècle*, ed. Caroline zum Kolk and Kathleen Wilson-Chevalier, 321–337. Villeneuve-d'Ascq: Presses Universitaires du Septentrion.

Ghirardo, Diane Yvonne. 2001. The Topography of Prostitution in Renaissance Ferrara. *The Journal of the Society of Architectural Historians* 60 (4): 402–431.

———. 2005. Lucrezia Borgia's Palace in Renaissance Ferrara. *The Journal of the Society of Architectural Historians* 64 (4): 474–497.

———. 2008a. Lucrezia Borgia as Entrepreneur. *Renaissance Quarterly* 61 (1, Spring): 53–91.

———. 2008b. Lucrezia Borgia, imprenditrice nella Ferrara rinascimentale. In *Donne di potere nel Rinascimento*, ed. L. Archangeli and S. Peyronel, 129–143. Rome: Viella.

———. 2009. *Le duchesse le bufale e l'imprenditoria femminile nella Ferrara rinascimentale / Duchesses, Water Buffaloes and Female Entrepreneurship in Renaissance Ferrara*. Ferrara: Di Scaranari.

Gorris, Rosanna. 1997a. 'D'un château l'autre': la corte di Renata di Francia a Ferrara (1528–1560). In *Il Palazzo di Renata di Francia*, ed. Loredana Olivato Puppi, 139–173. Ferrara: Il Corbo Editore.

———. 1997b. 'Un franzese nominato Clemente': Marot à Ferrare. In *Clément Marot, "Prince des Poëtes françois", 1496–1996. Actes du Colloque de Cahors, 1996*, ed. Gérard Defaux and Michel Simonin, 339–364. Paris: Honoré Champion.

———. 2011. La bibliothèque de la duchesse. De la bibliothèque en feu de Renée de France à la bibliothèque éclatée de Marguerite de France, duchesse de Savoie. In *Poètes, princes & collectionneurs. Mélanges offerts à Jean Paul Barbier-Mueller*, ed. Nicolas Ducimetière, Michel Jeanneret, and Jean Balsamo, 473–525. Geneva: Droz.

Guidoboni, Francesco. 2013. Gli edifici di Ippolito II d'Este a Ferrara e gli interventi dopo il terremoto del 1570. In *Ippolito II d'Este cardinale principe mecenate*, ed. Marina Cogotti and Francesco Paolo Fiore, 17–65. Rome: De Luca Editori d'Arte.

Guillaume, Jean, ed. 2010. *Jacques Androuet du Cerceau "un des plus grands architectes qui se soient jamais trouvés en France"*. Paris: Picard.

Hall, J.T.D. 1973. Three letters of Primaticcio. *Burlington Magazine* 125: 35–38. with a commentary by Anthony Blunt.

Hamon, Étienne. 2011. *Une capitale flamboyante la création monumentale à Paris autour de 1500*. Paris: Picard.

Jaffé, Michael. 1966. The Picture of the Secretary of Titian. *The Burlington Magazine* 108: 114–127.

Jimenes, Rémi. 2017. *Charlotte Guillard. Une femme imprimeur à la Renaissance*. Tours and Rennes: Presses universitaires François-Rabelais and Presses universitaires de Rennes.

Joubert, Fabienne. 1987. *La Tapisserie médiévale au musée de Cluny*. Paris: RMN.

Knecht, R.J. 1994. *Renaissance Warrior and Patron. The Reign of Francis I*. Cambridge: Cambridge University Press.

Laureati, Laura. 2002. Da Borgia a Este: due vite in quarant'anni. In *Lucrezia Borgia*, edited by Laura Laureati, 21–75. Ferrara: Ferrara Arte. Exhibition catalog.

———., ed. 2002. *Lucrezia Borgia*. Ferrara: Palazzo Bonacossi, 2002–2003. Ferrara: Ferrara Arte. Exhibition catalogue.

Lemerle, Frédérique. 2000. *Les* Annotations *de Guillaume Philandrier sur le* De Architectura *de Vitruve Livres I à IV*. Paris: Picard.

———. 2011. *Les* Annotations sur L'Architecture *de Vitruve Livres V à VII*. Paris: Classiques Garnier.

Losito, Maria. 1997. Il palazzo tra definizioni e manomissioni. In *Il Palazzo di Renata di Francia*, ed. Loredana Olivato Puppi, 97–131. Ferrara: Corbo Editore.

Maffei, Francesca. 2012. Celio Calcagnini, Terzo Terzi e la cultura architettonica a Ferrara nel primo Cinquecento (1513–1539). *Arte lombarda* 166 (3): 40–61.

———. 2013. *Eterodossia e vitruvianesimo: Palazzo Naselli a Ferrara 1527–1538*. Rome: Campisano.

Manson, Michel. 1982. Diverses approches sur l'histoire de la poupée du XVe au XVIIe siècle. In *Les Jeux à la Renaissance. Actes du XXIIIe colloque international d'études humanistes (Tours–juillet 1980)*, ed. Philippe Ariès and Jean-Claude Margolin, 525–551. Paris: Vrin.

Marchesi, Andrea. 2010. Il busto di Ercole II d'Este dello Spani. *Ferrara. Voci di una città* 32: 63–66.

——— 2011. *Delizie d'archivio. Regesti e documenti per la storia delle residenze estensi nella Ferrara del Cinquecento. I: Dimore suburbane e extraurbane*. Ferrara: Le Immagini edizioni.

———. 2015. *Delizie d'archivio. Regesti e documenti per la storia delle residenze estensi nella Ferrara del Cinquecento. Tomi I-II: dimore urbane*. Ferrara: Le Immagini edizioni.

Marescotti, Elena, et al. 2008. *Gli Estensi a Consandolo. La Delizia ritrovata*. Consandolo: Associazione Ricerche Storiche di Consandolo.

———. 2013–2017. *La vita di Renata di Francia a Consandolo dal 1540 a 1560*. Consandolo: Associazione Ricerche Storiche Consandolo.

Matarasso, Pauline. 2011. *Le Baptême de Renée de France en 1510. Compte des frais et préparatifs*. Paris: CNRS Éditions.

Mezzetti, Amalia. 1977. *Girolamo da Ferrara detta da Carpi*. Milano: Silvana.

Michon, Cédric. 2011. *Les Conseillers de François Ier*. Rennes: Presses universitaires de Rennes.

Occhipinti, Carmelo. 1998. La Villa d'Este a Fontainebleau e le sue stufette. Documenti su Serlio e il Cardinale di Ferrara. *Prospettiva* 89–90: 169–183.

Olivato, Loredana. 1971. Per il Serlio a Venezia: documenti nuovi e documenti rivisitati. *Arte Veneta* 25: 284–291.

———., ed. 1997. *Il Palazzo di Renata di Francia*. Ferrara: Corbo Editore.

Orth, Myra Dickman. 1983. "The Prison of Love": A Medieval Romance in the French Renaissance and Its Illustration (B.N. MS fr. 2150). *Journal of the Warburg and Courtauld Institutes* 46: 211–221.

———. 2015. *Renaissance Manuscripts. The Sixteenth Century*. 2 vols. London and Turnhout: Harvey Miller.

Pattanaro, Alessandra. 2000. *Girolamo da Carpi Ritratti*. Cittadella (PD): Bertoncello Artigrafiche.

———. 2008. Per la *Dama in verde* dello Städelsches Kunstinstitut di Francoforte. Un problema di rapporti nord-sud. In *Culture figurative a confronto tra Fiandre e Italia dal XV al XVII secolo Nord/Sud*, ed. Anna De Floriani and Maria Clelia Galassi, 136–145. Cinisello Balsamo: Silvana Editore.

———. 2011. I pittori di Ercole II a Belriguardo: modelli giulieschi e tradizione vitruviana. *Prospettiva* 141–142: 100–123.

Peebles, Kelly D., ed. and trans. 2014. *Jeanne Flore. Tales and Trials of Love.* Toronto: Centre for Reformation and Renaissance Studies.

———. 2018. Embodied Devotion: The Dynastic and Religious Loyalty of Renée de France (1510–1575). In *Royal Women and Dynastic Loyalty*, ed. Caroline Dunn and Elizabeth Carney, 123–137. Cham, Switzerland: Palgrave Macmillan.

Petris, Loris. 2002. *La Plume et la tribune. Michel de l'Hospital et ses discours (1559–1562).* Geneva: Droz.

Pollard, John Graham. 2007. *Renaissance Medals. The Collections of the National Gallery of Art Systematic Catalogue.* 2 vols. Washington, DC: National Gallery.

Potter, David. 2018. The Life and After-Life of a Royal Mistress Anne de Pisseleu, Duchess of Étampes. In *Women and Power at the French Court, 1483–1563*, ed. Susan Broomhall, 309–334. Amsterdam: Amsterdam University Press.

Prosperi, Adriano, with Christian A. Arseni. 1997. Zwischen Mystikern und Malern: Überlegungen zur Bilderfrage in Italien zur Zeit Vittoria Colonnas. In *Vittoria Colonna Dichterin und Muse Michelangelos*, ed. Sylvia Ferino-Pagden, 283–295. Vienna: Kunsthistorisches Museum. Skira editore. Exhibition Catalog.

Rajchenbach-Teller, Élise. 2012. De 'ceux qui de leur pouvoir aydent et favorisent au publiq' Guillaume Rouillé, libraire à Lyon. In *Passeurs de textes Imprimeurs et libraires à l'âge de l'humanisme*, ed. Christine Bénévent, Anne Charon, Isabelle Diu, and Magali Vène, 99–116. Paris: Publications de l'École nationale des chartes.

Ribouillault, Denis. 2009. Le ville dipinte del cardinale Ippolito d'Este a Tivoli: l'architettura di fronte all'antico, la tradizione ferrarese, e un nuovo documento su Belriguardo. In *Delizie Estensi. Architetture di villa del Rinascimento italiano ed europeo Ferrara Paesaggio Estense 4*, ed. Francesco Ceccarelli and Marco Folin, 341–371. Florence: Leo S. Olschki.

Righini, Giulio. 1964. *Due donne nel destino di casa d'Este: Marchesella degli Adelardi, Laura Dianti.* Ferrara: Deputazione Provinciale Ferrarese di Storia Patria.

Rodocanachi, Emmanuel. 1895. *Renée de France, une protectrice de la réforme en France et en Italie.* Paris: P. Ollendorf.

Rolet, Anne. 2015. *Les Questions symboliques d'Achille Bocchi. Symbolicae quaestiones, 1555.* 2 vols. Rennes: Presses universitaires François-Rabelais de Tours, Presses universitaires de Rennes.

Samaran, Charles. 1966. Georges d'Armagnac, ambassadeur de François Ier à Venise, peint par le Titien en compagnie de son secrétaire Guillaume Philandrier. *Comptes rendus des séances de l'Académie des Inscriptions et Belles-Lettres* 110: 38–44.

Sambin de Norcen, Maria Teresa. 2004. I miti di Belriguardo. In *Nuovi antichi. Committenti, cantieri, architetti, 1400–1600*, ed. R. Schofield, 17–66. Milan: Electa.

———. 2006. 'Ut apud plinium': giardino e paesaggio a Belriguardo nel Quattrocento. In *Delizie in Villa. Il giardino nel Rinascimento e i suoi committenti*, ed. Gianni Venturoli and Francesco Ceccarelli, 65–89. Florence: Leo S. Olschki.

———. 2009. Nuove indagini su Belriguardo e la committenza di villa nel primo Rinascimento. In *Delizie Estensi Architetture di villa nel Rinascimento italiano ed europeo*, ed. Francesco Ceccarelli and Marco Folin, 145–180. Florence: Leo S. Olschki.

Santrot, Jacques. 2017. *Les Doubles funérailles d'Anne de Bretagne. Le corps et le cœur (janvier-mars 1514)*. Geneva: Droz.

Scailliérez, Cécile. 1992. *François Ier et ses artistes dans les collections du Louvre*. Paris: Réunion des musées nationaux. Exhibition catalog.

Scher, Stephen K. 1994. *The Currency of Fame: Portrait Medals of the Renaissance*. New York: Harry N. Abrams, Inc. & The Frick Collection.

Smith, Pauline M. 1966. *The Anti-courtier Trend in French Literature*. Geneva: Droz.

Snyder, Jon R. 2009. *Dissimulation and the Culture of Secrecy in Early Modern Europe*. Berkeley, Los Angeles, and London: University of California Press.

Stras, Laurie. 2018. *Women and Music in Sixteenth-Century Ferrara*. Cambridge, UK: Cambridge University Press.

Strinati, Claudio, and Bernd Wolfgang Lindemann, eds. 2008. *Sebastiano del Piombo 1485–1547*. Rome: Federico Motta Editore. Exhibition catalog.

Tafuri, Manfredo. 1989. Ipotesi sulla religiosità di Sebastiano Serlio. In *Sebastiano Serlio. Sesto seminario Internazionale di Storia di Architettura, Vicenza, 31 agosto-4 settembre, 1987*, ed. Christof Thoenes, 57–66. Milan: Electa.

Tallon, Alain. 2017. *La France et le concile de Trente (1518–1563)*. Rome: École française de Rome.

Thorel, Mathilde. 2012. La première réception du *Peregrin* en France: lecture éditoriale et recontextualisation culturelle. *Réforme, Humanisme, Renaissance* 75: 87–105.

Torboli, Micaela. 2010. Erasmo da Rotterdam alla corte di Ferrara. *Ferrara. Voce di una città* 32. https://rivista.fondazionecarife.it/it/2010/2010.

Tuohy, Thomas. 1996. *Herculean Ferrara. Ercole d'Este (1471–1505) and the Invention of a Ducal Capital*. Cambridge: Cambridge University Press.

Verdon, Timothy. 1990. Guido Mazzoni in Francia: nuovi contributi. *Mitteilungen des Kunsthistorischen Institutes in Florenz* 34 (1–2): 139–164.

Viennot, Eliane, and Kathleen Wilson-Chevalier, eds. 1999. *Royaume de fémynie. Pouvoirs, contraintes, espaces de liberté des femmes, de la Renaissance à la Fronde*. Paris: Honoré Champion.

Visser Travagli, Anna Maria, Giordana Mariani Canova, and Federica Toniolo, eds. 1998. *La miniatura a Ferrara dal tempo di Cosmè Tura all'eredità di Ercole de' Roberti*. Modena: Franco Cosimo Panini. Exhibition catalog.

Vitale, Andrea. 2002. Lucrezia, il mestiere di principessa. In *I Borgia*, ed. Alfano Carla and Felipe V. Farin Llombart, 241–247. Milan: Mondadori Electa. Exhibition catalog.

Wardropper, Ian. 1981 (1983). Le voyage italien de Primatice en 1550. *Bulletin de la Société de l'histoire de l'Art français* 30 (73): 27–31.

Watson, Elizabeth See. 1993. *Achille Bocchi and the Emblem Book as Symbolic Form*. Cambridge: Cambridge University Press.

Weber, Gregor J.M., ed. 2002. *Il trionfo di Bacco. Capolavori della scuola ferrarese a Dresda 1480–1620*. Torino, London, and Venice: Umberto Allemandi & Co. Exhibition catalog.

Welch, Evelyn. 2009. Art on the Edge: Hair and Hands in Renaissance Italy. *Renaissance Studies* 23 (3): 241–268.

Wieck, Roger, and Cynthia J. Brown. 2010. *The Prayer Book of Claude de France MS M.1166. The Pierpont Morgan Library, New York*. Lucerne: Quadernio Verlag.

Wieck, Roger, Cynthia J. Brown, and Eberhard König. 2012. *The Primer of Claude de France. MS 159, The Fitzwilliam Museum, Cambridge*. Lucerne: Quadernio Verlag.

Wilson-Chevalier, Kathleen. 2018. Claude de France and the Spaces of Agency of a Marginalized Queen. In *Women and Power at the French Court, 1483–1563*, ed. Susan Broomhall, 139–172. Amsterdam: Amsterdam University Press.

Wilson-Chevalier, Kathleen, ed., with the collaboration of Eugénie Pascal. 2007. *Patronnes et mécènes en France à la Renaissance*. Saint-Étienne: Publications de l'Université de Saint-Étienne.

Woods-Marsden, Joanna. 2007. The Mistress as 'Virtuous': Titian's Portrait of Laura Dianti. In *Titian: Materiality, Likeness, Istoria*. ed. Joanna Woods-Marsden, 53–69. Turnhout: Brepols.

Zarri, Gabriella. 2006. *La religione di Lucrezia Borgia. Le lettere inedite del confessore*. Rome: Roma nel Rinascimento.

Zum Kolk, Caroline. 2007. Les difficultés des mariages internationaux: Renée de France et Hercule d'Este. In *Femmes et pouvoir politique. Les princesses d'Europe XVᵉ–XVIIIᵉ siècle*, ed. Isabelle Poutrin and Marie-Karine Schaub, 102–119. Rosny-sous-Bois: Éditions Bréal.

CHAPTER 11

Renée de France as Dowager Duchess and Epistolary Diplomat

Kelly Digby Peebles

In his 1580 *Ecclesiastical History of the Reformed Church in France*, Théodore de Bèze, author, reformed theologian, and Jean Calvin's successor as the religious figurehead of Geneva, praises Renée de France for her lifelong study of and dedication to the reformed religion. She publicly favored reformed views, writes Bèze, "nonobstant qu'elle fust belle mere du sieur Duc de Guyse" (despite the fact that she was the mother-in-law of the Duke of Guise).[1] The latter's marriage to Renée's daughter, Anne d'Este, had been negotiated by Renée's nephew, King Henri II, in 1548. Their match was socially brilliant and politically expedient, for Guise, who came from one of the most prominent families at court, was a distinguished military hero, then later Grand Master of France and close advisor to his niece, Mary Stuart, and her husband François II, during their brief

---

[1] Théodore de Bèze, *Histoire ecclesiastique des églises reformees au royaume de France, tome II* (Anvers: Jean Remy, 1580), 463. Translations throughout are my own.

K. D. Peebles (✉)
Clemson University, Clemson, SC, USA
e-mail: kpeeble@clemson.edu

K. D. Peebles, G. Scarlatta (eds.), *Representing the Life and Legacy of Renée de France*, Queenship and Power, https://doi.org/10.1007/978-3-030-69121-9_11

reign.[2] In Bèze's view, which was widely held throughout the Protestant network in Europe, Guise's personal ambition was extreme, and his influence—bolstered by that of his brother, the Cardinal-Legate Charles de Lorraine—was tyrannical, earning him the reputation of "ennemi capital d'icelle Religion" (archenemy of this [reformed] Religion).[3]

While Renée's close family ties to the French crown as a *fille de France* gave her sufficient socio-political clout to become a unifying figurehead for the Protestant network, her equally close family ties to the staunch Catholic Guise family represented a significant embarrassment to overcome in the eyes of Protestant leaders.[4] Indeed, correspondence between Jean Calvin and Renée reveals a marked tension between her image as a "mere nourriciere des povres fidelles"[5] (mothering caregiver of

[2] In the mid-sixteenth century, the rival houses of Lorraine and Montmorency were at the forefront of the political scene of the French court. François de Guise and Cardinal Charles de Lorraine were at the head of the former, while the Constable of France, Anne de Montmorency, and his nephews, the brothers Admiral Gaspard de Coligny, Cardinal Odet de Châtillon, and François d'Andelot, led the latter. The families' associations with opposing religious factions further added to the rivalry. See *Histoire et dictionnaire des guerres de religion*, ed. Arlette Jouanna, Jacqueline Boucher, Dominique Biloghi, and Guy le Thiec (Paris: Éditions Robert Laffont, 1998), 17. See also contemporary historian Jacques de Thou, who concedes that Guise was respected by all despite the polarizing nature of his persona: "ce fut de l'aveu même de ses ennemis, le plus grand homme de son siécle, digne de toutes sortes de loüange" (even his enemies admitted that he was the greatest man of his century, worthy of all sorts of praise). *Histoire universelle de Jacque Auguste de Thou, depuis 1543, jusqu'en 1607. Traduite sur l'édition latine de Londres, Tome Quatrieme, 1560–1564* (London: n.p., 1734), 518. Pierre de Bourdeille, sieur de Brantôme, offers another contemporary account of Guise, describing him as "bon et genereux" (good and generous) and highlighting his unflagging confidence: "[…] il garda tousjours sa preheminance et ce qu'il luy apartenoit, sans s'estonner de rien" (he always maintained his rank and what was due to him, without ever becoming flustered). *Recueil des Dames, poésies et tombeaux*, ed. Étienne Vaucheret (Paris: Gallimard, 1991), 44, 40.

[3] Bèze, *Histoire ecclesiastique*, 463.

[4] Throughout this chapter, I rely on the admittedly imprecise term of Protestant in order to speak more broadly about European heterodox movements, including not only those in France, but also in England and Geneva. Although Théodore de Bèze and Jean Calvin tend to use the term "of the religion" to refer to their followers, often adding the adjective "true," the terms "Huguenot" and "Lutheran" appear in print and manuscript texts from the time. On the origin and use of the term "Huguenot," see Hugues Daussy, *Le Parti Huguenot, chronique d'une désillusion (1557–1572)* (Geneva: Droz, 2015), 9–15. See also Jouanna et al., *Histoire et dictionnaire*, 68–69.

[5] Letter dated May 10, 1563, in *Ioannis Calvini opera quae supersunt omnia, Volumen XX*, ed. Edouard Cunitz, Johann-Wilhelm Baum, and Eduard Wilhelm Eugen Reuss (Brunsvigae: Schwetschke et filium, 1879), 16.

downtrodden believers) and that of her son-in-law as the figure who "avoit allume le feu,"[6] (had lit the flame) of the Wars of Religion. However, other contemporary accounts, including Renée's own correspondence, ambassadorial dispatches, and published historical anecdotes, demonstrate that Renée's family and religious loyalties were not necessarily at odds.[7] On the contrary, she drew strength from her loyalties despite their apparent incongruity, and she actively worked to bridge differences by mediating among political figureheads, foreign ambassadors, and family representatives from both religious factions. As Tracy Adams explains in her study of the relationship between Renée's mother and godmother (Anne de Bretagne and Anne de France), the public and private lives of late medieval and early modern noblewomen overlapped a great deal, and they strategically projected character traits and actions to accomplish specific goals.[8] For these reasons, relationships must be contextualized within broader networks in which women embodied the roles of "mediators, patrons, and brokers."[9] To better understand Renée's religious and family loyalties, this chapter first examines the historical context surrounding her arrival at the French court in the early 1560s, including her relationships with key players in politico-religious happenings of the time: Jean Calvin, François de Guise, and Elizabeth I's ambassador to the French court, Nicholas Throckmorton. I will then discuss how she leveraged her image and relationships in order to influence political policy and protect the loyalties that formed the core of her personal and public identity: her royal roots, her alliance with the Este, and her religious convictions, all of which were intricately intertwined, yet potentially at odds with one another.

[6]Undated letter, Cunitz et al., *Ioannis Calvini, Vol. XX*, 246. On Guise's involvement in the Massacre of Wassy, which Calvin implicitly identifies in this letter, see Daussy, *Le Parti Huguenot*, 283–286.

[7]On depictions of Renée's loyalties in literary works by Antoine Couillard and Théodore de Bèze, see Kelly D. Peebles, "Embodied Devotion: The Dynastic and Religious Loyalty of Renée de France (1510–1575)," in *Royal Women and Dynastic Loyalty*, ed. Caroline Dunn and Elizabeth Carney (Cham, Switzerland: Palgrave Macmillan, 2018), 123–137.

[8]Tracy Adams, "Rivals or Friends? Anne de Bourbon and Anne de Bretagne," *Women in French Studies* Special Issue 3 (2010): 46–61. On Anne de Bretagne's influence on Renée, see Kathleen Wilson-Chevalier, chapter two in this volume. See also Cyril Cvetkovic, chapter twelve.

[9]Adams, "Rivals or Friends," 51.

RENÉE'S RETURN TO FRANCE

Following the death of her husband, Ercole II d'Este, in late 1559, Renée began to contemplate leaving Ferrara, where she had resided for over thirty years, and returning to her native France, where she would be in closer proximity to the royal family and to her first-born child, Anne, who by that time had become a prominent personality at the French court as a lady-in-waiting and confidante of Queen Catherine de Médicis.[10] In early 1560, Renée wrote to Catherine, who by that time was Queen Mother to the reigning François II, of her plans to travel to France. She received a response in February of that year indicating that the court would be honored by her presence and welcome her warmly.[11] Renée's return to France was of sufficient importance at court to merit a mention in the correspondence of Nicholas Throckmorton, the astute and opportunistic English ambassador with whom she would soon discuss sensitive politico-religious strategies.[12] In August 1560, Throckmorton comments to Queen

---

[10] Renée writes in French to her son, Alphonse, on October 1, 1559, indicating the seriousness of his father's illness and urging him to return home from France, where he and his sister were well connected socially and politically. Two days later, she writes again, this time in Italian, informing him of Ercole's death. See Odette Turias, *Renée de France, Duchesse de Ferrare, témoin de son temps: 1510–1575, Tome I* (PhD diss, Université de Tours, 2005), 285–287. On May 6, 1560, Renée informs the French ambassador to Venice, François de Noailles, of her preparations to return to France, and on September 3, 1560, she announces to Alphonse that she has arrived in Modena, indicating the beginning of her journey. Additional letters follow until her arrival in Orléans. See Turias, 331–341. On Anne d'Este's position at court, see Una McIlvenna, *Scandal and Reputation at the Court of Catherine de Medici* (New York: Routledge, 2016), especially chapters five and six.

[11] Catherine writes: "[…] je conoysès que vostre présance feut nésésére ysi que aytes preste à y venir, chause qui nous sera tousjour très agréable et que vostre présanse nous sera à grent contentement et hauneur; […] vous suplirions croyre que c'est cet que désirons le plus que de vous voyr haurdinérment en sete compaignie […]" (I knew that your presence here was necessary and that you are ready to come here, which will always be very agreeable to us, and your presence will be a great pleasure and honor to us; […] we entreat you to believe that it is this that we desire the most, that is, to regularly see you in our company). *Lettres de Catherine de Médicis, Tome Premier. 1533–1563*, ed. Hector de la Ferrière (Paris: Imprimerie Nationale, 1888), 131.

[12] Tracey A. Sowerby elucidates Throckmorton's central role in facilitating the flow of information between the English court and those of France, where he was Elizabeth I's first resident ambassador, and Spain, where Sir Thomas Chaloner was stationed. See "Elizabethan Diplomatic Networks and the Spread of News," in *News Networks in Early Modern Europe*, ed. Joad Raymond and Noah Moxham (Leiden: Brill, 2016), 305–327. See also Sebastian Walsh, "Most Trusty and Beloved," *History Today* 55, no. 9 (September 2005): 39–45.

Elizabeth I on Renée's family connections, noting that she "had secretly sent word to the Duke of Guise [...] that she would come into France and end her life there, and be as his mother."[13] Three months later, Renée writes with transparent glee to inform her son Alphonse of her arrival and warm reception in Orléans: "l'honneur et faveur et affection qu'il [le roi] m'a demonstree, [étaient] tant qu'il ne se pourroict dire" (the honor and favor and affection that he [the king] showed me [was] greater than one could possibly express).[14]

While Pierre Brantôme, the often outrageous court chronicler, also professes to have personally witnessed Renée's arrival, what is most interesting about his brief account is his description of Renée's role as an unofficial court diplomat.[15] In fact, almost immediately upon rejoining the court, following an absence of over three decades, Renée began mediating between families and religious factions, first attempting to diffuse a politically charged situation between her son-in-law, Guise, and his first cousin, Louis de Bourbon, the Prince de Condé.[16] Just days before Renée's arrival, Condé had been imprisoned and was awaiting execution for treason due to his alleged participation in the failed Amboise Conspiracy, an attempt by the reformed faction, of which he was the figurehead, to remove King

Walsh explains that Throckmorton's "object was for the English to maintain the balance between Protestant and Catholic factions [...]," and his "ability to speak frankly to Elizabeth, to frame proposals around her priorities, and to extract commitments from her, made him a formidable actor within the circle concerned with English foreign policy," 41–42.

[13] "Elizabeth: August 1560, 21–25," in *Calendar of State Papers Foreign: Elizabeth, Volume 3, 1560–1561*, 253. Hereafter referred to as *CSP, Vol. 3*.

[14] Turias, *Renée de France*, 341. Throckmorton also confirms Renée's arrival at court. See *CSP, Vol. 3*, 395.

[15] Pierre de Bourdeille, sieur de Brantôme, *Recueil des Dames, poésies et tombeaux*, ed. Étienne Vaucheret (Paris: Gallimard, 1991): "[...] la vis arriver. Le Roy et toute la Court estant allez au devant, et receue aveq' ung très-grand honneur, comme il luy apartenoit" ([I] saw her arrive. The King and all the court had ridden out ahead and received her with the greatest honor, just as was befitting her rank), 176.

[16] Antoine de Bourbon, who was King of Navarre through his marriage to Jeanne d'Albret, and his younger brother, Louis de Bourbon, Prince de Condé, were Princes of the Blood (*princes du sang*) through their father, Charles IV de Bourbon. As such, they were of comparable royal status to Renée, but as male descendants through the male line, they were also first in line to the throne after Catherine de Médicis's children. François de Guise and his brother, the Cardinal de Lorraine, were the children of the Bourbon brother's paternal aunt, Antoinette de Bourbon, but as they were descended through the female line, they did not have the same claim to the throne.

François II from the influence of the Catholic Guise family.[17] According to Brantôme, Renée was quick to scold her son-in-law, stating: "quiconques avoit conseillé au Roy ce coup avoit failly grandement, et que ce n'estoit peu de chose de traitter un Prince du sang de ceste façon" (whoever had advised the king to take this action had committed a grievous mistake, for it is no small thing to treat a Prince of the Blood in this manner).[18]

Following the untimely death of François II on December 5, 1560, Condé was released within two weeks; the Duc de Guise and Cardinal de Lorraine lost much of their political clout, and Catherine de Médicis consolidated her power as mother of the young Charles IX. She soon began seeking a *rapprochement* between the recently weakened Bourbon and Guise families, and was able to exercise her power, as Katherine Crawford observes, through her facilitation of social relationships, or in other words, through "a natural outgrowth of female deference," as such actions were in keeping with traditional gender roles of daughter, wife, and mother.[19] This strategy, paired with the absence of an adult male monarch, allowed Catherine to protect her young son's reign. Crawford explains: "Catherine was free to utilize a carefully accumulated reservoir of positive sentiment about her capacity as a good woman, widow, and mother to construct her political claim."[20] Similarly, Renée adeptly exploited her lifelong political status as a royal, recently acquired social status as a widow, and growing spiritual status as protector of religious refugees and dissidents in order to manipulate her public image and effect a sort of damage control in response to increasing criticism of her son-in-law's character. Even Calvin observes the apparent incongruity between Renée's Guise connections and her altruism, noting in his correspondence that her charitable activities and religious faith belie the public's view of her relationship with her son-in-law. Calvin writes:

[17] The Guise brothers suspected Throckmorton of colluding with Condé and other reformers in the Amboise Conspiracy. For that reason, "he [Throckmorton] returned to France in 1560, as a *persona non grata* [...] his prior departure for London being to inform Elizabeth [about the plot]. Such was their rage that Throckmorton feared for his life." Walsh, "Most Trusty," 41–42.

[18] Brantôme, *Recueil des Dames*, 176.

[19] On Catherine's consolidation of power in the days after François II's death, see Katherine Crawford, "Catherine de Médicis and the Performance of Political Motherhood," *Sixteenth-Century Journal* 31, no. 3 (2000): 643–673. Hugues Daussy also discusses the challenges that Catherine faced during the Estates General in Orléans, *Le Parti Huguenot*, 189–197.

[20] Crawford, "Catherine de Médicis," 653.

les gens de bien vous aient eu en haine ou horreur, pour estre belle mere de feu monsieur de *Guise*, qu'ils vous en ont tant plus aymee et honoree, voiant que cela ne vous destournoit point de faire droicte profession et pure de chrestienté, et non seulement de bouche, mais par effectz si notables que rien plus.[21]

(good people may have felt hatred and revulsion for you due to your being the mother-in-law of the late Monsieur de Guise, they loved and honored you all the more seeing that this fact did not deter you in the least from your upstanding vocation and pure Christian faith, which you made clear not only through your speech, but through actions that could not be more honorable.)

VISUAL AND TEXTUAL REPRESENTATIONS OF RENÉE AT THE ESTATES GENERAL OF ORLÉANS

Renée was not only ideally poised to shape and to exploit this new, female-centric political landscape, but she also carefully crafted her image in order to pursue her lifelong charitable activities and reform-minded agenda, both from her own domain of Montargis and from within the French court. She is depicted as a central figure in one of the first political actions to take place after her arrival: the December 1560 meeting of the Estates General in Orléans (Fig. 11.1).[22] This particular illustration was conceived by the Protestant wood and copper engravers Jacques Tortorel and Jean Perrissin in their *Quarante Tableaux*, published from Geneva in 1569 and 1570.[23] As Philip Benedict explains, for Protestants seeking representations of valor and victimization, this collection became "an important building block of Huguenot historical memory," allowing the reader to visualize events associated with the buildup and outbreak of the first Wars

---

[21] Cunitz et al., *Ioannis Calvini, Vol. XX*, 279.

[22] See Philip Benedict, "L'assemblée des trois Estats, tenus à Orléans au mois de Janvier 1561," in *Graphic History: The Wars, Massacres and Troubles of Tortorel and Perrissin* (Geneva: Droz, 2007), 251–254.

[23] For the precise date of the Estates General in Orléans, December 17, 1560, see *Collection des Procès-verbaux des assemblées-générales du Clergé de France Depuis l'Année 1560, jusqu'à présent* (Paris: Guillaume Desprez, 1767), 4. On the location, which was destroyed just two years later, see François le Maire, *Histoire et Antiquitez de la ville et duché d'Orléans*, "à la prise de la ville d'Orléans par le Prince de Condé en Avril 1562, les Huguenots ayans fait dresser dans le Convent un Arsenal et mis leurs munitions et poudres, le feu s'y prit qui brusla le Convent et l'Eglise" (Orléans: Maria Paris, 1648), 104–105. I thank Kathleen Wilson-Chevalier for her assistance with this image.

Fig. 11.1 Jacques Tortorel. *L'Assemblee des trois estats, tenus a Orleans au mois de Jannier.* [sic] 1561. Paris, Bibliothèque nationale de France, département d'estampes et photographies. Réserve FOL-QB-201 (5). Source: BnF

of Religion.[24] Renée is pictured at the heart of this gathering, seated with the royal family to the left of Charles IX and Catherine. A prose description, published soon after the event, clearly distinguishes the hierarchical relationships among the attending personalities by pointing to specific spatial locations: physical steps create distances that correspond closely to figurative steps of the social hierarchy. For example, the king is depicted in the center of the illustration and described in prose as seated "en lieu fort eminent, pour estre veu de tous" (in a very imminent position, in order to be seen by all). While his mother is seated to his left and described as being

---

[24] *Graphic History*, 180. Benedict also discusses a prefatory address to the reader where the engravers define their overarching goal. In his assessment, "at best, the *Quarante Tableaux* represent the efforts of a group of people working in Geneva to imagine what events at which they were not present might have looked like and to develop effective strategies of visual representation to narrate what they were able to learn about them," 123.

"en mesme hauteur" (at the same height) as her son, in the woodcut illustration, she appears to tower over him. Also on the king's "main senestre" (sinister side), "mais un degré plus bas" (but one step lower), are the king's sister, Marguerite de France, and his great-aunt, Renée, referred to in the woodcut's legend and in the prose pamphlet as "madame la Duchesse doüairiere de Ferrare" (Madame the Dowager Duchess of Ferrara), the title by which she was typically addressed after her return to court.[25] On the king's "costé dextre" (heraldic right), and also one step lower at the same level as Marguerite and Renée, are the male members of the royal family: Charles's younger brother, the Duc d'Orléans (who would later become King Henri III), and the King of Navarre, Antoine de Bourbon. To honor King Charles's very recently deceased brother, François II, the prose description specifies that all members of the royal family are in mourning dress. While this isn't visibly evident in the illustration, the engravers do offer other visual clues about the interpersonal relationships of the participants. The diminutive age of the king and his younger siblings is clearly represented in scale, for all three appear much smaller than the adults in the room. Furthermore, the position of Renée's son-in-law, Guise, is carefully crafted in both documents. In the prose pamphlet, he is described immediately after the royal family, before any other participants are mentioned, and although he is depicted in the woodcut at the center of the event, his position is significantly lower than that of the king, as he is located two steps below the dais and described in prose as "aux piedz du Roy sur les degrez en sa main le baston de Grand Maistre" (at the King's feet, on the stairs holding the Grand Master's baton).[26] The illustration and complementary prose clearly distinguish Guise's social and political prominence within this assembly, but also his distance from the royal family. That hierarchical distance is further underscored, and his political prominence is further tempered, by the fact that Constable Anne de Montmorency and Chancellor Michel de l'Hospital are seated in chairs, just as the royal family, whereas Guise rests directly on the step of the dais. Additionally, the Constable and the Chancellor, though described as "trois ou quatre pas plus loing" (three or four steps further away), also benefit from a "vis-à-vis" (face-to-face) position in

---

[25] *La Description du plant du theatre faict à Orléans, pour l'assemblée des trois Estatz: avec un brief discours de la seance des tenans & representans lesdictz Estatz* (Lyon: Anthoine du Rosne, 1561), A2r.

[26] *La Description*, A2r–A2v.

relation to a member of the royal family: the Constable is seated before the King of Navarre, and the Chancellor before Renée. While Guise is at equidistance between both, his position also reflects his unequal status. A neat triangle is formed among Renée, Michel de l'Hospital, and Catherine, with its parallel formed among Antoine de Bourbon, Anne de Montmorency, and Charles. Similarly, one might trace a triangular relationship among Guise and Charles's two siblings, all of whom are depicted in smaller scale. Interestingly, the symmetry between Renée's and Antoine de Bourbon's position in the woodcut seems undermined by her erect seated posture when compared to the latter, who is illustrated as slumping in his seat. Renée appears to lift herself head and shoulders above her hierarchically superior male counterpart, as he is closer in line to the throne despite his relatively distant family connection, and the hierarchically superior Marguerite de France, seated directly to her right. In other words, Renée's visibility in the woodcut illustration remarkably supersedes her rank and positioning.[27]

The overarching goal of the prose description is to articulate the event's theatrical and public nature. The very design of the scaffolding—the *plant* referred to in the original French title—on which these strong personalities are either standing or seated, as is the case of the most hierarchically privileged participants (some of whom even rest their feet upon cushions to signify their royal status), was constructed to inform the reader or viewer of their respective roles as the event played out.[28] In other words,

---

[27] While neither the prose description nor the *Quarante Tableaux* explains Renée's perceived role in this assembly, the Protestant background of the engravers and of the collection's readership could possibly account for her apparent prominence in the woodcut. By the time of its publication (1569), two central figures in the French Calvinist movement had already published dedicatory epistles to her in their works. See Théodore de Bèze, *Receuil des opuscules. C'est à dire. Petits Traictez de M. Jean Calvin. Les uns reveus et corrigez sur le Latin, les autres translatez. Nouvellement de Latin en Français* (Geneva: Baptiste Pinereul, 1566), *2r–*5r, and Pierre Viret, *De l'Estat, de la conférence, de l'authorité, puissance, prescription & succession tant de la vraye que de la fausse Église, depuis le commencement du monde, & des Ministres d'icelles & de leurs vocations & degrez* (Lyon: Claude Senneton, 1565), *iir–*viiiv.

[28] See also Mimi Yiu, *Architectural Involutions: Writing, Staging, and Building Space, c. 1435–1560* (Evanston: Northwestern University Press, 2015): "the term *platform* already suggests a conceptual slippage between architecture and theatre in this period: as a flat (plat) structure, a *platform* in early modern usage indicates a stage, scaffold, or draftsman's sketch. A *platform* thus switches—with the blink of a mind's eye—from a static drawing into a vibrant piece of theatre, subsuming the bones of architecture into something rich and strange," 4.

the assembly, and the temporary structure on which it took place, were deliberately constructed so that the participants might perform their relationships and signal their outwardly projected identities. Likewise, the prose description was deliberately crafted so that its readers might deduce those relationships and assess the public roles of those involved. Not long before this particular event, Calvin uses the same vocabulary to write of Renée's hierarchical status and the social responsibility that derived from her rank: "[...] je vous prie de vous esvertuer à donner tel exemple que vous saves que Dieu le requiert de vous en tel degré quil vous a eslevee, tellement que les bons y prennent courage, et les meschans en soyent confus" (I beg of you to strive to set the type of example that you know God requires of you due to the rank to which he raised you so that upstanding individuals might be edified by you and the villainous might be admonished).[29] Thus, for Calvin, Renée's hierarchical rank provides her with a figurative platform on which her charitable actions become a veritable theater of example.

Much as Adams observes Anne de Bretagne and Anne de France consciously constructing their images by acting out relationships in public, so Ellen Welch describes early modern diplomacy, that is, ambassadors' duties to negotiate and to represent their monarch on the international stage. These activities required acute knowledge and adept navigation of "a theoretical hierarchy of prestige," that served as a "mirror-image of the system of rank that governed interactions among barons, dukes, and marquises within individual court societies."[30] Just as male leaders often used these kinds of strategies to control public image, so, too, did their female counterparts. Indeed, Welch credits Catherine de Médicis for having promoted the Florentine tradition of court spectacle in France after her marriage to Henri II.[31] Furthermore, archival evidence demonstrates

---

[29] Although this letter is undated, Cunitz, Baum, and Reuss place it just prior to Renée's arrival in France, *Ioannis Calvini opera quae supersunt omnia, Volumen XVIII* (Brunsvigae: Schwetschke et filium, 1863), 315.

[30] Ellen Welch, *A Theater of Diplomacy. International Relations and the Performing Arts in Early Modern France* (Philadelphia: University of Pennsylvania, 2017), 3.

[31] Welch, *A Theater of Diplomacy*, 8. This broad issue is developed at length from a French point of view in the work of Monique Chatenet. See, for example, *La Cour de France au XVIᵉ siècle. Vie sociale et architecture* (Paris: Picard, 2002) and *Le prince, la princesse et leurs logis. Manières d'habiter dans l'élite aristocratique européenne (1400–1700)*, ed. Monique Châtenet and Krista de Jonge (Paris: Picard, 2014). Thanks to Kathleen Wilson-Chevalier for this reference.

that certain male leaders were aware of women's mastery of these tactics and even encouraged them to do so.

IMAGE-MAKING THROUGH CORRESPONDENCE

On hearing of Renée's return to France, Calvin urgently reminded her that her newfound widowhood presented an opportunity to live out her faith. But with that opportunity came a responsibility, for in his correspondence, he imagines Renée not only on a path toward her own salvation, but also demonstrating that path to a wider audience. As Charmarie Blaisdell points out, Calvin "understood very well that the successful conversion of France depended on the support of the powerful French noble families."[32] Due to his increasingly ill health and geographical distance from the happenings at French court, from 1557 on, Calvin communicated primarily via letters with numerous French noblemen and noblewomen. He also conducted from afar, as Hugues Daussy argues, a veritable orchestra of diplomatic missionaries, sending newly converted pastors, recruited almost exclusively from noble families, from Geneva into France and elsewhere in Europe as ambassadors of his cause.[33] And the dowager duchess is a central node in Calvin's network of epistolary and missionary diplomats, a true linchpin with far-reaching social and political connections.

Calvin's epistle to Renée dated July 5, 1560 (when she was still residing in Ferrara), elucidates these strategies, the potential dangers surrounding written communication, and the extent of his caution and suspicion in utilizing this diplomatic network. Indeed, this letter suggests that Renée had frequently requested pastoral care from Calvin, for he opens it by stating, "[…] jay esté souvent requis et solicité de vostre part" (I have often been needed and solicited by you). However, he declines her most recent request that he deploy a pastor to Ferrara, stating concerns that the information he had received in her name could possibly have been a forgery, or otherwise influenced by someone with ill intent.[34] Instead, Calvin offers counsel on two other topics: a pledge made on her late husband's

---

[32] Charmarie Jenkins Blaisdell, "Calvin's Letters to Women: the Courting of Ladies in High Places," *The Sixteenth-Century Journal* 13, no. 3 (1982): 67.
[33] Hugues Daussy, "L'action diplomatique de Calvin en faveur des Églises reformées de France (1557–1564)," *Bulletin de la Société de l'Histoire du Protestantisme Français (1903–2015)* 156 (avril–mai–juin 2010): 197.
[34] Cunitz et al., *Ioannis Calvini, Vol. XVIII*, 147–148.

deathbed to cease all further communication with Calvin and her desire to return to France now that marriage no longer tied her to Ferrara. Renée's correspondent seizes this opportunity to test Renée's firmness of faith by first reminding her that since that pledge had been extracted under duress and within the confines of marriage (from which she was now freed), God would certainly absolve her. After assuring Renée that she now has the freedom to act as her conscience dictates, he continues to manipulate her conscience in the direction that best suits his cause. He first sympathizes with her plight and then appraises the politico-religious situation in France:

> Du voyage lequel vous avez entreprins, combien que la captivité en laquelle vous estes et aves esté par trop detenue, soit dure et pitoyable, toutesfois si fault il que je vous declare, Ma Dame, que vous n'aures pas beaucoup gagné destre sortie dun abysme pour entrer en lautre.[35]
>
> (As for the journey that you are considering, while the captivity in which you have been detained for far too long—and in which you still find yourself—may be difficult and deserving of pity, I must nevertheless declare to you, Madame, that you will not gain very much by escaping one chasm and entering into another.)

Calvin's argument against Renée's potential displacement evokes his perennial worry about the "religious constancy or backsliding"[36] of his noble correspondents, albeit a lucid and realistic assessment of a worsening situation. Through a sustained series of hypothetical situations, arguments, and counter arguments, his prose betrays a calculated effort to weigh the extent to which he should invest in cultivating Renée as an ambassador of the reform movement in France. Calvin warns Renée, for example, that "le gouvernement auquel on pretend vous mesler est aujourdhuy si confus que tout le monde en crie a larme" (the government in which they wish to entangle you is currently in such turmoil that everyone is threatening to take up arms).[37] On the one hand, he notes, "quand vous y series, et qu'on vous escoutast, je croy bien, Ma dame, que les choses niroyent point du tout si mal" (if they listen to you once you arrive, Madame, I think that it could be possible that things would no longer go so poorly at all).[38] But on the other hand, he concedes that "ce n'est point

---

[35] Cunitz et al., *Ioannis Calvini, Vol. XVIII*, 147–148.
[36] Blaisdell, "Calvin's Letters to Women," 70.
[37] Cunitz et al., 148.
[38] Cunitz et al., 148.

ce quon cherche. On se veut couvrir de vostre nom pour nourrir le mal qui ne peult estre plus enduré" (this is not what they seek. They wish to exploit your good name in order to cultivate the evil deeds that can no longer be endured).[39] In Calvin's view, this situation would expose her to the height of temptation, and he purportedly wants above all for Renée to thrive during this stage of her life and affirms that "Dieu par la viduité vous a rendue plus franche et libre, à fin de vous retenir du tout à soy" (through widowhood, God has increased your freedom and movement in order to bring you closer within his fold).[40] However, Calvin remembers all too well her past transgressions and chides her in a patronizingly conditional statement: "Si vous esties bien resolue de vous porter franchement, et en autre Magnanimité que n'aves fait jusqu'icy, je le prieroye de vous avancer bien tost en plus grand maniement quon ne vous presente" (if you were resolved to carry yourself unambiguously and with greater magnanimity than you have done to date, I would pray to Him that an opportunity present itself for you to be moved quickly to carry out greater actions).[41] Ever skeptical of his reader's devotion, Calvin incites further tension from the figurative pulpit of the page: "Mais si c'est pour dire Amen à tout ce qui est condamné de Dieu et des hommes, je ne say que dire sinon que vous gardies bien de tomber de fiebvre en chauld mal" (if it is to accept with complacency all that has been condemned by God and by man, then I know not what to say to you other than to take care not to harm yourself by playing with fire).[42]

Ultimately, Calvin concedes that it is Renée who must make her own decision, and he advises her to expand her horizons by looking forward rather than dwelling on the confines of her past. Calvin's letter closes with one final exhortation: "Seulement je vous prie de changer tellement que ce soit pour servir à Dieu à bon escient, et tendre au droit but, nomplus vous envelopper en des filets quil vous seroit difficile de rompre" (I only beg you to change so significantly that you are able, with a clear conscience, to serve God and follow a steady path, no longer getting yourself tangled up in knots that will be difficult to unravel).[43] The carefully chosen language in these passages demonstrates Calvin's strategy to manipulate

---

[39] Cunitz et al., 148.
[40] Cunitz et al., 147.
[41] Cunitz et al., 148.
[42] Cunitz et al., 148.
[43] Cunitz et al., 148.

his correspondents by alluding to potential guilt over past shortcomings, juxtaposing worldly political desires with eternal spiritual ones, and calling on their responsibility to serve as an example for the future.[44] In his voluminous correspondence, especially that with women, he persistently insists that his correspondents tow a narrow line and publicly declare their adoption of his teachings.[45] In other words, he urges them to step onto and exploit the platform that their social status allows—a role visible in Tortorel's and Perrissin's image— all the while taking care not to deviate from his script. Though he never explicitly identifies Renée's past offenses, Calvin justifies his reticence in supporting her return to court on past equivocations, likely referring to the impossible situation she faced when placed before the Inquisition six years earlier. In fact, he labels the charitable activities of her dowager years as the "[…] arreraiges que vous luy [Dieu] debviez a cause de vostre timidité du temps passé" (arrears that you owed him [God] to compensate him for your timidity in the past).[46]

While Renée had begun to exploit her social status by relying on the protection and resources that it afforded her in order to pursue social justice, she was always careful to maintain respect for the crown and to safeguard her place within the royal family. Her correspondence related to her 1554 experience with the Inquisition, the event to which Calvin implicitly refers in his letter, illustrates this poignantly. Due to her perceived heresy and support for heterodox religious views, her nephew Henri II sent Dr. Mathieu Ory, Inquisiteur Général de France, to Ferrara in order to encourage her confession and conversion.[47] Her prose from this difficult time

---

[44] Daussy observes a similar strategy in Calvin's letter to François d'Andelot, written during his imprisonment in 1558. "L'action diplomatique," 207–208. For the letter Daussy discusses, see Cunitz et al., *Ioannis Calvini opera quae supersunt omnia, Volumen XVII* (Brunsvigae: C. A. Schwetschke, 1863), 192–193.

[45] Blaisdell considers letters to other noblewomen and underscores Calvin's consistent "exhortation to remain firm in their newly acquired faith no matter what adverse circumstances they might face. His sympathy for their enduring persecution was overshadowed by his demand for their consistent and public adherence to 'the Cause.'" Blaisdell, "Calvin's Letters to Women," 72.

[46] Cunitz et al., *Ioannis Calvini, Vol. XX*, 16.

[47] On Renée's experience with Dr. Ory, see Emmanuel Rodocanachi, *Renée de France, duchesse de Ferrare* (Paris: Ollendorff, 1896), 237–252. See also the manuscript instructions sent by Henri II: "Instruction au Docteur Oriz allant devers Madame la duchesse de Ferrare pour le faict de la Religion" (Instructions given to Dr. Oriz, traveling to Madame the Duchess of Ferrara due to religious matters). Bibliothèque nationale de France, MS Français Dupuy 322, ff. 74r–75r.

betrays a marked insecurity and genuine fear of being permanently alien-
ated from the royal family. Following her interrogation, Renée writes to
Henri II on October 6, 1554, with the moving urgency of one who is
threatened with the loss of something that she holds very dear:

> Monseigneur, affin que mieulx je puisse mettre en effect ce desir naturel que
> j'ay de vous obeir et tousjours ensuivre les exemples tant honorables qui
> vous plaist par vostredicte laictre me aleguer, le plus pres que je pourray. Et
> affin qu'il me demeure moyen de vous faire service, je vous suplie tres hum-
> blement, Monseigneur, ne me vouloir abandonner sur mes vieulx jours,
> mais me avoir tousjours et pour le peu du reste de ma vie en vostre protec-
> tion et au lieu que je desire en vostre bonne grace […].[48]
>
> (Monseigneur, so that I might put into practice more effectively, and to
> the best of my ability, the natural desire that I possess to obey and always
> follow the most honorable examples that it pleased you to propose to me in
> your letter. And so that I might hold onto some means of serving you, I
> humbly beseech you, Monseigneur, please do not abandon me in my olden
> days, but keep me evermore under your protection for the little that remains
> of my life and in the place where I most desire to be: in your good
> graces […].)

Though separated from her king geographically, she nonetheless views
herself as falling under his political jurisdiction. It is the authority of his
crown and the sentiment of his good will toward her that make her feel
most secure. Renée closes this letter with an unusually effusive entreaty
that Henri retains his favor for her. She writes: "[je] vous suplie tres hum-
blemen et oir et croire et ressevoir mes tres humbles recommandations a
vostre bonne grace, et je suplie le Createur, Monseigneur, vous doner an
la sienne acomplissement de tous vos bons desirs" (I very humbly beseech
you to hear and believe and receive my very humble recommendation to
your good graces, and I beg the Creator, Monseigneur, to give you the full
realization of all your good desires in his [grace]).[49] The repeated emphasis in the original French on hearing (*oir*), believing (*croire*), and receiving
(*ressevoir*) is doubled by the poetic alliteration of the conjunction (*et*) and
the verbal ending (*-oir*). Through her written correspondence, Renée
explicitly calls on her nephew's emotions in order to influence his political
actions and to protect her economic well-being. In other words, an

[48] Turias, *Renée de France*, 213–214.
[49] Turias, *Renée de France*, 213–214.

ambassador relying on the affection and good will that her family ties generate, she engages in epistolary diplomacy and public relations strategies in order to manipulate both state-level policy, that is, the preservation of the Valois-Este alliance despite her perceived religious deviance, and her personal sense of self, that is, her continued inclusion within the Valois family and the possessions that her inheritance and dowry afforded her.[50] While for Calvin, Renée's firm attachment to family equates to a weak demonstration of her faith, it in fact demonstrates her skill at communicating emotion and affection that ends up being a powerful political strategy on both the macro and micro levels.

EPISTOLARY DIPLOMACY: EXPLOITING KINSHIP TO SHAPE PUBLIC POLICY

Ambassador Nicholas Throckmorton recognized this skill and urged Renée to exploit it. Within weeks of the Estates General held in Orléans, he reports to his sovereign on January 10, 1561, on a discussion that Renée had initiated with him four days earlier. Renée had summoned him to her lodgings, where in order to diminish their hierarchical distance and speak together as if two diplomats negotiating policy, she first "made him sit by her in a chair" before proceeding to appeal to his emotions, stating "that she owed the Queen of England great love because she was a Christian and virtuous Queen, and had in her realm set forth the true service, glory, and honour of God, by whose good example therein she trusts that other Princes will do the like."[51] Renée then points to the recently changed political landscape in France, describing "the great towardness that was in the young King," a situation that may well permit

---

[50] Renée engages in this same strategy in 1529, when the Paix de Cambrai threatens the diplomatic alliance that François Ier had sought to create between France and Ferrara through her marriage. See Kelly D. Peebles, "Renée de France's and Clément Marot's Voyages: Political Exile to Spiritual Liberation," *Women in French Studies*, Special Issue Volume 7 (2018), 40–42. Odette Turias discusses Renée's use of this strategy thirty years later, stating: "la fonction de Renée de France dans les rapports avec la Cour est essentielle puisque c'est elle qui incarne le lien d'alliance entre Este et les Valois" (Renée de France's function in relations with the court is essential because it is she who embodies the alliance between the Este and Valois families), 97. "Hercule d'Este et Renée de France: un rêve de mediation à la fin du règne de Charles Quint (1548–1555)," in *La Diplomatie au temps de Brantôme, Cahiers Brantôme no. 3* (Bordeaux: Presses Universitaires de Bordeaux, 2007), 87–100.

[51] *CSP, Vol. 3*, 489–490.

"the Queen of England [to] advance the religion of God in France, and consequently over all Europe."[52] Throckmorton draws on the religious kinship between Renée and Elizabeth, imagining that their shared beliefs would generate emotional kinship, as well, writing that "the Queen would most thankfully accept her good affections, the more so because it was grounded upon occasion of religion." Renée responds by putting forward a potential foreign policy that extends that religious and emotional kinship to a political one: Throckmorton "should offer [Elizabeth] some persuasions," she suggests, for she can imagine no other method "so certain for a perfect amity between France and England as a unity in religion," further lamenting that since "unity in the contrary religion did not always occasion amity," then perhaps shared beliefs could transform the nations' relationship, for "discord was not amongst those who professed the truth."[53] Ultimately, Throckmorton proposes an alternative method, one that valorizes Renée's role within the royal family, acknowledges the power of her personal relationships with both prominent figures from religious factions, and urges her to exploit this leverage in order to broker change. The English ambassador responds to Renée's policy suggestion with his own, stating that:

> it behoved an Ambassador to speak warily, and that he took himself not to be a fit instrument for that matter, but that she, being a near relative to all the great personages of the realm, might do so, that her words must be taken to proceed only of zeal of religion and tranquility of the realm, whereas an Ambassador's words might have another interpretation.[54]

At the end of Throckmorton's report of this conversation, we learn that Renée concluded their discussion by evoking "another cause which worked in her a goodwill towards the Queen," for as Renée reminds him, the two royal women have religious histories that are founded in a common source: "an old acquaintance between the Queen's mother [Anne Boleyn] and her [Renée], when the former was one of the maids-of-honour of the Duchess's sister, Queen Claude."[55] One month later, Renée also writes to Elizabeth I, alluding to a follow-up interview with Throckmorton and Francis Russell, Count of Bedford, the English

---

[52] *CSP, Vol. 3*, 489–490.
[53] *CSP, Vol. 3*, 489–490.
[54] *CSP, Vol. 3*, 489–490.
[55] See also Kathleen Wilson-Chevalier, chapter two in this volume.

sovereign's special envoy in France. The two had reported on Elizabeth's high opinion of Renée and her reciprocal feeling of good will, and Renée seizes that opportunity to affirm that she will "[s]'enploier pour elle en sorte que [elle] ne demeure ingrate ne redevable de tant d'honneste et bonnes parolles" (devote herself to her [Majesty] so that she will not seem ungrateful or beholden of such honorable and kind words).[56] By drawing on the shared ancestry of their faith, a heritage rooted in Renée's sister, she presents herself not only as a religious ally, but as a potential ally in the European political arena, as well. While the tight bond of family is a potential unifying theme in Renée's epistolary diplomacy with her English correspondents, it is one that complicates her relationship with Calvin. This fact becomes starkly apparent as the religious tensions at court break into outright war, and the central role of her son-in-law, François de Guise, within the Catholic faction led to the public defamation of his character and actions—and ultimately his death—and her equally public defense of her affection and loyalty to him.

"The death of the Duke of Guise has produced a deep sensation in this Court," states Guido Giannetti in a letter to Queen Elizabeth I on March 13, 1563.[57] Giannetti, an Italian Protestant, merchant of reformed books, and secret agent for the English court,[58] observes with interest the fear felt in France following Guise's assassination by the Protestant Jean Poltrot de Méré. Those in power at court understood the event's significance, for as Giannetti writes: "they see that there is no one capable of filling Guise's place [and] they know that the inclination of the French people is in favour of the Protestants."[59] Among the most prominent of Protestant figures was the Châtillon family, led by Admiral Gaspard de Coligny. His central role in the Catholic-Protestant debates is made visible in Tortorel's and Perrissin's image of the Estates General in Orléans, for he is depicted in an animated discussion with the Marshals of France, and he was publicly

---

[56] Turias, *Renée de France*, 345.

[57] "Elizabeth: March 1563, 11–15," in *Calendar of State Papers Foreign: Elizabeth, Volume 6, 1563*, ed. Joseph Stevenson (London: Her Majesty's Stationery Office, 1869), 204. *British History Online*, accessed August 9, 2019, http://www.british-history.ac.uk/cal-state-papers/foreign/vol6/pp198-205. Hereafter referred to as *CSP, Vol. 6*.

[58] M. Anne Overell, *Italian Reform and English Reformation c. 1535–c. 1585* (New York: Routledge, 2016), 78–80.

[59] *CSP, Vol. 6*, 204.

excoriated by Guise's widow, Anne d'Este, for allegedly encouraging the attempt on the duke's life.[60]

Venetian Marcantonio Barbaro reports to the Doge one day after Giannetti's missive to Elizabeth indicating that the Cardinal de Lorraine had been warned by Renée "to be well on his guard, as there were plots against his life on every side."[61] And Throckmorton, still serving at that time as the English ambassador, confirms Renée's continued effort to engage in family diplomacy, writing that "the old Duchess of Ferrara travails to compound this difference betwixt the houses of Guise and Châtillon."[62] But Calvin's correspondence reveals that her attempts to join together these increasingly dissonant groups did not earn his favor. He chides her display of affection toward her late son-in-law: "Jay apperceu en vostre lettre que laffection vous faict oublier ce qui aultrement vous seroit assez cognu" (I observed in your letter that affection causes you to forget that which otherwise would be apparent to you).[63] After all, Calvin reminds her, "Or si le mal faschoit a toutes gens de bien, Monsieur de Guise, qui avoit allume le feu, ne pouvait pas estre espargne" (since these troubled times cause everyone to suffer, Monsieur Guise, who lit the fire, could hardly be spared).[64]

Renée's desire to remain close to the crown and Calvin's entreaty to use that status to serve as a living example at times put her at odds with individuals with whom she shared both religious and family ties. For example, Jeanne d'Albret, Queen of Navarre and daughter of Marguerite de Navarre, openly declared herself for Calvin on Christmas Day, 1560, just weeks after Renée's arrival, François II's death, and Condé's release. Indeed, Jeanne also was taking advantage of the rapidly changing political landscape, which further highlights women's power within the French court at the time. Her husband, Antoine de Bourbon, was named

---

[60] On Guise's assassination, see Nicola M. Sutherland, "The Assassination of François Duc de Guise, February 1563," *The Historical Journal* 24, no. 2 (1981): 289–295.

[61] *Despatches of Michele Suriano and Marc' Antonio Barbaro, Venetian Ambassadors at the Court of France, 1560–1563*, ed. Sir Austen Henry Layard (Lymington: The Huguenot Society of London, 1891), 83.

[62] *CSP, Vol. 6*, 543.

[63] Cunitz et al., *Ioannis Calvini, Vol. XX*, 244–245. Though the letter is undated, the editors cite intertextual evidence pointing to early 1564.

[64] Cunitz et al., 246. Cunitz, Baum, and Reuss suggest that the fire Calvin refers to is the Massacre of Wassy. Tortorel's and Perissin's collection also suggests this, as their woodcut depicting the Massacre of Wassy highlights Guise's involvement.

Lieutenant Général on Charles IX's accession, and he found it politically expedient to fight for the Catholic Guise faction, threatening to repudiate his wife for her reformed beliefs and ultimately losing his life fighting against the Huguenots in 1562.[65] Renée is keenly aware of her precarious position as mother-in-law of Guise, and acknowledges this fact in her March 1564 letter to Calvin, written one year after Guise's death: "je sçay fort bien que je ay esté haye et abominee de plusieurs pour ce qu'il estoyt mon gendre, a qui l'on a voulleu charger les faultes de tous" (I know all too well that I am hated and excoriated by many because he was my son-in-law, the one whom they wished to hold accountable for everyone's wrongdoings).[66]

CONCLUSION

Renée's correspondence demonstrates that her family loyalty and personal autonomy took precedence over her concerns for public opinion. In 1548, as soon as she learned of the impending marriage between her daughter and Guise (then known as the Duc d'Aumale), she wrote to Henri II to express her gratitude. She begins this letter by referring to her future son-in-law's brother (the Cardinal de Guise, who would later become the Cardinal de Lorraine) as her own son. In other words, she writes him into her family. It was he who had transmitted this news to her, and she recognizes him as representing the king's person. In keeping with that role, she is resolved to obey his wishes, and she acknowledges the authority of the French crown. This letter reveals that Henri II had announced his continued high esteem for Renée—this letter predates the 1554 incident with the Inquisition—and she affirms that her devotion to the crown is carried forth by her children. They, too, are dedicated to his service, and most

---

[65] Jouanna et al. explain Antoine de Bourbon's religious ambivalence in the early days of Charles IX's reign: "son indétermination est l'une des conditions de la tolérance civile. S'il choisit l'un des camps, celui-ci aura à la fois la force et la légitimité" (his indetermination is one of the conditions of civil tolerance. If he were to choose one of the factions, it would give it both power and legitimacy). *Histoire et dictionnaire des guerres de religion*, 105. It was not until after the Edict of January, a decree of tolerance in early 1562, that he openly opted for Catholicism, 109. Daussy also explains the pressure Antoine de Bourbon felt from Philip II of Spain, whose ambassador insisted on distancing Jeanne d'Albret, Coligny, and Châtillon from the French court in order to limit their Calvinist influence. *Le Parti Huguenot*, 278–280.

[66] Turias, *Renée de France*, 372.

importantly, he has named them as his own. Through the verb *nommer*, he gives her children the specific attribute of belonging to the royal family. They are part of his *race*, which at the time represented a group of descendants sharing a common heritage.[67] As such, they, too, take on the burden of serving the crown. In closing, Renée comes back to her own extended family:

> le bien de parataie qu'il vous plaict ogmenter entre nous n'estre moindre en mon endroit que s'il estoit mon propre filx […] ossi mon filx monsr le marquis du Maine [Claude de Lorraine] qui m'a promis ne m'estre jamais moins affectionné de tous ces freres, et cant a mon filx monsr d'Aumale [François de Lorraine], je ne vous en diré aultrement […].[68]
>
> (the gift of lineage that it pleases you to extend among us is no less meaningful to me than if he were my own son […] also my son Monsieur le Marquis du Maine, who promised me never to be less affectionate to me than any of his brothers, and as for my son Monsr d'Aumale, I will express the same thing to you […].)

Over time, Renée writes routinely to Guise, both to ask for and to return help. Years later, her loyalty was tested. When the first War of Religion broke out, Renée's castle at Montargis became a strategic location for troop movements on both sides of the fighting. She writes to her son, Alphonse, in September 1562, telling him that the king (Charles IX at the time) had come through with his mother and the Duc d'Anjou (Charles IX's brother). Guise accompanied them, leading the troops. Renée, in addition to greatly enjoying their company, also comments on their respect. She writes: "jamais camp ne fut en lieu ou il se soyt faict moins de mal que en cestuy-cy, en sorte que apres qu'ilz furent passez, il ne sembloyt quasi poinct qu'il y eust passé personne" (never had a camp been set up in a place where less harm was done than in this particular one, to the point that after they had left, it seemed almost as though not a single person had passed through).[69] But the most noteworthy part of this letter is a statement that Renée makes about her own authority: "touttefois le tout soubz mon obeissance et commandement et n'entreprennent rien sans

[67] *Dictionnaire du moyen français*, s.v. "race," accessed August 4, 2019, http://www.atilf.fr/dmf/.
[68] Turias, *Renée de France*, 148. For the original French manuscript, see Bibliothèque nationale de France MS Clairambault 346, f. 172.
[69] Turias, *Renée de France*, 359.

m'en advertir" (furthermore, everything happened under my surveillance and command and nothing was undertaken without my knowledge).[70] Renée retained her authority as *châtelaine* of her domain and princess of the blood, allowing no one to come and go from her premises without her express permission.

Bèze offers another point of view in his *Histoire ecclésiastique*. At this later point in time, he writes, "ce fut la retraitte de plusieurs povres fugitifs avec leurs femmes et enfans, [...] mesmes de plusieurs de la religion Romaine fuyans le tumulte de la guerre" (this was the sanctuary for many poor refugees with their wives and children, [...] even for many of the Roman Catholic religion fleeing the turmoil of war).[71] And this very public display—and equally public acknowledgment—of Renée's ability to bridge the divide between antagonistic belief systems offers further evidence of her unofficial, yet highly effective, diplomatic prowess.

Tortorel and Perrissin, the Protestant engravers who pictured the 1560 meeting of the Estates General of Orléans, emphasize that the overarching goal of their *Quarante Tableaux* is to highlight the "admirable" nature of these events, which through its Latin root implicitly points to the importance of visual representation.[72] They encourage viewers to wonder and marvel at what is before their eyes, just as did the original "tesmoins occulaires," the eyewitnesses on whose descriptions the engravings were based. Likewise, Calvin exhorts Renée to craft the public image of her household at Montargis so that she may provide outwardly visible edification to his followers and admonishment to his detractors. On January 8, 1564, five months before his death, he writes: "que vostre maison soit ung miroir pour donner exemple a ceulx qui se rendent aucunement dociles, et rendre confus ceulx qui sont incorrigibles et endurcis du tout" (may your household be a mirror to set an example to those who are somewhat susceptible to learning and to chastise those who are impertinent and unbending).[73] This is precisely what Renée accomplished: the embracing of both sides of her family and both sides of the politico-religious divide, though she did so in her own tolerant, generous, and autonomous manner despite the heightened violence of civil war.

[70] Turias, *Renée de France*, 359.
[71] Jouanna et al., *Histoire ecclésiastique*, 52.
[72] Benedict, "To the Reader/Au Lecteur." *Graphic History*, 217–218. See also *Online Etymology Dictionary*, s.v. "admire," accessed August 4, 2019, https://www.etymonline.com.
[73] Cunitz et al., *Ioannis Calvini, Vol. XX*, 231.

BIBLIOGRAPHY

PRIMARY SOURCES

BnF MS Clairambault 346, f. 172.

BnF MS Français Dupuy 322, ff. 74r–75r.

Brantôme, Pierre de Bourdeille, sieur de. 1991. *Recueil des Dames, poésies et tombeaux*. Edited by Étienne Vaucheret. Paris: Gallimard.

Calendar of State Papers Foreign: Elizabeth, Volume 3, 1560–1561. 1865. Edited by Joseph Stevenson. London: Her Majesty's Stationery Office. *British History Online*. Accessed June 4, 2019. http://www.british-history.ac.uk/cal-state-papers/foreign/vol3.

Calendar of State Papers Foreign: Elizabeth, Volume 6, 1563. 1869. Edited by Joseph Stevenson. London: Her Majesty's Stationery Office. *British History Online*. Accessed August 9, 2019. http://www.british-history.ac.uk/cal-state-papers/foreign/vol6.

Calvin, Jean. 1863a. *Ioannis Calvini opera quae supersunt omnia, Volumen XVII*. Edited by Edouard Cunitz, Johann-Wilhelm Baum, and Eduard Wilhelm Eugen Reuss. Brunsvigae: Schwetschke et filium.

———. 1863b. *Ioannis Calvini opera quae supersunt omnia, Volumen XVIII*. Edited by Edouard Cunitz, Johann-Wilhelm Baum, and Eduard Wilhelm Eugen Reuss. Brunsvigae: Schwetschke et filium.

———. 1879. *Ioannis Calvini opera quae supersunt omnia, Volumen XX*. Edited by Edouard Cunitz, Johann-Wilhelm Baum, and Eduard Wilhelm Eugen Reuss. Brunsvigae: Schwetschke et filium.

Collection des Procès-verbaux des assemblées-générales du Clergé de France depuis l'Année 1560, jusqu'à présent rédigés par ordre de matieres, et réduits à ce qu'ils ont d'essentiel. Tome Premier. 1767. Edited by Monsieur l'Évêque de Mâcon. Paris: Guillaume Desprez.

de Bèze, Théodore. 1566. *Receuil des opuscules. C'est à dire. Petits Traictez de M. Jean Calvin. Les uns reveus et corrigez sur le Latin, les autres translatez. Nouvellement de Latin en Français*. Baptiste Pinereul: Geneva.

———. 1580. *Histoire ecclesiastique des églises reformees au royaume de France, tome II*. Jean Remy: Anvers.

Despatches of Michele Suriano and Marc' Antonio Barbaro, Venetian Ambassadors at the Court of France, 1560–1563. 1891. Edited by Sir Austen Henry Layard. Lymington: The Huguenot Society of London.

La Description du plant du theatre faict à Orleans, pour l'assemblée des trois Estatz: avec un brief discours de la seance des tenans & presentans lesdicta Estatz. 1561. Lyon: Anthoine du Rosne.

Lettres de Catherine de Médicis. Tome Premier, 1533–1563. 1888. Edited by Hector de la Ferrière. Paris: Imprimerie Nationale.

Thou, Jacques de. 1734. *Histoire universelle de Jacque Auguste de Thou, depuis 1543, jusqu'en 1607. Traduite sur l'édition latine de Londres, Tome Quatrieme, 1560–1564.* London: s.n.

Viret, Pierre. 1565. *De l'Estat, de la conférence, de l'authorité, puissance, prescription & succession tant de la vraye que de la fausse Église, depuis le commencement du monde, & des Ministres d'icelles & de leurs vocations & degrez,* *iir–*viiiv. Lyon: Claude Senneton.

SECONDARY SOURCES

Adams, Tracy. 2010. Rivals or Friends? Anne de Bourbon and Anne de Bretagne. *Women in French Studies* Special Issue 3: 46–61.

Benedict, Philip. 2007. *Graphic History: The Wars, Massacres and Troubles of Tortorel and Perrissin.* Geneva: Droz.

Blaisdell, Charmarie Jenkins. 1982. Calvin's Letters to Women: The Courting of Ladies in High Places. *Sixteenth-Century Journal* 13 (3): 67–84.

Châtenet, Monique, and Krista de Jonge, eds. 2014. *Le prince, la princesse et leurs logis. Manières d'habiter dans l'élite aristocratique européenne (1400–1700).* Paris: Picard.

Crawford, Katherine. 2000. Catherine de Médicis and the Performance of Political Motherhood. *Sixteenth-Century Journal* 31 (3): 643–673.

Daussy, Hugues. 2010. L'action diplomatique de Calvin en faveur des Églises reformées de France (1557–1564). *Bulletin de la Société de l'Histoire du Protestantisme Français (1903–2015)* 156: 197–209.

———. 2015. *Le Parti Huguenot. Chronique d'une désillusion (1557–1572).* Geneva: Droz.

DMF: Dictionnaire du Moyen Français, version 2015. ATILF—CNRS and Université de Lorraine. http://www.atilf.fr/dmf.

Harper, Douglas. *Online Etymology Dictionary*, version 2019. https://www.etymonline.com.

Jouanna, Arlette, Jacqueline Boucher, Dominique Biloghi, and Guy le Thiec, eds. 1998. *Histoire et dictionnaire des guerres de religion.* Paris: Éditions Robert Laffont.

Le Maire, François. 1648. *Histoire et Antiquitez de la ville et duché d'Orléans.* Orléans: Maria Paris.

McIlvenna, Una. 2016. *Scandal and Reputation at the Court of Catherine de Medici.* New York: Routledge.

Overell, M. Anne. 2016. *Italian Reform and English Reformation c. 1535–c. 1585.* New York: Routledge.

Peebles, Kelly D. 2018a. Embodied Devotion: The Dynastic and Religious Loyalty of Renée de France (1510–1575). In *Royal Women and Dynastic Loyalty*, ed. Caroline Dunn and Elizabeth Carney, 123–137. Cham, Switzerland: Palgrave Macmillan.

———. 2018b. Renée de France's and Clément Marot's Voyages: Political Exile to Spiritual Liberation. *Women in French Studies* Special Issue 7: 33–60.

Rodocanachi, Emmanuel. 1896. *Renée de France, duchesse de Ferrare*. Paris: Ollendorff.

Sowerby, Tracey A. 2016. Elizabethan Diplomatic Networks and the Spread of News. In *News Networks in Early Modern Europe*, ed. Joad Raymond and Noah Moxham, 305–327. Leiden: Brill.

Sutherland, Nicola M. 1981. The Assassination of François Duc de Guise, February 1563. *The Historical Journal* 24 (2): 279–295.

Turias, Odette. 2005. *Renée de France, Duchesse de Ferrare, témoin de son temps: 1510–1575, Tomes I & II*. PhD diss., Université de Tours.

———. 2007. Hercule d'Este et Renée de France: un rêve de mediation à la fin du règne de Charles Quint (1548–1555). In *La Diplomatie au temps de Brantôme, Cahiers Brantôme no. 3*, ed. François Argot-Dutard and Anne-Marie Cocula, 87–100. Bordeaux: Presses Universitaires de Bordeaux.

Walsh, Sebastian. 2005. Most Trusty and Beloved. *History Today* 55 (9): 39–45.

Welch, Ellen. 2017. *A Theater of Diplomacy. International Relations and the Performing Arts in Early Modern France*. Philadelphia: University of Pennsylvania.

Yiu, Mimi. 2015. *Architectural Involutions: Writing, Staging, and Building Space, c. 1435–1560*. Evanston: Northwestern University Press.

CHAPTER 12

The Gardens of the Château de Montargis as an Expression of Renée de France's Identity (1560-1575)

Cyril Cvetkovic

Literary portraits of Renée de France have often celebrated the excellence of her royal lineage and the purity of the moral values that guided her actions during her lifetime.[1] Her desire to cultivate intellectual pursuits, but above all her great generosity and desire to help the needy in France and in Italy, have been presented as illustrating her virtues. In her own correspondence, Renée regularly evokes the principles of goodness, charity, justice, and peace, which contributes to the construction of an image faithful to her own ideal of a royal princess.[2] These qualities were per-

---

[1] Kelly D. Peebles, "Embodied Devotion: The Dynastic and Religious Loyalty of Renée of France (1510-1575)," in *Royal Women and Dynastic Loyalty*, ed. Caroline Dunn and Elizabeth Carney (Cham, Switzerland: Palgrave Macmillan, 2018), 123-137.

[2] Odette Turias, *Renée de France, Duchesse de Ferrare, témoin de son temps: 1510-1575*, 2 vols. (PhD diss., Université de Tours, 2004).

C. Cvetkovic (✉)
Centre d'études supérieures de la Renaissance, UMR/CNRS 7323, Université de Tours, Tours, France

© The Author(s), under exclusive license to Springer Nature Switzerland AG 2021
K. D. Peebles, G. Scarlatta (eds.), *Representing the Life and Legacy of Renée de France*, Queenship and Power,
https://doi.org/10.1007/978-3-030-69121-9_12

359

ceived both as a gift received through her illustrious birth and as an obligation to legitimize her high position in society. Renée's public comportment was characterized mainly by the high regard in which she held her royal rank and her loyalty to the French crown. However, the princess struggled to reconcile her family's socio-cultural heritage with her own heterodox religious beliefs.[3] This juggling act complicated Renée's ability to fulfill her duties of social representation, especially regarding her carefully constructed public image.

During the Renaissance, within a growing court society, more exacting obligations were imposed upon the nobility in matters of appearance, so as to assert and legitimize their dominant position in society.[4] The Aristotelian notion of magnificence propounded, for example, that a beautiful, richly furnished palace was a fundamental element of an aristocrat's reputation and social importance.[5] For several years, researchers have been highlighting Renée's expenditure on clothing, gold and silverware, jewelry, tapestries, and portraits, but also on architecture and gardens.[6] The two main projects that Renée ordered for her residences, first at the Villa di Consandolo from 1540 and then at the Château de Montargis from 1561, accorded particular importance to the design of the gardens. Although the duchess's two former homes are no longer standing, extant drawings by the architect Jacques Androuet du Cerceau offer precious insight as to the appearance of the Château de Montargis during Renée's lifetime, skirted by imposing semi-circular gardens.[7]

[3] Charmarie Jenkins Webb, *Royalty and Reform: the predicament of Renée de France* (PhD diss., Tufts University, 1969); Eleonora Belligni, *Renata di Francia (1510-1575). Un'eresia di corte* (Turin: UTET, 2011).

[4] The following analysis builds on the work of Marjorie Meiss-Even, *Les Guise et leur paraître* (Tours: PUFR, 2014).

[5] In the Middle Ages, the magnificence is a virtue of a prince who earns the respect of his subjects by using his wealth for the common good (organization of festivities, charitable acts, etc.). In the Renaissance, this notion is oriented toward a private domain of application that associates the social reputation to the possession of luxurious palaces and items.

[6] See especially Chiara Franceschini, "Tra Ferrara e la Francia: Notizie su orefici e pittori al servizio di Renée de France," *Franco-Italia* 19-20 (2001): 65-104; Rosanna Gorris, "'D'un château l'autre': la corte di Renata di Francia a Ferrara (1528-1560)," in *Il Palazzo di Renata di Francia*, ed. Loredana Olivato (Ferrara: Corbo, 1997), 185-214; Turias, *Renée de France*, vol. 2, 479, 557-564, 653-662. See also Kathleen Wilson-Chevalier, chapter ten.

[7] The Château de Montargis was almost completely dismantled during the first half of the nineteenth century. Today some vestiges of walls and buildings remain, including cellars, the crypt of the church, and parts of the garden's terrace.

During the sixteenth century in France, ornamental gardens became an essential feature of all châteaux and underwent important transformations, driven by architectural contributions from Italy. In France as in Ferrara, Renée lived in a socio-cultural context where the creation of gardens corresponded to new courtly norms and practices and the need for symbolic representation of a noble identity.[8] At Montargis, the renovation and embellishment of the former royal château also involved the construction of gardens that expressed the grandeur and magnificence of her rank. The affirmation of her status and authority was a question of strategic importance for Renée at the time of the first Wars of Religion. At Montargis, the duchess wished to live under the king's authority, but in accordance with her own religious ideas, offering protection on her estate to a Protestant community living on peaceful terms with the other inhabitants of the town who were predominantly Catholic.[9] Gardens are a powerful medium for representation, on which Renée could leave her imprint during a period of religious division that made her middle ground all the more precarious. This essay questions how the gardens of the Château de Montargis contributed to the public representation of Renée's identity. It will investigate the way in which the architectural program and the construction works in the gardens expressed the dowager duchess's royal rank and authority over the surrounding territory. Finally, it will offer some thoughts on how these gardens were compatible with Protestant views at her court.[10]

An Architectural Program to Express Renée's Royal Magnificence

The gardens at Montargis as designed by Renée seem to have had an ephemeral existence after her death in 1575. Plots of land were gradually ceded to private individuals as early as the sixteenth century, and the Wars

---

[8] *Jardins de château à la Renaissance*, ed. Élisabeth Latrémolière and Pierre-Gilles Girault (Paris: Gourcuff Gradenigo, 2014).

[9] See also Huguette Leloup-Audibert, *Les Dernières Dames de Montargis au temps des guerres de Religion. Renée de France, duchesse de Ferrare (1510-1575), Anne d'Este, duchesse de Guise, puis duchesse de Nemours (1531-1607)* (Châtillon-Coligny: Éditions de l'Écluse, 2014).

[10] Belligni, *Renata di Francia*, 355-390.

of Religion inflicted heavy damage on them.[11] Neither the descriptions of the seventeenth-century château nor eighteenth-century plans suggest the presence of important ornamental gardens.[12] The main source for describing and analyzing the sixteenth-century gardens remains the designs by Jacques Androuet du Cerceau, Renée's architect. These are available both in the first volume of *Les Plus excellents bâtiments de France*, printed in 1576, but also in a series of drawings on vellum, preserved in the British Museum in London. The latter contains additional details, including two extra views from the town of Montargis.[13] A comparison of these representations with Renée's household accounts and those of the castellany, as well as with notarial acts, confirms that the gardens were indeed laid out in the sixteenth century and provides additional information for their analysis.[14] I shall leave a detailed study of the Montargis architectural program to architectural historians and propose, rather, to analyze Renée's garden by tracing broader principles according to which ornamental gardens evolved during the Renaissance.[15]

---

[11] Archives départementales du Loiret (hereafter referred to as AD Loiret), 3E 17987, lease of the large garden at the Château de Montargis, September 19, 1597; 3E 7496, contract for the restoration of the château gardens, November 6, 1606.

[12] Inguimbertine Library of Carpentras, Ms. 1771, description of the Château de Montargis by Nicolas-Claude Fabri de Peiresc, seventeenth century, 198r-199v; Dom Guillaume Morin, *Histoire générale des pays de Gastinois, Senonois et Hurepois* (Paris: Chez la veuve Pierre Chevalier, 1630), 13-19.

[13] The British Museum (London), Prints and drawings, Inv. N. 1972, U. 814, 815, 816, 817, 818, 819. Published in *Jacques Androuet du Cerceau. Les dessins des Plus excellents bâtiments de France*, ed. Françoise Boudon and Claude Mignot (Paris: Cité de l'architecture et du patrimoine: A. and J. Picard, 2010). We unfortunately were unable to reproduce the original drawings and instead offer those found in a sixteenth-century imprint housed at the Bibliothèque nationale de France, RES V-390. See Jacques Androuet du Cerceau, *Le Premier volume des plus excellents bastiments de France. Auquel sont designez les plans de quinze bastiments et de leur contenu ensemble les elevations et singularitez d'un chascun, par Jacques Androuet Du Cerceau, architecte* (Paris: Pour Jacques Androuet du Cerceau 1576), f. 128v-129r.

[14] See the publications with notarial deeds by Huguette Leloup and Gaston Leloup in the *Bulletin de la Société d'émulation de l'arrondissement de Montargis*, in particular 46 (June 1979): 17-18; 119 (August 2002): 59; 139 (June 2008): 26; 151 (October 2011): 38-40; 163 (June 2015): 3-14.

[15] See particularly the work of Jean Guillaume, "Le jardin mis en ordre. Jardins et châteaux en France du XVe au XVIIe siècle," in *Architecture, jardin, paysage. L'environnement du château et de la villa au XVe et XVIe siècle*, proceedings from the symposium held in Tours, June 1-4, 1992, ed. Jean Guillaume (Paris: Picard, 1999), 103-123.

Contemporary norms for expressing the magnificence of her royal standing forced Renée de France to create large gardens in line with the architectural innovations of her time. At Montargis, gardens covering an area of about five *hectares* (twelve acres) were set around an egg-shaped castle, the grounds of which were comprised of buildings from different periods clustered around a central keep. The fortress was located on a high area of the limestone plateau overlooking the Loing valley and the town of Montargis, which grew up below. Having gardens spread around a princely residence was the first characteristic of the architectural evolution brought to bear upon the *hortus conclusus* during the Renaissance (Fig. 12.1). The semi-circular gardens of Montargis were made up of two parts, the first of

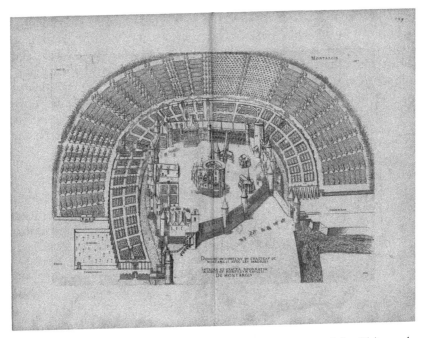

Fig. 12.1 Jacques Androuet du Cerceau. Perspective view of the Château de Montargis and its gardens, ca. 1570. *Le Premier volume des plus excellents bastiments de France. Auquel sont designez les plans de quinze bastiments et de leur contenu ensemble les elevations et singularitez d'un chascun*, par Jacques Androuet Du Cerceau, architecte. (Paris: Pour Jacques Androuet du Cerceau, 1576), f. 128v-129r. Paris, Bibliothèque nationale de France, RES V-390. Source: BnF

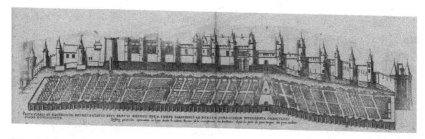

Fig. 12.2 Jacques Androuet du Cerceau. Upper gardens around the castle, ca. 1570. *Le Premier volume des plus excellents bastiments de France.* (Paris: Pour Jacques Androuet du Cerceau, 1576), f. 136v-137r. Paris, Bibliothèque nationale de France, RES V-390. Source: BnF

which was known as the "jardins d'en haut" (upper gardens), composed of fifty-two square beds, mazes, trellises, arbors, and walkways, resting on a monumental terrace running alongside the château's dry ditches. This large terrace, thirty-five meters wide and four to five meters high in places, followed the site's natural topography: it was flat in the center, while at its extremities it descended the limestone plateau toward the town (Fig. 12.2). The second part, called the "grand jardin" (large garden), spread out beneath the terrace and featured strips of parterres delimited by radial paths lined with trees, spanning seventy meters in width.

These gardens also testify to a gradual opening to the outside environment that was characteristic of the Renaissance. At Montargis, anyone strolling through the upper gardens would discover that the view playfully alternated between openness and concealment. Indeed, on the flat part, the trellises, arbors, and walkways were covered with climbing plants that partially masked the view, forcing visitors onward to discover what was obscured from view. The slope of the terrain, controlled by the monumental terrace, could provide an open or closed view, depending on whether the slope was approached from above or below. Finally, this game was subtly complemented by the walls of the large terrace that, depending on the rise of the land and the size of the square beds, were topped alternately with high sculpted merlons and embrasures through which the landscape and the large garden could be freely observed. The border of the large garden, which faced the paths on the large terrace, was materialized by a hedge and a ditch to avoid a visual break with the surrounding countryside.[16]

---

[16] AD Loiret, 3E 7476, purchase of land behind the château, February 17, 1571; 3E 17987, lease of the large garden, September 19, 1597.

This opening up of Renaissance châteaux to the outside environment extended to the buildings. Although we do not have any precise knowledge of the transformations Renée made to the buildings of the château, archival sources indicate she had a balcony overlooking the gardens added to her personal apartments (Fig. 12.3).[17] This served as the foundation for a "gallerie de nouvelle architecture" (new type of gallery), also described as "un cabinet de verre avec balustres de pierre" (glass room with stone balusters).[18] This balcony also sheltered beneath it a large aviary that was visible from the upper gardens. A few meters away, a "new doorway"[19] into the château was opened up in a wall that supported a passageway connecting two buildings. To reach it, visitors first had to pass through an imposing gateway, climb a large staircase, and walk along a path bordered

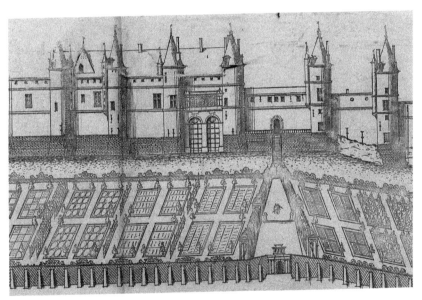

Fig. 12.3 Jacques Androuet du Cerceau. Detail of the glass room and the aviary, ca. 1570. *Le Premier volume des plus excellents bastiments de France.* (Paris: Pour Jacques Androuet du Cerceau, 1576), f. 136v-137r. Paris, Bibliothèque nationale de France, RES V-390. Source: BnF

[17] *Archivio di Stato di Torino, Sezioni Riunite* (hereafter referred to as ASTo, SR), Camerale Piemonte, Art. 806, para. 2, m. 37, 1569, March / Donations and Alms; April / Silverware.
[18] Morin, *Histoire générale*, 19; Inguimbertine Library of Carpentras, Ms. 1771, 198r-199v.
[19] ASTo, SR, Camerale Piemonte, Art. 806, para. 2, m. 36, 1568, September / Silverware.

Fig. 12.4 Jacques Androuet du Cerceau. Wooden gallery, ca. 1570. *Le Premier volume des plus excellents bastiments de France.* (Paris: Pour Jacques Androuet du Cerceau, 1576), f. 136v-137r. Paris, Bibliothèque nationale de France, RES V-390. Source: BnF

by high, wooden galleries that narrowed as the path approached the gate (Fig. 12.4), then cross a footbridge over the moat up to the new doorway. This was the main axis connecting the château to the gardens, whose progression and monumental staging symbolically recall the rank and authority of Renée de France.

Renaissance gardens increasingly appeared as extensions to the châteaux that they surrounded. At Montargis, for example, the beds of the upper gardens were aligned with the rooms of the seigneurial residence. Indeed, outside the large hall and Renée's private apartments was the flat part of the upper gardens, embellished with mazes, and several ensembles of four square beds separated by trellises. According to du Cerceau's drawings, each of these ensembles had its own visual and thematic coherence (Fig. 12.2). The most ornate part of the upper gardens corresponded to the most symbolic space within the château. The large, surrounding garden then made the château the center of the composition: its flower beds, alleys, and rows of trees prolonging the square beds, walkways, and trellises of the upper garden. In spite of their different designs, the organization of the spaces in the upper garden was extended through the large garden, transporting and stretching this design outwards toward the surrounding landscape (Fig. 12.1).

The architectural program of the Montargis gardens created a visual unity in which the château appeared as a central, organizing element of the surrounding countryside. The château attracted the visitor's gaze and projected itself onto its environment via radial pathways, some of which extended beyond the boundaries of the large garden.[20] Thus, by pointing outwards, the gardens symbolically recall Renée's power and domination over the surrounding territory.

To express the royal princess's magnificence, this program finds its source in the most famous ideal garden model of Renaissance literature: the island of Cythera, imagined by Francesco Colonna in his *Hypnerotomachia Poliphili* (*The Dream of Poliphilus*), published in 1499 and translated into French by Jean Martin in 1546. Descriptions in this book, illustrated by 159 woodcut prints, strongly and durably influenced the art of the ornamental garden, both in Italy and in France. This work's last chapter describes the island in the form of a vast, circular, geometrical garden, punctuated by patios and checkered by concentric and radial paths converging on a center that was occupied by an amphitheater, where Venus bathed in a fountain. The plan of Montargis, from the details of its pathways and terrace walls to its château, was obviously inspired by the island of Cythera, as described in the 1546 translation (Fig. 12.5).[21] In the 1560s, the aesthetics of *The Dream of Poliphilus* were considered by European courts to be the *summum bonum* of perfection, beauty, and refinement, inspiring many garden projects in the princess's entourage, in particular that of her brother-in-law, Ippolito II d'Este, at Tivoli. At the time, this was undoubtedly the most appropriate model to illustrate the Duchess of Ferrara's high position in society and the excellence of her values. The creation of such a garden, therefore, constituted a real act of power.[22]

THE CONSTRUCTION SITE: A DEMONSTRATION OF RANK AND POWER

Our knowledge of the building works undertaken at Montargis is truncated by the disappearance of the records—those made by the notary whom Renée employed to register her contracts, as well as the vast majority of the castellany's accounts that detailed the expenses incurred by the

---

[20] Guillaume, "Le jardin mis en ordre," 109-111.

[21] Francesco Colonna, *Hypnerotomachie, ou Discours du songe de Poliphile* [...], ed. Jean Martin (Paris: Jacques Kerver, 1546), 111r.

[22] See original map of the chateau and city of Montargis London, The British Museum, Prints and Drawings, Inv. N. 1972, U. 815.

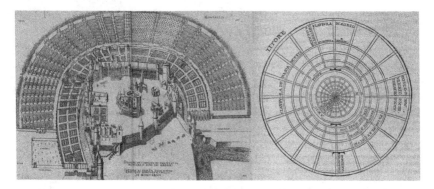

Fig. 12.5 Comparison between Androuet du Cerceau's castle plan and Cythera's plan. *Le Premier volume des plus excellents bastiments de France.* (Paris: Pour Jacques Androuet du Cerceau, 1576), f. 128v-129r. Paris, Bibliothèque nationale de France, RES V-390. Source: BnF

works carried out in the château and gardens.[23] Nevertheless, some information is dispersed in the duchess's household accounts and a few remaining notarial deeds. These few elements allude to certain aspects of the work and underscore the role that the construction works themselves played in shaping Renée's royal image. This vast undertaking of building an ideal garden was a demonstration of the princess's capacity to mobilize her socio-political and socio-cultural milieu for her project.

It would seem that the launch of the works on the gardens provoked a violent reaction on the part of the inhabitants of Montargis in 1561 or 1562. The parish priest Claude Haton reported in his memoirs that the townspeople rioted against Renée's project to seize the town cemetery in order to redesign it for incorporation in her future gardens.[24] The inhabitants not only undermined the workers' progress but also confronted and chased away the men-at-arms sent by their lady. This sedition was severely repressed with the help of royal commissioners who hanged the leaders. Claude Haton presents this case in the context of territorial struggle

[23] Two copies of the accounts from the castellany of Montargis are kept for the period 1560–1575: AD Loiret, A 301 (June 1564–June 1565); Archives nationales, Paris, R / 4 / 567 (June 1572–June 1573).

[24] *Mémoires de Claude Haton contenant le récit des événements accomplis de 1553 à 1582, principalement dans la Champagne et la Brie,* ed. Félix Bourquelot (Paris: Imprimerie Impériale, 1857), vol. 1, 200-201.

between Catholics and Protestants, but for the royal princess, it was also a matter of imposing her authority on the town. After thirty-two years of distant connections, the inhabitants of Montargis now had to submit to their lady's rule on a daily basis. According to later accounts, Renée intervened authoritatively in the town's affairs by appointing her own men as its leaders and appropriating public funds.[25] The creation of the gardens, therefore, took place within a context of territorial appropriation and the affirmation of her seigneurial power.

The different stages of the Montargis building works are difficult to establish. Work probably began firstly on the buildings, especially the interiors, in order to remedy the "quasi inhabitable" (almost uninhabitable) state of the château described by Jacques Androuet du Cerceau.[26] Work on the gardens seems to have started in 1561 or 1562, with the case of the cemetery. The lack of sources, however, means it is difficult to learn very much about the first three years of the Montargis building works (1561–1563).[27] In 1564, work on the château and gardens continued, but the account books teach us little of the work in progress.[28] The upper gardens were, however, apparently well advanced: the painter was applying mortar and paint to the merlons, and the gardener received many tools and plants. In 1565, Renée had her notary register twenty-nine purchase contracts for lands behind her château, which seems to indicate that work on the large garden was beginning.[29] In 1568, works were underway on the grand stairway leading from the upper gardens to the new doorway. Building work on the terrace and aviary was completed in March 1569. In April, a masonry purchase details the addition of a new tower to the château.[30] The first mention of the wooden galleries in the gardens appears in 1570, and a year later, a gardener from Paris was paid for having

[25] See Jenkins Webb, *Royalty and Reform: the predicament of Renée de France*, 463-466.

[26] *Le Premier volume des plus excellents bastiments de France* (Paris: Jacques Androuet du Cerceau, 1576).

[27] We know that in 1563 Renée received a quantity of glass for a new gallery for her château from one of her officers in Lyons. See Xavier Pagazani, *La Demeure noble en Haute-Normandie 1450-1600* (Tours: PUFR, 2014), 82.

[28] The following information is scattered in the household accounts from 1564 to 1565, 1568 to 1574 (ASTo, SR, Camerale Piemonte, Art. 806, para. 2, m. 35, 36, 37, 38, 39, 40, 41, 42, 55, 56-57) and in the castellany accounts (see note 23).

[29] A deed of sale from 1725 recalls all the owners of the plots of the former château gardens since Renée. Archives nationales, Paris, MC / ET / LXVIII / 365. We thank Frédéric Pige for this indication.

[30] AD Loiret, 3 E 17075, Masonry contract, April 21, 1569.

constructed "cabinets" (green rooms), about which no further details are provided. Throughout this period, the gardener was busy planting, and regular repairs were made to the terrace and the aviary.

It is difficult to assess the cost of the works due to the lack of sources. Nevertheless, the amount of expenses deducted from the castellany's revenues in 1564–1565 testifies to the extent of the work.[31] Renée called on the management skills of her manservant and *Maître de Fourrière*,[32] Nicolas Riguet, to oversee the construction work and pay a sizeable workforce. At first, the realization of the gardens depended on the services of Jérôme Teste, Renée's gardener of Italian descent.[33] This unknown man knew how to write, count, read a plan, recruit, and supervise a team of laborers with the help of another French gardener.[34] Jérôme Teste received the plants, the tools, and the finances to lay out and maintain the château gardens. The architectural program might have been the work of Jacques Androuet du Cerceau, the architect in the service of Renée at Montargis. Du Cerceau's role as an architect and master builder is difficult to establish with certainty, but some indications in the accounts attest to his responsibility on the site.[35] In 1564, he ordered the garden tables to be covered in slate, and in the same year, "Maistre Jacques" is recorded as having asked the gardener to fetch some trees from Paris. In 1565, du Cerceau noticed a young builder named Joseph Trigollot and obtained financial help from Renée on his behalf, probably to enable him to qualify as a master craftsman. In 1569, du Cerceau received new architectural instruments, and Joseph Trigollot is cited as one of the two master builders supervising the renovation works at the château.[36] Traces of collaboration between this craftsman and Renée's architect are again found much later in 1581, when together they appraise work undertaken at a gate and a bridge in the

[31] AD Loiret, A 301, 134r-188v. The expenses incurred by the building works represented 31% of the castellany revenues.

[32] This title denoted the servant in a French aristocratic household charged with procuring firewood and fodder.

[33] The gardener wrote and signed his name in Italian (see note 4).

[34] AD Loiret, 3 E 17977, Contract between Jérôme Teste and Laurent Bongards for the upkeep of the château gardens, October 1st, 1574.

[35] Relevant archival sources on Androuet du Cerceau may be found in the following: ASTo, SR, *Camerale Piemonte*, Art. 806, para. 2, m. 56-57, 1564, August / Silverware; m. 35, 1565, April / Donations and Alms; m. 37, 1569, March / Silverware. And in AD Loiret, A 301, f. 142v.

[36] See note 30.

town.[37] Du Cerceau was undoubtedly the key player in the realization of the Montargis program.

Through her patronage of Jacques Androuet du Cerceau, Renée hired the services of a talented architect who could boast solid experience and a fine reputation at the royal court.[38] He was a strategic player, able to facilitate the exchange of services within the family network and among the princess's supporters. Indeed, the sources indicate that the gardener of the Château de Montargis was regularly in contact with his counterpart from the neighboring château in Châtillon-sur-Loing, belonging to the Admiral Gaspard II de Coligny.[39] Renée had friendly relations with this French Protestant leader and his wife, Charlotte de Laval, and regularly took counsel from them when she was at Montargis. In addition to the correspondence between the Coligny family and Renée, the accounts have recorded an exchange of favors and servants for the improvement of their gardens.

Another relationship seems to have been maintained with the Château de Fontainebleau, where works on the buildings and gardens were directed by Francesco Primaticcio, an artist well known to Renée and du Cerceau. This Bolognese painter-architect, serving the king of France since 1532, was one of the leading Italian masters of Château de Fontainebleau's decoration and his superintendent of buildings since 1559. Primaticcio traveled to Italy to extend the royal collections with new treasures and allowed exchanges of portraits and news between the Duchess of Ferrara and her family in France.[40] After Renée's return to France, a letter from this artist, addressed to the duchess between 1561 and 1563, testifies to his role as

---

[37] Archives municipales de Montargis, DD 5, Expertise, August 30, 1581.

[38] Jacques Androuet du Cerceau was well known, thanks to his ornamental or architectural books which benefit a royal privilege since 1545. This architect was protected by the queen Marguerite de Navarre before he served Renée de France, and his notoriety was reinforced by the first of several volumes, *Livre d'architectvre de Jaques Androvet du Cerceau, contenant les plans et dessaings de cinquante bastimens tous differens [...]* (Paris: Benoist Prevost, 1559), and his likely involvement in several constructions, in particular that of Château de Verneuil commissioned by Philippe IV de Boulainvilliers. See Jean Guillaume, "Qui est Jacques Androuet du Cerceau?" in *Jacques Androuet du Cerceau, "un des plus grands architectes qui se soient trouvés en France,"* ed. Jean Guillaume (Paris: Picard, 2010), 17-33.

[39] The traces of these exchanges are in the household accounts: ASTo, SR, *Camerale Piemonte*, Art. 806, para. 2, m. 56-57, 1564, January / Donations and Alms, April / Silverware; m. 35, 1565, July / Donations and Alms; m. 36, August / Donations and Alms, September / Donations and Alms; m. 38, 1570, March / Donations and Alms; m. 39, 1571, August / Donations and Alms.

[40] Chiara Franceschini, "Tra Ferrara e la Francia."

adviser to a painter from Ferrara regarding the repair of a famous painting adorning a chimney in the Great Hall at the Château de Montargis.[41] This document also mentions a visit made by Renée's gardener to see Primaticcio in Fontainebleau, and the accounts for 1564 continue to mention trips made to fetch trees there. It, therefore, seems likely that the workshop at Fontainebleau would have provided support for the renovation of the interior decoration of the Château de Montargis, and perhaps also for the realization of its gardens.

Gardens were a subject of great interest, which in aristocratic circles resulted in acquaintances exchanging both services and servants and regularly sending one another fruit they had produced. Renée particularly enjoyed visiting the gardens of the châteaux where she was received during her travels and meeting the gardeners who worked there. Thus, work on the gardens at Montargis involved various actors, and Renée demonstrated her ability to mobilize her own resources by recruiting local laborers, as well as the resources of her broader network of relations and her territory, by employing well-established court artists. Involving all the strata of society in this way was characteristic of the expression of aristocratic magnificence in the sixteenth century.[42] Ever loyal to her rank and her family, creating the gardens at Montargis was a way for the duchess to affirm and maintain her place in court society and thus her closeness to the king. However, this expression of her royal identity could also be a source of tension with Protestant ideas, for the Calvinist approach to art was complex and subject to an imperative celebration of God. Indeed, the gardens invite a second level of reading, an analysis that demonstrates their compatibility with Renée's religious stance.

WERE THE GARDENS COMPATIBLE WITH RENÉE DE FRANCE'S RELIGIOUS STANCE?

Ornamental gardens were admitted by the French reformers because they celebrated the glory of God. For Protestants and Catholics alike, gardens were a place where the expression of the divine magnificence at the origin of creation combined with that of the aristocrat capable of rendering the divine perceptible by using landscape architecture to emphasize the

---

[41] J. T. D. Hall, "Three Letters of Primaticcio," *The Burlington Magazine* 115, no. 838 (January 1973): 35-36.
[42] Meiss-Even, *Les Guise*, 279-310.

beauties of nature. Recent research driven by the work of Yves Krumenacker has indeed highlighted that Calvinists did turn to artistic expression, especially if it celebrated God without representing him and if it was inspired by the Scriptures.[43] The art of combining materials and forms without any profusion of luxury was perceived as a gift designed to render God's presence in matter perceptible. Otto Schaeffer emphasizes the Reformer's great sensitivity to the beauty of Creation and how he encouraged his followers to reveal this spectacle of the glory of God present in nature for all to witness.[44] Iconoclastically, the vegetal aesthetic was put forward as a true representation of the divine, making God's invisible presence felt. For the French Reformers of the sixteenth century, nature was an object of appreciation, contemplation, and study, especially in the context of garden design.

The garden is thus a means by which Renée could represent herself as poised between the affirmation of her royal rank and the reformed precepts of divine celebration. The period during which the renovation works were carried out at Montargis coincided with a broader cultural context of Protestants searching for a form of garden that would be aesthetically compatible with the Reformation. Indeed, in 1563, in his book *La Recepte véritable*, the Calvinist artist Bernard Palissy imagined a garden that, in many ways, directly echoed Renée's stance in Montargis.[45]

Bernard Palissy's garden model is a free Protestant adaptation of the aesthetic model from *The Dream of Poliphilus*. Research has shown that this artist was indeed influenced by the work of Francesco Colonna.[46] However, the aesthetics of *The Dream of Poliphilus*, including numerous icons and enigmatic inscriptions, would clearly not have been suitable for Bernard Palissy, since they did not contribute to making the divine spectacle of nature directly intelligible.[47] On the contrary, he suggested creating a garden directly inspired by Psalm 104, which celebrates the bare

---

[43] Yves Krumenacker, ed., *Le Calvinisme et les arts, Chrétiens et sociétés*, Special Issue (2011).

[44] Otto Schaeffer, "'Théâtre de la gloire de dieu' et 'Droit usage des biens terrestres.' Calvin, le calvinisme et la nature," in *Calvin Naissance d'une pensée*, ed. Jacques Varet (Rennes: PUR, 2012), 213-226.

[45] Bernard Palissy, *Recepte véritable par laquelle tous les hommes de la France pourront apprendre à multiplier et augmenter leurs thrésors* (La Rochelle: B. Berton, 1563).

[46] Gilles Polizzi, "L'intégration du modèle: le Poliphile et le discours du jardin dans la *Recepte veritable*," *Albineana, Cahiers d'Aubigné* 4 (1992): 65-92.

[47] Franck Lestringant, *L'expérience huguenote au Nouveau Monde (XVIe siècle)* (Geneva: Droz, 1996), 242-249.

beauty of creation. He described a geometric Italian garden, located on the side of a mountain and bordered by eight "green rooms," where only plants, animals, and minerals were depicted, arranged, and aestheticized. There, man found himself face-to-face with creation, invited to contemplate nature without any intermediary.

The garden of *La Recepte véritable* is also Bernard Palissy's reaction to the violence unleashed against the Protestants during the First War of Religion. After the Peace of Amboise in 1563, the Calvinist artist sought to create a place of retreat that could also serve the pursuit of leisure activities, where victims of the civil war would be able to retire and find protection. He thus imagined that near his garden there should be "un palais ou amphithéâtre de refuge pour recevoir les chrétiens exilés en temps de persecution" (a palace or amphitheater to offer refuge to exiled Christians in times of persecution). This refuge would also be a place of peace, guided by wisdom: the garden and its flowerbeds would feature sentences derived from the *Wisdom of Solomon* and *Ecclesiasticus*. According to Marianne Carbonnier-Burkard, references to these two books, both of which Protestants considered apocryphal, indicate that Bernard Palissy did not intend to reserve his garden only for Calvinists. Rather, appalled as he was by the state of extreme division that reigned throughout the kingdom and the violence of the religious clashes, he sought to express a form of multi-denominational wisdom that would appeal to a wider humanist audience.[48] Palissy's reflections on a Protestant garden aesthetic, the creation of a place of refuge, and his multi-denominational wisdom closely echo Renée's aspirations in Montargis.

There is strong contextual proximity between the issues that Bernard Palissy was trying to address and Renée's situation in Montargis. In the midst of the Wars of Religion, the duchess was attempting to make her château and the surrounding town a place of peace, religious harmony, and a refuge for both Protestant and Catholic exiles.[49] This proximity is probably due to the fact that Palissy belonged to Renée's circle of acquaintances. This artist benefited from the protection of the Saubonne and Pons-Parthenay family, whose influence over Renée at Ferrara is well

---

[48] Marianne Carbonnier-Buckard, "Le jardin et le désert, ou le 'théâtre sacré' des protestants français (XVIe-XVIIIe siècle)," *Diasporas. Circulations, migrations, histoire* 21 (2013): 10-19.

[49] On Renée's protection of religious exiles, see also Kelly Peebles's contribution to this volume.

documented.[50] A little later, he worked for Catherine de Medici on the construction of the Tuileries, where the Duchess of Ferrara met with him in 1572.[51] In addition, he moved in the same milieu of court artists as Jacques Androuet du Cerceau, whose work he knew well. In Renee's service in Montargis, had du Cerceau, a Protestant himself, not found a refuge to build for himself, and many other persecuted Christians? Bernard Palissy's work must have been known to Renée and her entourage.

The sources do not directly testify to Palissy's concrete participation or his aesthetic influence over Montargis. Renée's accounts provide no details of the "green rooms" (cabinets) created in 1571 by a gardener from Paris. The fact that none of the documents describing the gardens mentions any statuary could be the sign of an aesthetic adaptation to the Calvinist ideas which held sway in the princess's court. Palissy's work in particular provides a testimony of the ideas and expectations which were in currency within Renée's entourage. The prism of this specific context can thus provide a second viewpoint from which to understand the Montargis gardens.

The circular shape of the Montargis gardens would seem to be indicative of a desire for refuge and wisdom, in line with Palissy's project. Circles symbolize the search for divine perfection, but also for universal harmony. Renée's garden plan is that of an ideal world modeled on the island of Cythera, a place of perfection, beauty, and love. It therefore expresses an ambition to return to a state of harmony between man and his environment, as in the early days in Eden. The shape of Montargis's gardens also includes an iconography used by Protestants to symbolize a refuge. Theodore de Bèze's *Emblems* symbolize the "true Church" in the form of a circular city closely resembling the plan of Geneva,[52] the city that embodies the idea of refuge *par excellence* for Calvinists.[53] It is traditionally praised

[50] Louis Audiat, *Bernard Palissy: étude sur sa vie et ses travaux* (Paris: Didier, 1868). See especially chapters 4 and 9.

[51] ASTo, SR, *Camerale Piemonte*, Art. 806, para. 2, m. 40, 1572, June / Donations and Alms.

[52] Theodore de Bèze, *Les Vrais pourtraits des Hommes illustres en piété et doctrine, du travail desquels Dieu s'est servi en ces derniers temps, pour remettre sus la vraye Religion en divers pays de la Chrestienté. Avec les descriptions de leur vie et de leurs faits plus memorables. Plus quarante quatre Emblemes Chrestiens, Traduicts du latin par Theodore de Besze*, A Genève, Par Jean de Laon, 1581, Embleme IX, p. 249.

[53] Theodore de Bèze (1519–1605) was one of Calvin's chief collaborators and his successor at the head of the Genevan Church. After the Reformer's death in 1564, Bèze continued a correspondence with Renée and dedicated to her the *Recueil des opuscules, c'est-à-dire, Petits traictez de M. Jean Calvin* (Geneva: Baptiste Pinereul, 1566).

for its impeccable order, as well as for its function as an international cross-roads.[54] Did du Cerceau not attribute a parallel role of acting as a cross-roads to Montargis, in a drawing that places the town at the center of its environment and international directions: Italy, Rome, Spain, England, Paris, and Germany?[55] The circular shape of the Montargis gardens is well suited to combine several modes of royal representation compatible with the Calvinist Reformation and to meet the expectations of divine celebration, refuge, peace, and religious coexistence expressed during the first Wars of Religion.[56]

CONCLUSION

The gardens of the Château de Montargis are the expression of the magnificence of Renée de France's royal rank. They are both a symbol and a means of respecting her socio-cultural obligations. The gardens reflect this daughter of France's loyalty to her family heritage and the care she took to maintain her place alongside the king at court. This image was conveyed partly through the construction of gardens obeying a model considered as the *summum bonum* of an ideal of perfection, beauty, and refinement in the sixteenth century. This program shows the château in the center of the landscape and symbolizes Renée's authority over the territory of Montargis. The protection she granted to Jacques Androuet du Cerceau afforded her the services of an architect who was renowned in the aristocratic milieu and a courtier capable of fostering exchanges with her network of relations. These gardens were realized, thanks to contributions from various groups of society, and demonstrated her ability to mobilize a vast set of resources. This strong assertion of her royal identity through her gardens is not, *a priori*, incompatible with the Calvinist precepts circulating within her court. The garden can also be perceived as an iconoclastic celebration of the glory of God through a directly intelligible staging of the beauty of

[54] Daniela Solfaroli Camillocci, "Refuge et migrations à Genève au miroir de polémistes, missionnaires et voyageurs (XVIᵉ-XVIIᵉ siècles)," *Revue de l'histoire des religions* 1 (2015): 53-81.

[55] The British Museum, Prints and drawings, Inv. N° 1972, U. 814. This drawing indicates main border regions with the Kingdom of France. Indications of Rome and Paris signal the most important cities in Europe, that of an ancient fallen empire and that of a new empire dominated by French power, according to the traditional concept of the *Translatio Imperii*.

[56] See original map of the city of Montargis and surrounding area. London, The British Museum, Prints and Drawings, Inv. N. 1972, U. 814.

creation. In addition, the contextual proximity between the renovation works at Montargis and the Protestant Bernard Palissy's *Recepte véritable* is a key to a different reading of the château gardens as a place of concord, peace, and refuge built by the Lady of Montargis. The different components of Renée de France's identity find their place in the image conveyed by her château gardens.

BIBLIOGRAPHY

PRIMARY SOURCES

MANUSCRIPTS

Archives nationales, Paris: MC / ET / LXVIII / 365; R / 4 / 567
The British Museum, Prints and drawings: Inv. No. 1972, U. 814, 815, 816, 817, 818, 819
Archivio di Stato di Torino, Sezioni Riunite (ASTo, SR), Camerale Piemonte: Art. 806, para. 2, m. 35, 36, 37, 38, 39, 40, 41, 42, 55, 56-57
Archives départementales du Loiret (AD Loiret): A 301, 3E 7496, 3E 17075, 3E 17987
Archives municipales de Montargis: DD 5
Inguimbertine Library of Carpentras: Ms. 1771

IMPRINTS

Androuet du Cerceau, Jacques. 1559. *Livre d'architecture de Jaques Androuet du Cerceau, contenant les plans et dessaings de cinquante bastimens tous differens: pour instruire ceux qui desirent bastir, soient de petit, moyen, ou grand estat. Auec declaration des membres & commoditez, & nombre des toises, que contient chacun bastiment, dont l'elevation des faces est figurée sur chacun plan*. Paris: Benoist Prevost.
———. 1576. *Le Premier volume des plus excellents bastiments de France. Auquelz sont designez les plans de quinze bastiments, & de leur contenu: ensemble les elevations & singularitez d'un chascun*. Paris: Jacques Androuet du Cerceau.
Bèze, Théodore de. 1566. *Recueil des opuscules, c'est-à-dire, Petits traictez de M. Jean Calvin*. Geneva: Baptiste Pinereul.
———. 1581. *Les Vrais pourtraits des Hommes illustres en piété et doctrine, du travail desquels Dieu s'est servi en ces derniers temps, pour remettre sus la vraye Religion en divers pays de la Chrestienté. Avec les descriptions de leur vie et de leurs faits plus memorables. Plus quarante quatre Emblemes Chrestiens, Traduicts du latin par Theodore de Besze*. Geneva: Jean de Laon.

Colonna, Francesco. 1546. In *Hypnerotomachie, ou Discours du songe de Poliphile, deduisant comme Amour le combat a l'occasion de Polia*, ed. Jean Martin. Paris: Jacques Kerver.

Haton, Claude. 1857. In *Mémoires de Claude Haton contenant le récit des événements accomplis de 1553 à 1582, principalement dans la Champagne et la Brie. Tome 1*, ed. Félix Bourquelot. Paris: Imprimerie Impériale.

Palissy, Bernard. 1563. *Recepte véritable par laquelle tous les hommes de la France pourront apprendre à multiplier et augmenter leurs thrésors*. La Rochelle: B. Berton.

Secondary Sources

Belligni, Eleonora. 2011. *Renata di Francia (1510-1575). Un'eresia di corte*. Turin: UTET.

Boudon, Françoise, and Claude Mignot. 2010. *Jacques Androuet du Cerceau. Les dessins des Plus excellents bâtiments de France*. Paris: Picard and Cité de l'architecture et du patrimoine.

Carbonnier-Buckard, Marianne. 2013. Le jardin et le désert, ou le 'théâtre sacré' des protestants français (XVIe-XVIIIe siècle). *Diasporas. Circulations, migrations, histoire* 21: 10–19.

Franceschini, Chiara. 2001. Tra Ferrara e la Francia: Notizie su orefici e pittori al servizio di Renée de France. *Franco-Italia* 19-20: 65–104.

Gorris, Rosanna. 1997. 'D'un château l'autre': la corte di Renata di Francia a Ferrara (1528-1560). In *Il Palazzo di Renata di Francia*, ed. Loredana Olivato Puppi, 185–214. Ferrara: Corbo.

Guillaume, Jean. 1999. Le jardin mis en ordre. Jardins et châteaux en France du XVᵉ au XVIIᵉ siècle. In *Architecture, jardin, paysage. L'environnement du château et de la villa au XVᵉ et XVIᵉ siècle, Proceedings from the symposium held in Tours from 1ˢᵗ to 4ᵗʰ June 1992*, ed. Jean Guillaume, 103–123. Paris: Picard.

———. 2010. Qui est Jacques Androuet du Cerceau? In *Jacques Androuet du Cerceau, "un des plus grands architectes qui se soient trouvés en France,"*, ed. Jean Guillaume, 17–33. Paris: Picard.

Hall, J.T.D. 1973. Three Letters of Primaticcio. *The Burlington Magazine* 115 (838): 35–36.

Krumenacker, Yves, ed. 2011. Le Calvinisme et les arts. Special issue, *Chrétiens et sociétés*.

Latremolière, Élisabeth, and Pierre-Gilles Girault, eds. 2014. *Jardins de château à la Renaissance*. Paris: Gourcuff Gradenigo.

Leloup-Audibert, Huguette. 2014. *Les Dernières Dames de Montargis au temps des guerres de Religion. Renée de France, duchesse de Ferrare (1510-1575), Anne d'Este, duchesse de Guise, puis duchesse de Nemours (1531-1607)*. Châtillon-Coligny: Éditions de l'Écluse.

Lestringant, Franck. 1996. *L'expérience huguenote au Nouveau Monde (XVIe siè-cle)*. Geneva: Droz.

Meiss-Even, Marjorie. 2014. *Les Guise et leur paraître*. Tours: Presses universitaires François-Rabelais.

Morin, Dom Guillaume. 1630. *Histoire générale des pays de Gastinois, Senonois et Hurepois*. Paris: Chez la veuve Pierre Chevalier.

Pagazani, Xavier. 2014. *La Demeure noble en Haute-Normandie 1450-1600*. Tours: Presses universitaires François-Rabelais.

Peebles, Kelly D. 2018. Embodied Devotion: The Dynastic and Religious Loyalty of Renée of France (1510-1575). In *Royal Women and Dynastic Loyalty*, ed. Caroline Dunn and Elizabeth Carney, 123-137. Cham, Switzerland: Palgrave Macmillan.

Polizzi, Gilles. 1992. L'intégration du modèle: le Poliphile et le discours du jardin dans la Recepte veritable. *Albineana, Cahiers d'Aubigné* 4: 65–92.

Schaeffer, Otto. 2012. 'Théâtre de la gloire de dieu' et 'Droit usage des biens terrestres.' Calvin, le calvinisme et la nature. In *Calvin Naissance d'une pensée*, ed. Jacques Varet, 213–226. Rennes: PUR.

Solfaroli Camillocci, Daniela. 2015. Refuge et migrations à Genève au miroir de polémistes, missionnaires et voyageurs (XVIe-XVIIe siècles). *Revue de l'histoire des religions* 1: 53–81.

Turias, Odette. 2004. *Renée de France, duchesse de Ferrare, témoin de son temps: 1510-1575*. 2 vols. PhD diss., Université de Tours.

Webb, Charmarie Jenkins [Blaisdell]. 1969. *Royalty and Reform: the predicament of Renée de France*. PhD diss., Tufts University.

CHAPTER 13

Epilogue: Future Directions for Studying the Life and Legacy of Renée de France

Kelly Digby Peebles and Gabriella Scarlatta

This volume's twelve chapters offer a comprehensive portrait of the historical, political, and religious circumstances that Renée navigated through time and space, from her early years as a young *fille de France* to her adult life in Italy, and her later years back in France as a dowager duchess. The many nuanced aspects and very often intricate and secreted details that made up her existence flesh out the portrait of a strong woman who never forgot where she came from or where she was going. From her upbringing, sheltered in the strong female Valois court crafted by her mother, Anne de Bretagne, and godmother, Anne de France, and supported by her family and household, including Michelle de Saubonne, to her years shared with the Angoulême women, Louise de Savoie and Marguerite de

K. D. Peebles (✉)
Clemson University, Clemson, SC, USA
e-mail: kpeeble@clemson.edu

G. Scarlatta
University of Michigan–Dearborn, Dearborn, MI, USA
e-mail: geschric@umich.edu

© The Author(s), under exclusive license to Springer Nature
Switzerland AG 2021
K. D. Peebles, G. Scarlatta (eds.), *Representing the Life and Legacy of Renée de France*, Queenship and Power,
https://doi.org/10.1007/978-3-030-69121-9_13

381

Navarre, to her husband's court and in her own, parallel ones, where she inherited a legacy of charity, patronage, and resilience from previous Este duchesses, this collection narrates the intricacies and events of a brave life journey and a substantial legacy. As Belligni maintains, the Duchess of Ferrara challenged the role of the most famous Italian religious patronesses by exporting a long-standing French pattern of simulated celibacy to Renaissance Ferrara.[1] Indeed, as several essays in this volume demonstrate, Renée exported deeply rooted values and traditions from the French court to her new home in Ferrara, her humanistic education, religious tolerance, and significant patronage, charity, and generosity, including her far-reaching protection of the persecuted and distressed.[2]

In Ferrara, she became an agent of integration and mediation between her own family and country of origin and those of her husband. In doing so, she skillfully crafted a cultural and intellectual continuum that would then be transmitted to her own children, consistent with her godmother's lesson: "Noblewomen are and should be a mirror, a pattern, and an example for others in all things."[3] Each chapter in this collection considers a different aspect of Renée's legacy, highlighting examples of her self-assurance in asserting her role as *fille de France* and sister-in-law of one of the most powerful kings in Europe, of her resilience in her role as wife of a duke struggling to keep control of his duchy (and wife), and of her determination in her role as the mother of five children who would perpetuate both the Valois and Este traditions. She challenged powerful men, inspired innovative writers, sheltered religious refugees, and endured isolation from her children and *maison*.[4] Despite these circumstances, she continued to shine her brilliant "light" as a "ricevitrice di buoni cristiani,"[5] attracting those from all walks of life to the sustaining influence of her

[1] See Chap. 9 in this volume.

[2] For example, eight years after returning to France, in a letter written to her son, Alphonse, on May 23, 1568, Renée requests that he use his authority with the local inquisitors, as did his late father, to deliver a certain Jean Courtault, one of her *officiers* who had been imprisoned. See Turias, *Renée de France*: "[…] je vous prieray plus particulierement […] d'user de l'auctorité que feu mons[r] vostre pere s'estoyt reservee devers les inquisiteurs, pour faire delivrer Jean Courtault, l'un de mes officiers qu'ilz detiennent en prison […]," 390.

[3] Anne de France. *Lessons for My Daughter*. Trans. and ed. Sharon L. Jansen, Cambridge: D. S. Brewer, 2004, 49.

[4] As in the case of the reformed preacher Fanino Fanini (1520–1550), for which Renata pleaded for his life. See her 1549 letter to Ercole II, in Fontana, *Renata di Francia*, II, 275–276.

[5] See Oratio Brunetto's dedication to Renata, in Scarlatta's Chap. 7.

courts in Ferrara and in Montargis. As this collection demonstrates, Renée de France embodies the strength and resilience of female patronage and power and the far-reaching influence of royal women's social networks.

This collection calls attention to the creative ways in which Renée de France was represented by artists, writers, playwrights, diplomats, clergy, and family members in order to elucidate her fascinating biography and actions. Far from exhaustive, these chapters aim to encourage new lines of inquiry into Renée de France's life journey and legacy. For example, contributor Cyril Cvetkovic's work contributes to an innovative digital project "Montargis 3D. Le Songe de Renée." Supported by the interdisciplinary research program Intelligence des Patrimoines, this three-dimensional virtual model invites the viewer to stroll through Renée's château and gardens in Montargis.[6] Transmedia storytelling such as this allows us to experience the narrative of her "universe" in different ways, though other digital methodologies also hold great promise. For instance, a digital edition of Renée's letters, which are widely dispersed in European archives and libraries, would allow for a prosopographical study of her correspondence that could elucidate her role and activities in the French Calvinist network and in courtly and diplomatic channels in ways that would not otherwise be possible.[7] Many avenues for further study remain promising and fruitful, such as Renée's broad social connections and correspondence throughout Europe, her family relationships—those with her sister, Claude de France, and cousins, Marguerite de Navarre and Jeanne d'Albret—her influence on the literary world of Ferrara, including theater and poetry, her direct intellectual legacy to her children, and her actions within the Calvinist networks of Ferrara and France. Indeed, this collection is meant to provide in equal measure a more comprehensive portrait of Renée de France, as well as new lines of inquiry and sources to continue the research into her life and legacy.

---

[6] On the projects and goals supported by Intelligence de Patrimoines, see https://intelligencedespatrimoines.fr. The project "Montargis 3D" will be made available by the Renaissance Transmedia Lab: https://renaissance-transmedia-lab.fr/rtl4/.

[7] See, for example, Early Modern Letters Online, a University of Oxford-based project that aims to reassemble widely dispersed manuscript correspondence through a searchable, open-source union catalogue. http://www.culturesofknowledge.org.

Bibliography

Anne de France. 2004. *Lessons for My Daughter.* Translated and edited by Sharon L. Jansen. Cambridge: D. S. Brewer.

Cultures of Knowledge. n.d. *Early Modern Letters Online.* University of Oxford. http://emlo.bodleian.ox.ac.uk/.

Fontana, Bartolomeo. 1889. *Renata di Francia, duchessa di Ferrara: sui documenti dell'archivio Estense, del Mediceo, del Gonzaga e dell'archivio segreto Vaticano.* 3 Vols. Rome: Forzani.

Intelligence des Patrimoines. n.d.. https://intelligencedespatrimoines.fr.

Renaissance Transmedia Lab. n.d. Montargis 3D. https://renaissance-transmedia-lab.fr/rtl4/.

Turias, Odette. 2005. *Renée de France, Duchesse de Ferrare, témoin de son temps: 1510–1575, Tomes I & II.* PhD diss., Université de Tours.

Index[1]

---

[1] Note: Page numbers followed by 'n' refer to notes.

Henri III, Duke of Orléans, King of
France, 341
Henri IV, King of France (Henri III,
King of Navarre), 263
The Heptameron, 261
Heresy, 142n34, 142n37, 144n43
Holy week ceremonies, 232
Hudson, Robert J., 12, 14, 198n26
Huguenots, 260, 261
See also Protestants

I
Idolatry, 129, 143, 144
Inquisition, 207, 207n59, 347, 353
See also Roman inquisition
Ippolita d'Este, 296
Ippolito d'Este, Cardinal, 222, 223,
228, 230, 230n32
Ippolito II d'Este, 367
Isabella d'Aragona del Balzo, 294
Isabella d'Este, 222, 227n19, 286,
303, 304, 309, 320
Italian Wars, 260

J
James V, King of Scotland, 134
Jamet, Lyon, 199, 270, 315
See also Ferrarese imbroglio
Jean de Parthenay-l'Archeveque,
Baron de Soubise, 260
Jeanne d'Albret, Queen of Navarre,
15, 261, 263
Jew, Jews, 196, 267
Jouanna, Arlette, 334n2, 353n65
Julius II, Pope, 31
Julius III, Pope, 248, 322

K
Kemp, William, 129n6

King Louis XI, King of France,
257, 258
Kinship, 349–353
Krumenacker, Yves, 373, 373n43

L
La Recepte veritable, 373,
373n46, 374
La Rochelle (Siege of), 275
La Vigne, André de, 259
Lansac, Jacqueline de, 305, 305n102
Latremolière, Élisabeth, 361n8
Lauro, Pietro, 322
Le Baud, Pierre, 23, 24n12
Leblanc, Paulette, 130, 130n11
Lefèvre d'Etaples, Jacques, 31, 33, 35,
44, 48, 51, 52, 259, 293, 314
Leli da Foligno, Gianantonio, 302
Leloup-Audibert, Huguette, 361n9
Lemaire de Belges, Jean, 41, 143, 259
Lent, 11, 99–102, 112, 118
See also Ferrarese imbroglio
Leo X, Pope, 33, 222
Leonello d'Este, 290
Lestringant, Franck, 373n47
Locus amœnus, 169, 175–181
London, Christie's, 20 November
2013, lot 56, 88n25
Louis XII, King of France, 1, 2, 2n2,
2n3, 21, 24, 26, 27, 31, 42, 70,
75, 87n22, 194, 290, 291
Louis XIV, King of France, 222
Louis de Bourbon, Prince of Condé,
337, 337n16
Louise de Montmorency, 263
Louise de Savoie, 3, 3n7, 7, 13, 22,
23n7, 24, 24n16, 28, 36, 39, 44,
47, 55, 57, 195, 290, 294, 299,
300, 381
Louise de Valentinois, Duchess of La
Trémoille, Luisa Borgia, 305

CPSIA information can be obtained
at www.ICGtesting.com
Printed in the USA
LVHW051631120323
741461LV00006B/823